OUTBACK AUSTRALIA HANDBOOK

SOUTH AUSTRALIA • WESTERN AUSTRALIA
NORTHERN TERRITORY

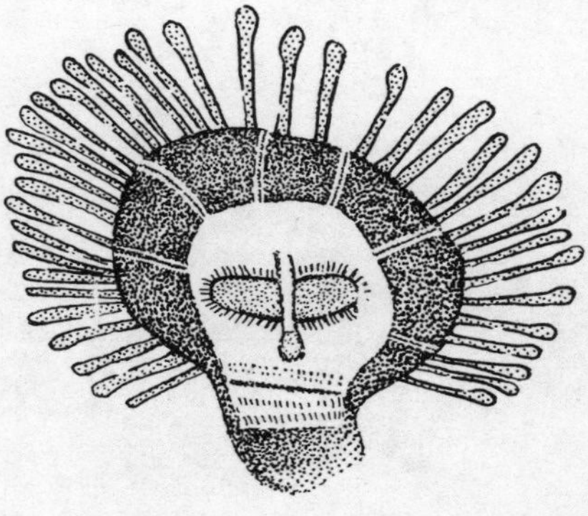

OUTBACK AUSTRALIA HANDBOOK

SOUTH AUSTRALIA • WESTERN AUSTRALIA NORTHERN TERRITORY

MARAEL JOHNSON

MOON
PUBLICATIONS INC.

Please send all comments,
corrections, additions,
amendments, and critiques to:
MARAEL JOHNSON
c/o MOON PUBLICATIONS
722 WALL STREET
CHICO, CA 95928 U.S.A.

Published by
Moon Publications Inc.
722 Wall Street
Chico, California 95928 U.S.A.
tel. (916) 345-5473

PRINTING HISTORY
First Edition—May, 1992

Printed by
Colorcraft Ltd., Hong Kong

All photos by Marael Johnson unless otherwise noted

Library of Congress Cataloging in Publication Data

Johnson, Marael
Outback Australia Handbook: South Australia, Western Australia, Northern Territory/
Marael Johnson—1st edititon
p. cm.
Includes bibliographical references and index.
ISBN 0-918373-79-4 : $15.95
1. Australia—Description and travel—1981—Guidebooks.
2. Western Australia—Description and travel—Guidebooks.
3. South Australia—Description and travel—Guidebooks.
4. Northern Territory—Description and travel—Guidebooks.
I. Title.
DU310.J64 1992 91-45970
919.404'63—dc20 CIP

Printed in Hong Kong

Cover photo: Bill Bachman

This book is dedicated to the Qantas Airways pilot
who allowed me to join him in the cockpit
as he landed his jumbo jet over Sydney Harbour—
sun rising on one side, full moon setting on the other—
enticing me to create my own Australian full moon (handbook).
Thanks for one of the most memorable experiences of my life!

TO MY READERS

I feel like your mother. Inside these pages I have told you where to go, how to get there, what to eat, and who to call in emergencies (which reminds me—keep telephone coins in your pocket at all time).

I have warned you about hitchhiking, crocodiles, macho men, and poisonous snakes. I have done a good job. (And what thanks do I get?)

Have lots of fun, don't drink too much, and call me once a week.

Love, Mom (Mum)

ACKNOWLEDGEMENTS

Thanks to everyone for helping me pull this masterpiece together: Ernie Beyl, Robert Kane, and Qantas Airways for generous help and support; my sister, Susan (aka The Good One), whose crackerjack contract negotiations almost made the Moon pale; Hamish Trumble and Macro The Wonder Dog for their magnificent contribution to this book's Introduction; Northern Territory Government Tourist Bureau; South Australia Tourism; Western Australian Tourism Commission; Australian Tourism Commission; Moon computer whiz, Asha Johnson, who accomplished the impossible by teaching me how to use a computer; my editor, Mark Morris, for having the good sense not to censor me; Taran March, who was left with the dirty work; artist and cartographer Bob Race, lay-out artist Nancy Kennedy, and all the other Moon beams; and all my mates Down Under and my pals Up Top who put up with my bad moods and midnight appetites during this intense project.

CONTENTS

MAPS

MAP SYMBOLS

WATER
DRY LAKE
NATIONAL HIGHWAY
STATE HIGHWAY
MOUNTAIN

STATE BORDER
BRIDGE
FREEWAY
MAIN HIGHWAY
OTHER ROAD
UNPAVED ROAD

C.P. CONSERVATION PARK
POINT OF INTEREST
CITY
TOWN

NOTE: CONDITION OF UNPAVED ROADS MAY VARY

ABBREVIATIONS

a/c—air-conditioning
B&B—bed and breakfast
BBQ—barbeque
Bldg.—building
C—centigrade
CWA—Country Women's Association
4WD—four-wheel drive
P.O.—post office
STA—State Transit Authority (South Australia)
Student Travel Association
tel.—telephone
YHA—Youth Hostel Association
YMCA/YWCA—Young Men's/Women's Christian Association

IS THIS BOOK OUT OF DATE?

Of course it is. What do you think—I wrote it last night, it was printed this morning, and you got the first copy hot off the press? Though we strive to be as accurate and current as possible, alas—things change.

If you discover an error, or something new and exciting (a walking trail, dinosaur footprint, cache of diamonds, a reflection of the man in the moon), please let me know. Other than routine updates, your contribution, if used, will be acknowledged. Also, send love letters and snapshots.

Marael Johnson
c/o Moon Publications, Inc.
722 Wall St.
Chico, CA 95928 USA

PREFACE

Almost every night, for ten years, I dreamed about the Outback. I was involved in every imaginable activity—walking about purposefully, running circles around myself, skipping down a long stretch of road. Time stopped still, eons flashed past—I was stuck in dreamtime, not Aboriginal, but my own. And it was sublime, like pop-out fairy tales suddenly come to life. When I finally did step onto Australian soil, I was not disappointed. I felt like Dorothy (or maybe Toto) in the wonderful land of Oz. (And I was not crying for Kansas or Aunt Em!)

The Outback is an adventure through some of the oldest, most wondrous places on earth—Oz-spots where perhaps your only constraint will be your imagination. This is where reality is dreamlike and Dreamtime is for real. You may have no idea of the mind-expanding and body-humbling experiences that await you in this land of unearthly enigmas and geological giants—but I do.

Other guidebooks will plunk you down in Sydney, Melbourne, or Brisbane—shadowing zillions of tourists before you. Give you a meat pie and a souvenir tea towel. Not this handbook. I want you to stand (and your spirits to soar) with brave warriors, "never say die" survivalists, Outback characters, and know-somethin'-we-don't natives. You'll come as close as you dare to man-eating crocs, and rub your unbelieving eyes at the sight of pink lakes and monolithic termite mounds. And when you want cities, well, I'll give you cities—serene Adelaide, cosmopolitan Darwin, sexy Perth, and a town like Alice—not unknown, but lesser known (and traveled) than the east coast hubs. If you like, I'll even feed you a pie and toss in the towel.

INTRODUCTION

Australian history . . . does not read like history, but like the most beautiful lies. And all of a fresh sort, no mouldy old stale ones. It is full of surprises and adventures and incongruities, and contradictions and incredibilities; but they are all true, and they happened.

—Mark Twain

THE LAND

Australia is indeed made of contradictions and conundrums. Is it the smallest continent or the biggest island on earth? Is it the oldest place in the world? Indeed it is, and you can stroll over rocks that were formed four billion years ago. But geologists will remind you that Australia, as a separate geographical entity, is a recent, almost modern, phenomenon, dating from a mere 50 million years ago.

Its isolation in the remote southern ocean meant that Australia was the last continent to succumb to human occupancy (Aborigines arrived about 40,000 years ago), but long before Europeans arrived, the existence of the "antipodes" was postulated by philosophers from Athens to Alexandria (on the theory that symmetry demanded a southern continent to balance the known world in the north).

Australia is a fragment of the ancient supercontinent Pangaea. Six hundred million years ago, South America, Africa, Antarctica, Australasia, and the Indian subcontinent were all hooked together. Over the millennia since, they have been drifting apart, as the massive tectonic plates float across the earth's mantle. Australia is riding in the middle of a plate whose leading edge in northern India is relentlessly smashing into central Asia, piling up the Himalayas. The eastern edge of the same plate runs alongside New Zealand, which experiences the volcanic consequences of two

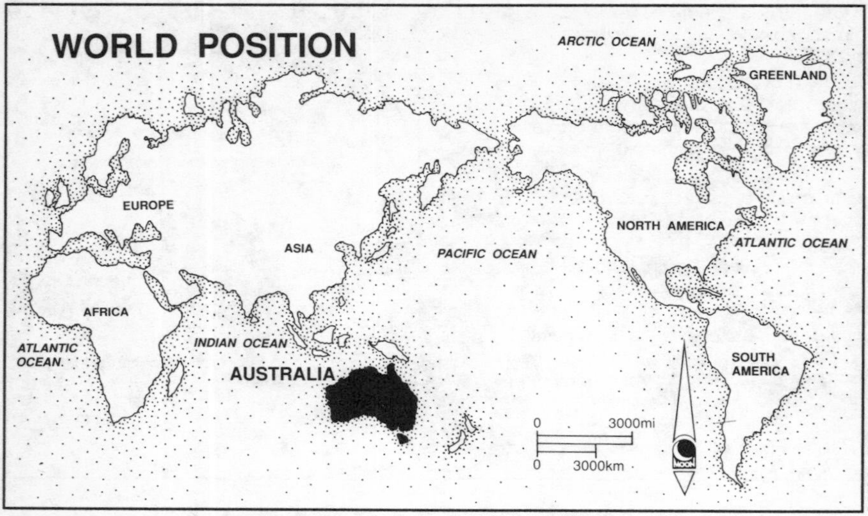

unimaginably vast slabs of rock grinding away at each other.

Being in the middle of this enormous plate has meant that the Australian continent has been comparatively free of volcanic and other cataclysmic upheavals. Consequently, Australia is the flattest of the continents; time and weather have eroded mountain ranges that once would have dwarfed Mt. Everest. Mount Kosciusko, Australia's highest mountain (2,228 meters above sea level), would barely pass muster as a respectable foothill elsewhere in the world. Australia has an average height of only 200 meters, and one of the most powerful impressions the traveler experiences in Australia is of awesome, mind-numbing flatness.

Another impression is dryness. Australia is the driest of the continents; some areas are subject to more evaporation than precipitation. While 40% of its landmass lies in the tropics, almost 70% is arid, with an annual rainfall below 25 centimeters. These parched conditions are accompanied by a *big* load of sand: The longest sand dunes in the world run parallel for up to 200 km in the Simpson Desert. Where the sandy deserts give out, they are replaced by stony "gibber" deserts, relics of an ancient inland sea.

GEOGRAPHICAL FEATURES

Australia has three main geographical zones. The "highlands" run parallel to the east coast, and are more commonly called the Great Dividing Range, although in places they only reach 300 meters. To the west are the "central eastern lowlands" which traverse the continent from north to south, and never rise more than a dizzying 350 meters. South Australia's northeastern corner is comprised in part of these lowlands. The "western plateau" covers almost three-quarters of the continent and is the true flat, arid, harsh, empty, knock-your-socks-off, and alluringly beautiful Outback.

Notable geographical features include Uluru (or Ayers Rock), the largest monolith in the world. Like an iceberg, most of its bulk lies beneath the surface, and it rears so dramatically out of the landscape that it is little wonder that Aborigines regard it as a sacred site. Lake Eyre, usually Australia's largest salt pan, is also the country's largest lake when it fills a couple times per century. The Great Sandy, Gibson, and Great Victoria deserts occupy much of the central Outback.

The lowlands that bisect the continent along the 140th meridian contain the Great Artesian Basin, a vast underground water source tapped by some 9,000 bores, or wells. At the southern edge of this basin is the Murray-Darling river system, really the only river system in Australia. Many of Australia's rivers run only seasonally, and in times of drought dry up, leaving stranded pools or lakes called "billabongs." Lake Eyre is at the center of the largest internal drainage system on earth, more than twice as big as the Great Basin of Utah, Nevada, and California. When it fills, only a few times each century, it transforms the landscape with a spectacular explosion of birds and plantlife.

The center of the continent is flat, sandy, and arid, except for the MacDonnell and Musgrave ranges. The sand and rock here are the color of terra-cotta, giving rise to the expression, the "Red Centre." More desolate yet is the Nullarbor Plain, which runs almost 1,500 km from east to west; it is famous for its utter flatness and for the limestone caves that lie hidden beneath its featureless face. The longest straight stretch of road in the world runs for 200 km across the Nullarbor. The southern edge of the Nullarbor drops abruptly into the wild ocean from spectacular vertical cliffs that run along the Great Australian Bight.

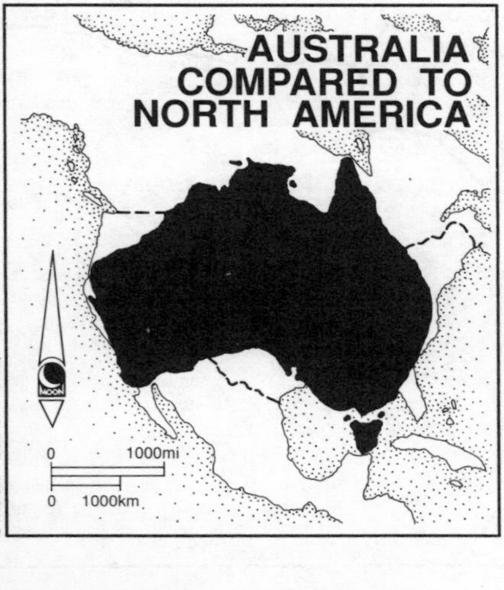

SEASONS

Seasons in the Southern Hemisphere are the reverse of those in the Northern Hemisphere:

Spring: September-November
Summer: December-February
Fall: March-May
Winter: June-August

CLIMATE

The Seasons

Visitors from the Northern Hemisphere will immediately be struck by Australia's topsy-turvy seasons: summer officially begins on 1 December and winter on 1 June. This means that the academic and calendar years coincide, and both end with the summer holidays, in December. It also means you may experience the morbid novelty of sitting down to a piping-hot Christmas dinner, perhaps of roast turkey or baked ham with all the trimmings, in the sweltering heat of high summer. And don't look for the mossy side of trees when you get lost, because here the sun rides across the northern sky, and new rules apply.

Australia straddles the Tropic of Capricorn, and climatic conditions range from temperate in the south to tropical in the north. Adelaide enjoys a mild, almost Mediterranean climate, with moderate winters and dry summers. South Australia's northern half shares the same hot, semiarid Outback conditions which characterize the Northern Territory's southern reaches. Top End weather, which occurs in the northern part of Western Australia and the Northern Territory, favors distinct wet (Oct.-March) and dry (May-Sept.) seasons. Perth's weather is some of the best: sunny, mild, and not too humid. Conditions are mild by run-for-the-thermal undies standards.

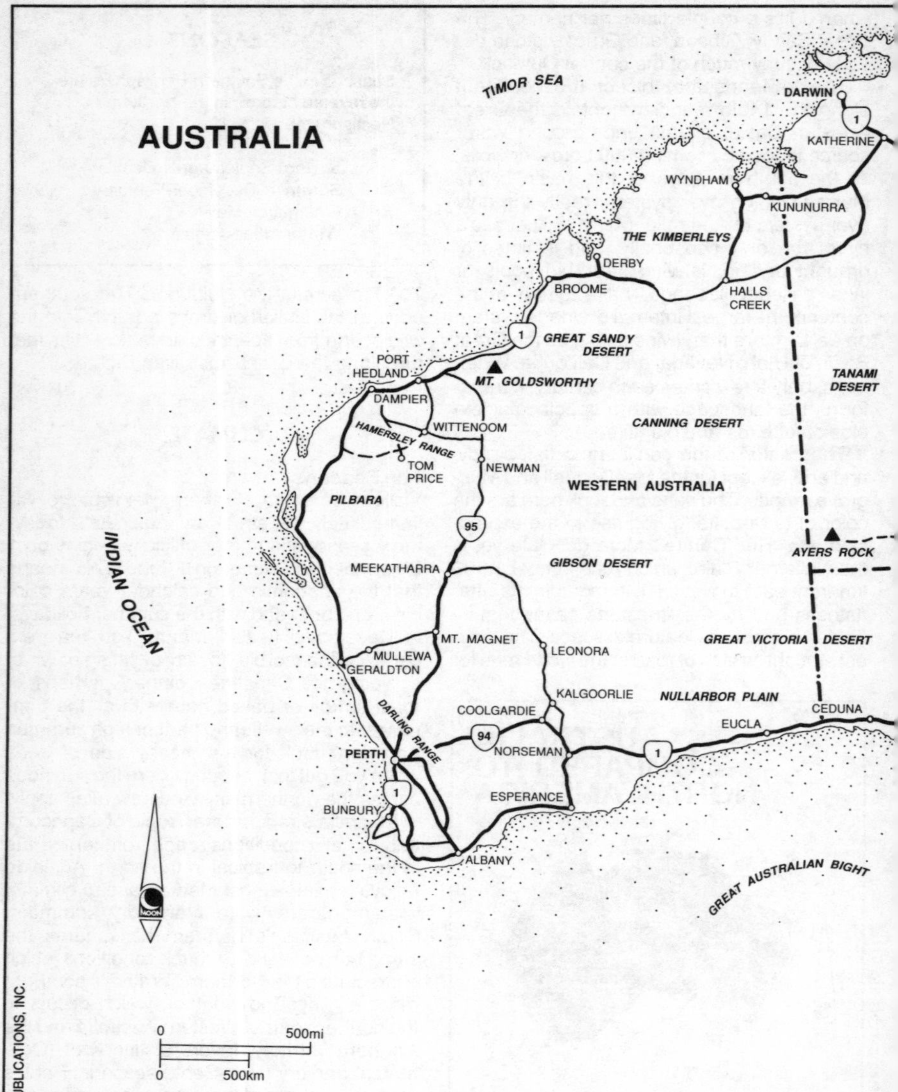
AUSTRALIA
TIMOR SEA
DARWIN
1
KATHERINE
WYNDHAM
KUNUNURRA
THE KIMBERLEYS
DERBY
BROOME
HALLS CREEK
1
GREAT SANDY DESERT
TANAMI DESERT
PORT HEDLAND
MT. GOLDSWORTHY
DAMPIER
CANNING DESERT
WITTENOOM
HAMERSLEY RANGE
TOM PRICE
NEWMAN
WESTERN AUSTRALIA
PILBARA
95
AYERS ROCK
INDIAN OCEAN
MEEKATHARRA
GIBSON DESERT
MT. MAGNET
LEONORA
GREAT VICTORIA DESERT
MULLEWA
GERALDTON
NULLARBOR PLAIN
KALGOORLIE
DARLING RANGE
COOLGARDIE
CEDUNA
EUCLA
94
PERTH
NORSEMAN
1
1
ESPERANCE
BUNBURY
ALBANY
GREAT AUSTRALIAN BIGHT
MOON
0
500mi
0
500km
© MOON PUBLICATIONS, INC.

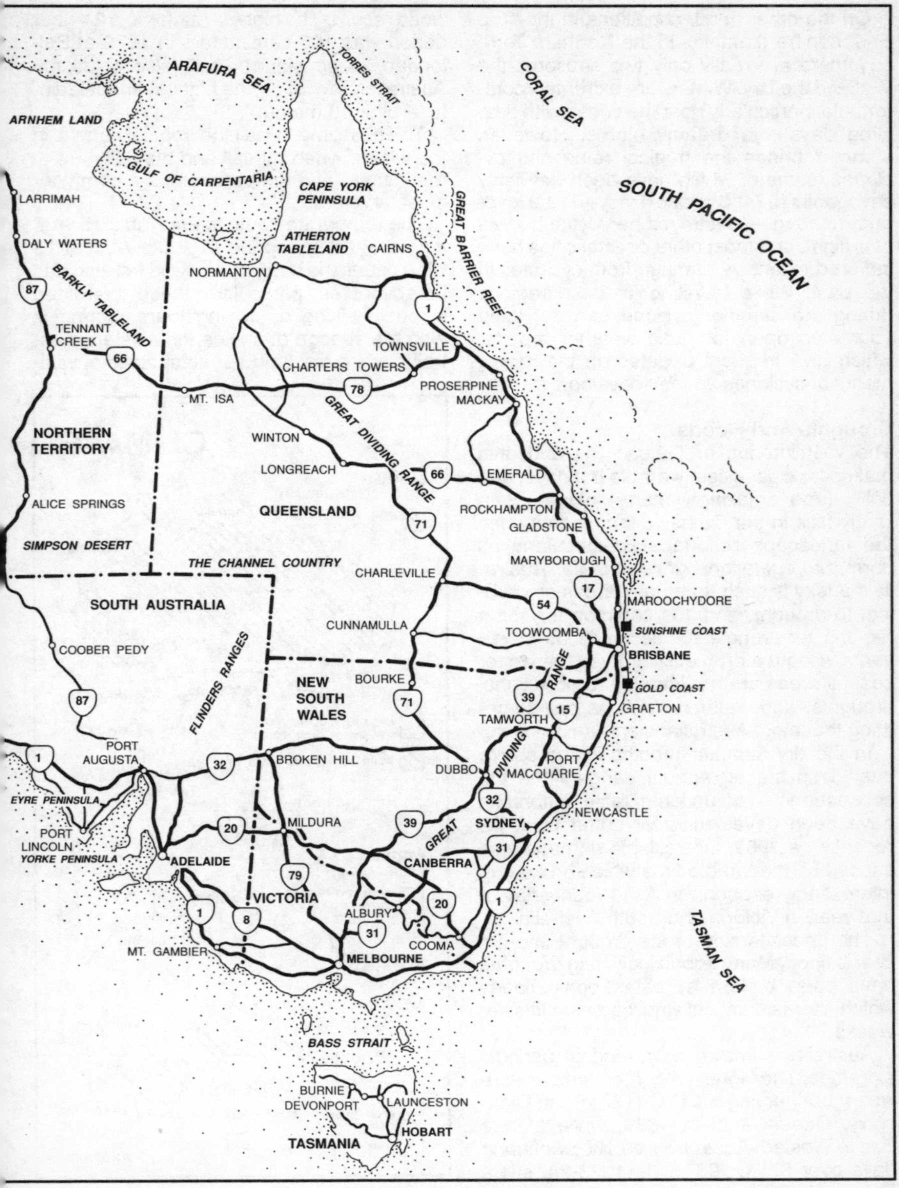
ARAFURA SEA
TORRES STRAIT
CORAL SEA
ARNHEM LAND
GULF OF CARPENTARIA
CAPE YORK PENINSULA
GREAT BARRIER REEF
SOUTH PACIFIC OCEAN
LARRIMAH
DALY WATERS
ATHERTON TABLELAND
CAIRNS
NORMANTON
BARKLY TABLELAND
87
1
TENNANT CREEK
66
TOWNSVILLE
CHARTERS TOWERS
78
PROSERPINE
MT. ISA
MACKAY
GREAT DIVIDING RANGE
NORTHERN TERRITORY
WINTON
LONGREACH
66
EMERALD
ALICE SPRINGS
QUEENSLAND
71
ROCKHAMPTON
GLADSTONE
SIMPSON DESERT
MARYBOROUGH
THE CHANNEL COUNTRY
CHARLEVILLE
17
54
MAROOCHYDORE
SOUTH AUSTRALIA
SUNSHINE COAST
CUNNAMULLA
TOOWOOMBA
BRISBANE
COOBER PEDY
FLINDERS RANGES
RANGE
NEW SOUTH WALES
BOURKE
GOLD COAST
39
87
71
GRAFTON
15
TAMWORTH
PORT AUGUSTA
1
32
BROKEN HILL
PORT MACQUARIE
DUBBO
DIVIDING
EYRE PENINSULA
32
NEWCASTLE
MILDURA
39
GREAT
SYDNEY
PORT LINCOLN
20
31
YORKE PENINSULA
ADELAIDE
CANBERRA
79
VICTORIA
20
1
1
8
ALBURY
TASMAN SEA
31
MT. GAMBIER
COOMA
MELBOURNE
BASS STRAIT
BURNIE
DEVONPORT
LAUNCESTON
HOBART
TASMANIA

On the other hand, conditions in the "Top End" can be dramatic. In the Northern Territory there are really only two seasons: the Wet and the Dry. Winters are extremely comfortable, particularly near the coast, with dazzling days and dreamy nights. However, summer brings the tropical rains and cyclones, some of which have been devilishly savage. In 1974, Cyclone Tracy—like a lover on a rampage—destroyed her victim Darwin overnight, and most other coastal cities have suffered extensive damage from cyclones in the past. While traveling in these regions during the summer cyclone season, keep your ears open for radio weather reports, which give frequent updates on the movements of cyclones as they develop.

Droughts And Floods

The vast interior, or Outback, is arid; this makes for clear skies, warm to hot days, and chilly (and amazingly starry) nights. Rain rarely falls in the Outback, but when it does the landscape responds spectacularly as dormant vegetation bursts into life. Australia's aridity is such that many areas are subject to drought, and it is common for some regions to struggle for as much as seven years without a drop of rain. Even the wetter coastal areas are not immune to occasional droughts, and water restrictions are something that most Australians are familiar with.

In the dry summer months in the south, bush fires are an annual danger, and the consequences of uncontrollable outbreaks have been devastating for some time. As recently as 1982, incalculable damage was caused by the terrible fires which broke out, interestingly enough, on Ash Wednesday of that year, in Victoria and South Australia.

The opposite side of the drought-and-fire coin is flood. Many agonizingly long droughts have been broken by catastrophic floods which can isolate outlying communities for weeks.

Australia is known as a land of periodic extremes. The highest recorded temperature was a brain-frying 53.1° C (127° F), in Cloncurry, Queensland, in 1889, while Marble Bar, in Western Australia, had 160 sweltering days over 37° C (98° F) in 1923-24, still a world record. The highest rainfall in a 24-hour period was 108 centimeters in 1979 at Bellenden, Queensland, which also holds the Australian record for the highest annual rainfall—over 10 meters.

The best time to visit the tropical north is in the winter, when rainfall and humidity are at a minimum and temperatures are comfy for most travelers.

The temperate south is enjoyable all year 'round although spring in south Australia's wine country is hard to beat and fall also has its advocates, particularly those interested in bushwalking or cycling tours. Spring is also the season of choice for Western Australia, when the 8,000 or so species of wild-

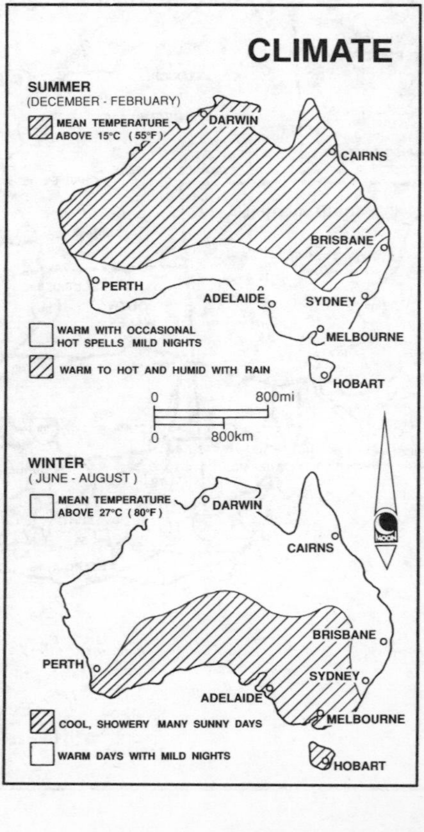

flowers, for which the state is famous, are in bloom. For more detailed information on local weather, see "Climate" in the Introduction to each state.

Sunshine And Ozone

Australia is exposed to more hours of sunshine than most countries. This has two important consequences. First, the anxiously observed hole in the protective ozone layer over the South Pole has extended at times to expose southern parts of the continent, and it is expected that the hole will only enlarge further. Scientific opinion about the negative effects of this startling development are divided. There is no doubt, however, about the consequences of exposure to high levels of sunshine on humans. Even before the rent in the ozone layer became a concern, Australia's rate of skin-cancer cases was abnormally high. The combination of a fashion for bronze suntans, an addiction to sunbathing, a beach culture, and a love of outdoor activities has led to a national health problem of major proportions. It is worth remembering the simple creed propounded in a recent public health campaign: Slip, Slop, Slap (slip on a shirt, slop on some sunscreen, and slap on a hat).

Harsh climatic conditions have helped to shape the national character, and, far from resenting the forces of nature that so often blight the lives of Australians, especially in the bush, many people have a strangely sentimental attachment to this rigorous and inhospitable land. The words of Dorothy Mackellar in this poem, which most Australians learn at school, sum up their ambivalent affection:

I love a sunburnt country,
A land of sweeping plains,
Of rugged mountain ranges,
Of droughts, and flooding rains.
I love her far horizons.
I love her jewelled sea.
Her beauty and her terror;
A wide brown land for me.

FLORA AND FAUNA

In wilderness is the preservation of the world. We need the tonic of wilderness, to wade sometimes in the marshes . . . we can never have enough of nature.

—Henry Thoreau

Australia's 50 million years of utter isolation has led to the evolution of a bewildering array of indigenous plant and animal life that has little in common with life-forms in relatively nearby parts of the world. It is one of the fascinations of travel in Australia to be continually confronted with animals and plants which might easily spring from the fevered brains of science fiction writers.

FLORA

"The great quantity of plants Mr. Banks and Dr. Solander found in this place occasioned my giving it the Name of Botany Bay." This laconic entry in Captain Cook's 1770 journal does little justice to the excitement the two botanical gentlemen in his company must have experienced. The flora they collected was certainly novel and was the subject of lively academic interest in Europe. The following overview highlights some of the botanic marvels that Banks and Solander probably observed.

The Bush

The term "bush," which Australians bandy about so loosely, covers a variety of terrains and broad vegetation types, including rainforests, both temperate and tropical, mangrove swamps, savannah, rolling scrub-covered hills, forests of eucalypt or conifer, grasslands, and desert. Australian plants and trees are generally non-deciduous, and many species bear fragrant blossoms. After a desert rainstorm, the air is cloyingly sweet, and sailors say they can smell the sharp medicinal scent of gums (eucalypts) far out to sea.

Myrtles And Gums

The largest and most famous of Australian plant groups is the myrtle family. It contains over 1,000 native species, from the ground-hugging heath-like kunzeas to the 500-odd species of eucalypt. It includes the tea-tree, so named by Captain Cook's crew who made a tea-colored drink from its leaves, as well as the picturesque paper-bark with its white papery trunk, and the brilliantly colored bottlebrush. The hundreds of species of eucalypt or gum tree, many with colorful scarlet, coral, and white blossoms, are now the most transplanted trees in the world. More than 100 years ago these fast growers, well-suited to arid climates, were planted in California and Arizona as windbreaks, and you can find Australian eucalypts in well over 70 countries, a tribute to their hardy adaptability.

In the mountains of eastern Victoria and Tasmania, you can see dense forests of giant gums, some standing over 300 feet tall. In drier climes the gums have developed an ability to resist heat and preserve moisture. Many gum trees have leaves that turn edge-on to the sun's rays to reduce evaporation (and incidentally making them poor shade on a scorching afternoon). Gum leaves are generally thick-skinned and equipped with oil glands to provide an oily film to resist the heat. Snow gums are adapated to the burdensome require-

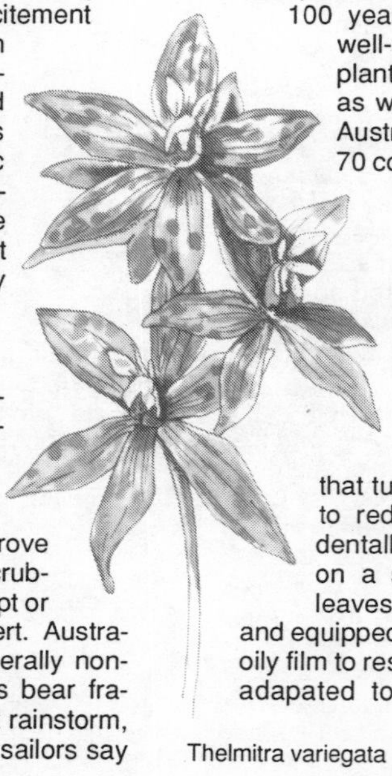

Thelmitra variegata KAREN WHITE

ments of their environment, and have supple limbs which can bend beneath their annual load of snow and ice.

Other Plants And Shrubs

The wattle, Australia's floral emblem, belongs to the acacia family, which is represented by some 600 species across Australia. In early days, colonists made wattle-and-daub huts, an ancient building technique involving interwoven saplings covered with mud, and the name "wattle" was attached to this profusely blooming species. Like a good Aussie football player, the wattle is extremely hardy and fast growing, and can thrive in the arid, bare interior where even eucalypts cannot compete, but its career is not long-lived. Some species have adapted to sand dunes drenched with salt spray, some to soggy ill-drained swamps, and others to stony exposed ridges. And like many Australian plants, they have adapted to fire.

The bush fire did not come to Australia with the Europeans. Since ancient times, lightning has started many a blazing inferno, and Aborigines used fire to flush animals out of dense foliage. Many species of Australian plants have developed a remarkable resistance to fire. Eucalypts have dormant buds beneath their bark which open immediately after a bush fire to restore foliage to a burnt tree. The seeds of other species of plants do not readily germinate until the first rains after a fire, when great quantities of acacia seedlings spring up from the charred earth. The woody fruits of *Hakeas* and *Banksias* actually require the heat of fire before they will burst open and release the seeds.

The ubiquitous *Banksia* trees and shrubs are named after Sir Joseph Banks, and they have a special place in the nightmares of Australian children after the artist May Gibbs created the wicked Banksia men for her popular bush fairy tales. *Banksias* belong to the Protaceae family, which has developed most abundantly in Australia. It is named after Proteus, the shape-changing Old Man of the Sea in Greek mythology, and it points to the enormous diversity of the family. Some *Banksias,* for instance, grow half submerged in the sand, while others grow into trees 50 feet tall. Leaves and flowers of this family vary tremendously from the so-called spider flowers of the *Grevilleas* genus to the dense heads of the waratahs. The most commercially valuable members of the family are the macadamia, which is grown in Queensland for its rich yummy nut, and the silky oak, which produces a fine cabinet wood.

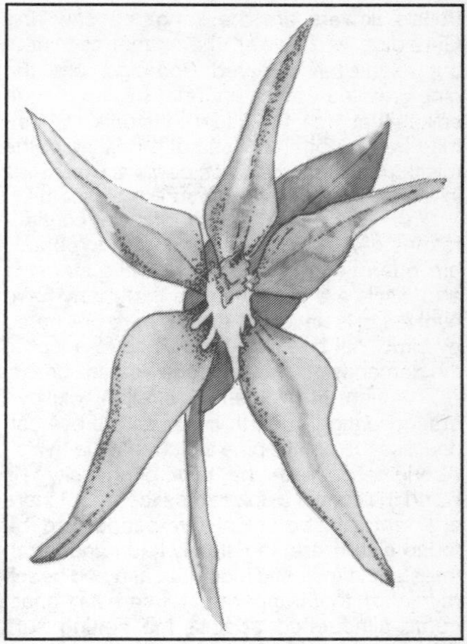

KAREN WHITE

Caladenia flava

Late And Early Bloomers

Australian native plants include profuse bloomers. Sturt's desert pea stretches like a red carpet across vast tracts of inland desert. More than 600 varieties of orchids, including the only two underground species in the world, lend their sensuous beauty to the steamy rainforests of the north.

Western Australia alone grows more than 6,000 species of wildflowers and flowering shrubs and trees. For many eons, the southwest corner of Australia was virtually a floral island, isolated from the world by the Indian Ocean and the deserts to its north and east. Among the most colorful of Western Australia's flowers are the kangaroo paw, the Geraldton wax flower, the scarlet coccinea, the exquisitely scented *Boronias,* and the pine grevillea with its enormous deep orange spikes that grow to 20 feet. Australia's Christmas tree is not a conifer, but a relative of the mistletoe, a parasite that blooms at Christmas in masses of orange balloon-like blossoms.

One reason for the very different configurations of Australian flowers, in which petals are often tiny or nonexistent while stamens and pistils are prominent, is that many have evolved in isolation where they are pollinated by birds, not bees, and have had to adapt to the demands of a host of honey-eaters' beaks.

The sight of Western Australian wildflowers, covering the earth as far as the eye can see, like the prolific blue Leschenaultia (which Aborigines called "the floor of the sky") is worth the cost of a dozen trips there. But there are fantastic botanical eye-poppers to be found elsewhere: the stately kauri and jarrah forests; the majestic mountain ash and beech myrtle of the temperate rainforests; ghost gums silhouetted against the setting sun; "blackboys" with their fantastic "spears"; primitive tree ferns slowly inching their way up from the mossy, mist-shrouded forest floor; the sparse but fascinating vegetation of the Nullarbor Plain—so inhospitable but so alive; and for the ghoulish, two carnivorous species, the pitcher plant and the rainbow plant. The isolation and stress of a harsh climate have created plant life in Australia that is unique, extraordinary, and well worth investigating.

FAUNA

The Extinct

Prehistoric Australia was inhabited by its own fair share of monstrous dinosaurs: carnivorous lizards standing nine meters tall, eight-meter ichthyosaurs (or fish lizards), and three-meter labyrinthodonts (or frog lizards). These creatures largely died out in the cataclysmic worldwide extinction of the dinosaurs, long before humans arrived. Their most dangerous descendants are the saltwater crocodile, the great white shark, and a gallery of some of the world's deadliest snakes. A class of creature known as megafauna, however, still roamed the land when the first Aborigines came ashore. The bones of gigantic wombats bigger than buffalos, huge saber-toothed marsupial lions, and outsized kangaroos that would dwarf their puny descendants have been found, and some of these creatures may well have entered the racial memory of the Aborigines, in the form of Dreamtime myths.

The Extraordinary

Some of Australia's native fauna which survived into the era of European colonization are candidates for *Ripley's Believe It Or Not.* The silver barramundi, found in Kakadu National Park, spends the first six years of its life as a male and the rest as a female. Australia has the world's largest and most ferociously destructive termites, some of which build nests as high as six meters. The grand champion of termite mounds is located near Hayes Creek in the Northern Territory. The world's most venomous snake is the taipan, which can grow up to three meters long and carry enough venom to kill over 20,000 mice.

The rather unsavory platypus frog deserves a mention; the female carries her young in her stomach and gives birth by regurgitating them. Scientific texts are not clear on how the young get into her stomach in the first place.

Marsupials

The most famous of Australian animals are the marsupials—mammals that lack a placenta, give birth to offspring still in the gestative stage, and carry them in a pouch. Almost all the 150-odd marsupial species, most notably kangaroos, wallabies, possums, koalas, and wombats, are found in Australia.

Kangaroos (or "roos") are the largest of the marsupials. They are also the most widespread; since the arrival of Europeans, their numbers have increased as pastoralists cleared land and drilled water bores for sheep and cattle. Australians now resort to "culling"—a polite euphemism for massacring large numbers of native animals which interfere with graziers' interests and thereby earn the title of pest.

Despite the increasing numbers of some kangaroo species, it is a misconception that kangaroos can be seen loping down the main street of any town in Australia. In fact, they are timid creatures, often most active at night, and they are seen about as often as a deer is in North America. Kangaroos are hunted for their skins and meat by Aborigines, for whom they form an important food source. At the time of writing, most culled kangaroos end up as dog food, but new initiatives are afoot to get kangaroo steaks onto the menus of sophisticated city restaurants. Evidently, kangaroo meat is highly nutritious, containing no cholesterol, and very little fat.

The largest recorded kangaroo was 3.2 meters tall and weighed nearly 100 kilograms. Far from being the harmless, inoffensive creature gazing doe-eyed from a glossy tourist brochure, kangaroos are ready and able to defend themselves. When attacked, by dingoes or a rival kangaroo, they use their forepaws to immobilize their opponent, and rearing up on their powerful tail, they attempt to rip open their adversary's belly with knife-like hind claws.

The kangaroo has evolved a remarkably efficient means of locomotion: jumping. It cannot walk or run, though it can swim surprisingly well, and it can achieve speeds of up to 50 km per hour by just hopping along. The sight of a group of kangaroos in full flight is overwhelming.

Kangaroos' powerful hind legs are cunningly structured with a system of counterweighted tendons and muscles which conserve the energy expended in motion, thus enabling the animal to travel at high speeds for prolonged periods. Some rural racetracks have stories to tell about kangaroos bounding onto the track and beating a field of thoroughbred race horses.

The female kangaroo, like some other marsupials, is able to control her reproductive cycle depending on the availability of food and water. A female can carry a "joey" or immature kangaroo in her pouch and one in her uterus. Should conditions become unfavorable, she will terminate her unborn joey in utero. The joey at birth is about one inch long and must drag itself from the birth canal to the mammary gland in the pouch, a perilous journey during which the mother offers no assistance. Hairs on the mother's belly grow in a pattern which give the joey directional aid, but should the joey fall off the mother, she will abandon it. Once the joey puts its mouth to the mammary gland, the nipple swells up and effectively locks the joey onto the teat until it has grown sufficiently to suck for itself. The joey will stay in the pouch for six to eight months until it is weaned, but it will continue to use its mother's pouch for safety and transportation until it is almost ridiculously big.

Kangaroo species range in size from the five-cm dusky hopping mouse to the giant two-meter red kangaroo. "Wallaby" usually denotes smaller kangaroos, while "wallaroo" usually denotes kangaroos that prefer a rocky or densely wooded habitat.

The sleepy, cuddlesome **koala,** beloved star of so many Australian tourist promotions, is not a bear but another marsupial. Despite its endearing good looks, koalas prefer not to be handled by kootchy-kooing humans, and frequently outrage distinguished visitors who pose for photo opportunities by piddling on them. They are also equipped with formidable claws and are really much better left dozing in the trees where they belong.

Koalas rarely drink water; they obtain their moisture from the 37 species of eucalypt leaves which form their sole diet. Their sleepy attitude is due in part to the sedative and hypnotic effect of a naturally occurring barbituate in the eucalypt leaves. Koala numbers have rapidly declined since European settlement, and they are a protected species. No longer hunted for their pelts, they are still under threat from loss of habitat and a venereal disease similar to chlamydia. Needless to say, that stuffed bear you take home will—hopefully—be a fake.

Wombats are stocky, thickset marsupials slightly bigger than the koala. They make their home in burrows on the forest floor. They are nocturnal animals, and consequently the headlights of cars upset their night vision. One disturbing sight for drivers

Don't call me cuddly!

on Australian country roads is passing countless carcasses of wombats and other native animals. Road signs warn motorists of frequent crossing points, and not just for the animals' protection. Many drivers have cracked a radiator—or worse—in a collision with a kangaroo.

Other marsupials include the tree kangaroo, the monkey-like cuscus, bat-like flying foxes, a host of tree-dwelling possums (which are really the only marsupial to have adapted to city life), marsupial rats and mice.

Monotremes

Monotremes are egg-laying mammals. There are only two in the world and they are both in Australia—the platypus and the echidna. The **duck-billed platypus** is perhaps the most intriguing of all Australia's odd creatures. The first specimens sent to the British Museum were dismissed as a hoax. Scientists thought that the web-footed, duck-billed creature with fur and claws had been intricately stitched together from the various parts of several animals, like so-called mermaids made of monkey heads attached to fish bodies, that travelers brought back from time to time from the East. However, the platypus is really genuinely odd. It represents a possible link in the evolutionary chain between reptiles and mammals, since it lays eggs and suckles its young.

The platypus is extremely shy and sensitive to pollution or disturbance to its habitat. Naturally its numbers are well down since European settlement and it is a protected species. It lives in burrows in the banks of streams, and feeds off the streambed. The platypus must close its eyes and ears under water and uses a mysterious electric sense to locate food. For protection against natural predators, the adult male carries venomous spurs on its hind legs. It's not too likely that you'll see a platypus in the wild, but if you do, remember that these creatures are enormously sensitive and their existence is utterly dependent on being left alone.

The other monotreme, the **echidna** or spiny anteater is much more accessible and a reasonably common sight in the bush. It is named after Echidna, a monster of Greek mythology—part beautiful woman, part voracious serpent—whose offspring were even more monstrous than her own sweet self. The echidna resembles a North American porcupine, with a spine-covered body, a protruding snout, and a distinctive waddling gait, as it rolls along on its knuckles. It also has sharp claws, but its usual response to disturbance is to roll into a ball with its quills flexed.

Dingoes, Tigers, And Bats

Australia's native dog is the dingo, which was actually introduced from Southeast Asia about 6,000 years ago, well after the Aborigines arrived. Traditionally, Aborigines used dingoes for several activities, including sleeping beside them for warmth on cold nights—hence the expression "a three-dog night" for a particularly cold night. Nowadays the dingo roams the Outback in packs, and it is a difficult, though not impossible, animal to domesticate. The dingo earned worldwide notoriety through the Azaria Chamberlain case (wherein a dingo allegedly snatched—and, later, gnawed to death—baby Azaria from her family's Ayers Rock campsite), which only reinforced the need to take precautions when traveling in the more remote regions of the Outback.

Australia is home to about 50 species of bat, including the colossal fruit bat. These large bats congregate in huge colonies, often in the tops of trees, and feed at night. Watching a colony wake up at sunset is a spectacle not to be missed: there is an all-pervading batty smell, and the sound of their bat cries as they fly in bat formation 'round the treetops is quite eerie. Gradually they disperse in search of fruit. The rare golden horsehoe bat can be viewed at the Cutta Cutta Caves south of Katherine in the Northern Territory.

Introduced Species

These are "the animals that ate Australia." Feral dogs, cats, pigs, horses, and a host of other nonnative species, introduced by a series of intentional and accidental blunders, have brought with them economic and environmental devastation and a wave of extinctions unparalleled in the 50 million years since Australian life has been cut off from outside influence. Scores of native animals have been driven to near or complete extinction by competition with or attack from introduced species. Unique and irreplaceable creatures like the eastern hare-wallaby, the golden bandicoot, and the short-tailed hopping mouse have disappeared forever.

Australia's 200-300 million rabbits were introduced by English colonists soon after settlement for the purpose of sport. The spry hippity-hops adapted marvelously to the semiarid areas which were cleared for pasture, and they soon out-ate the resident animals. Now, rabbit infestations regularly break out, producing tens of millions of rabbits at a time. Huge amounts of money and effort have been poured into the control and eradication of the rabbit, most notably for the construction of the "rabbit-proof fence" which extended for thousands of miles across the continent, and for the hideous virus myxomatosis which wiped out millions of rabbits in the 1930s. These days rabbits are largely immune to myxomatosis and vast research programs seek new and more virulent solutions to the rabbit problem.

An estimated 10 million feral pigs cause in excess of $100 million worth of damage annually and pose a nightmare threat to Australia's lucrative livestock industry, should they contract and spread diseases like foot-and-mouth disease or rinderpest.

Feral cats and dogs create havoc in national parks. In the trees, gorgeously colored native parrots, parakeets, and lorikeets are fighting a losing battle against introduced sparrows and starlings. Wild horses and feral goats roam at will, ravaging remote areas of wilderness. More than 70,000 feral donkeys are shot each year. Foxes—also introduced deliberately for sport—are a pest for farmers, but they are steadily wiping out native species as well. In the arid zones, wild camels (descendants of animals brought here for cartage purposes) are actually captured for export to Saudi Arabia; Australia now has the dubious distinction of being home to the last wild camels on earth.

Until the arrival of Europeans, Australia had never known a cloven-hoofed beast; the hard impact of hoofs breaks up the dry crusted earth in the arid regions so that annually millions of tons of topsoil simply blow away. In the Northern Territory, herds of wild buffalo and semiwild cattle roam across a fragile landscape which struggles to recover from the devastation.

Where feral animals encroach on the interests of agriculture, enormous efforts are made to control the situation. But where human population is thin, and livestock (and, consequently, livelihoods) are not affected, feral animal populations are quite literally out of control. Paradoxically, in areas that are declared national parks, feral animals often thrive because they are no longer subject to the control mechanisms of agriculture, and park authorities rarely have sufficient resources to take over.

BIRDS

Australia's birds are a wonderful and unexpected surprise for many visitors—about 700 species, of which approximately 500 are endemic and 200 migrate to all parts of the world. Watchers will spot exotic multicolored parrots (including the raucous cockatoo), budgerigars, lorikeets, rosellas, and galahs. Of the kingfishers, the largest is the kookaburra. Its infectious laughing cry has earned it the nickname "the laughing jackass." On the open plains the flightless emu roams; it's a biggy, slightly smaller than the ostrich. The male emu has sole responsibility in child-rearing from the time the eggs are laid.

When rain falls in the interior, and long-dry watercourses and lakes fill for a few months, millions of birds appear—from black swans, ducks, and geese to pelicans and cormorants—to feed on the long-dormant creatures that lie for years under the scorched clay.

KAREN WHITE

white-breasted wood swallows

Around the coast, seabirds congregate in large numbers; gulls and terns, the fairy penguins of Adelaide and Kangaroo Island, the mutton bird—even the lonely albatross—may be seen in the southern oceans.

The bowerbird constructs an elaborate "bower" or display for mating purposes. It collects all manner of shiny and colorful objects for inclusion in its display, from flowers and berries to jewelry stolen from campsites. Some bowerbirds mix various substances into a form of paint to enhance their overall concept of interior decorating. The females select their mate from the most resourceful and tasteful males. The lyrebird, so named after the fabulous lyre-shaped display feathers of the male, is a great mimic and will deliver prolonged concerts imitating the sounds of the forest, other birds' calls, and tricky impersonations like a tractor or a chainsaw. A single concert may contain up to 40 different calls.

The stately brolga (a large crane) is famous for its courtship dance, a spectacle of immense poignancy. Of the birds of prey, the wedge-tailed eagle is the largest, and hawks and kites are a common sight, hovering motionlessly above their prey or wheeling in pairs high over their territory.

A fashion for native gardens that swept Australia in the '60s has meant that many species of native birds have returned to the suburbs of Australian cities to feed on the flowering shrubs that replaced the hedges and annuals imported from Europe. Many previously unsighted species of native birds are now common in suburbs that once knew only sparrows and pigeons.

Unfortunately, many of Australia's exotic birds are highly prized by collectors overseas and, since the birds are protected, a cruel and illicit smuggling industry has developed. Snaring threatens to wipe out some species, especially of parrots, and the smuggling process itself kills more of these sensitive creatures than can satisfy this objectionable market.

REPTILES AND AMPHIBIANS

Fond of lizards and snakes? You can select from about 230 species of lizard, from the extraordinary frill-necked lizard to the lethargic two-meter-long goanna, plus 140 species of snake, and two species of crocodile. About four people are killed annually by snake bites and occasionally an incautious swimmer is taken by a crocodile—sometimes beside a sign warning against swimming (or, worse,

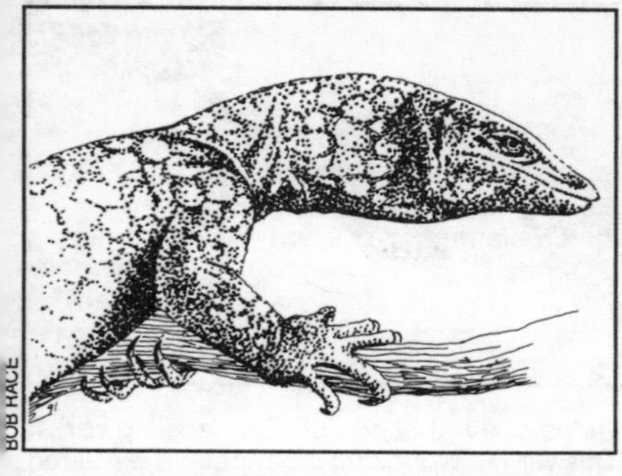

The Pilbarra's bugarra might make you feel like you're in a time warp!

beside a sign that *used* to be there but was pinched by a thoughtless tourist!).

Fewer than 20 species of Australian **snakes** have the potential to kill humans. The taipan is the deadliest, although it's bite is not necessarily fatal if an antivenin is administered soon enough. Other snakes to be wary of include the tiger snake, the copperhead, the death adder, the common brown, and the common black snakes. Additionally, more than 30 species of poisonous seasnakes frequent northern waters, though they are rarely encountered by humans. Remember that snakes are no more delighted to meet you than you are to meet them. Most snake bites are the result of humans trying to kill the snake, or stumbling across one suddenly and startling it into attack. When walking in the bush it's sensible to make some noise to alert snakes of your approach well in advance; most will simply move away.

The two types of **crocodiles** found in Australia—freshwater and saltwater, or "salties," are now protected since hunting severely depleted their numbers. The salties, inhabitants of tidal estuaries along Australia's northern coastline, occasionally creep into freshwater territory and are *extremely dangerous*. The freshwater Johnstone crocodile, found in the rivers of northern Australia, is comparatively harmless, although it grows to a length of seven meters. It has been known to attack humans and, more frequently, livestock. No matter how inviting the river or pool, and no matter how tantalizing the prospect of diving into its limpid depths, if there are crocodile warning signs, *always* resist the temptation to swim there. Most victims of crocodile attacks have ignored the warnings. It is worth going out of your way to see these magnificent creatures, but always treat them with the greatest respect and give them a wide berth!

Australian **lizards** are harmless to humans, but you might not believe that when you look at them. The very size of the giant perentie (almost 2½ meters long) is enough to keep most of its foes at bay. The thorny or mountain devil dragon can change color to a limited extent and is covered with spines so sharp that no predator would contemplate eating it. The frill-necked lizard is another whose hiss is worse than its bite; when threatened, it unfurls a vividly colored ruff of membrane—making it appear much larger—and sways menacingly from side to side, spitting and hissing with gusto.

Giant leatherback **turtles** (one of Australia's dozen or so species of freshwater tortoise and five types of marine turtle) breed on some northern beaches, but they are under threat from driftnet fishing and suffocation from floating plastic bags that impersonate their favorite kind of jellyfish.

You can pick out 130 species of **frogs,** but no salamanders or newts. In the arid claypans where rains come only once every few years, some croakers survive by filling their bladders with water and burrowing into the mud just before it dries. There they coat their bodies with a mucilaginous secretion which seals in their juices for the next few years until rain falls again. In this way they might live for 40 years—unless they are dug up by Aborigines who use them as a source of fresh water.

INSECTS AND ARACHNIDS

Just as there are numerous bird species across Australia, there are some 50,000 insect species for them to feed on. These include 350 species of butterflies, 7,600 varieties of moths, and 18,000 types of beetles.

southern right whale

New insect species are discovered with almost monotonous regularity.

Australia's 9,000 kinds of ants make it the mecca for ant scientists around the world. In some arid areas of Western Australia, there are more ant species in one acre than there are in the rest of the world. The various types of flies will soon become all too familiar to visitors with no interest in natural history, as will the staggering array of mosquitoes, midges, and other biting mites. Native bees and wasps are present as are the generally larger and more vicious European varieties. And, if the human race were to die out, cockroaches are already established in Australia, poised to take take our place.

Thousands of spider species reside here—many of them large and hairy enough to feature in the most horrific Hollywood fantasy—but the only two which pose a threat to life and limb are the infamous red back and funnel web spiders. Popular mythology places the red back squarely under the seats of outdoor lavatories, and uneasy thoughts of tiny red spiders haunt many Australians' more intimate moments. Scientists tell us that only the female red back is venomous, but it is hard to tell the difference in a creature so tiny. The funnel web spider is the most toxic in the world and is confined to Sydney and its environs. Still, only six people in Australia have died from spider bites in the last 15 years.

The most ubiquitous, infuriating, and unsavory creature in the Australian biosphere is without a doubt the fly. This noisome insect-seeks out your moistest orifice and irritates you until you resort to the ridiculous contrivance of a hat fitted out with dangling corks. This will not work, and other people will laugh at you anyway, so resort instead to waving your hand constantly in front of your face, like everybody else. This is known as the Great Australian Salute.

MARINELIFE

Australia's seas are filled with such diversity and abundance that this topic deserves a book of its own. The first sea creature that most Aussies would think of is the **shark;** Australians love the beach and the danger of shark attack is instilled into all swimmers from a tender age. Consequently, the shark has been hunted mercilessly and undeservedly, without regard to the vital part it plays in the overall marine ecology, and now some species are threatened. The largest sharks inhabit southern waters, the home of the white pointer which starred in *Jaws.* The best place to ogle these monsters is Dangerous Reef (hence the name) on the eyre Peninsula. Smaller sharks are the staple fish in fish 'n' chips shops, where they are called "flake."

Swimmers should also beware of the deadly **box jellyfish,** which is most prevalent Oct.-May.

Most coastal areas of Australia are visited by **dolphins,** and surfers often tell of schools of dolphins frolicking with them while they surf. An isolated beach in Western Australia called Monkey Mia has become quite famous for the intimacy of its regularly visiting dolphins. Humans flock to this remote spot in such droves that there is a danger of the dolphins being frightened away or getting sick from too much human contact.

Fishing addicts, don't worry that Australia's aridity will prevent you from finding a catch of the day (or year). Whether your taste runs to game fishing à la Hemingway or dropping a line off the end of a pier, a fish waits for you! Surfing beaches usually provide space enough for surf fishing, and the reefs, bays, estuaries, and Outback rivers and pools are full of fish. Among the most sought-after catches is the barramundi in northern Australia; abalone, crayfish, oysters, and prawns are also delicious and lucrative resources.

HISTORY

FIRST SETTLERS

Contrary to the assertion of most Australian school textbooks before 1980, Australia was not discovered by Europeans, and certainly not by the intrepid Captain Cook. Australia's first settlers were the Aborigines, who arrived from Asia at least 40,000 years ago, and possibly as much as 100,000 years ago.

At that time the sea levels were very much lower than they are today, and the Australian landmass was connected to Papua New Guinea in the north and Tasmania in the south. Nevertheless, the water distance separating what was then Asia from this extended Australian continent was 100 km at its very shortest. The sea journey necessary to reach and colonize Australia was a remarkable achievement, especially when you consider that early Europeans had not yet reached some Mediterranean islands where the distances involved were a lot shorter. Aborigines had arrived and populated the entire continent millennia before the great expansionary movements of either the Europeans or the Polynesians.

At least 1,800 generations of Aborigines have lived in Australia with a simple but appropriate technology—a stark contrast to the eight or nine generations of Europeans with their highly inappropriate mechanical and agricultural technologies.

Early Aboriginal Society

Much of the archaeological evidence revealing Aboriginal history comes from places like Lake Mungo in southwest New South Wales. Sites like this are natural treasures because their remoteness and aridity has left the fossil record undisturbed. Lake Mungo used to lie on the edge of a vast inland sea, even at the time of the earliest Aboriginal relics, and huge piles of discarded bones and seashells (known as "middens") found there provide a fairly detailed peek into the daily life of the Aborigines.

Aborigines dwelt in hunter-gatherer societies, following the kangaroos, wallabies, goannas, and fish and collecting "bush food" like witchety grubs, roots, seeds, honey, nuts, and berries as they went. Conditions in Australia seem to have been so favorable, and the bounties of nature so prolific, that Aborigines never developed permanent agricultural settlements as their cousins in Papua New Guinea did. Their main tools were three types of boomerang, spears, sharpened stones for digging and shaping wood, and a spear-thrower called a woomera, which can propel a spear 120 meters or more. Nets, traps, and hooks were used for fishing. Controlled fires were started to flush game and, it has been suggested, as a land-management practice, since some forests have adapted to periodic bush fires. The remnants of elaborate stone weirs designed to trap fish can be seen in parts of Victoria and New South Wales.

Parts of Australia contain the harshest and most inhospitable environments on the planet, yet the Aborigines developed an affinity with the land which is a testament to their knowledge and skill. As recently as the mid-1980s, an Aboriginal family arrived at a remote Outback station, never before having had contact with whites. Their only possessions were two

THE EDIBLE DESERT

These notes (provided by the Northern Territory Conservation Commission) are a brief introduction to the traditional lifestyle and bush foods of central Australian Aborigines.

You should not eat any bush foods unless they have been positively identified as being edible. The desert areas contain many poisonous plants, some of which look just like their edible relatives.

Aboriginal Lifestyle

Aborigines have survived the harsh conditions of semiarid and desert lands for thousands of years. The secret of their survival lies in their detailed knowledge of the plants, animals, and water sources available in the country.

The women and children gathered fruits, roots, witchety grubs, and small animals, while the men hunted larger game such as kangaroos and emus. Many of the traditional foods are still collected and eaten today.

Water

Knowledge of all available water sources is passed down from old to young. Water is not only found in local waterholes and under the dry surface of creekbeds, but also in a variety of plants and certain animals. The succulent leaves of the parakeelya plant can be eaten in time of emergency. The graceful desert oak tree holds a secret store of water in its roots and in hidden hollows amongst its upper branches.

cyclorana

The water-holding frog, ***cyclorana,*** burrows beneath the ground with an abdomen full of water and waits for the next heavy rains to fall. With their detailed knowledge of the land, the Aborigines can dig these frogs from their burrows and squeeze them for a thirst-quenching drink.

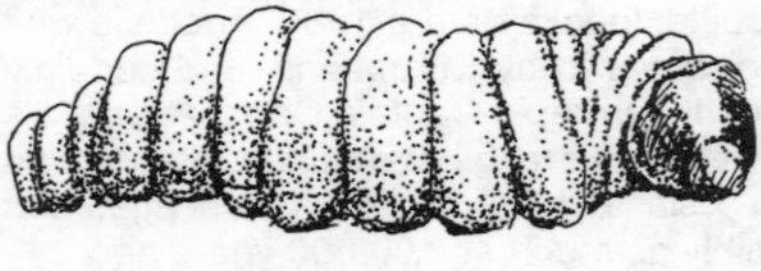

witchety grub

Protein

Witchety grubs live in the roots of certain acacia bushes. These grubs, the juvenile stage of a large moth, contain large amounts of protein and fat, and can be eaten either raw or cooked. When roasted, the grub has a pleasant nutty flavour.

Both the ***perentie*** and its eggs are valuable sources of protein. The perentie is roasted whole in hot coals with the eggs, which are pierced to remove the whites before cooking.

Flour

The seeds of the ***woollybut*** grass and ***hakea*** tree are just two of the many seeds that can be mixed with water to make damper or seed

2/BOB RACE

stone knives, two rubbing sticks to make fire, a container of dried worms, a boomerang, a spear, a woomera, and a dingo.

In contrast, automobile clubs today advise travelers in the same terrain to carry the following equipment in their 4WD vehicles: long-range fuel tanks, water tanks, food for twice the expected stay, two spare wheels and tires, spare battery, tools, medicine, cooking gear, mosquito nets, blankets, maps, compass, and a radio!

Long before Captain Cook sailed into Botany Bay and formally "took possession" of their land on behalf of the British Crown,

THE EDIBLE DESERT (CONT.)

hakea

cake. The seeds are dehusked, ground, mixed with water, and then baked on hot coals. The result is a highly nutritious seed cake.

Fruits And Vegetables
The arid lands of central Australia provide an abundant supply of native fruits. The ***ruby saltbush*** bears a small red berry that can be eaten. The yellow ***bush tomato*** is very high in vitamin C and can be dried and stored for long periods. ***Bush onions*** can be peeled and roasted on hot coals before being eaten, perhaps with seed cake or witchety grubs.

Honey
There are many sources of honey in the bush. The tiny lac scale insects that live on the branches of the ***mulga tree*** appear as red bumps that exude sweet sticky honeydew. The dew is usually sucked directly from the mulga branch.

The flowers of the ***honey grevillea*** produce quantities of sweet nectar, which can be sucked straight from the flower or mixed with water in a mimpu (wooden bowl) to make a sweet drink.

A different source of honey comes from ***honey ants.*** These ants live in nests several meters underground and have honey-filled abdomens the size of small grapes. The honey can be eaten by biting off the honey pot or by mixing the whole ant with flour to make a sweet damper.

there were 700 Aboriginal tribal groups using some 300 different languages. Their population then is estimated at anywhere up to a million people, distributed in subgroups of up to 40. By that time theirs was an ancient complex culture, rich and finely turned to their environment. Like their American Indian counterparts, the Aborigines lived in a spiritual communion with the land. Concepts of land ownership (like that icon of European social order—the fence) implicit in Captain Cook's first act of possession, are alien to Aborigines; "We don't own the land," says Aboriginal poet Oodgeroo. "The land owns us."

European Contact

Like white Americans, European Australians have historically accorded the native culture and heritage little or no value. This attitude was encapsulated in the earliest recorded commentary on the Aborigines by a European, the gentleman pirate William Dampier, when he wrote in 1688: "The Inhabitants of this country are the Miserablest People in the World . . . they are long visaged and of very unpleasing Aspect, having no one graceful Feature in their Faces."

The balance and harmony that Aborigines had developed and refined in their world was doomed to destruction with the first contact with land-owning Europeans who quickly "pioneered" beyond their first few coastal settlements. But the dispossession of the Aborigines came with brutal suddenness and more from epidemics of introduced diseases to which they had no immunity than from gunfire and violence. Aborigines died by the thousands from smallpox, sexually transmitted diseases, tuberculosis, measles, and influenza, all of which spread rapidly through the nonresistant native community. In addition there was a policy of "dispersal," in which Aborigines were cynically cleared like any other pest from areas valuable to the pastoralists—a sickening practice tantamount to massacre. Aborigines were even hunted "for sport" as recently as the 1950s in isolated parts of Australia.

The "tourist walk" up Ayers Rock—bet the Aborigines never dreamed up this *sight!*

The Tasmanian example illustrates the deliberate policy of genocide instigated by the invading Europeans. Aborigines were either killed or simply rounded up and shipped to small island colonies "for their protection," where they died of disease, malnutrition, and mistreatment. Tasmania's Aboriginal population declined from an estimated 4,000 to fewer than 500 between 1800 and 1830. By 1847 only 40 remained.

Truganini, the last Tasmanian, died in 1876. Her body was preserved and displayed in a museum. Hers was not the only body to receive such ignominious treatment. Scientists in the learned universities of Europe were excited by the search for a "missing link" to demonstrate Darwin's novel theories of evolution, and thought that the Tasmanian Aborigines might prove to be that link. Bodies were purloined from burial sites to enhance the collections of anthropological faculties from Dublin to Leipzig. In 1803, the governor of New South Wales presented the preserved head of the Aboriginal warrior Pemulwoy to botanist Sir Joseph Banks, who wrote that the head "caused some comical consequences when opened at the Customs House but when brought home was very acceptable to our anthropological collections." Today, the remains of some 3,000 Aborigines, together with objects of immense cultural value, lie moldering in British museums; Aboriginal groups have been negotiating for some time, with little success, to retrieve these bodies for proper burial.

Not everybody contributed to this genocide; there were well-meaning, sometimes enlightened, but usually ineffectual efforts to help. Reservations were created, rations issued, and religious missions established, many of which are still the focus of Aboriginal settlements today. However, by the beginning of the 20th century, most Aborigines were beggars in their own country, dependant on handouts of food and clothing (without which they were not allowed in the white man's towns), or working for white bosses without pay. (Recently I saw a newspaper photo of several Aboriginal entertainers on tour in America. Posing in costume—i.e., nearly naked—they were being presented with brand new suitcases!)

White society, if it thought at all about Aborigines, took a paternalistic approach which resulted in legislation aimed at the "benevolent" protection of an inferior race for its own good. Aborigines were under the control of official guardians in the bureaucracy until very recent times. Children were sometimes taken from their families to be raised within the "civilizing" influence of urban, Christian folk. A form of segregation, with limits to movement, property restrictions, separate employment conditions, and regulated marriage has existed in different forms from state to state until the last few decades. In fact, the infamous South African apartheid laws grew in part from the observations of a delegation to Queensland (where the treatment of Aborigines was at its worst) early this century.

Up until 1939, official policy was still predicated upon the inhuman thesis that the Aborigines were a self-solving problem, meaning that they would eventually die out. It was not until 1967 that Aborigines were granted the vote. Australians are traditionally suspicious of attempts to alter the constitution by referendum, and most referenda fail. It is to Australia's credit that one of the very few to succeed was this landmark 1967 vote to grant Aborigines the same status as the rest of the community. Too bad it had to take so long. The full horror of the dispossession of the Aborigines is difficult for many Australians to grasp, and there is still an enormous gulf that separates the lives of white Australians from the ugly realities that Aborigines are laboring under even today.

ABORIGINES TODAY

Why change our sacred myths for your sacred myths?

—Oodgeroo

Of the 17 million people who live in Australia today, fewer than one percent are Aborigines. Most Australians seldom ever see an Aborigine, but political pressure from Aboriginal groups means that they are no longer psychologically invisible. Issues like land rights, unlawful discrimination, and Aboriginal deaths in custody are much more likely to gain media attention today than just 10 years ago. Hand in hand with increased political struggle is a renaissance of Aboriginal identity through art, dance, and music. The 1988 Bicentennial celebrations, which marked two hundred years since the establishment of the first penal colony, saw protests and demonstrations from highly visible and vocal Aboriginal groups, who tried to point out that the country was a bit older than that.

The largest population of Aborigines (about 40,000) is in the Northern Territory where the first land-rights legislation returned some lands to their traditional owners, who are organized into land councils. Altogether there are some 300 Aboriginal reserves totaling about 286,000 square kilometers. Advances on the land-rights issue are slow but have gained momentum in the past 10 years.

Other issues are not proceeding quite as well. In most states, Aborigines make up 25-40% of prison populations, while infant mortality is twice the national average among Aborigines. In Queensland, 50% of the inmates in youth-detention centers are Aboriginal. Aboriginal children are affected by serious diseases like trachoma and hepatitis B at rates well above the national average. Aborigines are still more vulnerable to sexually transmitted disease, and have a life expectancy 20 years below the national average.

Unemployment among Aborigines is four times the national average. Access to education and health services in remote areas, where most Aborigines live, is minimal. Racial discrimination, while outlawed theoretically, is a constant reality for many Aborigines. Under these demoralizing conditions many are vulnerable to alcohol abuse, or worse, petrol-sniffing.

Recently a treaty has been proposed to finally acknowledge original ownership of the land by Aborigines. (Nothing of the kind was ever done in the past; Europeans, exercising a finders-keepers mentality, simply took what they wanted with no regard for the First Inhabitants.) It is a powerful idea that would, its proponents say, dramatically alter the relationship of all Australians to Australia, and put Aborigines in their rightful place in the common culture that has developed over the last 200 years. But then, it's *still* just an idea.

EUROPEAN SETTLEMENT

The concept of a large landmass in the Southern Ocean was proposed by the ancient Greeks, who were quite comfortable with the notion that the earth was round and who felt—without any concrete evidence—that a southern continent was necessary to preserve the earth's equilibrium. In the 2nd century A.D., the mathmatician Ptolemy mapped an area he called "Terra Incognita," the Unknown Land. It was not until the great age of European exploration more than a thousand years later that these intuitions were confirmed. Following the sea routes opened up by Magellan and Diaz, who

ABORIGINAL LEGENDS: THE DREAMTIME

Aborigines were explaining their existence by telling stories about the land and animals around them long before the ancient Egyptians built the pyramids. Cave paintings of animals and spirits here are at least as old as the earliest example of European cave art. The paintings and stories tell how the great spirits made the land, animals, and plants, and how they taught the people to find food, perform ceremonies, dance, sing, paint, and keep the laws.

Aboriginal thought is inductive; that is, general principles and laws are inferred from particular instances. Cause and effect have a more fluid relationship than Europeans are used to. Aboriginal spiritual mythology is totemic and is incorporated into the Dreamtime, a spiritual experience that extends into a vague and indefinite past—one which cements the deep spiritual connection between the land, Aborigines, and all living creatures.

In the Dreamtime, animal spirits existed in human form, eventually turning into the various animals we know today as kangaroo, snake, and so forth, while the spirits of their human descendants remain totemically related to them. To the Aborigine, the Dreamtime is not simply an ancient past, however, but a continuing present that is acknowledged, honored, and fortified with ritual.

Family groups or individual Aborigines have their own Dreaming, which can be a particular plant, animal, place, or natural force. Significant places where Dreamtime spirits lived or played out their destiny are marked by physical formations such as rocks, waterholes, trees, or the shape of the land. These are sacred sites, and recently some of these places have been protected from mining or other development by legislation.

An Aboriginal leader, Pat Dodson, describes the Dreaming this way:

> Our dreaming in this country travels thousands of kilometres. It comes from the sea in the north to Uluru in the centre, and it spreads out in all directions, east, north, south and west. We relate to other people through the Dreaming tracks which form paths among the sacred places, and there is not just one Dreaming line, there are many.

The complexity of the Dreamtime for most non-Aborigines is not simply that it is obscure. Many aspects of the culture are accessible only by initiation, and taboos forbid some ceremonial and spiritual practices to be even discussed. Men and women often have separate and exclusive ceremonies.

entered the Pacific while exploring South America, Portuguese navigator Cristoval de Mendonca made an unauthorized trip to map much of the north and east coasts of Australia before 1536. This expedition violated the treaty between Spain and Portugal which gave Spain all the lands west of Brazil, and so the discovery was kept hush-hush; no European saw the east coast until Cook's expedition 240 years later.

As early as 1606, the Spanish navigator Torres, approaching from the east around southern Africa, sailed through the straits that bear his name and separate Australia from Papua New Guinea. Willem Janzoon followed in the same year and entered the Gulf of Carpentaria. Seventeen years later, Jan Carstensz followed Janzoon's route and mapped the western coast of Cape York. In 1642, the Dutch almost completed the coastal surveillance of Australia when Abel Tasman circumnavigated Tasmania. He called it "Van Diemen's Land," but could see little potential for the mercantile interests which he largely represented.

By the end of the 17th century, the Dutch had poked about every part of Australia but the east coast. This was partly because they caught the prevailing westerlies as they rounded Cape Horn in Africa which would sweep them on to the lucrative markets in the East Indies; many of the Europeans who

ABORIGINAL LEGENDS: THE DREAMTIME (CONT.)

Non-Aborigines often can only guess at the real significance and experience that underlies the Dreamtime stories. Here is a world where giant marsupials carve out the hills, the hills themselves are age-old marsupials frozen in moments of significance, the rivers are the tracks of the rainbow serpent, and the Milky Way is the river of the sky where, after the rainbow serpent has swallowed the sun, people fish for stingrays and turtles, and the stars are their campfires.

The Southern Cross is an especially significant constellation for all Australians. One Dreamtime myth gives this account of its creation: A father had four daughters. When he was old, he told his daughters that they had no one else to protect them and that when he died they might have to marry men they did not like. They agreed to meet him in the sky after he was dead. With the aid of a sorcerer, he spun a silver rope from the strands of his hair, and when he died, his four daughters climbed the rope to take up their positions as the four bright points of the Southern Cross. Their father is the brightest of the nearby pointers, Alpha Centauri, still watching over them.

The spiritual inter-connectedness of all living things is very powerful for Aborigines. For example, among some central Australian tribes, the Kadaitja, an elder sorcerer who wears boots of emu feathers which leave no tracks, enforces the decisions of the community. He has only to take a certain bone and point it at a miscreant to punish him. "Pointing the bone" will cause an offender to withdraw from the tribe, pine away, and eventually die. In other examples, certain painted images are invested with such power that their misuse can result in the deaths of those to whom the paintings are sacred. Disputes have arisen as recently as 1989, when some sacrosanct tribal designs were incorporated in the decor of the new Parliament in Canberra, resulting in—if not pointing the bone—at least pointing the finger.

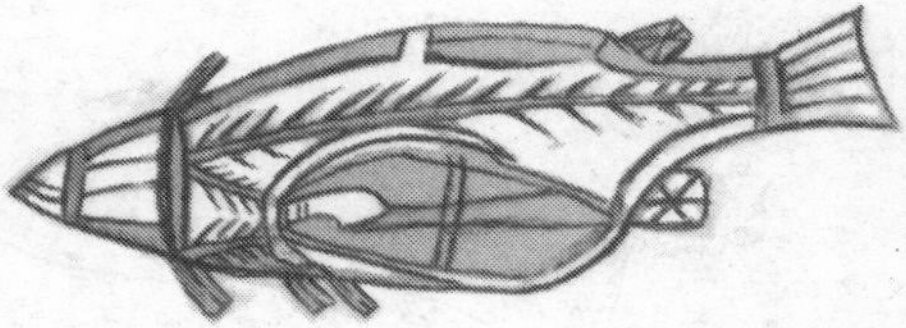

BOB RACE

found their way to Australia had simply overshot their mark on the way to the Spice Islands in the north.

The first Englishman to visit Australia, William Dampier, landed near King Sound on the northwest coast in 1688 with a rather disreputable company who had lost their way and needed to effect repairs. He was so unimpressed with the desolate country that he could see no good reason to return or to encourage his countrymen to do so.

It was not until 70 years later that the celebrated navigator Captain James Cook visited Australia and dragged it into the modern world. Cook had been sent to the South Pacific primarily to make astronomical observations of a transit of Venus and, while he was about it, to explore a region which was receiving more and more attention from the great powers of the day. After accomplishing his scientific mission, he returned, circumnavigating New Zealand; on 20 April 1770, he sighted the southeast coast of Australia. He turned north and charted the length of the east coast. His first landfall was "a fine bay," which Cook later called "Botany Bay" because of the numerous botanical specimens they were able to collect there.

Cook continued north for 3,000 km until his ship *Endeavor* ran aground on a coral reef near what is now Cooktown in north Queensland. It took his crew two months to repair the

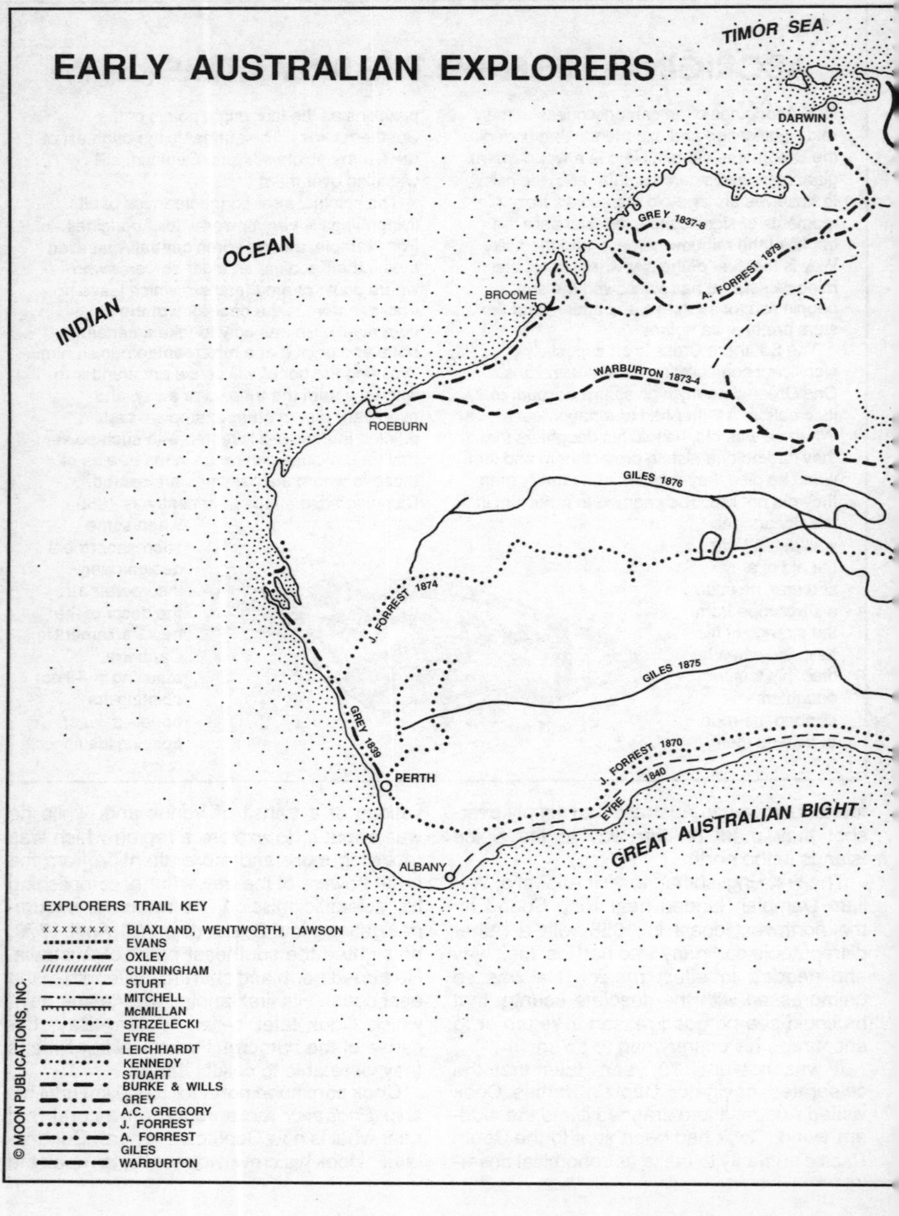
EARLY AUSTRALIAN EXPLORERS
TIMOR SEA
DARWIN
GREY 1837-8
A. FORREST 1879
OCEAN
INDIAN
BROOME
WARBURTON 1873-4
ROEBURN
GILES 1876
J. FORREST 1874
GILES 1875
GREY 1839
PERTH
J. FORREST 1870
EYRE 1840
GREAT AUSTRALIAN BIGHT
ALBANY
EXPLORERS TRAIL KEY
BLAXLAND, WENTWORTH, LAWSON
EVANS
OXLEY
CUNNINGHAM
STURT
MITCHELL
McMILLAN
STRZELECKI
EYRE
LEICHHARDT
KENNEDY
STUART
BURKE & WILLS
GREY
A.C. GREGORY
J. FORREST
A. FORREST
GILES
WARBURTON
© MOON PUBLICATIONS, INC.

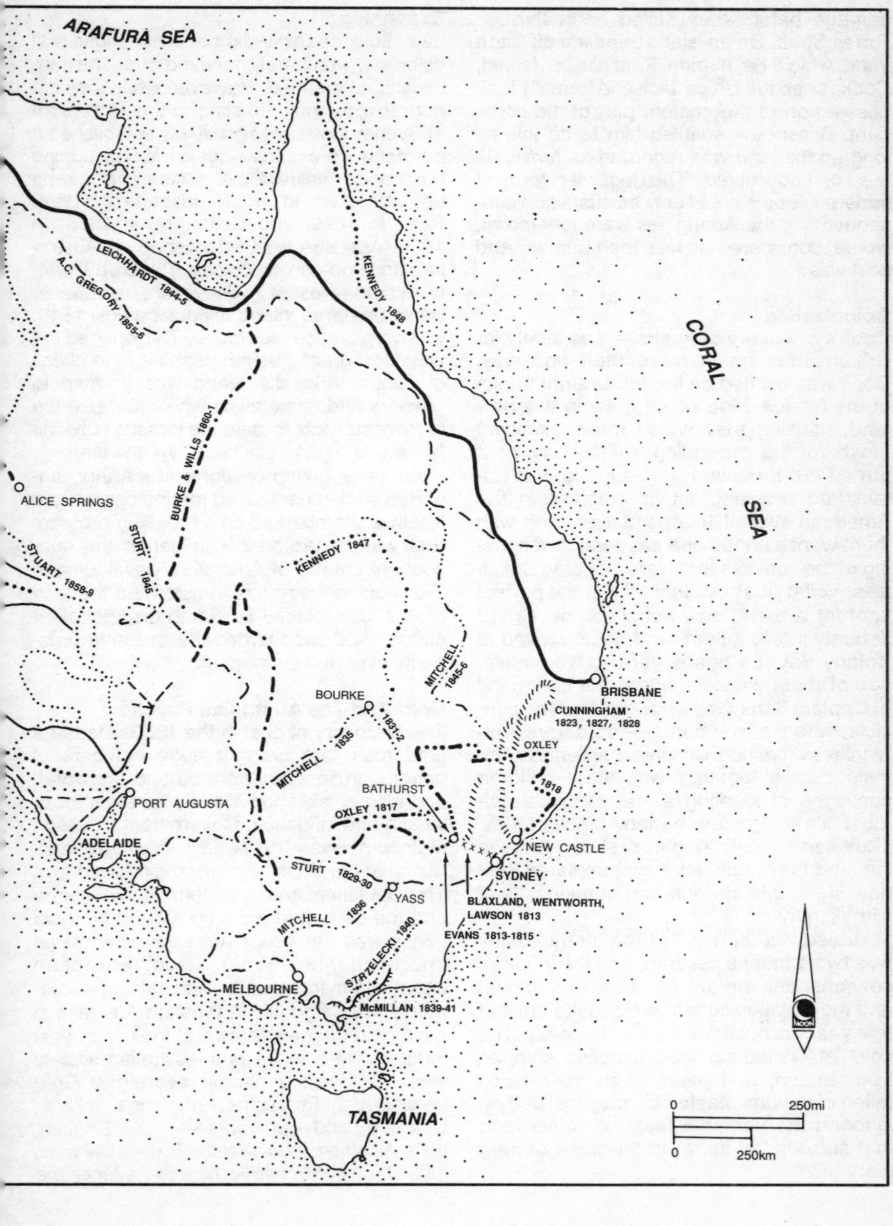
ARAFURA SEA
CORAL SEA
LEICHHARDT 1844-5
A.C. GREGORY 1855-6
KENNEDY 1848
BURKE & WILLS 1860-1
ALICE SPRINGS
STUART 1858-9
STURT 1845
KENNEDY 1847
MITCHELL 1845-6
BOURKE
1831-2
MITCHELL 1835
BRISBANE
CUNNINGHAM 1823, 1827, 1828
OXLEY 1818
BATHURST
OXLEY 1817
PORT AUGUSTA
ADELAIDE
STURT 1829-30
NEW CASTLE
SYDNEY
YASS
BLAXLAND, WENTWORTH, LAWSON 1813
MITCHELL 1836
STRZELECKI 1840
EVANS 1813-1815
MELBOURNE
McMILLAN 1839-41
TASMANIA
0 250mi
0 250km
MOON

damage before they sailed north through Torres Strait. On an island three km off Cape York, which he named Possession Island, Cook raised the Union Jack and formally took possession of the eastern part of the continent. British law enabled him to do this as long as the land was regarded as *terra nullius,* or unoccupied. This legalistic form of finders-keepers could only be sustained subsequently if the Aborigines were ignored or, worse, considered as less than human. And so it was.

Colonization

Cook's discovery of Australia was timely for British interests in more than one way. Cook was excited by the tall straight trunks of the Norfolk pine which grew in this new land, thinking they would make excellent masts for the expanding British navy. As it turned out they were not suitable, but Britain had recently lost its colonies in the American War of Independence, and with them went a cheap and easy way of disposing of the convicts that were clogging British jails. Voila! Australia looked like the perfect spot for a brand new penal colony. On 18 January 1788, a fleet of 11 ships arrived at Botany Bay; on board were 1,030 people, 736 of them convicts, under the command of Captain (later Governor) Phillip. The convicts were a mixed bunch—murderers, petty thieves, political radicals, hardened criminals thrown together with mere children convicted of stealing a loaf of bread—almost like things are in many places today. Their sentences varied from seven years to life, and they must have contemplated their new life in this strange and thankless land with dismay.

Indeed, the survival of the infant colony was by no means assured, and the inverted seasons, the unfamiliar flora and fauna, and the isolation conspired to make the first few years precarious to say the least. The colonists relied on food supplies shipped from Britain, and even when their crops failed in the unsuitable soil, they insisted on ignoring the veritable feast of native food that surrounded them, to the point of near starvation.

Expansion

Lady Luck certainly did not grace those first colonists, who barely survived from one supply ship to the next. However, while they did not prosper, they did cling to the settlement at Sydney Cove, and gradually established a permanent presence—not to mention upping the property value. Other settlements sprang up, at Hobart in 1803, Brisbane in 1824, Perth in 1829, and Melbourne in 1835. In 1836, Adelaide was established as Australia's first non-convict colony. The Blue Mountains to the west of Sydney were an impenetrable barrier to inland expansion until 1813, when a passage was found. This opened the way for a great western push into the plains of central Australia. Land was granted to graziers and pastoralists who could use the labor of convicts to clear the forests, build the fences, and generally "improve" the land.

An early governor, John MacArthur, imported some fine-fleeced merino sheep from Spain and embarked on a breeding program that was to profoundly influence the subsequent course of Australia's development. The wool industry has transformed the face of Australia, placed its stamp on Australia's culture, and shepherded the nation to prosperity over and over again.

Gold And The Australian Psyche

The discovery of gold in the 1850s started a gold rush that brought huge numbers of hopeful prospectors from around the world, and also established Victoria as a center of wealth and influence. Government House in Melbourne was the largest vice-regal residence in the British Empire (next to India's). The opulence and grandeur of Melbourne and the cities that grew up around the gold mines was the exuberant expression of an unprecedented boom. Great European opera stars traveled to wild mining settlements like Kalgoorlie in Western Australia to have gold nuggets thrown at their feet. Vast fortunes were made and Australian society was transformed almost overnight. Gold fever brought Prussians, Americans, Italians, Chinese, and—of course—more English, Irish, Scottish, and Welsh. Today, Darwin's mix of over 50 ethnic groups reflects the demographic wealth brought about by the gold rush. A tiny parochial society was inundated with intellectuals, merchants, entrepreneurs, professionals, artists, and adventurers ready to take advantage of new opportunities that seemed to be opening up everywhere.

As well as its economic and social consequences, the gold rush gave birth to a peculiarly Australian ethos, that of "mateship." In many other parts of the English-speaking world, "mate" means a marriage partner; in Australia it also means a friend, and as a form of address it carries an unspoken appeal to deep levels of devotion, loyalty, and affection that come from a tradition of interdependence that was born in the crucible of the goldfields. This fraternal tradition remains deeply entrenched in the Australian male psyche.

It was on the goldfields near Ballarat that the Eureka Stockade incident took place. As the easily extractable ore gave out, the "diggers" were forced to sink deeper and more expensive shafts. With gold harder to come by, the gold miners' license fee became the subject of outraged protest. The dispute between the miners and the government agents became so heated that a group of diggers who refused to pay the fee built a stockade at a place called Eureka, and fought government troops on 3 December 1854. Thirty diggers died and the incipient rebellion was put down, but the event remains significant as an expression of what author Thomas Keneally calls "that most Australian of birthrights, the Fair Go." This is a central concept for Australians, involving a sense of natural justice based on common sense, equality, and a healthy disregard for authority and ideology.

The Bushrangers

A passion for the "fair go" flows on as a sympathy for the underdog, the "battler." This accounts for the affection—almost reverence—rogues and outlaws command in the popular imagination, particularly the 19th-century bushrangers. The most famous of them was Ned Kelly, whose distinctive homemade helmet and suit of armor have become icons of Australian culture. Kelly came from an Irish family of small selectors—cockatoo farmers or "cockies"—whose frequent conflict with wealthy pastoralists or "squatters" and the authorities led them into a miniature revolt. After seeing their mother imprisoned and serving time themselves for uncommitted crimes, the Kelly brothers took to the bush and began a brief but spectacular career as bank robbers. Ned Kelly brazenly and single-handedly often captured entire townships for days at a time. His reputation grew until he was captured after a siege at Glenrowan in which he received 28 gunshot wounds. He was taken to Melbourne where, after a sensational trial, he was hanged. "Tell them I died game," he said, awaiting execution. On the gallows his last words summed up the battler's philosophy: "Such is life."

There were many other bushrangers—Bold Ben Hall, Mad Dog Morgan, John Cash (who was one of only a few to escape the infamous Port Arthur penal colony in Tasmania), Bogong Jack, Captain Moonlight—and it is interesting to note that much of the mythology that surrounds them concentrates on the unfair or treacherous circumstances of their capture and death. Traditionally, Australians have tolerated almost every kind of social aberration but they draw the line at the arbitrary exercise of power and privilege by the strong over the weak.

Social Reform

By the end of the 19th century the scene was set for further social upheaval. Labor was organizing itself and leading the world in a militant struggle for workers' rights. The Australian Labor Party was founded 100 years ago in 1891, and that same year a wave of strikes for better wages and conditions culminated in the famous shearers' strike, which was ruthlessly put down by the wealthy landowners who employed scabs or blacklegs to bring in the all-important wool clip (crop). Labor leaders were imprisoned, which led to the cry, "If they jail a man for striking, it's a rich man's country yet." If the cardinal virtue in Australia is Mateship, the two deadly sins are Scabbing and Dobbing—informing against one's mates.

On 1 January 1901, after a decade of debate and negotiation, the six Australian colonies were joined in a federation of states with the passage of the Constitution by the British Parliament. The new federal government met in Melbourne until the construction of a new capital, Canberra (designed by the fashionable architect Walter Burley Griffin) was completed in the '30s. Australia continued to pioneer policies of social reform that did not go unnoticed elsewhere in the world. For example, Australia was the first country to elect Labor representatives, and the first country to elect a Labor government. It was one of the first countries to grant women the vote.

These notable developments came to the attention of Lenin, who wrote a tract on the Australian Labor Party; his analysis was that it was a tool of the bourgeoisie. Nevertheless, a number of developments were enshrined in legislation in Australia long before they were achieved elsewhere. The old-age pension, the eight-hour workday, the right to strike—all these became realities in Australia when other nations would not even tolerate their advocacy.

While Australia achieved its independence from Britain without bloodshed, it has remained emotionally and psychically bound to the Mother Country even today, when talk of republicanism can cause fisticuffs on national television. Britain remained Australia's chief trading partner and military ally through two world wars. The decline of the British Empire and the emergence of the United States as a world power have meant merely that dependence has transferred from one to the other.

World Wars

The first world war brought with it the terrible scars that afflicted the generation that took part. Australia's first action was at Gallipoli in the Dardanelles, where, hopelessly outnumbered and outpositioned by a firmly entrenched Turkish army, thousands of young Australians were slaughtered. The incident was so profoundly shocking to a young nation that the sacrifice and suffering of those Anzacs (Australia and New Zealand Army Corps) has never been forgotten.

Perhaps the most moving story of that conflict concerns a young soldier, Simpson, who with his donkey rescued the injured and dying without regard for his own safety. Eventually he fell to a sniper's bullet, but Simpson and his donkey have an honored place in the national consciousness.

Australians went on to fight on the battlefields of Europe and, if nothing else, their experiences helped to open the eyes of an insular and isolated community to the wider world. This process was terribly gradual and, despite its proximity to Asia, Australia for years regarded itself as an outpost of the British Empire.

The '20s brought increased prosperity, largely through the export of primary produce. Refrigeration had made possible the shipment of frozen meat over the enormous distances necessary to reach markets in Europe; Australia was said to ride once again on the sheep's back. Unable to avoid the worldwide depression of the '30s, Australians suffered all the hardships that were familiar to people in America and Europe, and—with the outbreak of WW II—once again took up arms for king and country. This time, however, there was a direct threat from Japan and, while Australians fought in Europe and Africa, they also had to defend their own land. An air raid on Darwin by Japanese bombers created an unprecedented response and helped cement a military alliance with the United States that continues today. General Douglas MacArthur's proud boast that he would return to the Philippines was made possible in part by retreating and regrouping on the Australian mainland.

Changing Times

After the war, social change picked up tempo. A positive immigration drive replaced the infamous White Australia Policy, which had restricted entry to Australia largely to white Anglo-Saxons. Displaced refugees from Europe were recruited to come for a new start in the land of opportunity. For many, the realities did not measure up to the promise but nevertheless, ever-increasing numbers of Italians, Greeks, Yugoslavs, and peoples from a host of other countries began to make their presence felt.

It is often hard now for Australians to appreciate just how staid, unimaginative, and limited their society was only a few decades ago. In Melbourne 20 years ago, for example, no alcohol could be sold after six o'clock, which led to the degrading "six o'clock swill," as patrons rushed into hotels after work and downed as many beers as quickly as they could. "Wowserism," or puritanism, ensured that virtually no activity of any kind, bar church-going, could take place on Sunday. A combination of the influx of more sophisticated migrants and the liberating influence of the youth culture of the '60s has irreversibly transformed the face of Australian society over the past two or three decades.

During the same period, Australia's traditional allegiance to Britain became more and more irrelevant. Meanwhile, Britain has gradually divested itself of its colonial heritage and turned more and more toward a future in Europe. With Britain's entry into the Common Market, Australia lost automatic access to its traditional markets and was forced to face the reality of its location on the edge of Asia. The increasing numbers of European and, later, Asian migrants felt no sentimental attachment to the British institutions which had figured so largely in the minds of Anglo-Saxon Australians.

Finally, Australia's strategic position in the South Pacific brought it into the sphere of American influence. Since the 1950s, Australian troops have answered the call from Washington, not London, first in the Korean War and more disastrously in the Vietnam War. Australia's longest-serving prime minister, Sir Robert Menzies, once said of Queen Elizabeth, "I did but see her passing by, and yet I love her till I die," much to the dismay of independence-minded Australians. Nothing could better illustrate the dramatic shift in cultural focus that has taken place in Australia than the words of his successor, Harold Holt, at the height of the Vietnam War: "All the way with L.B.J."

AUSTRALIA TODAY

Australia describes itself as a multicultural society, and it is perhaps the most cosmopolitan society in the world, with almost one-quarter of its present population having been born elsewhere. The benefits of such a wide mix of peoples of various ethnic, cultural, and religious backgrounds are immense and, although the potential for social discord undoubtedly exists, somehow the friction that characterizes similarly heterogeneous communities has rarely occurred in Australia. Whether this is due to a tradition of easygoing tolerance, or to an ambience of apathy which infects all new arrivals, Australia's numerous ethnic communities have achieved a harmony that would be unthinkable in many parts of the world.

That is not to say that discrimination and prejudice do not exist, but most Australians have grown to appreciate the differences that succeeding waves of migrants bring to their society—from the novelty of new foods (Australia boasts a lot of good ethnic restaurants) to the challenge of learning new languages, customs, and ways of thinking.

It would be wrong to suggest that Australians are a race of Paul Hogans laconically tossing prawns onto barbies, or Greg Normans playing endless rounds of golf. Beneath the gloss of tourist promotions is a dark side—Australians consume more alcohol and pain killers per capita than does any other English-speaking country. Like other developed countries, Australia is plagued by recession, unemployment, a blowout of foreign debt, and pressing environmental degradation. Having a small population, and a tax base that is minuscule compared to that of larger industrialized countries, Australia is helpless in the face of international economic developments. For decades, the country has relied on the export of primary produce and now finds that its markets are increasingly unreliable, while prices are out of its control. A new drive to turn the "Lucky Country" into the "Clever Country" has been launched to stop the flight of its scientists and technicians to the universities and research companies of America and Europe, and at the same time develop the "sunrise" industries necessary for a high-technology future. New high-technology cities, or the "Multi-function Polis," are planned in partnership with the Japanese—the first having already been approved at a site near Adelaide.

Australians have developed a unique laissez-faire attitude, embodied in the expressions "no worries" and "she'll be right," and it seems difficult to rouse them to action. The advantage of this approach is that life in Australia is remarkably relaxed and stress-free, even in the cities. Violence and the social blight of drug abuse have not reached the heady heights that most Americans would consider normal. Access to a comfortable standard of living is easier in Australia than almost anywhere else on earth. The price for such a self-satisfied lifestyle is indolence, apathy, and procrastination, and Australians are only just beginning to realize how precarious their delightful existence is.

Australia is changing, and never more so than now. The past has forced Australians to be innovative and adaptable because of their extreme isolation. Air travel (which so many Australians helped to pioneer) and the information revolution have meant that Australia no longer must labor under the "tyranny of distance."

Despite its very real problems, there is still a refreshing overriding sense of optimism—a sense that "it will all come out in the wash." Even if the wash is dirty. (See also "History" under the Introduction to each state.)

GOVERNMENT

For a country of only 17 million people, Australia has an awful lot of government. It is a measure of Australians' political apathy that they have allowed themselves to become, according to some commentators, one of the most over-governed peoples in the free world. Australians labor under three tiers of government—federal, state, and shire or municipal. There are six state governments, two assemblies for the territories, and 900 local government bodies. All are accompanied by the appropriate bureaucracies, red tape, and seals of approval (or disapproval).

STRUCTURE

Australia follows the American example in the separation of powers, whereby the executive, legislative, and judiciary are independent. The federal government is an odd mix of the British Westminster system and the American congressional system. Australia's constitution is an Act of the British Parliament—passed in 1901—which provides for a House of Representatives, whose members are elected every three years, and an upper house, the Senate, whose function is to act as a house of review and provide equal representation for each state, thereby preserving state rights. The government is drawn from the majority in the House of Representatives and the prime minister is elected from within that majority. Mr. Paul Keating, former treasury minister, is the current prime minister of Australia.

The formal head of state is still the Queen of England, although her powers are invested in her representative, the governor-general, who is nominated by the Australian government of the day. Under the Australian Constitution, the governor-general is the chief executive, with the power to dissolve parliament, ratify legislation, appoint ministers of the government, command the armed forces, and appoint judges to the high court. Under an unwritten convention, the governor-general acts (in a mainly titular capacity) under the instructions and advice of the prime minister, as the queen does—but not always. Many Australians remember with outrage the events of 11 November 1975, when Governor-General Sir John Kerr dismissed the Labor government of Prime Minister Gough Whitlam. Whitlam was unable to pass supply bills (annual budget or money bills) through a hostile senate and the governor-general's intervention precipated a general election. The intricacies and implications of that decision still reverberate around the corridors of Parliament House and the case is still a hotly debated sore point for many Australians.

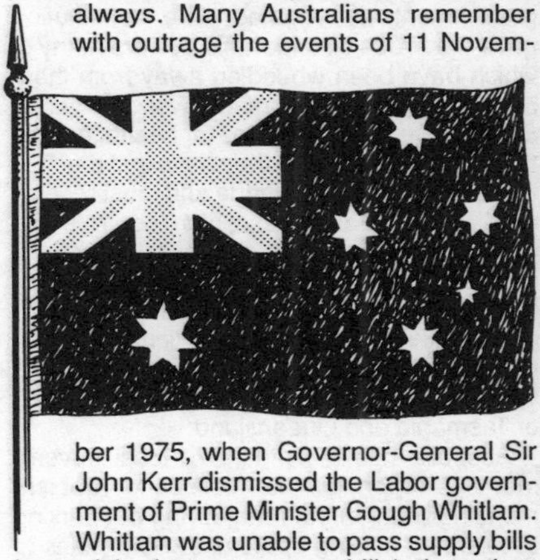

The Senate is made up of 10 senators from each state and two from each territory. Senators are elected for six years, but only half the Senate faces the electorate every three years. Because the popular mandate only affects those senators who stand for reelection, this has often led to the situation in which the House of Representatives faces a hostile Senate. The Senate, while theoretically a house of review, is able to block legislation—as it did in the crisis of 1975.

State governments are microcosms of the federal structure and are bicameral, with the exception of Queensland which disbanded its upper house as soon as it could. Numerous attempts in other states to follow that example have all been met with the in-built suspicion with which Australians treat politicians who start tinkering around with the system: it is axiomatic that politicians are not to be trusted, so if they want to do something it is much safer not to let them do it. Consequently, most states are lumbered with unwieldy edifices of government.

The struggle between the state and federal governments is ongoing. The constitution gave the states considerable powers many of which have been wheedled away from them by the federal government over the years. States have responsibilities for health, education, and transport, but they have lost much of their power to raise revenue and must receive grants from Canberra, which controls the power of taxation. The control of natural resources is under the jurisdiction of the states, but the federal government has used its powers to make foreign policy (particularly by entering the world Heritage Treaty) to block development in environmentally sensitive areas of Tasmania and Queensland.

Australia has a plethora of local governments, responsible for collecting rubbish, mending holes in the road, giving out parking tickets, and holding up homeowners' plans to renovate their kitchens. Councillors are mostly unpaid, except for the widely publicized case of the mayor of Brisbane who, it turned out, was earning more than the prime minister.

POLITICS

Parties

Australian politics has been effectively dominated for most of its history by a two-party system. The Labor Party has traditionally drawn its support from the union movement but in recent times has extended its base to white-collar workers and liberals. The Liberal Party, drawing its support traditionally from private enterprise, small business, and the professions, is the principal partner in a conservative coalition with the rural-based National Party. Recently, the Australian Democrats, a centrist party with a strong environmental platform, and various Green Independent parties, have made inroads into the two-party system. In 1990 the Democrats held the balance of power in the Senate, and Green Independents have formed a coalition with Labor in the Tasmanian State Parliament.

The push to make the final break with Britain and declare Australia a republic has recently intensified. It does seem inevitable that sooner or later the constitutional monarch will be replaced as head of state by an elected Australian. However, the movement to replace "God Save The Queen" with "Advance Australia Fair" as the national anthem was resisted stoutly by loyalists, and any attempt to remove the Union Jack from the Australian flag is met with ferocious opposition.

Voting

Because of the huge variations in population density across Australia, it has never been possible to achieve "one vote one value"; rural electorates can be quite enormous in area but still have fewer electors than inner-city seats, so there is an inevitable gerrymander that favors rural communities, traditionally the most conservative voting block.

Voting is mandatory for all citizens over 18; electors who fail to vote are liable for a fine. Voluntary voting was tried in the '20s, but the turnout was so abysmally low that it was abandoned. Voting is preferential and candidates on the ballot must be numbered in order of the elector's preference. This has made it necessary for political parties to produce "how to vote" cards and hand them out at polling booths, to instruct their supporters in the best manner of distributing their preferences. Some Senate ballot papers have had over 60 candidates, and voters have had to number each one for their vote to be valid. This system has given rise to the "donkey vote" in which a lazy, bored, or hurried voter will simply number the candidates in order down the page. So widespread did this practice become that it has decided the outcomes of several close ballots, and candidates with names at the beginning of the alphabet enjoyed such an advantage that they have been known to change their names to secure the donkey vote. To counter this practice, candidates' positions on the ballot are now determined by random selection.

International Relations

The Australian government is signatory to a number of international treaties including ANZUS, a joint-defense pact between Australia, New Zealand, and the United States. Recently, New Zealand was suspended from this arrangement because of its refusal to allow nuclear-armed ships into their ports. The United States maintains three top-secret military bases in Australia—at Pine Gap, the North West Cape, and Narungar. No rental is charged for these facilities (unlike U.S. bases in the Philippines), and while they are described as joint facilities, access for Australians is limited. Many Australians believe these bases are first-strike targets and have lobbied for their removal. The North West Cape facility is currently turned over to the Australians.

Australia is one of the senior members of the Commonwealth of Nations and has a long history of concerned involvement in international affairs through the United Nations and, more recently, the South Pacific Forum. Australia lays claim to the largest area of the Antarctic and has been instrumental in ensuring that Antarctic Treaty nations agree to prevent mining and damaging development of the continent. Australia has also campaigned vigorously against French nuclear testing in the Pacific and has gradually taken steps to enter into dialogue with its Asian neighbors, for example working dispassionately for a solution to the terrible problems that beset Cambodia. The good offices that Australia earned by being the first country to recognize the early '70s Peking government have been used to persuade the Chinese government to improve civil rights for its people. Similarly, in a pact ratified in 1991, ex-Prime Minister Bob Hawke recognized Timor's sovereignty and legitimacy as an Indonesian country.

ECONOMY

Australia entered the 20th century with an economy based largely on agriculture, more particularly, those divine and woolly sheep. There are still ten times as many "jumbucks" as people, and the Melbourne sheep sales are the biggest in the world, where a prize ram can fetch up to half a million dollars.

However, times are tough down on the farm these days, and not only because the world recession of the last few years has dragged Australia down with it. An international trade war is waging with disastrous consequences for the land of Oz. Australia's traditional markets are under increasing threat from subsidized produce from the warring trade blocks of Europe and the United States. Each cow in the European Community, for example, is subsidized by as much as a Third World farmer earns in a year. In August 1991, Australia's Foreign Minister, Senator Gareth Evans, described the sale of subsidized wheat by the United States to China and Yemen as "the act of a hostile nation." Extraordinary how the Europeans can achieve nuclear disarmament and pull down the Iron Curtain almost overnight but fail to dismantle the trade barriers that threaten to drive small free-trading countries like Australia into receivership!

Australia lobbied during the 1991 round of GATT (the General Agreement on Tariffs and Trade) talks in Uruguay for the removal of all agricultural trade barriers, and is allied in this endeavor with a number of free-trading nations—Canada, Argentina, and others—all primary producers striving for "a level playing field."

In a country where most of the population are city dwellers, and most of them wage and salary earners, the economy is the source of lively and usually well-informed debate. The booming '80s, which saw high-profile entrepreneurs shuffling worthless pieces of paper back and forth, have been replaced by the stark realities of the '90s. And in a country that boasts one of the highest levels of home ownership in the world, the disastrous legacy of soaring interest rates has become a national obsession. The pressure of international competition has inevitably eroded the hard-won conditions that a century of union activity had established; over 50% of the labor force belong to unions and industrial relations continue to be a thorny issue in Australian politics.

PRIMARY COMMODITIES

Almost 30% of the world's wool production comes from Australia (approximately 700,000 tons annually), which accounts for nearly 10% of Australia's export income. Unfortunately, the wool industry is facing its own crisis with world prices slumping below the cost of production.

Australia produces almost two million tons of meat products each year and is the world's largest exporter. Many of the cheap restaurant steaks in the United States are from Australian cows. Much of this beef comes from the huge Outback stations (ranches) in north and central Australia. The Anna Creek Station in South Australia is a measly 20,000 square km (12,000 square miles).

Other significant primary production includes dairy, sugar, fruit, fish, tobacco, cotton, and grain—especially wheat, about 15 million tons of which are exported annually. The down side of wheat production, however, is its environmental costs: increased soil salinity and the loss of precious topsoil. It's estimated that a ton of topsoil is lost for every ton of wheat harvested.

Wood Products

Forestry has become a contentious and divisive issue over the past decade. Three-quarters of Australia's native forests (mainly eucalypt forests, but significant areas of rainforest as well) have disappeared since the arrival of Europeans. Some of these forests have been destroyed by fire, but by far the

BOB RACE

An old mine attests to early settlers' interest in precious metals.

majority of forested areas has—as elsewhere—simply been logged. Plantation forests are usually pine, which offer no food or habitat to native bird and animal life. Logging in native forests and reserves, the "national estate," has been increasingly opposed by environmental groups on the grounds that such activities are unsustainable, and bitter disputes rage between Greenies and proponents of the timber industry, who see their jobs and livelihoods threatened. Much of the Australian hardwood forests still being harvested are not logged but chipped, and the resulting woodchip product is sold to Japan where there is a huge demand for paper. Some of the manufactured paper is sold to Australia. In case you're wondering why Australia hasn't established its own paper mills, it's because of resistance to the inevitable pollution they'd bring.

MINING

Australia has been mined for well over a century. Once the only mineral of any interest to the prospector was gold, gold, and more gold; this is still one of the principal targets of the mining industry, and gold miners have tax-exempt status. And there's still gold in them thar hills, pardner; every now and again some lucky fossicker stubs his toes on a nugget and sells it to a casino in Las Vegas for a million dollars.

Now miners have turned their attention to the host of other valuable minerals still underground. Prices fluctuate and mining has its booms and slumps, but the only check on mining activities for the past decade has been the combination of environmental and Aboriginal land rights issues.

Australia is the world's largest producer of bauxite, which is mined mostly in Cape York. The principal source of aluminum, bauxite is also a major player in the iron ore business, much of which is mined from the remote Pilbara region of Western Australia. Iron ore was the catapult that launched B.H.P. (Broken Hill Proprietary) on the path that has made it Australia's largest company and a multinational corporation. Australia has some of the world's largest reserves of brown coal, an energy source that becomes more significant as global supplies of oil are depleted. Like so many of Australia's raw materials, minerals are generally shipped offshore to the industrial powerhouses of Europe and Japan, there to be turned into consumer products like cars, television sets, and computers and sold back to Australia, aggravating the problems of foreign debt and balance of trade. After World War II, Australia enjoyed a 30:1 export advantage over Japan; today Japan securely holds the ball.

Australia is a major producer of copper, nickel, zinc, and the heavy mineral sands that contain titanium and zircon, minerals which are important in the development of new technology ceramics. These sands have traditionally been found and mined on the nation's beaches, and areas of pristine environmental importance have been ravaged in the past. Public pressure has resulted in the preservation of Fraser Island, Moreton Island, and other sensitive areas, while places like the Shelbourne Bay wilderness in Cape York, where mineral sands have been identified, are the subject of ongoing disputes.

Australia contains an estimated 25% of the world's known uranium ore. Current government policy is to allow three uranium mines to operate, and the raw "yellowcake" to be exported on the condition that it is used for peaceful purposes only. This is a dubious restriction when one buyer is the French government, which persists in a program of nuclear testing at Moruroa Atoll in the Pacific, at Australia's back door. Further exploration for uranium threatens parts of Kakadu National Park in the Northern Territory, where environmentalists and Aboriginal activists have joined to oppose development.

Other mining activities include extraction of lead, manganese, and most of the world's opals, the majority of which come from the underground township of Coober Pedy in South Australia.

ENERGY

Australia is ideally situated to take advantage of the development of solar energy; although progress in this field is slow, some five percent of Australian homes are equipped with solar hot-water units, and the figure is growing. In the Northern Territory and Western Australia, where cloudless days are as numerous as anywhere on earth, the figure is much higher. Locally developed silicon solar cells power remote railway crossings, and Telecom, the national telephone authority, has installed solar-powered telephones to service isolated communities in the Outback (as well as selling the phones to Saudi Arabia). Interest in solar power is strong in a land that is running low on traditional energy sources.

Most of Australia's energy requirements are still supplied by coal, which is also exported in the millions of tons, and Australia is roughly 60% self-sufficient in oil, from fields in Bass Strait and the proposed developments on the North West Shelf. However, the looming greenhouse effect from carbon gas emission is becoming more critical, even to the normally apathetic Australian public. Several neighboring nations in the South Pacific face the prospect of literally sinking beneath the waves should global warming cause sea levels to rise even a few feet. Australia has committed itself to reducing carbon dioxide emissions by 20% by the year 2000.

Substantial hydroelectric systems operate in Tasmania and the Snowy Mountains between New South Wales and Victoria, but it is unlikely that further development of this energy source will be acceptable to a public that, thankfully, is growing more environmentally aware. It was the planned flooding of the Gordon River for hydroelectricity that placed environmental issues firmly on the agenda of every political party in Australia in the early 1980s.

TOURISM

Respected travelers, *you* are the brightest stars in Australia's economic constellation. Over the past decade, tourism has boomed, driven by the success of Big Croc Dundee and an aggressive marketing campaign in which juicy shrimp were tossed on the barbies of Europe, Japan, and the United States. Tourism has consistently been the highest growth sector of the economy, and tourist bucks promise to be the country's largest source of foreign income. The setbacks of a crippling pilots' strike, which adversely affected many resorts in the late '80s, have now been largely overcome.

Australians are an amiable people and easygoing, but they've had to learn the rudiments of a service industry like tourism from the ground up. They have had to master the arts of commercial hospitality in a culture that does not readily distinguish between service and servility. Can you fault them if they don't do a kangaroo hop whenever a demanding tourist snaps his fingers? On the whole, tourists are treated with great openness and friendliness, and the keen interest that visitors generally take in Australia has boomeranged and turned the Aussies onto *themselves,* stimulating an interest in the natural wonders of their own country—wonders that had previously been taken for granted.

THE PEOPLE

Australia's population is estimated at 17 million, about the same as Texas. These millions are spread over a continent roughly the size of the United States, but they're concentrated along the east coast, and almost the entire population lives in six or seven cities. The breakdown for Outback regions is as follows: 1.4 million in South Australia; 150,000 in the Northern Territory; and 1.5 million in Western Australia. Aboriginals comprise about one percent of the total population, with the majority of them residing in the Northern Territory.

Australians are an urban people, despite their cherished image of themselves as a race of rugged individualists taming a savage wilderness. More specifically, they are a suburban people, having realized the Australian Dream (i.e., a home of one's own—preferably on a quarter-acre lot) more fully than any other Western society. Melbourne, a city of some three million, sprawls over an area the size of London, and most of that seems to be taken up by suburban backyards.

Australia has the world's newest people—one in three is a product of post-WW II migration, and one-quarter of the work force is foreign born. Waves of migration occurred in the 1850s, 1880s, early 1900s, and 1920s. The Great Depression and World War II restricted immigration and, a low birth rate made necessary a renewed migration drive in the 1950s. This campaign brought three million people to Australia between 1947 and 1974.

Before WW II, people of British and Irish origin made up 90% of all immigrants. That proportion has dropped rapidly since 1945 to less than 40% today. The scrapping of the White Australia Policy and Australia's humanitarian refugee program after the Vietnam War have seen a steady increase in Asian immigration. Hong Kong's reversion to China in 1997 is looming and many Chinese are looking to Australia as a possible new home. Other migrant groups to place their stamp on Australia since 1945 include Italians, Greeks (Melbourne is said to be the second-largest Greek city in the world, after Athens), Yugoslavs, Dutch, Germans, Lebanese, and Maltese.

Australia is an aging society. The combination of medical advances to prolong the average life expectancy, a falloff in the birth rate since the postwar baby boom, and an aggressive immigration program means that the average age is creeping higher each year. This has implications for the provision of welfare in the decades to come; a shrinking labor force (and, therefore, a shrinking tax base) will make it harder to provide pensions for the elderly. A government-led drive is underway to wean the young and middle-aged off the idea of a pension (which many anticipate will soon dwindle to insignificance) and encourage them to take out private superannuation insurance for their retirement.

RELIGION

To cast off the religion of the Aborigines in a paragraph or two (or a century or two) would be a real sacrilege; Australia's first inhabitants, in isolation, had a spirituality that was inseparable from their way of life. In a sense their religion was and is an all-encompassing experience in which their life, their tribe, the land, the plants and animals around them,

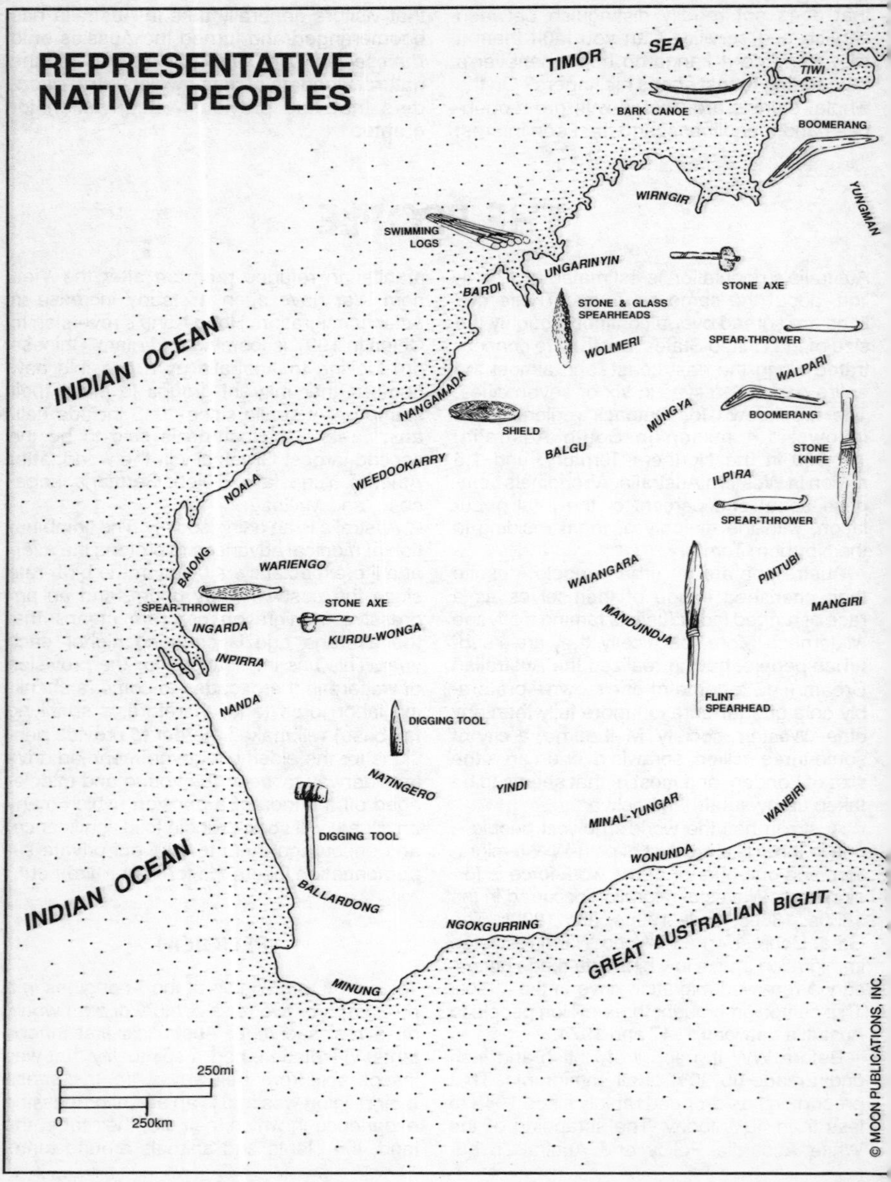
REPRESENTATIVE NATIVE PEOPLES
TIMOR SEA
TIWI
BARK CANOE
BOOMERANG
WIRNGIR
YUNGMAN
SWIMMING LOGS
UNGARINYIN
STONE AXE
BARDI
STONE & GLASS SPEARHEADS
INDIAN OCEAN
WOLMERI
SPEAR-THROWER
WALPARI
NANGAMADA
SHIELD
MUNGYA
BOOMERANG
STONE KNIFE
BALGU
WEEDOOKARRY
NOALA
ILPIRA
SPEAR-THROWER
BAIONG
WARIENGO
WAIANGARA
PINTUBI
SPEAR-THROWER
STONE AXE
MANGIRI
INGARDA
KURDU-WONGA
MANDJINDJA
INPIRRA
NANDA
FLINT SPEARHEAD
DIGGING TOOL
NATINGERO
YINDI
WANBIRI
MINAL-YUNGAR
DIGGING TOOL
WONUNDA
INDIAN OCEAN
BALLARDONG
GREAT AUSTRALIAN BIGHT
NGOKGURRING
MINUNG
0
250mi
0
250km
© MOON PUBLICATIONS, INC.

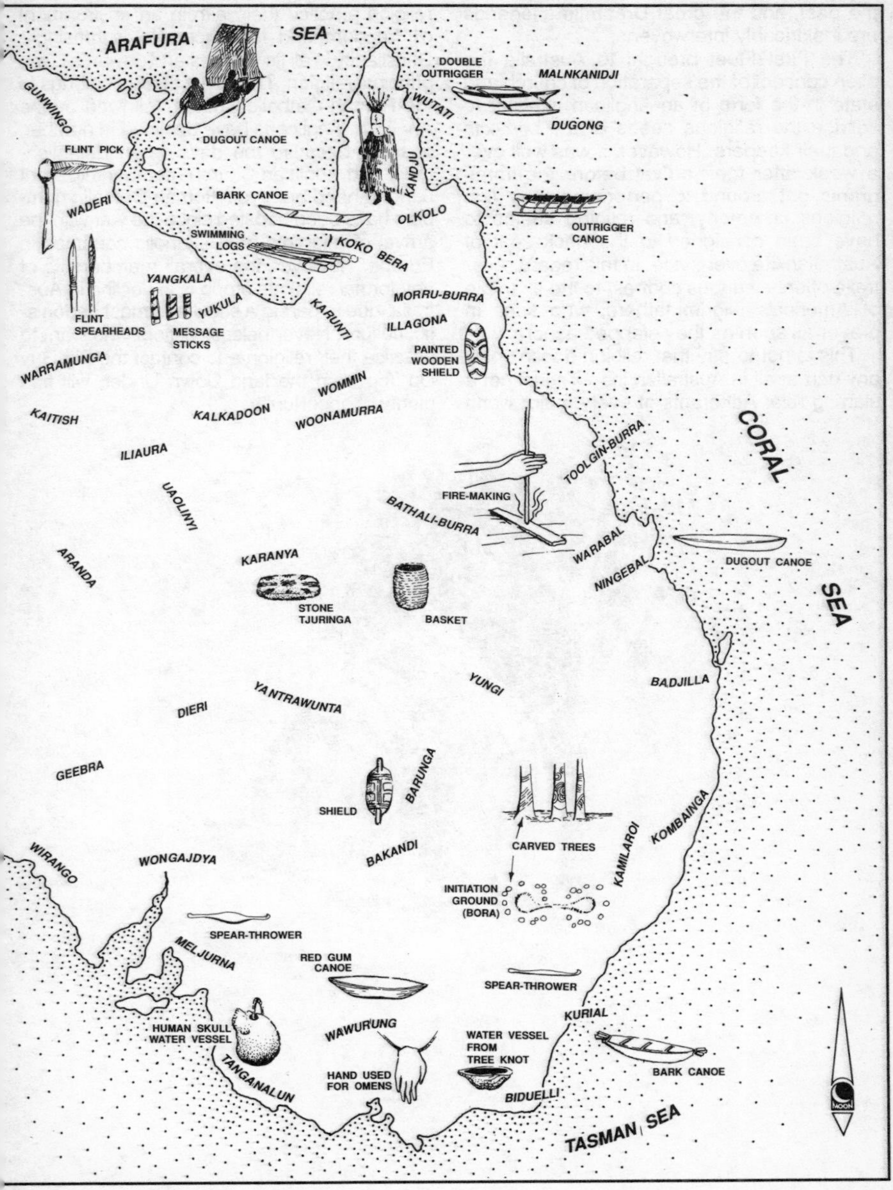
ARAFURA
SEA
GUNWINGO
DUGOUT CANOE
FLINT PICK
DOUBLE OUTRIGGER
MALNKANIDJI
WUTATI
DUGONG
KANDJU
WADERI
BARK CANOE
OLKOLO
OUTRIGGER CANOE
SWIMMING LOGS
KOKO BERA
YANGKALA
YUKULA
KARUNTI
MORRU-BURRA
ILLAGONA
FLINT SPEARHEADS
MESSAGE STICKS
PAINTED WOODEN SHIELD
WARRAMUNGA
WOMMIN
KAITISH
KALKADOON
WOONAMURRA
CORAL
TOOLGIN-BURRA
ILIAURA
UAOLINYI
FIRE-MAKING
BATHALI-BURRA
WARABAL
DUGOUT CANOE
ARANDA
KARANYA
NINGEBAL
SEA
STONE TJURINGA
BASKET
YUNGI
BADJILLA
YANTRAWUNTA
DIERI
GEEBRA
BARUNGA
SHIELD
CARVED TREES
KOMBAINGA
KAMILAROI
WIRANGO
WONGAJDYA
BAKANDI
INITIATION GROUND (BORA)
SPEAR-THROWER
MELJURNA
RED GUM CANOE
SPEAR-THROWER
KURIAL
HUMAN SKULL WATER VESSEL
WAWURUNG
WATER VESSEL FROM TREE KNOT
BARK CANOE
TANGANALUN
HAND USED FOR OMENS
BIDUELLI
TASMAN SEA
MOON

the past, and the great Dreamtime legends are inextricably interwoven.

The First Fleet brought to Australia the alien concept of the separation of church and state in the form of an Anglican minister to service the religious needs of the convicts and their keepers. However, it was well over a week after their arrival before the immigrants got around to performing their first religious ceremony, and religion seems to have been consigned to the back seat of Australian life ever since. In this regard, Australia offers a curious contrast to the example of America's pilgrim fathers, who knelt in prayer as soon as they stepped ashore.

This is not to say that religion doesn't play any part at all in Australian life—it's just not a starring role. Adherents of every major world religion practice their faith in an environment of freedom and tolerance. Not surprisingly, Christianity in all its variants and deviants is the principal religion. The largest group belongs to the Roman Catholic Church, followed by the Anglican. Anglicans have declined in number, possibly because the days when Establishment and Anglican Church membership went hand-in-hand are over. Roman Catholic numbers have been boosted since the war with the arrival of migrants from Catholic countries in Europe. However, the overall membership of any formal religious group is in decline in Australia, due in part to a secular, almost hedonistic, culture. Nevertheless, visitors who want to practice their religion and contact the Big Guy Up Top from the land Down Under, will find plenty of opportunity.

BOB RACE

LANGUAGE

English—sort of—is the predominant language spoken throughout Australia. Of course, that's aside from hundreds of Aboriginal languages and dozens of other languages spoken within various immigrant communities. As in other English-speaking countries around the world, Australians have developed a distinct accent and vocabulary.

One advantage to visitors is that regional variants are almost nonexistent, so if you can understand someone in Perth, you can understand someone in Cairns or Melbourne. Differences in both accent and idiom do exist, but they are very subtle. Class distinctions are more noticeable than regional ones; the upper middle classes affect a "plummier" accent closer to their English cousins, while the working classes are prone to exaggerate the idiosyncratic earthy tones that distinguish the Australian accent. However, even these distinctions are much less dramatic than those that Americans are used to amongst themselves.

However—be warned. The Australian accent can be tricky for American or British visitors, at least at first. Australians love to tell stories about their compatriots traveling overseas and failing to make themselves understood; tales of Australians trying to explain to bewildered American barmen that all they want is a beer, or British hotel receptionists calling for the house translator to cope with Australian tourists, are greeted with great hilarity.

One common misapprehension is that all Australians utilize a profusion of colorful idiomatic words and phrases, such as those that are regularly listed in travel books. Such words are well known to all Australians, but have a currency that may exist solely in the minds of the compilers of Australian slang dictionaries. Some Australians will live their whole lives without ever saying "fair dinkum" or "chunder," even though they know perfectly well what these terms mean. Treat such words with caution! People using them may be doing so facetiously or ironically. "Bastard," for example, may be the form of address for a dear personal friend, a complete stranger, or a mortal enemy, depending on the inflection and circumstances. "Mate" may be the cheery greeting of long-lost chums *or* the signal for a barroom brawl. With the proviso that these words are often the fossilized relics of an Australia that may never have existed, and that they can sound quite peculiar in an American accent, refer to this book's glossary.

Trans-Atlantic variations that exist between English and American usage often occur in Australia as well, where generally the English version is preferred. However, from being regularly bombarded by American film, music, and television, Australians are familiar with all things American, and most people will understand that when you say "cookie" you really mean biscuit, and so on.

In some parts of Australia a variant of the Cockney rhyming slang is used and this can lead to profound obscurity of meaning for the visitor. Often the rhyming part of the expression is left out altogether, which confounds the uninitiated even more. Examples are far too numerous to give more than a few of the most common and relevant instances:

Arra—Aristotle, bottle (of beer)
Captain Cook—a look
china—china plate, mate
rubbity—rubbity dub, pub
septic tank—Yank

If it seems from these examples that Australians talk about almost everything except alcohol and everyone except themselves in only the most insulting and derogatory terms, it is a function of the kind of language just discussed; for most Australians, the use of many of these expressions would be unthinkable. The visitor to Australia will find a language with its own unique flavor that is riddled with delightful idioms while remaining basically English.

ARTS AND CRAFTS

Australians have long been noted for a "cultural cringe," meaning they look to London and New York in matters of taste and style, slavishly following their lead. Although this attitude dies hard, Australians are making real advances in the creation of a national culture. Bolstered by the success of expatriates in all artistic endeavors (Dame Joan Sutherland, Nobel Laureate Patrick White, artist Sir Sydney Nolan—not to mention the Bee Gees and INXS), artsy Aussies are growing more confident and ready to take their work to the outside world.

Each state capital has its own symphony orchestra, opera company, ballet company, theater, and art gallery which are recipients of generous arts funding. Lovers of traditional Western artforms will be happily surprised at the high standards and support from a quite sophisticated public at the end of the earth.

Australia also is home to a lively "fringe" arts scene, mainly centered in the bohemian suburbs of Sydney, Melbourne, and Adelaide. Adelaide's Fringe Festival, which runs concurrently with the city's renowned and highbrow Festival of the Arts, honors the more avant-garde contibutions to theater, music, art, and literature. And while it isn't Times Square or Haight-Ashbury, the low-key local color can be a lot of fun. The cultural melting pot of Australia's cities has meant that artists no longer need to travel to Europe or America to eke out a penurious living in a squalid garret; they can do it here!

Aboriginal Art

Aboriginal art has its own aesthetics that reflect the profound experience of life in Australia. Recently "discovered" by the West, Aboriginal paintings can command substantial prices on the world market.

Most Aboriginal artforms are spiritually based and concerned with the myths and totemic beliefs of the Dreamtime. Painting on bark and more recently, canvas, Aboriginal artists employ a decorative dot technique which to Western eyes appears quite abstract, and even representational images of animals and spirits are painted in the style of an X-ray, revealing internal organs. These techniques are incredibly ancient, and extremely old examples are found on the walls of caves in Arnhem Land. Often the actual rendering of these works is accompanied by songs which instruct the artist in the progress of the work and invest him with spiritual power. The full significance of such works is sacred and available only to the initiated. Aborigines also craft exquisite implements, from the aerodynamically perfect boomerang to ceremonial belts and headdresses.

"Corroborees" are ceremonial dances accompanied by the unearthly music of the didgeridoo. Aboriginal dance is another resurgent artform, and new performances of established companies are eagerly awaited. It is possible to buy Aboriginal art from co-operatives run by local communities; these are often the best sources. Much of what is passed off as Aboriginal art in the cities is worthless imitation and souvenir schlock.

SHOPPING

Aside from Aboriginal arts and crafts, Oz is *not* shop-til-you-drop territory! I'm afraid it's basic and boring—malls, K marts, and a few chic international- and local-designer boutiques plunked about the major city centers. In all the cities and most smaller towns, you *will* be able to find everything you need, from flyscreens to condoms. The Outback, however, is another story—stock up on provisions before you start out. You'll find necessary and desired gear and clothing in most cities around Australia. Prices for most items are just a bit higher than in the U.S., but books and records are *much* more expensive. Either bring books with you or buy them secondhand.

A not-to-be-missed shopping experience is at the mostly outdoor, sometimes indoor markets held almost everywhere in the country. In Adelaide, the Central Market near Victoria Square is a prime example, as is Darwin's Big Flea Market, the city's oldest. These usually take place on weekends, though some city markets are open during the week. Depending on where you are and the type of market it is, you'll be able to pick up bargains on fruits and veggies, furniture, bric-a-brac, secondhand clothing, used tools and camping gear, and ubiquitous Asian imports like plastic fish and fake handcuffs.

Normal shopping hours are Mon.-Fri. 9-5, Sat. 9-noon. One night a week—usually Thursday or Friday—is often a designated "late shopping night" with doors staying open until 9 p.m. Darwin and Perth offer late-night shopping on Thursday; Adelaide's is Saturday.

ENTERTAINMENT

Like other Western industrialized nations, Australia is of course replete with the wonders of modern technology: television, films, popular music, and so on. Americans will find that much of their culture has preceded them and taken root to the point that Australia is beginning to export its own version of late-20th-century global techno-culture back to the United States. Filmmakers Peter Weir and Bruce Beresford and film stars Mel Gibson and Bryan Brown lead a coterie of expatriate Australian artists who have dazzled star-bright Hollywood. They learned their craft in the domestic Australian industry which, while offering entertainment with an Australian accent, leans heavily on the models provided in the United States.

However, this doesn't mean that visitors will only be entertained by copycats of American originals. Australia has a vital and dynamic music industry, centered on the pubs and clubs of Melbourne, but very much in evidence in the major cities and towns in the Outback. Hundreds of hopeful young musicians play nightly in every style you can name—and some you can't. Not long ago it was possible to see bands like Men at Work and the INXS playing in Melbourne's small suburban pubs, and you can bet the bands that play there now have big ambitions. Other cities have plenty to offer. Adelaide and Perth both have major international arts festivals (see "Holidays And Events").

Finally, Australia offers one superb entertainment that you won't see in the Northern Hemisphere—the brilliant glow of a million stars lighting up the unfamiliar constellations of a strange southern sky—an impossibly classy act to follow.

Gambling

Australians love to gamble. That's it in the proverbial nutshell. Care to bet? A huge industry has grown up around horse racing, harness racing (pacing or trotting), and greyhound racing. Billions of dollars are invested annually either with trackside bookmakers or off-course government-run Totalizators. Champion thoroughbred horses occupy as exalted a position in the galaxy of Australian sporting heroes as champion human athletes, and a racing subculture has long been established in which the uninitiated quickly find themselves lost in a strange land. The passion for horses culminates in the fabulous Melbourne Spring Carnival; the prized petunia of that meet is the Melbourne Cup, a race that few Australians fail to bet on—and a declared local holiday. But then, they will bet on almost *anything:* state lotteries, the poker machine clubs of New South Wales (which have grown rich on the gambling bug), and at casinos which—after years of opposition—are now springing up all over the country like mushrooms after the rain. Each of the three major cities in the Outback have their glitter-and-flash gambling meccas: the Adelaide Casino, Perth's Burswood Island Resort, and the Diamond Beach Hotel and Casino in Darwin.

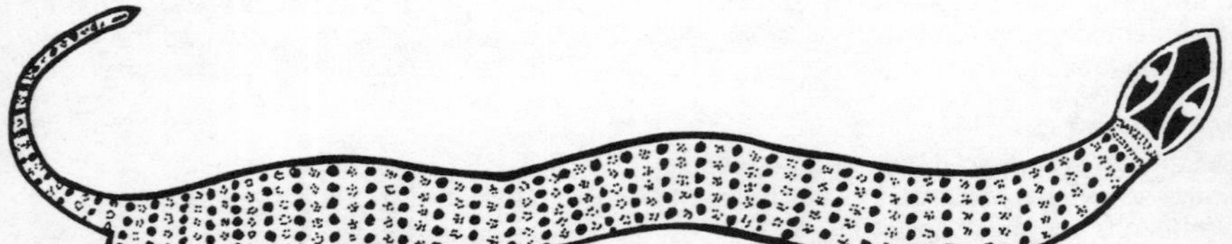

SPORTS AND RECREATION

Australians love sport. They love it so much that it's tempting to include this chapter under the "Religion" heading. They have a tradition of competitive sport that goes back to the earliest days of colonization, and they'll travel anywhere on earth if there's someone willing to play against them. Australia is one of the only countries to have been represented at every modern Olympiad, and the Olympic Games were held in Melbourne in 1956. At those games Australians won the third-most medals, an extraordinary feat for a nation with such a tiny population—yet that is a measure of how seriously Australians treat athletic achievement. Australian champions regularly crop up in sports as diverse as golf, tennis, weightlifting, squash, yachting, cycling, and swimming.

It cannot be emphasized too strongly that sport occupies a special, central place in the Australian mindset. A significant number of champion athletes enter public office after their sporting career is over and the former prime minister, Mr. Bob Hawke, is desperately interested in all sporting matters. Political leaders of all persuasions find it necessary to publicize their allegiance to particular sporting clubs, and personal appearances at matches are a prerequisite to a successful career in politics. The Grand Final of the Australian Football League in Melbourne drives all other news from the headlines for weeks beforehand. The Melbourne Cup is the occasion for a public holiday. Australians can name past or present world champions in almost every sport, a phenomenon that causes their chests to swell with pride, even though sporting involvement for many Australians is confined to watching their idols on the telly.

Watersports

Swimming is particularly important in a land where so much social activity takes place on the beach, and most Australian children are taught to swim very early. Let's face it—the country is filled with spectacular beaches. And, while the beaches are deserted and beautiful, the water may be dangerous. In surf areas, strong "rips" can sweep an unwary swimmer out to sea. Most popular beaches are patrolled by Surf Life Saving Clubs which post flags to indicate safe swimming areas. (Swim between the flags.) For specific recommendations for the Outback's virtually limitless swimming options, both coastal and freshwater, check the "Recreation" and "Sights" sections in the travel chapters.

Your author's first (and last) bull's-eye!

Once the Hawaiians introduced the surfboard to Australia, it was hang ten fever, and surfies soon made their own innovations to the clumsy Malibu, creating a generation of smaller, more maneuverable short boards. Superb surfing beaches surround the country, fronting the Pacific, Great Southern, and Indian oceans. And, like surfers almost everywhere, the Aussie variety has developed its own subculture, complete with fashion statements, lingo, morals, and surf-turf.

Australians are equally at home in boats, and the America's Cup created national heroes out of the team that wrested it briefly

NATIONAL PARK CODE

The National Parks and Wildlife Service asks you to follow a number of simple rules to protect both you and the parks.

Guard against fire. Use fireplaces where provided. Native timber is the home of small animals, so please preserve it by using a portable stove. No fires, including gas barbecues and stoves, may be lit when a fire ban is in force.

Do not disturb, collect, or damage animals, wildflowers, vegetation, earth or rock formations.

Do not disturb or collect artifacts from Aboriginal sites. Sites and items may have sacred, ceremonial, mythological, and historical significance to Aboriginal people, and have scientific value.

Firearms are not permitted.

Do not litter. Carry your rubbish out of the park when you leave, or use a litter bin.

Leave your pets at home. Dogs and cats are not allowed in parks, as they disturb both native animals and park visitors.

Drive carefully and observe all notices.

Use of registered off-road vehicles is restricted to existing designated roads and tracks.

Contact local rangers for camping permits and for information on local conditions for bushwalking.

from the grip of the New York Yacht Club. Most water-lovers have their sights set a bit lower than 12-meter racing, however, and are content to go fishing, skin diving, and water-skiing on the country's bountiful oceans, rivers, lakes, and streams.

Other Sports

The natural beauties of the Australian bush make bushwalking (or hiking) a popular activity for anyone who wants to see the wildlife up close. City, country, and Outback cycling is another favorite pursuit, and Australia has a history of producing champions in world competitions. Golf, tennis, horseback riding, hang gliding, even baseball all have their adherents and various Outback venues.

Spectator Sports

Australians love and excel at many competitive sports and flock in droves to watch their favorites. So important is sport in Australia that federal and state governments appoint quite senior ministers to Departments of Sport. The federal government sponsors a kind of athletic university in Canberra, called the Institute of Sport, where promising atheletes are coached. Tennis, golf, basketball, soccer, all are played and followed with keen interest, and the feats of champions are heralded on the television and analyzed in the press.

The most important game of all—and one which visitors must not miss—is Australian Rules football. Australian Rules (or footy) is the passion of all Australians except a few deadbeats who have lost their love of life. Developed on the goldfields of central Victoria well over a century ago, it is Australia's gift to the world.

Footy is an anarchic game, played with an oval ball on an oval pitch, with no offside rule—where the eternal verities of truth, courage, imagination, honor, and justice are acted out in front of an audience whose good taste and discernment are proverbial. Strongest in the cauldron of Melbourne, the game is currently in the throes of a titanic struggle to create a national league. Visitors can look forward to witnessing the game being played at the very highest levels in all the major capitals around Australia. The rival codes of rugby league and rugby union, while perhaps being more accessible to Americans used to gridiron football, are principally concentrated in New South Wales and Queensland and cannot claim the hearts of Australians in quite the same way as footy. Remember, footy is more than a game, it is a barometer of the culture of a particular society. Footy is life.

Unfortunately, footy is only played in the winter months, and Australians turn their attention in summer to their other great passion—cricket. Cricket is a relic of a colonial past and, although many Americans might be surprised to learn that the U.S. even has a national team, it is strongest in those Commonwealth countries like India, the West Indies, New Zealand, Sri Lanka, Pakistan, as well as Australia, which left the British Empire only this century.

Cricket is a leisurely, cerebral sport which ideally suits it to the thoughful and aesthetic Australian public. Important games can last five or six days without producing a result and, to the novice, whole days may pass with very little actually happening. This provides the spectator with ample time to chat (and drink) with a neighbor and discuss the Byzantine intricacies of past controversies. A livelier version of the game takes place in one day and is guaranteed to end in a result; this provides a more suitable introduction to the game.

HOLIDAYS AND EVENTS

Australia is partyland, folks, and *any* excuse for a long weekend or a raucous rage is welcomed. Most public holidays fall on Monday, allowing for what is called a "long weekend." You can pretty much count on everything being closed for all three (or, in some instances, four) days.

Major National Holidays
New Year's Day: January 1
Australia Day: last Monday in January
Good Friday, Easter Saturday, Easter Sunday, and Easter Monday: varies
Anzac Day: April 25
Queen's Birthday: a Monday in early June (Western Australia celebrates in late September-early October)
Melbourne Cup Day: first Tuesday in November (the whole country stops in its hooves for this all-important race meeting—Melbourne stops for the entire day!)
Christmas Day: December 25
Boxing Day: December 26

Regional Holidays
Labour Day: early March (Western Australia)
May Day: first Monday in May (Northern Territory)
Adelaide Cup Day: end of May (South Australia)
Foundation Day: first Monday in June (Western Australia)
Show Days: four days throughout July (Northern Territory)
Picnic Day: early August (Northern Territory
Labour Day: mid-October (South Australia)

School Holidays
These are scheduled four times a year and fall on different dates throughout all the states and territories. Basically they run mid-December to early February, mid-April to mid-May, late June to late July, and mid-September to mid-October. It is especially important to book transport and accommodations ahead during school holiday periods, as that's when most Aussies hit the road or take to the skies.

Festivals And Seasonal Events
January: The **Schuetzenfest** goes full guns in Hahndorf, South Australia's German community; at Lake Jabiru, in the Northern Territory, the **Jabiru Regatta** features offbeat games and races.

February: The two-day **Kangaroo Island Racing Carnival** comes to Kangaroo Island's Kingscote (South Australia). In the Northern Territory, **race meetings and rodeos** take place at Alice Springs, Tennant Creek, and Darwin.

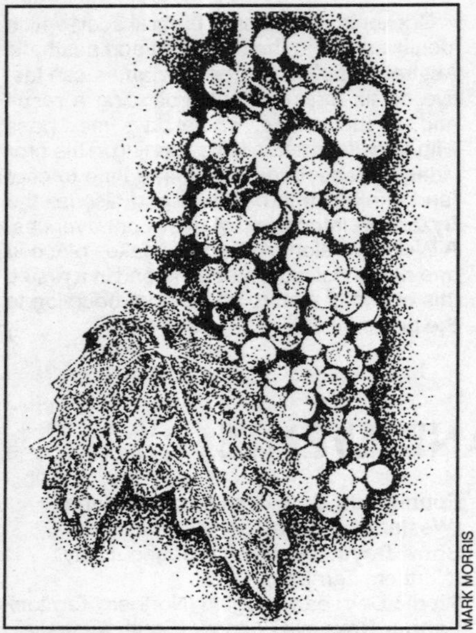

Grapes are the honored guests at the Barossa Valley Vintage and other wine festivals.

March: South Australia's famed **Adelaide Arts Festival** (even-numbered years) offers three weeks of premier theater, music, dance, arts exhibitions, and fringe events. The **Festival of Perth** is a similar cultural extravaganza in Western Australia, beginning the end of February and lasting a month.

April: In odd-numbered years, South Australia's **Barossa Valley Vintage Festival** is a major "taste till you waste" week-long celebration in honor of the local grapes and vintners. Coober Pedy hosts its **Opal and Outback Festival.**

May: In the Northern Territory, Alice Springs' **Bangtail Muster** features a float parade and other events. Other Alice Springs festivals include the **Alice Springs Cup** annual horse race and the **Lions Fosters Camel Cup** with races, fireworks, and—of course—camel races. **May Day** in Darwin signals the end of those treacherous box jellyfish and the beginning of beach parties.

June: Darwin is at the forefront again with its **Beer Can Regatta,** comprised of sailing "craft" constructed entirely from empty beer cans. Darwin's **Bougainvillaea Festival** offers two weeks of flowery events. The **Katherine Gorge Canoe Marathon** (Northern Territory), is a 100-km race along the Katherine River, organized by the Red Cross.

July: Almond-lovers will want to attend the **Almond Blossom Festival,** Willunga (South Australia), with assorted nutty activities.

August: Again it's all happening in the Northern Territory! The **Henley-on-Todd Regatta** in Alice Springs (late August or early September), features bizarre and creative mock-ups of boats, propelled by the racers' feet as they run along the dry Todd River bed. The **Darwin Rodeo** is a well-attended international competition. And Darwin's **Mud Crab Tying Competiton** is another must on the cultural calendar.

September: The **VFL Grand Final,** Australian football's final game, is located in Melbourne but religiously followed by almost everyone in the country. Watch it on the telly from your favorite pub.

October: South Australia's **McLaren Vale Bushing Festival** commemorates the release of a new vintage with a variety of events including the crowning of a Bushing King and Queen.

November: The **Australian Formula One Grand Prix** burns rubber through Adelaide's streets and parklands for four days (the race is on the last day).

December: And all's right with the world.

CONDUCT AND CUSTOMS

Rule number one: bring alcohol or flowers if you're invited to a dinner or party. Other than that, say "please" and "thanks," and you're in business—at least in the cities. In country and Outback areas, well—it's a different story. They take care of things *themselves,* if you catch my drift.

The concept of "fairness" is always a prime consideration. "Whatever's fair," "fair enough" and, yes, "fair dinkum." The only problem is, "fair dinkum" for the cocky or allegedly innocent (or downright guilty) foreigner can quickly become "fair dinkum stinkum." Play it by ear and don't get in over your head. It's fine standing up for principles and such but the reality is—when you're in the middle of nowhere with no one to jump to your aid—who cares? Tell them you'll sue and they'll laugh (tell them you'll call the cops and they *won't).* Think about survival first and foremost. This goes ditto for feminists; though it's tempting to barge into a redneck pub and demand equal rights, use common sense and a bit of restraint. (For those of you who have seen *Thelma and Louise,* I know you're going to ignore me anyway.)

My Aussie friends will hate me for saying this, but—all that hype you've heard about Australia being 20 or so years behind the U.S. is, in many ways, true. Not everyone is fast, fast, fast, nor is everything mega-modern or high-high-tech. But is that so bad? It also means that people still count, that in a country so far from other urban centers and with such a comparatively small population, human life is not so expendable.

Hitching

Use common sense. Outback areas are isolated and not well traveled—be prepared for *very* long waits. Best hitching combo is a man and a woman. Women should not hitch alone. If you're traveling solo, check hostel and backpacker lodging bulletin boards for partners and/or rides.

Tipping

Tipping is not mandatory in Australia—your waitperson will not follow you into the street, meat cleaver in hand, for the extra 15 or 20 percent. Normally, tipping is done only in an expensive restaurant, or when service has been extra good—and then 10% will suffice. Leave taxi drivers the extra change to make the tab an even amount and they'll be happy.

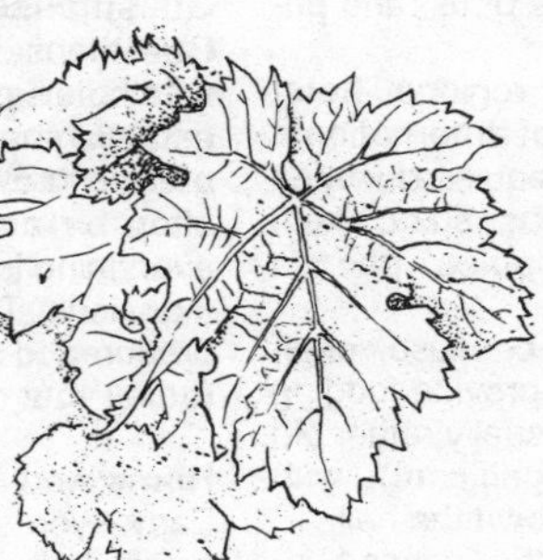

ACCOMMODATIONS

Australian lodging is well represented by the cliché "myriad of possibilities." Choices range from backpackers' dorms and youth hostels to penthouse suites in luxury hotels—with motels, pubs, guesthouses, bed and breakfasts, holiday flats, caravan parks, and Outback stations tossed in between. Accommodations guides with up-to-date prices can be obtained at branches of the automobile club or, often, at state tourist bureaus. It is advisable to book ahead during public and school holidays.

PRICES—USING THIS GUIDE

Here's the breakdown to accommodations costs listed in this handbook, give or take a few (Aussie) bucks either way:
Inexpensive—under $30
Moderate—$30-60
Expensive—$60 and way up (figure the big resorts and hotels in the $150 range)
YHA and backpacker hostels run about $10-12

Hotels

These come in a few varieties—the big Hyatt-type places, older-style pubs, and private hotels.

Worldwide, national, and regional **hotel chains and resorts** are of international standard and feature all the requisite luxuries and amenities—pools, saunas, spas, room service, complimentary toiletries, phones next to the toilet.

Pubs are called "hotels" because, originally, they were required to provide lodging for travelers. Thus they are usually rather old (and, in some cases, magnificent), with simple rooms and facilities down the hall.

The **private hotel** (versus the licensed hotel), does not serve alcohol, and is more like a guesthouse.

Motels

As in the U.S., motels are prevalent throughout Australia, owned either by independent operators or chain establishments (Flag Inns and Best Western are two biggies). Rooms—usually doubles—are serviced daily, and have private bathrooms, radios, televisions, fridges, and the ubiquitous electric jug accompanied by instant coffee packets and tea bags. Motels often have a swimming pool and attached restaurant, and some have family suites with cooking facilities.

Serviced Apartments And Holiday Flats

Serviced apartments are usually found in the cities, while holiday flats (or units) are located in resort or vacation areas. They range from basic motel-style rooms with kitchenettes, to full-on posh apartments with several rooms. Cutlery, dishes, and cooking utensils are provided but, unless you're staying in one of the upmarket pads with daily or weekly maid service, plan on doing the washing up yourself. Rented weekly or monthly, they cater mainly to those who plan an extended stay in one place, and can be exceptionally good value for a group traveling together.

Guesthouses

Guesthouses, bed and breakfasts, and private hotels are all basically the same—small establishments with shared facilities, and brekkie thrown into the deal. Other meals can often be arranged. Again, these comprise everything from simple residences to elegant mansions. This style isn't for everyone—be prepared to hear the other guests' life stories (or tell your own) over bacon and eggs.

Home And Farm Stays

Easy—you stay with Aussies in their homes or on their farms. In homes, you're treated like one of the family. You'll have a private bedroom, though you'll probably share bath-

HOME AND FARM STAYS

Book home and farm stays through state tourist centers or the North American representatives listed below:

Home Stays
At Home Downunder (Austravel), tel. (800) 544-0212; Australian Home Accommodation (ats/sprint), tel. (800) 423-2880, in the U.S. or (800) 232-2121, in CA; Away From Home Acommodation (ats/sprint), see above; Bed And Breakfast Australia (SO/PAC), tel. (800) 551-2012, U.S. or (800) 445-0190, CA; Quality Homestays (Swain Australia Tours), tel. (800) 227-9246.

Farm Stays
Australian Farmhost & Farm Holidays (ats/sprint or SO/PAC), see above; Countrylife Australia (Jet Vacations), tel. (800) 538-0999; Grand Country Estates (Pacific Destination Centre), tel. (800) 227-5317; Host Farms Association (SO/PAC), see above.

room facilities with your Aussie parents and siblings. Breakfast is usually included, and other meals can often be arranged.

Farm stays (usually on very large sheep or cattle stations) can mean anything and—if you're fussy—should be checked out thoroughly in advance. You might be lodged in the bunkhouse or shearers' quarters and expected to work alongside the jack-and jilleroos. Particularly on Outback stations, life is simple and often tough. Then again, you might arrange a motel-style farm stay, where you sit back on the veranda with a cold beer and breathe in the scent of cow and sheep dung.

Youth Hostels And Ys

If you're over the age of 12, don't let the word "youth" scare you off. Instead, think of it as meaning "young at heart." This type of lodging is the ultimate for budget travelers (about $10-12 per night), to say nothing of a superb clearinghouse for local information, job possibilities, ride-sharing, juicy gossip, et cetera. Accommodations are in dormitories or bunkrooms (though sometimes double rooms are available to couples), and usually offer communal cooking and laundry facilities. "Extras" might include bicycle, surfboard, and equipment rentals, as well as organized excursions and tour bookings.

YHA (Youth Hostel Association) hostels are internationally known, well organized, and efficiently run. They operate from an incredible variety of locations, including tiny shelters, railway cars, suburban mansions, and country churches. A number of rules and regulations are enforced—such as daytime lockout periods, evening curfew, and assigned chores. You must be a member ($18 per year, plus $14 to join), but you can sign up at any state office and at many individual hostels.

For more information, contact: YHA, 38 Sturt St., Adelaide, South Australia 5000 (tel. 08-231-5583); YHA, Darwin Hostel Complex, Beaton Rd. via Hidden Valley Rd., Berrimah, Northern Territory 0828 (tel. 089-84-3902); or YHA, 85 Francis St., Perth, Western Australia 6000 (tel. 09-227-5122). In the United States, contact the **YHA National Office,** Box 37613, Washington, D.C. 20013-7613 (tel. 202-783-6161). In Canada, contact the various regional offices: **B.C. Regional AYH,** 1515 Discovery St., Vancouver, B.C. V6R-4K5, tel. (604) 224-7177; **Ontario East Regional AYH,** 18 Byward Market, Ottawa, Ontario K1N-7A1, tel. (613) 230-1220; **Quebec Regional AYH,** 4545 Peirre de Coubertin, C.P. 1000 Succursale M, Montreal, Quebec H1V-3R2, tel. (514) 252-3117. In the UK, contact **YHA-Trevelyan House,** 8 St. Stephan's Hill, St. Albans, Herts. AL1 2DY, England (tel. 0727-55215). In Australia, book accommodations ahead with the **YHA Central Reservations Bureau,** Sydney (tel. 02-261-5727).

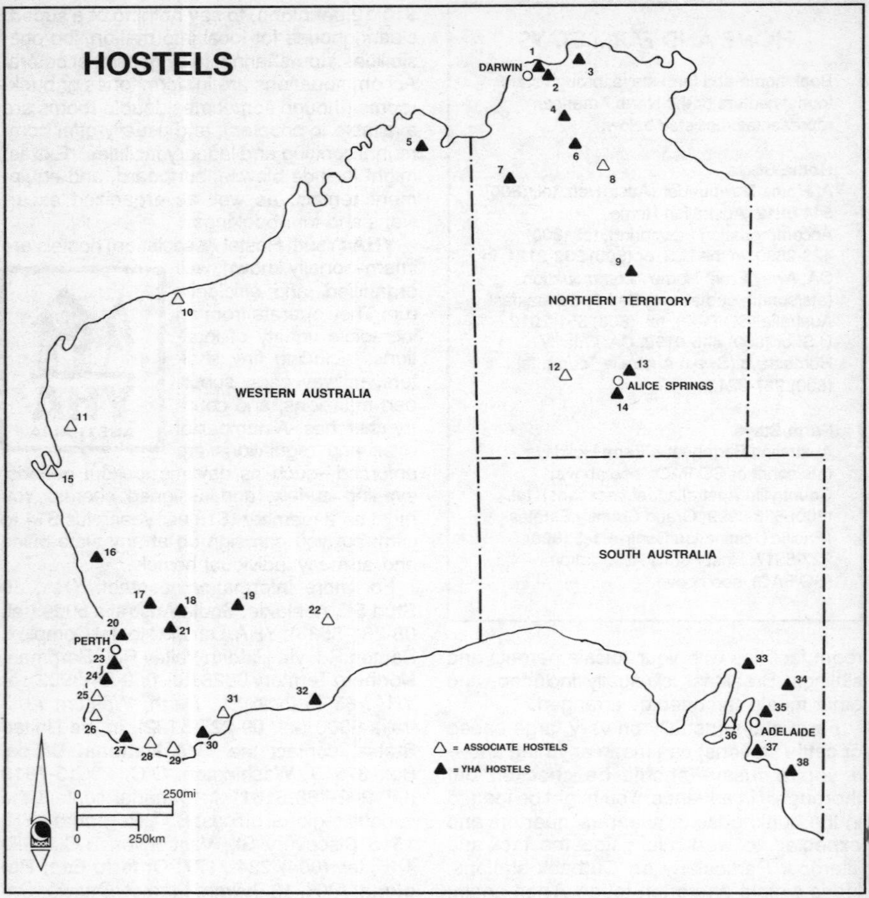

Non-YHA **backpacker hostels** vary in standards. They may have more relaxed hours, no membership requirements, and round-the-clock access, but they might also be a bit scruffy. Check out the other occupants before you bed down.

The **YMCA** and **YWCA** offer good-value city residences with plain rooms and shared bathrooms. Some Ys have dorm rooms for travelers; others are occupied mainly by permanent residents. You don't need to be a member to stay. The **CWA** (Country Women's Association), somewhat akin to the Y, has both city and country locations, and sometimes allows men and couples.

Camping And Caravanning

Australia has plentiful caravan (trailer) parks which offer powered and unpowered campsites, on-site vans (a caravan that stays on

HOSTELS

1. Darwin City
2. Darwin (Berrimah)
3. Kakadu
4. Pine Creek
5. Kununurra
6. Katherine
7. Timber Creek
8. Mataranka
9. Tennant Creek
10. Karratha/Dampier
11. Carnarvon
12. Glen Helen
13. Alice Springs (Parsons St.)
14. Alice Springs (Todd St.)
15. Monkey Mia
16. Geraldton
17. Toodyay
18. York
19. Coolgardie
20. Perth and Freemantle (Seven Backpacker Hostels)
21. Northam
22. Fraser Range
23. Bunbury
24. Dunsborough
25. Yallingup
26. Augusta
27. Pemberton
28. Valley of the giants (Tingledale)
29. Denmark
30. Albany
31. Stirling Range
32. Esperance
33. Wirrabara
34. Kersbrook
35. Adelaide
36. Port Vincent
37. Inman Valley
38. Beachport

its site), and cabins (a caravan without wheels). Parks are located along highways, near beaches and rivers, in country towns, and on the city fringes. Basic facilities include showers, toilets, hot and cold water; fancier sites might have swimming pools, playgrounds, and recreation rooms. Caravanning is a very popular travel mode for Aussies, so book ahead during peak periods.

Other Accommodations
During academic holidays (usually November through February, plus May and August), you might try scoring a room at one of the universities or colleges. It isn't that easy—you must book in advance and most of the places are inconveniently located. Students are given first preference and cheaper rates (about $15 for B&B, double for nonstudents).

FOOD AND DRINK

TUCKER

With the exception of major cities, food in the Outback is basic meat and potatoes fare. Just keep in mind that the "meat" may be crocodile, kangaroo, camel, or buffalo! Seafood, especially the prized barramundi, John Dory, yabbies (freshwater crayfish), and Moreton Bay bugs (a local crustacean), is popular around the coastal areas. Though most supermarkets are well stocked, don't expect to find very fresh fruits and veggies in the Red Centre.

Breakfast is an all-important meal Down Under, and Vegemite, a dark yeast mixture, is the national spread. Whatever you do, don't malign Vegemite in Australia—it's worse than desecrating the flag.

Although some progress has been made in recent years, this is *not* an easy country for cholesterol-watchers—many foods are fried, breaded, cheesed, and buttered. Food labeling is not very detailed. For example, a label may proclaim "100% vegetable oil" but won't elaborate on what *kind* of vegetable.

Favorite takeaway items include roast chicken, fish and chips, chips and chips, pies, pasties, and sausage rolls. And, thanks to the ethnic population, you'll find a large number of luscious Italian, Greek, Lebanese, Turkish, and Asian establishments for sit-down meals or takeaways. Takeaways are cheap, pub meals are cheap to moderate ($4-9), and restaurant meals run the price gamut ($10 and *way* up).

Restaurants

One of the best things about Australian dining is this: when you book a table in a restaurant, it's yours for the whole night. No one hovers vulture-like, intimidating you to gulp your meal so the table can be turned over to other diners. That's where the no-tipping stance really shines—no tips involved, no need to hurry the patrons. Consequently, dining out is popular entertainment for most Aussies.

Other things to know: a licensed restaurant serves alcohol (though sometimes only beer and wine), while a BYO restaurant, though unlicensed, allows you to bring your own bottle; dinner is often called "tea"; entrée means appetizer, and main course means entrée; pub counter meals (commonly veal, chicken, steak, sausages), are normally available 12-2 p.m. and 6-8 p.m., and do not have to be eaten at the counter; many pubs now have attached "bistros"—but be aware that the word "bistro" will probably add an extra digit to the tab!

DRINK

Australians love to drink. Walk into someone's house and the kettle is instantly put on the stove; make a deal and you'll inevitably seal it at the local pub.

Favorite nonalcoholic drinks include mineral waters, Coca-Cola, fresh juices, tea, and *lots* of coffee. "White" tea or coffee has milk in it; "flat white" or "flat black" coffee has milk in it, but no froth (as opposed to a cappuccino).

Australian Beer

Ice cold and plenty of it! Aussies love their beer, and each state and territory has its favorite brand, though Foster's is the best known worldwide. In addition, boutique breweries have popped up in the major cities, but you'll only be able to taste their efforts at the hotel where they're made. Beer comes in a dizzying variety of containers—tinnies, twisties, stubbies, middies, pots, schooners, ponies, goblets, and plain old glasses. Locals prefer draught (draft) beer straight from the tap. Keep in mind that Australian beer is higher in alcohol content than American varieties (even the Foster's you buy in the U.S. has been watered down), so gauge your consumption accordingly. Drunk-driving laws are *tough* in Australia; on-the-spot sobriety checks and mobile Breathalyzer vans are common in urban areas.

Australian Wine

South Australia's McLaren Vale, Barossa and Clare valleys, and Western Australia's Swan and Margaret River valleys produce excellent domestic wines. Barossa has some divine reds, and Western Australia excels with its dry riesling. Some common varietals are shiraz, hermitage, and cabernet (reds); riesling, semillon, chardonnay (whites). Australian champagne (oops—I mean *methode champenois)* is widely imbibed and good value. Tour the vineyards for free tastings, then buy a bottle or two of your favorite wine or bubbly.

Spirits

If you're on a budget, you'd best stick to beer and wine—spirits down here are expensive, at least compared to prices in the U.S. If money is no object, you'll find most of your favorite brands readily available at bottle shops and bars.

FOOD AND DRINK GLOSSARY

You say toe-mate-oh and I say toe-motto! Here are some common Aussie words, translated for your dining pleasure:

barbie—barbecue, natch
biscuit—cookie
brekkie—breakfast
BYO—Bring Your Own (booze)
chips—French fries
chook—chicken
cuppa—tea or coffee
damper—bush bread
floater—meat pie floating in pea soup
lollies—candy
middy—medium-size beer glass
milk bar—local convenience shop
piss—booze
pissed—drunk
plonk—wine, especially rotgut
pot—large mug of beer
schooner—large beer glass
serviette—napkin
takeaway—take-out
tea—evening meal
tinny—can of beer
tomato sauce—ketchup
tucker—food

Drinking Laws

You must be 18 or older to buy alcohol or consume it in public. Liquor licenses vary from state to state (and territory). Pubs normally stay open for 12 hours Monday through Saturday (10 a.m.-10 p.m., or variations thereof), with either limited or no Sunday hours. Other bars, clubs, and restaurants can offer alcohol until 2 or 3 a.m. Many establishments can serve you only if you're eating food. Beer, wine, and spirits can be purchased at bottle shops (often attached to a pub) or liquor stores. It is illegal to bring alcohol into an Aboriginal community or reserve.

ENTRY AND DEPARTURE

Keep up to date on current red tape by contacting the nearest embassy or consulate, as well as your country's customs service. See "Services And Information" below for addresses.

Passports And Visas

Every visitor must have a valid passport for entry into Australia. In addition, visas are required for everyone except holders of Australian and New Zealand passports. Visas are issued free of charge at Australian consulates and embassies and, for U.S. and Canadian citizens, are generally valid for one year. If you apply in person, a visa will probably be issued on the spot; if you apply by mail, be sure to enclose a stamped, self-addressed envelope large enough to accommodate your passport. Also, allow at least 21 days for processing. If you want special services, such as your documents returned via first class, certified, registered, or express mail, enclose the appropriate forms and postage. Mail that is marked "insufficient postage" will be returned, unprocessed.

Whether applying in person or by mail, you must present your passport, a signed application form, and a current passport-type photograph. If you're planning to take more than one journey in the next few years, request a "multiple-entry visa."

Within Australia, visas can be extended (often on the whim of the official you approach) at Department of Immigration offices in major cities. The application fee is $50, and it is *not* returned if your extension is denied. You may be required to have a personal interview and produce bank statements and other proof of financial solvency. Other visa possibilities are the **Working Holidaymakers' visa** and **student visa.** Inquire about qualifications *before* arriving in Australia.

Australian Customs

Visitors may bring personal clothing and effects into Australia duty-free. If you're over 18 years old, you're also allowed 200 cigarettes or 250 grams of cigars or tobacco, in addition to one liter of wine, beer, or spirits (you must carry these items on you to qualify). Other taxable goods (up to $400 per adult and $200 per child under 18 years old) may be admitted duty-free if included inside personal baggage.

Drugs, weapons, and firearms are prohibited or restricted in Australia. German shepherds will be sniffing you as you wait to clear immigration. Drug laws are strictly enforced. Also, certain quarantined items such as meats, vegetables, fruit, and flowers, are no-no's and will be confiscated. If you're not sure of something, *don't* try to smuggle it in—ask a customs agent. And if that doesn't suit you, drop the questionable article in the amnesty box.

Aside from international customs, quarantines on fresh fruit, vegetables, and plants are in effect between states and territories. Eat everything up before you reach the state line.

International Customs

Each family member is allowed to bring back up to US$400 in duty-free goods, if you're out of the country for a minimum of 48 hours and haven't taken any other international journey in 30 days. Family members may combine their exemptions. Goods between $400 and $1400 are assessed at a flat 10% rate. If you're at least 21 years old, your allowance may include 100 cigars (no Cuban brands), 200 cigarettes, and one liter of wine, beer, or spirits. You may mail gifts, valued under $50, duty-free to friends or relatives—but don't send more than one package per day to any one person.

Canadians who have been abroad for less than eight days may bring back up to C$100 of goods duty-free. Those who have been away for eight days or more are allowed up to C$300 of merchandise. The duty-free allowance for Canadians includes up to 1.1 liter of spirits, one carton of cigarettes, and fifty cigars. Tax rates vary by item.

AUSTRALIAN CONSULATES AND EMBASSIES

UNITED STATES

Chicago, Suite 2930, 321 N. Clark St., Chicago, IL 60610 (tel. 312-645-9440)
Honolulu, 1000 Bishop St., Honolulu, HI 96813 (tel. 808-524- 5050)
Houston, Suite 800, 1990 Post Oak Blvd., Houston, TX 77056 (tel. 713-629-9131)
Los Angeles, 611 N. Larchmont Blvd., Los Angeles, CA 90004 (tel. 213-469-4300)
New York, Suite 430, International Bldg., 636 Fifth Ave., New York, NY 10111 (tel. 212-245-4000)
San Francisco, 1 Bush St., San Francisco, CA 94108 (tel. 415-362-6160)
or the **Australian Embassy,** 1601 Massachusetts Ave. NW, Washington D.C. 20036 (tel. 202-797-3000)

CANADA

Ottawa, Suite 710, 50 O'Connor St., Ottawa, Ontario K1P 6L2 (tel. 613-236-0841)
Toronto, Suite 314, 175 Bloor St. East, Toronto, Ontario M4W 3R8 (tel. 416-323-1155)
Vancouver, Suite 602, 999 Canada Place, Vancouver, British Columbia V6C 3E1 (tel. 604-684-1177)

ASIA

Bali, Jalan Raya Sanur 146, Denpasar (tel. 25-997)
Hong Kong, 25 Harbour Rd., Wonchai (tel. 731-1881)
Japan, 1-12 Shiba Koen, 1-Chome, Tokyo 105 (tel. 435-0971)
Malaysia, 6 Jalan Yap, Kwan Seng, Kuala Lumpur (tel. 242-3122)
Singapore, 25 Napier Rd., Singapore 10 (tel. 737-9311)
Thailand, 37 S. Sathorn Rd., Bangkok 12 (tel. 287-2680)

EUROPE

Austria, Mattiellistrasse 2-4, 1040 Vienna (tel. 512-8580)
Belgium, Guimard Centre, 1040 Brussels (tel. 231-0500)
Czechoslovakia, Hotel Praha, Susicks 20, 166 36 Praha 6, Dejvice (tel. 333-8111)
Denmark, Kristianagade 21, 2100 Copenhagen (tel. 312-62244)
England, Australia House, The Strand, London WC2B 4LA (tel. 071-379-4334)
Greece, 37 Dimitriou Soutsou St., Ambelòkipi, Athens 11521 (tel. 644-7303)
Germany, Godesberger Allee 107, W5300 Bonn 2 (tel. 81-030)
Ireland, Fitzwilton House, Wilton Tce., Dublin 2 (tel. 76-1517)
Italy, Via Alessandria 215, Rome 00198 (tel. 83-2721)
Netherlands, Koninginnegracht 23, 2514 AB The Hague (tel. 363-0983)
Poland, Estonska 3/5, Saska Kepa, Warsaw (tel. 17-6081-5)
Portugal, 4th Fl., Avenida da Liberdade 244, Lisbon 1200 (tel. 52-3350)
Spain, Paseo de la Castellana, Madrid 28046 (tel. 579-8504)
Sweden, Sergels Torg 12, Stockholm (tel. 613-2900)
Switzerland, 29 Alpenstrasse, Berne (tel. 43-0143)
Turkey, 83 Nenehatun Caddesi, Gazi Osman Pasa, Ankara 06690 (tel. 136-1240)
Yugoslavia, 13 Cika Ljubina 11000, Belgrade (tel. 62-4655)

SOUTH AMERICA

Argentina, Avenida Santa Fe 846, Piso 8, Buenos Aires (tel. 31-268-418);
Brazil, SHIS Q.I.-9, Conj 16 Casa 1, Brasilia (tel. 61-286-7922)
Venezuela, corner of Avenida Luis Roche and Avenida 10, Altamira, Caracas 1060A (tel. 261-4632)

Travelers from the United Kingdom may bring home up to £32 of goods duty-free. In addition, goods such as wine, tobacco, and perfume are duty-free, and so is anything you've owned for longer than six months. The same regulations apply to items that are mailed home. The standard value-added tax rate for the UK is 17½%.

Departure Tax
Unless you're a transit passenger who's been in the country less than 24 hours, every person 12 years and older must pay a $20 departure tax when leaving Australia. Tax stamps must be paid in Australian currency and can be purchased at the airport or at any post office. Affix the stamp to your airline ticket.

MONEY, MEASUREMENTS, AND COMMUNICATIONS

All prices quoted in this guide are in Australian dollars (A$) unless otherwise noted.

Money
Australian currency is based on the dollars-and-cents decimal system (100 cents equal one dollar). Notes, of different colors, come in denominations of $5, $10, $20, $50, and $100. Coins are in denominations of 1¢, 2¢, 5¢, 10¢, 20¢, 50¢, $1, and $2 (though the one- and two-cent coins are being phased out).

You may bring in or take out any amount of personal funds however; if you're carrying or sending $5000 or more in Australian or foreign currency, you must file a form with the Australian Customs Service. You may also be required to furnish a report with customs agents in other countries.

Currency exchange facilities are available at all international airports, though many open only for incoming and outgoing flights. Larger hotels and most banks will also exchange foreign cash and traveler's checks (traveler's checks fetch a slightly higher rate). Traveler's checks are easily cashed, but have identification with you. Banks with automatic-teller machines are commonplace in major cities and many country towns.

The most commonly accepted **credit cards** are American Express, Bankcard, MasterCard, and Visa. Outback areas and smaller towns may only deal in hard cash.

Banking hours are generally Mon.-Thurs. 9:30 a.m.-4 p.m., Fri. 9 a.m.-5 p.m. A few of the larger city banks are open on Saturday morning—but don't count on it.

Measurements
Australia is on the meters/liters/centimeters system, like almost every other country in the world. Temperatures are in Celsius (C). (See the conversion tables at the back of this book.)

Electrical Voltage
Australia's electrical current is 240/250 volts, AC 50Hz. You'll need a three-pin adapter plug (*different* from the British three-pronger) for any 110 volt appliances you intend to bring, as well as the appropriate voltage converter. It's best to purchase adapter plugs and converters before arrival, though both

CURRENCY EXCHANGE

As of January 1992, the Aussie dollar was trading at about 74 cents to US$1. Travelers with currency other than the almighty greenback should be able to exchange funds at most banks and airport money-changing facilities without problem. Current exchange rates (per A$) for other major currencies are:

Yen 95
NZ$ 1.38
SFr 1.05
UK 41 pence
DMark 1.9

are available in the larger cities. If you're bringing a computer or other specialized equipment, be sure to check with the manufacturer for exact requirements.

Time Zones

Australia has three time zones: New South Wales, Australian Capital Territory, Victoria, Tasmania, and Queensland operate on **eastern standard time** (EST); South Australia and the Northern Territory use **central standard time** (CST); and Western Australia has its very own **western standard time** (WST).

Here is the confusing part: central standard time is half an hour behind eastern standard time, while western standard time is two hours behind eastern standard time. And all of the states except Western Australia and the Northern Territory go on **summer time** (daylight saving time) from October to March, when clocks are set ahead one hour. (No wonder the Aborigines keep to dreamtime!)

Communications

Australian Telecom is an efficiently operated **telephone** system. Local calls from pay phones (i.e., coin boxes) cost 30¢—and make that one 10¢ coin and one 20¢ coin. Almost all public phones are equipped for STD (subscriber trunk dialing) and ISD (international subscriber dialing). Just keep feeding coins into the slots (you can use one-dollar pieces, if you like). There is no three-minute minimum and unused change will be returned when you hang up. Don't forget to dial the "zero" before the city code when making STD calls, *then* dial the number you want. When placing international calls, dial 0011 (the international access code), the country code, the city code, and then the desired phone number (it's about $1.50 per minute to the U.S. or U.K.). Use the appropriate area code for long-distance calls between states in Australia.

Operator-assisted calls can be placed from any phone, though fees for reverse-charge (collect) and person-to-person calls run $6-8. Credit card phones are now installed in many airports, hotels, and post

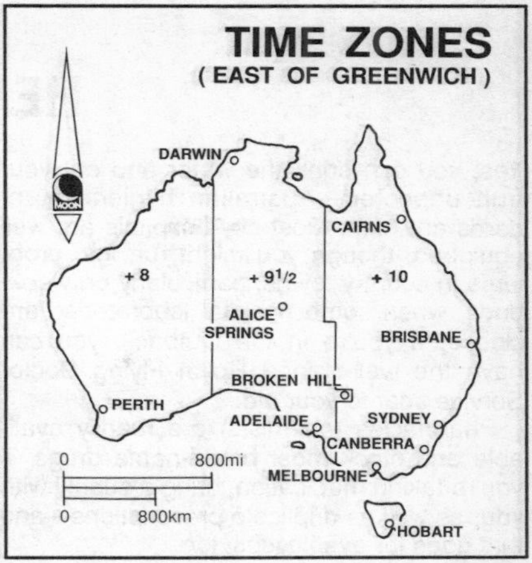

offices. Refer to the front pages of the local telephone book for dialing information and charges. Try not to make any long-distance calls from big hotels—the surcharges are usually astronomical and can double or triple the actual cost of the call.

In this land of few and far between, **fax** machines are used everywhere. Almost every post office provides a fax calling and receiving service.

In **emergencies,** dial 000 to summon help.

Mail

The mail averages a whopping seven to ten days or *longer* between Australia and North America or Europe—going either direction. Domestic service, however (barring postal strikes) is relatively efficient.

General post offices and branches will hang onto your mail in poste restante, free of charge, for up to a month. Alternatively, American Express cardholders can have mail sent to city American Express offices, to be held for later pick-up.

Post office hours are Mon.-Fri. 9-5 p.m. (There is no Saturday mail delivery.) Stamps can also be purchased at some hotels, motels, and newsagents (a domestic stamp costs 43¢). Main post offices have philatelic desks, which sell sets of souvenir stamps.

HEALTH

Yes, you can drink the water and eat your fruit unpeeled—Australian hygiene standards are high. Most city hospitals are well equipped, though you might run into problems in country towns, particularly on weekends, when some hospital laboratories are closed. If you're in the Outback, you can have the well-trained Royal Flying Doctor Service soar to your aid.

Pharmacies (chemists) are readily available and stock most brand-name drugs. If you're taking medication, bring a supply with you, as well as duplicate prescriptions—and that goes for eyeglasses, too.

Take it easy until you get acclimated, especially if the weather is hot or humid, if you're traveling into the Outback, or planning any strenuous physical activities. Go slow, and work up to a pace you're comfortable with.

The **International Association for Medical Assistance to Travelers** (IAMAT) provides a list of doctors worldwide with U.S. standards of medical training. For more information, contact IAMAT, 417 Center St., Lewiston, NY 14092 (tel. 716-754-4883). If you find yourself in a real medical nightmare, contact your country's consulate or embassy for emergency help.

Vaccinations

Vaccinations are not necessary if you're traveling from the United States, Canada or the United Kingdom. If you've visited a yellow fever-infected country within six days of your arrival in Australia, you'll need appropriate inoculations.

Aircraft Spray

All aircraft arriving in Australia on a first-port basis are given a three-stage fumigation, as a precaution against agricultural pests. This, naturally, is done with the disclaimer that the disinfectant spray will kill every living thing but is harmless to humans. The three-stage spray is as follows: a pre-spray in lockers and

Ain't no joke.

FIRST AID

Prevention

Be sensible! The ultraviolet rays are intense, the ozone hole wide, and the skin cancer rate *very* high. Even cloudy skies can cause a bad burn and—as for the super-bright Outback—wow! Wear a hat and sunblock, drink plenty of water to avoid dehydration, go easy on booze and fags, and you should be right, mates.

Exhaustion And Heat Exposure

It's *hot* in the Outback. Keep a slow pace until you get acclimated. Get lots of rest, fill up on water, make sure you have enough salt in your diet, and avoid overexposure to the harsh sun. Wear loose, cotton clothing (and your hat, of course). Beware of heatstroke—symptoms include increased body temperature, a reduction in sweat, and occasional vomiting or nausea. Heatstroke is an emergency situation: the victim should be taken to a cool place, then doused, fanned, and sponged with cold water until his body temperature has dropped to at least 39° C (102° F).

Traveler's Diarrhea

It doesn't matter how clean the place is—unfamiliar foods, overeating, too much drinking, and a variety of other factors can cause the runs. Again, be sensible until you get used to your new environment. If you do come down with Bali Belly or Montezuma's Revenge, ward off dehydration by drinking *lots* of fluids such as clear broth or soup, weak tea, or juice (*no* alcohol or coffee). Gradually add bland and boiled grub to your diet—rice, biscuits, bread, bananas.

Stings And Bites, Snakes And Beasties

Oz is renowned for its numerous evil snakes. Most won't attack unless provoked but exceptions are the tiger and taipan snakes (the most dangerous). For bites, apply a pressure bandage, keep the victim calm and immobilized, and get medical help fast.

Spiders to watch out for are the red back and the white tail. Place ice on the affected area and seek prompt medical attention.

Know your nasty sea critters *before* you wiggle your toes in the water. The box jellyfish can inflict a fatal sting. Douse the area with vinegar, pull out tentacles, and procure immediate medical attention. Some other poisonous marine dwellers are the sea snake, the blue-ringed octopus, the scorpion fish, and the stonefish (which masquerades as a harmless piece of rock). Treat stings as for snake bites.

Finally, if you're attacked by a saltwater croc, well . . . *adios.*

Sexually Transmitted Diseases

There is AIDS in Oz, and this includes the Outback. Use condoms. Period.

toilets (2% permethrin, 98% freon); top-of-descent spray inside the cabin prior to landing (2% d-phenothron, 98% freon); and a stronger and longer-lasting spray in the cargo hold (2% permethrin, 2% d-phenothron, 8% solvent, 88% freon).

If I didn't tell you, you'd probably only know about the top-of-descent spray. During that phase, flight attendants come up and down the aisles spraying. Keep a hanky, tissue, or blanket over your nose and mouth for as long as you can stand it.

Health Hazards

This is a country with one of the highest rates of skin cancer in the world. The sun is *intense* and the hole in the ozone layer is *wide*—wear sunblock and a hat whenever you're outdoors. Also, drink plenty of fluids to ward off possible dehydration. When traveling in Outback areas, check in first with the automobile club, local police, or park rangers.

Other potential dangers include Australia's infamous poisonous snakes, those faster-than-you'd-care-to-imagine saltwater crocs, a few poisonous spiders (the red back, funnel web, and white tail), and the box jellyfish. Obey all warning signs and, when in doubt, ask the locals.

Animals on the road, particularly at night, can also be deadly. When walking on coral reef, protect your feet with sturdy shoes. Seek prompt medical treatment for any coral cuts.

Health Insurance

Though a visit to the doctor's office might only cost $16 or so, other medical expenses can be quite hefty. Make sure you have health insurance to adequately cover possible accidents and illness before you leave home. Both Council Travel Services and STA offices, as well as most travel agents, can recommend reliable insurance companies. Coverage can also be obtained for emergency transportation, lost luggage, and trip cancellation. Holders of International Student Identity Cards receive automatic coverage up to certain limits.

Travel insurers include: **Travel Assistance International,** Suite 400, 1133 15th St. NW, Washington, D.C. 20005 (tel. 202-347-2025 or 800-821-2828); **TravelGuard International,** 1145 Clark St., Stevens Point, WI 54481 (tel. 715-345-0505 or 800-782-5151); and **WorldCare Travel Assistance Association,** Suite 1300, 605 Market St., San Francisco, CA 94105 (tel. 415-541-4991 or 800-666-4993).

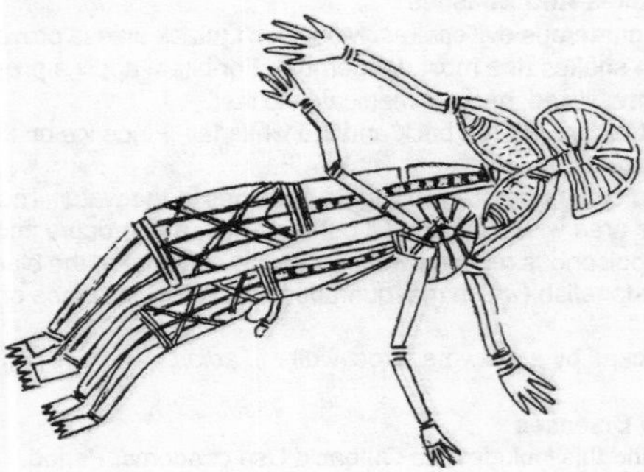

SERVICES AND INFORMATION

Tourist Information

There's no lack of tourist information centers in Australia. All of the states and territories have branch offices in major city centers—veritable treasure troves of details on tours, attractions, sports, accommodations, package deals, car and campervan rentals and local and interstate transportation. Most of these centers will make bookings for you, and all will load you with brochures. Additionally, almost every country town has an information center—albeit an office, petrol station, or museum—marked by the international "I" sign. Hours are usually Mon.-Fri. 9-5, Sat. 9 a.m.-1 p.m. Centers in heavily touristed areas are often open on Sunday as well.

For information on travel to Australia, contact the nearest office of the **Australian Tourism Commission. In the U.S.:** Suite 1200, 2121 Avenue of the Stars, Los Angeles, CA 90067 (tel. 213-552-1988); 150 N. Michigan Ave., Chicago, IL 60601 (tel. 312-781-5150); 489 Fifth Ave., New York, NY 10017 (tel. 212-687-6300). **In Canada:** Suite 1730, 2 Bloor St. West, Toronto, Ontario M4W 3E2 (tel. 416-925-9575). **In the United Kingdom:** Gemini House, 10-18 Putney Hill, London, England SW15 (tel. 081-780-2227). **In Germany:** Neue Mainzerstrasse 22, D6000 Frankfurt am Main 1 (tel. 069-23-5071).

For state tourist centers, see the "Information" section in the appropriate chapter.

Foreign Embassies

Diplomatic missions are located in Canberra, and the United States, New Zealand, and the United Kingdom have consular offices in various capital cities. Check under "Consulates and Legations" in the yellow pages. Major embassies are: **United States,** Moonah Place, Yarralumla, ACT 2600 (tel. 270-5000); **Canada,** Commonwealth Ave., Yarralumla, ACT 2600 (tel. 273-3844); **European Communities,** 18 Arkana St., Yarralumla, ACT 2600 (tel. 271-2777); and **Japan,** 112 Empire Circuit, Yarralumla, ACT 2600 (tel. 273-3244).

Automobile Associations

The **Royal Automobile Club** offers reciprocal rights to members of the American Automobile Club (bring your membership card with you). Services include free roadside emergency breakdown service (within certain city limits), route maps, touring information, and discounted travel guides, and accommodations and camping directories. Many offices will make tour and accommodations reservations for you. The main state offices are: **Royal Automobile Association of South Australia** (RAA), 41 Hindmarsh Square, Adelaide, S.A. 5000 (tel. 08-223-4555); **National Roads and Motorists Association** (NRMA), 151 Clarence St., Sydney, N.S.W. 2000 (tel. 02-260-9222); **Automobile Association of the Northern Territory** (AANT), 79-81 Smith St., Darwin, N.T. 0800 (tel. 089-81-3837); **Royal Automobile Club of Western Australia** (RACWA), 228 Adelaide Terrace., Perth, W.A. 6000 (tel. 09-421-4444).

National Parks

For information on Australia's more than 2,000 national parks, wildlife sanctuaries, and nature reserves, contact the following organizations: for **South Australia,** National Parks and Wildlife Service, G.P.O. Box 1782, Adelaide, S.A. 5000 (tel. 08-216-7777); for the **Northern Territory,** Conservation Commission, P.O. Box 496, Palmerston, Darwin, N.T. 0831 (tel. 089-89-4411); **Western Australia,** Dept. of Conservation and Land Management, 50 Hayman Rd., Como, W.A. 6152 (tel. 09-367-0333.

For countrywide information, contact **Australian National Parks and Wildlife Service,** 217 Northbourne Ave., Turner, ACT 2601 (tel. 062-46-6211).

Disabled Travelers

Many of Australia's accommodations, restaurants, and tourist attractions provide facilities and access for disabled travelers. Obtain the booklet, *Accessibility Guide for Disabled Travellers to Tourist Attractions in Australia,* from the **Australian Council for Rehabilitation of the Disabled** (ACROD), Box 60, Curtin, ACT 2605 (tel. 062-82-4333).

The following organizations offer free city guides: **Disability Information and Resources Centre,** 195 Gillies St., Adelaide, S.A. 5000; **C.A.D.P. Advancement Group,** Box 3280, Alice Springs, N.T. 5750; **City of Melbourne Council,** Swanston St., Melbourne, VIC 3000; **ACROD Western Australia,** Box 5558, Subiaco, W.A. 6008; **Council of the City of Sydney,** Town Hall House, Sydney Square, Sydney, N.S.W. 2000.

Media

The independent, government-funded Australian Broadcasting Corporation is the national television and radio network. Often its programs are all you will hear or see in rural areas, though the major cities and towns will feature two or three regionally based commercial stations. Stations frequently televise nearly first-run movies, as well as some excellent foreign films. American "lookalike" programming includes the "Today Show," "Good Morning Australia," "60 Minutes," and several genre dating game, newlywed, quiz, and love connection shows—plus MTV. You can also catch the U.S. "Today Show" in many locales, and—never fear—"L.A. Law," "All My Children," and "General Hospital" are part of the regular programming (although they're about a year or so behind).

Aside from city and regional newspapers, like Adelaide's *Advertiser, Daily News,* and *Sunday Mail,* Darwin's *Northern Territory News,* and Perth's *West Australian* and *Daily News,* Australia has two national dailies—*The Australian* and *The Australian Financial Review.* Australian editions of *Time, Vogue, Cosmopolitan,* and other international magazines, plus worldwide newspapers (like *USA Today)* and foreign-language press are sold at many news agencies.

WHAT TO TAKE

Clothing

Australians are casual dressers. Except in the major cities (especially Melbourne and Sydney) where you might wish to keep up with the trendy set, dress for comfort and climate. If you're going to the tropical north, take lightweight cottons, which are suitable year-round. (Shorts are okay most places.) The southern temperate regions also call for cottons and other natural fibers during summer months, while winters can be very cold; pack a heavy sweater and jacket. The Outback will be searing during the summer, giving way to chilly nights in winter. And rain can drop any time, unexpectedly, and in great torrents; you might want to include a light raincoat and an umbrella in your suitcase. It's always well advised to dress in layers, particularly due to rapidly changing weather conditions in many regions.

Photo Equipment

Film, processing labs, and photo equipment are easy finds in Australian cities. Bring your own 35mm camera and lenses. Unless you're coming in via Singapore or Hong Kong, it's unnecessary to stock up on film beforehand; Australian film costs about the same as in North America or Europe. You'll also find many "one-hour" photo shops with speedy processing for those on the move.

Special conditions to be aware of are: intensity of light, particularly in the Outback; temperature extremes (try to keep film cool and dry); Outback dust; and tropical humidity. And—a special **Note:** Do not photograph Aboriginals without their permission—which you probably won't get. They do not like having their photos taken.

As for those airport X-ray machines—if you're worried about your film (especially any over 400 ASA), carry it in a lead-lined bag and/or request hand inspection.

Et Cetera
Other articles to bring along are a sunhat, sunglasses, sunscreen, sturdy walking shoes (broken-in *before* arrival), and water-proof sneakers for coral reef-walking. You might also want to pack a voltage converter, adapter plugs, insect repellent, prescription medications, and an extra pair of eyeglasses or contact lenses. Most brands of cosmetics, toiletries, and over-the-counter medications are readily available at chemist shops.

GETTING THERE

Fly. It's the only way to get Down Under, unless you opt for an expensive cruise with a couple of one- or two-day port stops. Most international airlines operate wide-body aircraft to Australia. Gateway cities are Adelaide, Brisbane, Cairns, Darwin (from Asia), Hobart (from New Zealand), Melbourne, Perth (from Europe, Asia, and Africa), Port Hedland (from Bali), Sydney, and Townsville. Sydney and Melbourne are the two busiest international airports, and customs and immigration formalties can seem endless, particularly when many flights arrive around the same time. Try to avoid weekend arrivals.

Travel Agents
If you're looking for the most economical fare, make sure you have a travel agent who doesn't mind doing a little work on your behalf. **Council Travel** and **STA** usually offer the cheapest deals with the fewest restrictions, and student-status is not requisite for many of their fares. In London, bucket shops (advertised in *Time Out*) offer discounted fares; reliable agencies include **Down Under** (tel. 071-287-1566), **Trailfinders** (tel. 071-938-3366), and **Travel Cuts** (tel. 071-255-2082). Personally, I rarely use a travel agent. Instead, I call individual airlines myself; consequently, for about half a day's telephone inquiries, I have saved a *lot* of money by doing my own research. Important questions to ask include applicable standby fares, special promotions, allowed stopovers, and restrictions and penalties.

If you're not fussy about travel dates, *say so*. You can save plenty of bucks by traveling in the low or shoulder season instead of sky-high peak time. **Fare seasons** from the Northern Hemisphere are: 1 May-31 August, low; 1 December-28 February, high; everything else, shoulder. (Some airlines vary these periods by a few weeks.)

FARES

Scads of fares are available—from rock-bottom, off-season economy to super-luxe, super-bucks first class. Business class, an upgraded economy and downgraded first class, is available on most airlines. Advance-purchase excursion (APEX) fares are usually the best value, though some (and, occasionally, *many*) restrictions apply. These might include minimum and maximum stays, and nonchangeable (or heavily penalized) itineraries and arrival or departure dates.

Other travel options to consider are round-the-world or circle-Pacific fares. **Round-the-world tickets**—usually on two airlines—allow travel in the same direction (with no backtracking) around the world anywhere on their combined route systems. Tickets usually require that the first sector be booked in advance and that travel be completed within one year. The number of stops permitted may vary, and cancellation penalties may apply. **Circle-Pacific** tickets work pretty much the same as round-the-worlders except that they circle only the Pacific rather than the whole world. A sample itinerary might encompass San Francisco, Honolulu, Auckland, Sydney, Singapore, Bangkok,

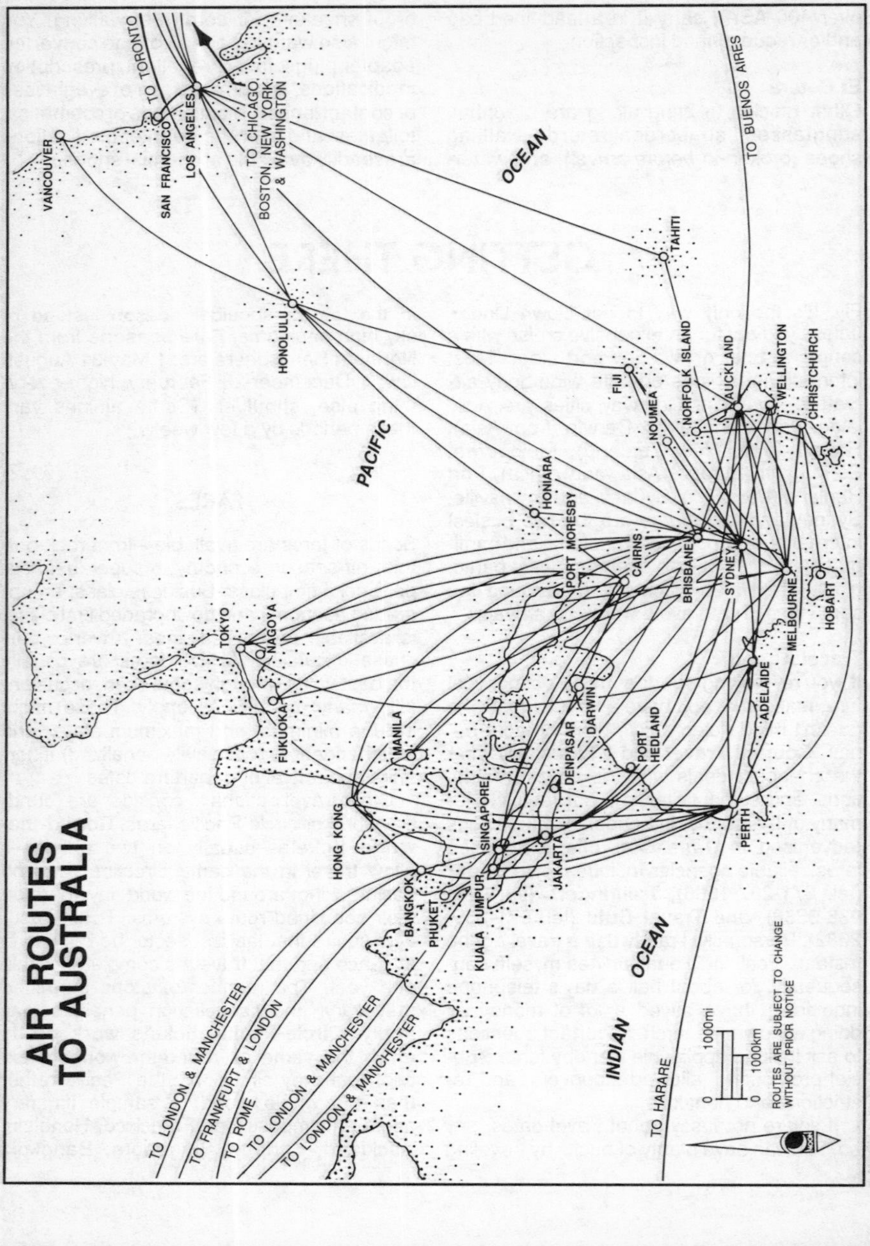
AIR ROUTES TO AUSTRALIA
TO LONDON & MANCHESTER
TO FRANKFURT & LONDON
TO ROME
TO LONDON & MANCHESTER
TO LONDON & MANCHESTER
TO HARARE
INDIAN OCEAN
PACIFIC OCEAN
VANCOUVER
SAN FRANCISCO
LOS ANGELES
TO TORONTO
TO CHICAGO, BOSTON, NEW YORK, & WASHINGTON
HONOLULU
TAHITI
TO BUENOS AIRES
FIJI
NORFOLK ISLAND
NOUMEA
AUCKLAND
WELLINGTON
CHRISTCHURCH
HONIARA
PORT MORESBY
CAIRNS
BRISBANE
SYDNEY
MELBOURNE
HOBART
ADELAIDE
PERTH
PORT HEDLAND
DARWIN
DENPASAR
JAKARTA
SINGAPORE
KUALA LUMPUR
PHUKET
BANGKOK
HONG KONG
MANILA
FUKUOKA
NAGOYA
TOKYO
0 1000mi
0 1000km
ROUTES ARE SUBJECT TO CHANGE WITHOUT PRIOR NOTICE

Hong Kong, Tokyo, and back to San Francisco. Contact travel agents for participating airlines and current fares.

At the time of this writing, the average low-season APEX fare from either Los Angeles or San Francisco—with three stopovers allowed—is $1130 to Sydney and $1731 to Perth; high season is $1592 to Sydney, and $2228 to Perth.

AIRLINES

Qantas Airways
Okay, I'm partial—I *love* flying Qantas (The Spirit of Australia) to Oz. You become an "old mate" the second you get on board. The crew is down to earth even while the plane is high in the sky. Nearing Australia, a news program is broadcast on the video system, informing passengers of national and regional events before they even get there.

From North America, Qantas flies out of Boston, Chicago, Honolulu, Los Angeles, New York, San Francisco, Toronto, Vancouver, and Washington D.C. For reservations in the United States, phone (800) 227-4500. In Canada, phone 684-8231 (Vancouver); (800) 663-3411 (Alberta and British Columbia); (800) 663-3421 (the rest of Canada).

International Carriers From North America
Air New Zealand, American, Canadian International, Continental, Northwest, and UTA French Airlines will also get you from the west coast of North America to the eastern shores of Australia, via a variety of routes. However, be forewarned: fares, airlines, and routes are continually changing. Call your travel agent or the individual airlines for up-to-date info and fares.

Currently, many nonstop flights operate between Los Angeles or San Francisco and Sydney (flying time about 15 hours). Other flights offer some attractive stopover possibilities: Honolulu-Papeete-Nadi-Rarotonga-Auckland (Air New Zealand); Honolulu-Papeete-Nadi-Auckland (Qantas); Papeete-Noumea-Auckland (UTA). American, Northwest, and United make stops in Honolulu, and Canadian International passengers transfer to Qantas or Air New Zealand flights in Honolulu. Air New Zealand flies to Adelaide, Cairns, and Perth. Qantas continues to Adelaide, Cairns, Darwin, and Perth.

COUNCIL TRAVEL OFFICES

In The United States

Berkeley, 2486 Channing Way, Berkeley, CA 94704 (tel. 415-848-8604)

Los Angeles, Suite 220, 1093 Broxton Ave., Los Angeles, CA 90024 (tel. 213-208-3551)

San Diego, 953 Garnet Ave., San Diego, CA 92109 (tel. 619-270-6401)

San Francisco, Suite 407, 312 Sutter St., San Francisco, CA 94108 (tel. 415-421-3473)

Washington, D.C., 3300 M St. NW, 2nd Fl., Washington, D.C. 20007 (tel. 202-337-6464)

Chicago, 1153 N. Dearborn St., 2nd Fl., Chicago, IL 60610 (tel. 312-951-0585)

Boston, Suite 201, 729 Boylston St., Boston, MA 02116 (tel. 617-266-1926)

New York, 205 E. 42nd St., New York, NY 10017 (tel. 212-661-1450)

Dallas, 3300 W. Mockingbird Ln., Dallas, TX 75235 (tel. 214-350-6166)

Seattle, Suite 210, 1314 Northeast 43rd St., Seattle, WA 98105 (tel. 206-632-2448)

Elsewhere

London, 28A Poland St., London W1 (tel. 071-437-7767)

Paris, 49 rue Pierre Charron, 75008 Paris (tel. 1-45-63-19-87)

Germany, 18 Graf Adolph Str., 4000 Düsseldorf 1 (tel. 211-32-90-88)

Japan, Sanno Grand Building, Room 102, 2-14-2 Nagata-cho, Chiyoda-ku, Tokyo 100 (tel. 3-581-7581)

Other International Carriers
From Asia: Air India, Air New Zealand, Alitalia, All Nippon Airways, British Airways, Cathay Pacific Airways, Garuda Indonesian Airways, Japan Airlines, KLM Royal Dutch

STUDENT TRAVEL ASSOCIATION OFFICES

In The United States
Berkeley, 82 Shattuck Square #4, Berkeley, CA 94704 (tel. 415-841-1037)
Boston, 273 Newbury St., Boston, MA 02116 (tel. 617-266-6014)
Cambridge, 1208 Massachusetts Ave. #5, Cambridge, MA 02138 (tel. 617-576-4623)
Los Angeles, 7202 Melrose Ave., Los Angeles, CA 90046 (tel. 213-934-8722) or 914 Westwood Blvd., Los Angeles, CA 90024 (tel. 213- 824-1574)
New York, 48 E. 11th St., New York, NY 10003 (tel. 212-986-9470)
San Diego, 5131 College Ave. #B, San Diego, CA 92115 (tel. 619- 286-1322)
San Francisco, 166 Geary St. #702, San Francisco, CA 94108 (tel. 415-391-8407)

In Canada
Toronto, Cuts Travel (S.T.A. affiliate), 44 St. George's St., Toronto, Ontario M5S 2E4 (tel. 416-979-2406)
Vancouver, Cuts Travel (S.T.A. affiliate), Room 108, 1425 W. Pender St., Vancouver, B.C. (tel. 604-682-9136)

In The U.K.
London, 74 Old Brompton, London SW 7 (tel. 071-937-9971)

In Australia
Adelaide, 33 Jetty Rd., Glenelg, S.A. 5045 (tel. 08-376-0730)
Brisbane, Shop 25, Brisbane Arcade, 111-117 Adelaide St., Brisbane, QLD 4001 (tel. 07-221-9388)
Cairns, 105 Lake St., Cairns, QLD 4870 (tel. 070-31-4199)
Canberra, Shop 208, Level 3, Westfield Shopping Mall, Belconnen, ACT 2616 (tel. 062-51-4688)
Darwin, Darwin Transit Centre, 69 Mitchell St., Darwin, N.T. 0800 (tel. 089-41-2955)
Melbourne, 222 Faraday St., Carlton, VIC 3053 (tel. 03-347-6911)
Sydney, 1A Lee St., Railway Square, Sydney, N.S.W. 2000 (tel. 02-212-1255)
Perth, 426 Hay St., Subiaco, W.A. 6008 (tel. 09-382-3977)
Townsville, 100 Stanley St., Townsville, QLD 4810 (tel. 077-72- 7382)

Airlines, Lufthansa, Malaysian Air System, Philippine Airlines, Qantas Airways, Singapore Airlines, Thai International, and UTA French Airlines. **From Europe and the United Kingdom:** Air India, Alitalia, Air New Zealand, British Airways, Cathay Pacific Airways, Japan Airlines, KLM Royal Dutch Airlines, Lufthansa, Malaysian Air System, Qantas Airways, Scandinavian Airlines, Singapore Airlines, and Thai International. **From South America:** Lan Chile and Aerolineas Argentinas, in conjunction with Qantas Airways. **From Africa:** Qantas (from Zimbabwe).

Qantas flies to Perth from Zimbabwe, and to Darwin from London, Frankfurt, and Rome (via Singapore and Bangkok).

GETTING AROUND

Australia is enormous. Distances between places are vast and destinations often completely isolated—don't try to see the whole continent on a 10-day tour. Australia is also not a dollar-a-day country, nor an especially good one for hitchhiking. Allow yourself plenty of time, plan at least a tentative itinerary, and budget your funds accordingly.

BY AIR

For the most part prices quoted here are full-price economy fares, but there is a wide range of other options. First off, Australian airlines were recently deregulated, resulting in a bevy of promotional, excursion, discount, and stand-by offers for domestic flights.

The main domestic carriers are Ansett, Australian, and East-West airlines; usually their prices and deals run neck-and-neck. Since deregulation, Compass Air, (the new kid on the block) had been giving them a run for their money until it went bankrupt in December, 1991.

Regional carriers, such as Ansett NT, Ansett WA, and Kendell airlines, provide regularly scheduled service between cities, provincial towns, and Outback areas.

If you plan to do a lot of domestic flying, inquire into Ansett, Australian, or East-West airlines' money-saving air passes. Passes also vary—some allow unlimited mileage, others restrict destinations and stopovers—and most need to be purchased outside Australia. Once you're in Australia, if you don't have an air pass but want to hop on a domestic flight anyway, international ticketholders are eligible for 30-50% discounts off regular economy fares (you have to show your ticket). International ticketholders are also permitted to fly domestic sectors on Qantas, no matter which airline they flew into Australia on (big discounts also apply).

North American contacts are: **Ansett Airlines and East-West Airlines** (tel. 800-366-1300, U.S. and Canada; book through Qantas in Europe); and **Australian Airlines** (tel. 800-922-5122, U.S.; 800-448-9400, Canada; 071-434-3864, U.K.). Within Australia, phone Ansett Airlines (tel. 13-1300) or Australian Airlines (tel. 13-1313). Both numbers are toll-free, countrywide (no area code is necessary).

BY TRAIN

Other than commuter and suburban trains that run from Adelaide and Perth, Outback Australia is not very well served by rail. **Railways of Australia** operates the transcontinental *Indian Pacific* (Sydney-Perth, 65 hours), the *Trans Australian* (Adelaide-Perth, 40 hours), the *Ghan* (Adelaide-Alice Springs, 22 hours), the *Prospector* (Perth-Kalgoorlie, eight hours), the *Overland* (Melbourne-Adelaide, 12 hours), and the *Daylink* and *Speedlink,* two train-coach combinations from Melbourne and Sydney (respectively) to Adelaide.

First- and economy-class seats and berths are available on all long-distance services and must be booked in advance. **Austrailpasses** allow unlimited rail travel (including metropolitan trains) and are good deals if you plan to do a lot of rail travel. They, too, must be purchased outside Australia. Costs are: 14 days ($690 first class, $415 economy); 21 days ($850/$535); 30 days ($1050/ $650); 60 days ($1460/$930); 90 days ($1680/$1070). Seven-day extensions on any pass is $350 first class, $225 economy. Passes do not cover charges for sleeping berths or meals.

For more information or reservations, phone **Railways of Australia:** (800) 423-2880, U.S.; (800) 232-2121, California; (416) 322-1034, Toronto; (604) 687-4004, Vancouver; (071) 828-4111, London.

If you want to catch a train but don't have a railpass, inquire about **Caper Fares.** If booked seven days ahead, they can save you some 30% off regular rail fares.

BY COACH

Modern air-conditioned coaches are an easy and comfortable way to see the country. Most of them have bathroom facilities, overhead video monitors, piped-in music, on-board hostesses, and drivers who double as tour guides. The big coach lines (Greyhound, Pioneer, and Bus Australia) travel to all capital cities, country towns, provincial centers, and most Outback regions; if there's a place they don't travel, they can usually hook up with a local bus system (which might be a mail truck) that will get you where you're going.

Coach travel is a good way to kick back and relax, see the countryside, and meet other Aussie and international travelers. On the downside, you might find yourself locked up with some madding crowd.

Again, you have an almost infinite assortment of bus passes—local, regional, national, and bus and train combination passes. Some you have to buy outside Australia; others you can only buy once you're there. Also, the companies have been changing names, going broke, and buying each other out. **Australian Coachlines** is the parent company of both Pioneer and Greyhound. For national reservations within Australia,

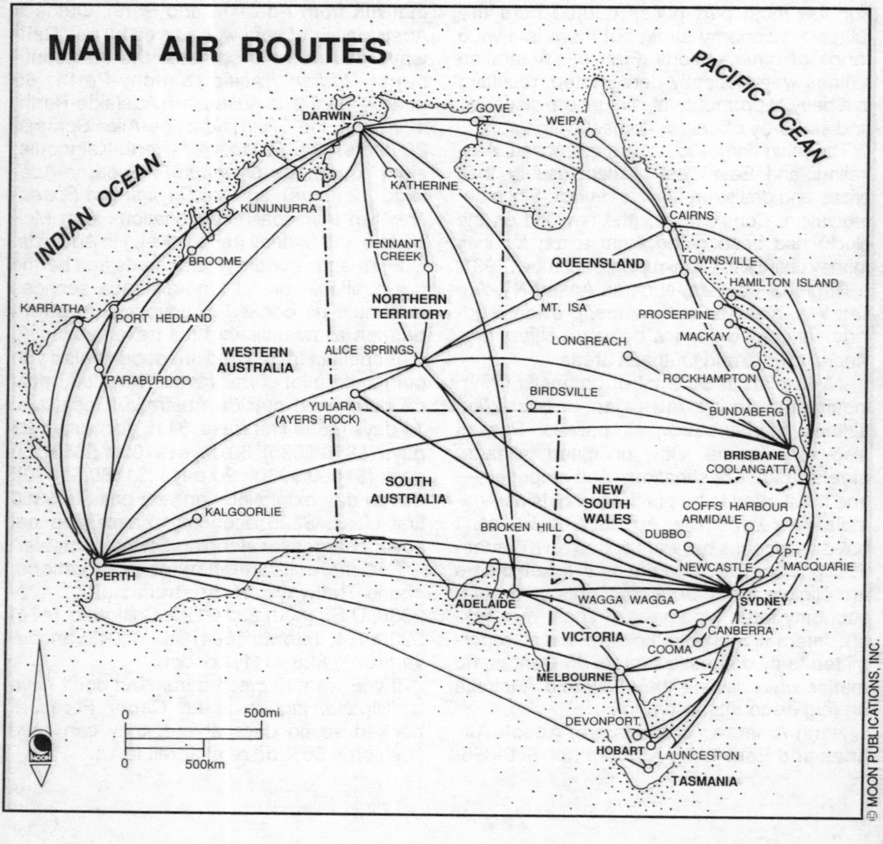

EQUIPMENT

The Royal Automobile Club suggests you take the following equipment on your Outback tour:

Vehicle Equipment
good condition spare wheel
spare tire
jack, jack base
tow rope
fan belt
radiator hose
extra ignition key
fuses, spark plugs
spare bulbs for headlights and tail lights
petrol in jerry cans
engine oil (sufficient for complete change)
container of brake fluid
lubricating spray
insulating tape
epoxy resin putty
tube of silicone rubber gasket
bottle Bars-Leak
tube Bostik
two meters bailing wire
welding wire or copper wire
set of disc brake pads (if fitted)
brass brake-lining rivets
spare air-cleaner element
spare engine oil/fuel filter cartridge
sufficient automatic transmission fluid for complete change

Minimum Tool Kit
hacksaw
hammer
set of ring and open-ended spanners and socket spanner set to suit your vehicle
cold chisel
set of screwdrivers
pliers
file
tire pump
wheel chocks
vulcanizing clamp and patches
tire levers
valve key
pressure gauge
jumper leads
two meters of 6.35 mm inside diameter reinforced fuel-resistant plastic hose
two meters of four-mm low tension wire

phone 13-1238 (toll free). For information within the U.S., phone (800) 828-1985.

Check with the Australian Tourist Commission office (see "Services And Information" for phone numbers) for current information and additional contact numbers.

BY CAR OR CARAVAN

First rule to remember: drive on the left side of the road! (And for you standard transmission types, this means you shift with your *left* hand!)

The major highways are sealed and well-maintained but are often only two-lane affairs. City expressways and thoroughfares are just about as hectic as everywhere else. For Outback travel you *must* follow special driving laws (a brochure detailing them can be obtained from any branch of the Royal Automobile Association) and have an appropriate vehicle with spare parts and other supplies in tow. Outback "roads" are like no others (off-roading in Baja on a summer weekend does not compare—or prepare you).

Rentals are not cheap. Avis, Budget, Hertz, and Thrifty are well represented and can be booked ahead from North America, but you'll often get a better deal from smaller, independent concerns after you've arrived.

WARNING SIGNS

SPEED LIMIT ENDS

One advantage of the big conglomerates is that you can pick up and return your car at the airport. Petrol, sold by the liter, comes in leaded and unleaded grades and works out to about $3 per gallon. Before renting a car ($40-70 per day), find out if it includes unlimited kilometers. If you take a car into Outback regions you will be charged a hefty premium. Four-wheel-drive vehicles are available for more adventurous travel, but they are much costlier than conventional cars.

Campervans (two to three berths) and **caravans** (four to six berths) range in price from $760 to $1200 per week, with unlimited mileage. Most come equipped with refrigerator, sink, gas stove, water tank, and some have showers and toilets.

Filling stations are plentiful in cities, suburbs, and townships, but can be few and far between in the Outback.

Whatever type of vehicle you rent, make sure you take out adequate insurance. If you're a member of the American Automobile Club, bring your membership card to receive reciprocal rights from the Royal Automobile Association.

Laws And Licenses

The maximum speed limit in cities and towns is 60 km, increasing to 100 km on country roads and highways (unless signs say otherwise). Seat belts are mandatory and must be worn by the driver and all passengers. Drunk-driving laws are strict and spot checks (including Breathalyzer tests) are commonplace.

International Driver's Licenses are recognized by all states and territories. Tourists can usually get away with using their valid overseas driver's license if driving the same class of vehicle.

CYCLING

Both long-distance and round-the-city cycling are popular in Australia. For route maps, trail suggestions, and information on bicycle touring, contact **Bicycle Australia,** Box 1047, Campbelltown, NSW 2560 (tel. 046-27-2186). This national touring organization is also developing an around-Australia route.

SOUTH AUSTRALIA

INTRODUCTION

License plates proclaim it The Festival State. Border crossing signs herald it The Grand Prix State (and, underneath, warn that speeding laws are strictly enforced). Fact decrees it the driest state in Australia. And the Tourism Commission slogan banners it—most accurately—The State of Surprise. The surprises are many for, dry as most of its 984,200 square km may be, South Australia is *definitely* not dull.

Flanked by Victoria and New South Wales on the east, by Perth on the west, and neatly tucked beneath the Northern Territory, this land has almost as many ripe attractions to pick from as it does grapes growing on its famous vines. Most people have heard about the Barossa and Clare valleys, famous for fine wines and the warm feelings that go with them—and about Adelaide, the "pretty" capital city, where nearly two-thirds of the state's 1.4 million inhabitants live from one festival to the next—and, without a doubt, the mere mention of the Outback probably sends shivers down the spines of those who dream of scorching in their boots. Coober Pedy, the opal-mining town so hot that homes and shops are built underground, has also received a share of the publicity (though it's often depicted as the end of the earth).

Not so popularized by films, jewels, or wine labels are South Australia's lesser known gems: Hahndorf, a German settlement where you can pick up streusel on the corner instead of meat pie; Burra, an exquisitely preserved copper center, with miners' dugouts, Cornish cottages, and the "monster mine"; Kangaroo Island, abundant in roos and other wild and woollies, with picnic areas that keep the humans fenced in so the animals watch *them* eat and perform; the Flinders Ranges—spectacular multicolored rock formations, about 1,600 million years old, with deep gorges and endless changing vistas; the Blue Lake, which is actually gray but turns to bright blue at the exact same time each year; Lake Eyre, a (usually) dry salt pan that is Australia's largest lake; and the mighty Murray, the country's most important river, which stretches more than 2,000 km from the Snowy Mountains to Lake Alexandrina.

These, of course, are just a few tidbits to whet your appetite. You will also discover heritage towns with exquisitely crafted sandstone buildings, little sleepy fishing villages, bustling beach resorts, reputed UFO landing sights, and Outback tracks to test the heartiest, nerviest, and possibly craziest souls. Naturally, there *are* some dry spots, but think of them merely as crackers to clear your palate between sips (or gulps) of the sweetest wine.

Most places are easily accessible by a variety of transport. Hop a vintage tram to the beach or catch the *Ghan* and train it up to the Red Centre. To get around cities, between towns, or across the Nullarbor Plain, hire an air-conditioned luxury car, a four-wheel-drive jeep, or use your thumb and your feet. Float along the Murray in your own houseboat, or sign up for a paddlesteamer cruise. (Incidentally, some of the gurgly ferries-'cross-the-Murray will pang the nostalgic hearts of early '70s travelers who once clutched a tattered copy of *Siddhartha* against their searching breasts.)

There is one new development, however, which may very well turn The State of Surprise into a State of Shock—the Multi-functional Polis, proposed for Adelaide's northwestern suburbs.

The MFP, as it is called, is billed a "city of the future." The 3,500-hectare building site will accommodate some very high-tech industries, housing for a hundred thousand people, as well as health, education, and recreation facilities—and it will be financed by those ubiquitous Japanese yen. The controversies are many and the committees of politicos, environmentalists, and Average Citizens are still being formed. Some of the pros: the MFP will give Australia prestigious international standing while providing a much-needed boost to the ailing economy. Opponents insist that the project will be an environmental nightmare, citing possible seepage of toxic chemicals, higher risk of earthquakes, and death of the all-important mangroves as just a few ramifications of filling in the land. *And* there is fear and consternation that the Japanese may well be using their yen only to satisfy their own cravings.

The project, originally slated for Queensland's Gold Coast area but nixed by that state due to problems with private land acquisitions, was shunted down to Adelaide, the alternate choice (don't ever say *second* choice —they're touchy about it!).

Amid all the hoopla comes this unique view expressed by South Australia's UFO expert, Colin Norris: "We must stop knocking the Multi-functional Polis because visitors from other galaxies are waiting for it. This is the sort of place that will attract other beings. It's the sort of place they've been waiting for to come to."

So, on that enticing note—welcome, aliens, to South Australia!

CLIMATE

There is good reason why more than 99% of the state's population live south of the 32nd parallel—it is the only part that isn't hot, harsh, and desolate.

Adelaide is frequently described as having a "Mediterranean-like" climate. The short, mild winters (June-Aug.) average 17° C (62° F). Even with occasional downpours and some very chilly nights, most days are bathed in plenty of sunshine. Summers, from Dec.-Feb., are very dry and range from a warm 29° C (87° F) to a downright hot 38° C (100°F). Autumn (March-May) and especially the spring months (Sept.-Nov.) are delightful times to visit the wine country or plan a bushwalk.

Adelaide's surrounding hills and vineyards are fertile and well irrigated. The southeast corner of the state, and Kangaroo Island, are cooler and greener yet. And, though snow is a rarity in South Australia, an occasional light spatter has been sighted atop the Mt. Lofty Ranges.

The Outback, which comprises most of the northern part of the state, blisters in summer. Searing temperatures of 51°C (132°F) have

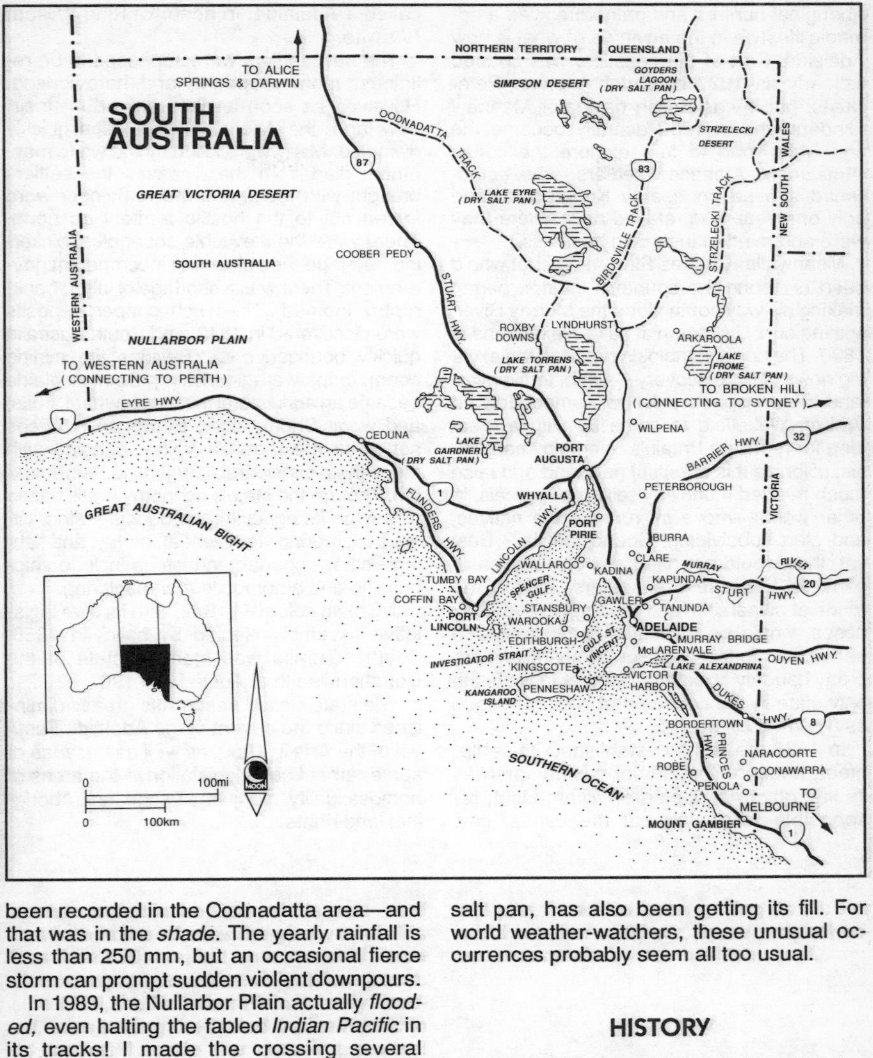

been recorded in the Oodnadatta area—and that was in the *shade*. The yearly rainfall is less than 250 mm, but an occasional fierce storm can prompt sudden violent downpours.

In 1989, the Nullarbor Plain actually *flooded,* even halting the fabled *Indian Pacific* in its tracks! I made the crossing several months after the rains and saw so many pools of water and bits of scrub popping up out of the normally cracked, parched, and stark earth that I feared I was hallucinating multiple oases. Lake Eyre, normally a huge salt pan, has also been getting its fill. For world weather-watchers, these unusual occurrences probably seem all too usual.

HISTORY

There was life before Light—Colonel William Light, that is, the British surveyor general who laid out the site for the capital city.

Thousands of years prior to Britain's colonization of South Australia, small tribes of

Aboriginal hunters and gatherers lived a nomadic lifestyle in the environs of what is now Adelaide. Part of the coastline was charted as early as 1627 by Dutch explorer Peter Nuyts, but it was British navigator Matthew Flinders who in 1802 actually became the first white man to fully explore the coast. (Amazingly, American sealers, who established a base on nearby Kangaroo Island only one year later, stayed right where they were and minded their own business.)

Meanwhile, Charles Sturt, a hotshot who'd been exploring the country's interior, began making his way south along the Murray River, spitting out of its mouth at Lake Alexandrina in 1830. The London tabloids reported the exciting news of his discovery—a rich, fertile riverland. This inspired a fellow named Edward Gibbon Wakefield to come up with a great idea for reducing Britain's unemployment crisis: colonize this bountiful new land and raise much-needed money by selling off parcels. In other words—move in, run out the natives, and start subdividing. Sound familiar? Best yet, they would not need any of those nasty convicts because the settlers, having the "pride of ownership" carrot dangling over their noses, would be motivated to do their own hard labor. To this day, South Australians are pretty haughty about the fact that theirs is the only state in the country that was not begun as a convict colony.

In 1836 the British established its settlement, naming Captain John Hindmarsh as its first governor. Colonel William Light, responsible for laying out the capital city, called it Adelaide, in honor of King William IV's wife.

The new settlers were supposed to be religious, morally upright, and hardworking. However, as soon as they arrived in "their" new land, the Aboriginal population quickly dwindled. Many were killed by the white men, others died from the diseases the settlers brought with them, and the remainder were forced out to the hostile territory up north. There were the inevitable squabbles, bickering, red tape, and claims of incompetent government. There was a shortage of labor; bankruptcy loomed. Then rich copper deposits were discovered in 1842, and South Australia quickly bounced back. Besides the mining boom, crops were flourishing. Soon Adelaide became an agricultural mecca for wheat, fruits, and wool. Shortly after, European refugees settled in the Barossa Valley, bringing with them their considerable talent for winemaking. Though the state's economy is still based mainly on its agricultural products—wine, citrus fruit, merino wool, wheat, barley, and fishing—other important industries include shipbuilding and automobile manufacturing.

A Crown colony in 1842, with its own legislative assembly elected by ballot in 1856, South Australia was made a state of the Commonwealth of Australia in 1901.

The state's staid image has greatly diminished since the advent of the Adelaide Festival of the Arts in 1960, as well as because of some rather liberal legislation in the areas of homosexuality, marijuana usage, and Aboriginal land rights.

ADELAIDE

> "Approaching Adelaide from Melbourne, we left the train and were driven in an open carriage over the hills and along their slopes to the city. It was an excursion of an hour or two and the charm of it could not be overstated.
>
> The road wound through gaps and gorges and offered all variety of scenery and prospect—color, color everywhere and the air fine and fresh, the skies blue and not a shred of cloud to mar the downpour of the brilliant sunshine.
>
> And finally the mountain gateway opened, and the immense plain spread out below, stretching away into the dim distance on every hand, soft and delicate and dainty and beautiful.
>
> On its near edge reposed the city; with wide streets compactly built; with fine houses everywhere, embowered in foliage and flowers and with imposing masses of public buildings nobly grouped and architecturally beautiful."
>
> —Mark Twain

Colonel William Light has practically been beatified for his foresight in planning South Australia's capital city. The man loved straight lines and broad boulevards. He wanted Adelaide to reflect both simplicity and elegance and he had a magnificent site on which to realize his vision: a flat plain, centrally located on the southern coastline, with the glorious backdrop of rolling hills and dales and the Mt. Lofty Ranges.

Light designed a one-square-mile central business district composed of grid-patterned streets bisecting at right angles and five perfect city squares interspersed at regular intervals. One of these, Victoria Square, is the designated heart of the city (you'll find the General Post Office across the street and the central bus station about a block away). Running north and south, skirting around Victoria Square, is King William Street, the center for business and commerce and supposedly the widest city street in any Australian capital. (Light named the main thoroughfare after his king, but it was his Queen Adelaide who took the whole city and, eventually, a wine label as well.)

Heading north up King William Street, you'll come to the intersection of Hindley Street on the west and Rundle Mall on the east—same street, but it changes names. Hindley Street is lined with restaurants, discos, and nightclubs, a couple of strip joints, and an adult book shop or two. This is Adelaide's "racy" quarter, if the odd street brawl, broken beer bottle, or risqué book jacket justify the term.

Rundle Mall is the no-cars-allowed main shopping promenade which sports arcades with specialty shops, art galleries, department stores, and occasional street vendors and buskers. One block farther, on your right, is the South Australian Travel Centre.

The city center is bounded in a neat little parcel by broad tree-lined terraces, aptly named North, South, East, and West Terrace. North Terrace, just another block up from the Travel Centre, is where you'll find most of the city's architectural and cultural attractions—Parliament House, the museums, Festival Arts Centre, University of Adelaide, and such. The terraces, in turn, are bordered by expansive parklands with lovely greenbelts, towering eucalyptus trees, picnic areas, and recreation facilities.

The River Torrens, navigated by rowboats, motor launches, and a variety of other putt-putts, separates the business district from North Adelaide, one of the oldest sections of the city. North Adelaide is yet another of Colonel Light's babies—the Chosen Suburb, an exclusive residential grid built around a perfectly regular town square, surrounded by lots of greenery.

Now, don't start thinking that all these well-organized grids and squares mean this is a metropolis full of unimaginative boxes. The architecture is *brilliant,* at least most of it—luscious stone churches, ornate and filigreed mansions, superb colonial buildings. As in most big cities, however, the old and beauti-

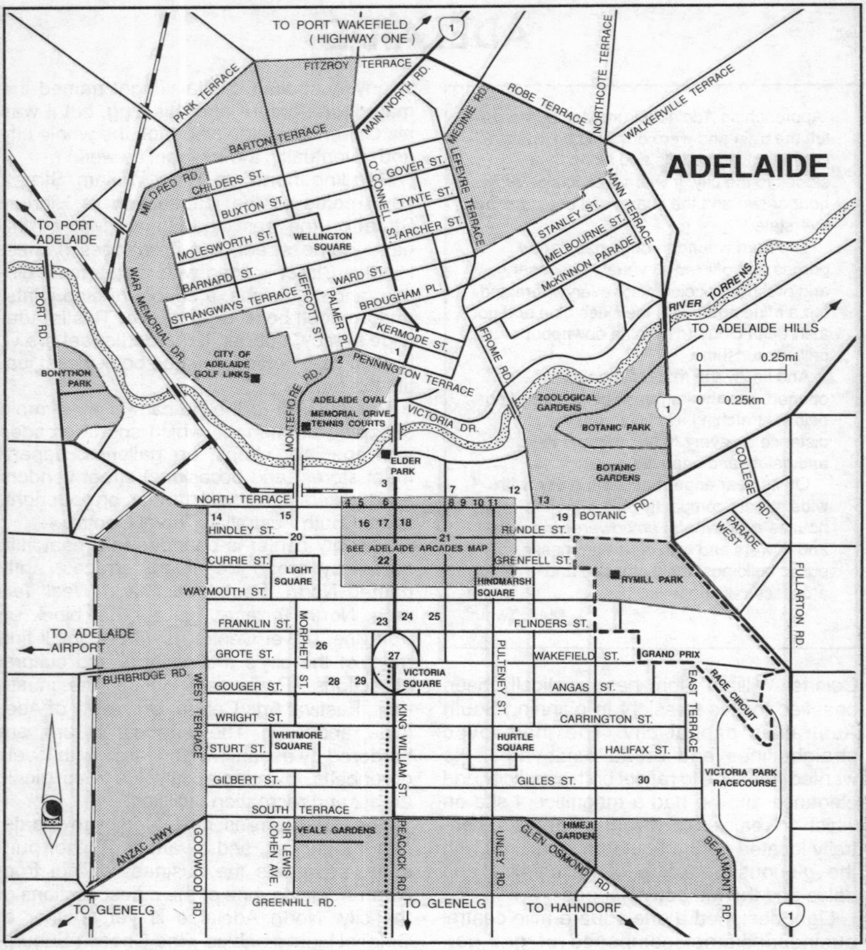

ful structures do sometimes sit side by side with new and tasteless office blocks, but a movement is well underway to preserve as much of the original architecture as possible, or at least to keep the original façades.

Because of its compactness and methodical layout, Adelaide is easy to explore on foot. And, though it lacks the street action of many major cities, the small town–ish atmosphere and almost pastoral spaciousness make this state capital unique.

You're likely to hear a string of adjectives rattled off whenever Adelaide is mentioned—"calm," "stately," and, occasionally, "staid." The slightly more than one million residents like to think of *themselves* as sophisticated, and infinitely more cultured than those beer-guzzling, telly-watching, footy-fiend louts

ADELAIDE

1. St. Peter's Cathedral
2. Lith's Vision
3. Festival Centre
4. Convention Centre
5. Adelaide Casino (and Railway Station)
6. Parliament House
7. Migration and Settlement Museum
8. State Library
9. Mortlock Library
10. South Australia Museum
11. Art Gallery of South Australia
12. University of Adelaide
13. Royal Adelaide Hospital
14. Newmarket Hotel
15. Living Arts Centre
16. Australian Airlines
17. Ansett Airlines
18. South Australian Government Travel Centre
19. Ayers House
20. Hindley St. Restaurant and Entertainment Area
21. Rundle Mall Shopping Area
22. Edmund Wright House
23. General Post Office
24. Adelaide Town Hall
25. YMCA
26. Central Bus Station
27. Glenelg Tram Terminal
28. Central Market
29. Hilton International Hotel
30. Adelaide Youth Hostel

who inhabit the rest of the country. In Adelaide *they* drink fine wines, follow the cricket matches, attend the theater, and on alternate years, put on a Formula One Grand Prix and world-class Festival of the Arts.

Calm, stately, staid? In 1988, Mick Jagger opened his solo world concert tour in Adelaide. Let someone try to grid and square *that* one.

ON THE TERRACE

North Terrace, wedged between the city hustle-bustle and the gentle River Torrens, is Adelaide's historic and cultural heart. This easy walk begins at the corner of West Terrace and North Terrace and ends at the corner of East Terrace. Conveniently, you start off at the **Newmarket Hotel** and finish up at the **Botanic Hotel,** two of Adelaide's most sumptuous pubs, which date back to the late 19th century.

Living Arts Centre

Many of the Adelaide Arts Festival fringe events are held in this old Lions Club building at the corner of Morphett Street. Performance stages, galleries, arts and crafts workshops, and casual eating areas are the core of this vibrantly renovated factory. It is usually open during the daytime for a wander or coffee and a sandwich, otherwise hours depend on scheduled events.

Holy Trinity Church

The foundation stone for the state's oldest Anglican church, beside the Morphett Street bridge, was laid by Governor Hindmarsh himself in 1838. The present building is actually about 50 years newer, but the original clock still remains.

Adelaide Casino

You can bet that more people cross the threshold of the swanky casino than the church across the street! Built atop the classic sandstone railway station with its majestic colonnades and balconies (still used by commuters), the casino offers two floors of gaming tables—roulette, craps, blackjack, baccarat—plus Keno, a Money Wheel, and Two-Up, an Aussie invention that has something to do with tossing coins in a ring. For those of you who prefer one-armed bandits, you're already out of luck: you'll find no poker or slot machines here. High rollers, however, can try to get a pass into the exclusive International Room. Even if you don't gamble, this is a good spot to people-watch. Also, there are five bars and two restaurants, The **Pullman** and the less formal **Carvery.**

Security is tight—photography is not allowed. In addition, a dress code is enforced—dressy or "smart casual," and guards will scrutinize you from head to toe as you cross the marble hall to the entrance, although I'm not at all sure they know what they're looking for.

The casino is part of Adelaide Plaza, which also houses the Adelaide Convention Centre and Festival Centre, as well as the Hyatt Regency Hotel. It is open Mon.-Fri. 10 a.m.-4 a.m., Sat.-Sun. 24 hours, closed Christmas Day and Good Friday (when you can probably lay odds that more people are over at the church).

Old Parliament House

Sandwiched between the casino and the new Parliament House, South Australia's original Parliament is one of the state's oldest and most historic buildings. In 1855 this was home to the first Legislative Council. Painstaking renovations were completed in 1980 and it is now the **Constitutional Museum,** which presents audiovisual displays and exhibits depicting the state's history, from Dreamtime to the present. The museum's **House of Assembly** is reputedly the world's oldest surviving chamber of democracy. A bookshop specializes in South Australian history, and there's a pleasant restaurant in the garden courtyard.

New Parliament House, next door, was a 56-year-long construction project, begun in 1883 and completed in 1939. Built out of grey Kapunda marble with high Corinthian columns in neoclassical style, it is a sharp contrast to its simpler predecessor.

Old Parliament House is open Mon.-Fri. 10 a.m.-5 p.m., Sat.-Sun. 11:30 a.m.-5 p.m. Admission is $3.50. For more information, phone (08) 212-6881.

The Adelaide Festival Centre

On King William Street, just behind the houses of Parliament and banking the River Torrens, the Adelaide Festival Centre, built in 1972, is home to the three-week Adelaide Festival of Arts, held in March of even-numbered years. Ranked as one of the world's top international multi-arts festivals, it draws diverse and big-name talents like Rudolf Nureyev, Yehudi Menuhin, the Royal Shakespeare Company, Japan's Kabuki Theatre, Twyla Tharp, and Mick Jagger. In addition, the Fringe Festival, which takes place simultaneously, presents innovative theatrical productions, performance events, poetry readings, art exhibitions, and a writers' week. Fringe events are held at the Living Arts Centre and a host of other venues around town. The local newspapers' daily listings will keep you informed of when and where.

The Centre is comprised of a 2,000-seat multi-purpose theater and concert hall, a drama theater (home to the State Theatre Company), an additional flexible performance space, an open-air amphitheater, a piano bar, and two restaurants. A variety of entertainment is presented year-round, including professional productions of successful musicals like *Cats* and *Evita,* chamber orchestra symphonies, and an informal late-night cabaret.

You can take a 45-minute tour of the Festival Centre every day except Sun. and Thursday. Monday through Wed. and Fri. tours depart 11 a.m., 1, 2, and 3 p.m., Sat. tours 11 a.m. and 2 p.m. Cost is $2 (which includes a cup of coffee in the **Bistro**), payable at the enquiry counter in the foyer. For more information, phone 213-4788.

Government House

Back on North Terrace and east across King William Street is the Regency-style official residence of South Australia's governor. The first governor, John Hindmarsh, lived on the same site in 1836—but not in the same house. Governor Hindmarsh lived in a mud hut. It was George Gawler, the second governor (1838-41), who decided it was time to build a more suitable residence and, in 1839, began construction of the East Wing. The midsection was added in 1855 and, by 1878, the house as you see it was completed.

On either side of Government House are two **war memorials**: to the west is a bronze infantryman, commemorating South Australians who died in the Boer War; to the east is the National War Memorial, honoring those who died in WW I; plaques along the wall of Government House pay tribute to the dead of WW II.

Royal South Australian Society Of Art

Across Kintore St., the Society, founded in 1856, exhibits at least six major members' shows per year, its own permanent collec-

Modern complexes and historic structures share Adelaide's Torrens River banks.

tion, and works of various individual artists. The archives and reference library are available for research. Hours are Mon.-Fri. 11 a.m.-5 p.m., Sat.-Sun. 2-5 p.m., closed Christmas, New Year's Day, and Easter weekend. Admission is free. For information, phone 223-4704.

State Library

This place is just a bit confusing: the State Library, which was originally in the old wing, is now in the Angaston white marble building next door; the **Mortlock Library,** restored to Victorian grandeur, is actually the original state library. To put it another way: the State Library carries all the regular books and overseas newspapers; the Mortlock has all the special collections—memorabilia relating to South Australiana, a Historic Treasures Room with Colonel Light's surveying equipment on display, and a family history research library. The Mortlock is open Mon.-Fri. 9:30 a.m.-5 p.m., Thurs. until 9:30 p.m. For information, phone 223-8911.

Migration And Settlement Museum

Next to the State Library, on Kintore Ave., is Australia's first multicultural museum. The building itself is Adelaide's restored Destitute Asylum. Exhibits and an audio visual program give a realistic picture of what life was like for the early settlers. You can even visit the dark cells built back in the 1870s after a riot. The bookshop specializes in South Australian history. **Mrs. Gifford's** is a cafe, located in the courtyard. The museum is open Mon.-Fri. 10 a.m.-5 p.m., Sat.-Sun. and public holidays 1-5 p.m. Closed Good Friday and Christmas Day. Except for special traveling exhibits, admission is free. Guided tours are available. For information, phone 223-8748.

Police Barracks And Armory

Tucked in a courtyard, near the Migration and Settlement Museum the small **South Australian Police Museum** displays 1860s law enforcement memorabilia. Open Sat.-Sun. 11 a.m.-5 p.m. Donations are requested.

South Australian Museum

A distinctive North Terrace landmark, with whale skeletons in the front window, this museum is especially noteworthy for its extensive collections of Aboriginal, New Guinean, and Melanesian native artifacts. The museum shop stocks natural history and anthropology books, as well as related gift items. The museum is open Mon.-Sat. 10 a.m.-5 p.m. (Wed. 1-5 p.m.), Sun. 2-5 p.m., closed Good Friday and Christmas Day. Admission is free, and free tours are available on weekends and holidays. For information, phone 223-8911.

Art Gallery Of South Australia
Next door to the museum, two wings of this really fine gallery house a comprehensive collection of Australian, European, and Asian art. Highlights include examples of Australian impressionists, colonial works (including furniture, silver, and other decorative arts), 20th-century works by important painters like Arthur Boyd, Sir Sidney Nolan, and Russell Drysdale, recent Aboriginal landscapes, and an interesting collection of Southeast Asian ceramics. Changing exhibitions of contemporary art, and Australian and international touring shows, are also on display. The bookshop has a good collection of art books, periodicals and cards, some jewelry, and other related items. A pleasant coffee shop in the rear sells small cakes and sandwiches. The gallery is open daily 10 a.m.-5 p.m., closed Good Friday and Christmas Day. Admission is free, but there is often a charge for special exhibitions. Daily tours leave from the front entrance daily at 11 a.m. For information, phone 223-7200.

Museum Of Classical Archaeology
The Mitchell Building, a striking Gothic edifice on the **University of Adelaide** campus, is a fitting site for this collection of Greek, Egyptian, and Etruscan relics—some more than 5,000 years old. The museum, on the first floor, is open Mon.-Fri. 12-3 p.m. during school terms. Admission is free. For information, phone 228-5226. (There are many fine examples of 19th-century architecture on this 10-hectare campus. Of particular interest is castle-like Bonython Hall.)

Ayers House
Across Frome Rd. and opposite the Royal Adelaide Hospital, this former residence of Sir Henry Ayers, former premier of South Australia, is now headquarters of the **National Trust.** Construction on the elegant bluestone manor was begun in 1846 and took 30 years to complete. Carefully preserved and refurnished, Ayers House is a lovely specimen of gracious Victorian living, with special displays of fine silver, crystal, nursery toys, and an early kitchen. You can inspect the house Tues.-Fri. 10 a.m.-4 p.m., Sat.-Sun. and holidays 2-4 p.m., closed Good Friday and 24-31 December. Admission is $2. For information, phone 223-1655.

OTHER CITY SIGHTS

King William Street
You'll find several more noteworthy attractions as you stroll along King William Street, between North Terrace and Victoria Square.

Edmund Wright House, 59 King Williams St., was built in 1876 for the bishop of South Australia. These days the ornate Renaissance-style residence is used for government offices and offical functions. Take a peek inside during normal business hours. Free lunchtime music performances are held here every Wednesday.

The **Telecommunications Museum,** in Electra House at 131 King William St., features working displays and original equipment which trace South Australia's technology from past to present. Open Sun.-Fri. 10:30 a.m.-3:30 p.m., closed Saturday. Admission is free. For information, phone (08) 225-6601.

Approaching Victoria Square, on the opposite side of the street is **Adelaide Town Hall.** Built in 1863, the freestone façade is carved with the faces of Queen Victoria and Prince Albert. You can take a free guided tour on Tues. and Thurs. between 10:30 a.m. and 2:30 p.m.

The post office, across the street, is another fine example of stately colonial architecture. For postal history buffs, the **Postal Museum** next door (on the Franklin St. side) has a reconstructed turn-of-the-century post office, as well as archival philatelic displays. Open Mon.-Fri. 11 a.m.-2 p.m. Admission is free.

More Museums And Manors
You can view historic transport vehicles as well as ride on restored trams at the **Australian Electrical Transport Museum,** in St. Kilda (about 30 km northwest of the city center). Open Sunday and public holidays 1-5 p.m. Admission is $2.40. For information, phone (08) 344-5998.

Carrick Hill, 590 Fullarton Rd., Springfield (a 10-minute drive from the city), was built in 1939 in the fashion of a late Elizabethan-era English manor house. Set on nearly 39 hectares of English gardens and surrounded by native Australian bush, the estate features a superb collection of Australian, English, and French paintings, as well as silver, pewter, and English oak furniture. The grounds also include a sculpture park and picnic area. Devonshire tea is served in the tearooms. The home and grounds are open Wed.-Sun. 10 a.m.-5 p.m., closed the month of July. Admission is $4. For information, phone 379-3886.

Botanic Gardens

The Botanic Gardens sit on 16 hectares near the junction of North and East terraces. Besides the usual and unusual Australian and exotic species, the Adelaide gardens house Australia's only **Museum of Economic Botany** and the newly opened **Tropical Conservatory,** the largest conservatory in the Southern Hemisphere. The museum, housed inside a Grecian-style heritage building, exhibits an array of plants used for commercial, medicinal, and artistic purposes. The conservatory, built with the help of NASA technology, has been designed to address ecological imbalance and the importance of preserving the rainforests. Built of steel and lens-shaped glass, the building—measuring 100 meters long, 45 meters wide, and 27 meters high—encompasses rainforest plants from Australia, Indonesia, Papua New Guinea, and other nearby Pacific islands. Gardeners will not disturb the growth of any plants (which eventually will number 4,000), allowing leaves and bits of bark to fall and heap on the ground. The workings of a tropical rainforest are clearly explained at two information centers within the conservatory.

The Botanic Gardens are open Mon.-Fri. 7 a.m.-sunset, Sat.-Sun. and public holidays 9 a.m.-sunset. Guided tours leave from the kiosk on Tues. and Fri. at 10 a.m. Admission is free. The conservatory is open daily 10 a.m.-4 p.m. Admission is $2. The garden complex also features a book and gift shop, and a lakeside restaurant. For information, phone 228-2311.

Adelaide Zoo

On Frome Rd., next to the Botanic Gardens, this is one of Australia's oldest zoos. Set on the banks of the River Torrens, the animals, birds, and reptiles are contained in grassy moat enclosures, walk-through aviaries (with 1,200 birds), and nocturnal and reptile houses. The zoo is acclaimed for its exhibitions of infrequently seen native animals, such as the yellow-footed rock wallaby (native of the Flinders Ranges), and for its breeding programs of rare species like the Persian leopard, red panda, Prezewalski's horse, ctontop tamarin, pygmy hippopotamus, and other roll-off-your-tongue types. The zoo is open daily 9:30 a.m.-5 p.m., closed Christmas Day. Admission is $5.50. For information, phone 267-3255 (ask what the feeding times are for the big cats, seals, bears, penguins, and pelicans).

Other Parks And Gardens

It would be impossible not to stumble onto the many expansive parks that virtually surround this city. **Elder Park,** which fronts the River Torrens, deserves a special mention within this section because it is the departure point for the *Popeye* motor launch, an alternate and cheap ($1.50) way of traveling between the Festival Centre and the zoo. You can also take a lunch or dinner cruise.

A short ride away aboard the Glenelg tram is **Veale Gardens,** a portion of the South Parklands with lovely flowerbeds, meandering streams, fountains, and a conservatory. Following the terrace east will bring you to **Himeji Gardens,** a traditional Japanese garden honoring Adelaide's sister city.

North Adelaide

Outstanding architecture and ritzy shops are the focal points of this exclusive suburb. Like everywhere else in the city, it's easy to get to—just continue north up King William St., a nice walk across Adelaide Bridge and the River Torrens (or you can walk up Frome Rd., from the zoo).

If you're coming up King William Street, the first place you'll notice is **St. Peter's Cathedral,** at the corner of Pennington Terrace. It is one of the few churches in the country with

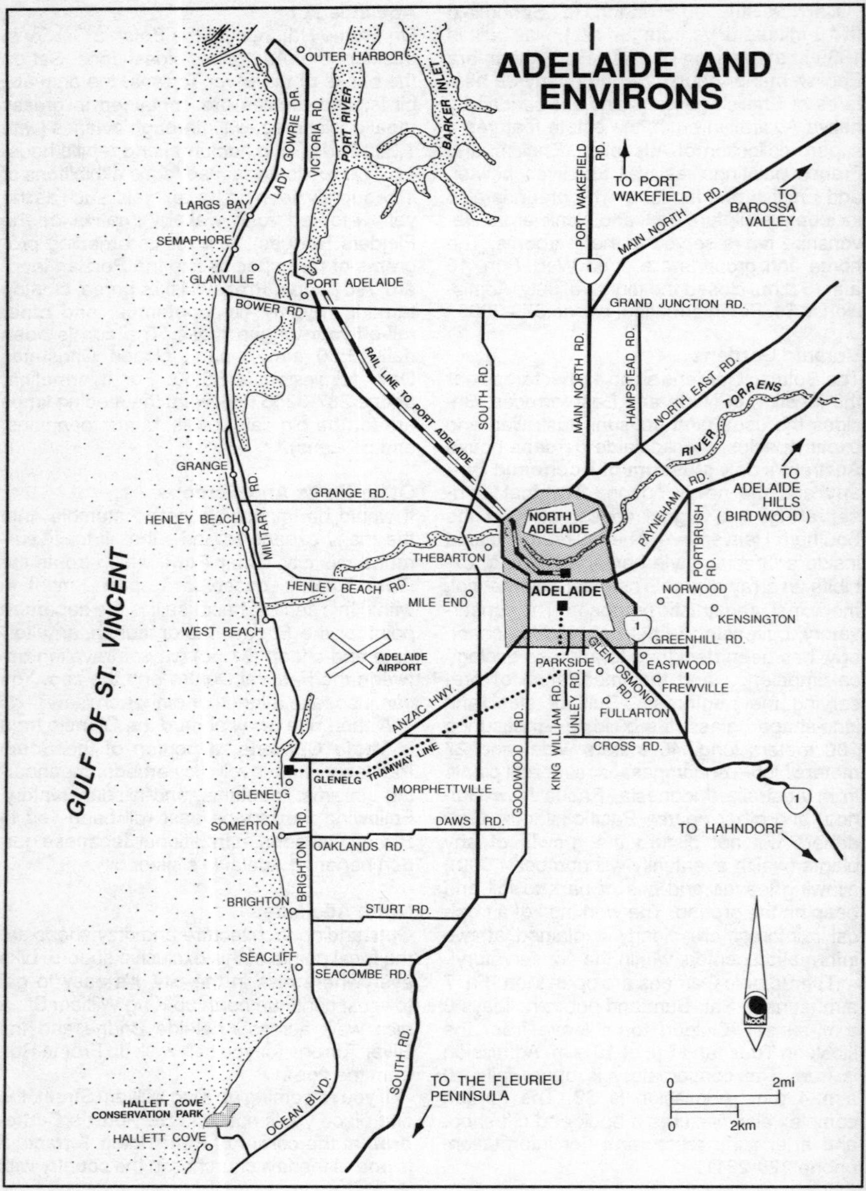
ADELAIDE AND ENVIRONS
OUTER HARBOR
LADY GOWRIE DR.
VICTORIA RD.
PORT RIVER
BARKER INLET
PORT WAKEFIELD RD.
TO PORT WAKEFIELD
TO BAROSSA VALLEY
MAIN NORTH RD.
LARGS BAY
SEMAPHORE
GLANVILLE
PORT ADELAIDE
1
GRAND JUNCTION RD.
BOWER RD.
RAIL LINE TO PORT ADELAIDE
SOUTH RD.
MAIN NORTH RD.
HAMPSTEAD RD.
NORTH EAST RD.
RIVER TORRENS
GRANGE
GRANGE RD.
MILITARY RD.
TO ADELAIDE HILLS (BIRDWOOD)
PAYNEHAM RD.
HENLEY BEACH
NORTH ADELAIDE
PORTBRUSH RD.
THEBARTON
GULF OF ST. VINCENT
HENLEY BEACH RD.
ADELAIDE
NORWOOD
MILE END
WEST BEACH
KENSINGTON
GREENHILL RD.
ADELAIDE AIRPORT
PARKSIDE
GLEN OSMOND RD.
EASTWOOD
FREWVILLE
ANZAC HWY.
UNLEY RD.
KING WILLIAM RD.
GOODWOOD RD.
FULLARTON
CROSS RD.
GLENELG TRAMWAY LINE
GLENELG
MORPHETTVILLE
TO HAHNDORF
SOMERTON
DAWS RD.
OAKLANDS RD.
BRIGHTON RD.
BRIGHTON
STURT RD.
SEACLIFF
SEACOMBE RD.
MOON
SOUTH RD.
TO THE FLEURIEU PENINSULA
0
2mi
0
2km
HALLETT COVE CONSERVATION PARK
OCEAN BLVD.
HALLETT COVE

above: whopper magnetic termite mounds near Litchfield Park (NORTHERN TERRITORY TOURIST COMMISSION)
below: You can't lose these Devils Marbles! (NORTHERN TERRITORY TOURIST COMMISSION)

clockwise from top left: the Gap, Albany, Western Australia (WESTERN AUSTRALIA TOURISM COMMISSION); South Australia's Fleurieu Peninsula juts into the Indian Ocean; striated coastline, Western Australia (WESTERN AUSTRALIA TOURISM COMMISSION); Ayers Rock (NORTHERN TERRITORY TOURIST COMMISSION)

MIKE WELLINS

Adelaide's only tram chugs from Victoria Square to seaside Glenelg, where South Australia began.

twin spires, and though the church building itself was built between 1868 and 1876, the spires and towers were not erected until 1902. And here's a fun fact for your almanac—St. Peter's has the finest and heaviest bells in the Southern Hemisphere.

Continue west to Montefiore Rd., where atop Montefiore Hill stands **Light's Vision.** A statue marks the spot where Colonel William Light purportedly started blueprinting his plans for the city. Here you can see his beatific vision through your own eyes.

Walking about the North Adelaide "grid," you'll view many architectural wonders with their grand and fascinating touches. The pricey bluestone mansions are well kept, and most are quite ornate with eye-catching roof lines, iron lace verandas, towers, and filigree. Melbourne and O'Connell streets are the "smart" shopping districts, with equally pricey boutiques, restaurants, and hairdressing salons, along with some interesting little pubs peppered in between. Many of the commercial buildings are renovated Victorian workers' cottages.

Port Adelaide

Port Adelaide, about 25 minutes from the city center (bus nos. 154-157 from North Terrace), is South Australia's first heritage area. The 19th-century wharf district, an important hub for coastal steamers until World War II, has been preserved as the **Maritime Museum,** spread over seven historic sites. Main display galleries are inside the **Bond** (1854) and **Free** (1857) stores; **Weman's Building** (1864) is the old sailmaker's shop; the **Lighthouse** (1869), first erected at the entrance to the Port River, was shifted over to South Neptune Island in 1901, then, in 1986, re-sited to its present location. The **Customs House, police station,** and **courthouse** complete the museum buildings. You'll soak up lots of atmosphere just wandering the streets. Many of the façades—ranging from modest houses to ornate banks (particularly those along Lipson St.)—have been restored to old port-days splendor. At **No. 1 Wharf** you can hop aboard the *Nelcebee* (1883), an old coastal ketch, or the *Yelta* (1949), the last tug to steam in the port. The museum buildings are open Sat.-Wed. 10 a.m.-5 p.m. Admission is $6. For information, phone (08) 240-0200.

Port Dock Station Railway Museum, also on Lipson St., has one of the country's largest collections of locomotives and carriages, as well as lots of memorabilia, an audio-visual theaterette, and model railways. Go on the weekend when you can take a ride on one of two different steam trains. A railway cafeteria car houses tearooms. Admission is $5. For information, phone 341-1690.

Got your sea legs and find the salt air flaring your nostrils? You might want to take a cruise aboard the *Captain Proud* paddleboat. The two-hour luncheon cruise departs Port Adelaide Wharf, Berth 3, Wed. and Sun. 11:30 a.m.-1:30 p.m. Cost is $12.50. Four-hour dinner dances run $32. For information and bookings, phone 47-1170.

Glenelg

This is the most popular of Adelaide's suburban beaches. Though not equal to the famed beauties on the east and west coasts, there's water (sometimes blue), sand (at low tide), shark netting (to keep out South Australia's deadly white pointer), a water slide, amusement park, pie carts, and wienie wagons. What more do you want? History? Then you've come to the right place—Glenelg is where South Australia began, the landing place of

Governor Hindmarsh and the first settlers back in 1836. Over at the **Patawalonga Boat Haven,** you can climb aboard a replica of the HMS *Buffalo,* from which Captain Hindmarsh stepped ashore and proclaimed South Australia a colony. (Unlike the original, however, this buffalo is fitted with a restaurant, bar, and small museum.) Open daily 9 a.m.-12:30 p.m. and 2-5 p.m. Admission is $2.50. For information, phone (08) 294-7000.

The **Old Gum Tree,** on MacFarlane St., marks the exact spot where the Union Jack was raised.

The **Tourist Information Center,** on the foreshore (tel. 294-5833), provides walking and cycling maps. Open daily, weather permitting, 9-5.

Adelaide's only tram makes a sentimental journey from Victoria Square directly to Jetty Rd., Glenelg's main street, taking approximately 30 minutes. Cost is $1.80 one way.

Other Beaches

Favorite local beaches north of Glenelg are West Beach, Henley Beach, Grange, West Lakes, Glanville, Semaphore, and Largs Bay; south of Glenelg (where the surf is decent) are Somerton, Brighton, and Seacliff. Nude bathing is allowed at Maslin Beach, about 40 km south of the city. Between Seacliff and Maslin is **Hallett Cove Conservation Reserve,** where the landscape has been fabulously molded and colored by a glacial movement some 270 million years ago.

At Grange, you can visit **Sturt's Cottage** where the famous explorer, Captain Charles Sturt, lived between 1840 and 1853 (when he was home, that is). The house contains his family memorabilia and is furnished in period style. Sturt's Murray River campsite has been re-created on the grounds—in case you need some pointers. The home is open Wed.-Sun. 1-5 p.m. Admission is $2. For information, phone (08) 356-8185.

Fort Glanville, in Semaphore, was built in 1878 and recently restored. You can blast your ears out on the third Sunday of each month (Sept.-May), when reenactments of rifle drill and cannon firing (two 64-pounders!) are staged.

ADELAIDE PRACTICALITIES

ACCOMMODATIONS

As in most large cities, accommodations in Adelaide run the spectrum from cheap and basic to ritzy and plush—except here, quite often, the two ends sit side by side and back—to-back. It's usually easy to find a room *unless* you arrive at festival time. Keep in mind that the Adelaide Festival of the Arts (first three weeks of March, in even-numbered years), Formula One Grand Prix (five days in Oct. or Nov., every year), and the spillover from the Barossa Valley Vintage Festival (Easter week, in odd-numbered years) are peak periods. If you plan to attend any of these events, or to be in the Adelaide area at those times, you'd be well advised to book a room *way* in advance.

City Center

(Words of caution—if you or your traveling companions are unaccustomed to city noises, you may not want to bed down on occasionally rowdy Hindley Street.)

Inexpensive (under $30): Centrally located **West's Private Hotel,** 110B Hindley St. (tel. 08-231-7575), is cheap ($20 per room), and more of a guesthouse than a hotel—linen included, but not much else. Backpackers are welcome. The **Metropolitan Hotel,** 46 Grote St. (tel. 231-5471), near Victoria Square, has basic accommodations with shared facilities. Rooms come with washbasins over at the **Plaza Private Hotel,** 85 Hindley St. (tel. 231-6371). The Plaza is an old-timer, but nicely kept. Some of the costlier rooms ($50) have private facilities. The **Austral Hotel,** 205 Rundle St. (tel. 223-4660), has clean and simple pub accommodations with shared facilities. **The Clarice,** 220 Hutt St. (tel. 223-3569), is both a hotel and motel, near the East Terrace side of town. Rooms with shared facilities start low. It'll cost you $10-20 more to stay in the newer motel wing, with your own shower and toilet. Accommodations at **City Central Motel,** 23 Hindley St. (tel. 231-4049), have private facilities and include continental breakfast.

Moderate ($30-60): At the corner of Gawler Place and Flinders St., the **Earl of Zetland Hotel** (tel. 08-223-5500) offers good value in pub accommodations. Rooms are air-conditioned and have private showers and toilets. The pub downstairs puts out a decent buffet spread at lunch (about $6). Near the Festival Centre and casino, try the **Festival Lodge Motel,** 140 North Terrace (tel. 212-7877), or the **Grosvenor Hotel,** 125 North Terrace (tel. 231-2961). Both places have all the modern amenities. Deluxe rooms at the Grosvenor (the city's former grand dame hotel) can climb as high as $120.

Expensive ($60 and way up): If you're a big spender (or you've just hit it big at the casino), Adelaide's two luxury high-rise hotels are the **Hilton International,** 233 Victoria Square (tel. 08-217-0711), peacefully situated over the center city square, and the super-glitzy **Hyatt Regency** (tel. 231-1234) on North Terrace, smack dab in the middle of the fun-side. Basic doubles at either hotel are around $200, and go *way* upwards.

On The Outskirts

If you've got your heart set on staying in lovely North Adelaide, the moderately priced **Princes Lodge Motel,** 73 Lefevre Terrace (tel. 08-267-5566), on the outer edge of the suburban grid, is your best bet. The more deluxe **Meridien Lodge,** 21 Melbourne St. (tel. 267-3033), sits on North Adelaide's prestigious shopping street.

If you're coming in from the southeast, Glen Osmond Rd., which heads straight into the city, is Adelaide's motel row. Some good choices on this section of road include **Princes Highway Motel,** 199 Glen Osmond Rd., Frewville (tel. 379-9253); **Sands Motel,** 198 Glen Osmond Rd., Fullarton (tel. 379-

0079); and **Powell's Court,** 2 Glen Osmond Rd., Parkside (tel. 271-7995). (Don't be confused—the suburbs change names frequently along this thoroughfare!) All of these motels are in the moderate range. Powell's Court has cooking facilities. Just two km from the city, **Parkway Motor Inn,** 204 Greenhill Rd., Eastwood (tel. 271-0451), is well located, has a pool and restaurant, and costs slightly more than the others.

Glenelg And The Beaches

Glenelg has oodles of places to stay, most at reasonable prices—particularly during off-seasons, when many of the holiday flats offer attractive weekly rates. The tourist office on the foreshore can provide a list of available flats.

The **Oriental Private Hotel,** 16 South Esplanade (tel. 08-295- 2390), has rates of $30 per room and that includes breakfast. Dorm rooms are available for $10 per person. **Pier Hotel,** 2 Jetty Rd. (tel. 295-4116), is a wonderfully atmospheric old seaside establishment. Rooms with private facilities are moderately priced, and $10-15 cheaper if you don't mind sharing a loo. **Colley Motel Apartments,** 22 Colley Terrace (tel. 295-7535), opposite Colley Reserve, is another good mid-range choice.

In Glenelg South, the **Bay Hotel Motel,** 58 The Broadway (tel. 294-4244), not far from the beach, has rooms with color television and private facilities. The **Norfolk Motor Inn,** 71 The Broadway (tel. 295-6354), provides guests with free breakfast. Prices at both are moderate.

West Beach and Henley Beach are also packed with holiday flats. In West Beach, try **Cootura Holiday Flats,** 8 West Beach Rd. (tel. 353-3210), or **Marineland Village Units,** Military Rd. (tel. 353- 2655). A best bet in Henley Beach is **Seaside Holiday Apartments,** at 71 Esplanade (tel. 353-1041), with cooking facilities and color television. Holiday flats are moderately priced but often require minimum stays of two or more nights. Farther north in Semaphore, the **Semaphore Bed and Breakfast,** 128 Esplanade (tel. 49-5373), offers spotless seaside doubles for $35, including breakfast.

Hostels

Adelaide's hostels, like everything else in the city, are centrally located and easy to find. Three of the hostels are in the South Terrace district and can be reached by foot or by bus (nos. 191-198, from Pulteney St.). The 50-bed **Adelaide Youth Hostel,** 290 Gilles St. (tel. 08-223-6007), has a friendly atmosphere and helpful staff. The building is closed from 9:30 a.m.-1 p.m. **Backpackers Hostel Adelaide** is nearby at 263 Gilles St. (tel. 223-5680), and has two sections: one closes from 11 a.m.-3 p.m.; the other section stays open all day but costs a buck more. Office hours are 8-11 a.m. and 3-10 p.m. You can also get a bed next door at the **Backpackers International Hostel** (tel. 232-0823). All three of these hostels have kitchen facilities, as well as lounges where you can meet up with other travelers.

Another hostel, closer to the center of town, is **Backpackers Inn,** 112 Carrington St. (tel. 223-6635). This former pub is run by the same folks at Backpackers Hostel Adelaide and offers both dorm beds and double rooms ($20). **East Park Lodge,** 341 Angas St. (tel. 223-1228), is a private family-run hostel, also near the city center. Dorm beds, double rooms, and some meals are available.

Both men and women are welcome at the **YMCA,** 76 Flinders St. (tel. 223-1611), conveniently near Victoria Square and the central bus station. Dorm beds run $9, singles are $16, doubles are priced at $26. Office hours are Mon.-Fri. 9 a.m.-9 p.m., Sat.-Sun. 9 a.m.-12 p.m. and 4-8 p.m.

In Glenelg, **Backpackers Beach Headquarters,** 7 Moseley St. (tel. 295-7592), offers home-style accommodations with kitchen, laundry, and even car rental facilities. Dorm beds and some single and double rooms are available.

Homestays

The **South Australian Government Travel Centre,** 18 King William St., Adelaide 5000 (tel. 08-212-1644), will provide you with a list of homestay properties which include city homes, historic cottages, health resorts, villas, and farms. Prices range from budget to luxury.

Camping

South Australia has a large number of camping facilities, though some accept only caravans, not tents. Most provide a number of powered and unpowered sites, as well as on-site cabins and vans. The state's caravan parks are generally of a very high standard—clean and comfortable. Many have swimming pools, games rooms, and tennis courts. The South Australian Travel Centre can provide maps and brochures, and assist with bookings. The following is a sampling of some of the more convenient and interesting locales.

Adelaide Caravan Park, Bruton St., Hackney (tel. 08-363-1566) is the nearest park to city attractions. **Brownhill Creek Caravan Park,** Brownhill Creek Rd., Mitcham (tel. 271-4824), set in 120 acres of bushland, is only seven km from Adelaide. **Levi Caravan Park,** Lansdowne Terrace, Vale Park (tel. 44-2209), adjoins the River Torrens and is only five km from Adelaide.

West Beach Caravan Park, Military Rd., West Beach (tel. 356-7654), sits on a good swimming beach and is surrounded by playing fields and golf courses. And, for those of you who want to be near Fort Glanville's big cannons, there's **Fort Glanville Caravan Park,** 349 Military Rd., Semaphore Park (tel. 49-7726), on the beach front.

FOOD

Adelaide does not have the "foody" scene so prevalent in its sister capital cities, Melbourne and Sydney. Though there are some "nouvelle" gourmet establishments sprinkled about, the emphasis here is on casual, outdoor dining—a terrace restaurant along the river, a picnic in the park, takeaways to eat in one of the city squares. Many of the restaurants are licensed, no doubt to keep those famous South Australian wines flowing. Adventurous eaters will often find dishes made from kangaroo meat on the menu—so if you want to try it in some form other than an old Jumbo Jack, keep your eyes peeled. In fact, this is the only state where it's a common meal selection. If you prefer to pass on the braised 'roo, you'll find plenty of fresh fish and seafood. Especially commendable are King George whiting and the local crayfish (sometimes called lobster).

Most of the ethnic restaurants and cafés are on Hindley Street, lodged above, between, or beneath the strip joints and sex shops. Indian, Chinese, Greek, Lebanese—and American—meals average $6-$10. The center for Italian cuisine is on Rundle Street, between Rundle Mall and East Terrace. Try Gouger Street for seafood houses. Many Adelaide restaurants are closed on Sunday, so plan accordingly.

Inexpensive

The **Adelaide University** campus has two informal eating places that are popular with students, faculty, and travel types. Both are in the Union Building. The cafeteria, on the ground floor, serves all the typical "uni" fare—sandwiches, apples, weak coffee, a few miscellaneous hot meals. The **Bistro** offers better quality at higher prices, about $5-9 for main dishes. The cafeteria has the customary casual class-in class-out hours; the Bistro is open Mon.- Fri. 12-2:30 p.m. for lunch, 5:30-8:30 p.m. for dinner.

The vegetarian budget travelers mainstay —the Hare Krishna all-you-can-eater—is at **Crossways,** 79 Hindley St. The three-course bounty, costing $3, is served Mon.-Fri. 12-3 p.m.

You can get a plain, simple **counter meal** at pubs throughout the city. Usually there's a blackboard outside the door which states meal times (around 12-2 p.m.) and prices (as low as $3). Menus are fairly bland, occasionally heavy on the grease. Typical choices are fish and chips, chicken schnitzel, gravy-covered beef and lamb. Some best bets include: **Old Queen's Arms,** 88 Wright St.; **Hotel Franklin,** 92 Franklin St.; **Austral Hotel,** 205 Rundle St.; and the **Park Tavern,** corner of Hindmarsh Square, at Grenfell St.

Pick and choose from some of the city's international food centers where different eateries are positioned around one central dining area. You can mix and match Indian, Thai, Chinese, Australian, and other cuisines

Moored at Glenelg, this replica of the HMS Buffalo *features a restaurant and museum.*

for about $5 (more if you get carried away). Centrally positioned food centers are: **Hawker's Corner,** corner of Wright St. and West Terrace; **City Cross Arcade,** off Grenfell St.; **Gallerie of International Cuisine,** Renaissance Tower Center, Rundle Mall; **The Food Affair,** basement level, Gallerie Shopping Centre (between North Terrace and Gawler Place); and the **International Food Plaza,** on Moonta St. next to the Central Market. Most of the food stalls stay open during shopping hours.

The Central Market, between Grote and Gouger streets (near Victoria Square), is a great spot to put together a meal or a picnic. The many colorful stalls in this historic old building feature fresh fruit and vegetables, meat, bread, cheese, and a variety of other foods. Or you can get a ready-made cheap (under $6) meal at **Malacca Corner,** a restaurant housed inside the market. Market hours are Tues.-Thurs. 7 a.m.-6 p.m., Fri. 7 a.m.-10 p.m., Sat. 7 a.m.-1 p.m.

Just south of the city center in Goodwood, **The Bagel Boys** bakery at 134 Goodwood Rd. (tel. 08-271-0818) boasts Adelaide's only authentic New York-style bagels, baked daily on the premises. You can select a variety of tasty fillings and nosh away for under $5. Open Mon.-Sat. 9:30 a.m.-5 p.m., Sun. 9:30 a.m.-2 p.m.

Don't forget about the cafes at the historic sites on **North Terrace.** You can get snacks and simple meals at the Botanic Gardens, Art Gallery, Old Parliament House, and the Living Arts Centre.

Moderate

The **Bangkok,** 217 Rundle St. (tel. 08-223-5406), is a well-respected Thai restaurant. Main courses average $12, and are served Tues.-Fri. lunch, Tues.-Sat. dinner. Make sure you book ahead for this one. A few doors down, at 227 Rundle St., **Da Clemente** (tel. 223-2211) is one of Adelaide's most popular Italian restaurants. You can watch your meal being cooked in the open kitchen. Main courses are in the $12-15 range. Open Tues.-Fri. for lunch, Tues.-Sat. for dinner.

Jasmin Indian Restaurant, 31 Hindmarsh Square (tel. 223-7837), has terrific North Indian dishes for about $14. Specialties include tandoori oven dishes and biryani rice plates. Open Tues.-Fri. lunch, Tues.-Sat. dinner.

Satisfy your fish 'n' chips cravings for $10 at **Paul's,** 79 Gouger St. (tel. 231-9778). This old-time favorite is open Mon.-Fri. lunch, Mon.-Sat. dinner. **Matsuri,** at 167 Gouger St. (tel. 231- 3494), is the place to find all your favorite sushi à la carte dishes. The four-piece jumbo sushi roll is $8. Open Mon.-Fri. lunch, Mon.-Sat. dinner.

Discerning vegetarians will appreciate the harmonious ambience and quality of food at **Clearlight Nights,** 137A Wright St. (tel. 231-2318). Whole foods are the specialty for dinner Tues.-Sat. 6 p.m. until closing. Main courses are in the $10-14 range.

Burger kings and queens should definitely check out the "Dietician's Despair" at the **Unley On Clyde** pub, 25 Unley Rd., Parkside (tel. 271-5344). It's big and thick, covered with bacon, avocado, and melted cheese, and served with chips. It costs $9 and is available for lunch Mon.-Sat.

One of my special finds (which I hesitatingly share!) is the **Grecian Taverna,** 89 O'Connell St., North Adelaide (tel. 267-1446). This intimate restaurant provides beautifully presented, delectable Greek specialties in enormous portions *plus* it's open for lunch and dinner every day of the week (yes, *including* Sundays). Average cost for main courses is $10.

Also in North Adelaide, **Bells Restaurant,** at the Cathedral Hotel, 45 Kermode St. (tel. 267-2197), features American cuisine, including Cajun-style specialties. Main courses range from $10-15. Bells serves lunch Mon.-Fri. 12-2:30 p.m., dinner Tues.-Sat. 6-10 p.m.

If you have a party of four (or you can grab two or three people along the way), **Delphi Restaurant,** 127 Henley Rd., Mile End (tel. 352-6799), spreads an 11-course Greek dinner feast Tues.-Thurs., for $12.50 per head.

Expensive

Splurgers should head directly for **Chloe's,** 36 College Rd., Kent Town (tel. 08-363-1001), comprised of several grandly furnished dining rooms within a stunning, restored villa. Classic French food and a superb wine list are standout features here. Without wine, you can expect to pay about $50 per person. Book ahead for lunch Mon.-Fri., dinner Mon.-Saturday.

Duthy's, 19 Duthy St., Malvern (tel. 272-0465), south of the city and a little out of the way, is worth venturing to for its creative and well-reputed nouvelle-ish cuisine. Main courses cost $20-30. Dinner is served Tues.-Saturday. Next door, **Duthy's Too** (tel. 272-9150) is an upmarket *brasserie* with slightly less expensive meals served for lunch Thurs.-Fri., dinner Wed.-Sunday.

Jarmers, 297 Kensington Rd., Kensington Park (tel. 332-2080), just east of the city, is another $50-per-header (again, without wine). Jarmers presents creative Australian cuisine (watch for that kangaroo!) in an elegant atmosphere for dinner Mon.-Saturday.

If you're not keeping tabs on your pocketbook *or* your cholesterol, you'll likely enjoy **Café Violetta,** 99 Hutt St. (tel. 223-3533). This vegetarian establishment (no fish, fowl, or meat) is heavy-handed on the cream, eggs, and cheese. Specialties include pastas, pesto, risotto, tarts, rich sauces, and fine wines. You'll probably fork over $40-50 per person, including wine and dessert. Café Violetta is open for dinner Mon.-Friday.

Late-night Eats

It's slim pickings for late-night refrigerator-raiders. If you're desperate you might try the **pie carts** which set up outside the GPO and on North Terrace, near the railway station, every night from 6 p.m. until the wee hours. They sell that infamous Adelaide gastronomic *specialité,* the "floater"—an Australian meat pie floating (sort of like a rock) inside a bowl of thick green pea soup, topped with tomato sauce (catsup). An interesting aside about the floater is that it looks pretty much the same both before and after in- and di-gestion!

Maybe you'd prefer some harmless pancakes. The **Pancake Kitchen,** 13 Gilbert Place (tel. 08-211-7912), on the South Terrace side of the city grid, is open every day, 24 hours.

You're probably best off tucking some tucker in your backpack, satchel, or motel fridge to tide you over until morning.

ENTERTAINMENT

Adelaide has all the usual amusements of a city its size—cinemas, art galleries, discos, pubs and clubs with live music, theater and concert performances, plus a couple of extras—the hustle-bustle casino and a really special festival of the arts. Newspapers, particularly Thursday's *Advertiser,* provide up-to-date information. Another good source is the monthly *Adelaide Review,* with lots of reviews and announcements of literary, arts, and theatrical happenings. You can also call in at the South Australian Government Travel Centre, on King William St., for current entertainment listings and booking assistance. And don't forget about Adelaide University where, during school sessions, there's always something on.

Cinemas

If you're looking for commercial cinema (with releases that are ordinarily three to six months behind the U.S.), the four-, six- and eight-plexes are scattered around Hindmarsh Square, Hindley St., Rundle Mall, and on Jetty Rd. in Glenelg. For artier films, try the **Capri,** 141 Goodwood Rd., Goodwood (tel. 08-272-1177), the **Chelsea,** 275 Kensington Rd., Kensington (tel. 31-5080), or Adelaide University.

The annual **Adelaide Film Event,** held at the Chelsea from mid-July to mid-Sept., presents a good series of international films (in 1990 the program included the reconstructed version of *Lawrence of Arabia, Do The Right Thing, Jesus of Montreal, Roger and Me,* and a Glasnost Film Festival). You can either subscribe in advance for a series of tickets, or purchase a single admission ($10) on the night of performance, if seats are still available.

Or curl up in front of the telly and watch some really terrific classic, contemporary, and cutting-edge films on SBS. Check the newspaper for times.

Pubs And Clubs

You can do an easy pub crawl along **Hindley Street,** between King William Street and West Terrace. You'll find discos at **Jules,** 94 Hindley St., a "real Aussie Pub," and across the street at **Rio's,** 111 Hindley St., which also has a bistro and piano bar. City pubs that regularly feature music are: **Austral Hotel,** 205 Rundle St.; **Royal Admiralty Hotel,** 125 Hindley St.; **St. Paul's Entertainment Centre,** corner of Pulteney and Flinders streets; **Tivoli Hotel,** 261 Pirie St.; and, promising "no renovations, no bullshit," the **Exeter Hotel,** 246 Rundle Street.

A few of Adelaide's trendiest upmarket musical pubs (where you may well run into renovations and bullshit) are **Bull and Bear Ale House,** 91 King William St.; **General Havelock Hotel,** 162 Hutt St.; and, on Melbourne St. in North Adelaide, the **Old Lion Hotel.** Still trendier are the bars and discos housed inside the **Adelaide Hilton** and **Hyatt Regency** hotels.

You'll pay a cover charge of $3-6 to hear music in the city pubs; about $10-12 at the big hotels.

Theater And Concerts

The **Adelaide Festival Centre** is the city's major venue for theater, stage musicals, opera, concerts, and most other performing arts. For information, phone the box office at 08-213-4788, Mon.-Sat. 9:30 a.m.-8:30 p.m.; for credit card bookings, phone BASS at 213-4777, Mon.-Sat. 9 a.m.-6 p.m.; for 24-hour recorded information, phone 211-8999. The celebrated **Late Show,** in the Centre's Fezbah every Friday night from 11 p.m. until late, features cabaret acts. Free and casual jazz as well as classical and chamber music performances are often held on Sunday afternoons in the Festival Theatre Foyer.

The **Adelaide Symphony Orchestra** and **Australian Chamber Orchestra** perform at the old Adelaide Town Hall on King William Street. For information, phone BASS at 213-4777. BASS also handles bookings for many other events, including Baroque and Renaissance music concerts at St. Peter's Cathedral.

Adelaide has a very active performance and contemporary theater scene. If you don't find what you're looking for at the Festival Centre, check with the Living Arts Centre (tel. 212-1258).

Events

The **Adelaide Festival of the Arts,** the oldest in Australia and one of the best in the world, attracts top international talent. During the first three weeks of March, in even-numbered years, the festival brews such mixes as Shakespearean tragedies with avant-garde performances, Beethoven symphonies with fusion jazz, Yehudi Menuhin with Mick Jagger.

The Fringe Festival, which is often even more exciting, coincides with the main event. During festival time, the city is agog over theater, dance, music, and art. Writers' Week attracts a wide array of poets, novelists, playwrights, and journalists to swig and tipple as they excerpt and expound. Make bookings for the festival well in advance by writing Adelaide Festival, GPO Box 1269, Adelaide, South Australia 5001 (tel. 08-216-8600).

In late October or early November of each year, Adelaide hosts the **Australian Formula One Grand Prix.** The ear-splitting action around the city streets east of the city center lasts for five days (including practice races and such). The big race—the last of the year

MIKE WELLINS

Adelaide's annual Formula One Grand Prix draws loud cars and big crowds to city streets.

—takes place on the fifth and final day. The track is easily accessible and you'll be able to find a good viewing perch without having to pay for a grandstand seat. "Staid" Adelaide is sheer pandemonium while this event is on. Book accommodations as far ahead as possible—or be prepared to camp out in the park.

RECREATION

Locals take advantage of the mild weather, gorgeous parklands, and nearby beaches, and spend a lot of time outdoors—if not participating in something themselves, then watching others who are. The parklands, particularly, are full of recreational areas. Meander too long in one grassy spot and you'll probably be commandeered into a game of soccer or cricket. Walkers and joggers will take happily to the many park pathways with their peaceful vistas and gentle climbs. Those of you who are more interested in a hike or bushwalk, stay tuned for "Hills and Vales," below.

Cycling

Cycling about this nitty-gritty city, and the nine tracks that surround the parklands, is smooth and trouble-free. Rent bikes from **Super Elliott,** 200 Rundle St. (tel. 08-223-3946), Mon.-Sat., or from **Action Moped Hire,** 400 King William St. (tel. 211-7060), Mon.-Saturday.

Scuba Diving

Diving is best off Kangaroo Island and the Yorke Peninsula, but boat diving isn't bad at Port Noarlunga Reef Marine Reserve, 18 km south of Adelaide, or Aldinga, 43 km south. You'll need proof of diving experience before you can rent equipment. For information, contact the **Scuba Divers Federation of South Australia,** 1 Sturt St. (tel. 213-0666).

Swimming

Swim along the beaches of St. Vincent Gulf, or dip into the **Adelaide Aquatic Centre,** Jeffcott Rd., North Adelaide (tel. 344-4411), in the north parklands. The pool's open daily 5 a.m.-10 p.m.

Tennis

Both grass and hard courts, as well as tennis rackets, are available for rent at **Memorial Drive Tennis Club,** War Memorial Dr. (tel. 231-4371), and **Roseland's Tennis World,** 323 Sturt Rd., Bedford Park (tel. 231-3033). **Adelaide City Courts** are in the parklands.

Golf

Guests are welcome to tee off at **City of Adelaide Golf Links,** Memorial Dr., North Adelaide (tel. 231-2359). Equipment is available for hire.

Sailing

Adelaide's shoreline is fine for sailing. All the city beaches have yacht clubs, and most welcome casual visitors.

Skating And Skiing

You can ice skate 'round the rink or ski down the 12-meter-high indoor slope (covered in Permasnow, a real snow-like Australian product), at **Thebarton Ice Arena,** 25 East Terrace, Thebarton (tel. 352-7977). The rink costs $5 per session; the slope costs $6 per hour. Skate and ski rental is extra. Open daily.

Spectator Sports

Adelaide Oval, north of the city on King William St., is the main location for **cricket** matches, the country's favorite summer sport. International and interstate test matches are played Oct.-March.

The big winter sport, **Australian Rules football,** is played—usually on Saturdays—at both Adelaide Oval and Football Park, West Lakes. Soccer and other football codes (rugby, rugby union) are also played during the April-Sept. season.

You can play the ponies or the pups year-round. The **South Australian Jockey Club** conducts meetings at Victoria Park, Morphettville, and Cheltenham; **Adelaide Greyhound Racing Club** is the venue for those flying dogs. Check local newspapers for meeting times.

SHOPPING

It's doubtful you'll ever "shop 'til you drop" in this city, but you will find the basics, maybe a few bargains, and possibly some baubles. (**Warning:** Be especially careful when purchasing opals—take your time and shop around for reputable dealers.) City shopping hours are generally Mon.-Fri. 8:30 a.m.-5:30 p.m., Sat. 8:30 a.m.-12 p.m., late-night trading Fri. until 9 p.m. (late-night trading is held on Thursday in the suburbs).

Rundle Mall, and its branches of arcades, offer standard mall-isms—John Martin's and Myer department stores, specialty shops that are really nothing special, a handful of commercial art galleries, a cinema complex, photo developers, jewelry stores, sandwich shops, a few buskers, and flower carts.

For more chic and boutiques, North Adelaide's exclusive **Melbourne Street** will please and appease until you make it back to Rodeo Drive.

Markets

For far less sterile shopping, **Central Market** (see "Food" above) has colorful stalls stocked with food, produce, flowers, and bazaar items.

The **Brickworks Market,** 36 South Rd., Thebarton, is about three km from the city center. Hundreds of stalls sell everything from food and clothing to arts and crafts to junk and junque. Take bus nos. 12, 114, 116, or 118 from Grenfell and Currie streets in the city. The market is open Fri.-Sun. 9-5.

Crafts

Local craftspeople create and sell jewelry, fabric, leather, glass, wood, ceramics, and other handmade wares at the **Jam Factory Craft Centre,** 169 Payneham Rd., St. Peters, a few minutes from the city. The gallery features monthly changing exhibitions. Open Mon.-Fri. 9-5, Sat. 10 a.m.-5 p.m., Sun. and holidays 2-5 p.m.

Contemporary and traditional Aboriginal arts and crafts are sold and displayed at **Adelaide Gem Trading Company,** 26 Currie Street. **Quality 5 Crafts,** in City Cross Arcade, is another respected outlet for Australian crafts.

Rustic Revival, 31 Kensington Rd., Norwood (a few kilometers west of the city), sells and exhibits heritage toys and crafts, including custom-made dollhouses.

Bookstores

Murphy Sisters Bookshop, 240 The Parade, Norwood, specializes in books by, for, and about women, as well as nonsexist and nonracist children's books. This shop is an excellent resource and meeting place for women. Hours are Mon.-Sat. 9-5 (Thurs. until 8 p.m.), Sun. 1-4 p.m.

Adelaide University Bookshop, on the campus, sells textbooks, plus general fiction, nonfiction, and children's books. The shop is open to the public. For information and hours, phone (08) 223-4366.

Psychic sciences, astrology, women's spirituality, health, and healing, are some of the selections at **Quantum, The Metaphysical Bookshop,** 113 Melbourne St., North Adelaide. You can also pick up quartz crystals and relaxation music. Hours are Mon.-Fri. 9 a.m.-6 p.m. (Thurs. until 9 p.m.), Sat. 9:30 a.m.-5 p.m., Sun. 1-5 p.m.

Two levels of the **Third World Bookshop,** 103 Hindley St., are "literally" crammed with all subjects of secondhand books, radical literature, records, and alternative periodicals. The shop is open daily 9 a.m.-1 a.m.-ish.

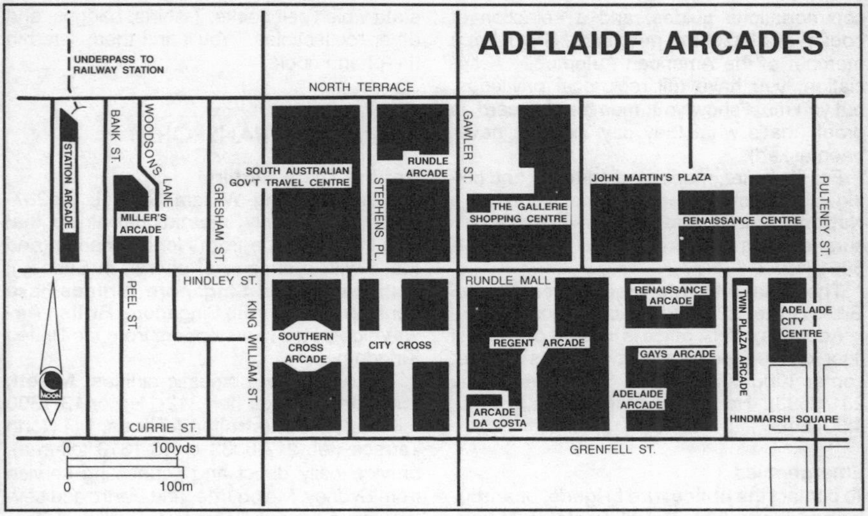

SERVICES

King William Street is lined with **banks** and other financial institutions. Business hours are Mon.-Thurs. 9:30 a.m.-4 p.m., Fri. 9:30 a.m.-5 p.m. When changing traveler's checks, be sure to carry your passport or driver's license for identification. Many city and suburban banking facilities have automatic teller machines that accept international credit cards.

The **General Post Office,** 141 King William St., provides the full range of **postal services,** including a philatelic bureau. Another convenient branch of **Australia Post** is in Rundle Mall. Hours of operation are Mon.-Fri. 8:30 a.m.-5 p.m.

The **U.S. Consulate,** 15 Nilpinna St., Burnside (tel. 08-332-8886), is open Mon.-Fri. 9-11 a.m.

Just about every hostel, motel, and hotel provides **laundry facilities** for guests. Launderettes are dispersed around the city and suburbs. **Adelaide Launderette,** 152 Sturt St. (tel. 231-4833), provides wash and iron service Mon.-Sat. 8 a.m.-8 p.m.

Stow your bags at any of the hostels, the YMCA residence hotel, the railway station, or central bus station—but not at the airport. The small fee will vary according to how many bags you stash and how long they're left.

Fruit pickers should have luck finding **casual labor** (during harvest time). Check at wineries in the Barossa and Clare valleys, as well as the Southern Vales, Riverland, and Coonawarra. The Murray River fruit-bearing districts of Berri, Renmark, and Loxton may also yield seasonal work.

INFORMATION

Bring an extra suitcase for all the literature you're sure to accumulate. Your first stop should be at the **South Australia Travel Centre,** 18 King William St. (tel. 08-212-1505), where you'll be handed an assortment of brochures, planners, maps, booklets, pamphlets, leaflets, and the like. The Centre is open Mon.-Fri. 9-5, Sat.-Sun. 9 a.m.-2 p.m. **The Royal Automobile Association,** 41 Hindmarsh Square (tel. 223-4555), is an invaluable source for detailed maps (particularly of Outback areas). They also have accommodations guides, and a selection of books available for purchase. If you're a member of the American Automobile Association, you have full reciprocal privileges, but you must show your membership card as proof (that's what they say, but I've never been asked).

For literature, maps, and camping and hiking information on specific parks, contact the **National Parks and Wildlife Service,** Insurance Bldg., 55 Grenfell St., Adelaide, SA 5061 (tel. 216-7777).

The **Disability Information Centre,** 195 Gillies St. (tel. 223-7522), is open Mon-Fri. 9-5.

Adelaide's **YHA** office is located on the first floor of the Recreation and Sports Centre, corner King William and Sturt streets (tel. 231-5583). Hours are Mon.-Fri. 9:30 a.m.-4:30 p.m.

Emergencies

To contact the **police, fire brigade,** or **ambulance,** phone 000. **Royal Adelaide Hospital,** corner of North Terrace and Frome Rd. (tel. 08-223-0230), is a full-service facility with 24-hour emergency services. Also on Frome Rd. is **Adelaide Dental Hospital** (tel. 223-9211). **Burden Chemist,** 41 King William St. (tel. 231-4701), is open daily 8 a.m.-midnight.

More Information

Read all about it on North Terrace—The Mortlock Library, and bookshops in the museums, historic sights, and Adelaide University, can provide inquiring minds with all they want to know about South Australian history, anthropology, archaeology, art, botany, politics—past and present.

Don't forget the **Third World Bookshop,** on Hindley St. (see "Shopping" above). Bibliophiles will be in hog heaven.

The coffee-and-newspaper crowd can choose from the morning *Advertiser,* afternoon *Daily News,* and the *Sunday Mail.*

The Wilderness Society is an Australian conservation group dedicated to addressing important and timely issues such as preservation of rainforests, harmful effects of logging, and other environmental concerns. They also operate wilderness shops in each state which sell books, T-shirts, badges, and other "collectibles." You'll find them listed in the phone book.

TRANSPORT

Getting There By Air

Qantas, 14 King William St. (tel. 08-237-8541), is the only international airline that flies into Adelaide from North America (and that's with a change of aircraft in Sydney); both Qantas and **Singapore Airlines** have nonstop service from Singapore; **British Airways** operates two-stoppers from the United Kingdom.

The two major domestic airlines, **Ansett,** 150 North Terrace (tel. 212-1111 or 13-1300 toll-free), and **Australian Airlines,** 144 North Terrace (tel. 217-3333 or 13-1313 toll-free), provide daily direct and connecting service from Sydney, Melbourne, and Perth, and several-times-a-week flights from Brisbane, Canberra, and Alice Springs. Sample fares to or from Adelaide are: Melbourne, $144; Sydney, $211; Brisbane, $260; Perth, $308; Alice Springs, $228; Darwin, $350. These prices reflect the 25% discount accorded international ticket holders, but you can get about the same fare by going standby. There are other passes and discounts available depending upon your route and length of time traveling. **STA Travel** is your best source for info and bargains. Phone 223-2426, or call in at one of six offices: 235 Rundle St., Adelaide; 55A O'Connell St., North Adelaide; Level 4, Union House, Adelaide University; Union Bldg., Flinders University (Adelaide); 154 The Parade, Norwood; 33 Jetty Rd., Glenelg.

Getting There By Train

Keswick Railway Terminal, on Railway Terrace, near the city center, is the arrival and departure point for interstate trains. The ***Indian Pacific,*** between Sydney and Perth, passes through both Adelaide and Broken Hill on its weekly run. From Sydney to Adelaide, the 30-hour journey costs $100 economy, $215 economy sleeper with meals, or $275 first-class sleeper with meals. From Perth to Adelaide you can take either the

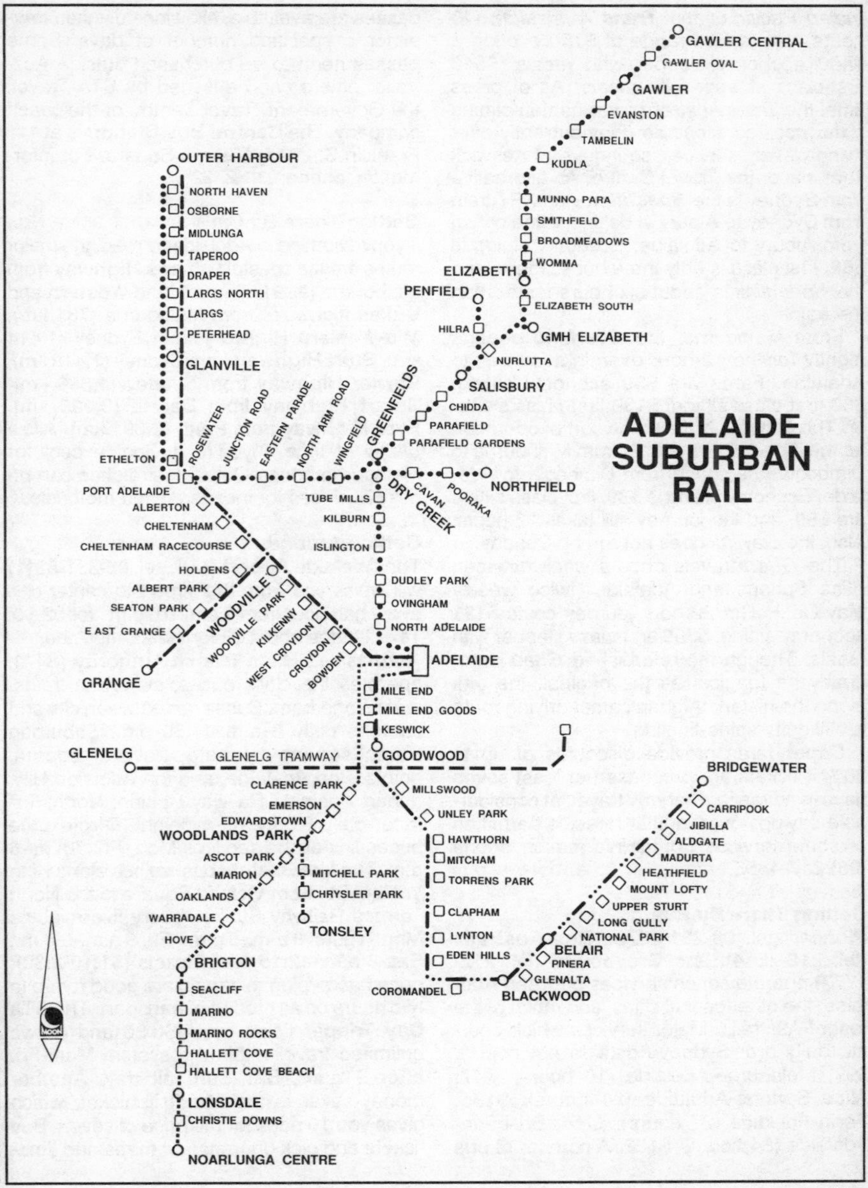
ADELAIDE
SUBURBAN
RAIL
GAWLER CENTRAL
GAWLER OVAL
GAWLER
EVANSTON
TAMBELIN
KUDLA
MUNNO PARA
SMITHFIELD
BROADMEADOWS
WOMMA
ELIZABETH
ELIZABETH SOUTH
GMH ELIZABETH
PENFIELD
HILRA
NURLUTTA
SALISBURY
CHIDDA
PARAFIELD
PARAFIELD GARDENS
GREENFIELDS
DRY CREEK
CAVAN
POORAKA
NORTHFIELD
OUTER HARBOUR
NORTH HAVEN
OSBORNE
MIDLUNGA
TAPEROO
DRAPER
LARGS NORTH
LARGS
PETERHEAD
GLANVILLE
ROSEWATER
JUNCTION ROAD
EASTERN PARADE
NORTH ARM ROAD
WINGFIELD
ETHELTON
PORT ADELAIDE
ALBERTON
CHELTENHAM
CHELTENHAM RACECOURSE
HOLDENS
ALBERT PARK
SEATON PARK
E AST GRANGE
GRANGE
WOODVILLE
WOODVILLE PARK
KILKENNY
WEST CROYDON
CROYDON
BOWDEN
TUBE MILLS
KILBURN
ISLINGTON
DUDLEY PARK
OVINGHAM
NORTH ADELAIDE
ADELAIDE
MILE END
MILE END GOODS
KESWICK
GOODWOOD
GLENELG
GLENELG TRAMWAY
CLARENCE PARK
EMERSON
EDWARDSTOWN
WOODLANDS PARK
ASCOT PARK
MARION
OAKLANDS
WARRADALE
HOVE
BRIGTON
SEACLIFF
MARINO
MARINO ROCKS
HALLETT COVE
HALLETT COVE BEACH
LONSDALE
CHRISTIE DOWNS
NOARLUNGA CENTRE
MITCHELL PARK
CHRYSLER PARK
TONSLEY
MILLSWOOD
UNLEY PARK
HAWTHORN
MITCHAM
TORRENS PARK
CLAPHAM
LYNTON
EDEN HILLS
COROMANDEL
BLACKWOOD
GLENALTA
PINERA
BELAIR
NATIONAL PARK
LONG GULLY
UPPER STURT
MOUNT LOFTY
HEATHFIELD
MADURTA
ALDGATE
JIBILLA
CARRIPOOK
BRIDGEWATER
MOON

Indian Pacific or the ***Trans Australian*** (40 hours) with a fare range of $150 economy, $400 economy sleeper with meals, $540 first-class sleeper with meals. As of press time, the *Trans Australian* was contemplating a downscaled schedule (they currently offer twice-weekly service), so inquire at Keswick Terminal or the Travel Centre. An alternative from Sydney is the ***Speedlink***—an XPT train from Sydney to Albury, a deluxe V-line coach from Albury to Adelaide. Economy sitting is $88, first class is only three bucks more, and the *Speedlink* is about six hours faster than the train.

From Melbourne, the ***Overland*** departs nightly for the 12-hour overnight journey to Adelaide. Fares are $39 economy sitting, $80 first-class sitting, $130 first-class sleeper. The ***Daylink*** is the same sort of operation as the *Speedlink:* the train from Melbourne to Dimboola, the coach from Dimboola to Adelaide. Economy sitting is $39, first-class sitters are $80, and the journey still takes 12 hours. Also, the *Daylink* does not run on Sunday.

The ***Ghan*** travels once a week between Alice Springs and Adelaide (twice weekly May-Oct.). The 22-hour journey costs $121 economy sitting, $360 first-class sleeper with meals. Though the refurbished *Ghan* is not nearly as magical as the original, the trek along the historic Afghan camel-driving route is still quite spine-tingling.

Caper fares provide discounts of up to 30% if tickets are purchased at least seven days in advance. Standby travel, at considerable savings over regular fares, is permitted on some services. For rail information, phone (08) 217-4455.

Getting There By Bus

Pioneer (tel. 08-231-2076), **Bus Australia** (tel. 212-7344), and **Greyhound** (tel. 212-1777) operate coach services between Adelaide, the other capital cities, and much of the rest of Australia. Major services which operate daily are: Sydney-Adelaide (24 hours), $97; Melbourne-Adelaide (10 hours), $47; Alice Springs-Adelaide (24 hours), $135; Perth-Adelaide (37 hours), $156; Brisbane-Adelaide (34 hours), $132. A number of bus passes are available, allowing unlimited travel for a specified number of days. Some passes need to be purchased outside Australia; others can be issued by STA Travel, the Government Travel Centre, or the coach company. The **Central Bus Station** is at 111 Franklin St., near Victoria Square. For information, phone 233-2722.

Getting There By Car

If you're coming to Adelaide by road, the major routes are the coastal **Princes Highway** from Melbourne (929 km), the inland **Western** and **Dukes** highways from Melbourne (731 km), **Mid-Western Highway** from Sydney (1,414 km), **Sturt Highway** from Sydney (1,418 km), **Barrier Highway** from Sydney (1,666 km), **Stuart Highway** from Darwin (3,026 km), **Eyre Highway** from Perth (2,691 km). Allow *plenty* of time if you're driving; except for Melbourne, these Outback stretches can be risky business for inexperienced motorists.

Getting Around

The **Adelaide Airport** (ADL, tel. 08-381-5311) will whisk you from the airport to center city, every half-hour from 7 a.m.-10 p.m., for $2.60. Taxis charge about $8 for the 25-min. ride.

Adelaide's **State Transit Authority** (STA), operates the city's buses, suburban trains, and its one tram. Buses run between city and suburbs daily 6 a.m.-11:30 p.m. Suburban trains serving Glenelg, several coastal points, Port Adelaide, and the Adelaide Hills depart Adelaide Railway Station, North Terrace, daily 5:30 a.m.-midnight. **Circle Line** buses link all the services Mon.-Fri. 7 a.m.-6 p.m. The free **Beeline** bus cruises along King William St., from Victoria Square to the North Terrace Railway Station, every five minutes Mon.-Thurs. 8 a.m.-6 p.m., Fri. 8 a.m.-9 p.m., Sat. 8 a.m.-12:15 p.m. Tickets ($1.10-2.80), priced according to zones, are good for up to two hours on all modes of transport. The STA **Day Tripper** ticket costs $3.30 and allows unlimited travel within the system Mon.-Fri. after 9 a.m., Sat.-Sun. all day. Another money-saver is the **Multitrip** ticket, which gives you 10 rides for the price of seven. Buy tickets and pick up transport maps and timetables at STA, 79 King William St. (tel. 210-1000), Mon.-Fri. 8:30 a.m.-5:30 p.m., Sat. 8-11:30 a.m.

Taxis are plentiful and can be hired at the airport, railway stations, city center taxi stands, or by phoning direct. Companies include **Amalgamated** (tel. 223-3333), **Suburban** (tel. 211-8888), and **United Yellow** (tel. 223-3111).

All the big-name car-rental firms are represented in Adelaide, with offices at the airport, the major hotels, and along North Terrace. Several lesser known, cheaper, and recommended firms are **Moke Rent-a-Cars** (tel. 352-7044), **Action Rent-a-Car** (tel. 352-7044), **Rent-a-Bug** (tel. 234-0911), and **Rent-a-Civic** (tel. 268-1879). **Action Moped Hire,** 269 Morphett St. (tel. 211-7060), rents mopeds for $15 per day, $6 per hour (be prepared to pay a $50 deposit). Action Moped Hire and **Super Elliott,** 200 Rundle St. (tel. 223-3946), rent bicycles for around $10 per day. Rent mountain bikes for $15 per day from **Bike Moves,** 1A White Ave., Fullarton (tel. 271-1854); 10-speeds are $12. In Glenelg, **Bayworld** (the tourist information center on the foreshore) rents bicycles by the day or the hour.

The **Adelaide Explorer Bus** departs the South Australian Government Travel Centre daily 9:20 a.m., 11:55 a.m., 2:05 p.m., and 4:15 p.m. (except Christmas Day, Good Friday, and Grand Prix day) for sightseeing trips to popular city spots, including Glenelg. One $12 ticket permits you to get on and off at will, so if one place strikes your fancy, you can spend as much time as you like, reboarding the bus next time around. Many tour operators offer City Sights, Adelaide Hills, Mt. Lofty Ranges, and Adelaide by Night junkets. Check with the tourist office for the current list of contenders.

Getting Away

Intrastate air carriers **Lloyd Airlines,** 144 North Terrace (tel. 08-216-1911) and **Kendell Airlines,** 9A Hindley St. (tel. 213-9567) will transport you to Coober Pedy, Ceduna, Mt. Gambier, Port Lincoln, Kingscote, and other South Australian destinations. **Airtransit** (tel. 352-3128) flies to American River, Parndana, Kingscote, and Penneshaw, all on Kangaroo Island.

The MV ***Philanderer III*** passenger ferry (tel. 0848-31-122, Penneshaw) operates service from Cape Jervis to Penneshaw, Kangaroo Island. Fares are $22, one way, for the one-hour journey. The **K.I. Connection** (tel. 384-6860), is a coach service connecting Adelaide with the Cape Jervis departure point. MV ***Island Seaway*** (tel. 47-5577) ferries from Port Adelaide to Kingscote (seven hours), and from Kingscote to Port Lincoln (11 hours). The fare is $26 for either sector, or $37 Port Adelaide-Kingscote-Port Lincoln. Phone either company for seasonal schedules.

Country trains depart Keswick Railway Terminal for Peterborough, Port Pirie and Mt. Gambier. For information, phone 217-4455.

Aside from the top four coach lines mentioned above, several smaller bus companies service the state's country towns, coastal villages, and remote stations. The **Country Passenger Depot,** 101 Franklin St., is next door to the Central Bus Station. For information, phone 231-5959.

If you're hitching to Melbourne, bus no. 161 from Pulteney St. will take you to Old Toll Gate on Mt. Barker Rd., a good thumb-and-sign post. If you're headed *far* away to Perth, across the very barren Nullarbor Plain, it's easiest to begin in Port Augusta, at the petrol station nearest to town. Bus no. 224 will get you from King William St. to Port Wakefield Rd., Gepps Cross, where you can walk to Carvans Petrol Station—your hitching point. Once you get to Port Augusta, be prepared to wait—sometimes *days.* Try to hit it on Friday night or Saturday morning when the truckies are coming through. **Warning:** Women should *not* hitch alone!

HILLS AND VALES

Less than half an hour's drive from grid-and-square-it Adelaide are rambling hills and rolling vales, secluded hollows and hideaway valleys, nook-and-cranny villages and lush green terrain smothered in wildflowers, delicate orchids, bold yellow wattle—bathed in the fragrance of almond, apple, pear, and cherry orchards, or scent from a strawberry patch. Euphoric names such as Happy Valley, Tea Tree Gully, Basket Range, Mount Pleasant, and Chain of Ponds will ring your ears with the distant echo of a near-forgotten, favorite fairy tale.

Adelaide is the perfect base for short excursions into the hills; or do the reverse—nestle into some cozy dell and day-trip down to the city.

ADELAIDE HILLS

The hills, part of the Mt. Lofty Ranges, can be explored by a number of meandering scenic routes. There's something for everyone—endless vistas for tourists in buses, scads of secluded picnic spots for lovers and loners, 1,000 km of walking tracks for hikers. One exceptionally pretty itinerary that leads you around and through conservation parks and lookout spots begins at **Windy Point** on Belair Rd. (reached from the city via Fullarton Rd.), for a bird's-eye view of the city. Skirt around Upper Sturt Rd. to **Belair Recreation Park,** one of the world's oldest national parks (established 1891). Facilities include tennis courts, football ovals, cricket pitches, a popular golf course, bushwalking tracks, and camping sites.

Continue along Upper Sturt Rd., cross the South Eastern Freeway, and you'll be on Summit Road. Take the turnoff to **Mt. Lofty,** the ranges' highest point (771 meters). At road's end, a monument pays tribute to Colonel Matthew Flinders, and a large lookout area affords a panoramic view of Adelaide and the surrounding hills and plains. Near the summit, **Mt. Lofty Botanic Gardens** cover more than 42 hectares with exotic cool and subalpine plants. The gardens are closed in winter, and are most colorful in autumn.

Cleland Conservation Park, on the slopes of Mt. Lofty, features koalas (cuddling daily 2-4 p.m.), emus, kangaroos, native birds, and other wildlife, as well as many enticing walking tracks along its 972 hectares of bushland.

Back on Summit Rd., you'll pass pear and apple orchards until you reach **Norton Summit,** where there's a restaurant and yet another view.

Turning toward the city will bring you into **Morialta Conservation Park**, noted for its waterfalls, deep gorge, and excellent bushwalking. Trails lead to the gorge and several of the waterfalls (and some pretty spectacular views), as well as to points like Pretty Corner, Kookaburra Rock, and the Giant's Cave.

Magill Rd. runs into Payneham Rd., which leads back to Adelaide. An alternate route is Marble Hill Rd. (turn off before Norton Summit) to Montacute, toward the city through Morialta and **Black Hill** conservation parks, to Payneham Road.

Para Wirra Recreational Park, 40 km northeast of Adelaide, is a wooded plateau with steep gullies, kangaroos, birds, spring wildflowers, and more good walking trails and picnic areas.

Accommodations

See the Adelaide **YHA** for information on its five limited-access hostels in the Mt. Lofty Ranges. Advance bookings are required.

Belair National Park (tel. 08-278-3540) rents inexpensive cabins with cooking facilities. Guest rooms at **Drysdale Cottage**, Debneys Rd., Norton Summit (tel. 390-1652), are moderate to expensive and include breakfast.

Big spenders and splurgers should consider a stay at **Mt. Lofty House,** 74 Summit Rd., Crafers (tel. 339-6777). The exquisitely furnished house, built between 1852 and

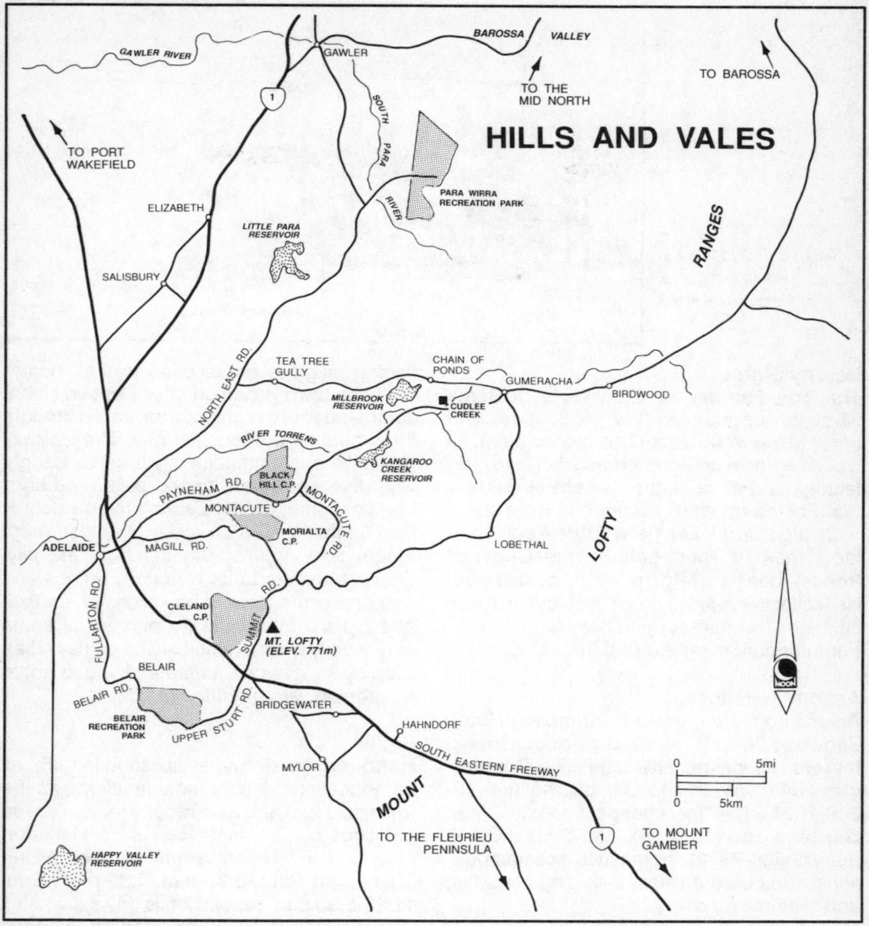

1858, has sumptuous bedrooms, sitting rooms, and two luscious restaurants. Prices are hefty—$225-400 per double—and the breakfast is light.

BIRDWOOD

Once upon a time Birdwood, less than 50 km northeast from Adelaide, was a gold-mining center. Today its claim to fame is the **National Motor Museum,** which displays more than 300 vintage, veteran, and classic motor cars and bikes. Housed inside an 1852 flour mill, the museum is open daily 9-5. For information, phone (085) 68-5006. Reached via Lobethal (and the River Torrens Gorge), or through Chain of Ponds and Gumeracha, Birdwood is both a convenient day-trip from Adelaide or a stop on the way to the Barossa Valley.

This 1860 Bridgewater Mill is the home of Petaluma winery.

Nearby Sights

The **Toy Factory** of Gumeracha features what is supposedly "the biggest rocking horse in the world" (about six stories high), as well as some nicely crafted wooden toys. The factory, and its coffeehouse, are open daily 9-5. For information, phone (08) 389-1085.

Cudlee Creek Gorge Wildlife Park, Cudlee Creek (a short detour from Chain of Ponds), boasts a large privately owned wildlife collection, with koalas just dying to be cuddled. The park is open daily 8 a.m.-dusk. For information, phone (08) 389-2206.

Accommodations

Across from the museum, **Blumberg Hotel**, Birdwood (tel. 085-68-5243), includes breakfast with its inexpensive tariff. The **Gumeracha Hotel**, Albert St., Gumeracha (tel. 08-389-1001), has the cheapest rooms. **Vega Gardens,** Holland Creek Rd., Cudlee Creek (tel. 08-589-2372), homestyle accommodations at moderate rates, including breakfast and swimming pool.

Transport

Torrens Valley Coach Lines provide regular service to Birdwood from Adelaide's Central Bus Station. Cost is $2.80 one way.

HAHNDORF

Hahndorf, 20 km southeast from Adelaide, is Australia's oldest survivng German settlement. Founded by East Prussian Lutherans fleeing religious persecution in their homeland, the town is named after Captain Hahn, commander of the ship *Zebra,* which brought them on their arduous journey. The typically (for its time) nightmarish voyage was fraught with disease, death, ripped sails, and killer heat; nonetheless the *Zebra* arrived safely at Port Adelaide in 1839. Today Hahndorf (pop. 1,300) is a popular day-trip from the city, drawing tourists to its historic buildings and well-preserved town to buy slices of streusel and *typisch* folk crafts, to partake of some oldy-worldy charm (albeit on the cutesy side). Stop by for a cuppa *kaffee* and you're apt to be greeted with a *"Guten tag,* mate."

Sights

Hahndorf Academy, established in 1857 as an educational facility, now functions as the town museum and a showcase for landscape paintings by Sir Hans Heysen, a Hahndorf favorite son. The museum is open Mon.-Thurs. and Sat. 10:30 a.m.-5:30 p.m., Sun. 11:30-5:30 p.m. Admission is $4.

View elaborate timepieces, a gigantic cuckoo clock, and buy your own authentic Black Forest cuckoo at the **Antique Clock Museum,** 91 Main Street. Open daily 9-5. Admission is $2. For information, phone (08) 388-7349.

Nearby Sights

Detour on Mt. Barker Rd. before you get to Hahndorf for an inspection of the 1860 stone **Bridgewater Mill,** restored and transformed into **Petaluma Winery.** View the huge waterwheel, taste the cabernet sauvignon and chardonnay, have lunch in the cavernous **Granary Restaurant.** Open daily 11 a.m.-5 p.m. For information, phone (08) 339-3422.

Warrawong Sanctuary, Williams Rd., Mylor, is another sidetrack to Hahndorf. See rare and endangered animals on organized dawn, daytime, and nocturnal walks. The property also has a nocturnal observatory, and craft and coffee shops. Open daily. For information, phone (08) 388-5380.

Accommodations And Food

Hochstens, 145 Main St. (tel. 08-388-7361), has a wide range of accommodations, from on-site caravans to luxury motel units and private chalets. Prices also vary from budget to expensive. **Hahndorf Old Mill Motel and Restaurant**, 98 Main St. (tel. 388- 7888), has moderate to expensive rooms with all the creature comforts.

You can get stick-to-your-bones German food all over town. The **German Arms Hotel,** 50 Main St., dating from 1834, serves pub meals in historic surroundings. Along Main St., **Otto's Bakery, Gretchen's Coffee Shop,** and the **Cottage Kitchen** will keep you going with good coffees and fresh cakes.

Events

The most interesting of the various festivals held in Hahndorf is the annual mid-January **Schutzenfest,** a traditional shooting festival with German folk dancing, entertainment, cuisine, and beer—*lots* of beer.

Transport

To get to Hahndorf, catch the twice-daily bus from Bowen St. in Adelaide, for $3 one way. For schedules, phone STA (tel. 08-210-1000).

THE BAROSSA VALLEY

South Australia's most famous wine district lies in a shallow valley just 29 km long and eight km wide, amid gently rounded hills, icy-cold brooks, neat-as-a-pin grape-staked fields, pseudo chateaus and castles, and authentic Lutheran churches.

Less than an hour's drive north of Adelaide, most of the 50 or so wineries are situated in the 20-km span from Lyndoch to Nuriootpa, with the town of Tanunda in between. Serious connoisseurs or occasional tipplers can follow their noses or their whims to commercial mega-complexes and family-run boutique wineries for a gargle or a swallow of full-bodied reds, crisp whites, sherries, ports, and sparkling wines.

Two routes will get you to the Barossa—a rather boring, but quicker and more direct road through Gawler, or the longer, winding, picture-postcard way via Birdwood and Torrens Gorge. Assuming that you'll start off on the scenic route and by day's end be wishing for the straight highway with the dividing lines, the following towns have been geographically arranged to reflect that. Also, not all of the wineries have been listed below, only some of the most historical and interesting. Well-placed signposts will lead you to others off the beaten path—it's fun to make a wrong turn here or there, up or down, to make your own vintage discoveries. You can do the Barossa in a day-trip from Adelaide, but if your feet get a little wobbly—or you haven't had your fill—consider bedding down for the night at a hostel, guesthouse, or motel along the way.

History

The Barossa was settled in 1842 by the same persecuted East Prussian Lutherans who arrived on the good ship *Zebra* with Captain Hahn. Their expedition had been funded by Englishman George Fife Angas, one of the original colonizers, in the hopes he was snagging good, hardworking folk whose skills would benefit South Australia. The new arrivals who didn't go to Hahndorf followed their pastor, August Kavel, to the Barossa Valley and put down roots in Lyndoch, Tanunda, Angaston, and Bethany. A few years earlier, the same region had been explored by Silesian mineralogist Johannes Menge, who passed the word that the area, similar to parts of Poland, was a grape-grower's heaven. By the late 1840s the new settlers had planted their vines, and were soon turning out vintages ambrosial enough to knock their *lederhosen* off. At the same time they constructed beautiful stone churches, cottages, and town buildings, which you'll see on your tour of the valley.

The actual name "Barossa" came from our man Colonel Light, back in 1837. Twenty-five years earlier he had squared off in a battle in Barrosa, Spain, under the command of Lord Lynedoch. Feeling nostalgic by the similar-looking terrain, Light named the Barossa "Barrosa" and the town of Lyndoch, "Lynedoch."

Springton

You've heard of the old woman who lived in a shoe? Well, pioneer settlers Caroline and Friedrich Herbig lived inside a gigantic hollow gum tree—even bore two of their children there—from 1855-1860. The **Herbig Gum Tree** is just before Hamiltons Road.

Springton Gallery, at Hamiltons Rd. (tel. 085-68-2001), has a selection of Australian and international crafts. The gallery (formerly the old settlers' store and post office) is open daily 11 a.m.-5 p.m.

Keyneton

This tiny village was once called "North Rhine" because of its resemblance to the settlers' homeland. **Henschke Wines** (tel. 085-64-8223), established 1868, is a small fifth-generation family-run winery with some of the oldest shiraz vines in the region. Specialties are premium-quality red and white table wines. Hours are Mon.-Fri. 9 a.m.-4:30 p.m., Sat. 9 a.m.-noon.

Angaston

Named for George Fife Angas, landholder and financial backer for the *Zebra* voyage, who settled near the town (pop. 1,820) in 1851. Fife's son built **Collingrove Homestead** (tel. 085-64-2061), where family members lived until turning it over to the National Trust in 1976. It now serves as a museum for Angas memorabilia, a restaurant, and elegant country accommodation. Open daily 10:30 a.m.-5 p.m.

Yalumba Winery (tel. 64-2423), established 1849, is built of Angaston marble and topped with a clock tower. Specialties are premium red and white table wines and champagnes. Open Mon.-Fri. 9-5, Sat. and holidays 10 a.m.-5 p.m., Sun. 12-5 p.m.

Angaston Galleria, 18 Murray St. (tel. 64-2648), features local and imported arts and crafts inside a 125-year-old former church building.

Saltram Winery (tel. 64-2200), founded in 1859, is another old-timer in the Barossa, featuring red and white table wines and ports. Hours are Mon.-Fri. 9-5, Sat.-Sun. 12-5 p.m., holidays 10 a.m.-5 p.m.

Nuriootpa

Once upon a time this town was an important Aboriginal bartering center (Nuriootpa translates to "A Meeting Place"). After William Coulthard, a pioneer settler, laid out his acre in 1854, the town grew around his red gum-slab hotel. Today, Nuriootpa (pop. 3,200), at the northern end of the Barossa Valley, is the district's commercial heart, with a wide range of facilities, services, and government agencies. Coulthard's hotel is gone, but his home has been preserved and serves as the main information center for the Barossa Valley. Aside from the many clusters of wineries, Nuriootpa has some lovely parks and picnic grounds banking the North Para River which meanders through town.

Penfolds Winery (tel. 085-62-0389), established in 1812, is a huge commercial complex (it recently merged with Kaiser Stuhl) specializing in a full range of red and white table wines and fortified wines. This property can store more than 22 million liters of wine! Hours are Mon.-Fri. 9 a.m.-5:30 p.m., Sat. and holidays 10 a.m.-5 p.m., Sun. 1-5 p.m.

Elderton Wines (tel. 62-1058), established 1906, has red and white table wines, sparkling wines, *and* bicycles and mokes for hire. Hours are daily 10:30 a.m.-5 p.m.

Wolf Blass Wines (tel. 62-1955), along the Sturt Highway, was only established in 1973, yet practically started out winning Australia's most coveted red-wine prize three years in a row. Specialties are premium red and white table wines and champagne. Hours are Mon.-Fri. 9:15 a.m.-4:30 p.m., Sat.-Sun. and holidays 12-4:30 p.m.

Marananga

Gnadenfrei ("Freed by the grace of God") was the original name given to this little town by its settlers in the 1840's. In 1918, when Germanic names were being changed, it was christened Marananga, Aboriginal for "My Hands."

It's worth making the turn off the main road to see the old schoolhouse, cottages, and splendid **Gnadenfrei Church,** begun in 1857, with additions in 1873 and 1913.

Heritage Wines (tel. 085-62-2880) is small, new (established 1984), with interesting dry red and white table wines. Hours are daily 11 a.m.-5 p.m.

Seppeltsfield

Take the out-of-place-looking, date palm-fringed road from Marananga to Seppeltsfield, founded by Silesian migrant Joseph Seppelt in 1851. Seppelt, who started off as a tobacco farmer, discovered that his crop was too rank for sale. He experimented with winemaking and the rest, as they say, is history. And history, as reported in the 1892 *London Gazette,* called Seppelt's cellars and stores "the most modern in the world." Those "modern" buildings have been carefully preserved and make for an interesting tour between sips of red and white table wines, fortified wines, and champagnes. Hours are Mon.-Fri. 9-5, Sat. 10:30 a.m.-4:30 p.m., Sun. 11 a.m.-4 p.m. For information, phone (085) 62-8028.

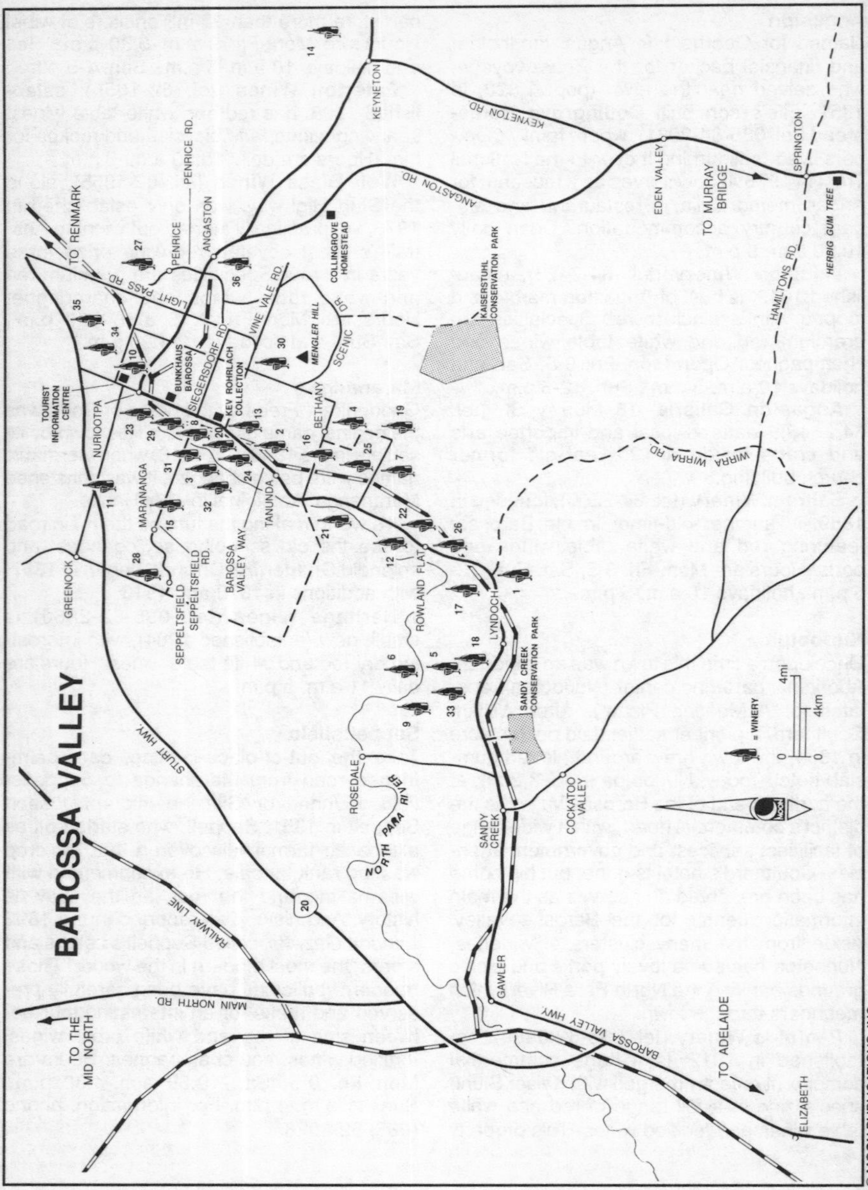
BAROSSA VALLEY
TO THE MID NORTH
MAIN NORTH RD.
RAILWAY LINE
STURT HWY.
GREENOCK
NURIOOTPA
TOURIST INFORMATION CENTRE
TO RENMARK
LIGHT PASS RD
PENRICE
PENRICE RD
ANGASTON
KEYNETON
ANGASTON RD.
KEYNETON RD
COLLINGROVE HOMESTEAD
EDEN VALLEY
TO MURRAY BRIDGE
SPRINGTON
HERBIG GUM TREE
HAMILTONS RD.
WIRRA WIRRA RD.
KAISERSTUHL CONSERVATION PARK
MENGLER HILL
SCENIC DR
VINE VALE RD.
BUNKHAUS BAROSSA
SIEGERSDORF RD
KEV ROHRLACH COLLECTION
BETHANY
TANUNDA
BAROSSA VALLEY WAY
MARANANGA
SEPPELTSFIELD
SEPPELTSFIELD RD.
ROWLAND FLAT
LYNDOCH
SANDY CREEK CONSERVATION PARK
ROSEDALE
NORTH PARA RIVER
SANDY CREEK
COCKATOO VALLEY
GAWLER
BAROSSA VALLEY HWY.
TO ADELAIDE
ELIZABETH
= WINERY
0 4mi
0 4km
MOON

BAROSSA VALLEY

1. Barossa Settlers
2. Basedow Wines
3. Bernkastel Wines
4. Bethany Wines
5. Burge Family Winemakers
6. Charles Cimicky Wines
7. Charles Melton Wines
8. Chateau Dorrien Wines
9. Chateau Yaldara Estate
10. Elderton Wines
11. Gnadenfrei Estate
12. Grant Burge Wines
13. Hardy's Siegersdorf
14. Henschke Wines
15. Heritage Wines
16. High Wycombe Wines
17. Kellermeister Wines
18. Kies Estate Cellars
19. Krondorf Wines
20. Leo Buring Wines
21. Lindner McLean Vineyards (St. Hallett Wines)
22. Orlando Wines
23. Penfolds Wines
24. Peter Lehmann Wines
25. Rockford Wines
26. Rovalley Estate
27. Saltram Wine Estates
28. Seppeltsfield Winery
29. Tarac Distillers
30. Tarchalice Wine Co.
31. Tolley Pedare Winery
32. Veritas Winery
33. Wards Gateway Cellar
34. Willows Vineyard
35. Wolf Blass Wines
36. Yalumba Winery

Barossa Valley Way

It only takes about five minutes to get from Nuriootpa to Tanunda along this stretch of road, but you'll probably get hung up for hours if you stop at the **Kev Rohrlach Collection** (tel. 085-63-3407), a private museum of science, transport, and technology. More than 3,000 mechanical exhibits collected by Mr. Rohrlach (a builder) from all over South Australia will amaze, amuse, confound, and confuse you. The transport collection alone includes a maharaja's barouche and the 1955 Australian Grand Prix-winning car. Don't miss it! Opening hours are Mon.-Sat. 9-5, Sun. 10 a.m.-5 p.m. Admission charge is $3.

Tanunda

Established in 1843, Tanunda (pop. 2,860) was the second German settlement in the valley. Many of the traditional early stone buildings line the main avenue, as well as **Langmeil Road,** one of the back streets. **Goat Square,** sight of the first town market, is bordered by original cottages, preserved and classified by the National Trust.

Tanunda is home to four of the valley's most exquisite Lutheran churches: **Langmeil Church,** on the main drag, has Pastor Kavel's remains buried in the adjacent cemetery; **St. John's,** Jane St., is home to life-size wooden statues of Jesus, Moses, and selected apostles; **Tabor Lutheran Church,** north end of Murray St., is notable for its orb-topped spire; **St. Paul's,** corner Murray St. and Basedow Rd., features fine stained glass.

Bethany

Bethany was the first German settlement in the Barossa, founded in 1842 by a group of Silesian families. This peaceful, pretty village is still home to old stone houses, cottage gardens, farmlets, as well as Australia's smallest hotel. The old village common has been transformed into **Bethany Reserve,** a haven for picnickers along bubbling Bethany Creek. The church bells still ring at dusk on Saturday to signal the end of the work week —in case anyone forgets. The **Landhaus,** on Bethany Rd. near the railway tracks, claims to be Australia's smallest licensed motel.

Opposite Bethany Reserve, **Bethany Art & Craft Gallery** (tel. 085-63-2614) is an outlet for handmade textiles, pottery, glass, and wooden wares. The gallery is open daily, 10 a.m.-5 p.m.

Rowland Flat

Commercial winemaking began at Jacobs Creek in 1847 when Johann Gramp planted his first vines. Nowadays the **Orlando Winery,** which dominates the town, pays its tribute by carrying an excellent claret with the Jacobs Creek label. The complex is enormous and pretty sterile, but it does offer a very good, educational $1 winery tour. If you visit February through April you'll get to view the grape-crushing process. Red and white table wines and champagnes are the specialties. Hours are Mon.-Fri. 9:30 a.m.-5 p.m., Sat.-Sun. and holidays 10 a.m.-4 p.m. For information, phone (085) 24-4500.

Rockford Wines (tel. 63-2720) is on Krondorf Rd., about three km from Rowland Flat. If you've just been to Orlando, this tiny establishment, with its tasting room inside a former stable, may underwhelm you—but the spectacular vintages won't. Specialties are traditional full-bodied Australian wine styles (premium regional wines). Hours are daily 11 a.m.-5 p.m.

Lyndoch

Lyndoch (pop. 705), at the southern edge of the valley, was originally settled in 1839 as a farming community; the first winery was installed in 1896 in a converted flour mill. All of the ten or so wineries in this district are family-owned. The largest is **Chateau Yaldara** (tel. 085-24-4200), established in 1947 on the remains of that same converted flour mill. Besides red and white table wines, sparkling wines and port, the "chateau" displays a collection of porcelain and antiques. Hours are daily 9-5.

Along the Barossa Highway, the **South Australian Museum of Mechanical Music** (tel. 24-4014) features antique music boxes, automatic accordions, barrel pianos, player organs, an 1840s musical church, and singing birds. The museum is open daily.

Cockatoo Valley

Detouring off the Barossa Highway, you'll pass through this small village with a general store (for petrol and provisions), remnants of goldfields, and an 1870s miner's cottage (converted to accommodations). The big attraction, down the road, is Barossa Reservoir (built in 1898) and its famed **Whispering Wall,** a retaining wall with peculiar acoustics which enable you to stand on one side and hear whispers all the way from the opposite side of the dam.

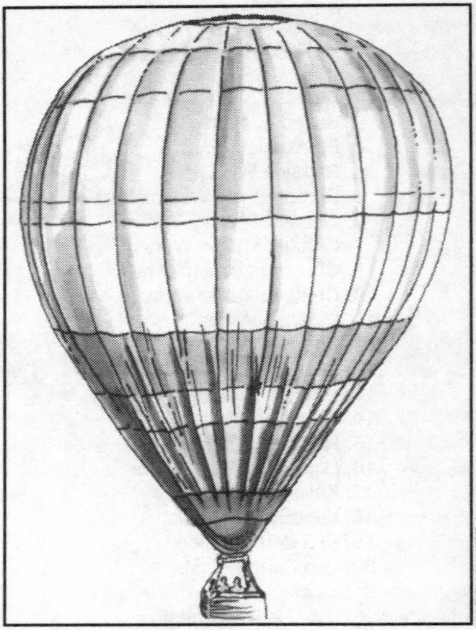
KAREN WHITE

ballooning over Barossa Valley vineyards

Gawler

Gawler (pop. 11,300), founded in 1839, was South Australia's second country town after Port Adelaide. Superb bluestone architecture, dating from the late 19th and early 20th centuries, is reflected in the town hall, post office, and various churches. Other fine buildings are the Old Telegraph Station, constructed of One Tree Hill sandstone, and homes and fences crafted from local limestone.

PRACTICALITIES

Accommodations

Angaston: Barossa Brauhaus Hotel, 59 Murray St. (tel. 085-64-2014), has both a cozy dining room and a saloon bar. Historic Angaston Hotel, 59 Murray St. (tel. 64-2428), is known for the Bacchus mural in its lounge. Both hotels are inexpensive. **Collingrove**

Homestead, Eden Valley Rd. (tel. 64-2061), is the Angas family ancestral home where guests can spend the night in converted servants' quarters. Prices are moderate and include continental breakfast.

Nuriootpa: Barossa Gateway Motel, Kalimna Rd. (tel. 085-62-1033), has plain, inexpensive rooms. **Karawatha Guest House,** Greenock Rd. (tel. 62-1746), is a much homier environment. Moderately priced rooms include breakfast. The modern **Vine Inn Hotel/Motel,** 14 Murray St. (tel. 62-2133), is in the center of town. Rooms run moderate to high and include continental breakfast.

Marananga: The **Hermitage of Marananga,** corner Seppeltsfield and Stonewell roads (tel. 085-62-2722), features spacious suites overlooking the property's vineyards. Expensive rates include breakfast in the popular country restaurant.

Seppeltsfield: You have your choice between the comfy, modern, and inexpensive **Holiday Cabins,** Seppeltsfield Rd. (tel. 62-8240) for $41-50 double, or the sumptuous Lodge, Main Rd. (tel. 62-8277), where for about $200, you can live in the old Seppelt family digs. (That rate does *not* include breakfast!)

Barossa Way: Bunkhaus Barossa, Barossa Highway (tel. 085-62-2260), is a friendly backpackers' hostel with kitchen facilities, TV room, swimming pool, and bicycle rental. Dorm beds cost $9 per night. **Barossa Junction Resort,** Barossa Highway (tel. 63-3400), offers motel-style accommodations inside converted railway cars, including lounge and dining carriages. Rates, with continental breakfast, are inexpensive to moderate.

Tanunda: Broadoak, 6 Murray St. (tel. 085-63-3054), is an old bluestone cottage with guesthouse accommodations and shared facilities. Inexpensive rates include breakfast. **Tanunda Hotel,** 51 Murray St. (tel. 63-2030), is also inexpensive and has a restaurant and swimming pool. **Weintal Hotel/Motel,** Murray St. (tel. 63-2303), with bars, a bistro, restaurant, underground cellar, tennis courts, swimming pool, and sauna, is moderately priced, as is rural **Lawley Farm,** Krondorf Rd. (tel. 63-2141), where the farm cottage and barn have been converted into lovely country rooms.

Bethany: The **Landhaus,** Bethany Rd. (tel. 085-63-2191), may be Australia's smallest licensed motel, but the price is a big $100, including breakfast.

Lyndoch: About 20 km south of Lyndoch, **Kersbrook YHA Hostel,** Roachdale Farm (tel. 08-389-3185), rents bunks for $5, but there is no public transport to the facility. **Yaldara Barossa Motel,** Barossa Valley Highway (tel. 085-24-4268), has a restaurant and swimming pool. Moderate rates include continental breakfast.

Cockatoo Valley: The old 1870 **Miner's Cottage,** Middleton Rd. (tel. 085-24-6213), has private accommodations comprised of living room with open fireplace, bedroom, and bathroom. Rates are expensive and include continental breakfast.

Gawler: Prasad's Gawler Motel, 1 Main North Rd. (tel. 22-5900), features good rooms, a swimming pool, spa, and sauna. Rates are inexpensive, but *double* during festival season. **Gawler Arms Hotel,** 102 Murray St. (tel. 22-1856), doesn't have all the fancy amenities, but the moderate prices are steady.

Camping

Barossa Valley Tourist Park, Penrice Rd., Nuriootpa (tel. 085-62-1404), is a very large park with swimming pool, barbecue, playground, tennis courts, a recreation lake, and reserve. **Tanunda Caravan Park,** Barossa Valley Way, Tanunda (tel. 63-2784), features full-service grass sites in a sheltered setting. **Barossa Caravan Park,** Lyndoch (tel. 24-4262), is fairly plain, but near the Whispering Wall and other hot spots. **Hillier Park,** Hillier Rd., Gawler (tel. 22-2511), has a quiet rural setting, with swimming pool, playground, sheltered picnic and barbecue areas.

Food

You mean you want something besides bread and cheese? You'll easily find tearooms, coffee shops, pub meals, bakeries, and takeaways, as well as some gourmet restaurants with food to match the local wines.

Collingrove Homestead, an elegant country manor

KAREN WHITE

Angaston: Angas Park Fruit Co., Moculta Rd. and North St. (tel. 085-64-2052), has a wide selection of dried fruit and nuts for your picnic basket. The **Angaston Hotel,** 59 Murray St. (tel. 64-2428) is a favorite for counter meals as well as more expensive à la carte dining.

Nuriootpa: Family-owned **Linke's Bakery,** 40 Murray St. (tel. 085-62-1129), has been turning out cakes and breads for more than 50 years. The tearooms serve sandwiches and other lunch items. The dining room at the **Vine Inn Hotel/Motel,** Murray St. (tel. 62-2133), puts out a smorgasbord salad bar. Big splurgers hunting interesting game dishes should book at **Pheasant Farm,** off Seppeltsfield Rd. (tel. 62-1286), where menu choices include glazed kangaroo, rabbit-stuffed sausage and, naturally, pheasant. The restaurant is closed during February.

Marananga: Marananga Restaurant, Seppeltsfield Rd. (tel. 085-62-2888), serves large portions of simple food inside a one-room rustic stone cottage with open beams and a fireplace. Prices are middle-of-the-road.

Tanunda: Stock up on delicious bakery items any day but Sunday at **Apex Bakery,** Elizabeth St. (tel. 085-63-2483). **Zinfandel Tearooms,** 58 Murray St. (tel. 63-2822), feature inexpensive light lunches and cakes. Moderately priced German cuisine is the specialty at **Die Gallerie,** 66 Murray St. (tel. 63-2788), where you eat in the courtyard when it's warm, or next to the open fire when it's cold. **Tanunda Hotel,** 51 Murray St. (tel. 63-2030), serves hearty counter meals at reasonable prices.

Lyndoch: Get your counter meals at **Lyndoch Hotel,** Gilbert St. (tel. 085-24-4211).

Events

With all that wine around, you can well imagine that denizens of the Barossa Valley are ready to party at the drop of a grape. The big event, of course, is the **Barossa Valley Vintage Festival,** held over Easter week in odd-numbered years. Activities and amusements that fill the valley include grape-picking and crushing contests, brass bands, maypole dancing, tug-o'-wars, gourmet dinners, arts and crafts exhibitions, and winetastings up the shiraz. For information, phone (085) 62-1866.

Some other prominent annual events include January's **Oom Pah Festival** in Tanunda (tel. 65-2674), the March **Essenfest** in Tanunda (tel. 63-2211), **Seppeltsfield Balloon Regatta** in May (tel. 08-389-3195), and **Barossa Classic Gourmet Weekend** also in May (tel. 62-1866). Needless to say all of these events feature *a lot* of food and grog!

Information

Barossa Information Centre, 66 Murray St. (inside Coulthard House), Nuriootpa (tel. 085-62-1866), is the regional information hub for the entire Barossa Valley. You can pick up maps to the vineyards, inquire about guided tours, etc., Mon.-Fri. 8:30 a.m.-5:30 p.m., Sat.-Sun. 9:30 a.m.-4:30 p.m. The **Gawler Tourist Association,** Murray St. (tel. 22-6814), is open daily 10 a.m.-4 p.m. (Heritage bus tours of Gawler leave from the tourist office at 10 a.m. every Tuesday.)

For police, medical, and fire **emergencies,** dial 000. **Hospitals** are located at Angaston (tel. 64-2065), Tanunda (tel. 63-2398), and Gawler (tel. 22-1677). **Police stations** are at 61 Murray St., Nuriootpa (tel. 62-1111) and 23 Cowan St., Gawler (tel. 22-1088).

Transport
If you're driving, the scenic route can be reached via Chain of Ponds, through Birdwood, to Springton. The direct route is straight up Main North Rd. from Adelaide, through Elizabeth, to Gawler.

Barossa Adelaide Passenger Service (tel. 085-65-6258) leaves Adelaide's Central Bus Station for Lyndoch, Tanunda, Nuriootpa, and Angaston. Departure times are Mon.-Fri. 9:30 a.m., 1:30 p.m., 5 p.m.; Sat. 12:15 p.m. and 5:45 p.m.; Sun. 5:45 p.m. The fare is about $5 one way.

Rent bicycles by the day or the hour from the **Bunkhaus,** corner Barossa Valley Highway and Nuraip Rd., Nuriootpa (tel. 62-2260), **Elderton Winery,** Nuriootpa (tel. 62-1058) or **Keil's Gift Centre,** 63 Murray St., Tanunda (tel. 63-2177).

Hertz cars and mopeds can be rented from **Caltex Tanunda** (tel. 63-2677). Elderton Winery rents mini-mokes.

FLEURIEU PENINSULA

The Fleurieu bills itself "South Australia's Holiday Playground." Like the Adelaide Hills and the Barossa Valley, the Fleurieu is easy day- tripping distance south of the city center. Aside from rolling hills, clustered vineyards, and pastoral farmlands, there are beaches—lots of beaches—from the Gulf St. Vincent, around Cape Jervis, along the pounding Southern Ocean, to Encounter Bay and the mouth of the Murray River—beaches to surf at, fish from, swim off, jog along, glide above, sail aside, and sun worship on.

Bushwalkers and nature lovers can explore more than 20 coastal, wetland, and woodland parks inhabited by native birds and animals. Hiking trails are plentiful, particularly within Deep Creek Conservation Park between Cape Jervis and Victor Harbor, where you super-adventurous hikers can hit the Heysen Trail and follow it all the way to the Flinders Ranges! Cape Jervis is also the jumping-off spot for Kangaroo Island, or you can island-hop to Granite Island, off Victor Harbor, for a glimpse of the fairy penguins, or Hindmarsh Island, off Goolwa, to boat, fish, or water-ski.

Less sporty travelers will enjoy tasting and tippling at the Wine Coast vineyards (especially noteworthy for reds), admiring early buildings, browsing the many antique shops and crafts cottages, holing up in a secluded cove, or maybe taking the plunge at clothing-optional Maslin Beach.

According to regional tourist literature, the Fleurieu "abounds" in fine beaches, "abounds" in fine wines, "abounds" in fun, history, and just about everything else—so abounding we shall go.

History
All the big-name explorers traversed the Fleurieu—Sturt, Light, Barker—but it was French explorer Nicholas Baudin who, in 1802, named the area for Napoleon's Minister of the Navy, Charles Pierre Claret Comte de Fleurieu. In the same year, Baudin "encountered" rival Matthew Flinders at a site which was appropriately named Encounter Bay—the Encounter Coast becoming a natural tangent thereof. It was at Encounter Bay, in 1837, that South Australia's first whaling station (and first successful industry) was created. Interestingly, neither Baudin nor Flinders spotted the sand-covered mouth of the Murray, Australia's largest river, a stone's throw away.

THE WINE COAST

About 20 km south of Adelaide, the Wine Coast stretches from old Reynella, home of Cellar Number One, to Old Willunga, with its own share of historic buildings.

Most of the Fleurieu wineries sprouted in the 1850s when individual farmers harvested

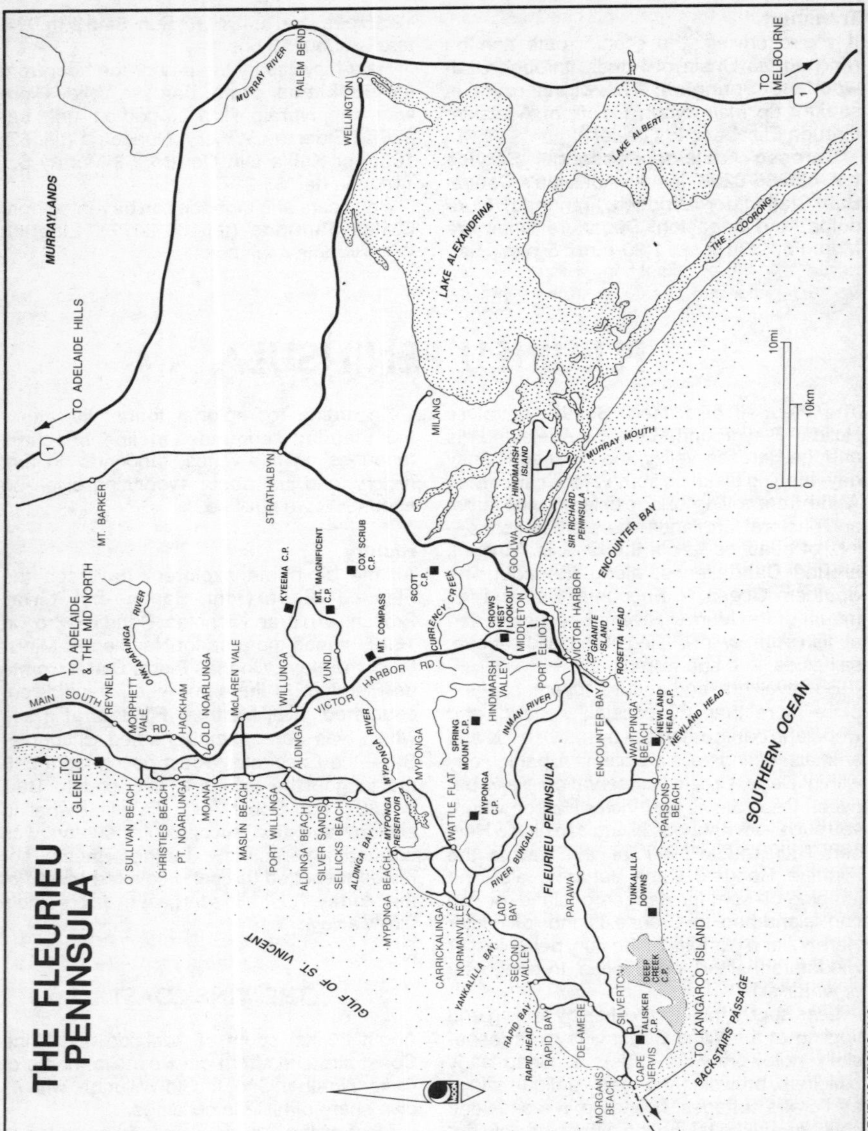
THE FLEURIEU PENINSULA
TO GLENELG
TO ADELAIDE & THE MID NORTH
TO ADELAIDE HILLS
MURRAYLANDS
TO MELBOURNE
1
MAIN SOUTH RD.
REYNELLA
MORPHETT VALE
ONKAPARINGA RIVER
HACKHAM
OLD NOARLUNGA
McLAREN VALE
WILLUNGA
MT. BARKER
STRATHALBYN
MURRAY RIVER
TAILEM BEND
WELLINGTON
LAKE ALEXANDRINA
LAKE ALBERT
THE COORONG
MILANG
HINDMARSH ISLAND
MURRAY MOUTH
SIR RICHARD PENINSULA
ENCOUNTER BAY
GOOLWA
KYEEMA C.P.
MT. MAGNIFICENT C.P.
COX SCRUB C.P.
SCOTT C.P.
CURRENCY CREEK
YUNDI
MT. COMPASS
VICTOR HARBOR RD.
CROWS NEST LOOKOUT
MIDDLETON
PORT ELLIOT
VICTOR HARBOR
GRANITE ISLAND
ROSETTA HEAD
HINDMARSH VALLEY
INMAN RIVER
ENCOUNTER BAY
WAITPINGA BEACH
NEWLAND HEAD C.P.
NEWLAND HEAD
SOUTHERN OCEAN
O SULLIVAN BEACH
CHRISTIES BEACH
PT. NOARLUNGA
MOANA
MASLIN BEACH
PORT WILLUNGA
ALDINGA
ALDINGA BEACH
SILVER SANDS
SELLICKS BEACH
ALDINGA BAY
MYPONGA RIVER
MYPONGA
MYPONGA RESERVOIR
MYPONGA BEACH
SPRING MOUNT C.P.
WATTLE FLAT
MYPONGA C.P.
RIVER BUNGALA
FLEURIEU PENINSULA
PARSONS BEACH
CARRICKALINGA
NORMANVILLE
LADY BAY
PARAWA
TUNKALILLA DOWNS
YANKALILLA BAY
SECOND VALLEY
GULF OF ST. VINCENT
DEEP CREEK C.P.
SILVERTON
TO KANGAROO ISLAND
RAPID BAY
DELAMERE
TALISKER C.P.
BACKSTAIRS PASSAGE
RAPID HEAD
CAPE JERVIS
MORGANS BEACH
0
10mi
10km

small vineyards for their personal use. It was Thomas Hardy who, in 1876, put the area on the map with his purchase of Tintara Vineyards (which subsequently evolved into a dynasty) in McLaren Vale. In the early 1900s, after the all-important London market accepted the Australian wines into their cellars and down their gullets, the local vintners began growing vines with a more serious bent. In 1973, the first annual bushing festival, celebrating the release of the year's vintage, furthered the Wine Coast's popularity. Today the district is comprised of more than 40 (mostly family-owned) wineries.

Reynella

Old Reynella, at the turnoff from Main South Rd., marks the start of the Wine Drive.

This is the town where John Reynell, South Australia's first commercial winegrower, planted his vines in 1839 and created Cellar Number One (also known as the Old Cave Cellar). See Reynell's original cellar and his home, Chateau Reynell, on the grounds of **Hardy's Reynella Winery,** Reynell Rd. (tel. 08-381-2266). The winery, established in 1853, is open daily 10 a.m.-4:30 p.m., except Christmas Day and Good Friday.

Reynella's first school, erected in 1858, is on Peach Street.

Morphett Vale

South Australia's first Roman Catholic church, St. Mary's, was built here in 1846. To view other historic buildings, turn off of Main South Rd., at the Noarlunga turnoff, for **Pioneer Village** at Hackham, where there's a rather hokey re-creation of other old structures, furnished in period style. Hours are Wed.-Sun. 10 a.m.-5 p.m., including public holidays. Admission is $3.

Eat a pork pie, plum pudding, or traditional plowman's lunch at **James Craig Inn,** Main South Rd., Hackham (tel. 08-384-6944).

Old Noarlunga

This was the oldest concentrated settlement in the southern part of the state. Some of the heritage buildings that remain are **Horseshoe Hotel** (1840), the **market square** (1841), **Horseshoe Mill** (1844), **Church of St. Philip and St. James** (1850), and **Jolly Miller Hotel** (1850).

McLaren Vale

Explore the many surrounding wineries, but pay a special visit to **Hardy's Wines,** Main Rd. (tel. 08-323-8676), whose purchase by Thomas Hardy in 1876 changed the course of Wine Coast winemaking. (Author's favorite is Hardy's black bottle pot still brandy.) Hardy's is open daily 10 a.m.-4:30 p.m., closed Christmas Day and Good Friday.

Chapel Hill Cellars, Chapel Hill Rd. (tel. 323-8429), formerly the Sir Samuel Way church and school, has a superb stained-glass window, plus excellent good dry red and white wines and ports. Hours are daily 11 a.m.-5 p.m.

The **World Thru Dolls,** Chalk Hill Rd. (tel. 323-8624), displays antique dolls, portrait figures, nursery rhymes, fairy tales, Bible stories, and other toys and dollies. Open Wed.-Fri. 1-4 p.m., Sat., Sun., and holidays 1-5 p.m.

Hotel McLaren, 208 Main Rd. (tel. 323-8208), has inexpensive room rates which include breakfast. Moderately priced **McLaren Vale Motel,** Caffrey St. (tel. 323-8365), has a swimming pool and spa.

Quite a few wineries have picnic and barbecue areas, as well as restaurants that feature a winetaster's lunch. **James Haselgrove Wines,** Foggo Rd. (tel. 323-8049), has good meals, as does **Oliverhill Wines,** Seaview Rd. (tel. 323-8922), with an Italian winemaker and Chinese chef.

McLaren Vale Bushing Festival (tel. 323-8999), celebrating the release of a new vintage, occurs over several days in October. Activities include tastings, tours, a ball, fairs, toasting and crowning of the Bushing King and Queen, and an Elizabethan feast.

For help contact **McLaren Vale Hospital** (tel. 323-8606), **police** (tel. 323-8330), or **fire brigade** (tel. 323-8393).

Willunga

Willunga, derived from Willa-unga, Aboriginal for "Place of the Green Trees," was first laid out in 1839. These days the town is one of Australia's most important almond-growing regions, with 4,500 acres planted. Several

Chapel Hill Cellars, formerly a church and school, produces fine local vintages.

old bluestone buildings preserved by the National Trust include the courthouse and police station, dating from 1855. Many of the roof slates have been quarried locally.

Pick your own strawberries at **Nicolle's Strawberry Fields,** California Rd. (tel. 08-323-8910), from mid-Sept. through January.

Vanessa's Restaurant Motel, 27 High St. (tel. 085-56-2379), has moderately priced rooms which include continental breakfast. The restaurant is on the expensive side.

Rosella Café, Upper High St. (tel. 085-56-2258), serves light lunches and homemade European cakes. The **Salopain Inn,** on Old Willunga Rd. before town (tel. 08-323-8769), features daily lunch in a restored 1861 hotel.

In late July, Willunga celebrates the start of spring with an **Almond Blossom Festival.**

Conservation Parks

South of Willunga, take the Hope Forest turn-off to **Kyeema Conservation Park,** with its active bird population and walking trails, including a special trail which explores park animals' homes.

Also southeast of Willunga, the Yundi turn-off will lead you to **Mt. Magnificent Conservation Park,** where a portion of the Heysen Trail makes a steep ascent to the top of the mount.

GULF ST. VINCENT BEACHES

Heading south of Adelaide, past Hallet Cove, the first beach you come to is **O'Sullivan's,** with its breakwater-protected swimming and boating facilities. Next is **Christies Beach,** a popular family resort with safe swimming, sailing, and reef fishing. **Port Noarlunga,** circled by steep cliffs and sandhills, features a lovely reef (at low tide), fishing jetty, and natural aquatic reserve, the **Onkaparinga River Recreation Park,** with many types of water birds.

A favorite with surfers is **Moana,** where you can drive (cautiously!) onto the beach. **Moana Beach Tourist Park,** on the Esplanade (tel. 08-386-2115), has on-site vans and campsites. The park has a boat ramp, tennis courts, gymnasium, sauna, and spa.

Maslin Beach, South Australia's first legal nude beach, is exceptionally popular for its, er, scenery and bodysurfing. Be aware that only the 1½-km southern strip of the beach is clothing-optional. **Maslin Beach Caravan and Camping Ground,** 2 Tuit Rd. (tel. 085-56-6113), rents campsites and on-site vans. Features include swimming pool, tennis court, coin-operated barbecue, and laundry facilities.

Port Willunga is a historic spot with off-shore reefs, occasional good surf, scuba diving to the shipwrecked *Star of Greece,* swimming, and sandy beaches.

Aldinga Beach also has good scuba diving, swimming, and sometimes surfing. Remnant plains scrub, wildflowers, and birdlife are features of **Aldinga Scrub Conservation Park,** off Cox Road. Walk through the scrub to the beach at **Aldinga Holiday Park,** Cox Rd. (tel. 085-56-3444). On-site vans and campsites are available, and there are also five "yurt-like" cottages, and a swimming pool.

There's good fishing from offshore boats at **Silver Sands,** swimming at **Sellicks Beach,** and decent surf at sheltered **Myponga Beach.** Three conservation parks near the town of Myponga are **Myponga,** nine km southwest, **Spring Mount,** 13 km southeast, and **Nixon-Skinner,** behind Myponga Reservoir.

Be careful of the rips at **Carrickalinga.** A better choice is **Normanville,** where there's excellent swimming, both jetty and boat fishing, snorkeling on the offshore reef, and paraflying during the summer. A river runs through the **Normanville Beach Caravan Park,** Jetty Rd. (tel. 085-58-2038). Rent an on-site van or campsite there, or at **Beachside Caravan Park,** Willis Dr. (tel. 58-2458). **High Country Trails,** Willis Dr., Normanville (tel. 58-2507), organizes horseback rides, from an hour's trot along the beach to three-day pack trips, for learners or experienced riders.

The beaches get pretty rocky from here on out. Try **Lady Bay** for snorkeling, **Second Valley** for boat and jetty fishing, and **Rapid Bay** for excellent scuba diving. (Rapid Bay was the site of Colonel Light's first landing.) In Second Valley, **Leonard's Mill** (tel. 085-98-4184), a restored 1849 stone mill, is open daily for à la carte meals, light snacks, and drinks at indoor or outdoor courtyard bars.

The tiny town of **Delamere,** inland along Main South Rd., has a number of historical buildings including the Uniting Church (1858), rural school (1861), St. James Church (1871), and council offices (1878).

CAPE JERVIS TO VICTOR HARBOR

Rounding the cape, the coast becomes more rugged as the waves of the Southern Ocean pound the shores and branch roads lead through weathered terrain to isolated and occasionally ferocious beaches below.

At the tip of the peninsula, **Cape Jervis** is both the jumping-off point to Kangaroo Island, 13 km across the Backstairs Passage, and the Heysen Trail, which passes through many different conservation parks on its faraway way to the Flinders Ranges. The coastal waters are noted for jetty and deep-sea fishing as well as scuba diving, and the tall cliffs and powerful breezes make it an ideal base for hang gliding. The **Cape Jervis Lighthouse** was in operation from 1871 to 1972. **Cape Jervis Tavern Motel,** Main Rd. (tel. 085-98-0276), has moderate rates which include continental breakfast.

Back on Range Rd., turn into **Talisker Conservation Park,** where you can fossick about the 1862 silver and lead mine. You'll pass through the old mining town of **Silverton** on your way to the park.

Deep Creek Conservation Park is nothing short of spectacular—rugged cliffs form sheer drops downward to the raging sea, profusions of delicate orchids and luxuriant ferns tangle along cool running streams, native birds and wildlife sweep from steep terrain to secluded coves. Accessed from Range Rd., Deep Creek offers a number of exciting trails for hikers—everything from casual strolls to challenging bushwalks. It is essential that you check in at Park Headquarters before embarking on any of the walks—particularly the strenuous, long-distance Heysen Trail (which is closed outside the conservation parks in summer). You can also pick up trail maps, camping permits, and other detailed information from **Deep Creek National Parks and Wildlife Service** (tel. 085-98-0263).

Due to powerful rips and changing currents, only very experienced surfers and strong swimmers should tempt their fate at isolated **Parsons** and **Waitpinga** beaches, both part of **Newland Head Conservation Park,** reached from Range Road. The park also has walking trails and camping facilities. **Rosetta Harbor,** on the northern side of the Bluff in Encounter Bay, has good snorkeling and scuba diving.

VICTOR HARBOR

Situated on the shores of Encounter Bay, Victor Harbor (pop. 5,300) is the largest town on the Fleurieu Peninsula. Being a close 83 km from Adelaide makes it exceptionally popular with city folk who invade the town during summer and school holidays. Two unique natural formations are the Bluff, a 100-meter-high headland, and—protecting the bay from the Southern Ocean's wild surf—Granite Island, connected by causeway to the shore.

History

Victor Harbor's whaling stations bustled with activity from 1837 (when the first station was established) until 1869, attracting both small and large vessels to its port, making it one of the state's most important export terminals. Assuming that Victor Harbor would not only become *the* river port, but possibly the state capital, a railway was built in 1864, linking the town to Goolwa, at the mouth of the Murray River. Unfortunately, big ship owners, scared off by the Southern Ocean's erratic and stormy seas, searched for safer spots to drop anchor and the port soon became obsolete.

Sights

The **Museum of Historical Art,** Yankalilla Rd., three km from Victor Harbor (tel. 085-52-1546), is a large private collection of shells, rocks, coins, medals, firearms, and miniature cars. Open Sundays and school holidays 1-5 p.m.

Historic buildings include the **Railway Station, Telegraph Station** (1867), **Newland Memorial Congregational Church,** Victoria St. (1869), **St. Augustine's Church of England,** on Burke St. (1869), and others. The **Victor Harbor Tourist Information Centre,** located in the original primary school on Torrens St., will provide maps and direct you.

If you climb to the top of the rather steep **Bluff,** you'll get a stupendous view of the bay where Baudin and Flinders had their famous meeting in 1802, and below to Rosetta Bay and Whale Haven, where the whaling stations operated.

Ride to **Granite Island** on Australia's only horse-drawn tram. Gentle giant Clydesdales commute from Victor Harbor to the island daily 10 a.m.-4 p.m. Fare is $1 one way (buy tickets at the causeway on Victor Harbor foreshore). During South Australian school holidays and good-weather weekends, chairlifts operate to the top of the peak for expansive views of the town and bay. Summertime visitors to the island might spy fairy penguins as they waddle toward their rocky homes each night after dusk.

Urimbirra Wildlife Park, Adelaide Rd., five km from Victor Harbor (tel. 085-54-6554), is a 16-hectare open-range park with dingoes, crocs (there's one named Aunty Jack), koalas, kangaroos, bats, wombats, bettongs, bandicoots, snakes, eels, and a nocturnal house. Hours are daily 10 a.m.-5 p.m.

Opposite Urimbirra, the one-hectare **Nagawooka Flora Reserve** is planted with almost 1,000 named trees, shrubs, and groundcovers from all over Australia. The park is open daily during daylight hours.

Safe swimming beaches are on either side of the Causeway to Granite Island, good snorkeling at **Oliver's Reef,** and bodysurfing at **Chiton Rocks,** between Victor Harbor and Port Elliot.

Accommodations

You have a choice of simple guesthouses, motel rooms, or fully equipped holiday flats. Check with the tourist office for long-term selections. If you're visiting during peak periods, book far in advance, and expect rates to increase (and often double).

Warringa Guest House, 16 Flinders Parade (tel. 085-52-1028), is an 80-year-old traditional establishment, set right on the sea with terrific views. Inexpensive rates include light breakfast. Both the **Grosvenor Hotel,** Ocean St. (tel. 52-1011), and **The Clifton,** 39 Torrens St. (tel. 52-1062), have inexpensive to low-moderate rooms. **Villa Victor,** 59 Victoria St. (tel. 52-4258), charges $30 single, including full breakfast and mah-jongg lessons!

Victor Harbor Holiday Centre, Bay Rd. (tel. 52-1949), has on-site vans and campsites, as well as moderately priced motel units with cooking facilities.

Food

You'll find the usual resort town takeaways. **Fine Foods International,** Coral St. (tel. 085-52-3732), has yummy imported picnic goodies, nuts, dried fruits, chocolates. **Higgy's Victor Harbor Bakery,** Albert Pl. (tel. 52-3515), bakes fresh pies and pasties and concocts custom-made sandwiches. The **Sub Station,** Ocean St., is another good sand-

top: preparing for a corroboree in central Australia (TOURISM SOUTH AUSTRALIA); bottom left: Jim Jim Falls, Kakadu National Park (NORTHERN TERRITORY TOURIST COMMISSION); bottom right: Aboriginal art near Katherine, Northern Territory (NORTHERN TERRITORY TOURIST COMMISSION)

above: coastline, Western Australia (WESTERN AUSTRALIA TORUISM COMMISSION); below: a slice of Western Australia's south coast (WESTERN AUSTRALIA TOURISM COMMISSION)

wich-maker. **Warringa Guest House** serves moderately priced home-style meals in historic surroundings. The **Ocean Chinese Restaurant,** Ocean St., serves meals for about $10. For finer and costlier meals, try the restaurants at **Apollon Motor Inn, Bayview Motel, Ocean Crest Motel,** or **Whalers Inn.**

Information

Victor Harbor Hospital (tel. 085-52-1066) and **police** (tel. 52-2088) serve the immediate area. For maps and other road information, contact the **Royal Automobile Association** (tel. 52-1033).

PORT ELLIOT

Farther along the Encounter Coast, on Horseshoe Bay, the historic township of Port Elliot (pop. 1,050) attracts body and board surfers to its fabled beaches and tourists to its picturesque shores with views of the Murray mouth and Coorong National Park.

History

Like neighboring Victor Harbor, Port Elliot did not fare very well as a port. Proclaimed a town in 1854—with the opening of South Australia's first iron railway on its inaugural Port Elliot-to-Goolwa link—Port Elliot was named by Governor Young after his buddy, Sir Charles Elliot. Though the first ship anchored in 1851, and traffic grew to a busy 85 arrivals in 1855, by 1864 seven ships had been sunk and strewn about the bay. So much for Port Elliot—in that same year, another railway link was built to Victor Harbor, and for a short time traffic was redirected.

Sights

Historic structures lining The Strand include the **police station** (1853), **courthouse** (1866), **Council Chamber** (1879), and nearby **St. Jude's Church** (1854). The National Trust has set up a historical display in the Port Elliot **Railway Station,** built in 1911.

For excellent **coastal views,** take the scenic walk from just above Horseshoe Bay and follow the cliffs to Knight's Beach, or look out from **Freeman Knob,** along The Strand at the Main Victor Harbor-Goolwa Rd. junction.

Boomer Beach, west of town, is where experienced bodysurfers come for large dumping waves. Small, sheltered **Green Bay,** on Freeman Knob, is good for sunbathing, but swimming is dangerous in the rocky bay with strong outcurrents. Swimmers will find very good facilities at **Horseshoe Bay,** with small surf at the Commodore Point end. **Middleton Beach,** on the way to Goolwa, is one of the best surfing beaches on the Encounter Coast. **Big Surf Australia,** Main Rd., Middleton (tel. 085-54-2399), sells bodyboards, swimwear, and accessories, rents quality gear, and is open daily. Flagstaff Hill Rd. leads from central Middleton to another inspiration point, a winery, and a mushroom farm.

Accommodations

Royal Family Hotel, 32 North Terrace (tel. 085-54-2219), has simple, inexpensive rooms with shared facilities. **Hotel Elliot,** The Strand, by the railway station (tel. 54-2218), also inexpensive, has more of a family-type atmosphere. Moderately priced **Cavalier Inn Motel,** The Strand (tel. 54-2067), has good views and a swimming pool. **Thomas Henry's House,** 8 Charteris St. (tel. 54-2003), offers 1930s-style B&B accommodation at high-moderate rates.

Port Elliot Caravan Park, Horseshoe Bay (tel. 54-2134), has on-site vans, campsites, and moderately priced cottages. **Middleton Caravan Park,** Middleton (tel. 54-2383) rents on-site vans and campsites.

Food

Royal Family Hotel and **Hotel Elliot** both serve inexpensive counter meals. **Sitar Indian Restaurant,** The Strand (tel. 085-54-2144), has moderately priced dinners and takeaways. **Arnella Restaurant,** North Terrace, on the main Victor Harbor-Goolwa Rd., has country-style dinners (lunch, in season, and on Sundays) in the higher price bracket. And, higher yet, is the continental cuisine at **Thomas Hardy's Restaurant.**

The **Middleton Fish Shop** (tel. 54-2688) and **Middleton General Store and Post Of-**

fice (tel. 54-2064) are both open daily for takeaway food and snacks.

GOOLWA

Situated where the Murray River mouth meets the Great Southern Ocean, Goolwa (pop. 2,360) draws railway buffs and river rats who come to ride Australia's first iron public railway, to cruise up or down the Murray or around Lake Alexandrina, or to laze away the days by the historic old wharf. Hindmarsh Island, a ferry ride away, sits between the mighty mouth and the entrance to Lake Alexandrina.

History

Prosperous paddlesteamer trade along the Murray River made Goolwa an important port from the mid- to late 1800s; the opening of the railway line to Port Elliot gave the town true, though short-lived, notoriety. Alas, a new line extending all the way to Adelaide and built in the 1880s caused Goolwa's final fizzle as port extraordinaire.

Over on Hindmarsh Island, an obelisk marks the place where Charles Sturt, in 1830, squinted past the sand hills and into the Murray mouth, as did Captain Collett Barker, another explorer, who must have opened *his* eyes a little too wide before he got speared to death by the natives.

Sights

The **Goolwa Hotel** (1853), Cadell St., **post office** (1857), Cadell St., **Corio Hotel** (1857), Railway Terrace, and **police station** (1859), Goolwa Terrace, are some of the old buildings that are still in use today. (The Goolwa Hotel has a figurehead from the wrecked ship *Mozambique* on its parapet.)

Other historic sights are the **Railway Superintendent's House** (1852), **Railway Horse Stables** (1853), **Goolwa Hotel** (1853), the **Saddlery** (1867), **Town Mechanics Institute** (1868), and **Church of England** (1867), all on Cadell Street.

The **Goolwa National Trust Museum** (1870), Porter St., is housed inside a former blacksmith shop. The museum has many exhibits which focus on Goolwa's early beginnings, including a "Port of Goolwa" room.

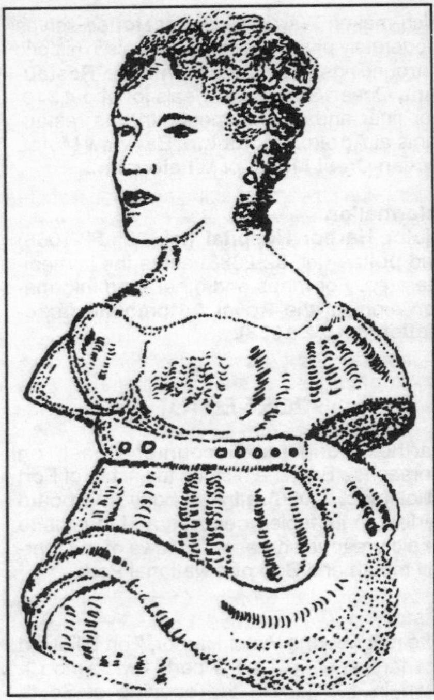

figurehead from the shipwrecked Mozambique

Signal Point, The Wharf (tel. 085-55-3488), opened in 1988 by the illustrious Prince of Wales, is the River Murray Interpretive Center. High-tech computerized displays show what the river was like before the Europeans came as well as the impact of modern industry and development on the important waterway. Climb aboard *Oscar W*, a restored paddlewheeler built in 1908, that sits alongside the wharf. Hours are daily 10 a.m.-5 p.m., except Christmas Day.

The only way to get to **Hindmarsh Island** is by the free 24-hour ferry near the wharf. Walking trails and lookouts enable you to see the Murray mouth on one side, Lake Alexandrina on the other. The Sturt Memorial granite obelisk is about three km from the ferry landing, on the right side of the main road. Boat ramps on the island will launch you into salt or fresh water.

Built between 1935 and 1940, **Goolwa Barrage,** an enormous concrete structure atop a multitude of wooden piles pounded into the riverbed, crosses the lower Murray—from Hindmarsh Island to Sir Richard Peninsula—which separates the salty sea from the fresh river water. A bird blind, off Barrage Rd., lets watchers view the area birdlife.

Currency Creek, an eight-km drive up Cadell St., has an Aboriginal canoe tree alongside the road, picnic areas, and a walking trail that will take you to a waterfall, old copper mine, and short detour to the cemetery.

Goolwa Beach often has big surf, cross currents, and some rips—recommended for experienced swimmers only.

Accommodations

Two of the town's oldest buildings, **Goolwa Hotel,** Cadell St. (tel. 085-55-2012), and **Corio Hotel,** Railway Terrace (tel. 55- 2011), have inexpensive rooms with shared facilities. **South Lakes Motel,** Barrage Rd. (tel. 55-2194), features moderately priced rooms with kitchenettes, swimming area, and adjacent golf course.

For moderately priced home-style accommodations, try **Graham's Castle,** corner Castle Ave. and Bradford Rd. (tel. 55-2182), and **Kenmaur House,** Saratoga Dr. (tel. 55-3494). **Goolwa Cottage,** 3 Hays St. (tel. 55-1021), in the heart of the wharf area, is a "smoke-free zone," with slightly higher rates.

Narnu Pioneer Holiday Farm, Monument Rd., Hindmarsh Island (tel. 55-2002), features self-contained cottages in a rural setting for $45-60 per double, with horseriding and aquatic equipment available.

On-site vans and campsites are available at **Goolwa Camping and Tourist Park,** Kessell Rd. (tel. 55-2144), and campsites only at **Hindmarsh Island Caravan Park,** Madsen St., Hindmarsh Island (tel. 55-2234).

Food

Counter meals and à la carte fare are served daily at both the **Goolwa** and **Corio** hotels. There's a coffee shop at **Signal Point** for light lunches, snacks, and cakes. **South Lakes Motel** has a comparatively pricey restaurant at the water's edge. Otherwise, it's the usual takeaways, chicken joints, and a Chinese restaurant.

Information

The **Goolwa Tourist and Information Centre,** Cadell St. (tel. 085-55-1144), open daily, provides information on all area facilities, as well as maps for historic walking tours.

Reach out and touch the **police** (tel. 55-2018), **ambulance** (tel. 52-2111), or **fire brigade** (tel. 55-2000). The **Royal Automobile Association** (tel. 55-2009) will assist with maps and driving-related questions.

STRATHALBYN

Approximately 30 km north of Goolwa, beautiful Strathalbyn (pop. 1,925), a designated heritage township, was settled by Scottish immigrants in 1839. Examples of architecture which reflect Scottish influence are the **Angus Flour Mill** (1852), **20 High Street Crafts** (1854), **London House** (1867), and **Argus House** (1868). **Saint Andrew's Church** (1848), overlooking the river, is one of Australia's most fabled country churches.

The River Angus, which flows through town, is bordered by **Soldiers Memorial Gardens,** a peaceful setting for picnicking, duck-feeding, swan-songing, and gentle strolls. Several Aboriginal canoe trees line the water's edge and gum trees hover above lush lawns and rambling bridges.

Many arts and crafts, antique, and second-hand shops are scattered about the town. A walking-tour book (80 cents) to Strathalbyn's two shopping areas is available at many locations. You can also pick up tourist literature at 20 High Street Crafts.

Milang, 20 km southeast of Strathalbyn, is another former river port, now used as a launching point for boating, windsurfing, and water-skiing on Lake Alexandrina. **Langhorne Creek,** 60 km northeast from Milang, is a grape and almond-growing district on the way to **Wellington,** farther east yet, on the banks of the Murray River. Don't miss a ride on the 24-hour free ferry, operating since

1839 (when it was the only access across the river between South Australia and the eastern states).

Accommodations

Two fine old pubs are **Robin Hood Hotel,** 18 High St. (tel. 085-36-2608) and the **Terminus Hotel,** 17 Rankine St. (tel. 36-2026). Both offer inexpensive rooms with shared facilities.

Strathalbyn Caravan Park, Coronation Rd. (tel. 36-3766), has on-site vans and campsites.

Food

Both the Robin Hood and Terminus hotels have reasonably priced counter meals. **Strath Eats,** 10 Dawson St. (tel. 085-36-3582), dishes up pizza, pasta, chicken, and chips. **Bonnie MacGregor's,** Dawson St. (tel. 36-3535), features gourmet foods and light meals at moderate prices.

Events

The **Penny Farthing Challenge Cup,** held annually in March, is an international event in which more than 30 riders race through the township on pennyfarthings and other vintage bicycles. Accompanying hooplah consists of parades, band performances, barbecues, a pancake brekky, arts and crafts displays, and Scottish street entertainment. For more information, phone (085) 36-2699.

Information

For assistance, phone the **police** (tel. 085-36-2044), **ambulance** (tel. 36-2333), **fire brigade** (tel. 36-2000), or local **Royal Automobile Association** (tel. 36-2066).

TRANSPORT

All buses to the Fleurieu Peninsula depart from Adelaide's Country Passenger Depot, 101 Franklin Street. **Premier Roadlines** (tel. 08-233-2777) travels the Adelaide-Willunga-Victor Harbor route three times daily Mon.-Fri., twice daily Sat. and public holidays, once on Sundays. Fare to Victor Harbor is about $9 one way. **Kangaroo Island Connection** (tel. 08-231-5959) departs twice daily for Cape Jervis via Aldinga and Normanville. Fare to Cape Jervis is $9.50 one way. **Johnson's Motor Service** (tel. 08-231-5959) provides transportation to Goolwa, twice daily, Mon.-Friday. Fare is $8.50 one way. **Mt. Barker Passenger Service** (tel. 08-391-2977) leaves for Strathalbyn three times daily, Mon.-Friday. Fare is $9 one way. The **State Transport Authority** (tel. 08-210-1000) serves outer suburbs within the Fleurieu area.

Railway buffs should board the steam-powered ***Cockle Train*** which follows the historic Victor Harbor-Goolwa route at least three times daily on school holidays, long weekends, and Sundays. The one-hour-and-45-minute roundtrip costs about $12. For information, phone (08) 231-1707.

The MV ***Philanderer III*** (tel. 008-01-3111, toll-free from S.A.) provides ferry service from Cape Jervis to Kangaroo Island up to five times daily for $22 one way.

Huck Finn-ers and river queens can choose from a variety of Murray River cruises departing from Goolwa. PS ***Mundoo*** makes 2½-hour paddlesteamer cruises to North Goolwa, Hindmarsh Island, and Currency Creek every Thurs. and Sat. at 11:30 a.m. Fare is $13, lunch is an additional $10. MV ***Aroona*** has a luncheon cruise downstream to the Murray mouth, Tues. and Sat., for the same rates, and a barbecue cruise, Sun. 11:30 a.m.-3:30 p.m., for $16. Cruises subject to demand are: Goolwa-Murray Bridge (all day, $43); Coorong (five hours, $20); and Milang (all day, $17). For information, phone Goolwa Cruises (tel. 085-55-2203). The super-luxurious 44-cabin ***River Murray Queen*** departs from Goolwa for six-night upriver cruises. Cost is about $750 per person, including all meals. For information, phone (08) 211-8333.

KANGAROO ISLAND

After Tasmania and Melville (off Darwin's coast), Kangaroo Island (pop. 4,000), approximately 145 km by 60 km, is Australia's third largest island. Though the climate is temperate, with only rare frosts and highs not usually exceeding 38 degrees C, the island is at its best (and most crowded) during the summer months.

Dramatic cliffs, sheltered beaches, untamed coastline, untouched scenery, and flourishing wildlife lure tourists to this popular holiday resort, a relatively close 113 km southwest of Adelaide and just a short hop off the Fleurieu Peninsula. Families enjoy swimming and sunning, camping and hiking in their choice of 16 conservation parks. Divers have a grand time exploring the 40-plus ships reported wrecked around the coastal waters, beginning with the *William,* in 1847. Anglers drop their lines from jetties, rocks, and boats, into surf, rivers, and the deep blue sea. Naturalists are enthralled by the plentiful wildlife—kangaroos, natch, plus koalas, seals, fairy penguins, emus, sea lions, echidnas, possums, and an occasional platypus—unscathed by such predators as foxes or dingoes, which are nonexistent on the island. (On the western side, you can still see the kin of wild pigs, reputedly set ashore by French explorer Nicholas Baudin as feed for shipwrecked sailors.) Besides all the critters, you can tiptoe through more than 700 native wildflower species, and about 150 others brought in from elsewhere in the world. *And,* if you're into the birds and the bees, keep your eyes and ears perked for crimson rosellas, purple-gaped honeyeaters, ospreys, sea eagles, the rare glossy black cockatoo, and the unique Ligurian honeybee.

Kingscote, on Nepean Bay, is the island's commercial center and the city nearest the airport. Other communities with holiday facilities are American River, Penneshaw, and Parndana. The north coast flaunts calmer waters, with stretches of beach for swimming, sunning, and lazy-day fishing. Dudley Peninsula, along the Backstairs Passage, boasts fairy penguins, pelicans, stunning views, and the Cornwall-style village of Penneshaw. The south coast is the wild side, with sand dunes, crashing waves, and three conservation parks. And Flinders Chase National Park, on the south and west coasts, is Kangaroo Island's spectacular wildlife sanctuary.

History

Not much is known about the Aboriginals who originally inhabited the island—stone tools thought to be more than 10,000 years old are about the only sign of their presence. Anyway, they were long gone by 1802, when Matthew Flinders, voyaging on the *Investigator,* "discovered" Kangaroo Island for himself (and his king). But French explorer Nicholas Baudin was also nosing about, doing some circumnavigating of his own. By the time the two sailor men faced off shortly afterward, in Encounter Bay, Flinders had named the island—this time in tribute to the many kangaroos he'd seen, instead of for a compatriot—while Baudin had christened the places *he'd* charted *à la française.* Consequently, you'll find French names attached to many island sights, reflecting the French vs. English "tug-of-words."

The island has an American influence also. In 1803, one year after Matthew Flinders had taken the island, a group of American sealers arrived at a site they named "American River." Using native pine they built the *Independence,* South Australia's first boat.

It wasn't until 1836 that the first 400 settlers, sponsored by the South Australian Company, arrived from England aboard the *Duke of York* to formally establish a township at Reeves Point, north of Kingscote. The lack of fresh water kept this from being a viable colonial settlement and, by 1840, except for a few lingering souls, most of the population had shifted over to the mainland. Fact is, though, Reeves Point was South Australia's first official European settlement, and the present inhabitants are tremendously proud of that bit of history.

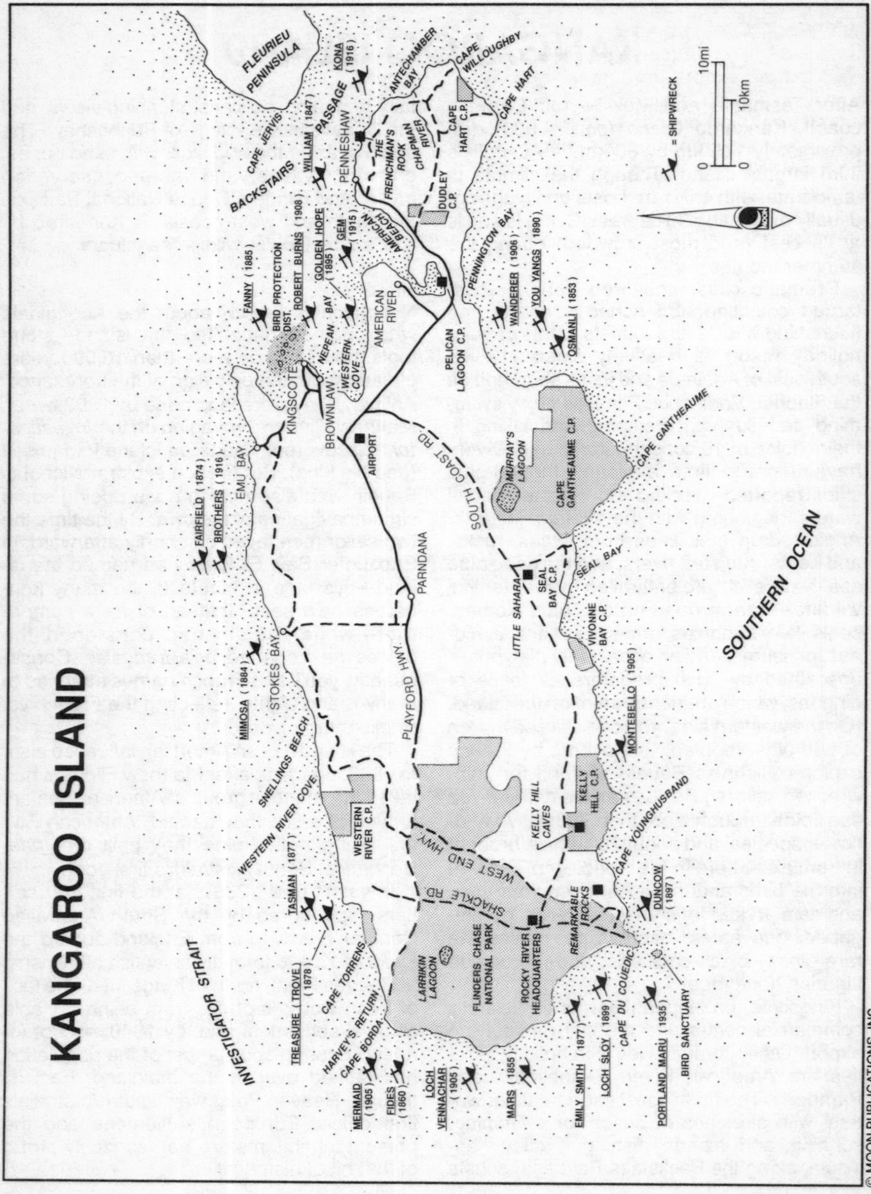
KANGAROO ISLAND
INVESTIGATOR STRAIT
FLEURIEU PENINSULA
CAPE JERVIS
BACKSTAIRS PASSAGE
KONA (1916)
WILLIAM (1847)
PENNESHAW
ANTECHAMBER BAY
CAPE WILLOUGHBY
CAPE HART
CAPE HART C.P.
CHAPMAN RIVER
THE FRENCHMAN'S ROCK
DUDLEY C.P.
AMERICAN BEACH
GEM (1915)
GOLDEN HOPE (1895)
ROBERT BURNS (1908)
BIRD PROTECTION DIST.
FANNY (1885)
NEPEAN BAY
AMERICAN RIVER
WESTERN COVE
KINGSCOTE
BROWNLAW
PELICAN LAGOON C.P.
PENNINGTON BAY
YOU YANGS (1890)
WANDERER (1906)
OSMANLI (1853)
AIRPORT
SOUTH COAST RD.
MURRAY'S LAGOON
CAPE GANTHEAUME C.P.
CAPE GANTHEAUME
SOUTHERN OCEAN
EMU BAY
FAIRFIELD (1874)
BROTHERS (1916)
PARNDANA
PLAYFORD HWY.
LITTLE SAHARA
SEAL BAY C.P.
SEAL BAY
VIVONNE BAY C.P.
MONTEBELLO (1905)
STOKES BAY
MIMOSA (1884)
SNELLINGS BEACH
WESTERN RIVER COVE
WESTERN RIVER C.P.
KELLY HILL CAVES
KELLY HILL C.P.
CAPE YOUNGHUSBAND
WEST END HWY.
SHACKLE RD.
REMARKABLE ROCKS
DUNCOW (1897)
TASMAN (1877)
TREASURE (TROVE) (1878)
CAPE TORRENS
HARVEY'S RETURN
CAPE BORDA
LARRIKIN LAGOON
FLINDERS CHASE NATIONAL PARK
ROCKY RIVER HEADQUARTERS
CAPE DU COUEDIC
BIRD SANCTUARY
MERMAID (1905)
FIDES (1860)
LOCH VENNACHAR (1905)
MARS (1855)
EMILY SMITH (1877)
LOCH SLOY (1899)
PORTLAND MARU (1935)
= SHIPWRECK
0
10mi
10km

Early industries on the island were yacca gum production, salt mining, and eucalyptus oil distilling (eucalyptus oil was Australia's first export product). Agriculture, however, was in a slump until the 1930s when cobalt and copper were added to the soil. After that, crops flourished and, before long, one-half the island had become productive farmland. Today Kangaroo Island's most vital industries are agriculture, fishing, and tourism.

KINGSCOTE

On the shores of Nepean Bay, Kingscote (pop. 1,400) blends its historical significance with modern-day necessities. Sheer cliffs to the north afford terrific views of the harbor and Western Cove, while cliffs to the south provide a languid drop to the Cygnet River swamp and bird lands. Kingscote is the island's major shipping port and trade center.

Sights

Reeves Point Historic Site, is where the *Duke of York* anchored in 1836 and South Australia officially began. You'll find remnants of the first post office, the state's oldest cemetery and, farther north, the state's oldest introduced tree—a mulberry, planted around 1836, that still bears edible fruit! (You can buy jam made from the berries.)

Hope Cottage, the National Trust Museum, is housed in an 1850s building built by two pioneering brothers. Displays include working exhibits, maritime history, family histories, photographs, and early newspapers. Open daily 10 a.m.-12 p.m. and 2-4 p.m.

St. Alban's Church, built in 1884, is Kingscote's oldest public building. Stained-glass windows, memorials to pioneer families, and graffiti from when the church was used as a schoolroom are worth seeing.

Memorial Park, on the seafront close to the town center, has memorials to Flinders and the war dead, as well as barbecue and picnic areas for when your nostalgia gives way to hunger pangs.

Fairy penguins parade to their homes at dusk on most nights. Best viewing places are between the swimming pool and jetty, or among rocks near the jetty. At **Bay of Shoals,** see pelicans and other birds fed daily at 4 p.m.

Heritage Walking Trails explore Kingscote's natural history and heritage sights. Pick up maps at the Tourist Information Office on Dauncey Street..

Family **beaches** with shallow swimming and wading facilities can be found in front of the Ozone Hotel and at Little Brownlow Beach, in front of the Yacht Club. Another spot for safe swimming is the rockbound **seawater pool.**

Accommodations

Be sure to book ahead, especially during school holiday periods. **Kangaroo Island Youth Hostel** (also known as Hillfarm Hostel), Brownlow Beach (tel. 0848-22-778), has dorm beds for $10 per night, plus bicycle rentals, transportation from Kingscote, and meal service.

Cygnet River Cottages, Camelback Farm, Cygnet River (tel. 23-020), near the swamplands, are inexpensive.

Kangaroo Island Holiday Village, 9 Dauncey St. (tel. 22-225), has self-contained family units with kitchens at moderate prices. Slightly higher-priced are the **Island Resort,** Telegraph Rd. (tel. 22-100), with an indoor heated pool, sauna and spa, and **Ellison's Seaview Motel,** Chapman Terrace (tel. 22-030), featuring seafront motel units or guesthouse rooms. Ozone Seafront Hotel, The Foreshore (tel. 22-011), at the high end of the moderate range, has great views.

Nepean Bay Caravan Park, the Foreshore, Brownlow Beach (tel. 22-394), rents campsites, on-site vans, and cabins.

Food

Good takeaways are **Pelican Pete's Takeaway Eats,** Main St. (tel. 0848-22-138), and **Nev's Tucker Box,** 3 Kingscote Terrace (tel. 22-585). **Port of Call Restaurant,** the Foreshore (tel. 22-834), serves seafood, steak, and pasta in an intimate setting overlooking Nepean Bay. The **Ozone Seafront Hotel** features an à la carte dining room, bistro, and informal coffee shop for meals at all prices.

THE DUDLEY PENINSULA

Kangaroo Island's eastern tip is a narrow neck that stretches from Pelican Lagoon Conservation Park and white-sand beaches to Cornish-influenced Penneshaw, around rugged Cape Willoughby, and Cape Hart and Dudley conservation parks.

American River

This tiny village, midway between Kingscote and Penneshaw, is named for the American sealers who lived here for four months in 1803. It's a favorite spot for fishermen who come not only for a fresh catch-of-the-day, but for the scenic beauty of gum and she-oak forested hills as they dip to meet the calm waters of Eastern Cove. Try to arrive at the end of August, when the freesias cover every knoll, dell, and pathway with brilliant blossoms.

The nearby aquatic reserve, Pelican Lagoon Conservation Park, is abundant with pelicans, swans, and Cape Barren geese.

Linnetts Island Club Resort (tel. 0848-33-053) has a choice of rooms, suites, villas, or holiday flats, ranging in price from inexpensive to expensive. **American River Motel,** Wattle Ave. (tel. 33-052), overlooks the American River and has a pool, spa, and sauna. Prices are moderate to expensive and include continental breakfast. Rates are the same at **Wanderers Rest,** corner Government and Bayview roads (tel. 33-140), a guesthouse on a hillside with sweeping views of American River. All of these accommodations have restaurants or dining rooms.

Pennington Bay

Just one km off the Kingscote to Penneshaw road, very near American River, Pennington Bay is a popular swimming and surfing beach —but only for the experienced. Otherwise, you can take a hike (more of a climb, actually) to the top of Mt. Thisby for views of both Pelican and Pennington bays.

Dudley Conservation Park, near Pennington Bay, is one of the island's many wildlife havens where you may see the dama wallaby, Kangaroo Island kangaroo, purple-gaped honeyeater, echidna, and the fairy wren.

Penneshaw

Passing along sandy white Island and American beaches, you'll come to Penneshaw, a Cornish-like hamlet, only 16 km across the Backstairs Passage from mainland South Australia. Tourists are drawn here for the safe bathing beach, excellent fishing off Hog Bay Jetty, and the parade of fairy penguins which nest (returning home each evening) in the cliffs and sand hills near town.

Captain Flinders landed near **Christmas Cove** in 1802. Also known as "The Basin," the granite boulders had a slightly earlier arrival than the good captain—they were deposited by a glacier more than 200 million years ago.

Frenchman's Rock, at Hog Bay, marks the spot where, in 1803, Captain Baudin (who'd just "encountered" Captain Flinders) came ashore to fill his empty water casks. The two seamen, unaware that their respective countries were waging war; unwittingly became water brothers.

Penneshaw Museum, housed inside the 1922 school, features maritime and other historic and folk exhibits. Hours are 3-5 p.m. Mon., Wed., and Sat. Sept.-June, daily in January.

Hog Bag Jetty, built 1902-09, is not only a famous fishing locale, but home port for the MV *Philanderer III*.

Bookings are essential at **Penneshaw Youth Hostel,** 43 North Terrace (tel. 0848-31-284, or 008-01-8258 toll-free), where dorm beds cost $9 per night. Facilities include scooter, bicycle, and boat rentals, kitchen facilities, launderette, swimming beach, nature walks, slide and video nights, and a range of organized tours of the island. **Sorrento Resort** (tel. 31-028), features modern motel suites, cottages with kitchenettes, or alpine chalets with kitchenettes, ranging from moderate to expensive. The resort, set on two acres of seafront gardens, has a safe swimming beach, swimming pool, poolside bar, half court tennis, spa, sauna, and offers a variety of island tours.

Penneshaw Caravan Park, Talinga Terrace (tel. 31-075), is opposite a safe beach and close to town.

Condon's Takeaway Foods, 43 North Terrace (tel. 31-173), serves breakfast, chicken, chips, and rooburgers. You can also buy souvenirs, gas, ice, bait and tackle, and get your laundry done here. The **Old Post Office Restaurant** (tel. 31-063), first corner away from the ferry, in one of Penneshaw's oldest commercial buildings, gives you a choice of à la carte dining or more relaxed (and inexpensive) bistro meals in the enclosed courtyard.

Antechamber Bay
This long, sweeping stretch of beach meets the ocean, backdropped by the mainland, bisected by Chapman River as it permeates Lashmar Lagoon. Though this area is famous for bream fishing and canoeing, you'll also find hiking tracks leading to bushland, sandhills, and lagoons.

Antechamber Bay Farmhouse (tel. 0848-33-020) provides inexpensive guest accommodations.

Cape Willoughby
The first flicker of light was emitted from Cape Willoughby Lighthouse (South Australia's first) in 1852. Built of local limestone, the tower measures 27 meters high and sits 73 meters above sea level. Just below the lighthouse the rocky, wild, crashing coastline is aptly named Devil's Kitchen. The lighthouse is open to visitors Mon.-Wed. and Fri. 1-3 p.m.

Cape Hart Conservation Park, four km southwest of Cape Willoughby, sports massive granite boulders and sandstone cliffs with drops to the Southern Ocean.

THE SOUTH COAST ROAD

From Kingscote to Flinders Chase National Park, ride the wild side in search of shells, shipwrecks, seals, and scenery, scenery, scenery.

Murray's Lagoon
Kangaroo Island's largest freshwater lagoon is encompassed within **Cape Gantheaume Conservation Park,** a favorite spot for birders. At D'Estrees Bay, on the east side of the park, you can catch fish or collect shells—both line the shores!

Seal Bay
Take the turnoff from South Coast Road to **Seal Bay Conservation Park,** a famous breeding colony of rare sea lions whose ancestors escaped the early sealers. Guided tours, led by the National Parks and Wildlife Service, will take you within a few meters of sunbathing sea lions. Tours run regularly year-round, and times are posted just off the road.

Little Sahara
Back on South Coast Road, the first road on the left (immediately before the bridge) will take you down to Little Sahara desert, where ridge upon ridge of bleached white dunes blend into the surrounding bushland.

Vivonne Bay
The only safe harbor on this side of the coast, Vivonne Bay has a long, curvy beach with dazzling scenery and a variety of activities—beach, boat, or jetty fishing, beachcombing, swimming, picnicking. Students of all ages can take part in the **Outdoor Education Living Classroom,** a series of guided tours to enhance knowledge of the island and its history.

Make inquiries before you take a dip. Normally, safe swimming areas are near the jetty, boat ramp, and Harriet River—other parts of the bay have an undertow.

Vivonne Bay Bush Cottage and **Vivonne Bay Coastal Cottage** (tel. 0848-33-020) are available at inexpensive rates.

Kelly Hill Conservation Park
An extensive network of limestone ridges, dense mallee, and coastal trail winds its way seaward; above, Kelly Hill shelters sinkholes, caverns, and caves molded from calcite sculptured into ornate shapes that cast eerie shadows in the tricky light. The largest cave is open to visitors.

At the park's western boundary, **Hanson Bay,** sheltered at each side by ocean reefs and rocky headlands, is another top spot for swimming and fishing.

Continuing along South Coast Road, you'll soon approach Rocky River Headquarters in Flinders Chase National Park.

FLINDERS CHASE NATIONAL PARK

South Australia's largest national park consists of 73,662 hectares of protected sanctuary for Kangaroo Island's rare and opulent wildlife. Taking up the entire western end of the island, Flinders Chase is a mecca of unspoiled wilderness for friendly kangaroos (the distinctive Kangaroo Island kangaroo has dark, sooty brown fur), emus, Cape Barren geese, koalas, glossy black cockatoos, and possums riding piggy on their mother's back. The natives are *so* plentiful and friendly that at Rocky River, humans picnic in enclosed areas while the animals scratch their chins and ogle at *them!*

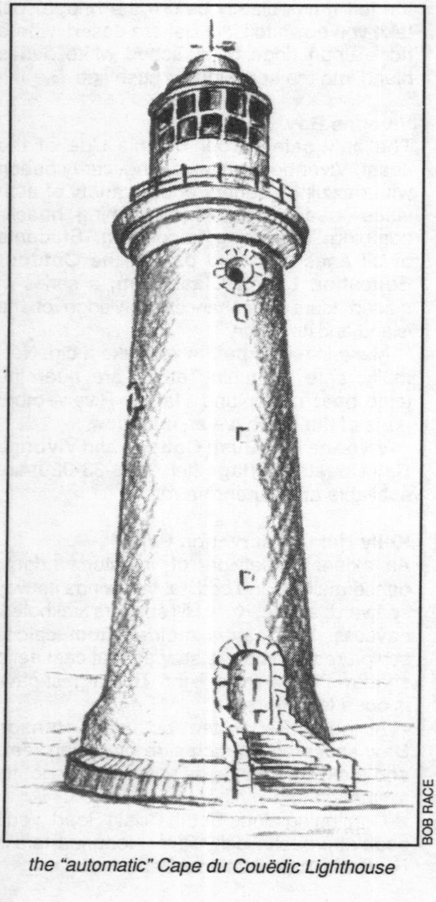

the "automatic" Cape du Couëdic Lighthouse

South of Rocky River Headquarters you can reach the huge, oddly sculpted **Remarkable Rocks, Admiral's Arch,** another intriguing formation, and **Cape du Couëdic Lighthouse,** an "automatic," opened in 1906. (The island's largest shipwreck, that of the *Portland Maru,* occurred near the cape in 1935.)

On the north side of the park, **Cape Borda Lighthouse,** opened in 1858, stands 155 meters above the sea. Before there was radio communication, the nearby cannon was used to signal ships of impending dangers. These days the meteorological station, also nearby, is a quieter guide—and, no doubt, preferred by the wildlife inhabitants!

The **Rocky River Headquarters** (tel. 0848-37-235) will provide you with maps, necessary permits, and all the information you require for your park visit. Be sure to check in with the rangers before embarking on any lengthy hikes along isolated trails. Camping in the park is permitted and, if you like, you can spend a night or two at the Cape du Couëdic and Cape Borda lighthouses (for a moderate fee).

THE NORTH COAST ROAD

The West End Highway, which borders the eastern edge of Flinders Chase National Park, will take you to the Playford Highway, a smooth run through grazing country back to Kingscote. The North Coast Road leaps and jogs off the beaten path to smooth beaches, rocky points, snug coves, and more stunning scenery.

Harvey's Return

This rugged, rocky cove, east of Cape Borda, was once a camp for American sealers. Later, after the lighthouse was built, it was used as a drop-off point for supplies. You can visit the graves of shipwrecked sailors and lighthouse-keepers at the nearby cemetery.

Cape Torrens Conservation Park
Towering cliffs hanging more than 200 meters above the sea make this a dazzling spot for bushwalkers who like trails with drop-dead views, or for birders in search of the rare glossy black cockatoo. Be sure to check in with the rangers at Rocky River Headquarters before setting out.

Western River Cove
This popular swimming and fishing beach, at the mouth of the Western River, is a steep descent from **Western River Conservation Park.** If you don't feel like hitting the beach, the park is full of stringy bark forests, wildlife, and excellent gorge, water, and valley views from its many high cliffs.

Snellings Beach
Swim, surf, dive, or fish at this peaceful protected bay, situated at the mouth of the Middle River (but be careful of the river's hidden snags and weeds). **Constitution Hill,** above the beach, affords great views of the area.

Accomodations at **Middle River Homestead** (tel. 0848-22-357), range from moderate to expensive.

Stokes Bay
Farther east along the coast road, this white sandy beach draws families to its secluded shores, reached by walking through a tunnel within enormous limestone boulders. Though Stokes Bay is an excellent surf spot and fishing hole, its special feature is the large rock-enclosed pool which provides a safe swimming area.

Paul's Place, between Stokes Bay and Amen Corner, has horse riding, a large aviary (on the off-chance you haven't seen enough birds in the wild), and a glass-fronted beehive where you can get a close-up look at the island's special Ligurian honeybee.

Stokes Bay Holiday House (tel. 0848-96-977) provides moderately priced accommodations.

Parndana
You have to head inland, back to the Playford Highway, if you want to visit this little farming community.

Though an experimental farm had been set up in 1938, development was hindered when the area became a soldiers' settlement during World War II. Eventually, 174 soldier settlement farms were established and, in 1950, a government research center was set up on the experimental property. Today, the area is used mainly for sheep and cattle grazing.

For inexpensive holiday house accommodations try **Kyalia Cottage** (tel. 0848-36-257), **Blue Gums Farmhouse** (tel. 96-115) or, 28 km west of Parndana, **Gosse Cottage** (tel. 33-020).

Emu Bay
In the early 1900s (and up until the 1970s) the town was named Maxwell. Once it was discovered that the bay was both too shallow and too exposed, the port was moved over to Kingscote. Emu Bay is now a top-notch spot for safe swimming and boat or jetty fishing.

INFORMATION

Kangaroo Island Tourist Information Centre, 27 Dauncey St., Kingscote (tel. 0848-22-381), can help with tours, trails, and treks, and direct you to dive shops and bait stores. Be sure to pick up maps which detail the roads branching off main highways. The center is open Mon.-Fri. 9-5, Sat. 9 a.m.-noon. (The public library and council office are in the same building.)

The information center can also provide brochures, issue permits, and arrange guided tours of the island's many conservation parks. Or, contact the **National Parks and Wildlife Service** at Murray's Lagoon Headquarters (tel. 28-233), Seal Bay Conservation Park (tel. 94-207), Rocky River Headquarters (tel. 37-235), Kelly Hill Conservation Park (tel. 37-231), or Cape Borda (tel. 93-257). Be sure to pick up a copy of the national park code, and follow all rules to protect the island's sacred wildlife.

Do not fish without first finding out regulations and acquiring necessary licenses. The tourist information center can help with these, as well as recommend and organize fishing expeditions. For more information,

Remarkable Rocks, near Flinders Chase National Park

phone the **Fisheries Officers** at tel. 22-130. At no time is fishing, or *any* disturbance of the seabed, permitted at the Pelican Lagoon and Seal Bay aquatic reserves.

Most of the island's emergency facilities are based in Kingscote, though park rangers provide assistance within their jurisdiction. Contact the local ranger station or, in Kingscote, **ambulance** (tel. 22-028), **police** (tel. 22-018), and **fire brigade** (tel. 22-200).

Island Stationery, 9 Osmond St., Kingscote (tel. 22-625), stocks a selection of books on the island.

TRANSPORT

For information on getting to Kangaroo Island by plane or ferry, see "Getting Away" in the "Adelaide" section.

Getting Around

Airport Coach Service (tel. 0848-22-678) operates a bus from the Kingscote airport into town for $3.

Though there is no actual public transport on Kangaroo Island, **Kangaroo Island Transport** (tel. 22-640) has taxis as well as daily bus service between Kingscote, American River, Penneshaw, and Flinders Chase National Park. Advance bookings are essential. The Penneshaw and Kangaroo Island youth hostels also provide airport pick-up and some coach services for guests.

If you haven't brought a car over with you on the ferry, you can rent one once you arrive. The Kingscote tourist information center or your accommodation can help you, otherwise try **Kangaroo Island Car Hire** (tel. 22-390), or **Budget,** Dauncey St., Kingscote (tel. 22-511). Expect to pay $50 and up per day. Again, advance bookings are strongly recommended.

Rent bicycles at **Condon's Takeaway** (home of the rooburger), Penneshaw (tel. 33-173), **Penneshaw Youth Hostel** (tel. 31-284), or **Wisteria Lodge Motel,** Kingscote (tel. 22-707); mopeds at **Kingscote Combined Taxi and Tour Service** (tel. 22-640); rent scooters at both Condon's and the Penneshaw Youth Hostel.

With nearly 1,600 km of roads on the island, only the major highways are sealed. The extensive maze of off-the-beaten-paths range from bush tracks to gravel roads. The combination of dust and gravel makes driving at high speeds very hazardous. Even the most experienced cyclists can find road conditions exhausting. Allow *plenty* of time to cover the distance you expect to travel. Except during peak holiday periods, the roads have very little traffic, making it unwise to depend on catching a lift. If you're driving, keep your tank full of petrol (available at Kingscote, American River, Penneshaw, Parndana, and Vivonne Bay, year-round). Bushwalkers must inform rangers before embarking on remote or dangerous trails. And whether driving, hiking, or cycling, carry plenty of water with you.

For those who'd rather sit back and relax, sign up for an organized coach tour. Both youth hostels offer an interesting selection of one- and two-day jaunts.

THE SOUTHEAST

On the map, South Australia's southeast region doesn't appear to be more than a couple of major highways along the Adelaide-Melbourne route. Those in the know read between the thick black lines and head straight for the juicy parts—swamplands and wetlands, bird sanctuaries and wildlife preserves, sandy dunes and beaches, yawn-away fishing ports (including one marked by a giant walk-in lobster, named Larry), thick-as-thieves pine forests, pastoral farmland, weathered limestone caves, volcanic lakes and craters, a right-regular share of "ye old-y" buildings, and some downright extraordinary red wines.

Aside from bountiful fishing (especially Oct.-April, when it's lobster season) and delectable wines produced from rich terra rossa soil, this area also sustains timber and farming industries. Good annual rainfalls yield lush landscapes and, combined with neighboring western Victoria, this district is known as the Green Triangle.

TAILEM BEND

Both the Dukes and Princes highways, principal routes between Adelaide and Melbourne, converge at Tailem Bend, along with the less traveled Ouyen Highway. The inland Dukes Highway (which becomes Western Highway at Victoria's border) passes through a lot of flat farmland and is often referred to as the "boring road." The Princes Highway, running along the coast, is the preferred passage—as coastal roads usually are. If you're not in any rush to get to Melbourne, or if you're not going there at all, you can make a complete tour of the southeast by taking Princes Highway from Tailem Bend to Mt. Gambier; then, detouring north through wine and cave country, join up with the Dukes Highway at Keith and loop back to Tailem Bend.

Sights

Tailem Bend's most noteworthy attraction is **Old Tailem Town,** another one of those authentic turn-of-the-century villages. The township, five km north of Tailem Bend, features the usual pioneering cottages, butcher, barber, and bootmaker shops, emporium, church, one-room schoolhouse, and "real" general store. Old Tailem Town is open daily 10 a.m.-5 p.m.

Accommodations

If you need more time to decide which road to take, inexpensive **River Bend Motel,** 110 Princes Highway (tel. 085-72-3620) will put you up for the night. **Westbrook Park River Resort,** Princes Highway (tel. 72-3794), on the banks of the Murray, has campsites and on-site vans. **Tailem Bend Riversedge Caravan Park,** Princes Highway (tel. 72-3307), also on the Murray, features a boat ramp and canoe hire.

MENINGIE

At the northern edge of the Coorong National Park, and the southern side of Lake Albert, Meningie (pop. 800) offers water sports, birdwatching, and easy access to the Coorong. The town is nothing special, but it is a decent place to overnight and stock up on provisions for your Coorong exploration. From Trigg Hill you can look out on Lakes Albert and Alexandrina, which comprise 746 square km of fresh water.

Accommodations

The selection of motels along Princes Hwy. are all in the inexpensive to low-moderate range. **Lake Albert Caravan Park,** Narrung Rd. (tel. 085-75-1411), offers bike, canoe, and sailboard hire, and a nice lakeside location.

THE COORONG

If you've seen the film *Storm Boy,* the poignant tale of a boy and his pelican, then you should have no trouble visualizing the Coorong, for it was filmed here. If you missed the flick, well, imagine a long, narrow, and shallow saltwater lagoon stretching 132 km from the Murray mouth to that big lobster Larry's mouth, just north of Kingston. Separated from the Southern Ocean by the shimmering sand dunes on Youngblood Peninsula (an average of two km wide), the Coorong is a haven for approximately 400 species of birds, including cormorants, terns, shags, ducks, swans, *and* pelicans. You can get from the Coorong across to the peninsula at Salt Creek during summer months; otherwise there's a year-round road about 75 km south, towards Kingston.

A large Aboriginal tribe lived on the Coorong for thousands of years (the name is derived from "Kurangh," Aboriginal for "Long Neck of Water"), sustaining themselves on fish, seafood, reptiles, birds, kangaroos, and wombats. You'll also come across wells, built in the 1800s by Chinese immigrants who landed in Robe and, instead of joining their compatriots headed for Victoria's goldfields, strayed northward to Adelaide. Australia's first oil well was drilled near Salt Creek in the 1890s, after Coorongite (a derivative of surface algae) was discovered.

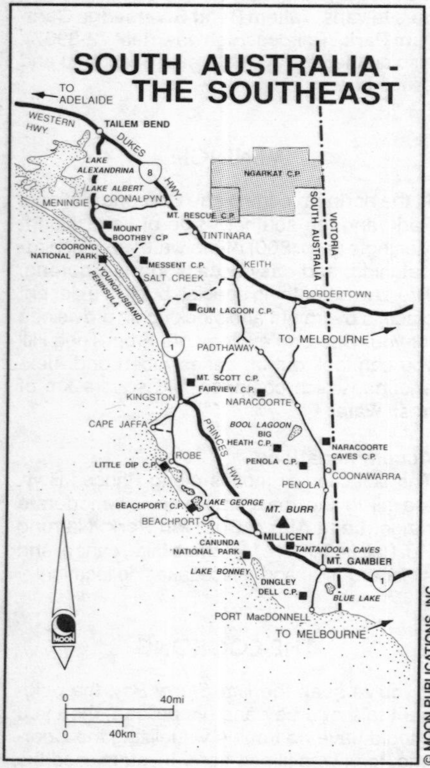

In 1966, the Coorong was designated a national park and since then the National Parks and Wildlife Service has been responsible for its 43,500 hectares, as well as for **Messant Conservation Park,** six km northeast of Salt Creek.

The Coorong is an ideal location for fishing, boating, and hiking. Walking trails are marked throughout the park (try the three km Lakes Nature Trail at Salt Creek) and, during Easter, Christmas, and New Year's holidays, rangers lead informative walks. Camping is permitted in the park, but you must obtain a permit first. The **National Parks and Wildlife Service** has offices at Salt Creek (tel. 085-75-7014) and Noonameena (tel. 085-75-1200).

KINGSTON

When you come upon a 17-meter-tall, four-ton pre-fab lobster named Larry, you've arrived in Kingston (pop. 1,370), "gateway to the southern ports." Larry, presumably "the world's biggest lobster," stands watch over the entrance to this popular fishing port and beach resort. The town was established in 1856 by the Cooke brothers, who had procured government land grants near Maria Creek (so named for the vessel *Maria,* which wrecked near the Cape Jaffa Lighthouse in 1840; the crew and the passengers survived the shipwreck, only to be massacred by Aboriginals after they went ashore). The original jetty was too short and too shallow to make it useful for loading goods and, in 1876, was replaced by another—much longer, sitting in much deeper water—but even that one ceased being practical with the advent of modern roads and railways.

Pelicans and hundreds of other bird species find sanctuary in The Coorong.

Sights

The **National Trust Museum,** originally a timber mill built in 1872, presents items of local interest, including nautical memorabilia. **Cape Jaffa Lighthouse,** moved from its 100-year-old post on Margarent Brock Reef, has been re-erected nearby and is open to visitors. Other historic buildings are the post office, courthouse, and police station (now an antique shop).

Aside from the Coorong to the north, Kingston is near three other national parks. **Butchers Gap Conservation Park,** six km southwest, off Wyomi Rd., is another natural bird sanctuary where coastal vegetation thrives in the wetlands. Part of a former coastal dune, **Mt. Scott Conservation Park,** 20 km east of Kingston, on Keith Rd., has good bushwalks through stringy bark forest inhabited by mallee fowl, sugar gliders, and wombats. **Jip Jip Conservation Park,** 50 km northeast of Kingston, features a variety of wildlife amid big exotically shaped granite boulders. You can also see unusual rock formations much closer to town at the **Granites,** off the highway north of Kingston, along the beach.

The fish are jumping in Kingston—anglers can cast lines from beach, boat, or jetty (either at Kingston or Cape Jaffa, a wee fishing village to the south). The foreshore and Wyomi and Pinks beaches provide safe swimming, while Lacepede Bay is popular for sailing.

Accommodations

Crown Inn Hotel, Agnes St. (tel. 087-67-2005), has simple, inexpensive pub-style rooms. Moderately priced **Bee Hive Motor Inn,** Marine Parade (tel. 67-2444), is near the jetty on the foreshore. **Kingston Caravan Park,** Marine Parade (tel. 67-2050), is situated on a sand beach.

Events

If you're visiting the area in January, you can catch the annual **Yachting Carnival** and Cape Jaffa-to-Kingston race.

Information

Larry, the Big Lobster (tel. 087-67-2555), is not just another pretty face, but a tourist complex with a bistro, cafeteria, takeaways, souvenir and bottle shops, *and* tourist information! You can also pick up tourist info at **Wood Hut Craft Shop,** Kingston District Hall, Agnes St. (tel. 67-2151). Both places are open daily.

For emergencies, contact the **police** (tel. (087) 67-2009), **ambulance** (tel. 67-2672), or local **hospital** (tel. 67-2477). The **Royal Automobile Association** can be reached at tel. 67-2129.

ROBE

In 1802, French explorer Nicholas Baudin cruised this area and bestowed Guichen Bay with its name. The town of Robe (pop. 740) was officially established in 1847, growing to South Australia's third major port (before the downfall of shipping in 1864), exporting wool and horses, and importing about 15,000 Chi-

Larry the Lobster welcomes visitors to Kingston.

nese immigrants. The Chinese, on their way to Victoria's goldfields, had found an ingeniously simple way to avoid the £10-per-head poll tax charged by Victorian officials—they landed in South Australia and quietly made their way across the state line.

Sights

Robe is a peaceful and picturesque village with many heritage buildings. The **National Trust Museum,** in the old Customs House (1863), will give you all the skinny on the town's early history.

From **Beacon Hill,** you can get a great view of Robe, Guichen Bay, and the Southern Ocean. Or look out from the **obelisk,** right or left, to shimmering expanses of coastline.

Little Dip Conservation Park, four km south of Robe, is comprised of sand dunes, coastal strips, and salt lakes, through which waterbirds and wildlife roam, as can you—along the bushwalking tracks. Rangers lead guided walks during the summer months.

Long Beach, a 17-km stretch of calm white sands along Guichen Bay, is noted for excellent swimming and windsurfing (the National Championships were held here in 1989). In the summer, you can drive along the beach and discover your own nook and cranny. Guichen Bay is also popular for sailing.

Anglers can get a bite just about anywhere. Crayfish lovers should visit from Oct.-April, when the fleet brings in a fresh catch each day.

Accommodations

You'll find all kinds of atmosphere-y accommodations in and around Robe. **Bushland Cabins,** Nora Criena Rd. (tel. 087-68-2386), have kitchen facilities and are inexpensive. The **Caledonian Inn,** Victoria St. (tel. 68-2029), built in 1858, offers newer cottages and rooms in the restored original section for moderate prices. **Flinders Rest Cottages,** Powell Ave. (tel. 68-2100), in the Long Beach area, are fully equipped two-bedroom cottages with open fires, and also moderately priced.

Or, choose from three caravan parks in the area. **Lakeside Select Caravan Park,** Main Rd. (tel. 68-2193), is on a safe swimming lake. **Long Beach Tourist Park,** The Esplanade (tel. 68-2237), is just 200 meters from the Long Beach water sporting area. **Sea-Vu Caravan Park,** Squire Dr. (tel. 68-2273), is near beaches and attractions.

Events

The Sunday before 1 October is the annual **Blessing of the Fleet.** Afterwards, local fishermen invite tourists to join them for a jaunt around the bay.

Information

Robe Historical Interpretation Centre, in the library building (tel. 087-68-2465), can provide additional tourist information.

Emergencies are handled by the **police** (tel. 68-2118), **medical centre** (tel. 68-2012) and, for breakdowns (the motoring variety!), the **Royal Automobile Association** (tel. 68-2006).

BEACHPORT

Beachport (pop. 410) is another seaside lobster, crayfish, and one-time hustle-bustle port. Set at the northern edge of Rivoli Bay, this former whaling station, established by the Henty brothers in the 1830s, became a township in 1878—the same year a Beachport-Mt. Gambier railway line was built, instantly turning the town into a train-trip-away holiday resort. And, though the trains no longer run, Beachport is still a desirable destination for the family-excursion set.

Sights

If you're coming from Robe, follow the detour to impressive **Woakwine Cutting,** a drainage project constructed by one farmer and his helper in less than three years. You can ooh and aah from the specially built viewing platform.

See fishing, farming, and whaling displays, as well as local relics, at the **National Trust Museum,** inside the old wool and grain store on Railway Terrace.

Bowman's Scenic Drive, from Foster St. to Wooleys Rocks, takes in terrific views of the town and Lake George on one side, the ocean on the other. You'll find lookout points at Backlers Lookout and Salmon Hole.

If you've got a four-wheel-drive vehicle you can drive past Wooleys Rocks, along sand dunes into **Beachport Conservation Park;** otherwise access is from Railway Terrace North. The park includes tracks through sand dunes and coastal vegetation, and around Wooleys Lake. The eight km drift, accessible only by four-wheelers or two feet, offers safe sailing and windsurfing.

Swimmers will do well around the jetty, scuba divers enjoy the **Back Beach** reef areas, and surfers like a spot known as the **Blowhole.** The **Pool of Siloam,** a *very* salty (six times more than the sea) lake near Beachport, is thought to have therapeutic waters.

Accommodations

Beachport Hotel, Railway Terrace (tel. 087-35-8003), has inexpensive pub accommodations, but for the same price you can get a motel unit at **Beachport Motor Inn,** Railway Terrace (tel. 35-8070). Try the Beachport **YHA Hostel** (tel. 35-8197) for dorm beds at $6 per night.

Beachport Caravan Park, Beach Rd. (tel. 35-8128), is situated on the foreshore with a jetty. **Southern Ocean Tourist Park,** Somerville St. (tel. 35-8153), is close to the beach and has open fireplaces. This park is also the local tourist information center.

MILLICENT

Bordered on the north and southeast by thick, fragrant pine forests, Millicent (pop. 5,075) is big timber country. From Kingston to Millicent, coastal travel is along Alternate Highway One; here it re-connects with the main highway.

This mini-city, begun in 1870 as a rural community, shifted to a timber center after pines were cultivated in nearby ranges, and sawmills and paper mills moved in—followed by a steady stream of workers (including a large European population).

Sights

Millicent Museum, 1 Mt. Gambier Rd. (tel. 087-33-3205), is one of the region's most extensive facilities, with natural history and Aboriginal displays, restored horse-drawn vehicles, farm implements, tools, machinery, and a coin-operated waterwheel. The museum also houses **Admella Gallery,** which exhibits and sells local arts and crafts. Hours are Mon.-Sat. 10 a.m.-4 p.m., Sun. 1-4 p.m.

Tantanoola Caves, on Princes Highway, 21 km from Millicent, are located inside a dolomite marine cliff beside the highway. Take one of the hourly guided tours of the single chamber, or sign up for a "wild cave tour" that explores the underground system (by appointment). At the nearby town of Tantanoola, you can view the stuffed carcass of *the* Tantanoola tiger, at—where else?—the **Tantanoola Tiger Hotel**. Load up on brew to go along with all the bull you'll hear about this legendary beast.

If you'd rather climb than cave, coastal **Canunda National Park,** beginning at Southend, 27 km west of Millicent, has a system of huge, wondrous sand dunes for you to sink your feet into. You can also camp here and, in the summer, take informative ranger-guided walks.

Accommodations

Sportsmans Hotel, 72 George St. (tel. 087-33-2017), has inexpensive rooms but facilities are shared. Other motels, all in the inexpensive to low-moderate range, are **Diplomat Motel,** 51 Mt. Gambier Rd. (tel. 33-2211), **Millicent Motel,** 82 Mt. Gambier Rd. (tel. 33-2854), and **Somerset Hotel Motel,** 2 George St. (tel. 33-2888).

Hillview Caravan Park, Dalton St. (tel. 33-2806), is less than two km from the town center. **Millicent Lakeside Caravan Park,** Park Terrace (tel. 33-3947), is adjacent to a swimming lake.

Information

Millicent Tourist Information Centre is located at the Millicent Museum. For information on Canunda National Park, contact the **National Parks and Wildlife Service** at Southend (tel. 087-35-6053). To sign up for cave walks at **Tantanoola Caves Conservation Park,** phone the park office at 34-4153.

Get emergency assistance from the **police** (tel. 33-3622), **hospital** (tel. 33-2244), or local **Royal Automobile Association** (tel. 33-3951).

MOUNT GAMBIER

The volcano has been extinct for 5,000 years, but Mt. Gambier (pop. 20,815), built upon its slopes and about halfway between Adelaide and Melbourne, is a busy commercial center, regarded as capital of the southeast. Big attractions of this city are the many crater lakes. Of these, mysterious **Blue Lake** is the largest (with a circumference of five km) and so famous that Mt. Gambier is often called the "Blue Lake City." The lake—which is actually gray—changes into an extraordinary blue each and every November, staying that color until late March when it reverts to gray. Long believed to be "bottomless," only recently did echo-sounding equipment dispell that myth by measuring a 77-meter maximum depth. Blue Lake also supplies Mt. Gambier with its domestic water.

In 1800, Lieutenant James Grant, in the HMS *Lady Nelson,* was sailing along the coast when he sighted two peaks which he named Mt. Schank (after Admiral Schank, who had invented the *Lady Nelson's* centerboard keel) and Mt. Gambier (for Lord Gam-

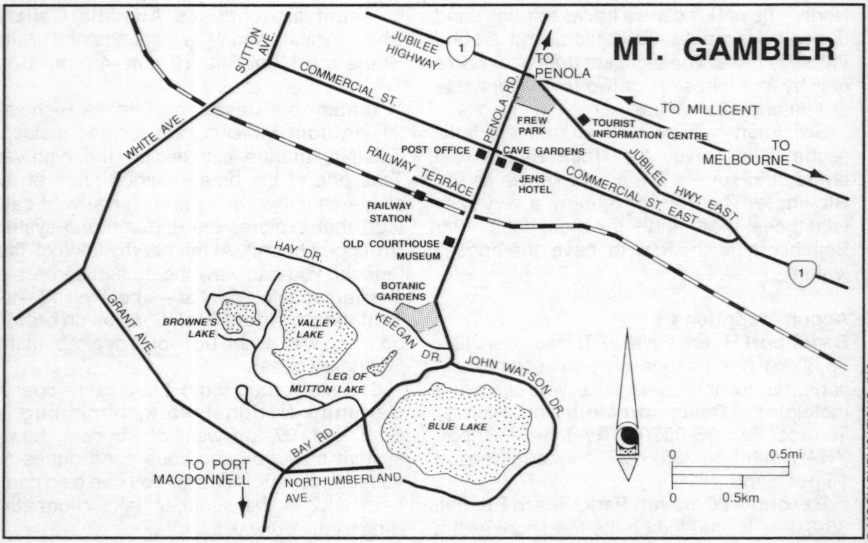

bier of the Royal Navy). Mt. Gambier developed as a township in 1841, when Stephen Henty and his companions, enticed by the rich volcanic soil and appreciable annual rainfalls, built their cottages between Valley and Brownes lakes, and brought their stock to graze on the fertile farmlands. Though agriculture is still important, the city's major source of employment is the forestry industry and the area's six large sawmills.

Sights

Besides Blue Lake, Mt. Gambier's other unique feature is **Cave Park,** an open cave in the city center, surrounded by lovely rose gardens. In complete defiance of Mt. Gambier's southern latitude, two banana trees rise from the cave and stretch toward the light. Other caves are **Umpherston Cave,** with terraced gardens and picnic grounds, and water-filled **Engelbrecht Cave,** an often-frequented diving spot. Other diving locations are **Little Blue Lake, Ewens Ponds, Picaninnie Ponds, Three Sisters,** and **Hell Hole.**

Historic buildings near Cave Park are the **post office, town hall,** and **Jens Hotel. Old Courthouse Museum,** Bay Rd., operated by the National Trust, displays the original courthouse furnishings and other local historic items. **Lewis' Museum,** Pick Ave. (across from the showgrounds), is jam-packed with Aboriginal, mechanical, industrial, and historical artifacts.

Accommodations

About thirty motels and hotels and six caravan parks are sprawled around the town. Prices for double rooms range from expensive to moderate, but none of the accommodations are exceptional. In this town, a room at the cheap end should do you just fine.

The **Jens Hotel,** Watson Terrace (tel. 087-25-0188), is a beautiful heritage property with inexpensive rooms.

Information

The **Lady Nelson Tourist and Interpretive Centre,** Jubilee Highway East, near the city center (tel. 087-24-1730), is a treasure trove of information. Besides the usual brochures and such, the centre books all types of accommodations, arranges tours (to sawmills, pumping stations, and dairies), provides everything you want to know about the lakes area (including issuing diving permits), and will even prepare a customized itinerary. While there you can view a full-size replica of HMS *Lady Nelson,* hear Lieutenant Grant (another replica, and *no* competition for Madame Tussaud!) give his spiel, and watch the volcano erupt in a blaze of neon! The center is open daily.

For emergencies, contact **police** (tel. 25-9333), **Mt. Gambier Hospital** (tel. 24-2211), and, for road mishaps or info, the **Royal Automobile Association** (tel. 25-4101).

PORT MACDONNELL

South Australia's most southerly port and crayfish center is 28 km south of Mt. Gambier. Once a bustling shipping center for freight being hauled between Adelaide and Melbourne, Port MacDonnell (pop. 650) these days is a quaint fishing village. On the way to Port MacDonnell, climb Mount Schank and follow walking tracks both inside and outside the crater, or just sit back and check out the grandiose view.

Sights

To the west of town, **Cape Northumberland Lighthouse,** reached by traveling through a petrified forest, affords a towering view of the rugged coastline below.

Dingley Dell Conservation Park, two km west of Port MacDonnell, is the restored 1860s home of horsey Scottish poet, Adam Lindsay Gordon (he was South Australia's big-time bard). Picnic on the grounds and soak up either some of Gordon's inspiration or his rays.

The large **Old Customs House,** on the foreshore, was built in 1860 to accommodate the sizeable freight loads of the time.

Accommodations

Get an inexpensive room with shared facilities at **Victoria Hotel,** 40 Meylin St. (tel. 087-38-2213), or anything from on-site vans to fully equipped holiday flats at **Sea View Motel,** 77 Sea Parade (tel. 38-2243).

Information

Gather tourist information at **Port MacDonnell District Council,** Charles St. (tel. 087-38-2437).

For emergencies, phone the **police** (tel. 38-2216) or **Royal Automobile Association** (tel. 38-2238).

PENOLA

North of Mt. Gambier, venture through the pine-forested communities of Tarpeena and Nangwarry to this tiny heritage town noted for its beautiful buildings and churches. Penola is also the gateway to the southeastern wine region.

Sights

Many 1850s cottages, built by the town's first settlers, still stand today. The **Penola Heritage Walk,** which departs from the tourist information center, takes in nearly 30 historic sites around Penola. **Petticoat Lane,** a sort of open-air museum of Penola's early architecture, features a number of traditional buildings, including the former Anglican rectory. Arts and crafts hounds will find galleries and gift shops inside many of the historic sites.

John Riddoch Interpretive Centre, Arthur St. (tel. 087-37-2855), in the former Penola Library and Mechanics Institute, pays tribute to the town's heritage as well as its most prominent citizens (including John Riddoch). **Yallum Park,** Riddoch's personal mansion, built in 1880, depicts the grand style of the upper crust.

Penola Conservation Park, 10 km west of town, features a signposted interpretive trail into this swampy wildlife sanctuary.

Accommodations

Book a variety of heritage accommodations, at moderate prices, through **Australian Country Cottages,** 33 Riddoch St. (087-37- 2250). Penola Caravan Park, 2 South Terrace (tel. 37-2381), has a few on-site vans for rent.

Information

Penola Tourist Information Centre, inside the John Riddoch Interpretive Centre, provides maps for scenic drives and heritage walks, as well as other local information.

In emergencies, contact the **police** (tel. 087-37-2315), **hospital** (tel. 37-2311), and **Royal Automobile Association** (tel. 37-2367).

COONAWARRA

It was John Riddoch, Penola mogul, who liked the looks of the grape vines in his Coonawarra Fruit Colony and, subsequently, established the district's first winery. Though Riddoch's winery was built in 1893, and the grape vines thrived, demand was low, and it wasn't until the 1960s that the industry really took off. Today, there are 15 wineries in the district (which runs for 16 km north of Penola), famed for the bold reds produced from rich terra rossa soil.

Accommodations

Coonawarra Country Cottages (tel. 087-36-3220) offer inexpensive country-style accommodations. **Chardonnay Lodge,** Penola Rd. (tel. 36-3309), is a moderately priced luxury motel, with an art gallery, swimming pool, good restaurant, and complimentary continental breakfast.

Information

For tourist info, see the Penola Tourist Information Centre, above.

NARACOORTE

Proclaimed a town in 1870 (though the first hotel and store were erected in the 1840s), Naracoorte (pop. 4,640) functions mainly as a regional service and commercial center, with lovely old dwellings scattered all about.

Sights

The **Sheeps Back Museum** (tel. 087-62-2518), in the old flour mill on MacDonnell St., run by the National Trust, traces the history of the wool industry. More interesting is the **Naracoorte Museum and Snake Pit,** Smith St. (tel. 62-2059), where more than 60 collec-

exploring Naracoorte's caves

tions of gemstones, clocks, weapons, butterflies, and other artifacts commingle with snakes and reptiles lounging about rocks and cacti.

Padthaway Estate, about 41 km north of Naracoorte, is a gracious country mansion, built in 1882. **Padthaway Conservation Park** features stringy bark and red gum forests where you can bushwalk or picnic.

Naracoorte Caves Conservation Park, 12 km southeast of town, features about 69 caves situated along a 25-km expanse of range. Daily tours explore Alexandra, Blanche, and Victoria Fossil caves and, during holiday periods, you can sign up for special wild-caving tours into undeveloped areas (be prepared to climb and crawl).

Bool Lagoon, a bit farther south, is a vast and diverse wetland with about 75 species of birds and other wildlife, plus both self-guided and organized walking tracks. A bird blind and boardwalks, built over the lagoon, allow for excellent birdwatching. **Mary Seymour Conservation Park,** near Bool Lagoon, is also a sanctuary for breeding birds.

Accommodations

Naracoorte Hotel Motel, 73 Ormerod St. (tel. 087-62-2400), has inexpensive rooms with shared facilities in the older hotel or, for 10 bucks more, you can stay in the updated motel section. **Country Roads Inn,** 28 Smith St. (tel. 62-3900), is more posh, with rooms in the moderate range. Big splurgers can spring for elegant accommodations at the historic **Padthaway Estate** (tel. 65-5037), where doubles run about $180, including continental breakfast.

Naracoorte Caravan Park, 81 Park Terrace (tel. 62-2128), is close to the town center. Camping is permitted at both **Naracoorte Caves** (tel. 62-2340) and **Bool Lagoon** (tel. 64-7541).

Information

The tourist information office is at Sheeps Back Museum. In an emergency, call **police** (tel. 087-62-2066), the **hospital** (tel. 62-2222), or the trusty **Royal Automobile Association** (tel. 62-2530).

BORDERTOWN

Situated 42 km northeast of Padthaway, along the Dukes Highway, Bordertown (pop. 2,320) isn't *on* but is *near* the Victorian border, 20 km away. Settled in 1852, along the route of the gold escort from Victoria to Adelaide, the area's rich farmlands produce wine grapes, small seeds, cereals, wool, meat, and vegetable crops. This is also the town where the former Australian Prime Minister Bob Hawke spent his early childhood. His home has been renovated, and his bust has been bronzed.

Adjacent Dukes Highway, **Bordertown Wildlife Park** has the usual native birds and animals, plus four specially bred pure white kangaroos.

Accommodations

Several good motels line Dukes Highway, with inexpensive to low-moderate prices. **Bordertown Caravan Park,** Penny Terrace (tel. 087-52-1752), is near the town center.

Events

The annual **Camel Racing Festival,** held each November, features camel and donkey races, parachute jumping and other antics, and camels from every state and territory in Australia.

Information

For tourist information, contact **Bordertown Council Office,** 43 Woolshed St. (tel. 087-52-1044). For emergency assistance, contact **police** (tel. 52-1355), the **hospital** (tel. 52-1166), or the **Royal Automobile Association** (tel. 52-1270).

KEITH

Keith (pop. 1,190), 46 km northwest of Bordertown, was proclaimed a township in 1889. At one time the region was part of the 90-mile Desert, but after zinc and copper were added to the soil, it became profitable grazing and farm land. Most of the old buildings sit along Heritage St., facing the Dukes Highway.

Sights

Mount Monster Conservation Park, 10 km south of Keith, has spectacular views from the lookout (a signposted walk will guide you), as well as a variety of natural vegetation, birds, and wildlife. Mount Monster, and others in a chain of granite outcrops, used to be islands about 40 million years ago!

Ngarkat Conservation Park, northeast of Keith, is perfect for bushwalks within its 5,000 hectares full of native animals and abundant flora. **Mount Rescue Conservation Park,** with 28,385 hectares of sand plains and dunes, containing rare species of birds and plants, is situated in the southwest corner, 20 km north of Keith.

Accommodations

Keith's only **hotel/motel** and **motor inn** both charge about $50 double. **Keith Caravan Park,** Naracoorte Rd. (tel. 087- 55-1957), has campsites and on-site vans.

Information

The **Tourist Information Centre** is inside the old Congregational church, on Heritage Street. In emergencies, contact **police** (tel. 087-55-1211), the **hospital** (tel. 55-1757), or **Royal Automobile Association** (tel. 55-1331).

BACK TO TAILEM BEND

Pass through more grazing land. **Tintara,** 38 km northwest of Keith, has a nice old post office and homestead (10 km west of town on Woods Well Rd.).

Mount Boothby Conservation Park, 20 km northwest of Tintara, features 4,045 hectares of heath, mallee, pink gum forest, and granite outcrops, where you can picnic or stretch your legs, between grazing scenes.

Coonalpyn is the last dot on the map before Tailem Bend.

TRANSPORT

Kendell Airlines, 9A Hindley St., Adelaide (tel. 08-213-9567), makes the 50-minute flight from Adelaide to Mt. Gambier, and on to Melbourne, several days a week. Fare is $130 one way from either capital city to Mt. Gambier. The standby fare runs about $25 less. **O'Connor Airlines** (tel. 087-25-6666) makes daily flights from Mt. Gambier to either Adelaide or Melbourne. Inquire directly to the airline for current fares, or book through Australian Airlines.

Catch **Mt. Gambier Motor Services** (tel. 08-217-0777) from Adelaide's Central Bus Station to Kingston ($25), Robe ($27), Millicent ($29), or Mt. Gambier ($31), or travel **Greyhound** (tel. 08-212-1777) along Princes Highway to Mt. Gambier ($38).

THE MURRAY RIVER

In these parts it's called the "Mighty Murray," and it conjures up all the romantic images a mighty river should—paddle steamers plying their trade, floating casinos and riverboat gamblers, dashing gents and bawdy women, a host of rascals, scoundrels, ne'er-do-wells, and free spirits, runaways aboard makeshift rafts, secret trysts along the banks . . .

Beginning in the Snowy Mountains, traveling along the border between New South Wales and Victoria, the river gains momentum as it reaches South Australia, makes a sharp turn seaward at Northwest Bend, and eventually empties into Lake Alexandrina where its mighty mouth meets the great Southern Ocean. And, though the Murray has often been called the "Mississippi of Australia," and the flavor is much the same, this river—at 2,575 km from source to mouth —is less than half the length of its American counterpart.

Within South Australia's 640-km section, the Murray is divided into two districts—the Riverland and the Lower Murray. The Riverland includes the Murray's six locks, the towns from Renmark to Blanchetown, bountiful citrus groves, and 17,000 hectares of vineyards. This, in fact, is Australia's biggest wine-producing region (yes—*more* than the Barossa, Clare, and Coonawarra, and even the Hunter Valley, in New South Wales), noted for high quality table wines and a variety of other products. The Lower Murray encompasses the span below Blanchetown to Murray Bridge, where you'll encounter more orchards, large granite outcrops, waterfalls, lagoons, and phenomenal bird life. Throughout the entire Murray area, you'll enjoy abundant sunshine with good fishing, swimming, waterskiing, and boating—including both paddle steaming and houseboating.

The annual flow of the Murray and its tributaries averages only 12.7 mm, the lowest runoff of any major river system, and it takes approximately one month for the Murray flow at Albury to arrive at South Australia. Furthermore—for all you riverphiles—the bed of the Lower Murray rests below sea level, thereby making it one of the few rivers on earth to run *uphill!*

History

In 1824, explorers Hume and Hovell were the first white men to sight the Murray. Six years later, Captain Charles Sturt steered a whale boat—while a group of soldiers and convicts rowed—some 2,735 km, from the Murrumbidgee and Murray rivers, to the sea and back again. Sturt named the river after Colonial Secretary Sir George Murray and, eventually, the Sturt Highway which runs through the Riverland was named for the brave captain himself.

Lady Augusta and *Mary Ann* were the first paddle steamers to navigate the river, making the journey in 1853, from Goolwa to Swan Hill in Victoria. Until the railway lines were built, river life was a-bustle, with trade being carted to and fro, and consummate river towns popping up along the banks (and with them a few rabble-rousers and river rats).

Then, in 1887, up in the Riverland, a fellow named Alfred Deakin, who'd been keeping tabs on irrigation in the California deserts, persuaded Canadians George and William Chaffey (experts in the field) to come to Renmark and set up Australia's first irrigation settlement. This project's success led to the high-grade citrus crops and wines produced in the region today.

MURRAY BRIDGE

Situated approximately 80 km from Adelaide, Murray Bridge (pop. 11,900) is the state's largest river town. This city should really be called Murray *Bridges,* since three of them cross the river here. Originally named "Edwards Crossing," the calm waters made this a favored spot for early settlers crossing the river—though at first they floated their wag-

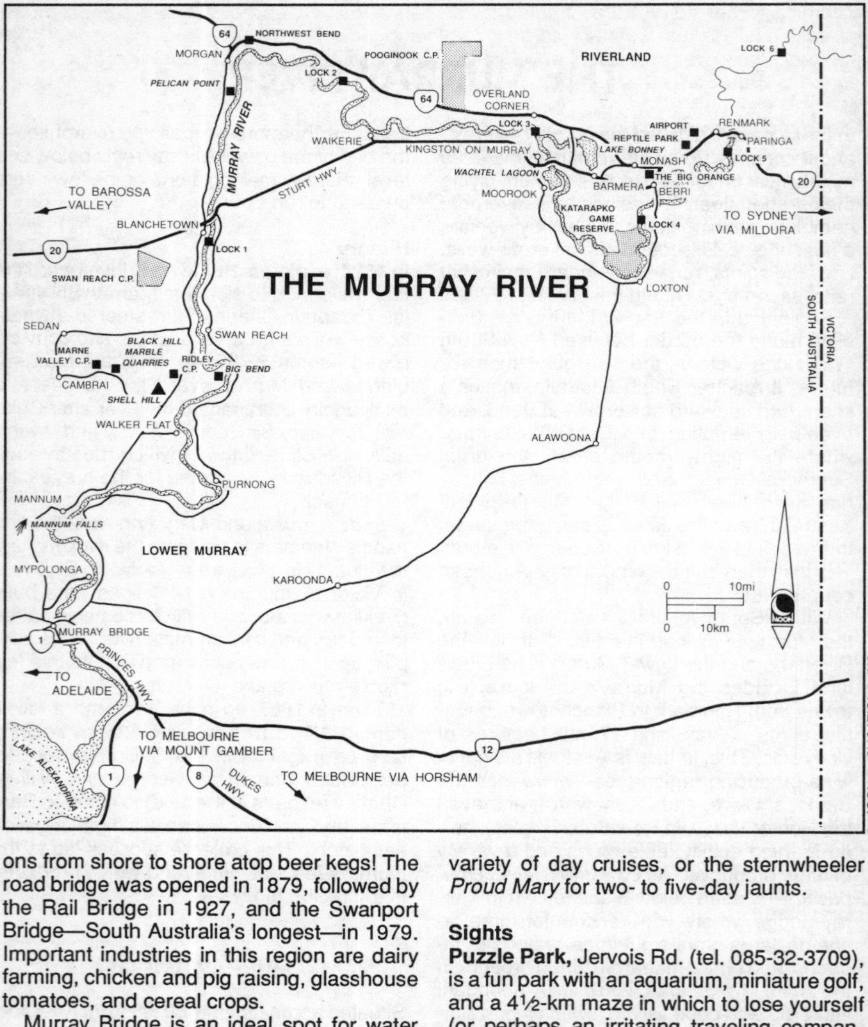

ons from shore to shore atop beer kegs! The road bridge was opened in 1879, followed by the Rail Bridge in 1927, and the Swanport Bridge—South Australia's longest—in 1979. Important industries in this region are dairy farming, chicken and pig raising, glasshouse tomatoes, and cereal crops.

Murray Bridge is an ideal spot for water sports, particularly water-skiing between White Sands and Willow Banks. Scads of picnic areas and reserves dot the riverfront, affording kick-back-and-relax opportunities for the road-weary. Or catch the Murray spirit and jump aboard the MV *Kookaburra*, for a variety of day cruises, or the sternwheeler *Proud Mary* for two- to five-day jaunts.

Sights

Puzzle Park, Jervois Rd. (tel. 085-32-3709), is a fun park with an aquarium, miniature golf, and a 4½-km maze in which to lose yourself (or perhaps an irritating traveling companion!). Hours are daily 10 a.m.-5:30 p.m. **Butterfly House,** next door (tel. 32- 3666), is the state's only place to prance with live tropical species. Hours are daily 9 a.m.-5:30 p.m.

Mary the Blacksmith, 41 Doyle Rd. (tel. 32-5526), spins a tale as she wields an anvil.

According to her ad, you'll be treated to "a yarn with a fair dinkum woman blacksmith as she forges iron over an ancient anvil." Mary "performs" Sat.-Sun. 10 a.m.-4 p.m.

Accommodations And Food

If you're staying the night, the bare-bones **Balcony Private Hotel,** 12 Sixth Ave. (tel. 085-32-3830) is inexpensive and includes breakfast. Also inexpensive, **Motel Greenacres,** Princes Highway East (tel. 32-1090), is a family-owned establishment five km southeast of the city center. Some rooms have kitchenettes. **Oval Motel and Caravan Park,** 4 LeMessurier St. (tel. 32-2267), near the river, also has inexpensive motel units as well as on-site vans. **Avoca Dell Caravan Park,** Loddon Rd. (tel. 32-2095), on the Murray, has campsites and on-site vans.

Pick up natural foods, vitamins, herbal teas, and grains at **Murray Bridge Health Foods,** corner Seventh and Fourth streets. (tel. 32-4383).

Information

The **Tourist Information Centre** is on Swanport Rd., between South and Mary terraces (tel. 085-32-8660). For emergencies, contact **police** (tel. 32-1888), **fire brigade** (tel. 32-1000), or **ambulance** (tel. 32-1122). The local branch of the **Royal Automobile Association** is on Railway Terrace (tel. 32-2022), and the **hospital** (tel. 32-1333) is at the corner of Swanport Rd. and Monash Terrace.

Transport

A local bus service operates Mon.-Sat. from the **Town Bus Terminal,** corner Sixth and Bridge (tel. 085-32-2022); there's a **taxi** stand off Bridge St., or phone 32-1818.

MYPOLONGA

Traveling eight km from Murray Bridge on Mannum Road brings you into this small farming community, an area of highlands and swamplands. Noted for its well-irrigated orange, apricot, peach and pear orchards, Mypolonga is another water sport and houseboat haven. The *Maratala,* a lock-maintenance vessel built here in 1970, cruises up- and downstream between locks one and nine, on the lookout for needed repairs.

MANNUM

Mannum (pop. 2,060), a wide spot in the river 21 km north of Murray Bridge, is the birthplace of Australia's paddle steamers. In 1853, Captain W.R. Randell (who had settled in the district some 10 years earlier) constructed *Mary Ann,* the first steamboat, and the following year sailed it up to Swan Hill in Victoria. In 1854, the busy captain also built Mannum's first house which, over time, was bought, sold, and transformed into the Mannum Hotel. Subsequent to the *Mary Ann's* inaugural voyage, Mannum became a busy shipbuilding center. Today Mannum is a peaceful community, known for its scenic beauty, rich heritage, and water activities.

Sights

Recreation Reserve (called the "Rec" by locals), lines the banks of the Murray with 350 meters of grassy picnic and barbecue areas, a boat ramp, and scenic lookouts to town, river, and valley.

The National Trust operates **Mannum Museum** (tel. 085-69-1303) inside the restored 1896 paddle steamer *Marion.* Moored at Randell's original wharf at Arnold Park, the floating museum contains river relics and other memorabilia. The museum is open Fri.-Tues. 10 a.m.-4 p.m., during the school term.

The **Bird Sanctuary,** on Halidon Rd., is home to ducks, swans, pelicans, and other beautiful water birds.

Mannum Waterfalls Reserve, 20 km south of town, offers picnic spots and walking tracks, but if you want to see the falls be aware they flow mainly in the winter.

Accommodations And Food

Stay at Captain Randell's inexpensive homestead-turned-**Mannum Hotel,** 15 Randell St. (tel. 085-69-1008), with shared facilities. **Leonaville,** 69 River Land (tel. 69-2073), offers bed and breakfast accommodations in

RULES FOR THE MURRAYLANDS

As part of a "Don't Muck up the Murray" campaign, aimed at preserving the river environment, the South Australia Department of Environment and Planning asks that visitors adhere to the following rules:

Protect Water Supplies
Do not bury excrement within 50 meters of the Murray.

Do not use pollutants, like soap, anywhere near the water.

Do not wash plates or utensils within 50 meters of the river.

Camp away from the river bank. Avoid blocking the access of stock or wildlife to the water; they need their water to live.

Respect Farmers, Their Property, And Stock
Leave machinery alone. Windmills, pumps, tractors, and generators are important for a farm's survival. Your interference could cause costly or ruinous breakdowns.

Do not frighten or disturb stock. Farm animals are valuable, easily disturbed, and some can injure you. They could be lambing or calving, so give them a go and keep right away.

Camp away from windmills and pumps and don't interfere with farm water supplies, except in an emergency.

Report vandalism. If you see any acts of vandalism, notify the landowner.

Respect And Keep To Roads And Tracks
Fences, gates, roads, and tracks represent important investments to farmers and property owners, so while you're a guest on their land, be considerate of your responsibilities.

Leave gates as you found them.

Avoid damaging fences and use gates and stiles where they are provided.

Keep to existing roads and tracks and do not widen them.

Contact the landowner if you propose to drive off a track or travel across his property.

Avoid vehicle travel when roads are wet.

If you see persons violating or polluting the river, you are asked to phone **River Watch,** the Murray's 24-hour watchdog, at (085) 82-2700.

an 1883 homestead for moderate prices. **Mannum Caravan Park,** Purnong Rd. (tel. 69-1402), is adjacent to the Bird Sanctuary.

Riverfront Coffee Spot, 67 Randell St. (tel. 69-1711), is open daily for cappuccino, croissants, cakes, and light meals.

THE MID MURRAYLANDS

The Mid Murraylands comprise the area from Bow Hill in the south (32 km from Mannum), to Swan Reach in the north, from Nildottie in the east to Sedan in the west. Just a 90-minute drive from Adelaide, this district offers lovely scenery and not-so-touristy river action where you can fish and boat in peace or just sit on the banks and float twigs downstream.

There's a stunning **scenic drive** along Younghusband Rd., on the way to Purnong, that takes in lagoons, lakes, stone quarries, and stupendous bird life. **Bow Hill,** before Purnong, is a popular water-skiing spot. **Purnong** is a slow-going holiday village but a barrage of river craft float past just the same. Great views can be enjoyed at **Caurnamont Landing,** a base for houseboat rentals. **Walker Flat,** sheltered by tall cliffs, is another location sought out both by water-skiers and water birds. Small, rural **Nildottie,** once an old paddle steamer landing, now bears citrus fruit and vegetable crops. **Big Bend** boasts big red river gums and sandstone cliffs which draw vast numbers of cockatoos to nest.

Surveyed in 1839, **Swan Reach** (pop. 200) is the Mid Murraylands's largest town and halfway point between the Barossa Valley and the Riverland. Again, it's another holiday and water sport mecca, as well as the finishing point for the *Murray River Queen's* uphill cruise. **Punuelroo,** seven km south, is a long time holiday hot spot, and *not* the place to hit if you want peace and quiet. **Ridley Conservation Park,** five km south of Swan Reach, is where you might glimpse hairy-nosed wombats and the rare striped honeyeater bird. **Swan Reach Conservation Park,** 11 km northwest of Swan Reach, is 1,900 hectares of grasslands, thick mallee, false sandalwood, open woodland, and roaming wildlife—including emus and western gray kangaroos.

Sedan, about 16 km west from Swan Reach Conservation Park, provides facilities for the surrounding farm community. Established in the late 1890s, the town has preserved many of its old buildings. From Sedan, you can take a number of scenic drives. Best is the route that winds from Cambrai through the Marne River Valley—taking in huge red river gums, a granite quarry, a pinnacle of fossils, and a myriad of wildlife—then swings north to Ridley Conservation Park and back to Swan Reach.

Accommodations

Pub-style rooms are inexpensive at **Swan Reach Hotel** (tel. 085-70-2003). **Punyelroo Caravan Park** (tel. 70-2021), on the riverbanks, has campsites and on-site vans.

BLANCHETOWN

This popular holiday resort—which begins the Riverland—sits 28 km north of Swan Reach and 134 km northeast of Adelaide, along the Sturt Highway. Governor R.G. MacDonnell named this town for his wife, Lady Blanche. There were high hopes for Blanchetown, begun in 1855 as an important commercial center and established as a port in 1863, but they fizzled after northerly neighbor Morgan won the much-sought-after railway line. In 1922, construction began here on the complex system of locks and weirs created to control fluctuations of the river's water level. If you stand atop Blanchetown Bridge, you might see a houseboat passing through Lock Number One.

Sights

Brookfield Conservation Park, 11 km west of Blanchetown, features 6,332 hectares of open scrub mallee, mallee box, and yorrell, through which wander red kangaroos, hairy-nosed wombats, fat-tailed dunnarts, and a variety of birds. Don't veer off marked walking trails without checking with the ranger station (three km inside the entrance); some areas are closed due to scientific hairy-nosed wombat research.

Accommodations

Riverside Caravan and Camping Park (tel. 085-40-5070) is a quiet riverfront park with a beach, also canoes available for hire.

Information

In an emergency, contact **police** (tel. 085-40-5013), **ambulance** (tel. 41-2444), or local **Royal Automobile Club** (tel. 41-2600).

MORGAN

At one time Morgan (pop. 400) was South Australia's second busiest port (Port Adelaide ranked first). Orginally known as "Northwest Bend," "Great Bend," and the "Great Elbow" (this is where the Murray makes its sharp turn), Morgan was officially named after Sir William Morgan by Governor Musgrave in 1878, the same year a railway line was opened. In the good old days Morgan used to have a veritable traffic jam of steamers and barges unloading cargo, which was then transferred by rail to Port Adelaide.

Sights

Reminders of the town's formidable history include the huge wharf, built in 1878, and the heritage buildings along Railway Terrace. **Port of Morgan Historic Museum,** on Railway Terrace, displays original river charts and trading-days artifacts.

Cross the river by ferry to **Morgan Conservation Park,** in the northwest bend, to view water birds in the wetlands or picnic under towering red gums.

Accommodations

Both the **Commercial Hotel** (tel. 085-40-2107) and **Terminus Hotel Motel** (tel. 40-2006), on historic Railway Terrace, have simple inexpensive accommodations. **Morgan Riverside Caravan Park** (tel. 40-2207) has on-site vans, with air-conditioning and telly.

WAIKERIE

Waikerie (pop. 1,600), reached from Blanchetown along the Sturt Highway, or from Morgan (passing river Lock Number Two), is the "citrus centre of Australia." Founded in 1880 by the Shepherd Brothers, the name "Waikerie" is a derivative of an Aboriginal word meaning "many wings or birds," no doubt because of the abundant colorful birds (and, nowadays, the glider flights), hanging around the district's lagoons and riverbanks.

Mild sunny winters and hot temperate summers, combined with modern irrigation, have turned this former desert into a citrus fruit oasis of more than one million bountiful trees, planted on over 5,000 acres (try to visit in Sept.-Oct. when they're abloom).

Sights

In the center of town is **Waikerie Producers Packing House,** the largest of its kind in Australia. You can arrange for a tour there or at the nearby **Crusta Fruit Juice Factory,** on Virgo Rd. in Cresta.

Pooginook Conservation Park, 12 km northeast of Waikerie, is home to a variety of animal and bird life, in environs ranging from open to dense mallee.

Accommodations And Food

The centrally located **Waikerie Hotel Motel,** McCoy St. (tel. 085-41-2999), has inexpensive to low-moderate rates, depending on which section you stay in. The restaurant offers both counter meals and à la carte dining. Air-conditioned on-site vans are available at **Gateway Caravan Park,** Ramco Rd. (tel. 41-2651).

Purchase local citrus, dried, and glacé fruits, honey, juices, and nonalcoholic wines at **The Orange Tree,** on Sturt Hwy. (tel. 41-2332). A viewing platform looks out over the river and town.

Sports And Recreation

Waikerie, sight of the 1974 World Gliding Championships, is the perfect place to soar and spiral the skies. **Waikerie Gliding Club** (tel. 085-41-2644) offers glider joy flights, as well as instruction.

Information

The Orange Tree also functions as the **tourist information center.** Hours are Sun.-Fri. 9 a.m.-5:30 p.m., closed Saturday.

Emergency numbers for Waikerie are **police** (tel. 085-41-2888), **ambulance,** (tel. 41-2444), and for road service, the **Royal Automobile Association** (tel. 41-2900).

BARMERA

Traveling 48 km east of Waikerie, past rural Kingston-on-Murray and the bird refuge at Wachtel's Lagoon (part of the Moorook Game Reserve), the Sturt Highway enters Barmera (pop. 1,900), dubbed the Murray's "aquatic playground." Set on the shores of freshwater Lake Bonney, this town draws like flies those who take to the water like fish. Joseph Hawdon discovered the lake while hauling stock overland from New South Wales to Adelaide. His pal Charles Bonney was with him, so he named the lake. Originally called Barmera by local Aboriginals, that title was transferred to the new township. Besides being a holiday resort, Barmera grows citrus and stone fruits, grapes, and vegetables.

Lake Bonney offers all types of water sports—swimming, fishing, windsurfing, yachting, water-skiing, speed boating (in 1964, Englishman Donald Campbell tried to break the world water speed record here). Or you can picnic, barbecue, and laze around on one of the sandy beaches (Pelican Point, on the western shore, is a nude beach).

Fresh fruit and veggies are sold along the roadside.

Sights

The **Overland Corner Hotel Museum,** 19 km from Barmera, on Morgan Road, built in 1859, was one of the Riverland's first stone buildings. This was where the weary overlanders and cattle drovers rested themselves and their bullock teams. Restored and run by the National Trust, the museum features pioneer exhibits and area artifacts. Hours are sporadic. For information, phone (085) 88-7021.

At Cobdogla, five km west of town, you can see the world's only operating Humphrey Pump and other historical displays at **Cobdogla Irrigation Museum,** Trussel Terrace. For information, phone 88-7031.

On the other side of Lake Bonney's Nappers Bridge, **Loch Luna Game Reserve,** set on 1,905 hectares, is another favorite fishing, canoeing, and waterfowl-breeding haunt. There's a picnic area at Lock Number Three, a few kilometers west of the reserve, where you can watch the action.

Accommodations

For lakeshore accommodations, **Lake Bonney Caravan Reserve,** (tel. 085-88-2234), has everything from on-site vans to holiday flats, all at inexpensive prices. This is a huge family-oriented complex, complete with a gym, sauna, squash courts, and jujitsu lessons! **Yatco Holiday Cottages,** Loxton Rd., near Moorook Game Reserve (tel. 83-9216), are fully equipped, self-contained cabins on the water's edge. Rates are inexpensive to low-moderate.

Camping is permitted at the Pelican Point nude bathing beach, but there are no facilities. To reach the beach, go three km along Morgan Road, turn right onto Ireland Road.

Sports And Recreation

Lake Bonney Aquatic Centre (tel. 085-88-2679) rents paddleboats, canoes, windsurfers, catarmarans, and single and tandem bicycles. The center is open during school holidays, and weekends from Sept.-May.

Information

For tourist information, drop by **Barmera Travel Centre,** Barwell Ave. (tel. 085-88-2289).

For emergencies, contact **police** (tel. 88-2122), **fire brigade** (tel. 88-2000), **ambulance** (tel. 88-2501), or **Royal Automobile Association** (tel. 82-1644). **Barmera Hospital** (tel. 88-2006) is on Eyre Street.

BERRI

The name is certainly appropriate for this wine and citrus growing district; however, it does not stem from "berry," but from "berri

berri," Aboriginal for "wide bend in the river." Established about 1870 as a riverboat refueling stop, Berri (pop. 3,500) is *still* a refueling stop—for wines and juices. The town also sports the customary riverfront parks and water activities. Get your bearings at the lookout tower on Fiedler Street.

Sights

Berri Estates is reputedly the largest single winery-distillery in Australia—if not the entire Southern Hemisphere; anyway, it's big enough to produce annually seven million liters of premium varietals, bulk, cask, and fortified wines, as well as brandies. The winery is open for tastings Mon.-Fri. 9 a.m.-5:30 p.m., Sat. 9-5. For information, phone (085) 83-2303.

When you're finished with the hard stuff, **Berrivale Orchards,** on McKay Rd., sells fruit juices, canned fruits, almonds, and gherkins, and presents a 15-minute video about the canning and juicing business. Hours are Mon.-Fri. 8:30 a.m.-4:30 p.m., Sat. 9 a.m.-noon. For information, phone 82-1455.

Grant's Super Playground, in the nearby community of Monash, houses more than 180 amusements for kids of all ages. Equipment includes roller coasters, flying foxes, earthmovers, multiple slides, and rotary cones. The park is always open and *free,* though donations are accepted.

The Riverland Big Orange, corner of Sturt Highway and the Monash bypass, is billed—in the spirit of Larry the Kingston Lobster—as the "largest orange in the world." You can pick up a bag of oranges and get your juices freshly squeezed. There's a small admission fee to the panoramic lookout. Hours are daily 9-5. For information, phone 82-2850.

Riverland Display Centre, adjacent to the Big Orange, houses a collection of vintage and classic cars, large-scale model airplanes, antique toys and dolls, as well as gem, mineral, and Aboriginal culture displays. Its hours are the same as the orange. For information, phone 82-2325.

Accommodations And Food

Rooms at the **Berri Hotel Motel,** Riverview Ave. (tel. 085-82- 1411), are inexpensive to low-moderate, and the pub serves cheap counter meals. You can get an on-site van with air-conditioning and television at **Berri War Memorial Riverside Caravan Park,** Riverview Dr. (tel. 82-1718).

If you enjoy fruit, you won't go hungry in these parts. **Berri Fruit Tree,** on Sturt Hwy. towards Glossop, sells fresh and dried fruits, nuts, jams, and honey.

Events

And, if you're into bronco bulls, pay a visit on Easter Monday for the annual **Berri Rodeo.**

Information

Berri Tourist and Travel Centre, Vaughan Terrace (tel. 085-82-1655), can arrange accommodations, provide winery maps and general information.

Emergency contacts are **police** (tel. 82-2488), **ambulance** (tel. 82-2555), **fire brigade** (tel. 82-1000), and the **Royal Automobile Association** (tel. 82-1644).

LOXTON

Berri's twin ferries, the main link to Loxton, will whisk you across the river in one and a half minutes; from there you pass around Lock Number Four and Katarapko Island into town. Settled in the 1890s and established in 1907, Loxton (pop. 3,370) is a picture-postcard township overlooking both the Murray and the game reserve. Named for William Charles Loxton, a boundary rider who worked on the original station property, irrigation methods turned the area into the same rich grounds as the rest of the Riverland.

Sights

Loxton's most famous attraction is the **Historical Village,** a riverfront collection of 25 fully furnished early buildings, including a replica of William Charles Loxton's pine and pug hut. Early farm equipment and machinery are also on exhibit. Hours are daily 10 a.m.-4 p.m. and Wed. evenings 7-9 p.m. For information, phone (085) 84-7194.

Penfold's Loxton Winery, Berri Rd. (tel. 84-7236), one of South Australia's largest bulk wineries, specializes in dealcoholized

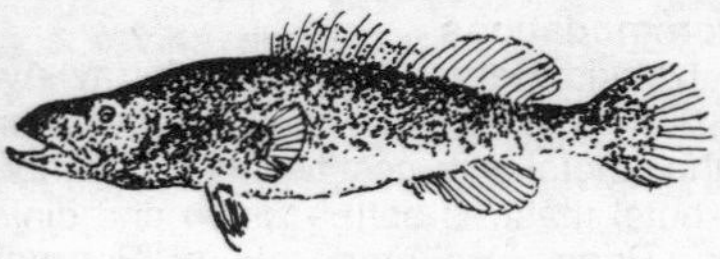

RESPECT THE RIVER AND ALL OTHER USERS

The Department of Environment and Planning has issued the following warnings to Murray River users:

On the Murray it's important to have consideration for other river users, so please observe all boating and fishing regulations. This includes bag limits and closures, because these are in force to prevent the depletion of fish life.

Before boating or swimming, check out the Murray. Get to know its waters. And watch out for snags.

When Swimming

Wear a buoyancy vest. It might look funny but it could save your life.

Don't even think about swimming the width of the Murray. With currents, snags, and power boats you might not make it.

Dive as shallowly as possible, especially if you're not certain of the depth. Steep dives have resulted in back or neck injuries.

Keep clear of busy boating areas. There's a chance the skippers might not see you.

When Boating

Carry all the required safety equipment on board.

Give a wide berth to other boats when overtaking.

Take care when turning and don't turn across the bow of another vessel.

Don't drink and drive. Swimming or driving a motorboat, when drunk, is setting a sure course for disaster. Alcohol, petrol, and water do not mix.

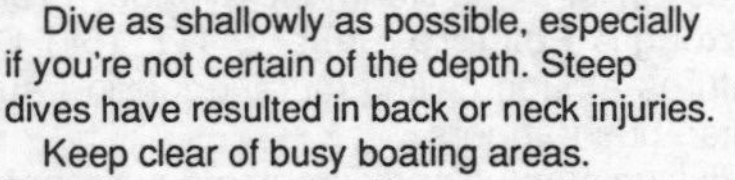

wines. Hours for sales and tastings are Mon.-Sat. 10 a.m.-5 p.m.

Katarapko Game Reserve is home to almost 150 species of birds. You can camp, fish, or bushwalk through red gum floodplain, explore horseshoe lagoons and gentle backwaters. **Kai Kai Nature Trail,** beginning at campsite 20, is a 40-minute walk encompassing a wide variety of Katarapko Creek birdlife and natural habitat.

Alawoona, 35 km south of Loxton, is the entry point for Mallee country. The 36,815-hectare **Billiatt Conservation Park** is home to the western grey kangaroo, hopping mouse, pygmy possum, and many mallee birds, including the endangered mallee fowl and red-lored whistler.

Accommodations

Loxton Hotel Motel, East Terrace (tel. 085-84-7266), has both old pub rooms ($21-30) and riverview motel suites at moderate prices. The restaurant serves counter meals and an à la carte menu. **Loxton Riverfront Caravan Park** (tel. 84-7862), on the Murray, has campsites and on-site vans, plus bicycle and canoe rentals. A 48-bed hostel is also available. At **Nadia Host Farm** (tel. 87-4362), 20 minutes from Loxton, you can experience life on a wheat and sheep farm. Moderate rates include breakfast.

Events

Wednesday night is party time as the *Murray Princess* cruises into Loxton and village minstrels perform in the Historical Village.

Information

Loxton Tourist and Travel, 45 East Terrace (tel. 085-84-7919), will assist with accommodations and tours, as well as canoe, bicycle, or houseboat rentals.

For emergency services, contact **police** (tel. 84-7283), **ambulance** (tel. 84-7565), or **Royal Automobile Association** (tel. 84-7393).

Getting Around

Rent **trail bikes** from Loxton Motorcycle Hire Centre, 10 Bookpurnong Terrace (tel. 085-84-7698).

RENMARK

Renmark (pop. 3,490) sits on a willow-lined Murray River bend, 255 km northeast of Adelaide and very near the Victoria border. Founded in 1887, Renmark is Australia's oldest irrigation district—thanks to Alfred Deakin's idea and the Canadian Chaffey brothers' expertise, the system spurred the Riverland's thriving citrus and wine industry. Ironically, the Chaffey brothers inserted a prohibition clause in their plans for the town's development. In 1897, the British Commonwealth countered the clause by erecting the Renmark Hotel, first of its kind within the Commonwealth. And we know who won!

Today Renmark is a busy commercial and holiday center, with *plenty* of wine to taste, houseboats to rent, and arts and crafts galleries to browse. Renmark is also home port to the 200-passenger PS *Murray Princess.*

Paringa, four km east from Renmark, is the location of **Lock Number Five** and, nearby, the quite wonderful **Headings Cliffs Lookout Tower,** the quite interesting **Lyrup Village** communal growing settlement (dating from 1894), and the quite dumb **Big Tyre.**

Sights

The **PS *Industry,*** built in 1911, serves as historical museum. Through a coin-in-the-slot operation, you can see how paddle wheels and other engine parts function. Moored on the Murray, between 9th and 10th streets, the museum is open daily.

Olivewood Homestead, Renmark Ave. and 21st St., the original home of Charles Chaffey, now operates as a National Trust museum. Hours are Thurs.-Tues. 10 a.m.-4 p.m., closed Wednesday. For information, phone (085) 86-6175.

Bredl's Reptile Park and Zoo, on the Sturt Highway, five km from town, has pythons, taipans, cobras, boa constrictors, rare yellow anacondas, lizards, alligators, crocs, and other reptiles. Hours are daily 9 a.m.-6 p.m., and there are special snake feedings Sun. 2-3 p.m. For information, phone 85-1431.

Accommodations

The historic **Renmark Hotel,** Murray Ave. (tel. 085-86-6755), has inexpensive rooms but their motel units cost twenty bucks more. The hotel features both a bistro and dining room. Prices are moderate at **Renmark Country Club,** Sturt Hwy. (tel. 85-1401) and include use of tennis court, swimming pool, spa, and 18-hole grass golf course.

Both **Riverbend Caravan Park,** Sturt Hwy. (tel. 85-5131), and **Renmark Caravan Park,** Patey Dr. (tel. 86-6315), are situated on the riverfront.

Sports And Recreation

Facilities at **Renmark Community Recreation Centre** include indoor tennis, indoor swimming pool, squash courts, weight-training equipment, spa and sauna, a suntan unit, and large multipurpose stadium for cricket, soccer, netball, badminton, volleyball, basketball, and roller skating. For information, phone (085) 86-6072.

Shopping

Most of the arts and crafts galleries are situated on or near Renmark Avenue. **Frank Harding's Folklore Gallery,** 117 16th St., features a huge ceiling mural depicting Australian bushrangers.

Pick up surplus and camping equipment at **Riverland Army Disposals,** Renmark Ave. (tel. 085-86-6767).

Information

The **Tourist Information Centre,** Murray Ave. (tel. 085-86-6703), distributes info and rents tandem or single bicycles (there's a good cycling track to Paringa).

TRANSPORT

Getting There

Sunstate Airlines (tel. 08-217-3333) flies daily from Adelaide to Renmark and on to Mildura. Book through Australian Airlines.

Murray Bridge Passenger Service (tel. 08-217-0777, or 085-32-1766 in Murray Bridge), operates daily coaches between Murray Bridge and Adelaide's Franklin Street Passenger Depot for about $10 one way. **Stateliner** (tel. 08-233-2755, or 085-86-6468 in Renmark), has daily coaches from Adelaide to Blanchetown ($14), Waikerie ($17), Barmera ($20), Berri ($22), Loxton ($24), and Renmark ($24). Many interstate coaches also serve the Lower Murray and Riverland.

There's regularly scheduled rail service between Murray Bridge and Adelaide. For information, contact **Murray Bridge Railway Station,** Railway Terrace (tel. 085-32-2344).

River Cruising

Why not feel the river rush through your veins by traveling *on* the Murray, instead of *along* it? In the Lower Murray, you can rent **houseboats** at Murray Bridge, Mannum, Younghusband, and Purnong; in the Riverland, houseboats are based at Morgan, Waikerie, Loxton, Berri, Paringa, and Renmark. Houseboats are completely self-contained, accommodate four to 10 berths, and are capable of traveling six to eight knots. Rental prices depend upon the size of boat, length of rental, and the season you rent it in—typically about $800 per week. However, keep in mind that this takes care of both transport and accommodations, as well as most meals—and, if you share the cost with others, it even becomes cheap. At any rate, it will be a delightful and memorable experience—floating along the Murray, in comfort, and at will. Use a little imagination and you may run into Tom Sawyer, Matthew Flinders, or Mr. Lucky.

Book houseboats *(well* in advance) at any South Australian Government Travel Centre, or through local tourist information centers. You won't need a boat operator's license, but a driver's license *is* required.

Or, leave the navigating to someone else. The 18-cabin *Proud Mary* luxury boat departs Murray Bridge for two- to five-day cruises. Cost is $250-625 per person. For information, phone (08) 231-9472. The glorious 44-cabin PS *Murray River Queen* makes six-night journeys from Goolwa to Swan Reach, at a cost of about $750 per person. For information, phone (08) 211-8333. The 60-cabin paddle steamer *Murray Princess* departs Renmark for six-night Riverland cruises, at $750 per person. For information, phone (085) 86-6703. All of the above prices include accommodations and meals.

Get a quick taste of the Murray on a lunch, dinner, or other short sail. Operators offering a wide range of tours (at a wide range of fares) include MV *Kookaburra* (tel. 35-4280) from Murray Bridge, *Lady Mannum* (tel. 69-1438) from Mannum, and MV *Barrangul* (tel. 86-6703) from Renmark.

THE MID NORTH

South Australia's Mid North lies north of the Barossa Valley, west of the Riverland, east of Yorke Peninsula, and just south of the Flinders Ranges. And it is special—touristed, but not *touristy*.

Just between you and me, the Mid North is my favorite part of the state. Burra, the historic copper mining town, was so awesome I dropped my camera, shattering it on the same cobblestone path once used by Cornish miners. Busted Olympus notwithstanding, I instamatically decided to live there for at least six months! And then there's Mintaro, a truly gorgeous heritage town. Down the road is Martindale Hall, a *very* chic B&B where *Picnic at Hanging Rock* was filmed.

Farther north is Peterborough, a railway junction, where buffs like me—with hearts that chug instead of beat—can all-aboard a narrow-gauge steam train through the Mid North countryside. Port Pirie, along the Spencer Gulf, is a mixture of heritage town, busy seaport, and commercial center.

You have a variety of options for exploring the Mid North. The Clare Valley is a 135-km zip north of Adelaide, along Main North Road.

From Adelaide, the Barrier Highway will lead you (with a couple of detours) to Burra and Peterborough. From Peterborough you turn westward to Jamestown, Gladstone, and Port Pirie, or continue north to the Flinders Ranges. At the junction of the Barrier and Sturt highways, be sure to take the Kapunda turnoff. The back road, through Hamilton, Marrabel, and Saddleworth—where you'll reconnect with the Barrier Highway—is one of my favorite day-in-the-country drives.

Highway One, also from Adelaide, travels to Port Wakefield (where you can cut over to Balaklava), up to Snowtown, Crystal Brook, and Port Pirie, then on to Port Augusta and the Eyre Peninsula, or across the Nullarbor to Western Australia.

Whichever road you follow, every once in a while veer off the beaten path—this territory is full of little surprises, marked by hand-lettered signposts, European-style back roads, an ornery cow, a stubborn mule, and unusual gusto in the breeze.

KAPUNDA

Located at the northern edge of the Barossa Valley, 75 km from Adelaide, Kapunda (pop. 1,620) was the location of South Australia's first significant copper find. An accidental discovery of green copper ore prompted the opening of one of the world's richest copper mines on 80 acres owned by the Dutton and Bagott families. The mine operated from 1844-1912, turning out approximately 14,000 tons of copper, and Kapunda soon grew into the state's largest country town. Though the community now lives off agricultural rather than mining products, many historic buildings, cottages, and churches still stand, and the town retains a lot of its original charm. Particularly stunning is the decorative iron lacework—known as "Kapunda lace," made locally at the turn of the century.

Sights

Kapunda Historical Museum (tel. 085-66-26902) is in the former Baptist church on Hill Street. Historical exhibits include colonial artifacts, memorabilia, and archival recordings. Hours are daily Sept.-May, and weekends June-Aug. 1-4 p.m.

The eight-meter-tall bronze sculpture of *Map Kernow* (Cornish for "Son of Cornwall"), at the south end of town, pays tribute to early Cornish miners.

Old Kapunda Copper Mine and Walking Trail is an easy 1½-km hike through the old mine workings for close-up investigation of shafts, tunnels, the open cut area, the mine chimney, and an early miner's cottage.

The **Heritage Trail** leads to 42 historical buildings along a 10-km route.

Accommodations And Food

Newly refurbished **Sir John Franklin Hotel,** Main St. (tel. 085-66-2106), has large inexpensive pub-style rooms. Across the street, **Ford House** (tel. 66-2280) is a beautifully renovated B&B with moderate prices ($10 less without breakfast). Excellent à la carte dinners are served at both accommodations, and Sir John Franklin's lively pub also has inexpensive counter meals.

Dutton Park Caravan Park, Baker St. (tel. 66-2094) rents campsites and on-site vans.

Information

Get maps for both walking trails mentioned above, as well as other information, from **Kapunda Tourist Centre** or Kapunda Historical Society—same address, same phone number. The tourist center is open daily 10 a.m.-1 p.m.

MINTARO

The entire tiny township of Mintaro (pop. 80) is on the heritage list. Of course, you'll find only a handful of streets, but they're lined with 1850s slate, stone, and wooden colonial structures—influenced by Italian, English, and German hands—constructed of such diverse materials as Baltic pine and Indian cedar. Most buildings incorporate the locally produced fine slate—a specialty of this district—in walls, floors, or fences, and many of the old cottages have been converted into accommodations houses. The town is thought to have been named by Uruguayan mule drivers who stopped there while carting copper ore between Port Wakefield and Burra.

Mintaro sits 130 km from Adelaide and about 14 km from Clare, burrowed amongst gentle hills and rolling pastures. It is a gorgeous, quiet, country village. Go there!

Sights

Robinson's Cottage (tel. 088-43-9029), a museum inside an original 1851 settler's cottage, features fire engine displays, fire appliances and memorabilia, classic and vintage cars, and other early equipment. Hours are daily 9 a.m.-4:30 p.m., closed Christmas Day.

Reilly's Cottage Gallery (tel. 43-9013) exhibits local and national art-and-craftworks in a 118-year-old cottage. Hours are Wed.-Sun. 10 a.m.-5 p.m.

Martindale Hall, on the outskirts of Mintaro, is the positively splendid Georgian mansion portrayed as "Appleyard College" in the film *Picnic at Hanging Rock.* A bachelor named Edmund Bowen had the house built in 1879, as an attempt to win the hand of a spoiled rich girl who promised to marry him if he built her a house as nice as her father's. Martindale Hall (which, in those days, cost the dear sum of £36,000) apparently wasn't up to snuff, for Edmund built the house but then lost the girl! The mansion is open for inspection daily 1-4 p.m., closed Christmas Day. It costs $6 admission, but you can visit the grounds for free.

Accommodations

All Mintaro accommodations are in converted historic digs. **Pay Office Cottage,** Hill St.

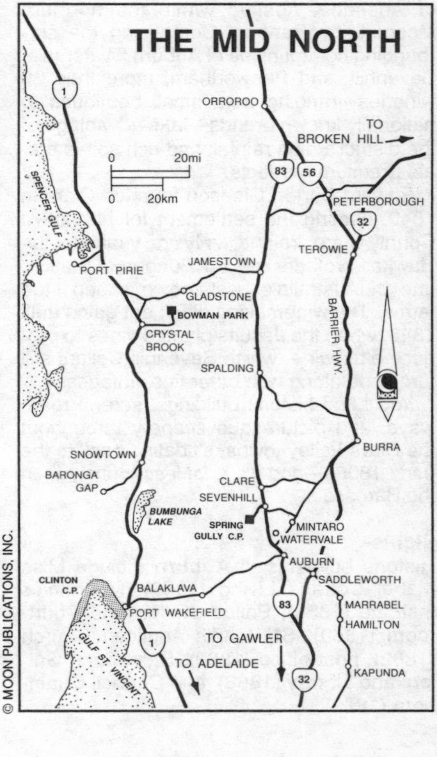

(tel. 088-43-9026), at low-moderate rates, is cheapest. **Mintaro Hideaway** (tel. 43-9011) and **The Teapot Inn** (tel. 43-9037), both moderately priced, include breakfast. **Mintaro Mews** (tel. 43-9011), offers two expensive, deluxe cottages with breakfast included. And, if you're a romantic or film-crazy, you'll pay the price to stay at the house Edmund built; **Martindale Hall** (tel. 43-9011) will give you a scrumptious room, pamper you with attention, and feed you delectable candlelight dinners for a whopping $150 per person (including breakfast and dinner). Even at that price, you'd better book way in advance!

THE CLARE VALLEY

The Clare Valley, famous for winemaking since 1851, is a 30-km stretch, 135 km north of Adelaide, nestled within the northern Mount Lofty Ranges. Comprising the surrounding communities of Auburn, Watervale, Sevenhill, and Penwortham, more than 20 wineries—ranging from small boutiques to nationally known brands—take advantage of the district's high rainfall and rich soil to create premium products.

Edward Burton Gleeson founded Clare in 1840, naming the settlement for his native County Clare, Ireland. Only one year later the Hawker brothers set up Bungaree Station, one of Australia's best-known sheep stud farms. The winemaking didn't get going until 1848, when the Jesuits planted vines to produce altar wine, which Sevenhill Cellars still turns out, along with other fine vintages.

You'll find historic buildings, serene roadways, and picturesque scenery throughout the Clare Valley towns, all dating back to the early 1800s—and it's a *lot* less touristy than the Barossa.

Sights

Historic buildings in **Auburn** include Miss Mabel Cottage Living (1859), Mechanics Institute (1859), Police Station and Courtroom (1860), St. John's Anglican Church (1862), post office (1862), Stonehurst Gallery and Library (1866), and Council Chambers (1879).

A painted cowboy rests against a real log.

Stanley Grammar School, Uniting Church of Australia, Watervale Primary School and the Methodist Church are National Trust buildings in **Watervale.**

The **Old Police Station Museum** (1850), corner Victoria Rd. and West Terrace, Clare (tel. 088-42-2895), run by the National Trust, was the valley's first courthouse and police station. Hours are Sat. 10 a.m.-noon, 2-4 p.m., Sun. and holidays 2-4 p.m.

Take a tour of **Bungaree Station,** dating from 1841 when the Hawkers established the famous merino stud farm, and *still* run by their grandsons! The self-sufficient community with church, council chambers, school, blacksmith shop, as well as wool shed, stable yard, and shearers quarters, are still in use. One- to two-hour conducted tours are arranged by appointment only, as the station is still going full-stud. Original knitting patterns and woolen yarns are sold on premises. For information, phone (088-42-2677).

Saint Aloysius Church and Sevenhill Cellars, College Rd., Sevenhill (tel. 43-

4222), is where the valley's first vines were planted. Father Aloysius Kranewitter, a young Jesuit priest, chose the site (patterned after the seven hills of Rome) as a cellar for his altar wines. Saint Aloysius Church was begun in 1856 and consecrated in 1875. Besides altar wines, Sevenhill specializes in dry red and white wines, and liqueur tokay. Hours are Mon.-Fri. 8:30 a.m.-4:30 p.m., Sat. and holidays 9 a.m.-4 p.m., closed Sundays, Christmas Day, New Year's Day, and Good Friday (you know where you can get their wine on *those* days!).

Wolta Wolta Homestead (tel. 42-3875) was one of the earliest settler's cottages. Unfortunately, it burned down in 1983's devastating Ash Wednesday fire. The homestead, now restored, features antiques, artworks, history, and memorabilia relating to the Hope family, owners of the property for four generations. Tours are conducted Sat.-Sun. 10 a.m.-4:30 p.m.

There're good picnicking and leisurely walks at **Pioneer, Christison,** and **Spring Gully** parks.

Accommodations And Food

You can stay inexpensively in the shearers' quarters at **Bungaree Station** (tel. 088-42-2677). Facilities include a large dining hall and modern kitchen. **Clare Valley Cabins** (tel. 42-3917) are seven two-bedroom self-contained cottages on a large property five km north of Clare. Rates are inexpensive to low-moderate. **Bentley's Hotel Motel,** 191 Main North Rd. (tel. 42-2815), rents moderately priced rooms in both units. **Clare Central Motel,** 325 Main North Rd. (tel. 42-2277), is down the street and runs about $20 more than Bentley's.

Spend the night in **Old Stanley Grammar School,** Commercial Rd., Watervale (tel. 43-0013), or at quaint **Stringy Brae Cottage** (tel. 43-4313), in Sevenhill. Both accommodations range high-moderate to expensive and include breakfast.

Christison Park Caravan Park, Main North Rd. (tel. 42-2724), near Clare, has campsites and on-site vans.

Cheap eats on the main drag are **Clare Valley Café, Salad Bowl,** and **Pantry Plus Coffee Shop. Bentley's Hotel** serves country-cooked meals at moderate prices. And more country cookin' is dished up at **Sevenhill Hotel** (tel. 43-4217), for Mon.-Sat. lunch and dinner. **Clare Dragon Restaurant,** 308 Main North Rd. (tel. 42-3644), is both a moderately priced licensed restaurant and an inexpensive takeaway.

Jones Bakery, 269 Main North Rd. (tel. 42-2473), bakes up buns and cakes, pies and pasties. Choose from more than 24 types of breads, as well as pastries and cakes at **Maurie's Patisserie and Hot Bread Bakery,** 292 Main North Rd. (tel. 42-3523).

Events

Similar to the Barossa event, the Clare Valley has its **Vintage Festival** during Easter of even-numbered years. The **Gourmet Weekend,** held every May, is when connoisseurs sip and sample, and foodies pig out on a progressive lunch at area wineries.

Recreation

Lakota Ranch (tel. 088-42-3875) organizes fully escorted horseback rides along the Clare Valley back roads and hills, as well as one-day cattle drives for beginners to advanced riders.

Information

Clare Valley Tourist Centre, Main North Rd., Clare (tel. 088-42-2131), has maps of the Clare Valley wineries and other local information. Hours are Mon.-Fri. 9 a.m.-4 p.m., Sat.-Sun. 10 a.m.-4 p.m. You can get tourist information in Auburn at **Miss Mabel Cottage Living,** St. Vincent St., Thurs.-Sun. and public holidays 10 a.m.-4 p.m.

BURRA

With the feel and flavor of a Down Under Bisbee, Arizona, Burra (pop. 1,900) is one of South Australia's most enchanting towns.

Originally, the community was a sheep-grazing area on the brink of bankruptcy. But in 1845, after shepherd William Streair discovered copper, followed by Thomas Pickett's find, the "Monster Mine" was created

bridge over Burra Creek

and Burra blossomed with prosperity. Named "Burra Burra" (Hindi for "Great Great") by Indian coolie shepherds, the district was collectively called "The Burra," and embraced several townships, all named according to their inhabitants' origins—thus Kooringa (Aboriginal), Redruth (Cornish), Aberdeen (Scottish), Hampton (English), and Llywchrr (Welsh).

Though the mine was one rich mother lode, operations ceased in 1877, when it became dried up. Agriculture (Burra was declared "Merino Capital of the World" in 1988) and tourism are the local revenue-takers these days. A leisurely 156-km drive from Adelaide, Burra draws visitors to its fascinating streets and dwellings to follow in historic footsteps along the copper trail.

Sights

Just about the whole town can be classified a sight, but you'll need a passport to cross many thresholds. The **Burra Passport** is a rental key, available from the tourist office, which allows you entrance to **Burra Creek Miner's Dugouts, Burra Open Air Museum, Redruth Gaol, Police Lock-up and Stables,** and **Unicorn Brewery Stables.**

Morphett's Enginehouse, built in 1858 and re-constructed in 1986, helped to dewater the mine. A 30-meter entry tunnel enables visitors to walk into the shaft to view original pump pipes.

Bon Accord Museum, on the site of the original Bon Accord Mine, serves as an interpretive center, with a working forge, six-meter by five-meter model of the Monster Mine, and tours of the old mine shaft. For information, phone (088) 92-2615.

Paxton Square Cottages are three rows of 1850s miners cottages, overlooking Burra Creek. The cottages are now visitor accommodations, but **Malowen Lowarth,** furnished as a mine captain's cottage, is open for inspection Sat. 1-3 p.m., Sun. 10:30 a.m.-12:30 p.m.

If you're into cemeteries, old **Burra Cemetery** is especially nice. If you're into diseases, it will be of interest that most causes of death at the time were typhoid, diphtheria, measles, and consumption.

Market Square Museum consists of a general store, post office, and private home, built 1870-1915. Nearby is the 13-meter ironbark and blue gum **Jinker,** which toted the huge Schneider's engine house cylinder from Port Adelaide to Burra Mine in 1852. Hours are Sat. 2-4 p.m., Sun. 12:30-2:30 p.m., or by arrangement. For information, phone (088) 92-2154.

Burra Gorge, 18 km east of town, has good walking trails through river gum forests and other scenic bushland.

Accommodations And Food

You can check into a pub for the night, but it's certainly more fun to stay in one of Burra's seeping-with-history heritage dwellings. The tourist center has all the skinny on these accommodations. The exquisite **Paxton Square Cottages** (tel. 088-92-2622), with fully equipped kitchens, are a very reasonable $30-40 double. **Bon Accord Cottage** (tel. 92-2615), the preserved mine manager's residence, is also available at the same rates. **Burra View House,** 7 Mount Pleasant Rd. (tel. 92-2648), is a B&B with excellent views and expensive rates. At **Miss Mabel Cottage,** (tel. 08-362-3306), you'll be greeted with fresh flowers and a bottle of Miss Mabel's wine for $75 double. Book all accommodations (especially Paxton Cottages) well in advance.

Reasonably priced places to fill your belly are **Polly's Tearooms** (tel. 92-2544), **Pickett's Pantry** (tel. 92-2530), and the counter at **Burra Hotel** (tel. 92-2389). Order hand-packed picnic baskets from **Hampers of Burra** (tel. 92-2069).

Information

Apply for "passports," and load up on brochures, at **Burra Tourist Centre,** Market Square (tel. 088-92-2154). Hours are daily 10 a.m.-4 p.m.

A number of historical books on the area are also sold here *(Discovering Burra* is included with your passport).

TEROWIE

Continuing up the Barrier Highway (be careful of kangaroos) for 63 km north of Burra brings you to Terowie, another historic town and a prominent part of the 1880s railway network. Horse and bullock teams from the surrounding country stations kept up a steady rush hour while loading or unloading produce, supplies, and stock. And—history buffs—get this: Terowie, site of a World War II army bivouac camp, was where General Douglas MacArthur (fresh from his Philippines escape), made his famous "I came out of Bataan and I shall return" statement.

It's a good wander down Main Street, where the original century-old shopfronts reflect times past.

Accommodations And Food

Stoker's Cottage, Mitchell St. (tel. 086-59-1092), is a fully equipped, century-old dwelling with inexpensive rooms.

Dusty Kitchen, Main St. (tel. 59-1073), serves meals, snacks, and cakes, daily.

Information

Terowie Information and Souvenir Shop, Main St. (tel. 086-59-1087), will organize visits to the Terowie Pioneer Gallery and Museum, as well as conducted tours of the town and buildings.

PETERBOROUGH

Turn off the Barrier Highway at Terowie for the 23-km ride into Peterborough—frontier town, historic railway depot, and gateway to the Flinders Ranges. Railway aficionados will thrill to find that Peterborough is one of the world's two known towns where three different rail gauges converge. This is still an important rail center on the Port Pirie-Broken Hill-Sydney main line. Get a good peek at the town (and the tracks) from **Tank Hill Lookout,** at the end of Government Road.

Sights

Don't miss a ride on the steam passenger train, along the narrow-gauge line, from Peterborough to Orroroo (about 38 km). The tourist center has schedules.

Round House Exchange, a unique railway turntable used for rerouting rolling stock, displays historic rail equipment.

Saint Cecelia, the former bishop's residence, is palatially furnished with paintings, antique pianos, polished mahogany, and stained-glass windows within its parlors, ballroom, 10 bedrooms, and library. The coach house now functions as an art center. Moderately priced accommodations are available in the main house, converted stables, coachman's room, or attached artist's studio, and include breakfast. Daily tours 1-4 p.m. are arranged through the tourist center. For information, phone (086) 51-2849.

The **Gold Battery** once extracted gold from locally mined crushed ore.

Information

You can't miss the **Peterborough Tourist Centre** (tel. 086-51-2708)—it's in a railway carriage along Main Street. Get your steam train tickets here and, if you're headed to the Flinders Ranges, inquire about roads and routes. Hours are daily 10 a.m.-4 p.m.

TO PORT PIRIE

Traveling coastward, on the back road southwest of Peterborough, Route 83 hooks up at Jamestown, drops a bit southward at Gladstone, then merges with Highway One to Port Pirie and beyond.

Jamestown

This wool-, wheat-, and barley-producing agricultural community, 44 km from Peterborough, originated back in the 1870s. The **Railway Station Museum** (tel. 086-65-2036) houses a collection of early memorabilia and historical relics. Hours are Sun. 2-4 p.m., or by arrangement.

South Australia's first government forest plantation, **Bundaleer Forest Reserve,** nine km south of Jamestown, affords a refreshing break-of-journey for walks and picnics. Climb up to the lookout tower and you'll see Mt. Remarkable in the distance.

Gladstone

This pastoral and grazing community, 28 km southwest of Jamestown and adjacent to the Rocky River, also dates back to the 1870s. In 1877, after the railway connected Gladstone to Port Pirie, the community became an important grain collection center. Eventually it became home to South Australia's largest inland silo (which now contains 82,500 tons). At the Gladstone railway yards, you can view one of the world's few places where narrow, standard, and broad gauges are interlaid in one siding.

Experience conditions withstood by "inebriates, debtors and other prisoners," at century-old **Gladstone Gaol** (tel. 086-62-2068). (Some of the "other prisoners" included Italians and Germans interned there during WW II.) Tours are conducted weekends, public holidays, and Mon.-Wed. on school holidays.

PORT PIRIE

Port Pirie (pop. 13,960), 210 km from Adelaide, is well-positioned on the eastern side and northern end of Spencer Gulf, shadowed by the Flinders Ranges. As the Mid North's largest center, Port Pirie (named after the colonial workhorse windjammer *John Pirie*), is notable for its enormous lead smeltery, capable of producing 280,000 kilograms of silver, 250,000 tons of refined lead, 90,000 tons of sulphuric acid, 45,000 tons of electrolytic zinc, as well as gold, cadmium, copper matte, and antimonial lead alloys—the annual turnout from rich Broken Hill mines.

As the closest port to Broken Hill, the precious metal is railed in and treated at the smeltery or exported internationally. Other products shipped from the port are large quantities of wheat and barley.

Obviously industry and shipping get top billing at Port Pirie, yet you'll also discover intriguing old buildings, excellent sports facilities, and a surprising variety of entertainment.

Sights

Port Pirie National Trust Museum, Old Ellen St., is comprised of the railway station, customs house, and police station. Displays include historical exhibits, a scale model of the smelters, railway and shipping exhibits, 10,000- to 20,000-year-old diprotodon bones, and a former shunting engine. Hours are Mon.-Sat. 10 a.m.-4 p.m., Sun. 1-4 p.m.

Historical home **Carn Brae,** 32 Florence St. (tel. 086-32-1314), belonged to the pioneering Moyles, soft-drink moguls. Aside from fine architecture, collections include turn-of-the-century furnishings, paintings, glassware, and porcelain, as well as more than 2,500 antique and contemporary dolls. Hours are daily 10 a.m.-4 p.m.

Fishermen's Jetty, with fishing and boat-launching ramps, is either busy or tranquil, depending on the tide. **Solomontown Jetty** provides a safe swimming beach, children's playground along the reserve, and sunbathing area. **Port Davis,** 15 km south of Port

Pirie, off Port Broughton Rd., has both jetty fishing and a boat launch.

Accommodations And Food

Rooms are inexpensive at **International Hotel Motel,** 40 Ellen St. (tel. 086-32-2422). Moderately priced **Flinders Range Motor Inn,** 151 Main Rd. (tel. 32-3555), offers videos, room service, beer garden, swimming pool, tennis court, and a Saturday night dinner dance. **John Pirie Motor Inn,** Main Rd. (tel. 32-4200), features a swimming pool and room service, with moderate to expensive rates. Both **Port Pirie Caravan Park,** Beach Rd. (tel. 32-4275), and **Range View Caravan Park,** Highway One (tel. 34-4221), have campsites and on-site vans.

Hungry? Hope you like Chinese food and fish 'n' chips!

Entertainment And Events

Northern Festival Centre, at Memorial Park, is patterned after the Adelaide Centre. Theater, films, exhibitions, and performances by both visiting and local entertainers are scheduled regularly.

The annual **South Australia Country Music Awards** are held in Port Pirie for four days in October. Aside from the actual award presentations, frivolities include a horse and cart street parade, fair booths, and a talent contest.

Information

Local details are provided by **Port Pirie Information and Tourism Centre,** Jubilee Place (tel. 086-32-3332). Hours are Mon.-Fri. 9 a.m.-4 p.m., Sat.-Sun. 10 a.m.-4 p.m.

ALONG HIGHWAY ONE

Up Highway One, beyond Gawler, the coastal road passes picturesque parklands, old copper ports, salty lakes, and sculptural rock formations.

Balaklava

A short 26-km detour east from Port Wakefield, Balaklava (pop. 1,365) was once a rest stop for bullock teams hauling copper ore from Burra to Port Wakefield. Nearby **Rocks Reserve,** with interesting rock formations, is a good picnic spot.

Port Wakefield

Port Wakefield, top of the Gulf St. Vincent, is a one-time copper and wool port with a lovely old wharf. Go bush at **Clinton Conservation Park,** just north of town. Back on Highway One and another 30 km north is **Bumbunga Lake,** a huge salt pan covering 3,530 acres. The lake changes color according to the weather—it's good weather if it's blue and unsettled when it's pink. You can tour the processing plant. The scenic drive along Lochiel-Ninnes Road affords a superb view of the inland lakes and countryside.

Snowtown

This primo sheep- and cattle-breeding township, 49 km north of Port Wakefield, was established in the 1840s by early settlers seeking greener pastures. These days Snowtown provides services for surrounding rural communities.

See what's left of **Burunga Gap Township,** 10 km west of Snowtown, established in 1873.

Crystal Brook

Scenic Crystal Brook (pop. 1,300), 52 km north of Snowtown, was declared a township in 1873, though it was named in 1839 by early explorer Edward John Eyre. It's a lovely town with tall river gums, picnic parks, water ponds and, of course, the crystal brook, which runs from the lower Flinders Ranges to the River Broughton.

Bowman Park, five km east of Crystal Brook, is a peaceful parkland for picnics and play, as well as a Mid North point for the Heysen Trail. The Native Fauna Zone houses crocodiles, koalas, kangaroos, waterfowl, goannas, pythons, eagles, and other critters. Hours are Mon.-Fri. 1:30 p.m.-3:30 p.m., Sat. 1-3:30 p.m., Sun. and public holidays 11 a.m.-4 p.m. For information, phone (086) 36-2116.

Make camp at either **Crystal Brook Caravan Park** (tel. 36- 2649), or the 22-bed lodge and tent sites for Heysen Trail trekkers (contact park manager at 36-2116).

TRANSPORT

Contact the **Country Passenger Depot** in Adelaide for coaches to Kapunda, Burra, Peterborough, and Port Pirie. For information, phone (08) 233-2722.

The major transcontinental rail lines stop at Port Pirie and Peterborough on journeys between Adelaide and Perth, Alice Springs and Sydney. For information, phone (08) 217-4455.

Or *walk!* **The Heysen Trail** passes from Tanunda (in the Barossa), through Burra, Mt. Bryan, Spalding, and Crystal Brook, in the Mid North.

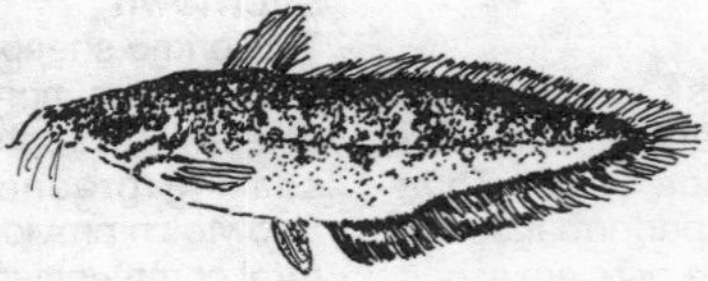

YORKE PENINSULA

Rich fields of golden wheat and barley, moody beaches and sandy coves, wildlife peeking from the bush, fluttering birds, cotton-puff skies, sparkling blue seas, spring wildflower blankets, and Cornish mining settlements, combined with close proximity to Adelaide, make the Yorke Peninsula an attractive holiday getaway. (Either that or travelers miss it altogether, ending up on the Eyre Highway and headed for Western Australia, having lost the whole Yorke with one blink!)

Set between Spencer Gulf and the Gulf St. Vincent, most of the peninsula's parks, beaches, and towns are not more than a two- or three-hour drive from Adelaide. The two sealed highways follow the east coast and midsection of the peninsula, converge at Warooka, and end at Stenhouse Bay in Innes National Park (right near the park headquarters). Gravel roads and dirt tracks spur off from the main highways, leading to hideaway beaches, rural communities, and patchwork farmlands. Yet, even on the inland route, you're never more than 25 km from the coast, with beaches to please anglers, divers, surfers, and sunners. So, if you're seeking a destination that lacks in the typical tourist trappings, is user-friendly rather than hard-sell, the Yorke offers a laid-back environment where you can set your own sights. The fishing is good year-round, but it's the spring months (Sept.-Nov.)—when the wildflowers serve up a visual feast of daisies, wattles, orchids, and red flame bush —that are exceptional.

Detour off Highway One, north of Port Wakefield (about 100 km from Adelaide), along the eastern coast, through the ports of Ardrossan and Edithburgh, down to Innes National Park, where the emus and kangaroos play. Take the scenic drive around Corny Point, meet the sealed highway at Warooka, pass through the "inland" communities of Minlaton and Maitland, up to the historic Copper Triangle towns of Moonta, Kadina, and Wallaroo, to Port Broughton, the seaside resort at the Yorke's northern tip.

History

Captain Matthew Flinders first sighted the Yorke Peninsula in 1802, the year he was exploring South Australia's coastline. Sheep farmers, looking for greener pastures for their stock, settled the region in the 1830s, but it was the 1859 discovery of copper at Kadina that made the Yorke prosper, *plus* provided a much-needed boost to South Australia's precarious economy. By 1861, extensive deposits were uncovered at Wallaroo and Moonta, and the copper rush was on. Cornish (and some Welsh) miners flocked to the Yorke, bringing their picks and shovels and leaving behind their heritage and pasties. Thus, the Copper Triangle towns of Kadina, Wallaroo, and Moonta also became known as "Little Cornwall." A bienniel festival pays tribute to the area's rich Cornish heritage.

The Yorke's copper mines operated up until the 1920s, when declining prices, combined with increased labor expenses and international competition, prompted closure (Poona Mine, at Moonta, reopened in 1988). Mines closed or not, the Yorke was hardly dried up. The flat plains of Australia's granary are considered one of the world's richest wheat and barley regions.

THE COPPER TRIANGLE

The historic Cornish townships of Kadina, Wallaroo, and Moonta are easily reached via the Kadina turnoff from Highway One, three km north of Port Wakefield. Otherwise, if you're exploring the entire Yorke Peninsula, you'll catch these towns on your way up the west coast. Most of the artsy-craftsy galleries are in this "tri-city" area, so if you're dying for a locally painted landscape, you'll probably find it here.

Kadina

This is the Yorke Peninsula's largest town. As one-time center of the copper action, Kadina

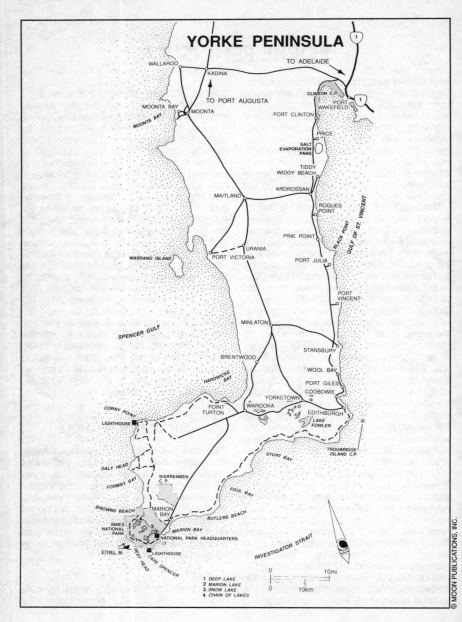

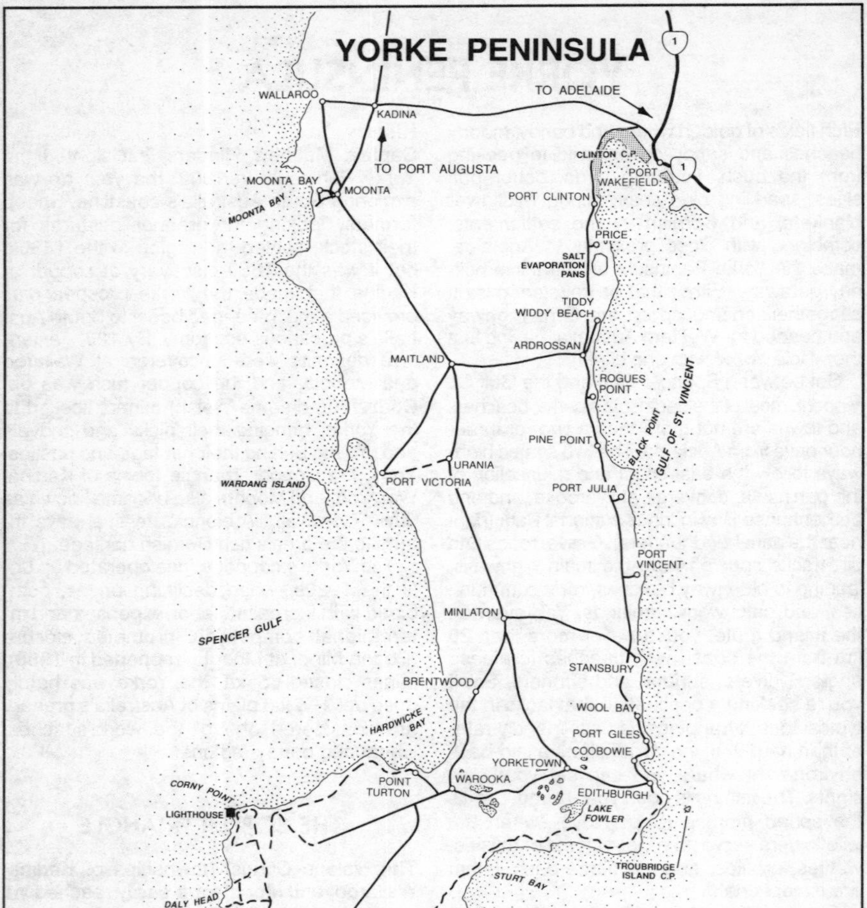
YORKE PENINSULA
1
TO ADELAIDE
WALLAROO
KADINA
TO PORT AUGUSTA
CLINTON C.P.
PORT WAKEFIELD
1
MOONTA BAY
MOONTA
MOONTA BAY
PORT CLINTON
PRICE
SALT EVAPORATION PANS
TIDDY WIDDY BEACH
ARDROSSAN
MAITLAND
ROGUES POINT
BLACK POINT
GULF OF ST. VINCENT
PINE POINT
URANIA
PORT VICTORIA
WARDANG ISLAND
PORT JULIA
PORT VINCENT
MINLATON
SPENCER GULF
STANSBURY
BRENTWOOD
WOOL BAY
HARDWICKE BAY
PORT GILES
COOBOWIE
YORKETOWN
POINT TURTON
WAROOKA
EDITHBURGH
CORNY POINT
LIGHTHOUSE
LAKE FOWLER
TROUBRIDGE ISLAND C.P.
STURT BAY
DALY HEAD
WARRENBEN C.P.
FORMBY BAY
FOUL BAY
BROWNS BEACH
MARION BAY
BUTLERS BEACH
INNES NATIONAL PARK
MARION BAY
NATIONAL PARK HEADQUARTERS
ETHEL M.
REEF HEAD
LIGHTHOUSE
CAPE SPENCER
INVESTIGATOR STRAIT
1 DEEP LAKE
2 MARION LAKE
3 SNOW LAKE
4 CHAIN OF LAKES
0
10mi
0
10km

(pop. 3,260) has a distinctively Cornish atmosphere, reflected in many of the old buildings.

Matta House Museum, 1½ km south of Kadina, off Moonta Rd., contains many relics and exhibits pertaining to the good old Matta Matta mining days, housed in the former mine manager's home. Hours are Wed., Sat., Sun., and holidays 2-5 p.m.

The **Banking and Currency Museum,** 3 Graves St. (tel. 088-21-2906), displays every type of Australian currency every issued, as well as other banking exhibits. The museum also buys and sells coins, notes, and medals. Hours are Fri.-Wed. 10-5; closed Good Friday, Christmas Day, and the month of June.

A heritage drive leads to **Wallaroo Mines,** one km west of Kadina, on Wallaroo Road. Signposts lead you on a walking tour of the old site, where you'll see ruins of the two-story-high engine building, and visit places named Jericho and Jerusalem.

Wombat Hotel, 19 Taylor St. (tel. 21-1108), has inexpensive pub-style accommodations. **Kadina Village Motel,** 28 Port Rd. (tel. 21-1920), has slightly higher rates, but includes breakfast. **Kadina Caravan and Camping Park,** Lindsay Terrace (tel. 21-2259), is close to all facilities.

Food? This is Cornish pasty country—they'll stick to your ribs but won't shrink your pocketbook. Buy 'em anywhere! Try **Cross's Cornish Bakeshop,** 20 Graves St., or **Wallis's Kadina Bakery,** 42 Graves Street. **Dynasty Room,** 4 Goyder St. (tel. 21-2829), offers Chinese, Thai, and Australian cuisine at moderate prices.

The Banking and Currency Museum is also the local tourist information center. In emergencies, contact **police** (tel. 21-1200), **ambulance** (tel. 21-1029), the local hospital (tel. 21-1544), or **Royal Automobile Association** (tel. 21-1111).

Wallaroo

Wheat and barley are shipped from this busy port (pop. 2,225), but it still doesn't equal the millions of tons of copper ore once trafficked over the jetty to destinations overseas.

Situated 10 km west of Kadina, Wallaroo was originally settled by the Welsh. The **Welsh Chimney Stack,** a Wallaroo landmark, contains 300,000 bricks in its huge square structure. (Did you know that for some reason Welsh masons built square stacks and the Cornish masons made theirs round?)

See an extensive pictorial display of sailing ships, exhibits related to the smelting industry, and postal and sporting relics at **Wallaroo Nautical Museum,** Jetty Rd., in the old post office (tel. 088-23-2366). Hours are Wed., Sat., Sun., public and school holidays 2-4 p.m. Other heritage buildings include **Harvey's Pumping Station,** the **Institute, General Store,** old **Methodist Church,** and original **Wesleyan Chapel.**

There's safe swimming at Wallaroo's sandy beaches, as well as excellent boating and jetty angling.

Wallaroo Hotel, 26 Alexander St. (tel. 23-2444), is pretty basic, but rooms are only about $21 double. **Sonbern Lodge Motel,** 18 John Terrace (tel. 23-2291), has inexpensive heritage accommodations, with rooms in the motel section costing $20 more. Campsites and on-site vans are available at both **Wallaroo North Beach Caravan Park,** North Beach (tel. 23-2531), and **Office Beach Holiday Flats and Caravan Park,** Office Beach (tel. 23-2722).

Dine on moderately priced local seafood at **The Seafood Corner,** corner Charles Terrace and Irwin St. (tel. 23-2288). For takeaway fresh and smoked fish, crayfish, and

THE CORNISH PASTY

The pasty was a traditional meal for the miners. Sometimes meat and veggies were placed at one end, fruit at the other. In all cases, there was crimping along the top. The crimping acted as a handle, so the men—hands filthy from work—could eat their meal and toss away the "handle." These days the crimped edge is devoured along with the contents.

The Original Cornish Pasty Recipe:
Pasty rolled out like a plate, filled with turmut, tates an' mait. Doubled up an' baked like fate. Tha's a Pasty.

prawns, try **G & KF Studt,** 35 Owen Terrace (tel. 23-3222).

Moonta

The third point in the Copper Triangle, Moonta (pop. 2,200) lies 10 km south of Wallaroo. Moonta is the nicest of the three mining towns—maybe because it was the richest. The dignified architecture, from tiny miners' cottages to the Gothic-esque Uniting Church, is a splendid reminder of times past.

After you've explored around town, head for the nearby mine site to investigate the old buildings and relics. The former schoolhouse, now **Moonta Mines Museum,** is a living history exhibit where you can experience what conditions were like for the miners, many of whom worked the 767-meter-deep Taylor Shaft. The museum will provide a self-guiding map. **Miner's Cottage,** adjacent to the museum, is a restored Cornish dwelling, open for public viewing. On weekends you can ride a narrow-gauge tourist railway around the mines complex. Hours are Wed., Sat.-Sun. 2-4 p.m., public and school holidays 11 a.m.-4 p.m.

Both the **Royal Hotel,** 2 Ryan St. (tel. 25-2108), and the **Cornwall Hotel,** 20 Ryan St. (tel. 25-2304), have inexpensive pub accommodations.

For your Cornish pasty fix, go to **Wither's Moonta Bakery,** 8 George St., or **The Cornish Kitchen,** 14 Ellen St. (tel. 25-3030). The historic **Cornwall Hotel,** serves home-style Australian meals, and the **Shaft Steak House,** Ellen St. (tel. 25-2981), specializes, obviously, in slabs of beef.

Events

Kerneweck Lowender, held in May of every odd-numbered year, is a festival commemorating the Copper Triangle's Cornish heritage. Activities include "A Golya" (Cornish feast with dancing and drinking), "A Fer Tref" (all the fun of a village green fair), "A Fer Kernewek" (a Cornish fair with traditional sports and the crowning of "Cousin Jack" and "Cousin Jenny"), and the Gorseth ceremony (a gathering of bands from Cornwall and Australia). Aside from Cornish pasties, revelers can sip on Swanky, a specially brewed ale.

THE EAST COAST

A sealed thoroughfare follows the coast to Edithburgh, where you either cut inland to Yorketown, Warooka, and Innes National Park, or continue along the coast on mix-or-match gravel and dirt roads.

Port Clinton To Ardrossan

Port Clinton, the east coast's northernmost seaside resort, has good crabbing beaches, and is a seashell's throw from Clinton Conservation Park. **Port Clinton Caravan Park,** on the Foreshore (tel. 088-37-7003), has campsites and on-site vans.

Tiddy Widdy Beach is a good spot for sunning and swimming, while **Price Beach** is located near a large salt refinery, harvesting from a vast area of pans pumped full of Gulf St. Vincent sea water.

Ardrossan, about 150 km from Adelaide, is not just the largest east coast port, with bulk grain-handling facilities; it's also home of the stump-jump plough. This particular tool, invented by Clarence Smith in 1876, enabled mallee scrubland to be turned into golden wheatfields all across the country. The folks over at the **Ardrossan Pioneer Museum,** on Fifth St., will be delighted to fill you in on more of the town's history. You can catch a scenic view of Gulf St. Vincent from the **BHP lookout,** or catch yourself some crabs from the jetty.

Royal House Hotel Motel, 1 Fifth St. (tel. 37-3007), charges inexpensive rates in the hotel, $20 more for motel rooms. **Adrossan Caravan Park,** Park Terrace (tel. 37-3262), offers campsites and on-site vans.

For emergencies, contact **police** (tel. 37-3017), **ambulance** (tel. 37-3295), or the local **hospital** (tel. 37-3021).

TO EDITHBURGH AND BEYOND

Continuing south, along the coast, you'll pass the fishing "villagettes" of **Rogues Point, Pine Point, Black Point,** and **Port**

Julia. Divers will want to check out the shipwrecked *Zanoni,* about 15 km southeast of Ardrossan.

Port Vincent, set on a sweeping bay 46 km south of Ardrossan, is an old ketch-landing place, and a popular swimming, yachting, and water-skiing resort. The **Vacationer,** corner Parsons Rd. and Kemp St. (tel. 088-53-7057), offers inexpensive holiday flats. **Port Vincent Seaside Flats and Caravan Park,** Minlacowie Rd. (tel. 53-7011), rents inexpensive flats as well as campsites and on-site vans.

Stansbury, 16 km away, is another sought-after holiday resort. Originally known as "Oyster Bay," it still offers some of the state's best oyster beds. Jetty fishing is also excellent here, and you'll find a decent selection of tourist facilities.

Stansbury Villas, Adelaide Rd. (tel. 52-4282), are inexpensive self-contained holiday flats. **Stansbury Holiday Motel,** Adelaide Rd. (tel. 52-4455), is on the deluxe side with moderate to expensive rates (every room has a sea view). Campsites and on-site vans are available at **Stansbury Caravan Park,** Foreshore Park (tel. 52-4171).

Past **Wool Bay, Port Giles,** and **Coobowie** lies picturesque **Edithburgh.** A former salt-producing township (and the first proclaimed settlement on southern Yorke Peninsula), Edithburgh is celebrated by divers, drawn to the many shipwrecks along its coastline. If you take the scenic drive up to **Troubridge Hill,** you'll be able to see part of the shipwreck *Clan Ronald.*

Swimmers will find a rock pool set into a small cove, while the jetty provides ideal conditions for anglers. The small **Edithburgh Museum** features maritime displays and artifacts.

Take a guided day-tour over to **Troubridge Island,** to view fairy penguins and other birds contained within the 14-hectare conservation park.

Motel accommodations in town are moderately priced. If you plan to stay awhile, you can get a self-contained unit for $110-195 per week, at **Ocean View Holiday Flats,** O'Halloran Parade (tel. 52-6029). **Edithburgh House,** Edith St. (tel. 52-6373), offers old-fashioned seaside guesthouse rooms for high-moderate to expensive rates, but they include dinner and breakfast. **Edithburgh Caravan Park,** corner South Terrace and O'Halloran Parade (tel. 52-6056), is situated on the Foreshore.

For **Troubridge Island Tours,** contact Chris Johnson, Blanche St., Edinburgh 5583 (tel. 52-6290).

Venture inland 16 km to **Yorketown,** one of the peninsula's earliest pastoral settlements. Surrounded by salt lakes where crystal formations decorate the shores, several of the lakes are pink and worth watching at sunset through rose-colored glasses. There's inexpensive accommodations at **Melville Hotel Motel,** 1 Minlaton Rd. (tel. 52-1019), or at **Yorke Hotel,** 1 Warooka Rd. (tel. 52-1221), but neither place is really comfy. Camping and on-site vans are available at **Yorketown Caravan Park,** Memorial Dr. (tel. 52-1563).

Beyond Edithburgh, the coast road turns to gravel (and occasionally to dirt) as it travels a sparsely populated route along scenic beaches and secluded bays, merging with the sealed highway about 10 km north of Innes National Park.

Hillocks Drive, 16 km east of Marion Bay, is a scenic road leading to **Butlers Beach,** set on a seven-km sea frontage. Privately run (by the Butler family), the property has two surf beaches, a number of fishing spots, camping facilities, and a small general store. The property is closed mid-June through mid-August. For information, phone (088) 54-4002.

INNES NATIONAL PARK

The main entrance to Innes National Park is four km southwest of Marion Bay. Situated at the southernmost tip of the Yorke Peninsula, this spectacular coastal park's 9,141 hectares stretch from Stenhouse Bay on the east coast, around Cape Spencer, to Browns Beach on the west coast. Just a three-hour drive from Adelaide, the park is a favorite with city dwellers who come to surf, fish, dive, and bushwalk.

The Yorke Peninsula offers secluded beaches and secret fishing holes.

Big sightseeing attractions are the shipwreck *Ethel M,* run aground in 1904 and now disintegrating near an isolated cove called The Gap, and the old ghost town at **Inneston** (follow the historical markers past the Cape Spencer turnoff).

Clean beaches, crystal-clear water, and colorful marinelife create a delightful environment for aquatic activities. There's good fishing at Chinaman's Beach, Salmon Hole, Pondalowie Bay, Browns Beach (terrific for year-round salmon), Little Browns Beach, Cape Spencer, and a host of rock fishing spots between Pondalowie and Stenhouse bays (be careful of those wet rocks!).

Bushwalkers can choose from a variety of tracks leading through such diverse terrain as low scrub, salt lake flats, coastal dunes, and rugged cliffs—with a good probability of running into a friendly emu or kangaroo!

Camping is permitted within the park, at several different areas. The main camping area is at Pondalowie Bay, where facilities were recently upgraded.

During Christmas holidays, park rangers conduct guided activities for children and young adults.

For camping permits and other information, contact **Park Headquarters,** Stenhouse Bay (tel. 54-4040), or the **Warooka District Council Office,** Warooka (tel. 54-5055).

UP THE PENINSULA

Going northward from Innes National Park, the sealed road brushes by **Warrenben Conservation Park,** 4,061 hectares of dense mallee, dryland tea tree vegetation, and native pines. The gravel road from Marion Bay sort of winds around the coast, with other gravel or dirt paths branching out to the beaches. **Daly Head** is yet another special fishing hole, as is **Corny Point,** at the northwestern tip. Corny Point also has a lighthouse and camping facilities.

At Point Turton, you can either continue zigzagging the beachy back roads to the top of the peninsula, or turn onto the seven-km sealed stretch that leads back to the main highway at Warooka.

In the tiny township of **Brentwood,** 17 km north of Warooka, visit **Brentwood Pottery** (tel. 088-53-4255) in the old general store/post office. Rent a **gypsy wagon,** pulled by a gentle Clydesdale, for overnight camping by the sea or for a longer and leisurely ride around southern Yorke Peninsula. Rates run about $100 per day, with a three-day minimum. For information, contact Stansbury Holiday Motel (tel. 088-52-4455), or Anthony Honner, Brentwood via Minlaton, SA 5575 (tel. 088-53-4201). The same people also arrange farm holidays in self-contained stone cottages.

Minlaton (pop. 815), about 14 km north of Yorketown, is referred to as the "Barley Capital of the World." It's also the home of Captain Harry Butler's "Red Devil," a 1916 monoplane flown by the pioneering aviator during World War I. Ostensibly, this is the world's only remaining Bristol fighter plane, and lucky you can see it at the glass-fronted **Harry Butler Hangar/Museum,** near the town center. Nearby, on Main St., the **National Trust Museum** exhibits photos, memorabilia, and farming implements, and, at the corner of Bluff and Maitland roads, **Jolly's Museum** features restored tractors and other machinery. **Gum Flat Homestead Gallery,** Stansbury Rd., two km east of Minlaton, is an arts and crafts center with locally made wares for sale. Rooms are inexpensive at **Minlaton Hotel Motel,** 26 Main Rd. (tel. 088-53-2014).

For Minlaton emergencies, contact **police** (tel. 088-53-2100), **ambulance** or local hospital (tel. 088-53-2200), and **Royal Automobile Association** (tel. 088-53-2243).

Turn off at Urania, for **Port Victoria,** "last of the windjammer ports," and now a busy little fishing resort. Sailing and water-skiing are popular around Wardang Island. See relics and curios of the nautical past at **Port Victoria Maritime Museum. Bayview Holiday Flats,** 29 Davies Terrace (tel. 088-34-2082), are fully self-contained units at inexpensive to moderate rates, depending on season. **Port Vincent Caravan Park** (tel. 088-53-7073), has campsites and on-site vans.

Maitland, the heart of Yorke Peninsula, is Colonel Light's vision at work again—a modern agricultural center, well laid out and surrounded by parklands. View agricultural artifacts and brush up on local history at **Maitland Museum,** corner Gardiner and Kikerran streets. **Maitland Hotel,** 33 Robert St. (tel. 088-32-2431), "where the beer is cold and the welcome warm," has inexpensive rooms. The pub serves good, home-cooked meals. **Eothen Farmhouse** (tel. 088-36-3210), near beaches and bush, is a fully equipped separate home, with kitchen, lounge, open fires. Moderate rates include continental breakfast.

Emergency numbers for Maitland are **police** (tel. 088-32-2621), **ambulance,** and local **hospital** (tel. 088-32-2626).

A 20-km jog westward from Maitland brings you to **Balgowan,** a century-old landing place for ketches making pick-ups and deliveries for local farmers. Today it serves as a serene retreat for fishermen.

Back on the main highway, it's a 35-km drive to Moonta, lower edge of the Copper Triangle, then about 60 km more through Kadina to **Port Broughton,** a seaside resort at the tippy-top of the peninsula. There's a safe swimming beach for children, a good fishing jetty for anglers. Spend the night at **Port Broughton Hotel,** on the Foreshore (tel. 086-35-2004). Built in 1888, this family-style establishment has inexpensive rooms, with breakfast included. Other facilities include a main bar, saloon bar, beer garden, large dining room, à la carte dining room, and bottle shop.

Port Broughton Charter Boats, 19 Harvey St. (tel. 086-35-2466), offers fishing trips ($22-60) or pleasure cruises ($6, for one hour) in the Spencer Gulf.

For Port Broughton emergencies, contact **police** (tel. 086-35-2255), **ambulance** (tel. 086-35-2544), the local **hospital** (tel. 086-35-2282), or **Royal Automobile Association** (tel. 086-35-2522).

INFORMATION

For more information on the Yorke Peninsula, contact **Yorke Peninsula Tourist Information Centre,** Victoria Square, Kadina 5554 (tel. 088-21-2093), or any South Australian Government Travel Centre.

TRANSPORT

Premier Coachlines (tel. 08-217-0777) operates daily service from Adelaide to Kadina, Wallaroo, Moonta, Port Hughes, and Moonta Bay. One-way fare for the three-hour trip to Moonta is $17.

Yorke Peninsula Bus Service (tel. 08-212-7999) travels daily from Adelaide to Ardrossan ($14), Port Vincent ($17), Edithburgh ($18), and Yorketown ($18).

All coaches depart Adelaide's **Country Passenger Depot,** 101 Franklin St. (tel. 08-231-5959).

There is no public transport south of Warooka and, if you're hitching, road traffic is pretty minimal.

EYRE PENINSULA

Wild coastlines with stupendous surf and isolated beaches, round-the-clock steel mills and busy grain terminals, phenomenal rock formations and ancient ranges, gentle sea lion colonies and great white shark breeding grounds are some of the Eyre Peninsula attractions that keep travelers coming (and going).

The peninsula is *wide,* stretching 469 km from Port Augusta in the east, across the Eyre Highway, past the Gawler Ranges, to Ceduna, last ample outpost before the Nullarbor Plain. Alternate Route 1 (called Lincoln Highway from Port Augusta to Port Lincoln, and Flinders Highway from Port Lincoln to Ceduna) traverses the peninsula, hugging the coast—and its bays, beaches, ports, and parks—along sheltered Spencer Gulf on the east, round the pounding Southern Ocean and the Great Australian Bight. The distance from Port Augusta back up to Ceduna is 668 km. Another option which enables you to see a sizeable chunk of this region is to follow the Eyre Highway, take a journey into the Gawler Ranges to the north, explore famed Mt. Wudinna Rock, cut through the center of the peninsula along the Tod Highway (258 km of sheep and cereal scenery), down to Port Lincoln and the adjacent national parks and offshore islands. Depending on which way you're headed, you can then follow the east coast up to Whyalla (and back to Adelaide or onward to the Northern Territory), or take the west side—skirt round the sea lion colony, through Streaky Bay to Ceduna, and the great *beyond.*

History

By now you've surely guessed that super-sailor Captain Matthew Flinders charted the Eyre Peninsula during his 1802 mega-voyage aboard the *Investigator.* He was not using his own charts, however, but those of Dutch explorer Pieter Nuyts who, in 1627, sailed his *Gulden Zeepaard* ("Golden Seahorse") as far as Streaky Bay. Nuyts, more inclined toward trade than homesteading, turned back when he got to the offshore islands now named Nuyts Archipelago.

By the time Flinders arrived, Abel Tasman and Captain Cook had already been there, Tasman circling the country and Cook glimpsing the peninsula's east coast. Flinders did a more thorough examination of the coastline, naming the majority of features after crew and family members, as well as locales around his hometown of Lincolnshire. The peninsula itself was named by Governor Gawler for Edward John Eyre, the explorer who in 1839-40 made a series of frustrating, obstacle-fraught overland expeditions, culminating in the first east-west crossing of Australia.

Bountiful golden grain harvests, iron ore deposits, a thriving steel industry, as well as an ocean bounty that makes this one of the country's largest commercial fisheries, are the region's money-makers. Port Lincoln and Thevenard, the two biggest seaports—both with road and railway connections—ship a steady flow of cargo worldwide.

Apropos of fish, the white pointer shark breeds around Dangerous Reef, off Port Lincoln's shores, and the underwater scenes in *Jaws* were filmed here.

PORT AUGUSTA

At the head of the Spencer Gulf, bustling Port Augusta (pop. 15,300) is the town at which Highway 1, the Eyre Highway (actually Highway 1 with a change of name and direction), and the Stuart Highway all converge. From this crossroad, travelers scurry and scamper north to the Flinders Ranges, south to Adelaide, east to Sydney, and west across the Nullarbor, or slightly southwest to the Lincoln Highway and the Eyre Peninsula coast. Besides that, it's on the main railway line used by the *Ghan, Trans Australian,* and *Indian Pacific.*

Established in 1852, Port Augusta, served as a wool port for nearly a century. Today its major functions are transporting goods to and from the isolated Outback and generating electricity for much of South Australia.

Sights

Wadlata Outback Centre, 41 Flinders Terrace (tel. 086-42-4511), features displays, videos, and models depicting Aboriginal Dreamtime (including a big fiberglass serpent storyteller). Other exhibits highlight the early explorers and the history of electricity and communications. Open daily.

Homestead Park Pioneer Museum, Elsie St. (tel. 42-2035), displays pioneer artifacts and machinery. Hours are daily 10 a.m.-4 p.m.

Australian National Workshops, south end of Carlton Parade (tel. 42-2611), allows you to view rail carriages as they're worked on. Tours are available Tues. and Thurs. 2 p.m. Be sure to wear closed footwear.

ETSA (Electricity Trust of South Australia) Northern Power Station, (tel. 42-0521), conducts one-hour behind-the-scenes tours of its new $500 million plant Mon.-Fri. 10 a.m. and 2 p.m. Turn off Highway 1 at Andy's Truck Stop, 2½ km east of Port Augusta.

Royal Flying Doctor Service, 4 Vincent St. (tel. 42-2044), provides medical care to Outback residents. The center is open for inspection Mon.-Fri. 10-11 a.m. and 2-3 p.m.

School of the Air (tel. 42-2695) offers educational programs to children residing in the Outback. Facilities are located at Central Primary School, southern end of Commercial Rd., and tours are conducted Mon.-Fri. 10 a.m., except holidays.

Accommodations And Food

Augusta Hotel, 1 Loudon Rd. (tel. 086-42-2701), has inexpensive pub rooms. **Myoora Motel,** 5 Hackett St. (tel. 42-3622), and **Port Augusta East Motel,** Highway 1 (tel. 42-2555), both offer comfy rooms at moderate rates. Also moderately priced is centrally located **Flinders Hotel Motel,** 39 Commercial Rd. (tel. 42-2544), with all the mod cons, family units, and good home cookin'.

Shoreline Caravan Park, Gardiner Ave. (tel. 42-2965), situated on the gulf, and **Fauna Caravan Park,** corner Highway 1 and Stokes Terrace (tel. 42-2974), set amidst peacocks and other birds, both rent campsites and on-site vans.

Eat at the pubs, where you'll probably catch a live band or dee-jay disco on weekends. **Ozzie's Coffee Lounge,** 22 Commercial Rd. (tel. 42-4028), in the Port Augusta Mall, serves coffee, croissants, paté, quiches, and sandwiches. There's a branch of the **Barnacle Bill Fish 'n' Chippery** at 60 Victoria Parade (tel. 41-0000). For that 24-hour truckin' experience, stop at **Andy's Truckstop,** Highway 1 (tel. 41-0700), 2½ km east of Port Augusta, for home-style meals, showers, and a laundromat.

Information

Wadlata Outback Centre, 41 Flinders Terrace (tel. 086-42-4511), is also home to Port Augusta's tourist information center.

Getting Around

Butler's Outback Safaris, 3 Prosser St. (tel. 086-42-2188), is an established company (run by Malcolm Butler, who was born in the Outback) and a safe and comfortable way to explore the desolate region north of Port Augusta. Four- to seven-day adventures include transport in air-conditioned four-wheel-drive vehicles, all meals, accommodations, and other necessary equipment.

WHYALLA

A big-time shipbuilding port until 1978, Whyalla (pop. 26,900) survives today on its round-the-clock steel production and shipments of ore from nearby Iron Knob and Iron Baron. As South Australia's largest provincial city—with a sunny, Mediterranean-style climate—facilities are good, and "pass-through" tourism gives yet another economic boost.

Originally called Hummock Hill by Captain Flinders, the township developed around 1901, after iron ore was discovered at Iron Knob. Trammed from mine to town, the ore was then barged over to the Port Pirie smelters. The flourishing community was renamed in 1914.

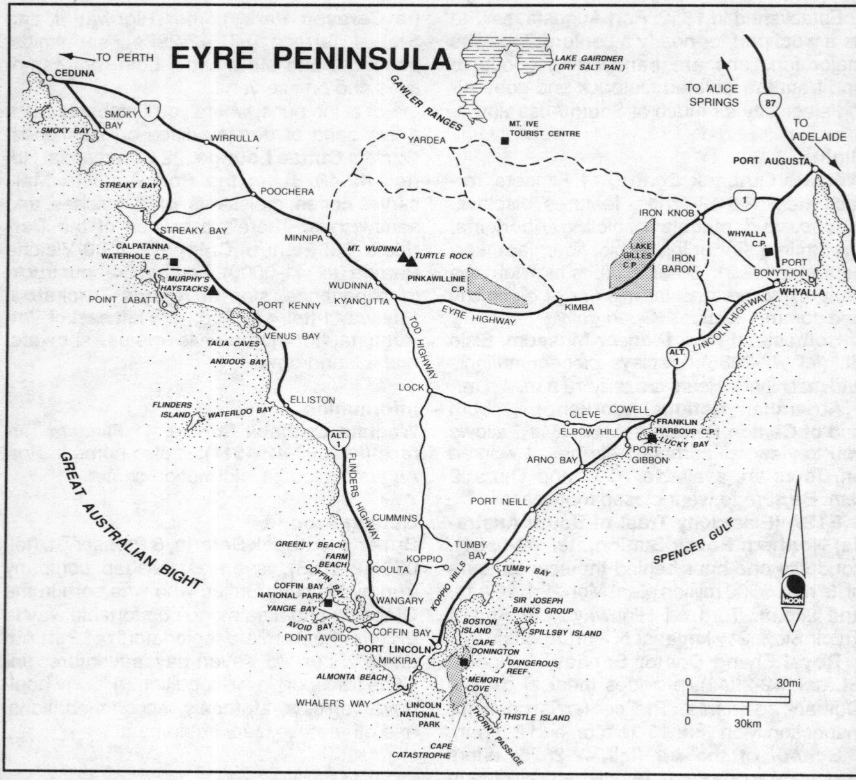

Whyalla had two major boom periods—the first in 1938 with the establishment of a blast furnace, and the second in 1958 when BHP Company (still the city's main employer) confirmed plans for building its completely integrated steelworks. In between was the creation of a deep-water port and successful shipyard, memorable days which still tug the hearts of the local old salts.

Sights

Whyalla Maritime Museum, Lincoln Hwy. (tel. 086-45-8900), is where you can climb aboard Australia's largest landlocked ship, the 650-ton corvette, *Whyalla* (aka HMA *Whyalla* and the *Rip*). Displays inside the Tanderra Building include shipping memorabilia, valuable BHP models, and one of the country's largest model railways. Hours are Wed.-Mon. 10 a.m.-4 p.m., closed Tuesday. Ship tours leave hourly 11 a.m.-3 p.m.

Mount Laura Homestead Museum, Eklom St., behind Westland Shopping Centre (tel. 45-9319), is the place to brush up on town history as well as view restored buildings and machinery. Hours are Sun., Mon., and Wed. 2-4 p.m., Fri. 10 a.m.-noon.

BHP Steelworks offers guided tours of their operations, including the blast furnace and steelmaking plant, coke ovens, railway line and one-km-long rolling mill. Tours last two hours or so and depart from Whyalla

Tourist Centre Mon., Wed., and Sat. 9:30 a.m. Be sure to wear closed footwear. For information and bookings, phone 45-7900.

Hummock Hill Lookout, site of a World War II gun battery, affords a dynamite view of Whyalla, the Foreshore, upper Spencer Gulf, Port Bonython, Point Lowly, and the Middleback Ranges. Follow the brown and white "Route 61" (Whyalla Tourist Drive) signs.

Whyalla Fauna and Reptile Park, Lincoln Hwy., across from the airport (tel. 45-7044), features koalas, wombats, dingoes, roos, emus, deadly snakes, and a walk-through aviary in natural bushland. Hours are daily 10 a.m.-6 p.m. (Nov.-April), 10 a.m.-4:30 p.m. (other months).

Port Bonython, about 10 km north of Whyalla, off the Lincoln Hwy., is the site of the massive SANTOS plant which distills liquid hydrocarbons that have passed from Moomba through a 659-km underground pipeline. Though you can't tour the facility, you can get a view of operations from along the roadway or shore.

Port Lowly, two km beyond SANTOS, offers beautiful gulf views, a popular summer beach, and the 110-year-old Port Lowly Lighthouse that often looks out upon playful dolphins.

The **Scenic Coastal Drive** is a 20-km combination sealed-and-gravel road along Spencer Gulf, from Fitzgerald Bay to Point Douglas. Take the marked turnoff before Port Bonython.

The **Whyalla Foreshore** redevelopment provides excellent facilities for swimming, jetty fishing, windsurfing, and picnicking. **Whyalla Marina** has a new four-lane launching ramp for all boating activities.

Murrippi Beach, off Eight Mile Creek Rd., 12 km south of Whyalla, is a legal nude beach (no facilities).

Accommodations And Food

As with most cities this size, you'll find pubs, motels, restaurants, and takeaways—all pretty standard. Most accommodations have their own dining facilities.

Pub rooms are inexpensive at either **Hotel Whyalla,** 9 Darling Terrace (tel. 086-45-7411), or **Lord Gowrie Hotel,** Gowrie Ave. (tel. 45-8955). **Airport Whyalla Motel,** Lincoln Hwy. (tel. 45-2122) and **Sundowner Hotel Motel,** Lincoln Hwy. (tel. 45-7688), both offer comfortable rooms at low-moderate rates. Campsites and on-site vans are available at **Whyalla Foreshore Caravan Park,** Broadbent Terrace (tel. 45-7474).

Entertainment And Recreation

Middleback Theatre, corner Nicolson Ave. and Racecourse Rd. (tel. 086-45-8022), presents live theater, musical performances and other stage presentations, as well as arts and crafts exhibitions. You can inspect the theater foyer, its mural, and stained-glass windows, Mon.-Fri. 9-5.

Whyalla Recreation and Leisure Centre, off Racecourse Rd., near the junction of Nicolson Ave. (tel. 45-5488), welcomes visitors to use the heated indoor swimming pool, squash courts, gymnasium, weightlifting equipment, sweat track, volleyball and tennis courts. Equipment is available for rental.

Information

Whyalla Tourist Centre (tel. 086-45-7900), next to BHP Steelworks on Lincoln Hwy., provides maps, tour bookings, and info on the local bus service (weekdays and Sat. mornings). Hours are Mon.-Fri. 9-5, Sat. 9 a.m.-4 p.m., Sun. 10 a.m.-4 p.m.

TO PORT LINCOLN

From Whyalla, the Lincoln Highway makes a slight inland jag, traveling for a short distance along the iron ore-rich Middleback Ranges, angling back to the coast (in about 111 km) at Cowell.

Cowell

Set on scenic Franklin Harbour, a protected bay noted for calm waters and great fishing, Cowell (pop. 692) is also famous for its huge jade deposits. Discovered in the nearby Minbrie Ranges in 1965, the area is thought to be the world's largest producer of green and black jade, as well as some interesting marble uncovered along with the jade boulders.

popular Redbanks Beach, near Arno Bay

Several operators offer mine tours, or you can visit the factory and showroom of **Gemstone Corporation of Australia,** Second St. (tel. 086-29-2111).

Other attractions include the **Franklin Harbour Historical Museum,** in the old post office, and the **Agricultural Museum,** on Lincoln Highway. Wildlifers can arrange for inspection of **Cowell Area School Fauna Park,** or **Lionel Deer's Camel Farm** (tel. 29-2082), on the outskirts of town.

Lucky Bay, 16 km north of town, is a popular beach resort with safe swimming, good fishing, and a boat ramp. **Poverty Beach,** just south of town, has good surfing.

Rooms are inexpensive at both the **Commercial Hotel,** 24 Main St. (tel. 29-2181) and the **Franklin Harbour Hotel,** 1 Main St. (tel. 29-2015). **Shultz Farm,** Smith Rd. (tel. 29-2194), offers home-style accommodations overlooking the coast, for moderate rates that include breakfast. **Cowell Foreshore Caravan Park** (tel. 29- 2307) has campsites and on-site vans. Don't miss a taste of the delicious locally harvested oysters.

Obtain local **tourist information** at District Council of Franklin Harbour, 6 Main St. (tel. 29-2019).

Continuing Southward

From Cowell, you can cut inland 42 km to the rural community of Cleve. The scenic Cleve-Cowell Hills drive provides great views of the countryside and Spencer Gulf. From Cleve, you can cut southeast 25 km back to the coast at Arno Bay. Or stick to the coast road and pass along the wide, lovely beaches at **The Knob, Port Gibbon,** and **Point Price Sandhills.**

Arno Bay, halfway point between Whyalla and Port Lincoln, is a tranquil fishing village in winter and a tourist mecca in summer. **Redbanks,** six km north of town, is a designated geological monument of rock pools and just-as-rocky cliffs. **Arno Hotel** (tel. 086-28-0001), near the beach, has country-style room. Low-moderate rates include breakfast.

Port Neill, 33 km south from Arno Bay (and two km off the main highway), is another attractive, clean, safe water-sporting haven. Check out the blue water/rolling hill view from **Port Neill Lookout,** one km north of town. **Fauser's Museum,** opposite the caravan park (tel. 88-9041), is a private collection of steam and stationary engines, motorcycles, vintage autos, and other relics. **Port Neill Hotel,** Peake Terrace (tel. 88-9006), has inexpensive rooms. **Henley's Holiday Flats,** Wallis St. (tel. 88-9001), are fully self-contained units, also inexpensive. **Port Neill Caravan Park,** Peake Terrace (tel. 88-9067), rents campsites and on-site vans.

If you wait until low tide to visit **Lipson Cove,** another 20 km south, you can walk across to **Lipson Island,** a coastal bird sanctuary.

Tumby Bay shelters fishing and boating waters and is also service center for the surrounding rural townships. **C.L. Alexander National Trust Museum** features local memorabilia in an original wooden schoolhouse. Head to **Island Lookout** to catch a good view of town, bay, and the **Sir Joseph Banks Group of Islands,** 15 km offshore. Named by Capt. Flinders for the renowned English botanist, the islands are bird sanctuaries for Cape Barren geese, pied cormorants, eastern reef egrets, crested terns, and many other species. If you don't have your own boat, sign on for a half- or full-day tour with **Sea Jade Charter,** 2 Pfitzner St. (tel. 88-2424).

Seabreeze Hotel, Tumby Terrace (tel. 88-2311), rents inexpensive rooms. **Tumby Bay Motel,** Berryman Crescent (tel. 88-2311), near the beach, has a swimming pool and is moderately priced. Campsites and on-site vans are available at **Tumby Bay Caravan Park,** Tumby Terrace (tel. 88-2208).

If you don't think you can live without another display of vintage implements, machinery, and artifacts (or if you just want to explore the hill country between Tumby Bay and Port Lincoln), take the 40-km detour to Koppio and the **Koppio Smithy Museum.** Try to get there for the annual Open Day, when all the machinery is turned on and huffs, puffs, toots, and honks in unison. For information, phone 84-4243. Hours are Tues.-Sun. 10 a.m.-5 p.m.

Back on the coast, **North Shields,** just 11 km north of Port Lincoln, is home of the **Karlinda Collection,** an amazing amassment of more than 10,000 shells, rocks, minerals, fossils, and other marine curios. It's all housed in the building next to the post office. For information, phone (086) 84-3500. You can live cheaply and simply at the historic 1868 **Wheatsheaf Hotel,** Government Rd. (tel. 84-3531), where rates include continental breakfast. The Wheatsheaf serves counter meals in the pub, or à la carte in the dining room overlooking Boston Bay.

Heading into Port Lincoln, you will pass through Australia's newest winegrowing region (vines planted in 1984, first harvest in 1987), and the cellars of **Boston Bay Wines.** Specializing in red and white table wines, the vineyard is open Sat.-Sun. 2-5 p.m., or by appointment. For information, phone 84-3600.

PORT LINCOLN

At the Eyre Peninsula's southern edge, Port Lincoln (pop. 11,550) is often referred to as "blue water paradise." Paradise?—Not quite, but there *is* plenty of blue water! Boston Bay, stretching from Point Boston to the tip of Port Lincoln National Park, is three times larger than Sydney Harbour. Mild winters and comfortable summers, combined with ideal conditions for boating, fishing, skin diving, and windsurfing (and great white shark breeding!), keep the tourists coming.

Named by Capt. Flinders after his home county of Lincolnshire, Port Lincoln was originally set to be South Australia's state capital. A lack of fresh water, along with Colonel Light's decided bent towards Adelaide, caused that plan to be withdrawn. The city didn't fare badly, though. Aside from a healthy tourist industry, Port Lincoln is home to Australia's largest commercial tuna fishing fleet as well as one of the country's busiest grain terminals.

Sights

Axel Stenross Maritime Museum, Lincoln Highway near Shaen St. (tel. 086-82-3889), features memorabilia from windjammer days, as well as early photos, a working slipway, and blacksmith shop. Hours are Tues., Thurs., Sat.-Sun., and public holidays 1-5 p.m.

A short distance from the maritime museum is the **First Landing Site.** See the freshwater spring that lured the early settlers—it's still bubbling and gurgling through the sand.

Mill Cottage and **Settler's Cottage** museums, located on the grounds of Flinders Park (at Lincoln and Flinders highways), both display artifacts and historical exhibits of Port Lincoln's early beginnings. Hours for Mill Cottage are Tues.-Sun. 2-4:30 p.m., closed Mon., Wed., Fri. during winter. Contact Port Lincoln Library to arrange entrance to Settler's Cottage.

Nearby, **Rose-Wal Memorial Shell Museum,** on the grounds of the Old Folks' Home, displays a large and valuable collection of shells and sealife. Hours are daily 2-4:30 p.m.

Apex Wheelhouse, Hindmarsh St. (across from the caravan park), is a restored tuna boat wheelhouse and interpretive center. Photos, charts, and a color video will brief you on the fishing industry. Hours are daily 9-5.

You'll find excellent lookout points at: **Winter's Hill,** five km northeast of town on Flinders Highway; **Puckridge Park,** on Angas St.; and the **Old Mill,** Dorset Pl., an 1846 flour mill (historic both because it's old *and* because it never operated).

A popular day-trip is the cruise to **Boston Island,** a working sheep station, discovered and named by Capt. Flinders. Select either the Boston Island Safari (a trip to the island, sightseeing, and historical commentary), or Bay Island Cruise (usually run only if a landing on the island is not possible). Departures are from the jetty at Tasman Terrace. Tours are operated by **Investigator Cruises** and can be booked at the tourist office or Kirton Point Caravan Park.

More daring souls who'd rather eyeball sharks instead of sheep can journey to **Dangerous Reef,** "home of the great white shark" and locale for *Jaws*'s underwater scenes. You can take a diving charter (good luck) or the *Dangerous Reef Explorer,* a high-speed commuter vessel (travel time about 40 minutes). A new feature for those who left their diving gear at home is a 30- by 12-meter underwater viewing platform with observatory and aquarium (and a dive cage). A large sea lion colony also lives on the reef. For info and bookings, contact the tourist office.

Accommodations And Food

If you plan to stay in a pub, I'm still partial to the old Wheatsheaf in North Shields (see p. 171). Most of the motels are on Lincoln Highway or Tasman Terrace. **First Landing Motel,** 11 Shaen St. (tel. 086- 82-2919), near the maritime museum, has moderately priced rooms with four-poster beds. **Westward Ho Holiday Flats,** 112 London St. (tel. 82-2425), are fully self-contained units at low-moderate prices. You can rent an inexpensive cabin at **Kirton Point Caravan Park,** Hindmarsh St. (tel. 82-2537). And, if you've got the bucks ($620-750 per week, for up to 12 guests), you can rent all of Boston Island. Tariff includes a six-bedroom home, fishing dinghies, tractor and trailer. For information, phone Peter Davis (tel. 82-1741) or contact the South Australian Government Travel Centre.

Tasman Mall has the best cheap eats in town. Aside from that, look to the local pubs for meals and nightlife.

Information

Port Lincoln Tourist Office, Civic Centre, Tasman Terrace (tel. 086-82-6666), books tours and accommodations and provides info on bicycle rentals, boat charters, and local coach service. Hours are Mon.-Fri. 9 a.m.-5:30 p.m., Sat. 9 a.m.-noon, Sun. (during holidays) 10 a.m.-noon.

Events

Port Lincoln's big blowout is the annual **Tunarama Festival,** held each January. Festivities include parades, cavalcades, roving musicians, a variety of competitions, fireworks displays, rock concerts, dinner dances, and the crowning of Miss Tunarama.

TIP OF THE EYRE

The southernmost edge of the Eyre Peninsula stretches from Lincoln National Park, leaning on Spencer Gulf, to Coffin Bay National Park, jutting into the Great Australian Bight.

Lincoln National Park, 20 km south of Port Lincoln, covers 17,000 hectares with open spaces, rugged cliffs, and peaceful bays. Catch panoramic views of park and town from Stamford Hill. Conventional vehicles can access scenic spots like Surfleet Point, Spalding Cove, Old Donington House, Cape Donington Lighthouse, and Taylor's Landing, but you'll need a four-wheel-drive to reach wilderness areas like Memory Cove and Cape Catastrophe. Check with the park ranger (tel. 086-82-3936) for camping information and road conditions.

You'll need a key and permit ($10) to enter privately owned **Whaler's Way,** a dynamically scenic cliff-top drive at the very tip of the peninsula. Magnificent lookouts, blowholes, caves, sparkling beaches, and roaring surf—as well as a wildlife and bird sanctuary—are some of the features. Get yet another special permit to camp at the Redbanks area. On the road to Whaler's Way, you'll pass **Mikkira Station,** an 1840s sheep station. Pick up keys and permits at Port Lincoln Tourist Office.

Continuing along Flinders Highway, you'll pass **Port Lincoln Fauna Park, Little Swamp, Big Swamp,** and **Wanilla Forest.** Turn off toward Coffin Bay, through **Kellidie Bay Conservation Park,** and the **Coffin Bay Lookout,** through the township, and straight into the national park.

Coffin Bay National Park, 46 km from Port Lincoln, is a massive 30,000 hectares of wilderness area, much of it accessible only to four-wheel-drivers or bushwalkers (there are some sealed roads for conventional vehicles). Hike the 25-km **Yangie Trail** to Almonta Beach, Avoid Bay, and Yangie Bay. The park is particularly spectacular early spring to early summer, when gorgeous wildflowers pop into bloom. Inquire about road conditions and pick up camping permits at the ranger's headquarters, near the park's entrance.

The town of **Coffin Bay** is literally surrounded by parks and offers sheltered waters for fishing, boating, swimming, skin diving, and windsurfing. Normally a teeny township of 350 residents, the population leaps to nearly 10 times that in summer. Oysters cultivated here are renowned across Australia. Pay a visit to **Coffin Bay Oyster Farm,** where the motto is "Eat fish and live longer, eat Coffin Bay Oysters and love longer."

Holiday flats, ranging from inexpensive to moderately priced, are lined up along the Esplanade. **Coffin Bay Caravan Park** (tel. 85-4170) has campsites and on-site vans.

Pick up **tourist info,** bus tickets, postage stamps, fishing tackle, and hot roasted chicken at Beachcomber Agencies, the Esplanade (tel. 85-4057).

UP FLINDERS HIGHWAY

Climbing up the peninsula, the highway makes gentle jags inward to pastoral land and country townships, then teases you back to sparkling bays and beaches along the Great Australian Bight.

Turn off at Wangary, 29 km north of Coffin Bay, to **Farm Beach** and Anzac Cove (sometimes called Gallipoli Beach), where the movie *Gallipoli* was filmed. You'll pass Mt. Dutton on the way, a good climb but get permission first, as the land is privately owned.

Back on Flinders Highway, it's mostly sheep and farm country. At **Coulta,** you can experience farm life for $24 d, at **Wepowie Farm,** Edilillie Rd. (tel. 086-87-2063). One- or two-day horseback trips and pack horse treks are offered, as well as customary farm activities. Close by are salty Lake Greenly, with hang-gliding at Mt. Greenly, and good surfing at Greenly Beach.

Elliston, 100 km from Coulta, is a small fishing village on Waterloo Bay, where the scenic coastline jumps from rugged cliffs to sheltered inlets. Unique geological specimens found here are "clogs"—fossilized cocoons of the *Leptopius duponti* weevil—thought to be nearly 100,000 years old. Both **Elliston Caravan Park,** Flinders Hwy. (tel. 87-9061), and **Waterloo Bay Caravan Park,** Beach Terrace (tel. 87-9076), have campsites and on-site vans.

Flinders Island, 35 km off the coast of Elliston, is a 3,700-hectare getaway with swimming beaches and picturesque views. Atmospheric accommodations in either a renovated cottage or shearer's quarters costs about $250 double, with a four-night minimum stay. For bookings and air charters ($60 return), phone (086) 26-1132.

Talia Caves, 40 km north of Elliston, has wonderful limestone caves, gnarly rock formations and bleached sand dunes to explore. **Venus Bay,** another 22 km north, is a small township popular with small boat and jetty anglers and, increasingly, with surfers. **Needle Eye Lookout** gives a great view of the pounding sea, intriguing rocks and arches, and towering cliffs. Turn off at **Point Labatt,** a designated national park, to view Australia's only permanent mainland colony of sea lions.

Back on Flinders Highway, east of Point Labatt, you'll be able to glimpse **Murphy's Haystacks,** sculptured rock formations rising out of the wheatfields. These huge granite *inselbergs* are reputedly more than 1,500 million years old.

Streaky Bay, 85 km north of Venus Bay (first sighted in 1627 by Dutch explorer Peter Nuyts), was named by Captain Flinders because of the seaweed streaks coloring the bay. This township (pop. 990), another of the myriad picturesque fishing villages, is also a service center for the local agricultural communities. Historical buildings of interest are the **Old Schoolhouse Museum,** full of local artifacts, and **Hospital Cottage,** built in 1864.

Koolangatta Farm, via Piednippie Rd., 25 km from town (tel. 26-1174), offers inexpensive country accommodations that include continental breakfast. **Streaky Bay Motel,** 7 Alfred Terrace (tel. 26-1126), features moderately priced self-contained units with cooking facilities. Rent a campsite or a cabin at **Streaky Bay Foreshore Tourist Park,** Wells St. (tel. 26-1666).

Sheltered **Smoky Bay,** about midway between Streaky Bay and Ceduna, is a teeny villagette, best known for its annual Easter rodeo.

THE EYRE HIGHWAY

From Port Augusta to Ceduna, the Eyre Highway (Highway 1) spans 469 km of industrial sights, wheat belts, wilderness, and geological wonders.

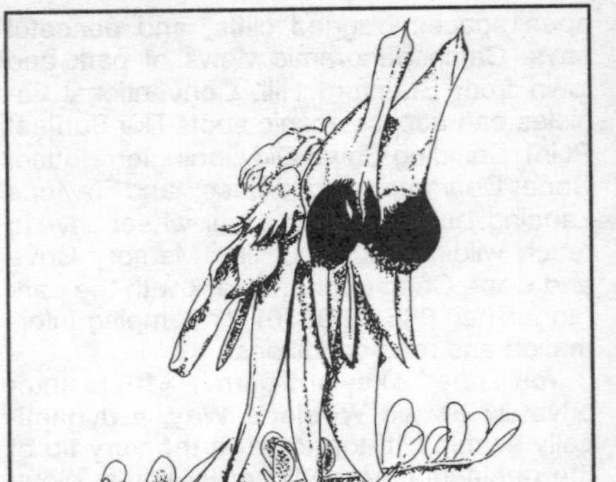

the Sturt Desert Pea, South Australia's state flower

Iron Knob, 68 km west of Port Augusta, is the birthplace of Australia's steel industry. Iron ore, discovered here in 1894, is quarried and shipped to the Whyalla Steelworks, along with supplies from the neighboring mines of Iron Monarch, Iron Baron, Iron Prince, Iron Queen, and Iron Duke (only Iron Knob is open to visitors). **Iron Knob Mineral & Shell Display,** Main St. (tel. 086-46-2130), features nearly 2,000 crystals from all over the world, as well as ore specimens from Iron Monarch mine. Rooms are inexpensive to low-moderate at either **Iron Knob Hotel,** Main St. (tel. 46-2013), or **Iron Knob Motel Roadhouse,** Eyre Highway (tel. 46-2058).

Kimba, 89 km from Iron Knob, is "Gateway to the Gawler Ranges" and, really, not much else. If you need a rest, **Kimba Community Hotel Motel,** High St. (tel. 27-2007), has inexpensive rooms ($20 higher in the motel section), as well as a bar, bistro, beer garden, and dining room.

At Kimba, turn off onto the winding gravel road that leads through the Gawler Ranges, gentle hills with unique rock formations, varied bird and animal life, and glorious spring wildflowers (Sturt's desert pea, the state flower, was first sighted here in 1839 by Eyre). You can camp at **Mt. Ive Station** (tel.

48-1817), near Lake Gairdner, in a range of very inexpensive facilities. A large part of the district is privately run and visitors are asked to stick to public roads, obtain permission before camping or hiking, to leave all flora and fauna, but take all rubbish with you. Conventional vehicles can access much of the area but, as in all wilderness and isolated regions, check regularly on weather and road conditions. **Gawler Ranges Wilderness Safaris,** P.O. Box 11, Wudinna, S.A. 5652 (tel. 80-2200), is an experienced operator offering two- to four-day 4WD safaris into the region.

Kyancutta, 89 km from Kimba, sits at the junction of the Eyre and Tod highways. **Wudinna,** 13 km farther, is the service center for the surrounding rural community, and the airstrip is used for regular service to and from Adelaide. Travelers stop here en route to see Australia's second largest granite outcrop, **Mt. Wudinna Rock** (261 meters high), 10 km northeast of town. Other weathered masses in this group are **Polda, Turtle, and Little Wudinna rocks. Wudinna Gawler Ranges Motel,** Eyre Hwy. (tel. 80-2090), has both moderately priced modern rooms and a caravan park.

More granite outcrops are located in the **Minnipa** area, 38 km from Wudinna. The Minnipa-Yardea road is another route into the Gawler Ranges. Pass through plains and grains country, the townships of **Poochera** and **Wirrulla,** to Ceduna.

CEDUNA

On the shores of Murat Bay, and at the junction of the Eyre and Flinders highways, Ceduna (pop. 2,880) is the last full-service town before the vast reaches of the Nullarbor Plain. As such, its name was quite aptly derived from "chedoona," Aboriginal for "a resting place."

Established as a town in 1901, Ceduna is the business hub of the far west coast and an important regional cereal-growing center (with an airport and regular service to Adelaide). The community was originally begun at Denial Bay, about 12 km to the west, where cargo ships pulled up close to shore, waited until low tide, then loaded wagons with provisions for the settlers. You can still see the ruins at **McKenzie Landing,** on the road to Davenport Creek. More recently, Thevenard (four km from Ceduna) serves as deep-sea port for the area, transporting grain, salt, and gypsum worldwide. (An interesting aside: according to map references in *Gulliver's Travels,* Gulliver encountered those little people of Lilliput on St. Peter and St. Francis islands, off the coast of Thevenard.)

Aside from being a supply and rest stop for travelers, Ceduna boasts a variety of local beaches for fishing, swimming, boating, and surfing.

Sights

The **Old Schoolhouse National Trust Museum,** Park Terrace (tel. 086-25-2210), displays historic relics of Ceduna's early days. **Overseas Telecommunication Earth Station** (OTC), 37 km northwest of town, is a global satellite system that channels approximately half of Australia's daily telecommunications with Asia, Africa, and Europe via Indian Ocean satellites. Guided tours of the facility are offered Mon.-Fri. 10 a.m., 11 a.m., 2 p.m., and 3 p.m. For information, phone 25-2505.

Accommodations And Food

The hotel section in **Ceduna Community Hotel Motel,** O'Loughlin Terrace (tel. 086-25-2008), is cheapest. Other motels, mostly along Eyre Highway, range moderate to expensive. (Face it—there's not a lot of price-choice way out here!) Campsites and on-site vans are available at **Ceduna Foreshore Caravan Park,** 5 South Terrace (tel. 25-2290).

Eats are at the pubs, motel dining rooms, coffee lounges, takeaways, or make your own from the supermarket.

Information

Stop in at **Ceduna Gateway Tourist Centre,** 58 Poynton St. (tel. 086-25-3155) for local and Eyre Peninsula information. Hours are Mon.-Fri. 9 a.m.-5:30 p.m., Sat. 9-11:30 a.m.

CROSSING THE NULLARBOR

Now that the road is sealed, this isn't *quite* the adventure it used to be (we'll get to the *authentic* Outback later). But, sealed highway or not, it is still a long, lonesome (and, sometimes, loathsome) trek across the Nullarbor Plain into Western Australia—480 km from Ceduna to the state line, and another 725 km to Norseman, end of the Eyre Highway, where you either take the high road or the low road *another* 725 km to Perth.

"Nullarbor" is Latin for "No Trees," but you'll see some timber, a few saplings, and a bit of scrub along the coastal part of the highway, particularly if you travel after the winter rains. It's the transcontinental railway line, several hundred kilometers north, that traverses the *really* plain Plains, a span 692 km long and 402 km wide. (By the way, that 478-km chunk of single track is the world's longest straight railway stretch.)

The usual Outback driving rules apply (familiarize yourself with the tips in this book). Also, you'll encounter quarantine stations at Ceduna, in South Australia, and Norseman, in Western Australia. Either have a picnic before reaching those two checkpoints or be prepared to surrender plants, fruits, veggies, nuts, grains, wool, animal skins, honey, soil, even used containers that held these products.

Another thing to remember (or discount altogether) is the time change between Balladonia and Nullarbor. Put your watch back 45 minutes at the border, unless it's Daylight Saving Time—then it increases to three hours. But, all in all, three hours either way are pretty insignificant when you're smack in the middle of nowheresville!

History

The Eyre Highway was named for Edward John Eyre who, in 1841, became the first fellow to cross the country from east to west—an agonizing five-month journey in which Eyre's buddy, John Baxter, bit the Nullarbor dust. Following Eyre's dusty footsteps came John and Alexander Forrest, brothers who mapped out much of the overland telegraph route which would connect Perth with Great

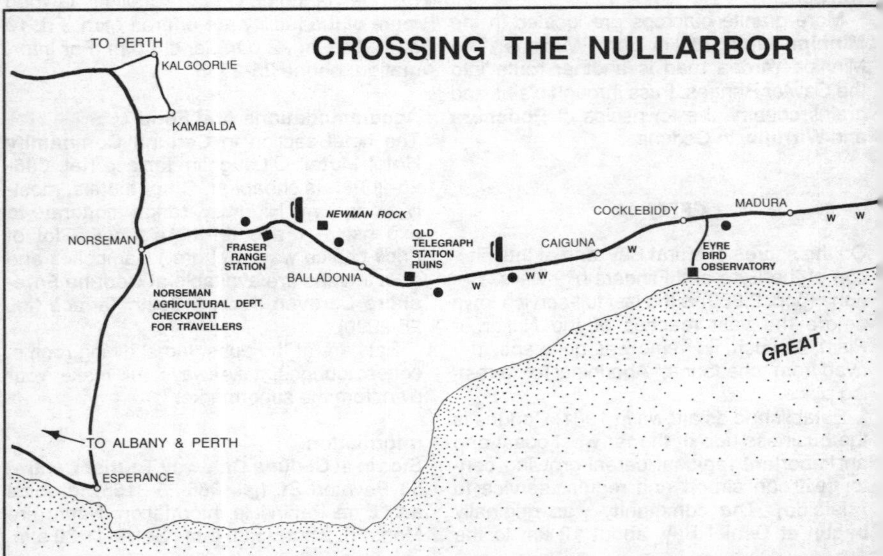

Britain. In 1877, the eastern and western sections of the telegraph line were linked up at Eucla, and in the 1890s those same bullock and camel tracks that helped build the line were followed by miners on their arduous trip to Western Australia's goldfields. After that, the Nullarbor was crossed by a succession of odd transport—camels, cycles, a 10 horsepower Brush car, a Citroen. In 1941, with the advent of World War II, army engineers commenced construction of the Eyre Highway. Cross country traffic, at first a trickle in the 1950s, grew (thanks to the Commonwealth Games in Perth) to more than 30 vehicles a day in 1962. The Western Australia section of the highway was sealed in 1969, and the South Australia portion was surfaced seven years later.

Ceduna To Border Village

Penong, 73 km west from Ceduna, is the "town of 100 windmills" and a good place to stop for petrol and supplies. Rooms are inexpensive at **Penong Hotel** (tel. 086-25-1050).

Cactus Beach, 21 km south of Penong, is famous worldwide for its three perfect surfing breaks ("Castles," "Cactus," and "Caves"). Other nearby attractions are **Point Sinclair** and **Pink Lake. Fowlers Bay,** on the turnoff to **Nundroo,** is a great fishing hole. **Scott's Bay, Mexican Hat,** and **Cabot's Beach** are popular camel-trekking points. The **Nundroo Hotel Motel** (tel. 086-25-6120) features moderately priced rooms. **Yalata Roadhouse,** another 51 km along, is a tourist complex run by the Yalata Aboriginal Community (you can buy locally made Aboriginal artifacts). Accommodations are moderately priced. From June through October **southern right whales** can be seen during their annual breeding migration along the coastline between Yalata and the border. In 1989, the largest group of these whales to visit the country's shores was spotted just off Yalata Reserve. Permits to enter the land can be obtained at Yalata Roadhouse.

From Nullarbor to the border, you'll pass along sheer coastal cliffs with plunging views of the rugged terrain and the Great Australian Bight. **Nullarbor,** 94 km from Yalata, is adjacent to the original **Nullarbor Homestead. Nullarbor Hotel-Motel** (tel. 086-65-6271) is

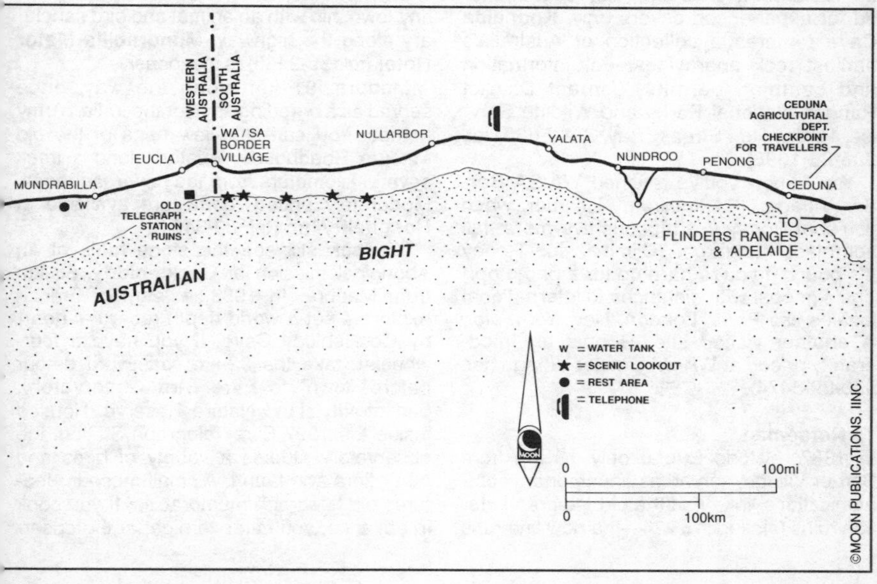

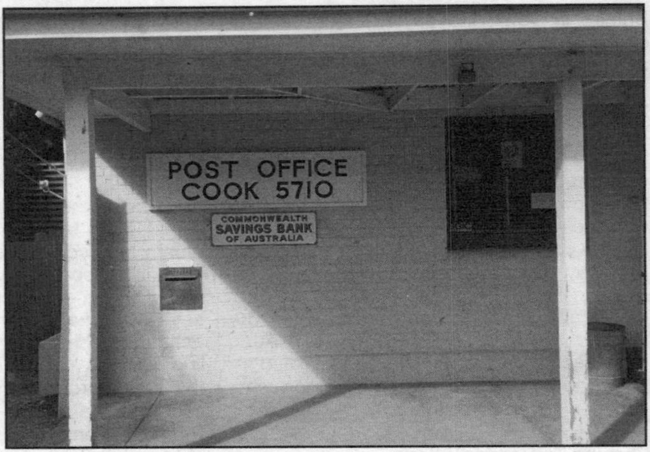

the South Australia-Western Australia border along the transcontinental rail lines

in the moderate range. The Eyre Highway transects **Nullarbor National Park,** where signs point the way to spectacular lookouts over the Bunda Cliffs, a 200-km stretch from the Head of the Bight almost to the Western Australia border. The area around the Nullarbor is cave-land, but recommended for experienced cavers only. **Koonalda Cave** features a collection of Australia's earliest rock engravings. For information and camping permits, contact District Ranger, National Parks and Wildlife Service, 15 Bay Rd., Streaky Bay, S.A. 5680 (tel. 086-26-1098).

You'll know you've reached **WA/SA Border Village,** 184 km from Nullarbor, when you spot *Rooey II,* a hideous five-meter-tall fiberglass kangaroo. (Climb inside Rooey II's pouch if you're hard up for a photo op.) The signpost with distances to international locales like Paris, London, New York, etc., is another visited site. Rooms are moderately priced at **WA/SA Border Village** (tel. 090-39-3474).

To Norseman

In 1887, historic **Eucla,** only 13 km from Border Village, served as an important communications link. Visit the old telegraph station ruins (closed in 1924—the new line runs along the rail line), the town jetty, as well as the nearby cliffs, caves and blowholes, and the sandhills at Eucla Pass. **Eucla Amber Motor Hotel** (tel. 090-39-3568) has inexpensive rooms, plus a swimming pool, beer garden, restaurant, and bar.

Mundrabilla, 66 km west from Eucla, is a tiny township with an animal and bird sanctuary along the highway. **Mundrabilla Motor Hotel** (tel. 39-3465) is inexpensive.

Madura, 91 km along the way, once served as a breeding spot for the Indian Army horses. You can still view ruins of the old Madura Roadhouse, located along a track several kilometers from the new roadhouse. Moderately priced rooms are available at **Hospitality Inn** (tel. 39-3464).

You can still see the stone ruins of an Aboriginal mission at **Cocklebiddy,** 66 km from Madura. In 1983, a team of French explorers set a world depth record at nearby Cocklebiddy Cave. If you have a four-wheeler, take the 32-km coastward detour before "town" to **Eyre Bird Observatory,** part of Nuytsland Nature Reserve. Housed inside the 1897 Eyre Telegraph Station, the observatory studies a variety of birds and other flora and fauna. A small museum features old telegraph memorabilia. If you book in advance, you can overnight at the observatory for about $60 (cheaper if you stay longer or have a YHA card) including room, full board, and roundtrip transport from Cocklebiddy. For advance bookings (mandatory), phone (090) 39-3450. In Cocklebiddy, **Wedgetail Inn** (tel. 39-3462) has a lounge, pub, dining room, and takeaway. Accommodations are in the moderate to expensive range.

It's another 66 km to **Caiguna,** with service facilities as well as an airstrip used both by charter planes and the Royal Flying Doctors. About 10 km south is the memorial to Eyre's buddy, Baxter, killed in 1841 by angry natives. **John Eyre Motel** (tel. 39-3459) has moderate to expensive rates.

The 182-km distance from Caiguna to **Balladonia** is one of the world's longest straight stretches of road. Those rock-hole dams you see just before Balladonia are called **Afghan Rocks,** for the Afghan camel driver who was shot dead for having the audacity to wash his tootsies in the water. **Balladonia Hotel Motel** (tel. 39-3453) offers moderately priced rooms, plus a bistro, pub, dining room, and takeaway.

Fraser Range Station (tel. 39-3457), almost midway between Balladonia and Norseman, is a family-operated sheep station that dates back to 1864. Pass through in July and you'll be in on the shearing; midwinter through midspring is wildflower season. This YHA associate offers a range of accommodations, including dorm beds ($12 per night) and campsites ($7 per night). If you're traveling by coach, phone ahead for pick-up from the nearest Eyre Highway drop-off.

You'll see mine shafts and tailings as you near Norseman, where—depending on mood—you'll either drop south to the coast, or north to the goldfields.

TRANSPORT

Air services operating to and about the Eyre Peninsula are: **Air Central Eyre** (tel. 086-80-2001 or 008-08-858), from Wudinna, Kimba, Cleve, and Adelaide; **Eyre Commuter** (tel. 086-86-2329), from Cummins to Adelaide via Tumby Bay; **Kendell Airlines** (tel. 08-233-332); **Adelaide,** (tel. 086-82-1933); **Port Lincoln,** (tel 086-45-8888); **Whyalla,** from Adelaide, Ceduna, Port Lincoln, Whyalla; **Lincoln Airlines** (tel. 086-82-5688), from Port Lincoln and Adelaide; **Lloyd Aviation** (tel. 08-224-7500 or 008-88-8250), from Adelaide, Whyalla, and Olympic Dam.

Greyhound, Pioneer, and **Bus Australia** operate daily coach service along the Eyre Highway on the Adelaide-Perth route, with stop-offs at Iron Knob, Kimba, Wudinna, Minnipa, Ceduna, and the Nullarbor. Coaches depart Adelaide's Central Bus Depot. **Stateliner** coaches serve all west coast towns—on the peninsula and along the highway—from Adelaide. The trip to Port Lincoln (eight hours) costs about $45, and to Ceduna (10 hours), $51. For information and bookings, phone (08) 233-2755.

The 88-passenger ***Iron Triangle Limited*** railway operates three times weekly between Adelaide and Whyalla ($27), stopping along the way at Crystal Brook, Port Pirie, and Port Augusta. For information, phone **Australian National Railway** (08) 217-4455, Adelaide; (086) 45-0422, Whyalla; (086) 82-1466, Port Lincoln.

For information on the **MV *Island Seaway*** vehicle and passenger ferry between Adelaide, Kingscote (on Kangaroo Island), and Port Lincoln, phone (08) 47-5577 Adelaide, or (086) 82-1011 Port Lincoln (see "Getting Away" in the "Adelaide" section).

THE FLINDERS RANGES

Photographers, painters, bushwalkers, and nature lovers travel to these desert range rock formations for hot shots, divine inspiration, colorful adventure, and a breath of fresh air.

The Flinders Ranges—broken into Southern, Central, and Northern sections—begin to jut between Crystal Brook and Peterborough (about 250 km north of Adelaide), then sweep and arc northward to a point 160 km east of Marree at the edge of the Outback.

Thrust up from the sea about 1,600 million or so years ago, these bent, twisted, buckled, and gorged ranges are best described as earth sculptures. Minerals embedded in the ancient plains and cliffs chameleon along with the sun or moon, the time of year, a turn of your head into delicate pink, salmon, mauve, purple, angry red, and sunshine yellow. These ranges aren't high, but they'll sure make *you* feel that way!

The scenery varies from woodsy slopes in the temperate south to rugged peaks in the dry north, with Wilpena Pound, the great natural amphitheater in the central region, ranking as the highlight of the Flinders Ranges. An abundance of wildflowers (including South Australia's state flower, Sturt's desert pea), wildlife, and birds can be seen throughout the area. In fact, you're bound to spot lots of interesting vegetation and pretty posies, but please help preserve this fragile and beautiful region by leaving your finds intact. As requested by the RAA: "If you must take something home—make it a photograph."

The most popular time to visit is April through October. Summer months are usually very hot and very cold. Rain, at any time of year, can cause flash flooding and render roads impassable. Be sure to follow Outback driving regulations and inquire about road and weather conditions along your journey. It is imperative that bushwalkers obtain detailed maps and information from park rangers or tourist information centers before embarking on either a short trail or lengthy trek. Heysen Trailers should note that the Flinders section is closed 1 Nov.-30 April due to fire restrictions.

The easiest way to reach the Flinders Ranges is via Highway 47 from Port Augusta. The road is sealed to Wilpena Pound, and also up to Lyndhurst (junction of the Strzelecki Track). After that it becomes gravel, dirt, and indescribable. A popular "circle tour" is to start at Port Augusta, pass through Quorn and Hawker to Wilpena, continue northward through Flinders Ranges National Park up to Blinman, swing west to Parachilna, then south back to Hawker.

History

This region is older than the hills—literally.

Captain Matthew Flinders undoubtedly thought he discovered the place when he visited in 1802—after all it was later named after him. Well, try telling that to the Aboriginals—though you won't find too many of *them* around anymore. You will find their paintings and rock carvings, some known to be 12,000 years old, scattered about the ranges. (*Please* do not tamper with paintings, carvings, or relics.)

There are a number of historical sites in and around the ranges—mostly old copper- and gold-mining towns, homesteads that served as resting spots for overland teams, remnants of the late 1800s wheat farming boom (nipped in the sheaf by bad weather, plagues, and hunger).

SOUTHERN FLINDERS RANGES

You can travel any of several sealed roads from the Mid North to tour the relatively more gentle and accessible southern region.

Telowie Gorge

Located 25 km northeast of Port Pirie, with access off Highway 1, Telowie Gorge (1,946 hectares) is the southernmost park of the Flinders Ranges. Steep red cliffs, open

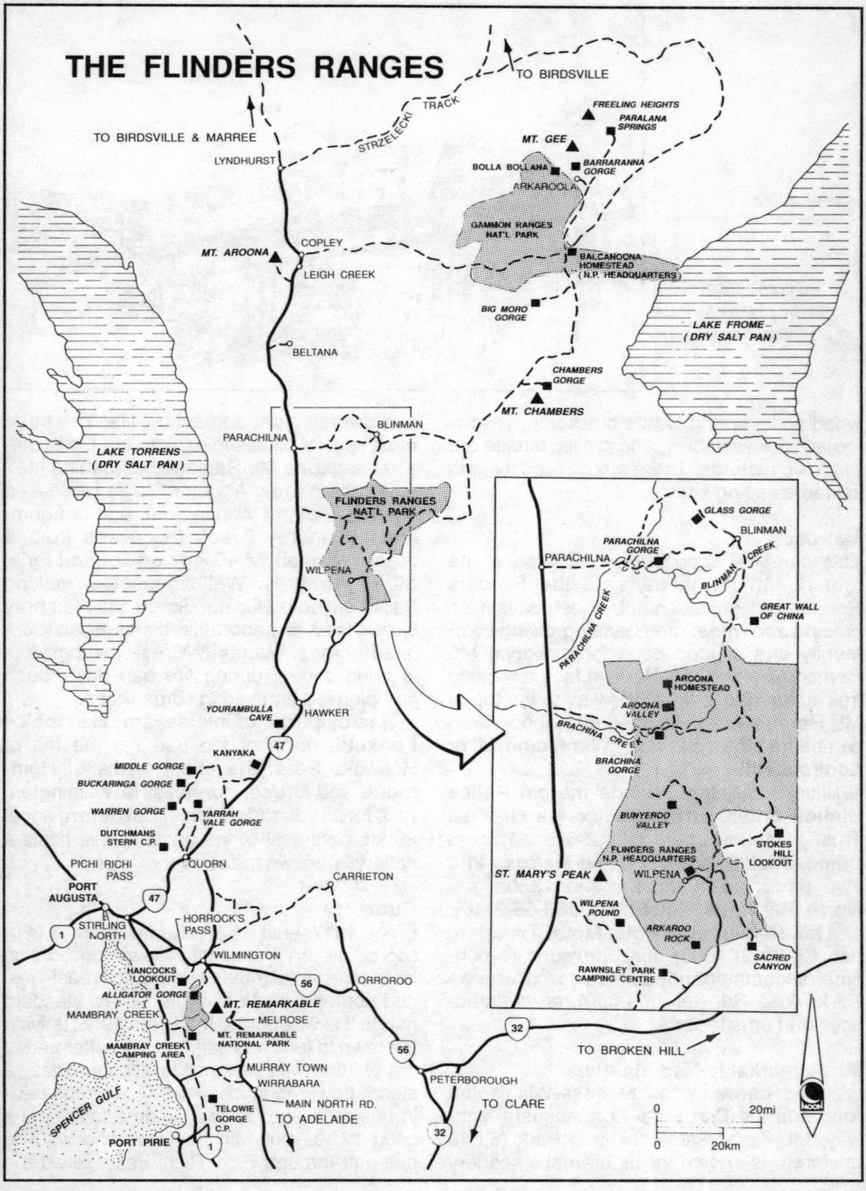
THE FLINDERS RANGES
TO BIRDSVILLE
TO BIRDSVILLE & MARREE
STRZELECKI TRACK
FREELING HEIGHTS
PARALANA SPRINGS
MT. GEE
BOLLA BOLLANA
BARRARANNA GORGE
ARKAROOLA
LYNDHURST
GAMMON RANGES NAT'L PARK
COPLEY
MT. AROONA
LEIGH CREEK
BALCANOONA HOMESTEAD (N.P. HEADQUARTERS)
BIG MORO GORGE
LAKE FROME (DRY SALT PAN)
BELTANA
CHAMBERS GORGE
MT. CHAMBERS
BLINMAN
PARACHILNA
LAKE TORRENS (DRY SALT PAN)
FLINDERS RANGES NAT'L PARK
WILPENA
GLASS GORGE
PARACHILNA GORGE
BLINMAN CREEK
PARACHILNA CREEK
GREAT WALL OF CHINA
AROONA HOMESTEAD
AROONA VALLEY
BRACHINA CREEK
BRACHINA GORGE
BUNYEROO VALLEY
STOKES HILL LOOKOUT
FLINDERS RANGES N.P. HEADQUARTERS
ST. MARY'S PEAK
WILPENA POUND
ARKAROO ROCK
SACRED CANYON
RAWNSLEY PARK CAMPING CENTRE
YOURAMBULLA CAVE
HAWKER
47
KANYAKA
MIDDLE GORGE
BUCKARINGA GORGE
WARREN GORGE
YARRAH VALE GORGE
DUTCHMANS STERN C.P.
QUORN
PICHI RICHI PASS
CARRIETON
PORT AUGUSTA
STIRLING NORTH
1
HORROCK'S PASS
WILMINGTON
HANCOCKS LOOKOUT
ALLIGATOR GORGE
56
ORROROO
MT. REMARKABLE
MAMBRAY CREEK
MELROSE
MT. REMARKABLE NATIONAL PARK
MAMBRAY CREEK CAMPING AREA
32
TO BROKEN HILL
MURRAY TOWN
WIRRABARA
PETERBOROUGH
SPENCER GULF
TELOWIE GORGE C.P.
MAIN NORTH RD.
TO ADELAIDE
TO CLARE
PORT PIRIE
0
20mi
20km
MOON

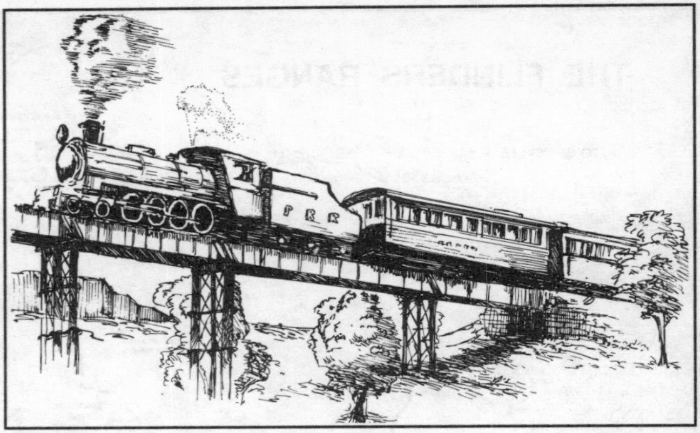

Quorn's Pichi Richi Railway takes tourists on a sentimental journey.

MIKE WELLINS

woodlands, spring wattle blossoms, yellow-footed rock wallabies, and prolific birdlife are the main features. There are no facilities and limited camping sites.

Melrose

This one-time copper town, situated at the foot of Mt. Remarkable, is the Flinders Ranges' oldest settlement. These days it's a grazing and wheat- and barley-growing community and a good base for exploring Mt. Remarkable National Park. In fact, a walking trail leads from town all the way to the top of Mt. Remarkable (956 meters). Good views can be had from either the **War Memorial** or **Lookout Hill.**

Historic buildings include the old **Police Station and Courthouse** (now a National Trust museum, open daily 2-5 p.m.), **post office, Jacka's Brewery,** and **Melrose Inn.** Two other oldies, built in the 1850s, are **North Star Hotel,** Nott St. (tel. 086-66-2110), and **Mt. Remarkable Hotel Motel,** Stuart St. (tel. 66-2119). Both offer inexpensive pub-type accommodations. **Melrose Caravan Park,** Joes Rd. (tel. 66-2060), rents campsites and on-site vans.

Mt. Remarkable National Park

Wedged between the Melrose-Wilmington road and the Port Pirie–Port Augusta highway, Mt. Remarkable National Park (8,649 hectares) is known for its dramatic scenery and diverse plant and animal life. The three most special places to explore are the somewhat separate Mt. Remarkable (behind Melrose), the narrow Alligator Gorge (accessed one km south of Wilmington), and red gum-lined Mambray Creek (accessed from a branch road about 45 km north of Port Pirie, off Highway 1). Well-signposted walking trails from both Alligator Gorge and Mambrey Creek lead to panoramic lookouts and isolated gorges. Mambray Creek campground is open except during fire ban days; bush camping is permitted in some areas.

Nearby points of interest are: **Hancock's Lookout,** north of the park, at the top of Horrocks Pass; the ghost towns of **Hammond** and **Bruce,** northeast of Wilmington; and, for all you rodeophiles, **Carrieton,** about 25 km northeast of the ghost towns, hosts a nationally known rodeo every October.

Quorn

From 1917 until 1937, Quorn (pop. 1,080) served as an important railway junction on transcontinental routes headed both east-west and north-south. Not so after a new standard gauge line was built to Marree in 1956, leaving the town to fend for itself. In 1974, after part of the old line was restored to accommodate a steam-powered tourist train, Quorn was back in business—not as the big-time rail depot it used to be—but with travelers who want to putt-putt through Pichi Richi Pass. Billed the

"Gateway to the Flinders Ranges," Quorn is about 40 km from Wilmington and a bit farther from Port Augusta.

The ***Pichi Richi Railway*** departs from old Quorn Railway Station for a picturesque 2¾-hour roundtrip journey (about $15) into Pichi Richi Pass, rolling over bridges, along the Pichi Richi River, and through the long-abandoned Pichi Richi township. The train only runs during school holidays and long weekends. Check at the tourist information office or Quorn Motel (tel. 086-48-6016) for schedules.

Quorn is full of historic buildings. Aside from the railway station, some of the best examples are the **public school, town hall, National Bank, Bank of Adelaide, courthouse, State Bank, Quorn Mill** (now the local museum), and the **Austral, Grand Junction,** and **Criterion hotels.** Accommodations in any of the three hotels, all on Railway Terrace, are inexpensive. You can stay in the old mill, also on Railway Terrace, for about $10 more.

Dutchman's Stern Conservation Park (3,532 hectares), five km west of Quorn, has sharp cliffs and steep gorges, a wide range of plant and bird species (this is the northern limit for Adelaide rosellas, scarlet robins, kookaburras, and the yellow-faced honeyeater). The park has marked walking trails (but only pro bushwalkers should attempt the climb to 800-meter Dutchman's Stern) and a picnic area. Camping is not permitted.

For Quorn emergencies, contact **police** (tel. 086-48-6060), **fire brigade** (tel. 48-6000), **ambulance** (tel. 48-6366), **hospital** (tel. 48-6200), or **RAA** (tel. 48-6012).

To Hawker

Take your pick—gorges, ruins, or caves. If you take the unsealed road, you'll pass through stunning **Yarrah Vale,** and the **Warren, Buckaringa,** and **Middle** gorges. Traveling the highway will bring you to **Kanyaka,** remnants of a large sheep station dating back to 1851. Though the station once supported 70 families, all that's left are bricks and pieces of the old stone buildings and graveyard. Farther along the road, behind a rise, is another group of ruins. Follow the track 1½ km to **Death Rock Waterhole**—road's end.

Other **historic ruins** in the area are Wilson, Gordon, Hammond, Saltia, Simmonston, and Willochra. Local information centers sell guidebooks to the sites.

About 10 km south of Hawker, and a 30-minute walk from the road, **Yourambulla Cave** features Aboriginal rock drawings and paintings. (Remember—*don't touch!)*

CENTRAL FLINDERS RANGES

At Hawker, you enter the heart of the Flinders and junction of the "Circle Tour" that will take you through the best parts of these ranges.

Hawker

Hawker (pop. 300) is another old railway community, bypassed when the standard gauge was built. Billed as a "typical Outback town," Hawker provides tourist facilities for travelers to nearby Wilpena Pound.

Historical buildings worth checking out are the **railway station, Hawker Hotel, Sightseer's Café, Post Office, Institute Building,** and **Hawker Motors** (formerly the Federal Boot Store, currently a teensie museum and tourist information center).

Hawker Hotel Motel, corner Elder and Wonoka Terrace (tel. 086-48-4102), has pub and motel rooms ranging from inexpensive to moderate. **Outback Motel,** 1 Wilpena Rd. (48-4100) is a modern motel that costs about the same as the Hawker. **Yappala Station,** 9 kilometers northwest of Hawker, off Leigh Creek Rd. (tel. 48-4164), provides a variety of accommodations on its working sheep station. A two-night minimum stay is required. **Hawker Caravan Park,** 44 Chace View Terrace (tel. 48-4006), has campsites and on-site van.

Emergency numbers are **police** (tel. 086-48-4028), **fire brigade** (tel. 48-4065), **ambulance** (tel. 48-4007), and **RAA** (tel. 48-4014).

Wilpena Pound

This natural amphitheater, 55 km north of Hawker, and encompassed within the 92,746-hectare Flinders Ranges National Park, is

Wilpena Pound in the Flinders Ranges

TOURISM SOUTH AUSTRALIA

the most popular attraction of the ranges. Once a wheat-farming and sheep-grazing area, this is now a wildlife refuge for many species, particularly kangaroos and a spectacle of birds ranging from wedge-tailed eagles to colorful parrots. The basin is a grandiose 80 square km, surrounded by a circle of sheer, splintered, multicolored cliffs (the highest point is 1,190-meter **St. Mary's Peak).** Within the circle, however, gentle slopes lead into the vast central plain. Wilpena Pound is a bushwalker's heaven—myriad trails guide you along everything from a casual one-hour stroll to a full-day's steep and stony climb. (Be sure to complete a log sheet at the park office, open 24 hours, before embarking on extended walks.) The only access into the pound is through the narrow gorge above **Sliding Rock,** near Wilpena Pound Motel.

The Pound is important in Aborginal mythology of the Flinders Ranges ("Wilpena" means "a kangaroo skin curled up on its edges") and tribal drawings, paintings, and carvings can be seen at **Arkaroo Rock,** near Moonarie Gap, and at **Sacred Canyon.** Both areas are about 19 km south of Wilpena (though on different roads).

Other points of interest within Flinders Ranges National Park are the **Bunyeroo** and **Brachina gorges** and **Aroona Valley,** where you can see ruins of the old homestead.

The only accommodations at the Pound are at **Wilpena Pound Motel** (tel. 086-48-0004). Upper-moderate to expensive rates include continental breakfast. Tent camping is permitted near the entrance to the Pound for about $10 per night. **Rawnsley Park Camping Centre** (tel. 48-0030), 20 km south of Wilpena, offers campsites, on-site vans, and moderately priced cabin accommodations, with a two-night minimum stay required.

To And From Blinman

You'll be traveling on gravel once you leave the pound. Engaging spots along the 59-km drive to Blinman are **Stokes Hill Lookout** and a long, ironstone-topped rock formation called the **Great Wall of China.**

Blinman (pop. 98), at the northern edge of Flinders Ranges National Park, was a hustle-bustle copper mining town from 1862 until 1890. Old mine machinery and relics are still in evidence, as are a few historic buildings. You can overnight at the 1869 **North Blinman Hotel** (tel. 086-48-4867) where moderate rates include breakfast.

Heading west and circling back to Hawker, two routes will get you to the highway junction at Parachilna: **Glass Gorge** is slightly out of the way along a dirt road, but the views are terrific, especially when the wild hops are in bloom; the gravel road goes through **Parachilna Gorge,** the tourist village at **Angori-**

china (where you can rent a campsite or a chalet), the spring-fed **Blinman Pools** (near Angorichina, reached from the Parachilna and Blinman creeks).

Rejoin the main highway at **Parachilna,** and either go north 70 km to Leigh Creek or south 89 km to Hawker. **Parachilna Hotel** (tel. 48-4895), a "typical bush pub," has moderately priced rooms with breakfast included.

About 70 km east of Blinman, along one route to the Northern Flinders Ranges, **Chambers Gorge** features 100 meters of Aboriginal rock carvings on its left wall. **Mount Chambers** (409 meters) provides dynamic views of Lake Frome on one side, Wilpena on the other.

NORTHERN FLINDERS RANGES

Rugged, arid, remote, and exquisite, the northern ranges are reached from either Leigh Creek or the Chambers Gorge road.

Leigh Creek

Leigh Creek (pop. 967), used to be 13 km north of where it is now. That's right—the whole town just up and moved when the original site was needed for additional coal mining. Beat *that* for town spirit! Leigh Creek South reopened in 1981 and grass (the kind you mow) has been banned. Like it or not, this is your northern ranges oasis, with shopping facilities, bank, post office, hospital, fuel, auto mechanic, as well as a regional office of the National Parks and Wildlife Service. **Aroona Dam,** four km west of town, is a popular picnic area.

If you're a coal enthusiast, you'll enjoy looking down at some of the mine workings from the visitor's viewing area, about three km from the turnoff to Leigh Creek Coalfields, on the Hawker to Marree highway. Free public tours are given March-Oct. and school holidays.

Arkaroola

Despite the harsh, occasionally hostile environment, Arkaroola's 60,000-hectare sanctuary harbors a large variety of plants and wildlife. This former mining area was only established as a privately run reserve in 1968. Since then it's been the buzz of naturalists, adventurers, and travel guiders.

At Arkaroola, see the art gallery, mineral and fossil museum, pioneer cottage, outdoor pastoral museum, and astronomical observatory (viewing is subject to light and weather conditions). Nearby points of interest are the Cornish smelters at **Bolla Bollana,** the dazzling view from **Mt. Painter** (790 meters),

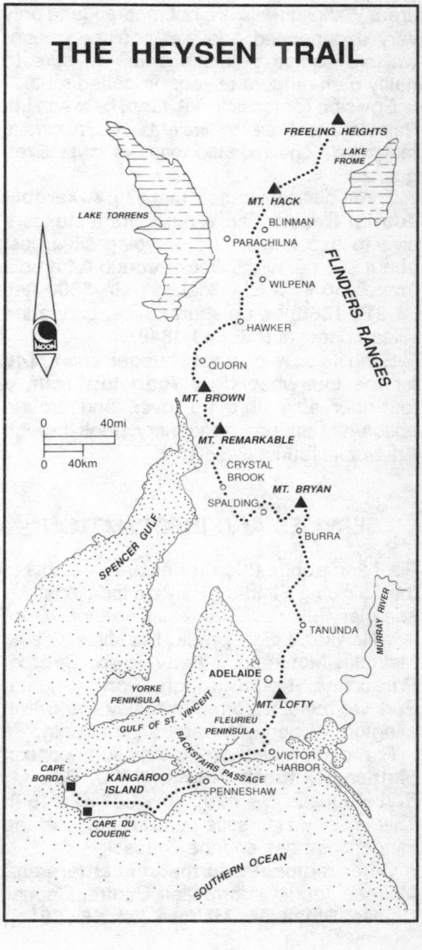

waterholes at **Bararranna** and **Nooldoonooldoona,** and **Sitting Bull, Spriggs Nob,** and **The Pinnacles** mountain tops. Radioactive **Paralana Hot Springs,** 27 km north of Arkaroola, is thought to be Australia's last site of volcanic activity, and is also an Aboriginal ceremonial spot.

Gammon Ranges National Park (128,228 hectares) is extremely rugged and isolated territory, accessed only by four-wheel-drive vehicles, except for the park headquarters area. Walking trails are not marked, and only very experienced and well-equipped bushwalkers should trek this area. Be sure to notify park rangers of your proposed route.

Envision (or fossick) **Mt. Gee,** between Mt. Painter and Freeling Heights. It's a crystal mountain—one gigantic mass of crystallized quartz.

Three different motels make up **Arkaroola Tourist Resort.** Tariffs range from inexpensive to expensive, and camping sites cost about $15 per night. Book through Arkaroola Travel, 50 Pirie St., Adelaide, SA 5000 (tel. 08-212-1366) or, on short notice, phone the village direct at (086) 48-4848.

Even if you're on a tight budget, spring $40 for the four-wheel-drive **Ridgetop Tour,** a four-hour adventure up, over, and around absolutely astounding scenery. Book through Arkaroola Tourist Resort.

SERVICES AND INFORMATION

Fuel and **public telephones** are available at the following Flinders Ranges locations: Arkaroola, Beltana, Blinman, Carrieton, Copley, Hawker, Leigh Creek, Mambray Creek, Melrose, Morchard, Murray Town, Orroroo, Parachilna, Peterborough, Port Augusta, Port Germein, Quorn, Rawnsley Park, Wilmington, Wilpena, Wirrabara, and Yunta.

For comprehensive information, contact **Flinders Outback Tourism,** P.O. Box 41, Port Augusta, SA 5700 (tel. 086-42-2469). This agency also sells detailed maps of the Flinders Ranges and the Outback.

Other **regional information centers** are: Melrose Tourist Information Centre, Council Offices, Stuart St., Melrose (tel. 66- 2014); Tourist Information Centre, Main St., Peterborough (tel. 51-2708); Port Augusta Tourist Information Centre, 41 Flinders Terrace, Port Augusta (tel. 41-0793); and Quorn Tourist Information Centre, Council Office, Seventh St., Quorn (tel. 48-6031). Most motels, caravan parks, and roadhouses also carry tourist information.

Information and **camping permits** for the national and conservation parks within the Flinders Ranges can be obtained from the following National Parks and Wildlife Service regional offices: 55 Grenfell St., Adelaide (tel. 08-216-7777); S.G.I.C. Building, Mackay St., Port Augusta (tel. 086-42-3800); and at Leigh Creek (tel. 086-75-2499).

Contact **park rangers** at Flinders Ranges National Park (tel. 086-48-0048), Wilpena (tel. 48-0048), Oraparinna (tel. 48-0017), Balcanoona Homestead (tel. 48-4829), and Mambray Creek (tel. 34-7068).

Obtain detailed maps of the **Heysen Trail** from the State Information Centre, 25 Grenfell St., Adelaide. Also collect maps and other motoring tips from RAA branches.

Northern Roads Condition Hotline (tel. 08-11-633) provides up-to-date info on Flinders and Outback road conditions.

TRANSPORT

Augusta Airways (tel. 086-42-3100) operates scheduled air service between Port Augusta, Adelaide, and Leigh Creek, Mon.-Friday.

Stateliner (tel. 08-233-2722, Adelaide; 086-42-5055, Port Augusta) provides coach service to Arkaroola, Beltana, Booleroo Centre, Copley, Hawker, Leigh Creek, Melrose, Murray Town, Mambray Creek, Parachilna, Port Augusta, Port Germein, Peterborough, Quorn, Wilmington, Wilpena, Wirrabara, and Yunta. Sample fares are: Adelaide-Quorn, $32; Adelaide-Wilpena Pound, $42; Adelaide-Arkaroola, $61.

Bushwalkers *must* carry detailed trail maps and adhere to all warnings. It is mandatory that you check in with park rangers before starting off. Heed rules for Outback travel and safety.

For travelers who'd rather leave rules and regulations in the hands of experienced guides, a wide variety of Flinders Ranges tours are available. Sightsee by air, coach, four-wheeler, horse, or camel. Any tourist information center can provide a list of recommended operators. Also inquire locally—often a shopkeeper or motel manager has a tour guide relative. A few old names in the tour biz are **Osprey Wildlife Expeditions** (tel. 08-370-9337); **Gawler Outback Tours** (tel. 085-22-2254); **Outback Camel Company** (tel. 086-48-4717); and **Butler's Outback Safaris** (tel. 086-42-2188).

THE OUTBACK

This region may be as close as you'll ever get to feeling like you're on another planet—one reason being that it's not particularly well-suited to human life.

In 1845, explorer Charles Sturt described the Outback as "a country I firmly believe has no parallel on earth's surface" (then he died). And that is precisely why 99% of the state's population live south of the 32nd parallel. Much of this area is no man's (or woman's) land. Peaceful, open space contrasts with harsh terrain, stony deserts, enormous salt pans, and eerie desolation. Then again, the challenge of surviving the elements is often what attracts travelers in the first place—that and thousands of native birds, fish jumpin' out of desert waterholes, the search for fiery opals, dry salt lakes, artesian springs, the odd spaceship, and a bunch of odd spaced-out characters.

Encompassing about 60 million hectares, the Outback presents a massive frontier to pioneering spirits, some pretty hazardous odds to those who gamble with nature, and breathing space galore for incurable claustrophobics. But pay attention to whose land you're on; vast areas are administered by the National Parks and Wildlife Services, others are Aboriginal reserves or part of the military's Woomera Prohibited Area. (Though *you* may feel free out here, the *land* is not!)

Choose from four Outback routes. **The Stuart Highway**, the sealed road which connects Port Augusta with Alice Springs, passes through the Woomera missile test site, Coober Pedy, and the opal-mining district. **Oodnadatta Track** is the old dirt road which follows the path of the old *Ghan* railway and overland telegraph lines, eventually meeting up with the Stuart Highway at Marla. Both the **Birdsville** and **Strzelecki** tracks are *long, hard treks* through remote desert into remote Queensland. Whichever route you take, at some point you'll cross the dingo fence—a protective wire stretching more than 3,000 km across central Australia—to keep those wild dogs from entering southern pastoral lands.

The best time of year for Outback travel is April to September, when the weather is usually mild and dry, though early mornings can be frosty (camping from June through October can be *very* cold and uncomfortable). Summers, as you'd expect, are scorching infernos when you can indeed fry your eggs (and seated body parts) atop any rock in this hard place. Rains, though infrequent, should be taken quite seriously, particularly if you're off the sealed highway. Dirt tracks can be washed away suddenly, leaving you stranded for what could be a deadly long time. But the Outback is exquisite after a rainfall, carpeted with wildflowers and exotic plants.

Make certain both you and your vehicle are well prepared for your journey. Follow Outback driving rules, inquire about road conditions, carry detailed maps, keep your car full of petrol and your body full of water.

History

If travelers think the Outback is challenging, imagine what the early explorers went through! In 1840, Edward John Eyre made the journey from Adelaide to Lake Torrens, crossing the Nullarbor the next year. Several years later, Charles Sturt—in a period of 18 months—

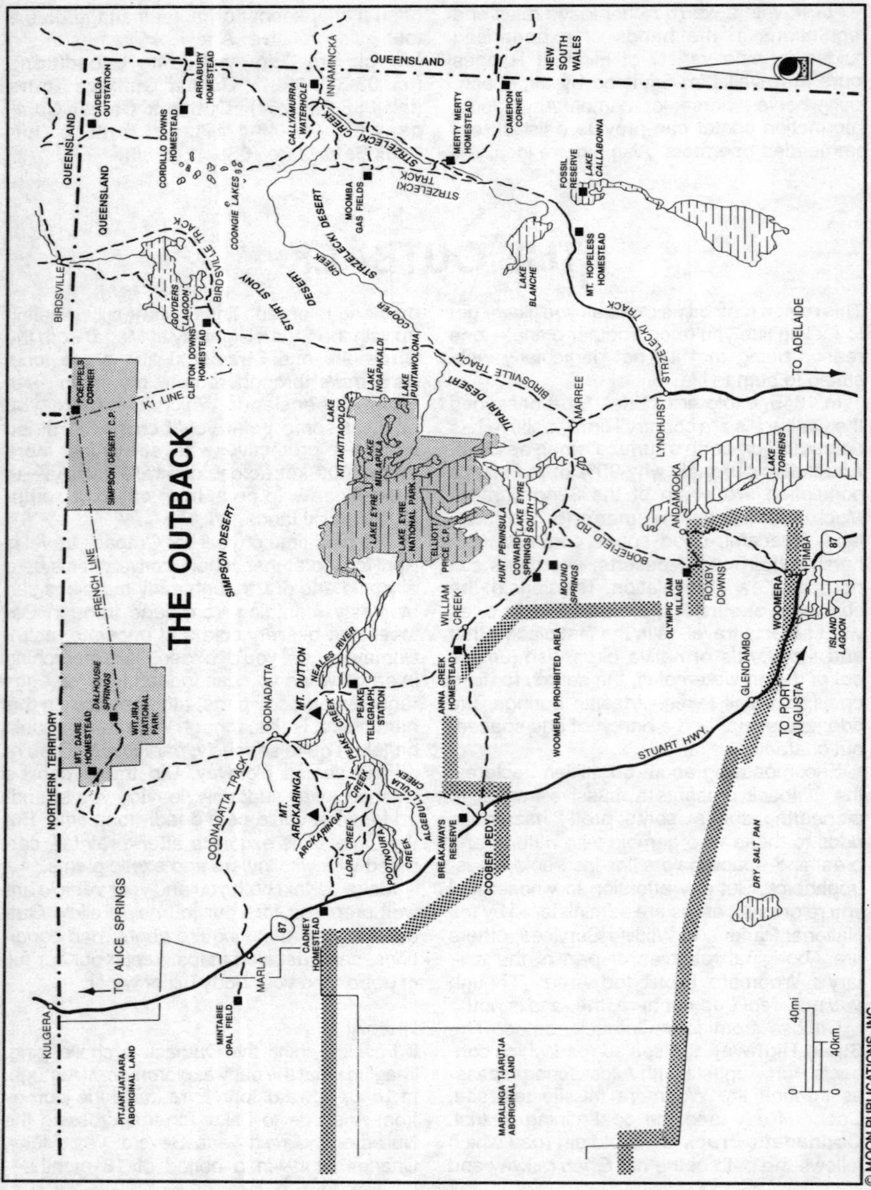
THE OUTBACK
NORTHERN TERRITORY
QUEENSLAND
NEW SOUTH WALES
TO ALICE SPRINGS
KULGERA
PITJANTJATJARA ABORIGINAL LAND
MINTABIE OPAL FIELD
MARLA
87
CADNEY HOMESTEAD
MARALINGA TJARUTJA ABORIGINAL LAND
OODNADATTA TRACK
OODNADATTA
MT. DARE HOMESTEAD
DALHOUSIE SPRINGS
WITJIRA NATIONAL PARK
FRENCH LINE
SIMPSON DESERT
SIMPSON DESERT C.P.
K1 LINE
POEPPELS CORNER
BIRDSVILLE
BIRDSVILLE TRACK
GOYDERS LAGOON
CLIFTON DOWNS HOMESTEAD
CADELGA OUTSTATION
CORDILLO DOWNS HOMESTEAD
ARRABURY HOMESTEAD
COONGIE LAKES
CALLYAMURRA WATERHOLE
INNAMINCKA
STURT STONY DESERT
COOPER CREEK
STRZELECKI DESERT
STRZELECKI CREEK
MOOMBA GAS FIELDS
STRZELECKI TRACK
MERTY MERTY HOMESTEAD
CAMERON CORNER
FOSSIL RESERVE
LAKE CALLABONNA
LAKE BLANCHE
MT. HOPELESS HOMESTEAD
LAKE PUNTAWOLONA
LAKE NGAPAKALDI
TIRARI DESERT
LAKE KITTAKITTAOOLOO
LAKE EYRE
LAKE MULAPULA
LAKE EYRE NATIONAL PARK
ELLIOTT PRICE C.P.
HUNT PENINSULA
LAKE EYRE SOUTH
MARREE
LYNDHURST
TO ADELAIDE
LAKE TORRENS
ANDAMOOKA
BOREFIELD RD.
OLYMPIC DAM VILLAGE
ROXBY DOWNS
COWARD SPRINGS
MOUND SPRINGS
WILLIAM CREEK
WOOMERA PROHIBITED AREA
ANNA CREEK HOMESTEAD
MT. DUTTON
NEALES RIVER
PEAKE TELEGRAPH STATION
PEAKE CREEK
MT. ARCKARINGA
ARCKARINGA CREEK
LORA CREEK
POOTNOURA CREEK
ALGEBUCKINA CREEK
BREAKAWAYS RESERVE
COOBER PEDY
STUART HWY.
GLENDAMBO
WOOMERA
PIMBA
ISLAND LAGOON
TO PORT AUGUSTA
DRY SALT PAN
0 40mi
0 40km
© MOON PUBLICATIONS, INC.

crossed the Cooper and Strzelecki creeks and Diamantina River, and discovered the Stony Desert (renamed Sturt Stony Desert), then fell sick and returned to Adelaide.

Robert O'Hara Burke and William John Wills made the first north-south continental crossing, only to die of malnutrition and exhaustion (near Innamincka, along the Strzelecki Track) on the return trip. John King, a member of their party, survived, thanks to nursing by local Aboriginals.

John McDouall Stuart, a member of Charles Sturt's expedition and no dummy, waited until the state Parliament gave him money to make the journey. In 1862, on his second try, he finally reached the sea in the northern end. Unfortunately, he also became ill on the return to Adelaide and he died a few years later, having lost his vision and his memory!

The first vehicle crossing from Adelaide to Darwin was made in 1908. Since then, historic journeys, in a wide assortment of transport, are still being made. *Yours* could be next!

ALONG THE STUART HIGHWAY

Unless you're desperate for petrol or a quick snack, pass by the ugly little town of **Pimba,** 173 km northwest of Port Augusta. In the 1950s-'60s, **Woomera,** off the highway a few kilometers from Pimba, was a test site for British experimental rockets. The most famous launching was that of the *Europa,* from 1964-70. About those same years NASA ran a deep space tracking station at nearby Island Lagoon. The testing range and "Narrungar" (the communications station) are controlled by the Australian Defence Department. Woomera still serves as a military base, and U.S. personnel continue to be stationed here (and the *stories* people tell about what goes on at this place! Spooky doings about spies, satellites, and alien spaceships!) The **heritage museum** at Woomera Village exhibits rockets, weapons, and aircraft. The Stuart Highway continues through part of the gigantic Woomera Prohibited Area, but permits are not necessary. Stay on the road and try not to think about the hush-hush plutonium accident that occurred here in the '50s.

For Woomera emergencies, contact **police** (tel. 086 73-7244), **ambulance** (tel. 74-3234), **hospital** (tel. 74-3294), or **RAA** (tel. 73-7715).

From Woomera, a detour travels north to newly established **Roxby Downs** township, built to house employees at the **Olympic Dam** mines, eight km away. Tours of dam operations depart from the visitor center at 10 a.m. daily.

Andamooka, 30 km east of Roxby Downs, is a small opal-mining site, known for high-quality gems. Claim owners often permit noodling on their claims, but be sure to ask first. You'll see a few dugout homes, as well as **Duke's Bottle Home,** a dwelling built from old beer bottles. **Andamooka Opal Hotel Motel** (tel. 086 72-7078) has inexpensive rooms. Campsites and on-site vans are available at **Andamooka Caravan Park** (tel. 72-7117).

For emergencies, contact the **police** (tel. 086 72-7072), **fire brigade** (tel. 73-7222), or **ambulance** (tel. 72-7087).

From Roxby Downs, Borefield Rd. (a dirt track) continues north, meeting the Oodnadatta Track near Lake Eyre South.

Back on Stuart Highway, **Glendambo,** 113 km northwest of Woomera, provides tourist facilities. **Glendambo Hotel Motel** (tel. 72-1030) has modern rooms at expensive rates, but campsites are available at the caravan park next door.

Coober Pedy (pop. 2,100), one of the world's leading opal-mining centers, was established in 1915 after a teenage boy discovered this gem while gold-prospecting with his father. It's so oppressively hot and dusty that most of the town works, lives, and prays in dugout dwellings underground. (Appropriately, the name "Coober Pedy" is derived from Aboriginal words which, put together, mean "White Man in a Hole.") It's a good pit stop (literally), 254 km northwest of Glendambo; otherwise this town is better suited to miners (about 40 different nationalities), would-be ants, and movie companies who choose this locale for lunar shots *(Mad Max III* was filmed here).

The best spot to noodle (pick through old diggings) is in the "jeweler's shop" area, near Faye's underground house. You don't need a permit unless you're on a pegged claim; you cannot use any sort of digging device—otherwise you must obtain a permit from the Department of Mines and Energy in Adelaide.

If you're in the market to buy, beware and shop around (there are more than 30 dealers in town). Highly regarded though expensive outlets are those at the Opal Inn and Desert Cave motels. You'll find scads of tours to dugout homes and opal outlets (it should be noted that some tour guides double as opal salesmen).

Radeka's Motel and Backpacker's Inn (tel. 72-5223) has an underground dorm for $15 per night; motel rooms are moderately priced. **Umoona Opal Mine, Museum and Motel,** Main St. (tel. 72-5288), has rooms with communal facilities for inexpensive rates that include a tour of the mine. **Underground Motel,** Catacomb Rd. (tel. 72-5324), in the moderate range, includes breakfast. Luxury digs are expensive at the **Desert Cave Motel,** Hutchinson St. (tel. 72-5688). Rent campsites or on-site vans at **Oasis Caravan Park** (tel. 72-5169), where facilities include a swimming pool.

Due to the multinational population, you'll find a wide range of ethnic eating spots. Pub-crawling, as you might imagine, can be rough here. Women should be particularly cautious.

For emergencies, contact **police** (tel. 086 72-5056), **fire brigade** (tel. 72-5000), **ambulance** (tel. 72-5009), or **RAA** (tel. 72-5036).

Breakaways Reserve, 28 km north of Coober Pedy, is a 40-square-km block of low hills which features a continually changing color landscape, unique flora and fauna, and walking trails.

The drive to **Cadney Homestead,** 153 km north of Coober Pedy, is fairly dreary. Refuel yourself and your vehicle and either cut east through Arckaringa Hills, Copper Hills, and the Painted Desert to Oodnadatta (160 km), or continue north on the Stuart Highway. Another featureless 81-km drive brings you to **Marla** (pop. 240), established in 1978 as a tourist service center. This is also where the highway meets the *Ghan* railway line. Rooms at **Marla Hotel Motel** (tel. 086 70-7001) are moderate to expensive; campsites at the caravan park are cheap.

The opal fields at **Mintabie,** 50 km west of Marla (along a gravel road), have proved to be richer than those at Coober Pedy. It's another 165 km to the Northern Territory border, 185 km to teensy Kulgera township, and 464 km to Alice Springs.

ALONG THE OODNADATTA TRACK

Marree (pop. 380), 379 km north of Port Augusta, is the beginning (and ending) point for both the Oodnadatta and Birdsville tracks. During the 1880s this mini-town was a big depot for camel drivers transporting goods to the Outback. (You can still see a couple of leftover date palms and a few Afghani names, as reminders.) Between 1960 and 1980, it was the changing-gauge station for the old *Ghan,* choo-chooing to Alice Springs. **Maree Hotel,** Main St. (tel. 75-8344), has inexpensive rooms. Campsites and on-site vans are available at **Marree Tourist Park** (tel. 75-8371).

It's 210 km from Maree to William Creek. The track edges along **Lake Eyre South,** where two lookouts adjacent to the roadway afford views of this salt pan which stretches 185 km north (and this is a baby compared with Lake Eyre North). A rough piece of track leads to the lakeshore.

At **Stuart Creek,** you can view a six-km piece of the original *Ghan* line, as well as a few preserved sheds, fettler's cottages, and a water tank. The oasis at **Coward Springs,** about 35 km farther north, includes railway ruins, an old plantation (now a bird refuge), some old date palms, and a warm, bubbling pond.

Bubbler and **Blanchecup** are mound springs, six km south of the track (you'll see fences around them), adjacent to Coward Springs. Bubbler is a bubbling pool of fine sand. Blanchecup is deceptively clear and clean-looking, but you have to dip in and out through a muddy, weedy stench. Either of the springs should open every pore in your body; stick your head in and you won't need a facial—or maybe even a shampoo—for years! (You'd pay a *fortune* for this in Europe!)

Other points of interest are the old **Beresford** railway siding and flowing bore (24 km north of Coward Springs) and, 11 km farther, **Strangways,** the old Overland Telegraph repeater, where there's also a flowing bore (a bare water pipe).

William Creek, 45 km north of Strangways, is touted as South Australia's (some say the world's) smallest town that lies within one of the state's (if not the world's) largest cattle stations—30,027-square-km Anna Creek. The big thing to do here is hang around the pub, soaking up local color and lore, or gawking at other travelers, usually crowded around the pay phone. Basic accommodations at that same **William Creek Hotel** (tel. 70-7880) are moderately priced; campsites cost $3 per person.

It's 206 km to Oodnadatta, a journey through gibber (Aboriginal for "stone") plains, ranging in color from sand to charcoal, and in size from pebbles to Frisbees. The gibbers also have a strange reflective quality. Sights along this section of track are **Edwards Creek** ruins and bore (you can take a shower here, but your hair will turn to Brillo), **Warrina Siding** ruin, a memorial to explorer Ernest Giles (in 1876 he crossed from Geraldton, Western Australia, to Peake Telegraph Station, east of the memorial), the **Algebuckina** siding ruin, one of the best old ***Ghan* railway bridges**, and **Mt. Dutton**.

Oodnadatta (pop. 160) sprang into being in 1891 with the arrival of the railway and then, in the 1980s, came close to disappearing when the rail line was moved and the Stuart Highway was sealed. This true Outback town has turned its old railway station into a museum, but the *real* attraction here is the **Pink Roadhouse,** which serves as social center, petrol stop, supermarket, "Oodnaburger" supplier, mechanic's garage, caravan park, info provider, tour organizer, and travelers' clearinghouse and meeting place. Both campsites and on-site vans are available. For information, phone 086-70-7822. Rooms at **Transcontinental Hotel** (tel. 70-7804) are moderately priced and include breakfast.

For emergencies, contact **police** (tel. 70-7805) or **ambulance** (tel. 70-7803).

The Oodnadatta Track continues northwest for 118 km, then turns west. From this junction, it's about 100 km to Marla and the Stuart Highway.

THE BIRDSVILLE TRACK

In the 1880s, the Birdsville Track was created so that stockmen could drive their cattle from the grazing grounds in southwest Queensland to the rail station at Marree, where they were loaded on a train. This border community kept busy during the days when interstate customs were charged. In 1901, after free trade was instigated, the cattle began traveling by truck along different routes.

The 517 km from Marree to Birdsville (in Queensland) pass by deserted homesteads and mission ruins, scalding bores and welcoming waterholes, and *phenomenal* amounts of sandy dunes and rocky plains—the Tirari, Simpson, Sturt Stony, and Strzelecki deserts. At Clifton Hills Homestead the road splits: the inside track which crosses Goyder Lagoon is closed; the Birdsville goes around it. Seek advice before picking up your fork—a wrong decision could be fatal. (Also keep in mind that the lagoon is a breeding ground for snakes.)

Birdsville, 12 km across the Queensland border, was established in 1882 to serve stockmen headed down the Birdsville Track. Today it caters to travelers following in the stockmen's tracks. Original buildings are the old pub and mission hospital. Even though this is a remote outpost town, after an arduous Outback trek Birdsville's simple tourist facilities seem like a limo ride down Rodeo Drive.

This route is for very well-prepared vehicles and bodies. Check in with police at either Marree or Birdsville, and follow all Outback driving rules and local advice.

For emergencies in Birdsville, contact **police** (tel. 00717-8220) or **ambulance** (tel. 8232).

THE STRZELECKI TRACK

For those with more larceny than cow pie in their souls, who'd rather follow in the bootsteps of outlaws than stockmen, the background on this route has a bit more juice to it.

The Strzelecki Track came into being in 1871 when bushman Henry Radford (aka Captain Starlight) used it to drive his herds of stolen cattle from Queensland down to the Adelaide markets. (Strzelecki Creek had been named earlier by Charles Sturt, for his fellow explorer Count Strzelecki.) Other drovers, legit and otherwise, used the track also, alternating the route a bit around Cooper Creek where there were more watering holes. The track fell into disuse for many years until the Moomba gas fields southwest of Innamincka were established. The Moomba section of this track (from Strzelecki Crossing to Innamincka) is better kept, but the original bit will appeal more to wanna-be rustlers.

Starting at **Lyndhurst** (193 km north of Hawker and 79 km south of Marree), the Strzelecki Track wends 459 km northeasterly to Innamincka, a tiny service town, then cuts north for 305 km, turning west in Queensland for the 110-km portion that leads into Birdsville. It's also possible to cross into Queensland from Innamincka and the Arrabury Homestead junction, and to travel 53 km east to Betoota and beyond, instead of going west to Birdsville (just keep in mind, you're still a long, long way from "civilization").

Pick up any necessary provisions at Lyndhurst; this is your last fuel stop until Innamincka (don't expect a petrol pump at the Moomba gas fields).

Following the northern edge of the Flinders Ranges, you'll pass ruins of several old homesteads, cruise through the Cobbler Desert between Lakes Blanche and Callabonna (incidentally, **Lake Callabonna** is the site of the fossilized diprotodon, the largest known marsupial), finally crossing Strzelecki Creek about 85 km north of Mt. Hopeless Homestead. From the creek crossing, you must choose either the track which passes the **Moomba gas fields** (no tourist facilities except a telephone at the security gate). The old road goes through **Merty Merty Homestead** where, if you're one of those people who likes to sprawl across different sides of borders at the same time (and have a photo taken!), you can drive 109 km southeast to **Cameron Corner,** a coming-together of South Australia, Queensland, and New South Wales.

Innamincka, another outpost town à la Birdsville, is also the place where explorers Burke and Wills bit the dust. Several historic spots are dotted about this bitsy service town, most of them memorials to the exploring dead—places where bodies were found, moved to, finally buried, where rescue parties set up camp, where the sole survivor was discovered by Aboriginals. On Cooper Creek, rock carvings by the Yantrwantas Aboriginal tribe can be seen at the eastern end of Cullyamurra waterhole. Fish can be found inside that very same waterhole as well as the waterholes along the northwest branch of Cooper Creek.

Find inexpensive accommodations at **Innamincka Trading Post** (tel. 75-9900).

The **Coongie Lakes,** 112 km northeast of Innamincka, a bird and wildlife refuge, also offer excellent fishing opportunities. It's a long, rough drive from Innamincka to Birdsville, past Cordillo Downs and Arrabury Homesteads (no facilities), and the ruins of Cadelga Outstation, used in the 1930s by the Royal Geographic Society to observe the transit of Venus.

Again, this is not an out-for-a-Sunday-drive road. Make sure you are well prepared, and check in with police at Lyndhurst.

OUTBACK PARKS

Only the most well-equipped and pre-informed travelers should explore the remote, arid Outback parks. Desert park passes must be obtained in advance from the National Parks and Wildlife Service. The issuing office will provide you with all necessary rules and regulations.

Lake Eyre National Park (1,228,000 hectares) encompasses Lake Eyre North (Australia's largest salt lake), adjacent Tirari Desert, and a desert wilderness conservation area. Lake Eyre, normally a huge dry salt pan, is where, in 1964, Sir Donald Campbell set a world land-speed record (640 kph) in Bluebird, his jet-powered car; when I visited a few years ago, the lake was full of water! Reaching a depth of 16 meters below sea level (where the

TOURISM SOUTH AUSTRALIA

Lake Eyre

salt crust measures 230 millimeters thick), the lake has filled only a few times since European settlement. Smaller salt lakes lie within the duney desert section, and fossil deposits have been discovered at Lake Ngapakaldi, on the far eastern edge.

The park has no facilities. Access is via Muloorina Homestead, 90 km north of Marree or, alternately, travel six km east of William Creek, then 51 km east to Belt Bay, on the lake's southwest corner.

Elliot Price Conservation Park (64,570 hectares), 105 km northwest of Marree on the southern edge of Lake Eyre North, was the first arid zone reserve, inhabited by red kangaroos, grass owls, and low sparse vegetation. Hunt Peninsula, within the park, is a long limestone arm reaching into Lake Eyre North. The park has no facilities.

Witjira National Park (776,900 hectares) 120 km north of Oodnadatta, comprises flat hills, salt pans, sandy dunes, desert and gibber plains, and numerous mound, thermal, and hot springs. Formerly Mt. Dare Homestead, this only became a national park in the 1980s. The most popular attractions here are the 60 or so **Dalhousie Springs,** Australia's largest artesian baths, in which visitors soak, bubble, and laze away in the tepid waters. This same mineralized bath water originated as rainfall in north Queensland about four million years ago!

Near the springs are ruins and relics of early farming days. After a rain, wildflowers spurt up around the pools. Native birds include brolgas, darters, gibbers, thrush, and cinnamon quail.

A campground is available near the springs. Mount Dare Homestead, 70 km northwest of the springs, has accommodations, camping, food, emergency repairs, fuel, and an airstrip.

Simpson Desert Conservation Park is an enormous (692,680 hectares) arid wilderness in the middle of the Simpson Desert. A large bird population, including zebra finches, budgerigars, black kites, and wedge-tailed eagles, shares the land with parallel red sand dunes, salt lakes, gidgi woodlands, and post-rain wildflowers.

The park has no facilities. More-than-adequate provisions, proper equipment, and a first-class 4WD vehicle are essential. Access to the park is via Dalhousie Springs from Oodnadatta, or via Poeppel Corner from Birdsville.

Large areas surrounding Innamincka, including Cooper Creek and the Coongie Lakes, have been declared a regional reserve, as has a huge portion of the Simpson Desert outside of the Witjira National Park and Simpson Desert Conservation Park boundaries.

Travelers who wish to make the hazardous trek across the Simpson Desert should do so only with experienced Outback drivers, in

Red-sand dunes paint the desert canvas.

top-condition 4WD vehicles, equipped with massive amounts of equipment, provisions, information, and stamina.

SERVICES AND INFORMATION

Fuel and **public telephones** are available at the following Outback locations: Andamooka, Birdsville, Cadney Homestead, Coober Pedy, Glendambo, Innamincka, Kulgera, Lyndhurst, Marla, Marree, Mintabie, Olympic Dam, Oodnadatta, Pimba, Tarcoola, William Creek, and Woomera.

See "Information" in the "Flinders Ranges" section for tourist information. Also obtain information at **Coober Pedy Tourist Information Centre,** Council Office, Hutchinson St. (tel. 72-5298). Purchase cards, maps, and local-interest publications at **Underground Books and Gallery** (tel. 72-5558), next to the Desert Cave Motel in Coober Pedy. Additionally, most pubs, motels, caravan parks, and roadhouses (particularly the Pink Roadhouse) carry information.

Desert Park Passes ($40 per vehicle, per year), can be obtained from National Parks and Wildlife Service offices. For further information, contact Information Officer, Desert Park Headquarters, P.O. Box 34, Leigh Creek, S.A. 5731 (tel. 75-2499).

FLINDERS RANGES AND OUTBACK RADIO STATIONS

Radio stations which broadcast into the Flinders Ranges and Outback are: 5CK 639; 5CL 729; 5AN 891; 5CS 1044; 5AU 1242.

TRANSPORT

Augusta Airways (tel. 42-3100) operates a "Channel Mail Run" between Port Augusta and Mount Isa (Queensland), with stops in Innamincka and Birdsville on the weekend. This company also offers charter and scenic flights. **Kendell Airlines** (tel. 231-9567, area code 08) flies a frequent Adelaide–Woomera–Olympic Dam–Coober Pedy route, and **Lloyd Aviation** (tel. 224-7500, area code 08) makes an Adelaide-Olympic Dam run. Fares are about $150 to Woomera, $230 to Coober Pedy.

Stateliner (tel. 233-2722, area code 08, Adelaide; 42-5055, Port Augusta) operates frequent coach service from Adelaide and some Flinders Ranges communities to Andamooka, Cadney Homestead, Coober Pedy, Glendambo, Lyndhurst, Marla, Marree, Olympic Dam, Pimba, Roxby Downs, Woomera, and on to Alice Springs. Fares are approximately $40 to Woomera, $60 to Marree, $70 to Coober Pedy.

See "Information" in the "Flinders Ranges" section for **organized tours.** Arrangements can be made for fishing and cruising trips along **Cooper Creek,** as well as other Innamincka area tours. For more information, phone (086) 75-9900.

BOB RACE

THE NORTHERN TERRITORY

INTRODUCTION

Ah, beware Australia's last frontier—take just one look and it's likely to itch clear through your bones and sting your spirit, and not even those venerable Royal Flying Doctors will be able to cure you. Long after the red dust has settled and you've put Aboriginal myths to rest, *your* dreamtime will be influenced forevermore by this superlative land with its big rocks, big crocs, and big thirst.

This barren-but-bewitching region, encompassing 1,346,200 square kilometers, is a veritable dynamo of contrasts—the tropical Top End and the arid Red Centre, sacred grounds and tourist meccas, Stone-Age culture and K marts—inhabited by fewer than one percent of Australia's population (about 150,000), a quarter of them Aboriginal, and the remainder residing mainly in Darwin or Alice Springs.

Despite inevitable infiltration by the 20th century, the Northern Territory, with its ancient lands, eerie geological formations, and 40,000 years of Aboriginal history, ceremony, and tradition, is still the ultimate magical mystery tour.

THE LAND

Orient yourself by the Aussie buzzwords: the Top End; the Track; the Alice; the Rock; and the Red Centre. The **Top End** refers to the northern part of the Territory comprised of Darwin (the cosmopolitan gateway with one of the world's highest consumptions of beer per capita), glorious Kakadu National Park (where *Crocodile Dundee* was born, or at least filmed, and real-life home to those man-eating saltwater crocs), the Aboriginals' Arn-

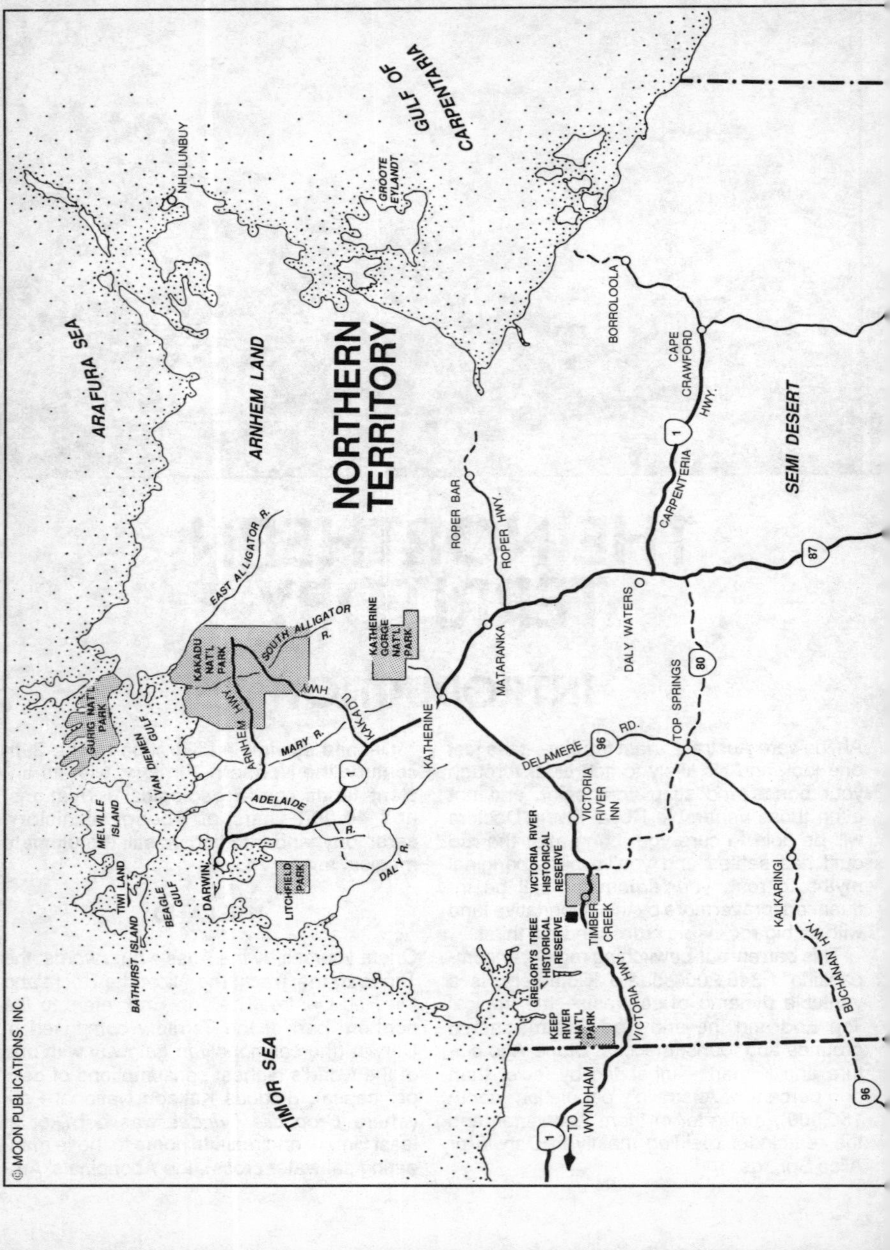
© MOON PUBLICATIONS, INC.
NORTHERN TERRITORY
ARAFURA SEA
TIMOR SEA
GULF OF CARPENTARIA
ARNHEM LAND
SEMI DESERT
NHULUNBUY
GROOTE EYLANDT
GURIG NAT'L PARK
VAN DIEMEN GULF
MELVILLE ISLAND
TIWI LAND
BATHURST ISLAND
BEAGLE GULF
DARWIN
LITCHFIELD PARK
KAKADU NAT'L PARK
EAST ALLIGATOR R.
SOUTH ALLIGATOR R.
MARY R.
ADELAIDE R.
DALY R.
ARNHEM HWY.
KAKADU HWY.
KATHERINE GORGE NAT'L PARK
KATHERINE
MATARANKA
ROPER BAR
ROPER HWY.
DALY WATERS
CARPENTERIA HWY.
CAPE CRAWFORD
BORROLOOLA
TOP SPRINGS
DELAMERE RD.
VICTORIA RIVER INN
VICTORIA RIVER HISTORICAL RESERVE
TIMBER CREEK
GREGORYS TREE HISTORICAL RESERVE
KEEP RIVER NAT'L PARK
VICTORIA HWY.
TO WYNDHAM
KALKARINGI
BUCHANAN HWY.
1
80
87
96

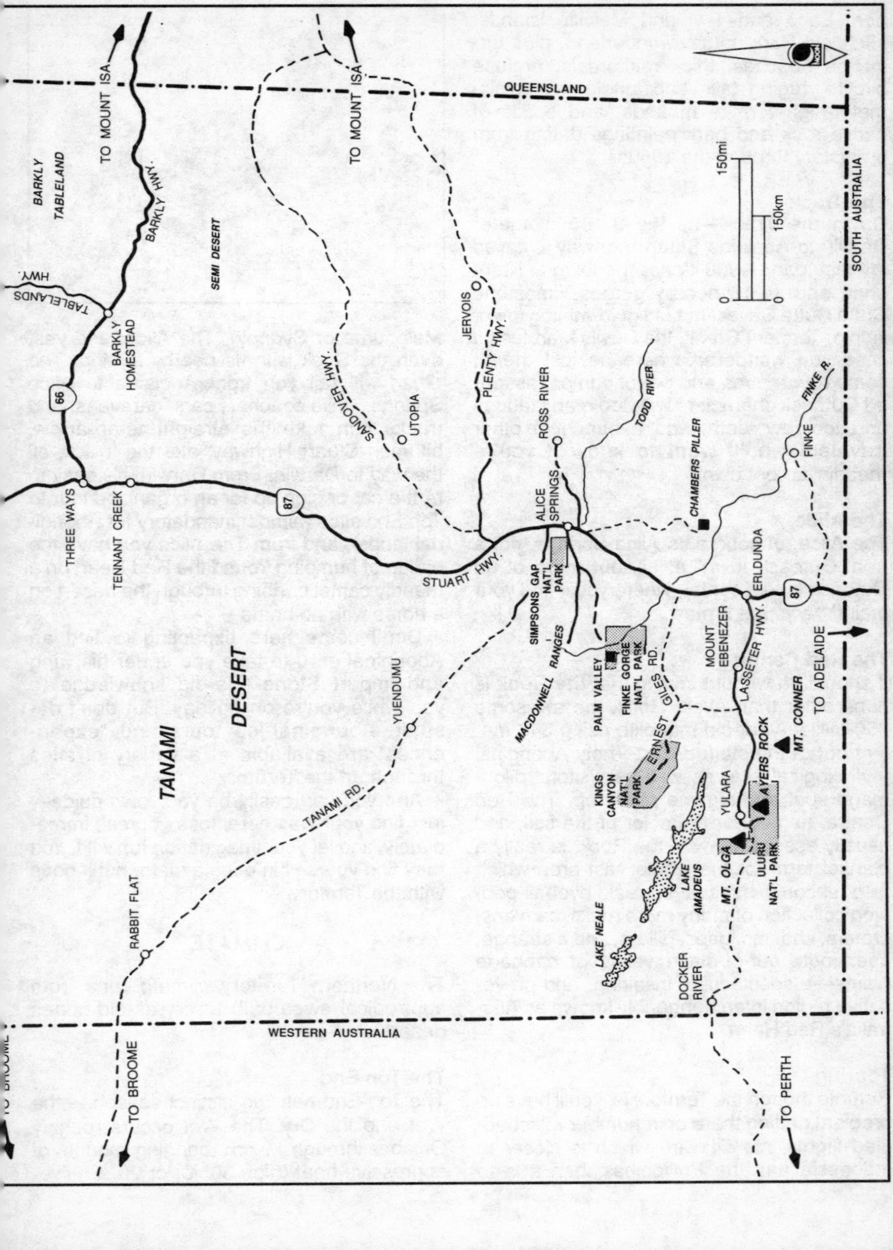
TO MOUNT ISA
TO MOUNT ISA
QUEENSLAND
BARKLY TABLELAND
BARKLY HWY.
SEMI DESERT
TABLELANDS HWY.
BARKLY HOMESTEAD
66
THREE WAYS
TENNANT CREEK
87
SANDOVER HWY.
UTOPIA
JERVOIS
PLENTY HWY.
ROSS RIVER
TODD RIVER
FINKE R.
FINKE
CHAMBERS PILLER
ALICE SPRINGS
STUART HWY.
SIMPSONS GAP NAT'L PARK
MACDONNELL RANGES
PALM VALLEY
FINKE GORGE NAT'L PARK
ERNEST GILES RD.
MOUNT EBENEZER
ERLDUNDA
87
LASSETER HWY.
TO ADELAIDE
MT. CONNER
AYERS ROCK
YULARA
ULURU NAT'L PARK
MT. OLGA
KINGS CANYON NAT'L PARK
LAKE AMADEUS
LAKE NEALE
DOCKER RIVER
TO PERTH
WESTERN AUSTRALIA
SOUTH AUSTRALIA
TANAMI DESERT
TANAMI RD.
YUENDUMU
RABBIT FLAT
TO BROOME
0
150mi
0
150km

hem Land and Tiwi and Melville islands, Litchfield Park nature wonderland, plus turquoise beaches, thick rainforests, profuse birdlife, raging falls and jungle rivers, six-meter-high termite mounds, and scads of native rock and bark paintings dating from prehistory through the 1960s.

MIKE WELLINS

The Track

Down the Track—as the 3,188-kilometer Darwin-to-Adelaide Stuart Highway is called in these parts—you'll pass the town of Katherine and its 13 nearby gorges, limestone Cutta Cutta Caves, the old gold-mining township of Tennant Creek, the Devils Marbles (in case you wondered where he lost them), some rough pubs and petrol pumps, assorted Outback characters with too many tattoos and too few teeth, and a bunch of other travelers who'll want to know if you're "headin' up or down."

The Alice

The Alice, of course, is Alice Springs, not a "real Outback town" at all, but more of an Outback tourist center, where you'll find your mall-fix *and* that K mart.

The Red Centre

It should go without saying that **the Rock** is none other than Ayers Rock, the awesome 650-million-year-old monolith rising 348 meters out of the stark desert—holy Aboriginal mythological site, as well as visitors' pilgrimage spot and bigtime photo op. The Red Centre, named for the color of the soil, and usually associated with the Rock, is really a blanket term for the whole vast area which also encompasses a surreal, eyeball-popping collection of many more rocks, canyons, craters, chasms, gaps, pillars, and a strange, seemingly out-of-place valley of cabbage palms—a spectacular, inspiring, and provocative region interchangeably known as Australia's Red Heart.

Touring

Remote though the Territory is, you'll have no problem getting there on a number of scheduled flights into Darwin (which is closer to Indonesia and the Philippines than it is to Melbourne or Sydney), The Alice, and yes, even the Rock with its nearby airstrip. The *Ghan* will rail you from Adelaide to Alice Springs, while coaches, cars, caravans, and trucks can take the straight-as-an-arrow, bitumen Stuart Highway, aka the Track, all the way to Darwin. From Darwin, it's easy to rent a car or sign up for an organized tour to Top End sites (almost mandatory for Aboriginal lands), and from The Alice you have the option of humping 'round the Red Heart on a friendly camel or riding through the desert on a horse with no name.

Don't come here expecting to find an Aboriginal guru to take you under his wing and impart Stone-Age-old knowledge to you while you're on holiday. But don't despair. Aboriginal-led tours and "experiences" are available at a variety of sites throughout the Territory.

And you can easily be your *own* guide—just find your way here, lose yourself immediately, and let your imagination run wild. You may find yourself in quite a state, but it goes with the Territory.

CLIMATE

The Northern Territory climate runs from subtropical sweatbath to dry-as-old-bones desert.

The Top End

The Top End has two distinct seasons—the Wet and the Dry. The Wet occurs roughly October through March, bringing months of oppressive heat (high 30° C, or 90° F), live-in-the-shower humidity, and monsoonal rains. The average rainfall of 1,500 mm occurs mainly from December through April, often causing roads, plains, and rivers to flood. Swimmers and divers should remember that from October to May northern waters are deluged with the dangerous box jellyfish.

May through September are the Dry, and probably the most comfortable months for travel, with only about 25 mm of rainfall and a lower daily temperature range of high 20s to low 30s C (high 70s to low 90s F).

The Centre

The Centre is a different story. Summer days are long and hot, from 35-40° C (95-104° F), with low humidity and warm nights. The Rock, the Olgas, and other heat-generating regions can reach 50° C (about 132° F) and strenuous treks (or even piggyback rides while twirling a parasol) should be avoided. Winter days are mild to warm, averaging 20° C (54° F), with plenty of clear skies and sunshine. Campers and bushwalkers, particularly, should come prepared for freezing nights.

Rainfall, though erratic, usually hits during summer months, occasionally flooding creekbeds and back roads, though normally the sealed Track stays open to motorists. Annual average downpour is 369 mm around Tennant Creek and 285 mm in the Alice area.

HISTORY

Prehistory

It's generally agreed that the Aborigines migrated from Indonesia at least 40,000 years ago, and some historians set the date even 80,000 years earlier, making the Aborigines quite possibly the world's oldest surviving race. Any way you look at it, they've been in Australia a long time, with Arnhem Land in the Territory's northeast corner marking the spot of tropical Australia's first human settlement.

For several centuries the Aborigines enjoyed a sort of love-hate relationship with Macassarese fishermen from Indonesia who visited regularly in search of trepang (sea slugs) until the early 1900s, when the Australian government told them to scoot.

Exploration And Colonization

In 1623, the Dutch ship *Arnhem* became the first recorded European contact, followed by Abel Tasman's exploration of the northern coast in 1644. Aside from naming some of the features, the Dutch didn't seem terribly interested in the region. Additional charting of the coast was undertaken by Matthew Flinders in 1803, and then navigator Phillip King 14 years later.

The British began the old colonial ball rolling when, in 1824, Captain Gordon Bremer—in the name of King George IV—claimed the land as part of New South Wales. After settlement attempts failed at Melville Island, Raffles Bay, and Port Essington (lousy climate, no trade), the northern coast was left alone for about 15 years. In 1863, on the heels of John McDouall Stuart's ground-breaking south-north continental crossing, the Northern Territory was vested in the colony of South Australia (and called Northern Territory of South Australia), and another settlement created by the first government resident, Colonel Boyle Finniss, at Escape Cliffs near the Adelaide River mouth. Another failure.

Finally, in 1869, Surveyor-General George Goyder decided to try out Darwin as a prospective site. Bingo! Good choice, especially when shortly thereafter gold was discovered at nearby Pine Creek—bringing with it a railway line—followed by the Overland Telegraph Line and, subsequently, the predictable array of cattle ranchers, Chinese laborers, pastoralists, and significant others. Additional mineral finds in the 1880s through early 1900s cinched the area as "a go." The Track, lifeline between Alice Springs and Darwin, was not constructed until the 1930s and not sealed for about another 20 years.

Recent History

The Australian Commonwealth government took over control of the Territory in 1911, and though the Northern Territory became self-governing in 1978, it still remains economically dependent upon the commonwealth. Agriculture, cattle-raising, mining (gold, bauxite, uranium), and booming tourism are the region's major money-makers.

The Aborigines
Wondering what happened to the Aborigines? Some tried to resist colonization of their land—in vain. The hunters and food gatherers who'd lived for so long in perfect harmony with the land and environment were, by the early 1900s, herded onto government reserves, introduced to Christian charities, forced into hard labor for low pay, left to rot on the fringes of towns, and given a taste of alcohol. Only those few who lived in the most remote areas were left alone to practice their age-old traditions.

It took some time but, in the 1960s, Northern Territory Aborigines began pressing for their rights—with various protests against mining, ranching, and other intrusions on their reserves—culminating with the passage of the 1976 Aboriginal Land (NT) Act, giving them control of their lands (i.e., designated reserves) and returning their sacred sites (including Ayers Rock). The Act also allowed for the appointment of Aboriginal Land Commissioners and the creation of administrative Aboriginal Land Councils. Presently the Aborigines own about one-third of the Territory. Many have returned to their traditional ways and stay on the reserves, out of white reach; others live in squalid conditions around townships, ravaged by the effects of racism and alcohol.

ABORIGINAL LAND ETIQUETTE

Permits To Enter
You need to obtain an advance permit from the traditional owners before entering Aboriginal land *and* you probably won't get one! Normally, permits are not granted to travelers, but if you are part of an organized tour or have a relative working on the land, authorization will probably be approved—allow *plenty* of time for the application process as communication is often difficult.

Permits are not required for travel on public roads that cross Aboriginal land, but if you might need to stop for fuel along the way, you'll still need a **transit permit,** though ordinarily those are given in 10 days or so. Entering Aboriginal land without a permit can result in a fine of up to $1000. Obtain an official application form from the appropriate Land Council.

Darwin, Nhulunbuy, And Katherine Regions
The Permits Officer
Northern Land Council
P.O. Box 39843
Winnellie, N.T. 0821
tel. 81-7011

BOB RACE

Alice Springs And Tennant Creek Regions
The Permits Officer
Central Land Council
P.O. Box 3321
Alice Springs, N.T. 0871
tel. 52-3800

Melville And Bathurst Islands
The Permits Officer
Tiwi Land Council
Nguiu, Bathurst Island via Darwin, N.T. 0822
tel. (089) 78-3966

Sacred Sites
Sacred sites are places or objects that hold special meaning for the Aboriginal people and, as such, are protected by law. Show respect for their significance and do not enter, damage, or deface these areas.

Photography
You'll need advance permission for any commercial photography on traditional lands, but not for personal snaps. However, *do not* snap away at individual Aborigines without asking first (and don't expect a jovial response, either).

Liquor
Liquor is restricted in many Aboriginal communities. Check with the permit-issuing Land Council for particulars.

DARWIN

The Northern Territory's capital city was named for Charles Darwin, a shipmate of harbor discoverer John Lort Stokes, and the place has been in a state of evolution ever since!

Australians commonly joke about this Top End tropical city—with its difficult climate, transient population, and fabled thirst. Though true, those elements have also inspired a thriving frontier town, lively cosmopolitan center and, yes, lotsa laughs as well as fisticuffs over that amazing intake of beer known worldwide as the Darwin Thirst. (Don't laugh —the Darwin stubby contains two litres of beer instead of the normal 375 milliliters; the average intake is 230 liters per year, and that's a *low* estimate.)

People don't stick around here long, that's a fact. The weather and the isolation take their toll. Heck, not even the *city* stays put! During WW II, more than 60 bomb attacks by the Japanese pretty much turned Darwin into a pile of rubble. Then, in 1974, Cyclone Tracy paid a surprise Christmas Day visit, leveling practically the entire city. With indomitable Territorian pull-together spirit (and no doubt *many* thirst-quenchers under their tool belts), Darwin was rebuilt into a durable, modern center, punctuated here and there by the few surviving historical structures, accented by flowering bougainvillea, frangipani blossoms, and swaying palms.

Today's Darwin, with a population of 76,000, is a conglomeration of 50 or so ethnic groups including descendants of the Chinese miners, Japanese pearlers, Europeans who sought escape from postwar oppression, a relatively new onslaught of refugees from Southeast Asia, barramundi fishers, and a steady stream of travelers and backpackers headed to or from Asia, Top End attractions, or the rest of Australia. Most of the people who "do time" here work within some element of this Territorial administrative center's government, mining, or tourism sectors.

The city center, compactly situated on a peninsula looking toward Darwin Harbour, is easily explored on foot. The Stuart Highway becomes Daly Street as it enters the city, bisecting Smith Street. Head one km toward the harbor to Smith Street Mall, the main shopping district and location of the Northern Territory Government Tourist Bureau. The majority of central Darwin sites and services—including Darwin Transit Centre, the General Post Office, and the Automobile Association of the Northern Territory—fall within a few blocks' radius of the mall. Noteworthy suburban attractions are mostly located at Larrakeyah, Palmerston, Fanny Bay, and East Point, all within 10 kilometers to the north and east of city center. Take a right turn off Smith St., onto Gilruth Ave. (which becomes East Point Rd.) to access most of these areas.

And, though you won't find the flair and sophistication of a high-falutin' metropolis like Melbourne or Sydney, easygoing and eclectic Darwin can hold its own. And it can certainly hold its beer!

THE HISTORICAL TOUR

Yes, acts of war and God aside, a few dear structures—or pieces thereof—still stand. *A Walk Through Historical Darwin,* a booklet published by the National Trust, is a good source of information. *This* particular stroll may move your spirit as well as your feet. It starts off at the Tree of Knowledge, on the east side of downtown, continues in a loop around the Esplanade, heads down Smith Street Mall, and winds up at the Chinese Temple.

Tree Of Knowledge

The ancient banyan behind the Civic Centre on Harry Chan Ave. is a longtime city landmark. Heralded as the "tree of knowledge" by Buddhists (Gautama received enlightenment while sitting beneath a bodhi tree—same

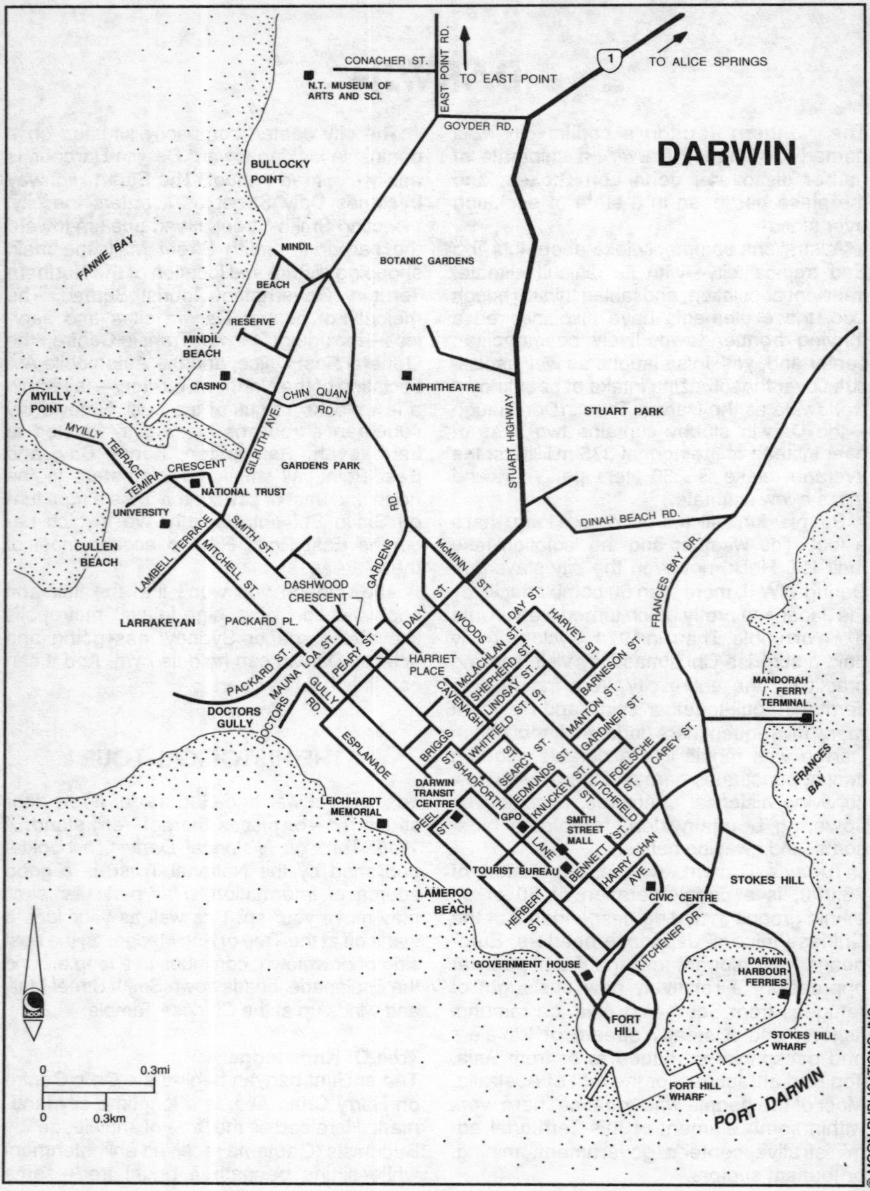
DARWIN
CONACHER ST.
EAST POINT RD.
TO EAST POINT
1
TO ALICE SPRINGS
N.T. MUSEUM OF
ARTS AND SCI.
GOYDER RD.
BULLOCKY
POINT
FANNIE BAY
MINDIL
BOTANIC GARDENS
BEACH
RESERVE
MINDIL
BEACH
CASINO
AMPHITHEATRE
MYILLY
POINT
CHIN QUAN
RD.
STUART PARK
STUART HIGHWAY
MYILLY
TERRACE
GILRUTH AVE.
TEMIRA CRESCENT
GARDENS PARK
NATIONAL TRUST
UNIVERSITY
CULLEN
BEACH
LAMBELL TERRACE
SMITH ST.
MITCHELL ST.
GARDENS
RD.
DINAH BEACH RD.
McMINN
ST.
FRANCES BAY DR.
DASHWOOD
CRESCENT
LARRAKEYAN
PACKARD PL.
PACKARD ST.
MAUNA LOA ST.
PEARY ST.
DALY
ST.
WOODS
DAY ST.
HARVEY ST.
HARRIET
PLACE
McLACHLAN ST.
SHEPHERD ST.
LINDSAY ST.
BARNESON ST.
DOCTORS
GULLY
DOCTORS
GULLY
RD.
CAVENAGH
ST.
MANTON ST.
MANDORAH
FERRY
TERMINAL
ESPLANADE
BRIGGS
ST.
WHITFIELD ST.
GARDINER ST.
CAREY ST.
FOELSCHE
SEARCY ST.
EDMUNDS ST.
KNUCKEY ST.
LITCHFIELD
ST.
FRANCES
BAY
SHADFORTH
DARWIN
TRANSIT
CENTRE
LEICHHARDT
MEMORIAL
PEEL
ST.
GPO
SMITH
STREET
MALL
LANE
BENNETT
ST.
HARRY CHAN
AVE.
TOURIST BUREAU
CIVIC CENTRE
STOKES HILL
LAMEROO
BEACH
HERBERT
ST.
KITCHENER DR.
GOVERNMENT HOUSE
DARWIN
HARBOUR
FERRIES
FORT
HILL
STOKES HILL
WHARF
FORT HILL
WHARF
PORT DARWIN
MOON
0
0.3mi
0
0.3km

genus, different species), this particular tree, survivor of cyclone and bombings, is serenely and defiantly spreading with age.

Brown's Mart

Follow Henry Chan Avenue and turn left onto Smith Street. The stone cottage on your left is a building with *a past*. Originally constructed in 1885 as a mining exchange, it changed hats several times to become a fruit and veggie market, a police station, and a brothel. The roof was blown off by two cyclones (though maybe it was a result of the action inside!). Today the reconstructed building—with exposed beams—is home to a well-regarded community theater.

Old Town Hall

The old town hall, across the street, didn't fare as well with Cyclone Tracy. The 1883 rectangular building, used during WW II for naval administration and later as an art gallery, was flattened by the cyclone. Its stone walls are all that remain, providing a memorable backdrop for outdoor theater performances.

Old Courthouse And Police Station

At the corner of Smith St. and the Esplanade, the old courthouse is a classic 1884 South Australian building, originally constructed to house that government's offices, with the police station and cellblock connected behind. Used by the navy from WW II through Cyclone Tracy, the reconstructed rubble retains its external charm and now serves as offices for the Northern Territory's Administrator.

Christ Church Cathedral

Set on the opposite corner, this post-Tracy modern Anglican church incorporates ruins from the 1902 original. The porch was part of a 1944 addition to the earlier building.

Government House

Farther south along the Esplanade, Government House (aka the Residency and House of the Seven Gables), first built in 1870, was a superb bit of colonial architecture ravaged first by white ants, then by two cyclones. Except for the white-ant demolition—after which timber was replaced with stone—the building and gardens have been continually restored to original splendor.

Hotel Darwin

Walk north along the Esplanade to Herbert St. and one of the city's oldest pubs. The original pub, known as the Palmerston, opened in 1883. The post-Tracy rebuild included lots of wicker, palms, and the tropically ubiquitious "just like a Somerset Maugham novel" slogan.

Old Admiralty House

Continuing up the Esplanade, at the corner of Knuckey St., Admiralty House, former home to North Australia's naval commander, is one of Darwin's last remaining 1920s tropical houses. Undamaged by Tracy, the cypress pine building, elevated on stilts, houses an arts-and-crafts gallery with works by Top End-ers, with an alfresco tearoom down below.

Lyons Cottage

The Georgian-revival-style bungalow across Knuckey St. was built in 1925 as a residence for the head honcho of the British Australia Telegraph Company (BAT), and later occupied by former Darwin mayor John Lyons. Now a BAT museum, the stone cottage features exhibits on Australia's history of telecommunications. Open daily 10 a.m.-5 p.m. Admission is free. For information, phone (089) 41-0341.

Victoria Hotel

Take Knuckey Street to the Smith Street Mall and turn right. Occupying a prime position in the center of the mall, the Victoria Hotel (called the Vic, locally) was originally built in 1894 and painstakingly reconstructed after each cyclone and war. Still Darwin's premier pub, the Vic's Verandah Bar, overlooking the mall and busker action, is a top spot for that big Thirst.

Star Village

Star Village, a shopping arcade across the mall from the Vic, was the site of The Star, Darwin's first open-air cinema. The original

1930s projection booth and entranceway have been incorporated within the arcade's facade.

Commercial Bank
At the mall's Bennett St. corner, only the 1884 stone colonnade was saved and restored when the bank's 1981 counterpart was built.

Chinese Temple
Continue along Bennett St. to Woods St., site of the post-Tracy temple which serves Darwin's large Chinese community. The original 1887 structure couldn't weather the storm, and only the floor, altar masonry blocks, and stone lions were spared. The current temple, built in 1978, has taken care to blend the old ruins within its steel and concrete replacement. Open Mon.-Fri. 8 a.m.-4 p.m., Sat.-Sun. 8 a.m.-3 p.m. Admission is free.

OTHER CITY SIGHTS

Aquascene
Located on the Esplanade, at Doctors Gully, this is one of Darwin's best attractions. Almost every day at high tide, throngs of catfish, mullet, bream, milkfish, and others come along to nibble bread from the hands of knee-deep, wading tourists! This bizarre ritual began about 20 years ago, when a local denizen tossed some scraps to passing mullet (who told their friends, who told *their* friends, who . . .). Anyway, talk about *wonder bread!* Open daily at high tide. Phone 81-7837, for each day's feeding time. Admission is $3.

Indo-Pacific Marine
This small aquarium, near the roundabout at Smith St. West and Gilruth Ave., is one of the few such facilities in the world with displays of isolated coral reef ecosystems. Other features include informative talks, a gift shop, and small garden café. Open Tues.-Fri. 9 a.m.-noon, Sun. 10 a.m.-5 pm. Admission is $4. For information, phone 81-1294.

National Trust
Consisting of four pre-WW II houses in the Myilly Point Heritage Precinct, just outside downtown, the National Trust buildings feature side-hung windows, louvres, feathered eaves, and other trappings of tropical architecture. Pick up booklets, brochures, good tips, and souvenirs at the information center and gift shop within. Open Mon.-Fri. 8:30 a.m.-4:30 p.m. Admission is free. For information, phone (089) 81-2848.

Botanic Gardens
Just outside the city center on Gardens Rd. (off Gilruth Ave.), Darwin's botanic gardens, wiped out by three cyclones and a fire since their creation in 1879, have returned to glory with collections of figs, palms (nearly 400 species), and other tropical flora. New additions include a rainforest and wetlands area, plus a greenhouse with ferns and orchids. The restored cottage of Dr. Maurice Holtze, the gardens' founder, houses a restaurant, and occasional live concerts are performed at the amphitheatre. Open daily 8 a.m.-sunset. Admission is free.

Aviation Museum
View more war paraphernalia such as wreckage of the Japanese Zero, (first enemy aircraft ever shot down over Australia), a Boeing B-52 bomber (a loan from the U.S. Air Force), Mirage and Sabre jets, and a host of other aviation memorabilia. The museum is located on Gardens Hill Crescent, Stuart Park (back near the botanic gardens). Open Mon.-Fri. 10 a.m.-2 p.m., Sat.-Sun. 10 a.m.-5 p.m. Admission is $2. For information, phone (089) 81-7617.

Northern Territory Museum Of Arts And Sciences
The Territory's major museum, on Conacher St., Fanny Bay, features exceptional Aboriginal, Southeast Asian, and Oceanian galleries with arts and crafts, maps, photos, and artifacts (including a pearling lugger and Vietnamese-refugee boat out front on the lawn). As a research and scientific institution responsible for cataloging plant and animal species, the museum also houses a comprehensive natural sciences section. One big attraction is Sweetheart, the five-meter, 780-kilogram saltwater crocodile which had terrorized trolling fishermen until its capture in the late 1970s.

The art gallery features works by important Australian artists such as Russell Drysdale, Sir Sidney Nolan, and Donald Friend, as well as touring exhibitions. The museum bookshop has a good selection of local lore as well as gift items. The fancy HMS Beagle Restaurant serves à la carte dinners and smorgasbord lunch.

Open Mon.-Fri. 9-5, Sat.-Sun. 10 a.m.-6 p.m. Closed Good Friday and Christmas Day. Admission is free. For information, phone (089) 82-4211.

Fanny Bay Gaol
Farther along East Point Rd., Darwin's main prison from 1883 to 1979 is now a museum where visitors can reminisce about life in the cells—1920s tax dodgers, WW II doings, and such—as well as view the gallows where the last hanging took place in 1952. Comprehensive exhibitions devoted to Cyclone Tracy's devastation include newspaper clippings and video-fied news footage from that time. Open daily 10 a.m.-5 p.m. Admission is free. For information, phone 41-0341.

East Point
The north shore of Fannie Bay affords dramatic harbor, city, and sunset views. This peninsular reserve, with good bushwalking and cycling trails, is a popular spot at sunrise or twilight when wallabies frolic in the nearby field.

Check out heavy artillery, small arms, and other military memorabilia and relics of WW II at the **Royal Australian Military Museum,** a former coastal defense complex adjacent to the reserve. Open daily 9:30 a.m.-5 p.m. Admission is $2. For information, phone 81-9702.

BEACHES

Watch your tootsies October to May when it's the deadly box jellyfish season! Though you'll be tempted by Darwin's sparkling beaches (and the ever-present humidity)—*don't chance it!* Nightcliff Beach, off Casuarina Dr. in north Darwin, has a protective stinger net.

Nude bathing is allowed on a strip of beach at **Casuarina Coastal Reserve,** a 1,180-hectare area which also contains rainforests and WW II gun emplacements.

The first Sunday in May is the official opening of Darwin's beaches and **Mindil Beach,** on Fannie Bay, is the place to be. Celebrations include rock bands, dancers, acrobats, foodstalls, fashion shows, and sandcastle-building contests. Mindil and nearby **Vesvey's** beaches stay crowded until the stingers return.

DARWIN PRACTICALITIES

ACCOMMODATIONS

This gateway city with a frontier heart has accommodations to suit just about any lifestyle or pocketbook. The central city and surrounding suburbs feature a good selection of hostels, hotels, motels, and holiday flats, while most of the campgrounds and caravan parks are situated on the outskirts of town. If you're seeking a roommate, check out the downtown cafés or around the mall, where you're bound to meet other travelers.

Getting a room is usually not a problem, but advance bookings are a good idea if you plan to arrive during the more crowded Dry season and at festival times. Rates during the Wet are usually cheaper or at least up for bargaining. The Northern Territory levies a 2.5% Tourism Marketing Duty on all accommodations, with the exception of caravan and campsites (on-site vans and cabins are taxed). Revenues are supposedly used to promote tourism to the Territory.

City And Suburbs

Inexpensive (under $30): **Darwin Transit Centre,** 69 Mitchell St. *inside* the coach transit center (tel. 089-81-9733), is one of the best deals in town—not to mention conveniently located. This former workers' residence has been given new life with refurbished rooms, cooking facilities, a pool, sauna, gym, laundry, and games room. Bathroom facilities are shared. Nearby **Larrakeyah Lodge,** 50 Mitchell St. (tel. 81- 2933), is a long-established place with a/c rooms, shared facilities, a pool, laundry room, and coffee shop.

Air Raid City Lodge (comforting name, eh?), 35 Cavenagh St., close to the GPO (tel. 91-9214), has plain but clean rooms, private facilities, a/c, TVs, communal kitchen, and laundry room. **Park Lodge,** 42 Coronation Dr., Stuart Park, two km north of city center (tel. 81-5692), is a 20-room guesthouse with four shared bathrooms, communal kitchen, dining room, TV room, laundry, pool, and spa.

Coolibah Resort, 91 Aralia St., Nightcliff, about 12 km from city center (tel. 854-166), is in the moderate price range but has a cheap, a/c, six-bed bunkroom with communal facilities and kitchen.

Moderate ($30-60): **Hotel Darwin,** 10 Herbert St. (tel. 81-9211), near the GPO, is the city's former grande dame. The colonial building is somewhat worn but still has some charm, as well as the requisite wicker and cane decor. Facilities include TVs, phones, pool, restaurant, pub, and laundry. **Tops Boulevarde,** 38 Gardens Rd., near the botanic gardens (tel. 81-1544), features a pool, tennis, and a restaurant. Costlier **Tops Crest Townhouses,** 88 Woods St. (tel. 81-1922), are centrally located holiday flats with cooking facilities. Both Tops properties provide airport transportation.

Ponciana Inn, corner Mitchell and McLachlan (tel. 81-8111), is a four-story motel with a pool in the center of town. **Paravista,** 5 MacKillop St., Parap (tel. 81-9200), near Fannie Bay attractions, also has a pool and barbecue area. Small and cozy **Palms Motel,** 100 McMinn St. (tel. 81-4188), is about one km north of the GPO.

Expensive ($60 and way up): All of Darwin's top-notch hotels provide the usual luxury range of restaurants, bars, recreational facilities, and business services. **The Beaufort,** the Esplanade (tel. 82-9911) has colorful desert architecture. **The Atrium,** Peel St. and the Esplanade (tel. 41-0755), features —natch—a beautiful seven-story, glass-roofed atrium. **Diamond Beach Hotel Casino,** Gilruth Ave., Mindil Beach (tel. 46-2666), features interesting geometric shapes, beachfront accommodations and, of course, an action-packed casino. The newer **Sheraton Darwin**, 32 Mitchell St. (tel. 82-0000), the city's highest rise, is near the business district.

Hostels

Darwin's hostels are perfect places to meet travelers from *everywhere* and pick up tips—and maybe a companion. Dorm beds average $10 per night.

Darwin's **YHA Hostel** (tel. 089-81-3995), next to the transit center on Mitchell St., features 182 beds in 90 rooms, shared bathroom and kitchen facilities, pool, courtyard, and a friendly atmosphere. New addition is an in-house travel office with discounted tour and bus tickets. There's another YHA branch with 50 beds on Beaton Rd., Berrimah, about 12 km outside the city (tel. 089-84-3902). Make sure you have your YHA membership card in hand.

Backpackers International Hostel, 88 Mitchell St. (tel. 81-5385), down the street from the YHA, has a/c dorm rooms, two communal kitchens, pool, barbecue, TV, video, and a helpful staff. **Sunset City Backpackers Haven,** 144 Mitchell St. (tel. 81-7326), is a small 16-room property with a pool and communal kitchen.

The popular **YWCA,** 119 Mitchell St. (tel. 81-8644), accepts both women and men at its 42-room facility with clean rooms, communal bathrooms and kitchens, TV lounges. Dorm beds and single or double rooms are available. The **YMCA** at Doctors Gully (tel. 81-8377) is on the shabby side and has a pool but no kitchen. It's okay digs for men and couples; however, women would do well to avoid this establishment. The **CWA Hostel** (Country Women's Association), corner Mitchell St. and Packard Place (tel. 41-1536), offers two four-bed rooms for both men and women, and four two-bed rooms for women only. Facilities include a communal kitchen, TV lounge, and large garden area.

Camping

Unfortunately all of Darwin's campsites are about 10-15 km outside the city. The following parks allow tents as well as caravans: **Leprechaun Caravan Park,** Sadgrove Crescent, Winnellie, across from the airport (tel. 089-84-3400); **Overlander Caravan Park,** McMillans Rd., Berrimah, 13 km east (tel. 84-3025); **The Palms Caravan Park,** Stuart Hwy., Berrimah, 17 km east (tel. 322-891); **Shady Glen Caravan Park,** Stuart Hwy. and Farrell Crescent, Winnellie, 10 km east (tel. 84-3330).

For additional camping opportunities in the Howard Springs area, 26 km from the city, see "Vicinity of Darwin" section.

Camping gear can be rented from U-Rent, 50 Mitchell St. (tel. 41-1280).

FOOD

What's your favorite nosh—buffalo, crocodile, camel, or kangaroo? You'll find such territorial specialties listed alongside fish 'n' chips in some restaurants. Tasty barramundi, fresh from local waters, is in plentiful supply also. And, as might be expected in this multinational city, ethnic foods are widely offered, with Asian cuisine ranking supreme. Supermarkets, small groceries, and takeaways are easy to spot throughout city and suburbs, and the Smith Street Mall area is full of coffee shops and lunch counters. Darwin's best dining value—and the most fun—is at the Asian-style markets held several times weekly.

Inexpensive

Head to Smith Street Mall, though keep in mind that most of the coffee shops shut down when the shops do, meaning 5 p.m. on weekdays (except for Thursday), Saturday afternoon, and Sundays. **Central City Café** is a popular breakfast and gathering spot. **Cosmopolitan Café,** in Anthony Plaza, serves up good breakfasts and lunches. Next door, the **French Bakehouse** is open daily for coffee and light meals. The historic **Victoria Hotel,** opposite Anthony Plaza, features a relatively cheap lunchtime carvery upstairs, and good-value counter meals downstairs.

Toward the Knuckey St. end of the mall, **Darwin Plaza** houses a glut of Lebanese, Thai, Chinese, and health food counters. The **Taco House,** within that same plaza, is where you can sample croc, buffalo, and roo burgers, along with tacos, of course (watch that filling!). The **Little Lark,** in Paspalis Centrepoint, across from Darwin Plaza, has developed quite a following for its Chinese lunches.

Shades of Ochre, 70 the Esplanade, in the Old Admiralty House, is an outdoor café with light meals, fruit juices, and smoothies. Open Mon.-Sat. 10 a.m.-5 p.m., Sun. 1-5 p.m. **Confetti's,** 85 Mitchell St., is open late for homemade ice cream, cappuccino, pancakes, and a variety of smoothies, sundaes, and snacks. Open daily 11 a.m.-late. **Fisherman's Eatery,** on Fisherman's Wharf, specializes in takeaway barramundi 'n' chips. Open Mon.-Sat. 8 a.m.-5 p.m.

Banyon Junction, next to the Darwin Transit Centre on Mitchell St., has an international food court with outdoor seating.

Moderate

Jade Gardens, on the mall, serves Chinese banquets and business lunches. Open Mon.-Fri. lunch, daily dinner. **The Noodle House,** on Knuckey St., specializes in freshly made Asian noodle soups and other dishes. Open Mon.-Sat. lunch, daily dinner. The **Maharaja,** 37 Knuckey St., features an extensive menu and excellent curries. Open Mon.-Sat. for lunch and dinner. **Arabian Nights,** 41 Cavenagh St., one of Darwin's better Lebanese restaurants, features a large selection of vegetarian dishes and special lunch banquets. Open daily for lunch and dinner.

Satisfy your pasta urge at **The Pasta Joint,** 21 Cavenagh St., with both regional and traditional Italian specialties. Open Mon.-Fri. lunch, Mon.-Sat. dinner. Traditional Swiss and international dishes are served at **Swiss Café and Restaurant,** 60 Smith Street. Open Mon.-Fri. for lunch and dinner. At the **Diamond Beach Hotel Casino,** the Lorikeet Lounge is open during casino hours for a range of meals and views of Fannie Bay.

Expensive

The **Asian Gateway,** 58 Aralia St., Nightcliff, is one of Darwin's best-respected Thai restaurants. Specialties include hot-as-you-please curries and boneless duck. Open daily for dinner. Fine traditional Chinese cuisine is featured at **Lee Dynasty,** Cavenagh Street. This establishment enjoys a long-standing reputation for excellent food and unhurried service. Open Mon.-Fri. lunch, daily for dinner. **Rock Oyster,** 17 Cavenagh St., features fresh seafood, mud crabs, oysters, and live crayfish in a garden setting. Open Mon.-Sat. for dinner.

Le Breughel, 6 Dashwood Crescent, has three intimate rooms (with Breughel prints on the walls) and a French provincial menu. Open Tues.-Sun. for dinner. Locals flock to **Genghis Khan Mongolian Barbecue Restaurant,** 44 East Point Rd., Fannie Bay, for its extensive selection of cooked-to-order meats and veggies. Open Sun.-Fri. lunch, daily for dinner.

Darwin's five-star hotels also feature some excellent restaurants, notably **Siggi's** at the Beaufort, **Flinders** at the Sheraton, and the **Orchid Room** at Diamond Beach Casino. Book ahead for all the restaurants listed above.

Markets

Darwin's thriving, colorful markets can be categorized equally under Food, Shopping, and Entertainment listings.

Foodaholics come early to set up folding tables and chairs beachside, watch the sunset, then tickle their tastebuds at the **Mindil Beach Market.** Foodstalls serve up Thai, Indian, Malaysian, Chinese, Indonesian, South American, and other ethnic cuisine, as well as cakes, breads, fruits, and veggies at very reasonable prices. The market is held Thursdays 6-10 p.m., during the Dry.

Other sniff-and-gobble markets are: **The Big Flea Market,** Darwin's oldest, held Sun. 8 a.m.-2 p.m. at Rapid Creek Shopping Centre; **The Parap Market,** held Sat. 8 a.m.-2 p.m. at Parap; and **Palmerston Markets,** held Fri. 5:30-9:30 p.m. at Frances Mall, Palmerston. Except for Mindil Beach, the markets are open year-round.

ENTERTAINMENT AND EVENTS

Don't expect Big City culture, but there is a range of theaters, cinemas, pubs, clubs, and the casino for amusement. On the other hand, special events in this isolated region can be a *whole* lot of fun. The *Northern Territory News* provides listings of all the current doings. Again, if you're looking for com-

The old Brown's Mart mining exchange now houses a community theater.

panionship for a night on the town, scout around the Smith Street Mall, surrounding coffee shops, or the hostels. This is an *easy* town to meet people in.

Cinemas
You can catch the usual commercial showings (several months or so old) at **Cinema Darwin,** on Mitchell Street. **Darwin Film Society** (tel. 089-81-2215) often hosts artier movies at the Museum Theatrette, Conacher St., Bullocky Point (tel. 82-4211).

Pubs And Clubs
The oldies are goodies. The **Vic,** on the mall, features live bands in the upstairs veranda bar, Wed.-Saturday. The **Darwin Hotel,** on Mitchell St., hosts live bands on Friday night, plus a poolside jazz barbecue on Sunday. You can alternate between indoor and outdoor bands, Sunday afternoons and Fri.-Sat. night, at the **Beachfront Hotel,** Rapid Creek. Or get down and grungy at the infamous **Nightcliff Hotel,** corner of Bagot and Trower, about 10 km north of city center. Depending on which night you visit, entertainment consists of live bands, wrestling females (covered in a variety of cooking sauces), *very* thirsty men, and wild women. The Nightcliff is what's referred to as a Darwin "experience."

Favorite discos, most open nightly, are: **Fannies Nightclub,** 3 Edmunds St.; **Dix,** 21 Cavenagh St. in the Hot Gossip Complex; and **Beachcombers,** corner Daly and Mitchell streets. Trendies should check out the array of nightclubs, piano lounges, and discos in the chichi hotels. Neat, casual dress is required.

Expect to pay a cover charge of about $4-6 in the pubs (when bands are on), $6-8 in the discos, and $10 or more at the five-star spots.

For those of you in the "Blowin' in the Wind" mood, the **Top End Folk Club** holds sessions at the East Point Gun Turret on the second Sunday of each month, from 8 p.m. Visitors and musicians are encouraged to join in the hoot. Admission is $5. For information, phone (089) 88-1301 or 41-1699.

The Casino
Depending on your inclination, wardrobe, luck, and budget (or *non*-budget!), the **Diamond Beach Hotel Casino** might be the only entertainment you need. All the games are represented, including the Aussie "Two-up." The 350-seat Cabaret Room hosts a variety of theatrical entertainment, along with bar service and elaborate buffets; a coffee shop is open round-the-clock. During the Dry, the casino puts on a Sunday afternoon poolside barbecue with live jazz.

Dress regulations are strict: neat, clean, tidy clothing at all times; no shorts, thongs, running shoes, or denim wear of any kind (not even your best hole-in-the-knee Levi's); and, it should go without saying—keep your shirt on your back, even if you lose it in the casino.

Diamond Beach is located on Gilruth Ave., Mindil Beach. Casino hours are daily noon-4 a.m. For information, phone 46-2666.

Corroborees
You're in your own dreamtime if you're waiting for an invite to an authentic Aboriginal corroboree. These sacred spiritual ceremonies are off-limits to the general public. You *will* be able to join tours that feature a kind of pseudo event, with traditional dancing, singing, and didgeridoo-ing.

Theater, Dance, And Concerts
The **Darwin Performing Arts Centre,** 93 Mitchell St., next to the Beaufort Hotel (tel. 81-1222), regularly stages theater, musical, and dance performances. The playhouse (capacity 1,070) also houses a rehearsal room, exhibition gallery, and dance studio.

Phone the center, or check the daily newspaper. The Centre can also provide details of upcoming events at the botanic gardens outdoor amphitheater.

Other theater groups with regular offerings are **Territory North Theatre Company** (tel. 46-6257), **Brown's Mart Community Arts** (tel. 81-5522), and **Darwin Theatre Group** (tel. 81-8424). Theater tickets can also be purchased through Tivoli Music House (tel. 81-6655) and Musicland (tel. 27-9979).

Events

This isolated laid-back city takes every opportunity to come together for just about any occasion. The Northern Territory Barra **Classic,** a premier "tag-and-release" tournament held by the Darwin Game Fishing Club, is held about the first of May. The **Mindil Beach Carnival** in May (see "Beaches" above) celebrates the departure of the box jellyfish and the opening of the beaches. More than a decade old, the **Bougainvillea Festival** is held for 18 days in late May or early June, the flower's peak blossoming time. Numerous festivities include a Mardi Gras, grand parade, concerts, photography contest, art exhibitions, music and film festivals, a food and wine fair, picnics, ethnic events, and daily doings on the mall. A weekend Festival Fringe Club produces alternative music, dance, theater, and literature events.

Darwin's famous **Beer Can Regatta** tailgates the bougainvillea Festival in early June, and is certainly an event to inspire the Darwin Thirst. Empty beer cans are used to construct rafts and boats, which then "race" in the local sea. Using full cans of beer to build the craft is strictly *verboten!*

Other big-turnout annual events—all falling in August—are the barefoot **Mud Crab Tying Competition**, the **Darwin Cup** horseracing meet, and the internationally known **Darwin Rodeo.**

The **Marratjila Festival** is a nine-day celebration of Aboriginal heritage which draws participants from both tribal communities and urban areas to join in dance and theater performances, contemporary and traditional music, and arts and crafts exhibitions.

SPORTS AND RECREATION

You'll find a wide range of sports and recreation ops in the city and suburbs, but bear in mind the heat and humidity if you're not fit or not used to the climate. Joggers and cyclists will find plenty of good, scenic tracks. Best bets are the waterfront area that follows the Esplanade, and the shoreline reserve from Fannie Bay to East Point.

Water sports and fishing are favorites here, but heed those box jellyfish and crocodile warnings! For information on any Darwin sport, phone the **Sports Hotline** (tel. 089 81-4300).

DANGER !

BOX JELLYFISH CAN BE DEADLY

OCT. to MAY
DO NOT SWIM

JUNE to SEPT.
TAKE CARE SWIMMING

FIRST AID:
Resuscitation + Vinegar
(poured on affected area)
+Transport to Hospital = LIFE

NT DEPARTMENT OF HEALTH AND COMMUNITY SERVICES

Scuba Diving

Divers can explore the litter of WW II wrecks, as well as the large coral reef off Darwin's shores. Good dive shops are **Fannie Bay Dive Centre,** 2 Fannie Bay Pl. (tel. 089-81-3049), and **Sand Pebbles Dive Shop,** De Latour St., Coconut Grove (tel. 85-1906).

Fishing

Top End waters are jumping with sport fish, particularly Australia's famous **barramundi.** The best time to score a catch is from Easter through May. The prime spots near Darwin are around the harbor arms, Leader's Creek, Bynoes Harbour, and in the creeks and estuaries of Shoal Bay. Other common species are queenfish, Spanish mackerel, longtail tuna, giant trevally, threadfin salmon, and barracuda. **Mud crabbing** in the estuaries is another favorite local activity.

For information on **licenses, regulations,** and **fishing tours,** contact the Department

Top End water lily

of Primary Industry and Fisheries, GPO Box 4160, Darwin, NT 0801 (tel. 89-4322). For **tidal charts,** contact the Port Authority, Henry Chan Ave. (tel. 81-6701).

Swimming Pools
Practically every hostel, motel, and hotel has its own pool. In addition, you'll find public pools at Darwin, Casuarina, Nightcliff, and Winnellie. One of the better locations is on Ross Smith Ave., Fannie Bay (tel. 089-81-2662).

Sporting Facilities
Tennis: Four courts are available for public use at the **Darwin Tennis Centre,** corner Bagot and Old McMillan (tel. 85-2844). Courts are also available outside the casino, near Mindil Beach. For information, phone 81-2181.

Golf: Darwin Golf Club, Links Rd., Marrara (tel. 27-1015), has the only 18-hole course in town. Nine-hole courses are available at **Gardens Park Golf Links,** opposite the casino, (tel. 81-6365), and **Palmerston Golf Club,** Dwyer Crescent, Palmerston (tel. 32-1324). Equipment can be rented on-site.

For information on other sporting facilities, phone the Sports Hotline, above.

Other Sports
Sailboards are available for rent in front of the Diamond Beach Hotel Casino at Mindil Beach. For **sailboat** hire, contact the Darwin Sailing Club (tel. 089-81-1700). For information about weekend **hiking** expeditions, contact Darwin Bushwalking Club (tel. 85-1484). **Darwin Gym,** 78 The Esplanade (tel. 41-0020), features workout and fitness equipment.

The most prominent spectator sport in Darwin is **horse racing,** with greyhounds placing, and an occasional touch football game making quite a show.

SHOPPING

Darwin's major shopping areas are **Smith Street Mall,** with more than 200 specialty shops, and **Casuarina Shopping Square,** 247 Trower Rd., in the northern suburbs. Just about any creature comfort or service can be purchased at either place (and Casuarina has a K mart, too). City shopping hours are Mon.-Fri. 9:30 a.m.-5:30 p.m., Sat. 8:30 a.m.-1 p.m., late-night trading Thurs. until 9 p.m. Casuarina shopping hours are daily 9 a.m.-5:30 p.m., late-night trading Thurs. and Fri. until 9 p.m.

Markets
Darwin's markets have a lot more than just foodstalls. You can pick up crafts, books, plants, dolls, knicknacks, Indian and Balinese clothing, and other goodies (see "Markets" in the "Food" section).

Crafts

Aboriginal art collectors will find a large variety of arts and crafts. **Aboriginal Artists' Galleries,** 153 Mitchell St., is the place to pick up Top End and central Australian bark paintings, sand paintings, weavings, didgeridoos, baskets, clothing, and Aboriginal literature (including books for children). Open Mon.-Fri. 9-5, Sat. 10 a.m.-1 p.m. Hours may vary during the Wet. The **Raintree Gallery,** 29 Knuckey St., sells similar wares, specializing in items made by the Tiwi people from Bathurst and Melville islands. Purchase T-shirts printed with Aboriginal designs, as well as Tiwi printed fabrics, at **Riji Dij-Australian and Original,** 11 Knuckey Street.

Weavers Workshop, Parap Place, Parap, sells locally made handknits, pottery, natural soaps, and toiletries. **Shades of Ochre** (in the Old Admiralty House), 70 The Esplanade, displays and sells fine local arts and crafts.

The Green Turtle, housed inside Darwin's Environmental Centre, at 24 Cavenagh St., features local crafts, cards, and other gifts with a nature theme. Proceeds support environmental issues.

Darwin Shipstores, Frances Bay Dr., sells flags from all over the world, including the Boxing Kangaroo and Northern Territory state flags.

Other Shops

Photo supplies: You'll find camera houses at just about every turn in this photo-op territory. **Camera World,** in Darwin Plaza, Smith Street Mall, offers fast passport service, a good range of photo supplies, and one-hour film processing. **Palm Photographics Drive-in Transit Shop,** on Mitchell St., right next to the Transit Centre, provides film processing and sales daily 8:30 a.m.-10 p.m.

New Age: Center yourself at **Inner Dreams Book and Gift Shop,** Parap Shopping Village, for quartz crystals, incense, flower essences, oils, books, tapes, and videos.

Gear: Everything you need for going bush is stocked at the **Northern Territory General Store,** 42 Cavenagh St. (tel. 81-8242). Inventory includes tents, boots, maps, compasses, knives, tarps, sleeping bags, mosquito nets, etc.

Surf Wear: Purchase top Australian brands at **Fannie Bay Beach Bums,** 2/5 Fannie Bay Pl., Fannie Bay. Open daily 10 a.m.-6 p.m.

Book Exchange: Nearly 20,000 books are stocked at **J.R. Book Exchange,** in Central Arcade, Smith St. Mall. You can also pick up good used clothing at this shop.

SERVICES

Branches of national and territorial banks are located on and around the Smith Street Mall. Many have suburban offices and automatic teller machines. Banking hours are Mon.-Thurs. 9:30 a.m.-4 p.m., Fri. until 5 p.m. Be sure to take your passport or other identification.

Darwin's glossy new **General Post Office,** 48 Cavenagh St., has instigated computerized postal services including self-selection service, electronic counters, and digital readouts. Postal officers stand by to assist with any problems. Operating hours are Mon.-Fri. 8:30 a.m.-5 p.m.

For visa and work permit inquiries, call on the **Department of Immigration,** 40 Cavenagh St. (tel. 46-3100).

Casual labor opportunities fluctuate. Check with the hostels or other travelers for the up-to-date skinny.

INFORMATION

The **Northern Territory Government Tourist Bureau,** 31 Smith Street Mall (tel. 81-6611), will quite likely be your one-stop-shop for any information about the Territory. The bureau also provides free maps, informative booklets, and arranges accommodations, car rentals, and a variety of tours to fit all budgets. Hours are Mon.-Fri. 8:45 a.m.-5 p.m., Sat. 9 a.m.-noon. In addition, there's a visitor office at Darwin's airport.

Walking maps and other historic information can be obtained from the **National Trust,** 52 Temira Crescent, Myilly Point (tel. 81-2848). The **Darwin Region Tourism Association,** 59 Woods St. (tel. 81-4300), provides local information and several brochures.

above: downtown Fremantle (WESTERN AUSTRALIA TOURISM COMMISSION);
below: Fremantle Markets (WESTERN AUSTRALIA TOURISM COMMISSION)

above left: A resident of Seal Bay, Kangaroo Island, enjoys a sunbath. (TOURISM SOUTH AUSTRALIA); above right: wild camel, South Australia (TOURISM SOUTH AUSTRALIA); bottom: a face only a mother could love (NORTHERN TERRITORY TOURIST COMMISSION)

The **Northern Territory Government Information Centre,** 13 Smith St. (tel. 89-7152), is a good source for specialized government publications. Hours are daily 9 a.m.-4 p.m. The **Australian National Parks & Wildlife Service,** Smith St., between Lindsay and Whitfield (tel. 81-5299), provides information about the Territory's parks, regulations, and required permits.

The **Disabled Persons Bureau,** Shop 7, Group floor, Casuarina Plaza, Casuarina (tel. 20-3213) offers an information and referral service for disabled visitors.

Tidal charts are essential if you plan to fish or boat and are available from the **Port Authority,** Harry Chan Ave. (tel. 81-6701).

Maps, up-to-date road information, and camping and accommodation guides can be obtained from the **Northern Territory Automobile Association,** 81 Smith St. (tel. 81-3837). The NTAA has reciprocal arrangements with both Australian and overseas automobile associations. Bring your membership card for free and discounted services.

Emergencies: Dial 000, or contact **police** (tel. 27-8888), **ambulance** (tel. 27-9000), **fire brigade** (tel. 41-0000), or **NTAA** road service (tel. 41-0611). For **marine stinger emergencies,** phone (008) 07-9909. **Darwin Private Hospital**, Rockland Dr. (tel. 20-6011), has a 24-hour accident and emergency center, as does **Royal Darwin Hospital,** next door (tel. 22-8888). **Night and Day Medical and Dental Service,** Bradshaw Terrace, Casuarina Shopping Square (tel. 27-1899), is open Mon.-Fri. 8 a.m.-9 p.m., Sat.-Sun. 9 a.m.-9 p.m. **Central Darwin Dental Surgery,** 59 Smith St., CML Bldg. (tel. 41-1899 or 41-1717), also handles dental emergencies. For **Travel and Immunization Services,** phone 81-7197.

Other Information

The **State Reference Library of the Northern Territory,** 25 Cavenagh St. (tel. 89-7177), has shelves full of books, photos, and other documents relating to the Territory. Interstate and international newspapers are available for browsing. Open Mon.-Sat. 10 a.m.-6 p.m. (come for free lunchtime entertainment Feb. to Nov.). The **city library** is in Paspalis Centrepoint arcade on Smith St. Mall.

Despite the name, **Budget Souvenirs and Gifts,** 20 Knuckey St., also carries a range of Northern Territory magazines, postcards, travelogues, and other literature. **Tivoli Book Centre,** 27 Cavenagh St., and **Book World,** on Smith St. Mall, are good central bookshops.

Darwin's local daily newspaper is the *Northern Territory News.*

The **Northern Territory Conservation Commission** has an information desk inside the Government Tourist Bureau on Smith Street. The Green Turtle, Darwin's **environmental center,** disseminates all types of "green" literature and can put you in contact with local groups and other related organizations.

GETTING THERE

By Air

The only airline serving Darwin from North America (with a change of planes in Cairns) is **Qantas,** corner Smith St. Mall and Bennett St. (tel. 089-46-4666). Other international carriers are **Garuda** (Garuda has a Los Angeles-Biak-Bali-Darwin route) and **Merpati,** from Indonesia, and **Singapore**, **Qantas,** and **Royal Brunei** from Asia.

From other Australian states, Darwin is easily reached on **Ansett, Ansett NT,** and **Ansett WA** airlines, Shop 14, Smith St. Mall (tel. 80-3333, or 13-1300 toll-free), and **Australian Airlines,** 16 Bennett St. (tel. 82-3333, or 13-1313 toll free).

All international and domestic flights arrive and depart from **Darwin Airport,** just eight km north of city center. Services include rental car desks, money exchange, and a visitor center. **Darwin Airport Bus Service** (tel. 41-1402) will shuttle you to or from the city for $5. Taxis are ready and waiting; fare to the city is about $10. Hang onto $20 for departure tax.

By Bus

Coach companies serving Darwin are **Bus Australia** (tel. 81-3377), **Greyhound** (tel.

81-8700), and **Pioneer Express** (tel. 81-6433). The three routes into the city are: up the Track from Alice Springs, with stops at Tennant Creek and Katherine; the Barkly Highway from Townsville, Queensland, via Mt. Isa, joining the Track at Three Ways; and the Victoria Highway from Western Australia through Broome, Derby, and Kununurra. One or more of the coach companies make daily runs along all routes. On Queensland routes it's sometimes necessary to change coaches at Tennant Creek or Three Ways.

Fares vary little among the coach lines and they all offer stopovers and money-saving passes (some need to be purchased outside the country). Sample fares are: Tennant Creek-Darwin (13 hours), $85; Alice Springs-Darwin (21 hours), $150; Mt. Isa-Darwin (22 hours), $120; Townsville-Darwin (34 hours), $165; Perth-Darwin (59 hours), $245.

All intercity coaches arrive and depart at **Darwin Transit Centre,** 69 Mitchell Street.

By Car

Same way as you get there by bus! The main highways are sealed with asphalt and have roadhouse facilities. But remember—it's a long way to the Territorial Tipperary: 350 km from Katherine, 978 km from Tennant Creek; 1,482 km from Alice Springs; 3,215 km from Adelaide; 2,489 km from Townsville; and 4,430 km from Perth. Don't venture off the main roads without a good 4WD vehicle, emergency supplies, and a phone call to the nearest police facility.

GETTING AROUND

By Air

Due to recent airline deregulation, flying within the country has become much more affordable. Check with both the YHA and the Northern Territory Government Tourist Bureau, as well as the airlines, for complete information on package, advance-purchase, student, and standby fares.

Air North (tel. 81-7188 or 85-4518) is a small commuter airline with services between Darwin and Kakadu, Arnhem Land, Tennant Creek, Katherine, and Bathurst and Melville islands. Ansett NT connects Darwin with Katherine, Tennant Creek, Alice Springs, Yulara (Ayers Rock), Gove, and Groote Eylandt.

By Bus

Darwin Bus Service operates weekdays and Saturday morning, entering the city along Mitchell St. and departing by way of Cavenagh Street. Routes no. 4 (to Fannie Bay, Nightcliff, Rapid Creek, and Casuarina) and no. 6 (to Fannie Bay, Parap, and Stuart Park) will take you to most of Darwin's attractions and other points of interest. Fares, based on zones, range from 70 cents to $1.50. The city terminal is on Harry Chan Ave., near Smith Street. For information, phone 89-6540.

By Car

Taxis are available at the airport, or phone **Darwin Radio Taxis** (tel. 81-8777).

Major **car rental** firms such as **Budget, Hertz,** and **Thrifty** have airport and city locations. Better deals might be had at **Cheapa Rent-a-Car** (tel. 81-8400), **Rent a Rocket** (tel. 81-6977), or **Rent a Dent** (tel. 81-1411). Rates start at about $35 per day, no kilometer charge. Rates are higher if you take the car more than about 50 km outside Darwin. Be sure to inquire about weekend specials or extended-rental deals. Cheapa, **Brits** (tel. 81-2081), and **Territory Rent-A-Car** (tel. 81-8400) have 4WDs, starting at $75 per day, plus kilometer charges.

By Bike

Top End Motorcycle Hire, 5 Knuckey St. (tel. 81-2661), offers a range of mopeds, motor bikes, scooters, road bikes, and trail bikes. Prices run $25-40 per day.

Hire **bicycles** by the hour, day, or week from **U Rent,** 50 Mitchell St. (tel. 41-1280), or **Darwin Bike Rentals,** 57 Mitchell St. (tel. 41-0070). Rates are about $2 per hour, $8 per day. Rent a Rocket also has bicycles and mopeds.

By Boat

Take a ride across the harbor to Mandorah on **Darwin Harbour Ferries.** Service operates Mon.-Fri., year-round, from Stokes Hill Wharf. Fare is $14 roundtrip, and the journey takes 30-40 minutes each way. Two-hour sunset and harbor cruises are also available. For information and schedules, phone 78-5094.

Tours

The organized tour offerings in and around Darwin are numerous—Litchfield Park, Kakadu Park, Cobourg Peninsula, Arnhem Land, Bathurst and Melville islands, crocodile farms, and other destinations and activities can be explored by plane, boat, jeep, canoe, or foot, for one day or longer. Pick up a copy of the *Northern Territory Holiday Planner* from the government Tourist Bureau, with pages and pages describing tours and operators, including prices and departure days. The **YHA** travel office also makes recommendations and bookings (note: my girlfriend went on a Litchfield Park outing with Coo-ee Tours, and reports a frightening experience with a male tour guide). Contact **Darwin Bushwalking Club** (see "Sports") for info on short or extended bushwalks. Some tours operate infrequently, or not at all, during the Wet.

The Darwin Tourist Circle, operated by the Darwin Bus Service, is a 40-minute tour of the city's major sites, and is charged only by the zones traveled (i.e., *cheap).* The tour operates May-Sept. at 9 a.m. and 2 p.m. For information, phone 89-7513. **Billy J Harbour Cruise** is a popular two- to three-hour harbor excursion, with commentary on WW II history and the pearling industry. Cost is $22, including tea and tropical fruits. Billy J's four-hour evening cruise ($54) features Aboriginal dancing on the shores of Mandorah, followed by a seafood smogasbord. Another longtime favorite is the **Adelaide River Queen Coach Tour and Crocspot Cruise,** a five- to six-hour coach trip to Fogg Dam and cruise to view jumping crocodiles. Cost is $55. Day-trips to Kakadu average $85-110, Litchfield Park $75-90, and Katherine Gorge $85-90.

GETTING AWAY

Due to its close proximity, Darwin is a popular gateway to Indonesia. **Merpati** flies twice weekly between Darwin and Denpasar and once a week between Darwin and Kupang, in Timor, with onward flights to many other Indonesian cities. Tickets can be purchased from the Indonesian government travel agency, **Natrabu,** 16 Westlane Arcade, beneath the Victoria Hotel on Smith St. Mall (tel. 81-3694). Sample fares are $175 one way from Darwin, with stops in Kupang, Maumere, Ruteng, Labuhanbajo, Bima, and Ampenan; $125 one way from Darwin to Kupang, a bargain for island-hoppers headed toward Bali. Scour the newspaper listings and check with travel agents about the many APEX and excursion fares and package deals available to Indonesia.

Garuda International, corner Bennett and Cavenagh (tel. 81-6422), has twice-weekly service between Darwin, Denpasar, and Jakarta. A Darwin-Denpasar return ticket runs about $580. Also check out special deals with **Singapore Airlines,** 48 Smith Street Mall (tel. 41-1799).

Unless you're in the big bucks, cruises are not a practical option. For current information about cruises and freighters, contact **Darwin Port Authority,** GPO Box 390, Darwin, NT 0801.

Hitching

It ain't so easy. Track traffic is sparse outside cities and towns. Many hitchhikers report long waits at Three Ways, junction of the Track and the road to Mt. Isa.

THE TOP END

Keep your hat on and knock your socks off. Ever since ad-rep Paul Hogan was reincarnated as *Crocodile Dundee,* the Northern Territory's tiptop has become one of Australia's most popular tourist destinations. Most of the moviedom believers head straight for Kakadu National Park and its realer-than-film-reel glories, with the spillover forging onward, upward, and backward to Arnhem Land, the Cobourg Peninsula, Litchfield Park, and Bathurst and Melville islands. Most of these spots can be visited on day-trips from Darwin but at some you'll no doubt want to stay longer. Make the most of your visit to this ancient and extraordinary region —there will be no sequel.

VICINITY OF DARWIN

Mandorah

Situated 10 km across the harbor from Darwin, this small resort on the northeast tip of Cox Peninsula is noted for its sandy beaches, superior fishing, and the tourist-oriented Aboriginal corroborees performed by the local Kenbi community and hosted by Mandorah Inn (tel. 089-81-6744). If you're not a guest of the resort, you can get in on the corroboree by taking a **Billy J** tour (see "Getting Around" under "Darwin"). Otherwise, hop on a Darwin Harbor ferry for an easy day-trip from the city. If you're driving up the Cox Peninsula road, you'll encounter magnetic anthills on the way into town. (By the way, they're called "magnetic" because they point north.)

Howard Springs

This nature park, 27 km southeast of Darwin along the Stuart Highway, features a refreshing spring-fed pool set amid lush rainforest and is often crowded with city escapers. Additional features include a fish-viewing area, short bushwalking tracks, birds and wildlife, a kiosk, and barbecue facilities. The facilities are open daily 7 a.m.-5 p.m. For information, phone (089) 83-1001.

Campsites are available at **Coolalinga Caravan Park,** Stuart Hwy. (tel. 089-83-1026) and **Howard Springs Caravan Park,** 290 Whitewood Rd. (tel. 83-1169). **Nook Van-O-Tel,** Morgan Rd. (tel. 089-83-1048) has campsites and on-site vans.

Darwin Crocodile Farm

I hate to tell you—many of the thousands of saltwater and freshwater crocs you see here are annually killed. But don't despair! You'll soon be able to admire them on someone's designer feet, slung over a fashion-setting arm, or inside tomorrow's burger. Come at feeding time when these beasts display their feelings about the future! Located 40 km from Darwin, on the Stuart Highway, the farm is open daily 9-5, with tours at 11 a.m. and 2 p.m. Feeding time is daily at 2 p.m., with an extra on Sunday at 11 a.m. For information, phone (089) 88-1450.

Berry Springs

Two top attractions make this spot worth the 56-km journey (take the turnoff from Stuart Highway). **Berry Springs Nature Park** offers spring-fed, croc-free swimming with fewer people than Howard Springs, plus rainforest, picnic areas, and barbecue facilities. The springs are open daily 8 a.m.-7 p.m. year-round, except after extremely heavy rains. For information, phone (089) 88-6030.

Territory Wildlife Park, next door, is a 400-hectare open-range sanctuary housing kangaroos, wallabies, water buffalo, dingoes, and other Northern Territory species, as well as a 20-meter-high walk-through aviary, an aquarium, natural lagoon with water birds and a viewing blind, and a nocturnal house. A motor train transports visitors along a four-km link road. Open daily 9 a.m.-6 p.m. (no admittance after 4 p.m.), except Christ-

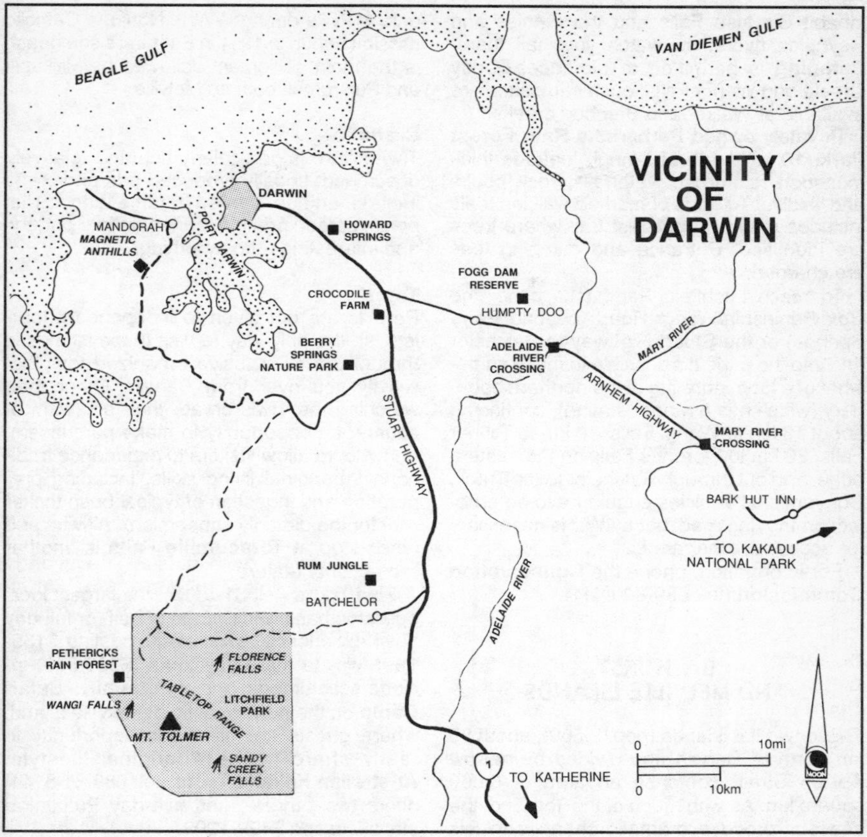

mas Day and Good Friday. Admission is $8. For information, phone 88-6000.

Litchfield Park

Long overshadowed by Kakadu, this newly developed 65,700-hectare reserve, just two-hours' drive from Darwin, has recently catapulted into the tourist limelight.

Dominated by the vast sandstone Tabletop Range and escarpment, some of the notable features of this awesome region include four major waterfalls cascading over the plateau (each with its own swimming pools and rainforest), creeks, caves, abundant flora, birds, and other wildlife, gigantic magnetic termite mounds, and numerous excellent bushwalking trails.

The **Lost City,** about six km east of Tolmer Falls, is a mysterious area of gigantic sandstone outcrops that resemble buildings, pillars, humans. Adding to the mystique is the fact that no Aboriginal settlement has been traced here. The "city" is accessible by foot or 4WD.

Swimming is safe in the falls area of the park (i.e., no crocs), but saltwater crocs *do* inhabit Surprise Falls and the Finniss and Reynolds rivers, so watch your tail there. **Camping** is permitted at Florence, Sandy Creek, and Wangi Falls; bush campsites are available at Walker and Bamboo creeks.

Privately owned **Pethericks Rain Forest Park,** 10 km north of Wangi, features thick monsoon rainforest, waterfalls, rock pools, and wildlife. A series of marked walking trails includes a special botanist trail where trees are identified. Entrance and camping fees are charged.

To reach Litchfield Park, take either the Cox Peninsula/Wangi Road (beyond Berry Springs) or the Stuart Highway to Batchelor and into the park. It's possible to make somewhat of a loop, entering at the northern boundary (which has a ranger station), continuing about 18 km to Wangi Falls, 10 km to Tolmer Falls, 20 km to Florence Falls on the eastern edge, and out through Batchelor to the Track. Conventional vehicles should have no problem on the ring road, but a 4WD is necessary for access to other areas.

For information, phone the **Conservation Commission** (tel. 089-89-4411).

BATHURST AND MELVILLE ISLANDS

These two flat islands (pop. 2,500), about 80 km north of Darwin and divided by narrow Apsley Strait, comprise an area of 8,000 square km. As with much of the Top End, the seasons produce dramatic changes in this region as well. In the Dry, grass burns, withers, and turns to straw; the Wet brings monsoon rains and lush greenery.

History

Strange as it seems, these islands and their Tiwi owners not only had little contact with Europeans but, until the late 1800s, had limited dealings with mainland Aborigines. The British attempted to establish their first settlement on Melville Island in 1824, but disease, isolation, and the animosity of the Tiwis sent the new residents quickly packing. Other visits were made by Macassarese fishermen, possibly the Portuguese, and a Japanese pilot who crashed onto Melville during WW II. Nguiu, a Catholic mission begun in 1911 in Bathurst's southeast, is the main settlement, followed by Milikapiti and Pularumpi, both on Melville.

Crafts

Tiwi culture is particularly rich and relatively unscathed. Locally produced arts and crafts include unique carved totems and burial poles, screen printing, bark painting, pottery, and interesting ethnic clothing.

Tours

Permits are not given to independent tourists, so the only way to visit these islands is through an all-inclusive organized tour that will fly you over from Darwin. Other than watching the Tiwis create their art (with, of course, an opportunity to make purchases), many tours allow visitors to experience traditional Aboriginal living skills, including preparation and ingestion of typical bush tucker *(not* for the dietarily squeamish). A swim and lunch stop at **Turacumbie Falls** is another recreational feature.

Tiwi Tours (tel. 81-5115), the largest local operator, has a wide range of half- or full-day "Tiwi experience" excursions, costing $135-199; two- to three-day tours ($399-549) include accommodations at **Putjamirra Safari Camp** on the northwest tip of Melville Island, where guests are given the opportunity to really share in the Aboriginal lifestyle. **Australian Kakadu Tours** (tel. 089-81-5144) offers two-, three-, and five-day Putjamirra stays, costing $499-1099.

It's best to bring necessities with you from Darwin. Stores stocking incidentals are located at Nguiu and at Barra Lodge at Port Hurd. Except for the bar at Barra Lodge, no alcohol is permitted on the islands.

ALONG ARNHEM HIGHWAY

The Arnhem Highway joins the Stuart Highway 34 km southeast of Darwin, traveling 217 km to Jabiru in the heart of Kakadu National Park. City buses go out as far as Humpty Doo, but you'll have to rely on the Kakadu-bound coaches or a car for other sites.

NORTHERN TERRITORY TOURIST COMMISSION

mmm . . . bush tucker. Bon appetit!

Humpty Doo
You can't miss this little service town (pop. 3,000) 10 km into this stretch—a massive replica of a croc decked out with red bulb-eyes and boxing gloves signals your arrival.

Turn west four km to **Graeme Gows Reptile World,** where you can see one of Australia's largest collections of snakes and lizards. Informative talks are given each day. Open daily 8:30 a.m.-5 p.m. Admission is $5. For information, phone (089) 88-1661.

Stop in at **Humpty Doo Hotel,** home of the annual Darwin Stubby Drinking Competition (31 July). Any time of year this pub is full of local color, serves counter meals, has an occasional live band, and is adorned with Territorial memorabilia.

Fogg Dam
Once an experimental rice farm, this 1,569-hectare conservation reserve, 11 km east of Humpty Doo, is an important refuge for water birds such as magpie geese, herons, ducks, egrets, brolgas, and rainbow pitta. Other wildlife includes jabirus, wallabies, frilled-neck lizards, file snakes, and pythons. Dawn and dusk during the Dry are the best viewing times. Camping is not allowed.

Adelaide River Crossing
Another eight km along the Arnhem Highway, the *Adelaide River Queen* departs from the western bank for 2½-hour upstream cruises to view crocs (who leap for morsels being dangled from poles), as well as buffalo, pigs, and birds. The two-story vessel has an a/c lower deck and snack bar. Cruises operate Tues.-Sun., Feb.-Oct., less frequently Nov.-Jan. Cost is $28. For information, phone 32-2892.

Leaning Tree Lagoon
Off the highway, some 13 km from the river crossing, Leaning Tree Lagoon Nature Park (101 hectares) is another water bird refuge during the Dry. The locals come here to picnic, canoe, and camp (no facilities).

Mary River Crossing
Continue another 25 km to this 2,590-hectare reserve, shelter to barramundi, saltwater crocs, and water birds during the Dry, as well as wallabies who peek from the granite outcrops. Boating, fishing, and camping are permitted.

Bark Hut Inn
Built in the 1970s, this favorite roadside pub (two km beyond Mary River Crossing) is the replica of a 1918 Annaburroo Station homestead and is decorated with all the Territorial trappings. An on-site wildlife enclosure houses dingoes, donkeys, kangaroos, wallabies, emus, buffalo, and pigs. Accommoda-

tions are in the moderate range, but campsites are also available. For information, phone 76-0185.

KAKADU NATIONAL PARK

Hallelujah—you've arrived at one of Australia's most majestic, mystical natural wonderlands, a tropical wilderness encompassing 1,307,300 hectares and six major topographical regions stretching some 100 km to the western border of Aboriginal-controlled Arnhem Land. Listed as a World Heritage site for its important wetlands and cultural significance, Kakadu's spectacles include a fortress-like sandstone escarpment, thick-as-thieves woodlands and forests, magnificent rock formations, lowland savannah, wide floodplains, mangrove-carpeted tidal flats, amazing birds and wildlife, gorges, waterfalls, caves, lagoons, mangrove-covered tidal flats, plentiful fish, flowers, and crocs, as well as an exquisite collection of Aboriginal rock art—some dating back 30,000 years or more.

It is recommended that, if possible, visitors experience the park during both the Wet and Dry seasons as features undergo drastic metamorphosis. During the oppressively humid Wet, rain falls in thunderous sheets over the weathered Arnhem Land escarpment, causing floodplains to swell, landscapes to green, posies to blossom, birds to breed, fish to jump, and all the beasties of the jungle to send out invites to fertility rites. In the height of the Dry, however, the searing sun cracks the earth, plants wither away, the fish die off, the abundant birds fight over the last bit of feed. (Secret: shaded gorges and billabongs off the main roads are still green and filled with wildlife.)

Nature lovers will have a hard time getting bored here at any time of year. Kakadu is home to a staggering variety of flora and fauna, with species numbering 1,000 plants, 50 mammals, 75 reptiles, 25 frogs, 275 birds (check out the massive flocks of magpie geese), 55 fish, and 10,000 insects (bring lots of repellent). Many are rare or endangered, and new species continue to be identified. One interesting fish is the silver barramundi, which makes a sex change from male to female at the age of about six.

Wanna-be croc hunters should have no problem spotting some of the thousands of freshwater and saltwater dinosaur cousins inhabiting the park. It's the saltwater croc ("saltie," in Aussie parlance) that's the big threat and **be forewarned:** salties do not live only in salt water but wherever they damn well please *and* they are masters of camouflage. Also, do not ignore any crocodile-warning signs (don't steal them, either!), and don't leave food scraps anywhere near the water. A safe way to see these prehistoric descendants is on a Yellow Water or South Alligator River boat cruise.

Approximate distances to and through Kakadu are 120 km from the Arnhem and Stuart highways junction to the park entrance, another 100 km east along sealed roadway to Jabiru. From Jabiru, the Ranger Uranium Mine is about 10 km southeast; Ubirr is 38 km north on mostly dirt road; and, just before Jabiru, turn onto the sealed Kakadu Highway 21 km south, and then another 12 km southeast, to Nourlangie. The sealed portion of the Kakadu Highway ends near Mardukal camping area, Cooinda, and Yellow Waters; it's unsealed from there to Pine Creek and the Stuart Highway (about 160 km), and impassable during the Wet. It's 20 km along the Kakadu Highway from the Nourlangie turnoff, to the Jim Jim Falls detour—60 km of 4WD only track.

History

Aboriginal settlement has been traced back at least 25,000 years. Derived from "Gagadju," name of one of the area's first tribes, today the park is back under Aboriginal control, with many Aborigines serving on the staff and as park rangers!

Wouldn't you just know that the Kakadu lands hold about 10% of the whole world's top-grade uranium ore? Three major mine sites—Ranger, Jabiluka, and Koongarra—sitting near the eastern edge, were leased to outside companies before the establishment of either the park or Aboriginal land rights. Land rights granted in the 1970s did not include the yea or nay of mining on sacred

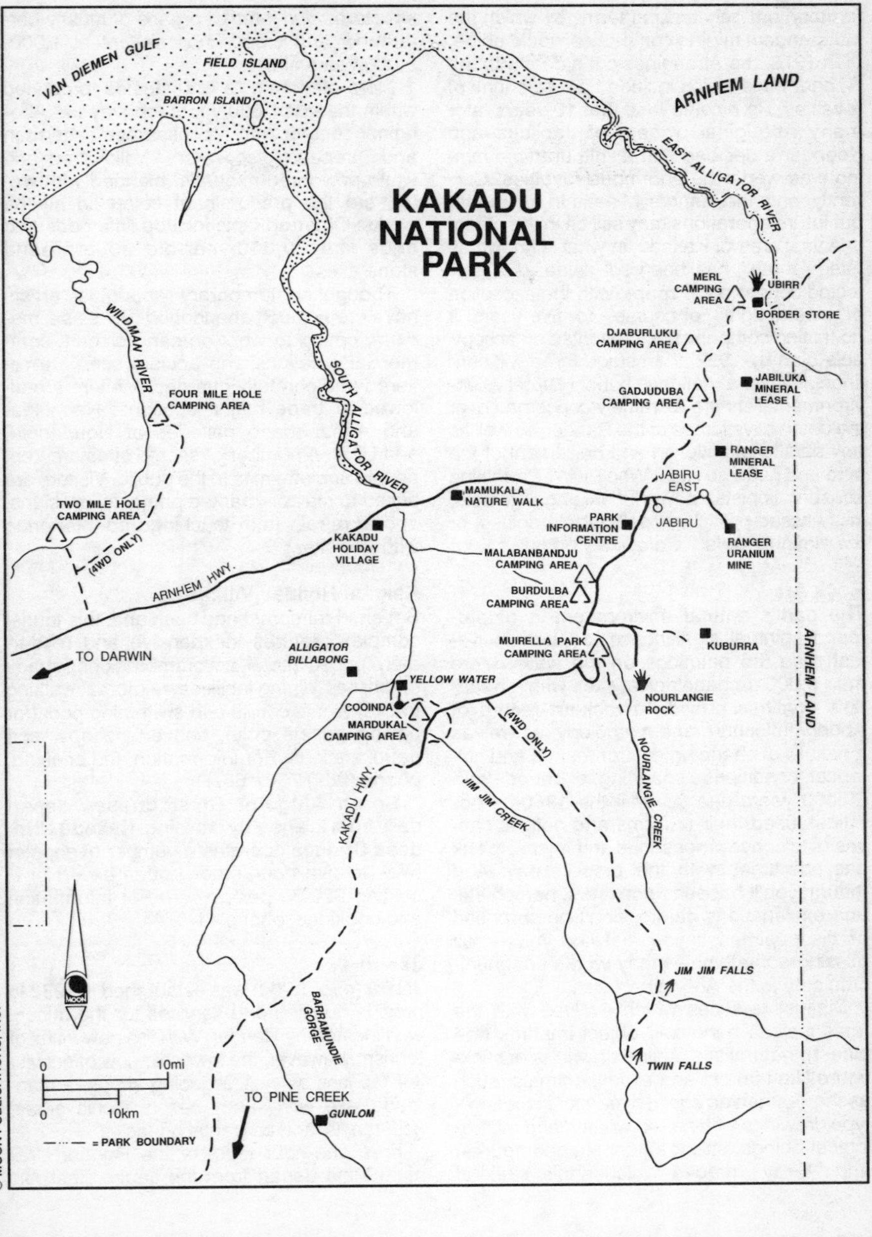

KAKADU
NATIONAL
PARK
VAN DIEMEN GULF
FIELD ISLAND
BARRON ISLAND
ARNHEM LAND
EAST ALLIGATOR RIVER
SOUTH ALLIGATOR RIVER
WILDMAN RIVER
MERL CAMPING AREA
UBIRR
BORDER STORE
DJABURLUKU CAMPING AREA
JABILUKA MINERAL LEASE
GADJUDUBA CAMPING AREA
RANGER MINERAL LEASE
JABIRU EAST
JABIRU
FOUR MILE HOLE CAMPING AREA
TWO MILE HOLE CAMPING AREA
(4WD ONLY)
MAMUKALA NATURE WALK
KAKADU HOLIDAY VILLAGE
PARK INFORMATION CENTRE
RANGER URANIUM MINE
MALABANBANDJU CAMPING AREA
BURDULBA CAMPING AREA
ARNHEM HWY.
MUIRELLA PARK CAMPING AREA
KUBURRA
ARNHEM LAND
TO DARWIN
ALLIGATOR BILLABONG
YELLOW WATER
COOINDA
MARDUKAL CAMPING AREA
NOURLANGIE ROCK
(4WD ONLY)
NOURLANGIE CREEK
JIM JIM CREEK
KAKADU HWY.
MOON
BARRAMUNDIE GORGE
JIM JIM FALLS
TWIN FALLS
0
10mi
0
10km
TO PINE CREEK
GUNLOM
= PARK BOUNDARY

territory, but only leasing terms by which the independent mining companies would abide.

In 1978, the Aborigines cut a deal with the Ranger Mine which included a nice chunk of royalties. So nice, in fact, that 10 years later many Aboriginal owners of Jabiluka and Koongarra decided that a little uranium mining was worth the enormous royalties. Currently, only the Ranger Mine is in full swing, but future operations may still be in the offing.

A vast area of Kakadu, in what is known as "stage three," has been set aside as a protected conservation zone—with the exception of mineral rights, of course—for five years. If no mining company has presented an acceptable plan by 1992, then stage three will continue life as a national park. Naturally, environmentalists are extremely concerned over the destructive forces of the Ranger, as well as any additional pollution and defilement of the land and heritage sites. Who'll win? Protesting conservationists, powerful mining interests, kissy-assed politicians, sell-out Aborigines, or the almighty dollar? Care to lay odds?

Rock Art

The park's natural environment is of profound spiritual significance to Aborigines—just read the paintings on the walls. More than 5,000 archaeological sites within Kakadu's confines provide a rock-art record of Aboriginal culture and mythology, as well as a picture of changing environmental and historical conditions, spanning a period from 20,000 years ago up until the 1960s. Aborigines used their artforms and natural canvases to convey messages and myths, to link past centuries with the present day. And though you'll happen upon tours, pamphlets, and explanations galore, don't be surprised or disappointed if you feel like you're still missing something—many works communicate only to the Aboriginal heart.

Distinctive styles which evolved with the ages include hand and object imprints (the oldest), naturalistic outline drawings of stick-figure-like hunters and extinct animals (such as the Tasmanian tiger), dynamic "in motion"-type drawings with naked women and mythological beings, strange yam-shaped figures, and "X-ray" images which show skeletal structures and internal organs of mostly barramundi and crocs (most recent at 1,000-9,000 years old).

More elaborate "X-ray" studies, produced within the last 1,000 years, convey the Aboriginal contact with Macassarese fishermen and European "discoverers." Yellow, red, and white powdered minerals, blended with water, are the predominant colors in all the works. Other artifacts include little odds and ends like 20,000-year-old edge-ground stone axes.

Though contemporary Aboriginal artists have pretty much abandoned rocks as a medium, opting to work on sand or bark commercial creations, the ancient sites are revered and carefully guarded. Visitors are allowed at three major locations: Nangoloar and Anbangbang galleries at Nourlangie, and Ubirr. A number of sacred sites are kept private and off-limits to the public. Visitors are asked to stay on marked paths, follow signs, and to refrain from touching and interfering with any site.

Kakadu Holiday Village

Set amid rainforest and bushland, this tourist complex features inexpensive and moderately priced motel accommodations, shady campsites, dining facilities, rainforest walking tracks, tennis courts and swimming pool (for paying guests only), souvenir shops, and petrol stations. For information and booking, phone (089) 79-0166.

South Alligator River cruises depart daily from the nearby crossing. **Kakadu Princess Cruises** operates a number of popular two- to five-hour croc-spotter excursions, costing $20-50 per person. For information and bookings, phone 41-0744.

Jabiru

Jabiru (pop. 1,300) was established in 1982 to provide housing and services for the miners working nearby Ranger. With the new influx of tourism, however, the township now offers visitor facilities as well, including shops, a man-made lake with sandy beach, picnic areas, golf, tennis, and car-rental agencies.

Free one-hour tours of the Ranger Uranium Mine depart from the Jabiru East Air-

NORTHERN TERRITORY TOURIST COMMISSION

Mount Brockman at Kakadu escarpment

port, six km east. For times and other information, phone 79-2031.

Jabiru is also the location of **Four Seasons Kakadu,** Flinders St. (tel. 089-79-2800). This is the new crocodile-shaped *expensive* hotel where guests enter through the "jaws," then pay through the nose to sleep and eat inside the belly and brains. The croc "head" houses shops, restaurants, and bars. It's definitely worth a look just for the reptilian kitsch angle.

For emergencies, contact **police** (tel. 79-2122), or **medical aid** (tel. 089-79-2018 or 79-2102).

Ubirr

Also known as Obiri Rock, this major rock-art site is home of some of the country's most important works contained within six different sheltered areas. A one-km path leads visitors to all of the sites, but most impressive is the main gallery with its exquisitely preserved "X-ray" paintings which depict king o' the jungle and sea wildlife as well as several haughty white boys in a 15-meter frieze. Another path leads to the top of the rock and magnificent views of Kakadu and Arnhem Land (some *Crocodile Dundee* scenes were shot up here).

Facilities include picnic grounds and a park headquarters with interpretive display and informative brochures. Park rangers lead guided tours during the Dry. Near Ubirr there's a border store and 20-bed **Manbiyarra Youth Hostel,** closed during the Wet. For information and opening dates, phone (089) 84-3902. Keep in mind that the gravel road to Ubirr is impassable for conventional vehicles—and often 4WDs—during the Wet.

Nourlangie Rock

The other major art site, reached via a short jog off the Kakadu Highway, is open year-round. The Aborigines call this rock Burrunggui, and the surrounding area Nawulandja, both of which somehow were bastardized into Nourlangie.

Rising from the Arnhem Land escarpment, this massive weathered sandstone, sheer-cliffed outcrop features several formidable areas: **Anbangbang,** an Aboriginal shelter for at least 20,000 years, where mythological figures such as Namarrgon, "Lightning Man," are friezed in time; **Anbangbang Gallery,** behind the shelter, with works created by Najombolmi (aka Barramundi Charlie) as recently as the 1960s; and **Nangaloar Gallery,** reached by a three- to four-km walk, with styles including "X-ray" paintings, hand stencils, and stick figures with subjects ranging from mythical beings and fish to European ships.

On the way back to the highway, a turnoff to the left leads a short walk's way to **Nawu-**

landja lookout, where park rangers will guide you to the only known blue paintings.

Facilities include interpretive displays, guided walks, and picnic area.

Jim Jim Falls

It's 4WD only, then a one-km walk across boulders, to reach these dramatic falls which plunge 200 meters over the Arnhem Land escarpment, thundering during the Wet and, in comparison, trickling during the Dry.

Visitors trek here for the majestic scenery, deep-plunge pool, freshwater crocs, sandy beach with shallow swimming area, breathtaking bushwalks, and good camping.

Twin Falls

It's not quite so easy to reach Twin Falls, 10 km south of Jim Jim Falls, where access is gained by fording Jim Jim Creek. Take your choice of two double-dare routes: make a few short swims and rock climbs up the gorge and hope you don't run into any freshwater crocs (no one said they were *safe,* just saf*er*); or scramble, climb, and walk your way across. On arrival you'll be rewarded by the glorious vision of the crystal falls (yes, two of them), lush ferns and greenery, and a sandy palm-lined beach.

Yellow Water

Don't get scared—despite its name, this billabong derives its color from an algae which, when concentrated, produces a distinctive yellow tinge. These wetlands are a sanctuary for a large number and variety of water birds (whistling ducks, jabiru, egrets, pelicans, magpie geese, spoonbills, etc.), as well as crocs, and boat trips on the mangrove-lined billabong are one of the park's highlights.

Access to Yellow Water is through Cooinda, about four km off the Kakadu Highway, 48 km from its junction with the Arnhem Highway. Accommodations at Cooinda are either at the expensive **Four Seasons Cooinda** (tel. 089-79-0145), or at the adjacent caravan park which also has campsites. Other facilities in the tourist complex include a restaurant, bistro, bar, takeaway, small supermarket, souvenir shop, petrol station, tourist information center, car rental agency, and airstrip.

Four Seasons Cooinda Tours operate daily two-hour Yellow River cruises departing at 6:45 a.m., 9 a.m., and 4:30 p.m. Cost is $18.50. If you can keep your eyes open at that hour, shoot for the 6:45 a.m. trip when birdlife is most active (you know who catches the worm . . .). Advance bookings are essential for this popular outing. Phone the hotel for information.

To Pine Creek

Just past the Cooinda turnoff, the Kakadu Highway becomes mostly dirt for the 208-km, southwesterly "back way" to Pine Creek on the Stuart Highway. The road is often closed during the Wet; check with park rangers or police at either end for current status. **Barramundie Gorge,** about 35 km along the highway from Cooinda, then a 10-km turnoff on 4WD track, is a-lush with rainforest patches, gorge pools and beaches, freshwater crocs, and abundant birdlife. Camping is allowed.

Farther south and west, and often inaccessible during the Wet, **Waterfall Creek** (also known as Gunlom, and once known as Uranium Development Project Falls) is part of that iffy stage-three region, and another site locale for *Crocodile Dundee.* Features include a 100-meter waterfall, interesting flat rocks, a large pool bordered by paperbark and pandanus, freshwater crocs, aerobic bushwalks, camping, and picnic areas.

Camping

Aside from the privately run campgrounds mentioned above, Kakadu has a variety of campsites under jurisdiction of the Australian National Parks and Wildlife Service. Major sites with showers, flush toilets, hot water, and drinking water are at **Merl** (near the border store), **Muirella Park** (south of Nourlangie Rock), and **Mardukal** (just south of the Cooinda turnoff). Other camping areas are Djaburluku, Gadjuduba, Melabanbandju, Burdulba, Jim Jim Falls, Barramundie Gorge, Gunlom (Waterfall Creek), Alligator Billabong, Black Jungle Spring, Two Mile Hole, and Four Mile Hole.

All of the campgrounds except Mardukal are subject to Wet-season closures. Permits (get 'em at park headquarters) are required for bush camping outside of designated areas. Camping fees (pay at the park headquarters) are $5 per night for caravans, and $2 per night for tents plus an additional $2 per night per person at developed campgrounds. Bushcamping is free.

Information

The **Kakadu National Park Information Centre** is a few kilometers south of Jabiru on the Kakadu Highway. The center provides extensive literature, guide maps, and tour info (particularly the ranger-led art and nature tours), as well as audiovisual displays ($3 admission) and video screenings. The center is open daily 8 a.m.-5 p.m. For information, phone park headquarters at (089) 79-2101, or write: Superintendent, Kakadu National Park, Box 71, Jabiru, NT 5796.

Tourist information is also available at Jabiru Airport and the hotels. In Darwin, contact the **Australian National Parks and Wildlife Service,** Box 1260, Darwin, NT 5794 (tel. 81-5299).

Entry fee to the park is $5 and is good for two weeks' stay. You can buy an annual ticket for $30, entitling you to unlimited access to both Kakadu and Uluru (Ayers Rock) national parks.

Getting There And Around

Both **Air North** (tel. 089-81-7188) and **Kakadu Air Services** (tel. 79-2731) provide regular service between Darwin and Jabiru.

Ansett Pioneer and **Greyhound** coach lines travel daily between Darwin and Kakadu, stopping variously at Humpty Doo ($10), Bark Hut ($18), Kakadu Holiday Village ($28), Jabiru ($33), Nourlangie Rock and Cooinda ($40). Service may be delayed or suspended during the Wet.

Rental cars can be procured in Darwin or within the park from Budget, Four Seasons Kakadu (tel. 79-2858), or Territory Rent-A-Car, Jabiru Airport (tel. 089-79-2552). Both companies have 4WD vehicles. For visitors arriving by bus or conventional vehicle, **Sundowner Safaris** (tel. 85-3465) provides 4WD shuttle service between accommodation centers and otherwise inaccessible waterfalls for $45.

CROCODILES

Know your crocs and take those warning signs *seriously!* There are two kinds: saltwater ("salties") and freshwater. The smaller freshwater croc is usually harmless unless provoked, while the larger saltie poses a definite danger. Worse, the saltie also inhabits fresh water! My opinion—don't trust either of 'em. They're smart and *fast!*

Aside from the obvious swimming hazards, you should avoid hanging out around water's edge, cleaning fish, or leaving food waste near the water. Also, crocs seem to get upset around dogs and teasing boaters.

Tours

The **Northern Territory Government Tourist Bureau** in Darwin has an exhaustive listing of Kakadu tour operators. The Park Information Center, Kakadu Holiday Village, Four Sea-

Cape Arnhem—really away from it all!

sons Kakadu and Four Seasons Cooinda, all book a number of excursions within the park.

Westcoast Helicopters NT (tel. 41-0400) and **Kakadu Air Services** (tel. 089-79-2441) schedule a wide variety of scenic air tours, lasting from 10 minutes to one hour. Prices range from $45-210.

For **boat trips,** see "Kakadu Holiday Village" and "Yellow River" above.

ARNHEM LAND AND BEYOND

Within this huge region (pop. 5,000), comprising the entire eastern half of the Top End, scattered groups of Aborigines keep their traditional fires burning in a homeland filled with escarpment and plateaus, gorges and rivers, an abundance of rock-art sites and birdlife.

The district was named by Matthew Flinders in 1803 for one of the Dutch ships that "discovered" the coast in 1623—though earlier discoverers were most likely visiting Malaccans, Indonesians, and Portuguese.

Don't even try to go onto these designated Aboriginal lands without the necessary permit—and don't count on getting one very easily either. Permits are seldom given to curious tourists, but several tour operators can take you up to the Cobourg Peninsula and to Bathurst and Melville islands, and a couple of companies offer trips deep into Arnhem Land. (Stop in at any Northern Territory Government Tourist Bureau for a free copy of *Come Share Our Culture, A Guide to Northern Territory Aboriginal Tours, Arts and Crafts.*) If flying in, you won't need a permit to visit Gove Peninsula, at the northeast tip.

Gurig National Park

Isolated on the Cobourg Peninsula, 200 kilometers northeast of Darwin, Gurig National Park (220,700 hectares) embraces exquisite virgin wilderness, important wetlands, protected coral reefs and marinelife, vast numbers of migratory birds, relics of the Macassarese trading days, and, of course, rich Aboriginal culture. The park is operated by the Conservation Commission, in conjunction with traditional owners (the Gurig people, made up of about 40 clans), many of whom live near Black Point and work within the tourist sector.

The Cobourg Peninsula was the location for several of those pre-Darwin, failed European settlements. Ruins of **Victoria Settlement,** the 1838 British garrison community at Port Essington, include building foundations, walls, stone chimneys, and a half-buried powder magazine. An interpretive walking track incorporates many sights; pick up informative pamphlets at the **Visitors Centre and Museum** at Black Point.

The British left more than just their ruins—imported livestock still roaming the peninsula include Indian sambar deer, Timorian ponies, Balinese banteng cattle, and Javanese buffalo and pigs. Saltwater crocs, turtles, sea cows, and numerous tropical fish inhabit the coastal waters (though we won't credit the Brits for *those.*) Along the sandy shores, beachcombers are apt to walk away with some primo shells for their collections. Fishing is idyllic year-round, but swimming is not recommended (unless you don't mind playing Russian roulette with the sharks, saltwater crocs, and box jellyfish).

A small **campground** is located near the shore at Smith Point. Facilities include showers, toilets, picnic and barbecue area, jetty, and a nearby store with sporadic hours.

The peninsula is about a nine-hour drive from Darwin along the Arnhem Highway, turning northwest from Jabiru. It's 4WD only from East Alligator River to Gurig, and the road is closed during the Wet. Advance permits to enter Arnhem Land are mandatory. For information, contact the **Northern Territory Conservation Commission** (tel. 089-22-0211). Be forewarned: only 15 vehicles per week are allowed access, and bookings are now running one to two years behind!

An **organized tour,** all-inclusive of air or land transport, accommodations, and necessary permits, is really the easiest way to go. Darwin-based operators specializing in the Cobourg Peninsula include Cobourg Marine (tel. 41-0734), Nimrod Safaris (tel. 47-0388), and Wimray Safaris (tel. 41-0015).

Gove Peninsula

This remote region on Arnhem Land's *very far away* northeastern tip, was first charted in 1803 by Matthew Flinders, but only settled at Nhulunbuy as late as 1969—when the bauxite mining began. The local Yirrkala Aborigines protested the intended rape of their traditional land and, though mining proceeded anyhow (surprise, surprise), a government inquiry and subsequent compensation award attracted national attention, planting a seed for the future land rights movement.

Visitors come to this balmy, tropical region expressly because it is so isolated and untouristy. White-sand beaches, birds and wildlife, reef and big-game fishing, varied sports facilities, and saltwater croc and buffalo safaris are the big attractions. In addition **Yirrkala,** a former mission, displays and sells art and artifacts produced by local Aborigines. Free half-day tours of the **Nabalco Mine** are given on Thursday mornings.

The only practical way to get up to Gove is by air. Australian, Ansett, and Ansett NT all fly from Australian capital cities into Nhulunbuy, and no permit is necessary. The cheapest fares are in conjunction with land packages, which usually include accommodations at moderately priced **Hideaway Safari Lodge** (tel. 87-1833). Driving up here is not practical due to the long distances (800 km of pretty lousy road from Katherine) plus a number of complicated permits involved. Coastline explorers who fly in can rent cars in Nhulunbuy. (Be sure to get a permit from the local Northern Land Council before setting out on the road.)

Arnhemland Adventure Safaris (tel. 87-1833) offers a wide range of local tours including 30-minute scenic flights ($75), half-day Nhulunbuy excursions ($55), full-day wilderness adventure tours ($110), and two-day Wigwam Island traditional-living "dreamtime" safari camps ($1100).

DOWN THE TRACK

It's about 1,500 km from Darwin to Alice Springs on the Stuart Highway (National Route 87). Closely paralleling explorer John McDouall Stuart's path (its namesake) and the 1872 Overland Telegraph Line, the Track has grown from a pre-WW II dirt stretch to a two-lane, sealed, all-weather highway. Sights on or near the road add interest to the long drive.

DARWIN TO KATHERINE

See "Vicinity Of Darwin" for towns and attractions on the Track within about 50 kilometers south of Darwin.

Manton Dam

This huge reservoir, 42 km down the Track from Darwin and another few kilometers along the turnoff, was originally built for WW II military personnel stationed in the Territory. The 440-hectare recreation area features sailing, swimming, water-skiing, and barbecue facilities. Open Mon.-Fri. 9-5, Sat.-Sun. 8 a.m.-7 p.m.

Lake Bennett

Situated 80 km down the Track and then seven km east, this 404-hectare manmade lake provides a large range of water activities, including windsurfing, swimming, sailing, canoeing, and fishing. Other features include prolific birdlife, tropical wilderness areas, bushwalks, and barbecue facilities. Accommodations at **Lake Bennett Holiday Park** (tel. 089-76-0032) consist of campsites or camp-o-tels (a combination tent and motel).

Batchelor

This Litchfield Park gateway (pop. 600) and former service town to the defunct Rum Jungle uranium and copper mine lies 84 km from Darwin and another 13 km to the west, in a lush forest setting with colorful birdlife. Nearby is an old airstrip, used from time to time by General Douglas McArthur during WW II, as well as other wartime memorabilia. **Karlstein Castle,** a miniature replica of a Bohemian castle, sits oddly out of place across from the police station. **Rum Jungle Lake,** six km from town, is a popular center for sailing, swimming, and canoeing. This town is also the site of an **Aboriginal Teacher Training College** and base for the **Top End Aerial Sports Association's** parachuting and gliding activities.

Moderately priced accommodations are available at **Rum Jungle Motor Inn,** Rum Jungle Rd. (tel. 76-0123). **Batchelor Caravillage,** Rum Jungle Rd., (tel. 76-0166) offers on-site vans and campsites, and also arranges tours of the Rum Jungle Mine.

Adelaide River

Located on the Adelaide River (but not the Crossing on Arnhem Highway), 110 km south of Darwin, this tiny township (pop. 200) was a hub of WW II military activity, undoubtedly due to its railway depot and prominent position. Relics and armaments still in evidence include the **Snake Creek Arsenal,** a major armaments depot and wartime military camp; **Adelaide River War Cemetery,** Australia's largest such graveyard where most of the Darwin dead have been laid to rest; and a host of old airstrips smattered around the Track. The restored **Railway Station** (built 1888-89) is a designated National Trust property, housing a **Tourist Information Centre,** open Mon., Wed., and Fri. 4-5 p.m. The **Railway Bridge,** built the same year as the station, occasionally doubled as a road bridge during the Wet!

Adelaide River Inn, Stuart Hwy. (tel. 089-76-7047), offers inexpensive rooms, and **Shady River View Caravan Park,** War Memorial Dr. (same phone), has campsites.

For emergencies, contact **police** (tel. 76-7042), **fire brigade** (tel. 76-7047), or **ambulance** (tel. 27-9000).

The Scenic Route

From Adelaide River you can continue on the Track or take the scenic Old Stuart Highway, an extra 14-km jog slightly to the west, for a variety of interesting attractions—though during the Wet, access is sometimes impossible.

First stop is **Robin Falls,** 17 km southwest of Adelaide River and a short walk from the road. Aside from the 12-meter-high falls (which are but a few drips and trickles during the Dry), this spot features a monsoon-forested gorge, good swimming, and, for those up to the climb, excellent views from the top.

The **Daly River** area is a bit of a detour (109 km southwest of the highway at Adelaide River), but worth the drive for several attractions. The town of Daly River (pop. 250), an 1880's copper mine, was the scene of a bloody race riot between Aborigines (who opposed the mine) and white miners. Though the mine did not stick around for long, the Jesuit mission, established around the time of the conflict, did—today it is run by the local Aboriginal council. The town has a variety of services, including a supermarket, Aboriginal art center, roadside inn, takeaway food, and petrol and camping gas.

Nearby attractions are: **Daly River Nature Park,** a 60-hectare reserve with barramundi fishing, boating, picnic and camping facilities; **Bamboo Creek Rainforest Park** (tel. 089-75-3410), 13 km from Daly River on Wooliana Track, features fishing, canoeing, guided motorbike and boat tours, camping, and moderately priced cottage accommodations; and **Mango Farm Safari Camp** (tel. 089-75-3464), five km south of Daly River and another seven km from the turnoff, offers a variety of scenic, wildlife, croc-spotting, fishing, and hunting tours, plus safari tents, campsites, and moderately priced cabins. Be sure to inquire at the Aboriginal council office in Daly River as to allowed access on local tribal lands.

Travel back to the old highway and turn another 35 km southwest (just before the junction with the Track) to reach **Douglas Hot Springs Nature Park.** The top attraction of this 3,107-hectare park is the thermal pools, particularly **Hot Springs Lagoon,** with 40° C bathtub water. Swimming, bushwalks, and camping are also popular here. **Butterfly Gorge Nature Park,** 17 km farther along a 4WD track, is a 104-hectare tranquil woodland reserve with swarming butterflies, deep rock pools, and a high-cliffed gorge ideal for bushwalking, fishing, and swimming. As crocs may be present, check first with the **ranger station,** located about five km from the park's turnoff. Next to the ranger station, **Corn Patch Riverside Holiday Park** (tel. 089-75-3479) offers a variety of facilities including general store, petrol, bar, restaurant, takeaway, camping gas, and campsites.

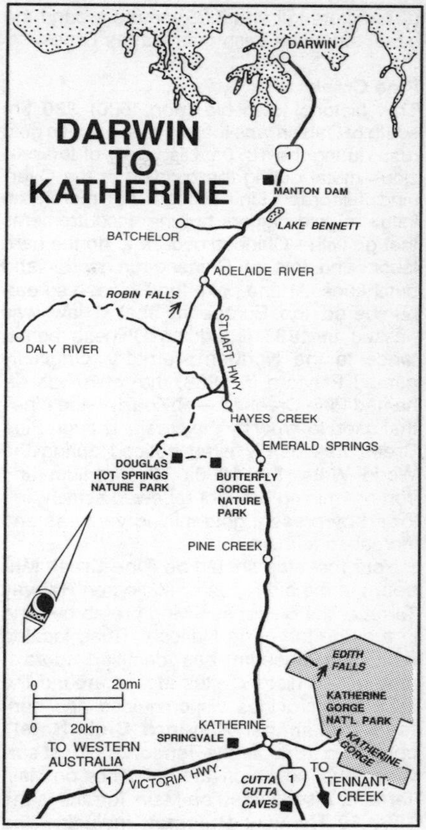

Back on the Track, keep your eyes peeled for one of Australia's largest **termite mounds**

(6.7 meters tall and 7.35 meters around the base) set in the bush near **Hayes Creek.**

Pine Creek

This historic township (pop. 500) 230 km south of Darwin was the site of a massive gold rush during the 1870s. Discovery of the precious metal during the building of the Overland Telegraph Line brought not merely an influx of gold diggers but the accoutrements that go with—Chinese coolies to do the hard labor, and lots of Chinese-run stores and butcheries. At one point the Chinese so outnumbered the Europeans that a law was passed in 1888 forbidding Chinese admittance to the Northern Territory. Originally named Playford in 1888, the town was renamed Pine Creek for—obviously—the pines that used to grow by the creek. Though Pine Creek was hardly even noticed during the World Wars, the 1960s-'70s uranium and iron ore mining brought renewed activity, followed by present gold-mining ventures and increased tourism.

Your first stop should be **Pine Creek Museum** in the old repeater station on Railway Terrace, the oldest surviving prefab building in the Territory. The National Trust, located within the museum, has identified approximately 140 historic sites in and around the town and provides visitor guides and heritage trail maps. **Playford Club Hotel,**, opened in 1889, is the Territory's oldest surviving pub, now a private residence on Main Terrace. Also located on Main Terrace is the 1888-89 **Railway Precinct,** including the station, weigh bridge, crane, water tank, sheds, and employee housing. **Miners Park,** next door, features assorted mining relics.

In case you forgot—or haven't read that part yet—Pine Creek is also the "back road" gateway to Kakadu Highway and Kakadu National Park. Pine Creekers fish for barramundi, black bream, and catfish at Mary River, at the park's edge.

Pine Creek Hotel/Motel, Moule St. (tel. 089-76-1288), has moderately priced rooms. **Pine Creek Caravan Park,** Moule St. (tel. 089-76-1217), features campsites as well as a fully equipped bunkhouse. A *very* basic **Youth Hostel** (tel. 76-1254), formerly an 1880s railway workers' housing, is located near the station on Main Terrace.

KATHERINE

This third-largest Northern Territory center, 350 km south of Darwin, has practically doubled in population (from 6,200 to about 10,000) with the 1988 opening of RAAF Tindal, Australia's largest air base. Other than military activities, Katherine is a booming tourist town renowned for nearby Katherine Gorge and Cutta Cutta Caves as well as a service town and turnoff point for the Kimberley region in Western Australia.

Set amidst tropical woodland and along the Katherine River banks, the town grew up in conjunction with installation of the Overland Telegraph Line and railway. World War II brought a number of airstrips to the area and, more recently, regional administration, agriculture, cattle stations, and service facilities have added prosperity to this middle-of-nowhere tourist center.

Katherine Museum and Historical Park, on Giles St., opposite the hospital, features a variety of local history displays and architectural relics in a former airport terminal building. Hours are Mon.-Fri. 10 a.m.-4 p.m., Sat. 10 a.m.-2 p.m., Sun. 2-5 p.m. Admission is $1.50.

Katherine Railway Station, on Railway Terrace, houses railroad memorabilia as well as the local branch of the National Trust. Pick up a self-guided tour brochure to 10 heritage sites. Hours are Mon.-Fri. 11 a.m.-3 p.m. Watch teachers in action with their Outback students at **School of the Air,** Giles Street. Admission is $4. The **O'Keefe Residence,** on Riverside Dr. across from Campbell Terrace, is an exceptional example of Territorial architecture, built of bush poles, corrugated iron, and asbestos(!).

Katherine Low Level Nature Park, a 104-hectare section of the Katherine River, is a local favorite for fishing, swimming (safe mainly during the Dry), and picnicking. Check locally about the possibility of freshwater crocs.

Knotts Crossing marks the site of Katherine's beginnings. Accessed via a turnoff past the hospital, the original settlement included a pub, store, telegraph, and police station. The old pub, located at the top of the riverbank, is now a private residence.

Springvale Homestead

Located eight km southwest of Katherine, on Shadforth Rd., Springvale, established in 1878, is reputedly the Territory's oldest original station homestead. Now a tourist facility, the homestead's features include period-costumed staff, walking tours, canoeing, croc-spotting, swimming (in the Dry), fishing, and Aboriginal corroborees (in the evening). Free tours of the homestead are given daily during the Dry at 9 a.m. and 3 p.m. (historical reenactments coincide with the afternoon tour). Croc cruises and corroboree nights cost $29. Canoe hire is $5 per hour or $20 for the day. For information, phone (089) 72-1044.

Lazy L Stables, at the homestead's entrance, offers trail rides and pony rides. For information, phone 72-2618.

Katherine Gorge

This glorious park (180,352 hectares), 32 km northeast of Katherine township, ranks third—after Ayers Rock and Kakadu National Park—among the Territory's most visited attractions. Recently returned to the Jawoyn Aborigines, its traditional owners, the park is administered jointly by the Conservation Commission and the Jawoyn people.

A total of 13 gorges, carved by the Katherine River through Arnhem Plateau sandstone merely 25 million years ago (though the base material is some 2,300 million years old), are geological marvels with sheer rock faces rising 75 meters high, exquisitely patterned stone floors, and weathered canyon walls adorned with Aboriginal paintings and engravings. Aside from the magnificent gorges, the landscape encompasses rugged escarpment and plateaus, a superb variety of flora, fauna, birds, and aquatic life. This is an area of mosses and ferns, pandanus and paperbark, freshwater crocs and long-necked tortoises, red-winged parrots and blue-winged kookaburras—and bat caves. Ten **bushwalks,** taking from two hours to several days, cover approximately 100 km of always scenic, sometimes rugged, track. The longest walk is the 76-km trek to **Edith Falls,** a series of low falls and cool rock pools at the extreme western edge of the park. In case you're contemplating a swim, be forewarned: freshwater crocs inhabit these waters. Katherine Gorge is another place that changes markedly with the seasons, becoming thunderous during the Wet, drying into deep pools as the rains subside.

The **visitor center,** near the park entrance, provides area and bushwalking maps, informative displays, literature, and also issues the required permits for long-distance or wilderness hikes.

Cutta Cutta Caves

Situated west of the Track, 27 km south of Katherine, this series of limestone caverns dates back 500 million years, give or take a year or so. Classic stalactite and stalagmite formations and tower karsts are the primary characteristics of this protected nature park (1,499 hectares). Rare and strange cave dwellers include blind shrimp and the golden horseshoe bat. Though Katherine tour operators often include these caves in their excursions, if you come on your own you can sign up for an informative ranger-led tour (you can only enter the caves while on a guided tour). Ninety-minute ranger-led tours operate daily at 10:30 a.m., noon, and 1:30 p.m., except during the Wet, when caves are closed. Cost is $4.

Accommodations

Springvale Homestead, Shadforth Rd. (tel. 089-72-1355), offers inexpensive rooms in historic surroundings. For moderately priced accommodations, try **Katherine Hotel Motel,** corner Katherine Terrace and Giles St. (089-72-1622), or **Beagle Motor Inn,** corner Fourth and Lindsay St. (tel. 089-72-3998). The 51-bed **YHA Hostel, 1 Victoria Hwy.** (tel. 089-72-2942), has dorm beds for $7 per night, and **Palm Court Backpackers Lodge,** corner Giles and Third (tel. 089-72-2722) charges $12 per person for shared rooms. **Kookaburra Lodge,** corner Lindsay and Third (tel. 089-71-0257), features $10-per-night dorm rooms.

Campsites are available at **Katherine Gorge Caravan Park,** Katherine Gorge National Park (tel. 72-1253), **Katherine Low Level Caravan Park,** Shadforth Rd. (tel. 089-72-3962), and **Riverview Caravan Park,** 440 Victoria Hwy. (tel. 72-1011).

Events

Though Aboriginal lands are normally off-limits to the public, everyone is invited to the big **Barunga Festival** at Beswick Aboriginal Land Trust, 130 km south of Katherine and an additional 29 km off the highway. Held over the Queen's Birthday weekend in June, it draws Aborigines from throughout the Territory for a four-day celebration of dancing, sports, arts and crafts, plus bush-tucker stalls. Sunday is the best day, with fire lighting, and boomerang- and spear-throwing competitions.

Information

Pick up heaps of local info and maps at the **Northern Territory Government Tourist Bureau,** corner Stuart Hwy. and Lindsay Ave. (tel. 089-72-2650).

Getting There And Around

Both **Ansett NT** and **Australian** airlines have regularly scheduled flights between Katherine, Alice Springs, and Darwin. All the Darwin-to-Alice Springs coach lines stop in Katherine. Fare from Darwin (3½ hours) is about $36 one way; from Alice Springs, $108 one way.

A **"commuter bus"** runs several times daily between Springvale Homestead, the YHA Hostel, and the Katherine bus station, and twice daily to Katherine Gorge. Check at the tourist bureau for information and schedules. **Rental cars** are available from Budget (tel. 72-1280), Hertz (tel. 72-1201), Territory Rent-A-Car (tel. 72-3183), and Thrifty (tel. 71-0923).

Inquire at the tourist bureau for best local tours. **Travel North** (tel. 089-72-1044) operates a variety of Katherine Gorge excursions, including river cruises ($13-82). **Scenic flights** over Kakadu National Park are offered by **Air North** (tel. 72-1711), **Brolga Air** (tel. 72-2141), **Kakadu Air Services** (tel. 79-2411), and **Mataranka Heli-Tours** (tel. 089-72-3349). Prices range from $40-400.

Bill Harney's Jankangyina Tours (tel. 72-2650) are excellent two-day, one-night Aboriginal adventures including rock-art sites, bush foods, and campfire stories. Prices range $195-220.

TO WESTERN AUSTRALIA

It's 513 km southwest from Katherine to the Western Australia border along the **Victoria Highway.** Though the road is bitumen all the way, it's extremely narrow and impassable during the Wet, when torrential rain causes rivers to flood and overflow bridges and roadways. Exercise caution when driving this route—if another vehicle approaches, so does an impending barrage of stones; slow down and pull as far off the road as possible.

It's 125 km along the Victoria Highway to the **Delamere Road** turnoff. **Top Springs** (pop. 15), 164 km south at the Buchanan Highway junction, features a popular beer-guzzler (an average of nine tons per week!) roadhouse, pools for swimming, moderately priced accommodations, campsites, and the usual range of services. For information, phone (089) 75-0767. The Buchanan continues 170 km southwest to **Kalkaringi** (pop. 250), a service town for the Daguragu Aboriginal Land Trust, and another 222 km to the Western Australia border. Four-wheel-drives are recommended for this highway, which is often flooded during the Wet.

Back on Victoria Highway, **Victoria River Wayside Inn** (tel. 089-75-0744), 196 km southwest of Katherine, sits at Victoria River Crossing, backed by smooth ranges and rugged cliffs. Known as the "friendliest pub in the scrub," facilities include a general store, supermarket, restaurant, pub, takeaway, petrol station, tourist information center, mechanic and towing service, petrol station, campsites, and moderately priced motel rooms. **Red Valley boat tours** depart from here or Timber Creek three times daily (April-Oct.) on cruises of the scenic river and gorges. Cost is $10-20. Barramundi and bream fishing is good in these parts, but both freshwater crocs and salties live in the water as well, so stave off your temptation to swim.

Surrounding the Wayside Inn and Victoria River and stretching all the way to Timber Creek is newly established **Gregory National Park** (10,000 square km) which encompasses much of the surrounding scenery, plus traces of Aboriginal and European presence, several historic homesteads, a few excellent camping spots (with no facilities), rare flora and fauna, abundant birdlife, and bushwalking trails. **Kuwang Lookout** offers spectacular views of Stokes Range. Access, at present, is mainly by four-wheel-drive. Park headquarters is located in Timber Creek.

Historic **Timber Creek** (pop. 100), 91 km from the Wayside Inn, was noteworthy for its Victoria River Depot and massive cattle stations. The old port, established in 1891, is now a historical reserve, located about eight km from town. The **Police Station Museum** presents displays, artifacts, and an occasional informal talk, relating to police action and racial turmoil in the 1880s (tip: don't ask about those subjects *today!)* **Gregory's Tree Historical Reserve,** west of town, features a baobab tree carved with early explorers' initials.

Campsites and moderately priced accommodations are available at **Circle F Motel and Caravan Park,** Victoria Hwy. (tel. 75-0722). A 16-bed **youth hostel** is located behind the police station.

Most basic services are available at Timber Creek. For emergencies, contact **police** (tel. 75-0733).

Keep River National Park (59,700 hectares) is 190 km from Timber Creek, at the Western Australia border. The park, known for its extraordinary land formations and distinctive geology, also is characterized by tropical savannah, dramatic escarpment and plateaus, enormous baobab trees, Aboriginal art sites, volcanic rocks, profuse plantlife, birds, and reptiles. Before embarking on bushwalks, make sure you are prepared for the searing heat and have plenty of water on hand. Check in with the park ranger located near the park entrance at Waters of Cockatoo Lagoon. **Camping areas,** with marked interpretive walking tracks, are located at **Gurrandalng** (15 km from Victoria Hwy.), and **Jarrnarm** (28 km within the park). Conventional vehicles can access the park, though roads may be closed during the Wet.

TO TENNANT CREEK

Mataranka

Heading south on the Track, Mataranka (pop. 150) is 109 km from Katherine. Tropical bushland, crystal-clear thermal pools, a *very* colorful pub, and a chunk of literary history are the celebrated characteristics of this small cattle and service community.

Historic **Mataranka Homestead,** nine km east of town, is a wooded tourist resort bordering Waterhouse River. Adjacent is **Mataranka Pool Nature Park,** a four-hectare reserve with relaxing thermal pools, plentiful birdlife, as well as palm, paperbark, pandanus, and passion fruit forest.

Near the homestead stands a replica of **Elsey Station Homestead,** a set for the 1981 film *We of the Never Never,* based on the well-known Outback novel of the same name in which author Jeannie Gunn relates the life and times at the remote station which she managed for a brief time. **Elsey Cemetery,** 13 km south of Mataranka and eight km east of the Track, is the dust-to-dust, ashes-to-ashes home of *Never Never* characters including Jeannie and Aeneas Gunn, Fizzer the mailman, and Muluka.

Old Elsey Roadside Inn, the colorful pub on the Track (tel. 75-4512), features inexpensive accommodations and counter meals. **Mataranka Homestead** (tel. 089-75-4544) offers moderately priced motel rooms, a **YHA youth hostel,** and campsites. Another choice in the moderate range is **Territory Manor,** Martin Rd. (tel. 75-4516), with both motel rooms and campsites, and a pool.

Canoes can be rented ($5 per hour) at Waterhouse River jetty. Historic **homestead walking tours** are available daily at 11 a.m. **Brolga Tours** (tel. 75-4538) offers a highly recommended four-hour tour of the Roper River, historic Elsey Station (the *real* one is at

remnants of Never Never Land

McMinns Bar on the Roper River), and Red Lily Lagoon ($50).

In emergencies, contact **police** (tel. 75-4511) or **ambulance** (tel. 72-1200).

Roper Highway

The Roper Highway intersects the Track seven km south of Mataranka. Another 185 km east—on mostly sealed road—is Roper Bar, a small tropical outpost (pop. 6) popular for boating and barramundi fishing (not swimming, though—both salties and freshwater crocs call this place home!). Facilities at "The Roper" include general store, takeaway, picnic and barbecue area, visitor information, boat ramp, airstrip, petrol station, Aboriginal art tours, moderately priced rooms, and campsites. For information, phone (089) 81-9455.

Private Aboriginal lands begin just past Roper Bar.

Larrimah

Lots of WW II activity took place in this former railhead township (pop. 25), 68 km south of Mataranka. Apart from being a supply base, a top-secret airfield was located here (from where General Douglas McArthur made some heavy-duty decisions). The original settlement was actually five km away at Birdum but, except for the 1920s Birdum Hotel which was moved to Larrimah, the rest of the town was abandoned after the war. The railway closed down in 1976, due to lack of funding and Cyclone Tracy's devastation, but its remains, as well as those of the Overland Telegraph Station and old post office, are nearby the hotel. **Larrimah Hotel,** another old bush pub, is not to be missed for its dining specialties—how do boar's tits on toast tickle your taste buds?

Campsites and cheap rooms are available at **Larrimah Wayside Inn,** Stuart Hwy. (tel. 089-75-9931). **Shell Roadhouse Caravan Park,** Stuart Hwy. (tel. 75-9932), offers campsites and more moderately priced accommodations, and is also a good clearing house for local information.

Daly Waters

First stop is **Daly Waters Pub,** 89 km from Larrimah and another three km off the highway. Known as one of the Territory's best and oldest Outback pubs, visitors are certain to soak up any color they desire amid a setting of Australian bush and traditional architecture, surrounded by tropical forest. The front bar "museum" displays pioneer and Aboriginal artifacts. A sign above the bar offers free credit to any 80-year-old woman who is with her mother. Inexpensive rooms and campsites are available. For information, phone (089) 75-9927.

Daly Waters (pop. 20), two km beyond the pub, is a former campsite for Overland Telegraph Line workers and cattle drovers, as well as a refueling stop for Qantas Airways'

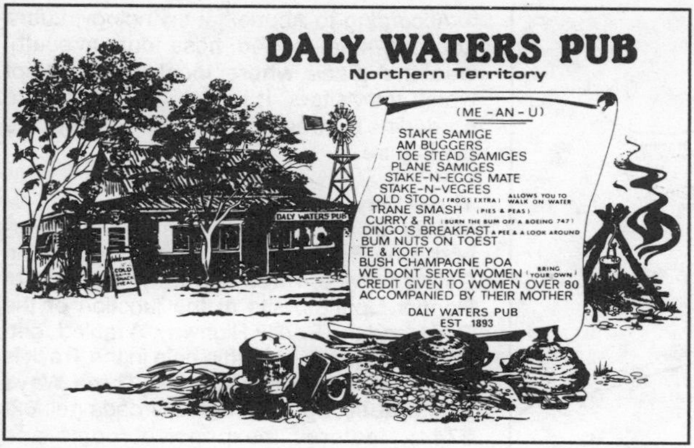

some daily fare at the Daly Waters Pub

first international route between Brisbane and Singapore in the 1930s.

Carpentaria Highway

Often mistaken for the *real* Daly Waters, **Daly Waters Junction** is another four km south, where the Stuart and Carpentaria highways meet. The **Hi-Way Inn** roadhouse only dates back to 1974—thus many of us can well imagine both its history *and* the origins of its name! All the usual Outback roadside facilities are offered, including inexpensive accommodations, campsites, restaurant, shop, pub, beer garden, and petrol station. For information, phone (089) 75-9925.

From the junction, the bitumen Carpentaria Highway travels 391 km east to Borroloola within the Narwinbi Aboriginal Land Trust, passing **Cape Crawford** (and the Heartbreak Hotel) 275 km along the way. The **Heartbreak** (tel. 75-9928) offers inexpensive rooms, campsites, restaurant, takeaway, shop, bar, picnic area, camping gas, and petrol station. From Cape Crawford, you can either turn south on the **Tablelands Highway** (also sealed), 378 km to Barkly Homestead on the Barkly Hwy., or continue on the Carpentaria Hwy., 116 km northeast to Borroloola.

Once a booming, colorful 1880s frontier town, today's **Borroloola,** set along the McArthur River, is a famous barramundi fishing hole and site of the Easter **Barra Classic** barramundi fishing competition. Some of the old building ruins, including the former police station, can still be seen. Inexpensive bunkhouse accommodations are available at **Borroloola Holiday Village** (tel. 75-8742), and **McArthur River Caravan Park** (tel. 75-8734) offers on-site vans and campsites. Camping along the riverbanks is not advisable due to croc danger.

Dunmarra

It's 36 km along the Track from Daly Waters Junction to the Buchanan Highway turnoff (another route to Top Springs), and another eight km to Dunmarra, a WW II staging camp for southbound convoys from Larrimah. **Shell Wayside Inn** (tel. 75-9922) offers moderately priced accommodations, campsites, travelers' services and facilities.

Elliott

The landscape gets drier as you near this Darwin-Alice Springs near-halfway point, 120 km south of Dunmarra and 23 km beyond **Newcastle Waters** historic cattle station. Also a former WW II staging camp, Elliott (pop. 600) is a low-key regional service center for the surrounding cattle-raising community. **Elliott Hotel** (tel. 089-69-2069) has moderately priced rooms. **Halfway Caravan Park** (tel. 69-2025) offers campsites, and **Midland Caravan Park** (tel. 69-2037) has campsites and an inexpensive bunkhouse.

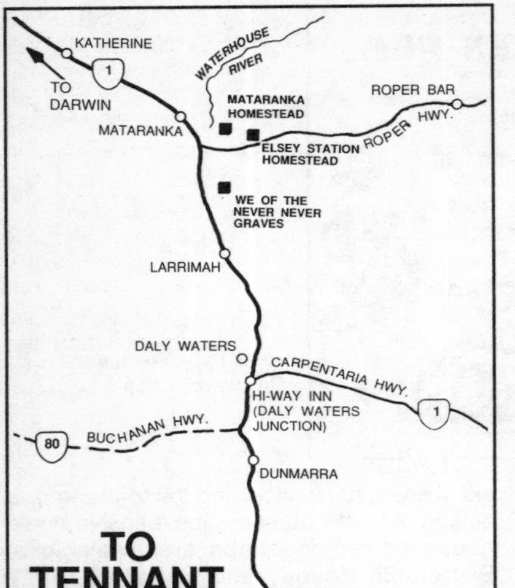

For emergencies, contact **police** (tel. 089-69-2010) or **ambulance** (tel. 69-2060).

Renner Springs

The pub building is a typical example of post-war roadhouse architecture and the pub interior is a primo example of wayside ambience—a few growls and a few giggles. Moderately priced rooms, campsites, dining, takeaway, petrol, and mechanical services are offered. For information, phone (089) 64-4505.

According to Aboriginal mythology, Lubra Lookout, a flat-topped mesa four km south, was the place where local women kept watch for visitors. It is also considered the borderline between the wet Top End and the dry Centre.

Three Ways

Marked by a large stone memorial to Reverend John Flynn, founder of the Royal Flying Doctor Service, Three Ways, 134 km south of Renner Springs, sits at the junction of the Track and the Barkly Highway. A fabled "getting stuck" place, this little hole in the Track is also known as hitchhiker hell. **Three Ways Roadhouse,** right at the crossroads (tel. 62-2744), features inexpensive rooms and campsites, as well as a sign warning hitchhikers not to loiter.

Barkly Highway

From Three Ways, the Barkly Highway travels 643 east to Mt. Isa, in Queensland. **Barkly Homestead,** 185 km along the way, is a modern roadhouse which provides basic facilities, including accommodations and petrol. For information, phone (089) 64-4549.

TENNANT CREEK

Other than Katherine, Tennant Creek (pop. 2,240) is the biggest town between Alice Springs and Darwin. Situated 675 km south of Katherine and 507 km north of Alice Springs, Tennant Creek is a modern Outback cattle and tourist town as well as an important past and present gold-mining center.

According to legend, the town's location is attributed to the breakdown of a beer cart—instead of crating the beer and building materials back to the intended site, the camp was moved to where the beer had fallen! Another tribute to laziness is that the shops and pub were supposedly built closest to the creek because the miners didn't want to walk any farther than necessary.

After gold was discovered here in 1932, 100 mines sprung up before WW II (though most were small producers), followed by copper mining in the 1950s which continues to

Allow plenty of room to pass!

the present day, along with gold and silver. The Tennant Creek area, home to Warumungu Aborigines, features some interesting historic structures, working mines, and unique geological formations.

Sights

The **National Trust Museum,** Schmidt St., originally a World War II army hospital, features early memorabilia and historical displays. Open Mon.-Fri. 4-6 p.m., during the Dry.

Church of Christ the King, Windley St., a classified historic corrugated-iron and wood structure, was originally built in Pine Creek in 1904 and eventually moved to its present location.

The 1872 stone **telegraph station,** 10 km north of town, is presently being renovated as a museum.

Watch the ongoing action of gold-bearing ore being crushed and flushed at the **government stamp battery,** about two km along Peko Road. Established in 1958, this mine-museum also features historical displays, artifacts, and a barbecue area. Tours are offered Mon.-Fri. 9 a.m., 10:30 a.m., 3 p.m., 4:15 p.m., Sat.-Sun. 9 a.m. and 4:15 p.m., April-October. Admission is $1.

Nobles Nob Mine, 16 km east along Peko Rd., once one of Australia's richest gold mines, used to be underground but was converted to a large open-cut mine after the crown pillar collapsed. Milling operations are still in full force. If you want to fossick for your own gold, the government battery area and Moonlight Rock Hole are two rich districts. Check with the local government tourist bureau.

One of Tennant Creek's best views is at **One Tank Hill Lookout,** two km east along Peko Road. Eleven significant local sites are depicted on plaques embedded in a semi-circular wall. **Purkiss Reserve,** corner of Ambrose and Peko roads, has a shady barbecue and playground area, and a swimming pool. A better recreation spot is at **Mary Ann Dam,** six km north of town, with a manmade lake perfect for swimming and boating. Bicycle and bushwalking tracks plus boat and sailboard rentals are also offered.

Devils Pebbles, 11 km north on the Track and another six km left onto a dirt road, are rounded boulders—weathered from a 1,700-million-year-old granite mass—heaped across the landscape. Come at sunset when the combination of minerals and evening sun produces exquisite colors. Camping is permitted, but there are no facilities.

Accommodations And Food

Moderately priced accommodations are available at **Eldorado Motor Lodge,** Paterson St. (tel. 62-2402); **Goldfields Motor Hotel,** Paterson St. (tel. 62-2030); **Safari Lodge,** Davidson St. (tel. 62-2207); and **Tennant Creek Motor Hotel,** Paterson St. (tel. 62-2006). Campsites and on-site vans can be rented at **Outback Caravan Park,** Peko Rd. (tel. 62-2459), and **Tennant Creek Caravan Park,** Paterson St. (tel. 62-2325).

A 26-bed **YHA Hostel** is located on Leichhardt St. (tel. 62-2719).

Most restaurants and takeaways are on or around Paterson Street. **The Dolly Pot Inn,** Davidson St., is supposed to have the best food in town ($6-14).

Services And Information

The **Northern Territory Government Tourist Bureau,** corner Paterson and Davidson (tel. 089-62-3388), provides literature and information and books tours and accommodations.

In emergencies, contact **police** (tel. 62-2606), or **fire brigade and ambulance** (tel. 62-2000).

Getting There And Around

Ansett NT operates regular flights into Tennant Creek.

All the major coachlines stop in Tennant Creek on daily services between Darwin and Alice Springs.

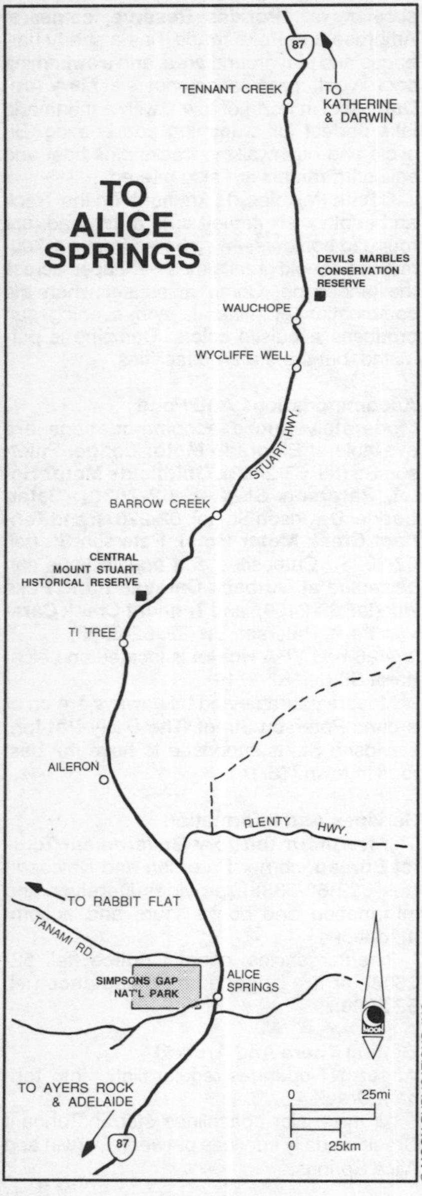

Ten Ant Tours (tel. 62-2358) offers a two-hour fossicker and plant-lover expedition to Kraut Downs. Cost is $15.

TO ALICE

Devils Marbles Conservation Reserve (1,828 hectares), 104 km south of Tennant Creek, is situated on both sides of the Track. These magnificent, precariously balanced granite boulders, spread across a wide shallow valley, were created from a single granite mass (similar to the Devils Pebbles). The Warumungu Aborigines believe the marbles are eggs that were laid by the Rainbow Serpent. Sunrise and sunset are the optimal visiting times to this Stonehenge-esque region. A short walking trail has signposts explaining the marbles' origins. Camping is allowed.

Wauchope, 113 km south of Tennant Creek, is a 1938 characteristic bush pub, full of tall tales and imaginative stories. A one-time post office and store, Wauchope offers inexpensive rooms, campsites, and roadhouse facilities. For information, phone (089) 64-1963.

Wycliffe Well (tel. 64-1966), 18 km south of Wauchope, is another roadhouse rest, boasting one of Australia's largest selections of foreign beers.

The oldest roadhouse on the Track is **Barrow Creek** (tel. 56-9753), another 88 km south. Its widely known "bush bank" is a wall covered with all types of notes and currency, signed by patrons to ensure they'll never go broke. (No withdrawal has ever made it beyond the bar.) This combination pub, art gallery, museum, and community center is definitely one spot where you'll meet some "real locals."

Barrow Creek was not always the site of jovial goings-on: in 1874 the old telegraph repeater station was attacked by local Aborigines, resulting in the deaths of the stationmaster and linesman (graves nearby the pub), as well as a number of Aborigines. Inexpensive accommodations, campsites, restaurant, takeaway, tourist information, six-hole golf, petrol, camping gas, and other necessary services are provided.

Ti Tree, 76 km from Barrow Creek, serves both the tourist sector and the surrounding Aboriginal community with a range of facilities including **Ti Tree Roadhouse** (tel. 56-9741) and the adjacent **Aaki Gallery,** which sells locally produced arts and crafts.

Last roadhouse stop before Alice Springs is **Aileron** (tel. 56-9703), which provides the necessary services.

Another 65 km farther, the Track meets the **Plenty Highway,** a part sealed, part gravel, and part dirt track to the Queensland border and Mt. Isa. The first portion of the Plenty is a popular fossicking area. The **Sandover Highway** links up to the Plenty 27 km off the Track, heading farther north through Aboriginal land to a dirt track which eventually connects to the Barkly Highway.

The **Tanami Road** turnoff, 48 km past the Plenty Highway junction, travels 604 km northwest to Rabbit Flat in the Tanami Desert, near the Western Australia border. Fascinating plant and wildlife inhabit this region, but most of it sits on Aboriginal lands. Check with the government tourist bureau in Alice Springs regarding necessary permits and other preparation. The Tanami Road is suitable only for 4WD vehicles.

ALICE SPRINGS

Va-va-va-voom—welcome to Alice (the Alice, as it's also known), the Red Centre. The thought can send chills up the straightest spine even in the most brain-meltdown heat. But, if you're thinking of the frontiersy Outback depicted in Neville Shute's slap-on-the-back novel *A Town Like Alice,* you'll be disappointed. However, The Alice ain't so bad, and, enclosed as it is within the MacDonnell Ranges, the surrounding area is downright astonishing. Just keep in mind that this is no longer an Outback town but a convenient tourist center for exploring the real Outback.

History

Originally "a town called Stuart" (after explorer John Stuart) and site of an important 1871 telegraph station built alongside normally dry Todd River (after telegraph superintendent Charles Todd) and its permanent spring (named Alice, after Todd's wife). When the repeater station was shifted into town in 1933, Stuart was renamed "Alice Springs." The town's growth was slow-going, particularly as supplies were delivered only once yearly by Afghan camel teams. Though the railway arrived in 1929, the European population was only about 250. Cattle and mining industries, as well as establishment of a government seat from 1926-31, still barely doubled Alice's population.

It was war and the WW II Darwin bombing that created a comparable population explosion. As a major military base, postwar rumors about the area's attributes were leaked, creating tourist interest and subsequent development. Presently the Alice Springs area is home to approximately 24,000 inhabitants. Besides being a service center to the neighboring Aboriginal and pastoral communities, and its obvious importance as a tourist base, nearby Pine Gap is home to a major (and controversial) hush-hush U.S. communications base.

A WALKING TOUR

Alice proper is easily explored on foot. The city center (including most accommodations and restaurants) is bordered by the Track (Stuart Highway) on one side, the Todd River (creekbed) on the other, Anzac Hill on the north, and Stuart Terrace on the south—about a five-square-block grid! Todd Street and its pedestrian mall between Wills and Gregory terraces is the main shopping street and site of the General Post Office and Northern Territory Government Tourist Bureau. The bus terminal is adjacent.

Old Telegraph Station

The original settlement site is now a 570-hectare historical reserve, featuring *the* Alice spring (you can swim in it), a small museum, several restored buildings, a walking trail to Trig Hill Lookout, picnic areas, and a wildlife enclosure. The reserve is an easy walk from town center along the path on the western edge of the Todd River bank. Open daily 8 a.m.-9 p.m. Oct.-April, 8 a.m.-7 p.m. May-September. Free ranger-guided tours are given Sun. 10 a.m., but book ahead. For information, phone 50-8211.

Anzac Hill

Just north of the town center, Anzac Hill provides superb views of Alice and the surrounding ranges. Sunset and sunrise are the best viewing times. Walk up via "Lions" walk opposite the Catholic church on Wills Terrace.

Spencer And Gillen Museum

On Todd Mall, at the corner of Parsons St., this museum of central Australia features natural history, Aboriginal culture, and early pioneering displays relating to the local region. Open daily 9-5. Admission $2. For information, phone 52-1001.

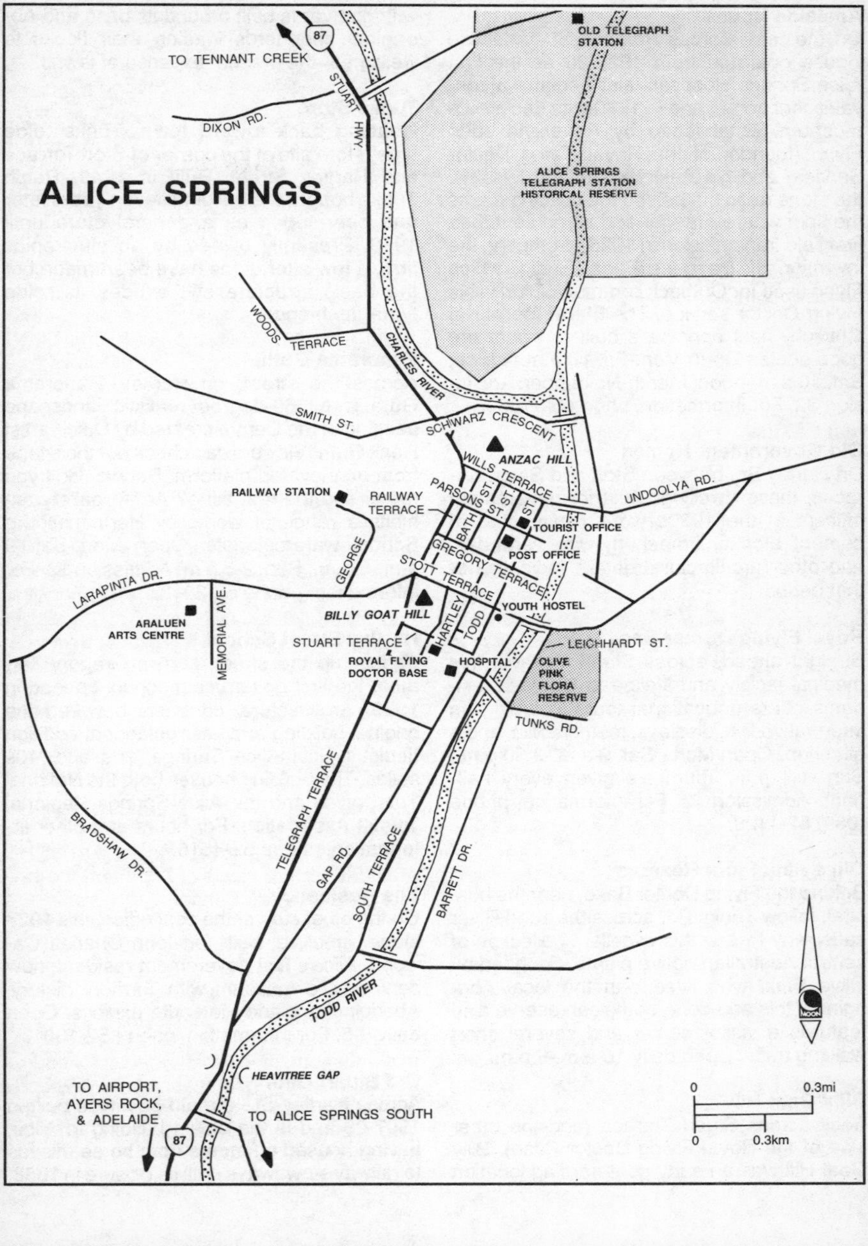
ALICE SPRINGS
OLD TELEGRAPH STATION
ALICE SPRINGS TELEGRAPH STATION HISTORICAL RESERVE
TO TENNANT CREEK
87
STUART HWY.
DIXON RD.
WOODS
TERRACE
CHARLES RIVER
SMITH ST.
SCHWARZ CRESCENT
ANZAC HILL
WILLS TERRACE
UNDOOLYA RD.
RAILWAY STATION
RAILWAY TERRACE
PARSONS ST.
BATH ST.
ST.
ST.
TOURIST OFFICE
POST OFFICE
GEORGE
GREGORY TERRACE
STOTT TERRACE
LARAPINTA DR.
MEMORIAL AVE.
ARALUEN ARTS CENTRE
BILLY GOAT HILL
HARTLEY
TODD
YOUTH HOSTEL
LEICHHARDT ST.
STUART TERRACE
ROYAL FLYING DOCTOR BASE
HOSPITAL
OLIVE PINK FLORA RESERVE
TUNKS RD.
BRADSHAW DR.
TELEGRAPH TERRACE
GAP RD.
SOUTH TERRACE
BARRETT DR.
TODD RIVER
HEAVITREE GAP
TO AIRPORT, AYERS ROCK, & ADELAIDE
TO ALICE SPRINGS SOUTH
87
MOON
0
0.3mi
0
0.3km

Adelaide House
On the mall, across Parsons St., Adelaide House operated from 1920-26 as the first Alice Springs Hospital, later became a convalescent home, and in 1980 was declared a museum. Established by Reverend John Flynn (founder of the Royal Flying Doctor Service) and his Australian Inland Mission, the stone radio hut behind the building marks the spot where Traeger and Flynn sent their first field transmission in 1926, prompting the invention of Traeger's Pedal Radio, which Flynn used for Outback communication in his Flying Doctor service. The **Flynn Memorial Church,** next door, was built to honor the good doctor. Open Mon.-Fri. 10 a.m.-4 p.m., Sat. 10 a.m.-noon, March-November. Admission $2. For information, phone 52-1856.

Old Government Homes
On Harley St., between Stott and Stuart terraces, these dwellings built for government officers in the 1930s were constructed of cement blocks, timber, fly-wire verandas, and other architectural details indicative of that period.

Royal Flying Doctor Base
Straight ahead, across Stuart Terrace, this medical facility and lifeline to Outback residents offers educational tours including an informative film, displays, memorabilia, and a gift shop. Open Mon.- Sat. 9 a.m.-3:30 p.m., Sun. 1-4 p.m. Tours are given every half-hour. Admission $2. For information, phone (089) 52-1129.

Olive Pink Flora Reserve
Behind the Flying Doctor Base, near the hospital, follow Tunks Rd. across the Todd River causeway to see this excellent collection of central Australian native plants. Founded by Olive Pink, who lived with the local Aborigines, this arid-zone botanical reserve also features a visitor center and several short walking trails. Open daily 10 a.m.-6 p.m.

Billy Goat Hill
Back across Stuart Terrace (and the other side of the Royal Flying Doctor Base), Billy Goat Hill was an early goat-herding location with goatyards built around its base and Aboriginal shepherds leading their flocks to wells near the present expanse of lawns.

Tunks Store
Heading back toward town, Tunks "olde type" store sits at the corner of Stott Terrace and Hartley Street. Built in 1940, Ralph Tunks bought the building seven years later and operated it as a general store until 1979. Presently owned by an electronics firm, a few alterations have been made but the basic structure still exudes its "olde tyme" ambience.

Panorama Guth
Across the street, on Hartley, Panorama Guth is a 360-degree realistic landscape painting of the Centre created by Dutch artist Henk Guth. Viewers can check out the scene from an elevated platform. But wouldn't you rather see the real thing? An art gallery exhibits a range of works by Hermannsburg School watercolorists. Open Mon.-Sat. 9 a.m.-5 p.m., Sun. 2-5 p.m. Admission $2. For information, phone 52-2013.

Hartley Street School
Farther up the street, across Gregory Terrace, the first government school opened in 1929. Architectural contrasts between the original building and later octagonal addition depict typical Alice Springs '20s and '40s styles. The building houses both the National Trust office and the Alice Springs Regional Tourist Association. For hours and other information, phone 52-4516.

The Residency
On the other side of the post office, this 1927 stone structure, built for John Charles Cawood, Alice's first government resident, now serves as a museum with Territory history, Aboriginal art, and meteorite exhibits. Open daily 9-5. For information, phone 52-1001.

Old Stuart Gaol
Across Hartley St., the old gaol was built in 1907-08 and is the oldest building in Alice, having housed offenders from horse thieves to railway stowaways until its closure in 1938.

Open Tues. and Thurs. 10:30 a.m.-12:30 p.m., Sat. 9:30-11:30 a.m. Admission $1.

Old Court House
Across Parsons St. diagonally from the gaol, this courthouse served as Administrator's Council Rooms from 1926-31, and operated as Alice Spring's primary court until 1980, when a new facility was constructed. Viewing is from the outside only.

Railway Terrace
Continue along Parsons St. to Railway Terrace. Toward your right, three 1920s cement-brick **railway cottages** can be viewed. Turn to the left to see the **Wild Dog** (Gnoilya Tmerga) sacred site, which depicts an Aboriginal legend about a great white Dog Man.

LARAPINTA DRIVE SIGHTS

Across the railway tracks from Billy Goat Hill, Stott Terrace becomes Larapinta Drive, a winding road with several additional attractions.

Pay your respects to some of the early pioneers at **Pioneer Cemetery** (the original Stuart Town graveyard) on George Crescent, off Larapinta Drive.

The **Aviation Museum,** on Memorial Drive, just off Larapinta, is housed inside the former Connellan Hanger, site of Alice's first airport. Besides the predictable early aviation memorabilia, exhibits include a couple of (previously) missing aircraft and a road train. Open Mon.-Fri. 9 a.m.-4 p.m., Sat.-Sun. 10 a.m.-2 p.m. Free admission.

Next to the Aviation Museum, also on Memorial Drive, **Memorial Cemetery** contains a few more interesting graves—most notably those of Aboriginal artist Albert Namatjira and Harold Bell Lasseter. (Lasseter was the fellow who claimed to have found a gold reef near Docker River on the Northern Territory/Western Australia border. The resulting hoopla was astounding and has continued from the 1930s to the present day, with the gold reef being lost, found, and lost again, many times over. Lasseter's reef may be folly, but his grave is well marked!)

Back on Larapinta Drive, **Araluen Arts Centre** houses two art galleries, a craft center, restaurant and bar, and presents a variety of performances. Open Mon.-Fri. 11 a.m.-4 p.m., Sat.-Sun. 1-4 p.m.

Beyond the arts center, **Diorama Village** features gaudy displays of Aboriginal Dreamtime legends. Open daily 10 a.m.-5 p.m.

SOUTH ALICE SIGHTS

Yet another group of sights is clustered around the Stuart Highway, on Old South and Emily Gap roads, south of the town center.

Pitchi Ritchi Sanctuary
This open-air museum, south of the Heavitree Gap causeway, showcases a large collection of vintage machinery and other early relics, as well as Aboriginal sculptures by noted Victorian artist William Ricketts (most of Ricketts's work is in his sanctuary, outside Melbourne), and a wide variety of birdlife. A kiosk on the premises sells souvenirs. Open daily 9-5. Admission $2.

Stuart Auto Museum
See restored vintage cars and motorcycles, as well as old phonographs, telephones, steam engines, and exhibits relating to Territorial motoring history (including the saga of the first car to cross the Territory back in 1907). A restaurant serves light meals and refreshments. Open daily 9-5. Admission $3.

Mecca Date Gardens
Australia's only commercial date farm features more than 20 different varieties of this ancient tree crop, introduced to the area by the Afghan camel drivers. Dates are available for purchase, and tours are given hourly. Open daily 9 a.m.-4:30 p.m. Closed Nov.-January.

Frontier Camel Farm
And Graeme Gow's Reptile World
Wow, what a combo! This strange-in-one site includes a camel museum, camel rides and tours, and a big reptile house filled with goannas, lizards, and desert snakes. The staff offers informal talks. Open daily 9-5. Admission is $6, but includes a short camel ride. For information, phone 53-0444.

one bone-dry riverbed

Weethalle Mohair Farm And Farm Animal Zoo

Unless you're shopping for mohair to knit up a spiffy winter pullover *or* you've got kids (the human variety) along, you could pass on this place. Right next to the camel farm, Weethalle sells a great selection of knitting wools and raw fleeces, and has a "cute" collection of kangaroos, pigs, sheep, and birdies. Open daily 10 a.m.-4 p.m. Admission $2. For information, phone 52-1892.

Old Timer's Museum

If you haven't had enough pioneering-day reminders, then stop in, pay a buck, and get another fix. Open daily 2-4 p.m., except summer months.

***Ghan* Preservation Society**

Okay, now we're talking *my* fix—trains. Come watch other railway aficionados at this MacDonnell Siding site (built to original design specs), as they restore and preserve classic 1929 *Ghan* locomotives and carriages along a 26-km stretch of the old train track. The *Old Ghan* (named for the Afghan camel drivers) operated between Alice and Adelaide for 51 years, until it was replaced by the *New Ghan* in 1980. Open daily 10 a.m-5 p.m. Admission $2. Daily one-way journeys are also offered, with return by coach. For information, phone (089) 55-5047.

Chateau Hornsby Winery

Take the Colonel Rose Drive turnoff from Stuart Hwy., then hang a left at Petrick Rd., to visit central Australia's only winery where you can sip and taste shiraz, cabernet sauvignon, riesling, semillon, and chardonnay varieties. A restaurant is open for lunch (with wine, of course). Open most days 11 a.m.-4 pm. For information, phone 52-5771.

Next to the winery, a commercial carnation farm offers sales and tours on weekdays.

above: the dingo . . . *nice* puppy! (NORTHERN TERRITORY TOURIST COMMISSION);
below: the hairy-nosed wombat, South Australia's fauna emblem (TOURISM SOUTH AUSTRALIA)

above: Katherine Gorge (NORTHERN TERRITORY TOURIST COMMISSION);
below: Murphy's Haystack, Eyre Peninsula (TOURISM SOUTH AUSTRALIA)

ALICE PRACTICALITIES

ACCOMMODATIONS

Most Alice accommodations are conveniently located smack-dab in the center of town, while campsites and caravan parks are scattered around the fringes. If possible, book ahead—especially at the most and least expensive places. Rates are usually somewhat lower during the hotter-than-hell summer months.

Inexpensive (Under $30)
Melanka Lodge, 94 Todd St. (tel. 089-52-2233), is a large 205-room property with modern rooms, pool, and rec room. The **Old Alice Inn,** on Todd Mall (tel. 52-1255), features simple accommodations as well as a cheap backpacker's dorm. Situated across from a park, **Alice Lodge,** 4 Mueller St. (tel. 53-1975), is a small seven-room establishment with weekly rates and a four-bed dorm. Facilities include a communal kitchen and laundry, plus pool and barbecue area. **Toddy's Holiday Accommodation,** 41 Gap Rd. (tel. 52-1322), offers budget and deluxe cabins, an eight-room bunkhouse, pool, communal kitchen, and laundry facilities.

Hostels
Backpackers will find plenty of options in Alice. Dorm beds average $8-10 per night and should be booked ahead during peak holiday periods. The **YHA Hostel,** corner Todd St. and Stott Terrace (tel. 089-52-5016), is a busy 64-bed operation right in the center of town. Facilities include communal kitchen, recreation room, and laundry. Travelers will pick up all sorts of helpful information on the local scene.

Alice Springs Backpackers Lodge, 94 Todd St. (tel. 52-2233), also in the town center, has 230 rooms with communal facilities and weekly rates. **Toddy's Backpacker Resort,** corner Lindsay Ave. and Warburton St. (tel. 52-3188), has 12 four-bed rooms and a bunkhouse that sleeps 10. The **YWCA Stuart Lodge,** Stuart Terrace (tel. 52- 1894), accepts both men and women, though many of the 31 rooms are occupied by permanent guests.

Dorm and bunkhouse beds are also available at **Glen Helen Lodge,** Namatjira Dr. (tel. 56-7489), and **Red Centre Resort,** N. Stuart Hwy. (tel. 52-8955).

Moderate ($30-60)
Alice Sundown Motel, 39 Gap Rd. (tel. 089-52-8422), features modern rooms with TVs, pool, barbecue area, and courtesy coach. One of Alice's best values is **Desert Palms Resort,** Barrett Dr. (tel. 52-5977), with large rooms, cooking facilities, pool, and half-court tennis. For longer stays, **Alice Tourist Apartments,** corner Gap Rd. and Gnoilya St. (tel. 52-2788), are also good value, with a variety of rooms particularly well suited to groups of travelers who pool their resources. Pool, laundry, cooking and barbecue facilities are available.

Outback Motor Lodge, South Terrace (tel. 52-3888), offers clean, simple rooms with kitchen facilities as well as a pool and barbecue area. Fully equipped, self-contained units with TVs and pool are available at **The Swagmans Rest,** 67 Gap Rd. (tel. 53-1333). A good choice near Alice South attractions is **Overland Motor Inn,** corner Palm Circuit and Ross Highway (tel. 52-7655). TVs, pool, and cooking facilities are included.

Expensive ($60 And Way Up)
The top choice for big budgets is **Sheraton Alice Springs,** Barrett Dr., about 1½ km from town (tel. 089-52-8000). This 243-room property with pastel decor and manicured grounds offers all the luxury comforts including TVs, videos, room service, pool, spa, sauna, tennis court, health club, restaurants, bars, live entertainment, and boutiques. **Four Seasons Alice Springs,** Stephens Rd. (tel. 52-6100), is about twice as far from town

as the Sheraton, half the size, but not quite half the price. Amenities include a pool, tennis court, rental bicycles, gift shop, restaurant, and bar.

Camping

All of the following parks allow caravan and tent camping, and many rent on-site vans as well: **G'day Mate Tourist Park,** Palm Circuit (tel. 089-52-9589), near South Alice sights; **Greenleaves Tourist Park,** Burke St. (tel. 52-8645), two km northwest of Todd River causeway; **Stuart Caravan Park,** Larapinta Dr. (tel. 52-2547), near the arts center; **Wintersun Gardens Caravan Park,** Stuart Hwy. (tel. 52-4080), two km north of the post office; **Carmichael Tourist Park,** Tmara Mara St., off Larapinta Dr. (tel 52-1200); **Heavitree Gap Caravan Park,** Emily Gap Rd. (tel. 52-2370), adjacent to the Todd River; **MacDonnell Range Tourist Park,** Palm Pl., off Ross Hwy. (tel. 52-6111), also near Alice South attractions; and **Ross River Homestead,** (tel. 56-9711), at the end of Ross Highway.

FOOD

Foodies who'll die without nouvelle cuisine better steer clear of Alice—'cause steer is exactly what you'll find on most menus, and well-done, shoe leather steer at that. Along with the frozen barramundi and other occasional fish, it's good old meat and taters in mid-Oz—just like it is in middle America. (By the way, that Kentucky Fried Chicken place is at the corner of Todd St. and Stott Terrace, across from the youth hostel!)

Inexpensive

Todd Street Mall is lined with coffee shops and takeaways and most are open seven days a week. **Jolly Swagman,** opposite Flynn Church, is open daily from 5:30 a.m. for breakfast, homemade cakes and dampers, vegetarian and Asian-style meals. The **Fish and Chips** shop, on Lindsay Ave., near the corner of Undoolya Rd., is highly recommended by locals. Next door, **Le Coq en Pâté** is a French-style deli—operated by French proprietors no less—with lots of goodies available for eat-in or takeaway meals. Open Tues.-Sun. for lunch and dinner.

Eranova Cafeteria, 72 Todd St., offers continental-style dining and good value. Open Mon.-Sat. for breakfast, lunch, morning and afternoon teas. **Aussie Tucker,** corner Leichardt Terrace and Parsons St., dishes up a mean bowl of kangaroo soup on the site of one of Alice's first outdoor cinemas. At Diorama Village, on Larapinta Dr., **Alice Springs Eating Centre** features a variety of indoor/outdoor fast-food restaurants.

Moderate

Lilli's, at Heavitree Gap Motel, Ross Hwy., specializes in Australian delicacies (watch out for that witchety grub sauce). **La Casalinga,** 105 Gregory Terrace, is an Alice favorite for pizza and Italian specialties. Open daily for dinner. **Camel's Crossing,** in Fan Arcade, off Todd Mall, features Mexican and vegetarian cuisine with Mexican smorgasbords on Thursday. Open daily for lunch and dinner.

For Chinese meals, try **Chopsticks,** in Yeperenye Shopping Centre on Harley St., or **Golden Inn,** 9 Undoolya Road. Both are open daily for lunch and dinner. The big, barn-like **Hindquarter Steakhouse,** 94 Todd St. (in Melanka Lodge), has a bar and barbecue and a range of steak meals (including buffalo). The **Overlanders Steakhouse,** 72 Hartley St., serves up genuine Aussie tucker including buffalo, camel, and kangaroo steaks. Both steakhouses are open daily for dinner. Filling counter meals are available for both lunch and dinner at the **Stuart Arms Bistro** and the **Old Alice Inn,** both on Todd Mall.

Expensive

The Legend, 4 Traeger Ave., offers intimate dining (if you can *be* intimate while stuffing your face with croc, roo, and buffalo) amid photos, sculptures, and pioneering memorabilia. Open Mon.-Sat. for dinner. Lighter, more modern cuisine is featured at elegant **Mr. Pickwick's,** 20 Undoolya Rd., where patrons select from a changing menu which includes seasonal produce. Open daily for lunch, Mon.-Sat. dinner. Also on Undoolya Road, **Puccini's** (at the rear of the Verdi Club), offers fine Italian cuisine.

ENTERTAINMENT AND EVENTS

Cinemas

Films screen regularly at **Araluen Art Centre,** Larapinta Road. The **Alice Springs Film Society** presents cinema programs at Totem Theatre, Anzac Oval, on the second and fourth Tuesday of each month. For information, phone (089) 50-2383.

Pubs And Clubs

The pub scene is somewhat limited. The **Old Alice Inn,** corner Todd St. and Wills Terrace, features live piano bar entertainment Thurs.-Sat., disco Thurs.-Sat., Monday night jam sessions, and Sunday night folk concerts. **Stuart Arms Bistro,** Todd Mall, presents occasional cabarets and live weekend entertainment.

Simpsons Gap Bar, in the Sheraton Hotel, offers live entertainment Mon.-Sat. nights. Popular discos are located at **Alice Springs Gap Motor Hotel,** 115 Gap Rd. (Wed.-Sat.), and **Alice Junction Tavern** (AJ's), at Heavitree Gap Tourist Resort, off Ross Highway (Fri.-Sat.). **Bojangles Restaurant and Nightclub,** Todd St., also has occasional late-night disco.

Bush Entertainment

Chateau Hornsby Winery presents the long-running **Ted Egan Outback Show,** with tall tales, bush lore, and Outback songs. Performances are Tues., Thurs., Sat., and Sun., 8 p.m. Cost is $12. For bookings, phone (089) 55-5133. **Bush Tucker Night,** Monday and Thursday at the Sheraton Hotel, features a three-course campfire meal cooked up by Outback entertainer and storyteller Rod Steinert. Cost is $45. For bookings, phone 52-8000. The **Overlanders Steakhouse,** 72 Harley St., features nightly local entertainers, including sing-alongs and bush bands.

Theater And Music

Araluen Arts Centre, Larapinta Dr., is Alice's venue for cinema, musical and theatrical performances, and visual arts. For schedules and ticket information, phone (089) 52-5022.

Events

Alice hosts a variety of strange and colorful events, usually during the cooler winter months.

The end of April or early May brings the **Camel Cup,** a series of camel roundups and races on the Todd River bed, commemorating the old Afghan camel train days. A **Food and Wine Festival** takes place the day after Camel Cup on the lawns of Verdi Club, Undoolya Road.

The **Bangtail Muster,** held the first Monday in May, once glorified the cutting of horses' tails before they were shipped out, but today is an excuse for a colorful and satirical parade.

In June, the **Finke Desert Race, Taps, Tubs and Tiles** is a 500-km, two-day endurance race for trail bikes and off-road vehicles.

Rodeo lovers will revel in August's week-long **Alice Springs Rodeo,** with heaps of events and cowboys and wanna-bes parading around town in full drag.

The **Henley-on-Todd Regatta,** in late September, is Alice's most famous event: competitors "race" along the dry riverbed in an amazing variety of bottomless boats, racers' legs poking out as they pick up their craft and speed along on foot. The series of peculiar events is followed the next day by the **Annual Beer Festival,** featuring live entertainment, children's activities, food and *many* beer stalls.

SPORTS AND RECREATION

Swimming Pools

Almost every hotel and motel has its own pool. Alice Springs Swimming Centre, Speed St. (tel. 52-3757), also has a waterslide, trampoline, and aquarobics classes. Open daily, mid-Sept. through April.

Sporting Facilities

Squash: Guests are welcome at Alice Springs Squash Centre, 13 Gap Rd. (tel. 52-1179). Equipment is available for rent.

Tennis: Public courts and private coaching can be hired at Traeger Park, off Traeger Ave. (tel. 52-4320).

one-stop shopping at the Alice Springs mall

Golf: Alice Springs Golf Club, Cromwell Dr. (tel. 52-1921), welcomes visitors.

Spectator Sports
Australian Rules **football** and **baseball** are played at Traeger Park, Gap Road. **Rugby League** meets at Anzac Oval, and Larapinta Oval, Memorial Dr., is the **softball** venue. The season for most sports is April to September.

Bond Springs Airstrip, North Stuart Hwy. (tel. 089-52-1417), is the site of weekend gliding.

SHOPPING

You've got a humongous K mart, Woolworth, and a mall—those will take care of most immediate shopping needs. But Alice's big consumer draw, of course, is Aboriginal art. Alice is the place to pick up a didgeridoo or boomerang for that special someone. Distinctive works include Papunya sand paintings, batiks from the local Utopia settlement, as well as a good selection of weavings, carvings, and bark paintings.

One highly recommended outlet is the government-sponsored **Aboriginal Art Gallery,** 86-88 Todd Street. Other good shops are the **Dreamtime Art Gallery,** Todd Plaza, Todd Mall, and the **Arunta Art Gallery,** Todd St. (with a good selection of books relating to Aboriginal culture).

The **Art Mart,** 54 Todd St., features local pottery, paintings, silk screens, batiks, candles, and weavings. You can also purchase craft supplies in case you're inspired to do a little dabbling of your own. Opal buyers might enjoy the gems and jewelry at the **Gem Cave,** 85 Todd Street Mall.

SERVICES

Branches of national **banks** and automatic teller machines are located on Todd Mall, Todd Street, and Parsons Street. Almost all banks will change overseas traveler's checks, usually for $2 per transaction.

The **General Post Office,** Hartley St., is open Mon.-Fri. 9-5. For information, phone (089) 52-1020.

The **Wash-house Launderette,** corner Stuart Hwy., Parsons St., and Railway Terrace, provides coin-op machines for do-it-yourself washing and ironing, daily 8 a.m.-8 p.m.

INFORMATION

The **Northern Territory Government Tourist Bureau,** Ford Plaza Building, Todd Mall, dispenses information, maps, and literature, and books tours and accommodations. Open Mon.-Fri. 8:45 a.m.-5 p.m., Sat.-Sun. and holidays, 9 a.m.-12:30 p.m. and 1:15-4 p.m.

For information, phone (089) 52-7404. The **Alice Springs Regional Tourist Association,** Old Hartley School, Hartley St., publishes *This Month in Alice,* a free booklet crammed with local info. For information, phone 52-5199.

Pick up maps, books, and information on ranger-led tours at the **Conservation Commission of Northern Territory** on Todd St., south of Stuart Terrace. For information, phone 51-8211. Disabled travelers might want to check in with the **Disabled Person's Bureau,** Helm House, corner Bath St. and Gregory Terrace, for information pertinent to special needs. For information, phone 52-6499.

In emergencies, contact **police** (tel. 50-1211), **fire brigade** (tel. 52-1000), **ambulance** (tel. 52-2200), or **Automobile Association of Northern Territory** (tel. 52-1087). **Alice Springs Hospital,** Gap Rd. (tel. 50-2211), provides 24-hour emergency service, plus an outpatient walk-in clinic Mon.-Friday.

For details about local driving conditions (including those rough, unpaved "roads"), contact **Road Conditions Information** (tel. 52-3833).

The **public library,** near the corner of Leichhardt and Gregory terraces, is open Mon.-Fri. 9 a.m.-5:30 p.m., Sat. 9 a.m.-3:30 p.m. A branch of the **Angus and Robertson Bookshop** chain is located in Ford Plaza on Todd Mall. Also on the mall is **Alice Springs Newsagency,** which stocks *The Centralian Advocate* (Alice's local paper, which comes out Wed. and Fri.), as well as a large selection of air-freighted national dailies and mags.

TRANSPORTATION

Getting There By Air

Alice Springs Airport, 12 km southeast of town center, is served by **Ansett** (tel. 089-52-4455, or 13-1300 toll-free) and **Australian Airlines** (tel. 50-5211, or 13-1313 toll-free) with daily scheduled flights from all capital cities. Offices are located opposite each other at Todd and Parson streets. Recent airline deregulation has spurred a number of attractive fares and packages; additionally, 30% discounts are offered to persons holding international air tickets, and **Qantas** offers up to 50% discounts to overseas passengers traveling on that airlines' domestic sectors. In case you'd like to skip Alice and fly directly to the Rock, direct flights are available from both Sydney and Adelaide.

Alice Springs Airport Shuttle Service (tel. 53-0310) meets all flights and provides transport to the city center for $6. Book ahead for service *to* the airport. **Taxis** into the city cost about two bucks more. Taxi ranks are located at the airport, or phone Alice Springs Taxis (tel. 52-1877).

Left luggage lockers are available at the airport.

Getting There By Bus

Interstate coaches arrive and depart from the terminal on Hartley St., near Wills Terrace. Daily services between Alice, Darwin, and Adelaide are operated by **Bus Australia** (tel. 53-1022), **Greyhound** (tel. 53-1022), and **Pioneer Express** (tel. 53-1222). You can also pick up a daily connection to the Rock and the Olgas. Approximate fares are $150 from Darwin or Adelaide.

Getting There By Train

The ***Ghan*** does not have quite the same flair and sense of adventure as its famous predecessor, but it's a terrific ride all the same. Half the fun of the original train was the dreadful track, frequent flooding, and the good chance of being stuck in the middle of nowhere and having emergency supplies parachuted in!

These days, darn it, the new track is fairly flood-proof, the train carries twice as many passengers in half the time (24 hours from Adelaide, instead of *50),* and probably nothing exciting will happen along the trip. The scenery, however, and the ability to take a shower while choo-chooing through the central Australian desert, make this one of the country's great rail journeys.

Trains depart Adelaide on Thursday, arriving in Alice on Friday, and return to Adelaide on Saturday. If you purchase a railpass, the *Ghan* journey is included. Otherwise, one way fares run about $280 economy class or $360 first class, with meals included. A coach seat costs $121 (no meals). For information

searching for water in the Centre

RUSSELL PETHERBRIDGE

and bookings, phone **Australian National Railways** (089-52-1011).

Getting There By Car, Thumb, Hook, or Crook

Basically it's the straight and narrow Track all the way from Adelaide or Darwin. Be careful hitching (see "Hitching" in Darwin's "Getting Away" section); traffic is light. Women should not hitch around the Outback without a male companion. Check the Alice YHA notice board for possible rides.

Getting Around

Other than taxis, Alice has no public transportation. **Alice Springs Taxis** (tel. 52-1877) and **Alice Radio Cars** (tel. 52-3700) offer transport and tours.

Rental cars will cost $25-50 per day, plus insurance and per-km charges; a 4WD is about $15 more. Mokes, as a rule, cannot be taken outside a 50-km radius of town or on dirt roads.

Rental companies include **Avis NT** (tel. 52-4366), **Brits Rentals** (tel. 52-8814), **Budget** (tel. 52-4133), **Cheapa Rent-a-Car** (tel. 52-9999), **Territory Rent-a-Car** (tel. 52-9999), and **Thrifty** (tel. 52-6555). For campervan and motorhome rentals, try **Budget Campervans** (tel. 52-7644) or **Go Touring** (tel. 52-9633). Most of the above offices are located on or near Todd Mall.

Rent **bicycles** (about $12 per day) or mopeds ($18 per day) at **Heavitree Gap Tourist Resort** (tel. 52-2370), **Shell Todd Service Station** (tel. 52-2279), Toddy's (tel. 52-1322), or **Sandrifter Safari Lodge** (tel. 52-4859).

Tours

As with Darwin, you can choose from a seemingly endless array of organized tours to the Rock and other Red Centre sites, traveling by air-conditioned coach, 4WD, camel, balloon, or airplane. Call into the Northern Territory Government Tourist Bureau for advice and bookings, according to your specific interests. The Alice YHA also arranges tours.

The Mbuntarinya people (traditional owners of Alice), lead half-day bushwalks, including preparation of bush tucker. Tours run Mon., Wed., Fri., and Sat., May-March. Cost is $45. For bookings, contact the **Camp Oven Kitchen** (tel. 53-1411).

Rod Steinert offers a variety of outings, including his ever-popular **Aboriginal Dreamtime Tour,** a half-day excursion that'll give you a taste of Aboriginal culture including bush food preparation, boomerang- and spear-throwing, and a "quicky" Dreamtime explanation. Cost is $55.

Tourists also flock to Alice for camel treks —everything from a quick ride, to breakfast and dinner outings (yes, *on* the camel), to treks of several days. The tourist bureau will provide details and bookings.

Sunrise **hot-air balloon** rides are particularly mesmerizing over the Red Centre. Costs range from $150-200 (including silver service breakfast) and are offered by **Outback Ballooning** (tel. 52-8723) and **Red Centre Ballooning** (tel. 52-8723).

The **Alice Wanderer** (tel. 53-0310) makes daily rounds to 20 places of interest in Alice. For $15, passengers can get on and off the bus at whim. A running commentary explains each point of interest.

VICINITY OF ALICE

Weathered gorges, rocky walls, and sheer cliffs of the ancient MacDonnell Ranges run east and west of Alice, with many of these scenic and mysterious spots an easy day-trip or overnight away from the town center.

About the same age as Ayers Rock (650 million years old, give or take a few years), the mostly sandstone MacDonnells reach 400 km east to west and 160 km north to south. As babies, the ranges stood more than 3,000 meters above sea level, eroding over the millennia to an average height today of under 500 meters. The rocky crags, crevices, and chasms are variegated with ferrous red, olive, and forest green—made even more evident by sparse vegetation. In spring, wildflowers provide an even more spectacular sight, while shy wildlife such as black-flanked rock wallabies are a bit more difficult to spot (try early morning or late afternoon). Whichever direction you travel in this majestic and meditative region, you'll end up gorged and centered.

TO THE EAST

Emily And Jessie Gaps

These two gaps, just east of Alice on the Ross Highway, form a 695-hectare nature park noted for its scenic river red gums and waterholes. The area was also significant to Aborigines, who have left rock paintings along the eastern face of Emily Gap. The area is popular with picnickers.

Corroboree Rock

Located 46 km east of Alice on the Ross Highway, this limestone rock outcrop was used by local Aborigines both for manhood rituals and as a storage area for sacred stones used in Dreamtime storytelling. The seven-hectare conservation reserve features a short walking trail, picnic and barbecue facilities. Camping is allowed.

Trephina Gorge Nature Park

A few km north of the Ross Highway, and 80 km east of Alice, this 1,770-hectare nature park features two contrasting gorges: scenic Trephina Gorge with its tall river gums, gentle pool, and wide sandy creekbed; and, a few kilometers west, shady and secluded John Hayes Rockhole, an area especially rich in birdlife.

The park offers grand campsites and walking tracks (one leads to John Hayes Rockhole); access to conventional vehicles may be limited in some areas.

Ross River Homestead

Situated about 12 km east of Trephina Gorge, this 1898 whitewashed homestead (the original headquarters of Loves Creek Station), features a variety of tourist pleasures including moderately priced accommodations, a budget bunkhouse, country walking trails, horse and camel rides, a restaurant, and pub. Keep in mind that tour buses love it here also—even so, it's worth a stop. For information and bookings, phone (089) 56-9711.

N'Dhala Gorge Nature Park

Continue about 10 km southeast of the homestead (4WD is necessary) to this 501-hectare park noted for its thousands of prehistoric rock carvings (at least 35,000 years old) decorating the gorge walls. Mystery fact: present-day Aborigines have no inkling what the designs mean or who the artists were! A short trail leads to the engravings. Picnic and barbecue facilities are available and camping is allowed, but you have to bring your own water.

Arltunga Historical Reserve

Set along the eastern edge of the MacDonnells, 44 km northeast of Ross River Homestead, Arltunga preserves the remains of this particularly isolated gold-mining town that was in operation from 1887-1912, and only

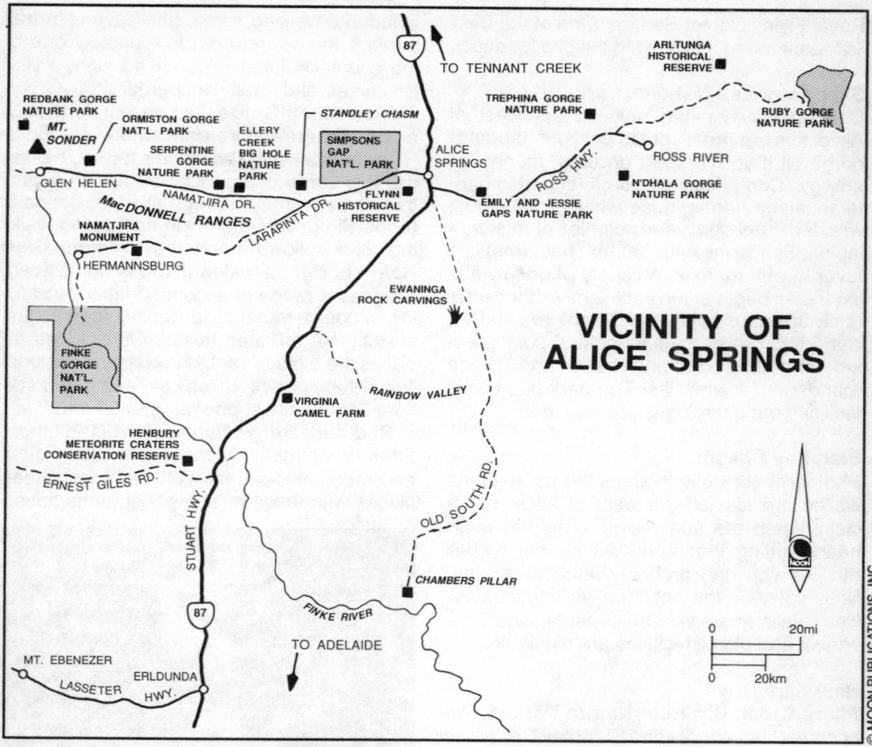

held a population of about 75 people during that period. Ruins within the 5,506-hectare reserve include mine offices, miners' graves, police station, gaol, assayer's residence, the old stamp batter and cyanide works, and many other sites. Walking tracks and picnic facilities are provided within the park. **Arltunga Tourist Park,** referred to as the "loneliest pub in the scrub," has a small campground and shop. The graded track to Arltunga is recommended for 4WD only, as is the 111-km northwest loop back to the Stuart Highway.

Ruby Gap Nature Park

If you're in a 4WD, head 39 km southeast to Ruby Gap (also known as Ruby Gorge), an unusual geological site composed of ribbon-like quartz and limestone strata along glorious, rugged gorges that parallel the winding Hale River. Bush camping is allowed along the river, but take care of your own waste.

TO THE WEST

Two different routes lead to sights in the western MacDonnell Ranges. You start off on Larapinta Drive and, about 54 km out of Alice (past Standley Chasm), either continue along Larapinta or turn onto Namatjira Drive.

John Flynn Historical Reserve

What historical reserve? It's a half-hectare gravesite on Larapinta Drive, where rest the ashes of Reverend John Flynn, founder of the

Royal Flying Doctor Service. One of the Devils Marbles was imported to the site for effect.

Simpsons Gap National Park

Conveniently located only 18 km west of Alice, this is a great spot to get your gap-and-gorge fill if you're short on time, money, or energy. Comprised of purple-tinged mountains, steep ridges, huge white ghost gums, wooded creekbeds, and colonies of rock wallabies, Simpsons Gap (30,950 hectares) is a favorite with tourists. A variety of good walking tracks begin at the excellent visitor center (pick up maps and other literature) and include short easy trails to lookout points, 20-km unmarked climbing treks, and 18-km roundabout bushwalks. The park has picnic facilities but camping is not allowed.

Standley Chasm

Photographers love to shoot this steep rusty-walled crevice, 50 km west of Alice, especially when the sun provides natural overhead lighting that turns the chasm fireball red. As you can probably imagine, it's not likely you'll be the only one clicking away. A kiosk sells snacks, refreshments, and souvenirs, and picnic facilities are available.

Namatjira Drive

Ellery Creek Big Hole Nature Park (1,766 hectares), 43 km beyond Standley Chasm, is another exquisite gorge with steep red cliffs and a large river red gum-shaded waterhole. This is an especially popular location for picnickers and energetic bushwalkers who climb to the ridge-tops for majestic views.

Another 11 km west will bring you to narrow, winding **Serpentine Gorge Nature Park** (518 hectares), which is actually two gorges with high rock walls, waterholes, and palm-like cycad vegetation. Picnicking and camping are allowed.

Next stop, 28 km down the road, is **Ormiston Gorge and Pound Nature Park** (4,655 hectares). The dominant two-km-long red cliff, rugged wilderness, permanent waterhole, and towering ghost gum and cypress pine forests, have earned Ormiston its reputation as one of the most scenic and colorful gorges in the western MacDonnells. Features include wonderful walking tracks (the seven-km trail through the pound area is reputedly one of the country's finest wilderness treks), a visitor center, and small campground.

Glen Helen Gorge, just one km farther, is a 386-hectare nature park where the Finke River (supposedly the world's oldest, having run this same course for 350 million years) begins its journey through the MacDonnells to the Simpson Desert. An interesting walking track follows along the riverbed. **Glen Helen Lodge,** a restored 1930s homestead, provides a range of accommodations including modern motel-style rooms, campsites, and a YHA-affiliated hostel. Other lodge facilities are a restaurant, bar, bistro, occasional live entertainment, takeaway, and petrol station. For bookings, phone (089) 56-7489.

Redbank Gorge Nature Park (1,295 hectares) is situated 30 km west of Glen Helen, and recommended for 4WD vehicles. Steep slopes with those mighty ghost gums hover-

NORTHERN TERRITORY TOURIST COMMISSION

Feel the walls closing in?

Huh? What are these palms doing in the middle of the Red Centre?

ing above this remote site provide the scenic beauty. If you intend to jump into one of the deep pools, be forewarned that the walls are slippery and the water is icy cold. Redbank also makes a good base for those experienced climbers who wish to scale nearby **Mt. Sonder** (1,380 meters). Picnicking and camping are allowed.

CONTINUING ALONG LARAPINTA DRIVE

The first sight you'll come to, about 100 km from Standley Chasm, is **Namatjira Monument,** which honors Albert Namatjira, one of Australia's most noted Aboriginal artists, famous for his central Australian landscape paintings.

Hermannsburg, another 30-40 km along, is the site of an 1880s mission brought to the Aranda people by Lutheran pastors. Though the Aranda own the mission now, this township still retains links with the Lutheran church. Historic buildings include the original church, Bethlehem church, schoolhouse, and smithy. A museum and tearooms are housed within two of the old residences.

Finke Gorge National Park (36,000 hectares), 12 km south of Hermannsburg, can be reached only via 4WD vehicle. Within its protected wilderness, the park straddles the southward-bound Finke River and contains large waterholes, bird refuges, sculpted rock formations, more sandstone gorge, and a very comprehensive collection of central Australian plants. The park's most famous attraction, however, is **Palm Valley,** a strange and bizarre tropical area encompassing approximately 400 plant species, including the red cabbage palm *(Livistona mariae),* found nowhere else in the world. The valley is thought to be a remnant from the days (about 10,000 years ago) when the Centre supported a moister climate. An information and ranger station is near the entrance to Palm Creek. Picnicking and camping are allowed.

TO THE ROCK

Back on the Track and aiming toward Ayers Rock, more fascinating center-of-Oz sights await travelers willing to steer off the very well-beaten path. One route will take you along the Old South Road, which parallels the *Old Ghan* line shortly past the Ross Highway junction; the other is the Kings Canyon turnoff (Ernest Giles Road), a gravel road which cuts into the Track about 145 km south of Alice. (Be careful if driving this road during or after rains—it gets very slippery!) Or you can just keep on the Track all the way to Lasseter Highway (200 km south of Alice), and turn west 241 km to the Rock.

Along Old South Road

Ewaninga Rock Carvings are located within a six-hectare conservation reserve, 39 km south of Alice. As with the N'Dhala Gorge site, these prehistoric engravings contain symbols so ancient that not even today's

Aborigines can figure them out. Other features here include abundant plants, birds, and wildlife. Visitors are asked to not climb on the boulders.

With a 4WD you can access **Chambers Pillar Historical Reserve,** 104 km south of the carvings. This impressive sandstone pillar rises 58 meters out of the surrounding flat plain, casting a phenomenal glow at sunrise and sunset. Used as a landmark by early explorers, the pillar still bears the evidence of pioneers who scratched their names onto the surface. (Don't *you* do this!)

Still On Track

Virginia Camel Farm, 93 km south of Alice along the Stuart Hwy., is run by breeder Noel Fullerton, founder—and ofttimes winner—of the Camel Cup. Noel runs the outfit that can take you humping through the center on short rides or long safaris. He even arranges packages in which you can take your camel to breakfast, lunch, or dinner. Longer expeditions tour nearby **Rainbow Valley Nature Park** (2,483 hectares), a sublime region of richly colored, broken sandstone gorge. You can camp here on your own, but you'll need to bring a 4WD *and* your own water. For information about the camel farm and Rainbow Valley tours, check with the tourist bureau or phone (089) 56-0925. Virginia Camel Farm is open daily 7 a.m.-5 p.m.

Along Ernest Giles Road

About 13 km from the Track (144 km southwest of Alice), follow the signpost to **Henbury Meteorite Craters,** a 16-hectare conservation reserve which encompasses 12 separate craters, thought to have been created by a meteor shower 5,000 years ago. The craters range in size from two to 180 meters across, and one is a whopping 15 meters deep! An easy walking track offers explanatory signs. This is another "look but *don't* touch" site.

Next stop along this road—and probably a welcome one—is **Wallara Ranch,** about 85 km west of the meteor craters and about halfway to Kings Canyon. This rambling local pub is a winner with tourists who stop to soak up the local atmosphere and stock up on supplies. Facilities include moderately priced motel accommodations, bunkhouse, campsites, dining room, takeaway, swimming pool, petrol station, and day-tours of the canyon. For information, phone (089) 56-2901. From Wallara Ranch, you can take an alternate route 70 km south to the Lasseter Highway or keep going to the canyon, at road's end.

Kings Canyon, often called Australia's Grand Canyon, is a dramatic gorge and escarpment situated 100 km past Wallara Ranch. Now called **Watarrka National Park,** some of the more unusual natural features of this 106,000-hectare area include the **Garden of Eden** palm shelter and the **Lost City,** a strange grouping of weathered outcrops that look like domed houses. A somewhat strenuous walking trail leads to most of the sights, or try the steep climb to the plateau for terrific canyon views. Park facilities include a ranger station and visitor center, plus picnic and camping areas.

Lasseter Highway

You're almost there! **Erldunda Desert Oaks Resort,** at the junction of the Track and Lasseter Highway, offers roadhouse facilities including a range of motel accommodations, caravan park, campsites, dining room, pub, takeaway, souvenirs, pool, tennis court, petrol station, and tourist information. For information, phone (089) 56-0984.

Mt. Ebenezer is another roadhouse, 55 km west, which is owned by the neighboring Imanpa Aboriginal people. Aside from the normal roadhouse features, Mt. Ebenezer also houses a gift shop which displays and sells local artifacts and paintings. For information, phone 56-2904.

Another 100 km will bring you to the **Curtin Springs** roadhouse, which is also a working cattle station. Founded in 1943, this inn exudes local atmosphere while providing necessary services. For information, phone 56-2906.

Travel 82 more kilometers west to Yulara, gateway to Ayers Rock and the Olgas.

AYERS ROCK AND THE OLGAS

Uluru National Park (126,132 hectares), encompassing Ayers Rock and the Olgas, contains one of the world's great natural wonders and one of Australia's top tourist destinations. It is also the heart of Australia—the big red heart.

Uluru National Park encompasses more than 400 plant species, 150 types of birds, and about 25 mammal varieties in a sensitive geological landscape that contrasts drastically from sandy flat plains to those big old rocks. Though Uluru has been returned to its Aboriginal owners, the park was leased to the Australian National Parks and Wildlife Service, and is presently co-managed by that office and the Anangu people.

Blissfully, all the "civilized" trappings are located in **Yulara,** a tourist village built in

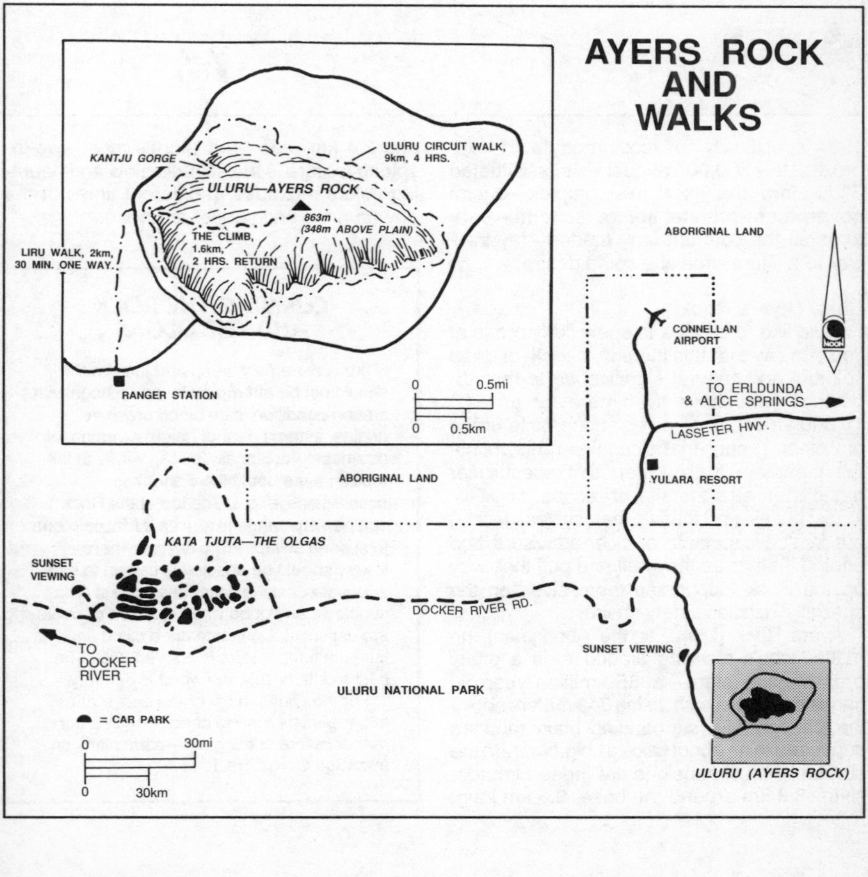

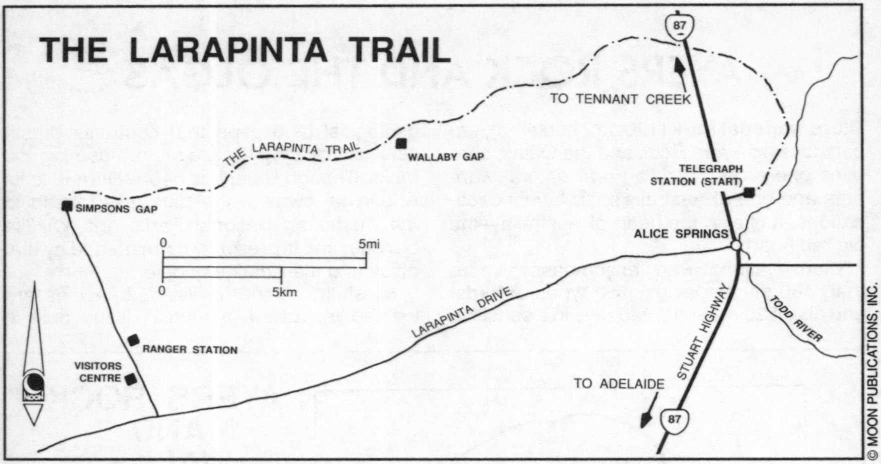

1984 specifically to accommodate the approximately 300,000 annual visitors. Situated 20 km from the Rock, this complex—a joint government-private sector scheme—features all the comforts any modern-day traveler to a Stone-Age site could desire.

Uluru (Ayers Rock)
I would like to be able to spew fluffy prose at you—to say that this incredible rock, of deep spiritual and cultural significance to the Aborigines (who have lived here for at least 10,000 years), is a sacred shrine quite unlike any other. Though that is certainly no lie, it's not the complete truth either; this spectacular monolith is also the site of resorts, facilities, tourist buses, and tourists themselves, decked out in straw sunhats or beer-ad visors and printed T-shirts as they huff and puff their way up the Rock (supporting themselves on the specially installed safety chain).

Ayers Rock (Uluru, to the Aborigines), no matter who's crawling around it, is a pretty breathtaking sight—a 650-million-year-old sandstone behemoth, rising 348 meters above the pancake-like surrounding plain (and it's supposed to be about twice as big *beneath* the surface!). Its dimensions are indeed impressive—8.8 km around the base, 3.6 km long, and 2.4 km wide—but Uluru's most awe-inspiring feature is the ecstatic glow and haunting colors it exudes at different times of the day (sunrise and sunset are best).

CLIMBING THE ROCK AND THE OLGAS

Uluru is extremely steep and the climb should not be attempted by any person with a heart condition, high blood pressure, angina, asthma, fear of heights, vertigo, or dizziness. Additionally, strong winds at the top can send both hikers and their possessions aflight. The top of the Rock can be very dangerous, with surfaces prone to sudden collapse into deep ravines. Hikers should be absolutely certain to carry adequate drinking water at all times. A hat, sunblock, and good walking shoes or boots are essential. Don't attempt a climb any time the temperature is above 38° C. The best month is July, the worst is January.

For the Olgas, most of the above rules apply, plus be sure to check in with a park ranger before starting out—particularly on that Olga Gorge Track.

mystical Ayers Rock

The Rock also features weathered gullies, eerie caves, and Aboriginal carvings and paintings (some 10,000 years old). The public is not permitted access to some declared sacred sites.

If you want to climb The Rock, you are supposed to be in excellent physical condition (a real chuckle once you check out some of the climbers). Also be aware that the higher slopes are often hit by gale-force winds (climbers have died while trying to retrieve a Foster's visor). Check with the park rangers for necessary equipment. Another option is the three- to four-hour walk around the base, fringed with caves, waterholes, and a variety of desert vegetation.

The Olgas

The Olgas (Kata Tjuta, or "Many Heads," to the Aborigines) lie about 27 km to the west and are also part of the protected Uluru National Park. These huge rocks, just as old and once much larger than Ayers Rock, are a jumble of more rounded monoliths, separated by gorges, valleys, and chasms. Many visitors enjoy exploring the Olgas more than the Rock because they have more hidden areas to discover, are a bit less intimidating, *and* less touristed.

A favorite attraction is deep, narrow **Olga Gorge,** which runs between 546-meter-high Mt. Olga and slightly shorter Mt. Wulpa. The Olgas's three main **walking trails** are the two-km track from the carpark to Olga Gorge, the four-km route up to **Kata Tjuta Lookout,** and a four-km circular track around the mysterious **Valley of the Winds,** on the north side. Another option for *very fit* walkers is the two-km track which joins up with the Valley of the Winds track from Kata Tjuta Lookout. Make sure you carry plenty of water for these excursions. It's also recommended that you check in with the ranger station before exploring the Olgas on your own. Rangers will advise you on accessible areas and necessary equipment.

PRACTICALITIES

Accommodations And Food

The cheapest place you'll find out here is the bunkhouse at **Red Centre Hotel** (tel. 089-56-2170). Two dorms, each with 40 beds, run $18.50 per person. "Budget" cabins are already in the expensive range, as are the rooms with small kitchenettes—and shared facilities—at **Yulara Maisonettes** (tel. 56-

the many heads of the Olgas

2131). If you're not bothered by room rates almost as high as the Rock, your choices are **Four Seasons Ayers Rock** (tel. 56-2100), or the **Sheraton Ayers Rock Hotel** (tel. 56-2200). All the luxuries come with the price tag (in the $150 bracket).

Ayers Rock Campground (tel. 56-2055) has campsites and on- site vans, plus a pool. Camping is not allowed anywhere within Uluru National Park.

Both the Four Seasons and the Sheraton offer dining options from snack bars to upscale restaurants. **Ernest Giles Tavern** features both counter and bistro meals. **Red Centre Hotel** has simple fare and takeaways. A **kiosk** at the campground sells a variety of foodstuffs, but there's a better selection at the **supermarket** in the shopping square. **Yulara Coffee Shop** is open daily for snacks, light meals, and takeaways.

Shopping

The **shopping square complex** has a news agent, supermarket, T-shirt shop, travel agency, and photo processor. Pick up Aboriginal handicrafts and paintings at the **Maruka Arts and Crafts Centre** (owned by the Anangu people), and souvenirs at the **Ininti Store, Ranger Station,** or the **Sheraton Gift Shop.**

Services And Information

A **bank, post office, police,** and **fire station** are located in Yulara Village.

The **visitor center,** near the Four Seasons Hotel on Yulara Drive, features informative displays on the area's history, geography, flora and fauna, and also presents regular slide shows. A variety of literature is available, including walking maps, visitors guides, and *The Yulara Experience* newsletter. Open daily 8 a.m.-10 p.m. For information, phone (089) 56-2240.

The ranger station, at the Rock, also dispenses maps, information, and helpful advice. For information, phone 56-2299.

In emergencies, **contact police** (tel. 56-2166), **fire brigade** or **ambulance** (tel. 56-2077). An emergency alarm is located at the base of the Rock.

TRANSPORTATION

Getting There

Yulara's Connellan Airport, six km north of the village, is served by **Ansett NT, Ansett WA, Ansett NSW, East West,** and **Kendell** airlines. For information from Yulara, phone (089) 56-2155. Direct flights are available from Alice Springs, Cairns, Sydney, and

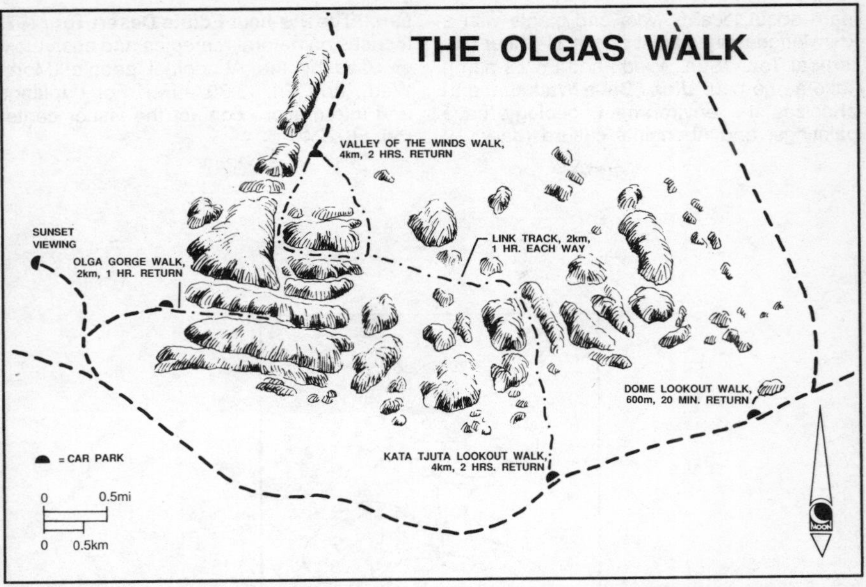

Perth. **AAT Kings** (tel. 56-2171) operates shuttle coaches between the airport and the village for $7. Taxi service, at about the same fare, is available from **Sunworth Taxi Service** (tel. 56-2152) or **Yulara Taxi Service** (tel. 56-2283).

All major coach lines operate between Alice Springs and Ayers Rock (450 km). Roundtrip day tours cost about $100, and a one-way bus ticket costs around half that. Most coachlines offer longer tours which include accommodations. For information in Yulara, contact **Bus Australia** (tel. 56-2170), **CATA** (tel. 56-2075), or **Greyhound** (tel. 56-2170). Holders of bus passes should book ahead as coaches fill up quickly.

Getting Around

It can cost big bucks to rent a car in Yulara—maybe $60-80 per day, including the "remote surcharge." **Rental companies** are Avis (tel. 56-2266), Brits (tel. 56-2131), Budget (tel. 56-2121), Hertz (tel. 56-2177), and Territory Rent-a-Car (tel. 52-9999). The taxi companies listed above also provide service to the Rock.

The Red Centre Hotel (tel. 56-2170) rents **bicycles** (including safety helmet) for $10 half day, $15 full day. Current identification and $40 deposit are required. **Mopeds** are available for $20 half day, $25 full day. Petrol, helmet, insurance, and 50-80 km are included in the rate, but you'll need to leave $100 on deposit. For bookings, phone 56-2152.

If you're planning to head out to the Olgas, the road is *miserable!*

Organized Tours

Zillions are available but some of the best are the **ranger-conducted** tours, organized by both the Australian National Parks and Wildlife Service or the Conservation Commission—and most of these are free. The two-hour **Liru Walk** led by Aboriginal rangers offers a traditional perspective of the land (Tues., Thurs, and Sat., 9:30 a.m.). See and learn about local flowers and plants with a knowledgeable botanist on the 1½-hour **Botanical Tour** (Sun., Wed., and Fri., 3 p.m.). Take a one-hour **Uluru Base Walk** that emphasizes the environment, geology, cave paintings, and Aboriginal culture (daily, 10 a.m.). The 2½-hour **Edible Desert Tour** ($7) focuses on natural remedies and bush tucker used by the Aboriginal people (Mon., Wed., and Fri., 8:30 a.m.). For bookings and information, contact the visitor center (tel. 56-2240).

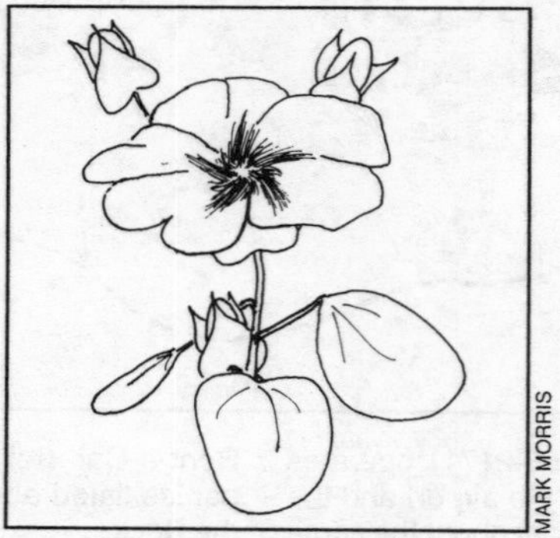

Sturt's desert rose, the territorial flower, is drought resistant.

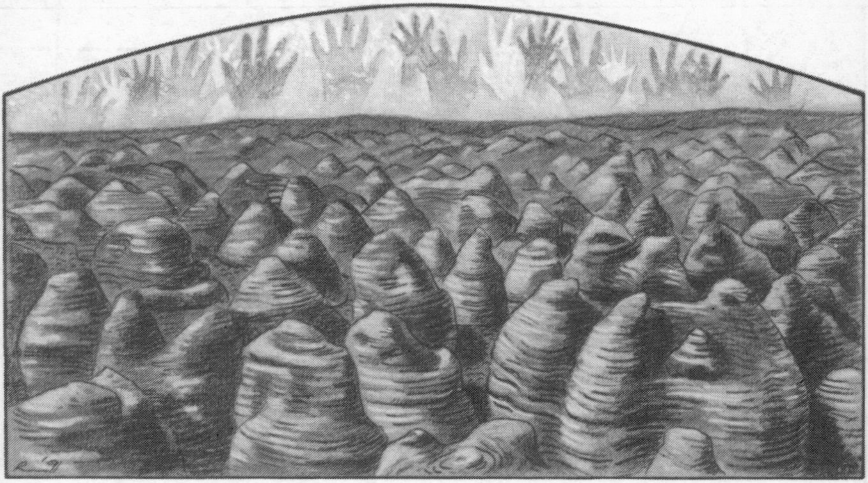

BOB RACE

WESTERN AUSTRALIA

INTRODUCTION

Recently I overheard a travelin' man refer to Western Australia as the "sexy" state. What could he be thinking of? Those rising pinnacles and deep cuts that come in all shapes and sizes? The fabulous sea with its ebb and flow of wave upon endless wave? The veritable orgy of this state's famous wildflowers, blossoming from well-pollinated pouches of fertile seeds? Fact is, W.A. (as the Aussies call it) is as sexy as your own wanderlust.

THE LAND

Western Australia is not merely big, it is *humongous*. Its 2½ million square kilometers—taking up about one-third of the Australian continent and boasting an area more than triple the size of little ol' Texas—are comprised of the harsh, desolate expanses of the Great Sandy, Gibson, and Great Victoria deserts sandwiched like dry toast between the Kimberley Plateau and the Nullarbor Plain. Yet within all this space dwell a mere 1½ million inhabitants (approximately 10% of the country's total population), most of them in or around Perth, the relaxed and youthful state capital, or along the southwest coastal sections.

Western Australia is divided into eight regions: the **South Coast,** famed for its wineries, beach resorts, and surfer and sailor havens; the **Southwest** (or Great Southern), for more swimming, surfing, and wave-pounded coastlines, as well as forests, wildflowers, coves, and capes; the **Wheatlands,** notable not only for the obvious grain and wheat fields, but for its unusual rock formations; the **Goldfields,** with its street of "sin" and "pound their chest" miners; the **Midwest,** with more wildflowers, coastal hideaways, and the port city of Geraldton; the **Gascoyne,** with sights ranging from tame dolphins at Monkey Mia to relatively unknown Mount Augustus, the

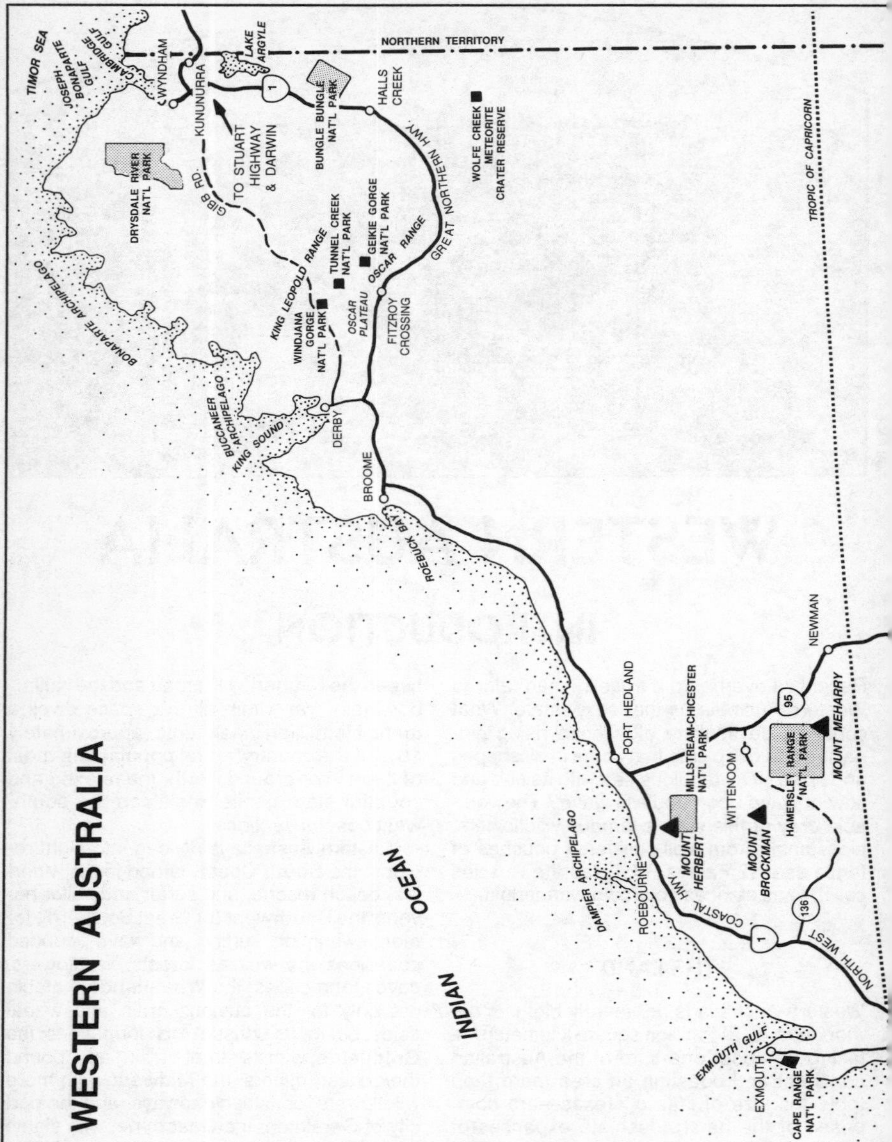
WESTERN AUSTRALIA
TIMOR SEA
JOSEPH BONAPARTE GULF
CAMBRIDGE GULF
WYNDHAM
KUNUNURRA
LAKE ARGYLE
NORTHERN TERRITORY
1
BUNGLE BUNGLE NAT'L PARK
HALLS CREEK
WOLFE CREEK METEORITE CRATER RESERVE
DRYSDALE RIVER NAT'L PARK
GIBB RD.
TO STUART HIGHWAY & DARWIN
BONAPARTE ARCHIPELAGO
KING LEOPOLD RANGE
TUNNEL CREEK NAT'L PARK
GEIKIE GORGE NAT'L PARK
OSCAR RANGE
GREAT NORTHERN HWY.
WINDJANA GORGE NAT'L PARK
OSCAR PLATEAU
FITZROY CROSSING
BUCCANEER ARCHIPELAGO
KING SOUND
DERBY
BROOME
ROEBUCK BAY
TROPIC OF CAPRICORN
INDIAN OCEAN
PORT HEDLAND
NEWMAN
95
MOUNT MEHARRY
HAMERSLEY RANGE NAT'L PARK
WITTENOOM
MILLSTREAM-CHICESTER NAT'L PARK
MOUNT HERBERT
MOUNT BROCKMAN
DAMPIER ARCHIPELAGO
ROEBOURNE
COASTAL HWY.
136
NORTH WEST
EXMOUTH GULF
EXMOUTH
CAPE RANGE NAT'L PARK

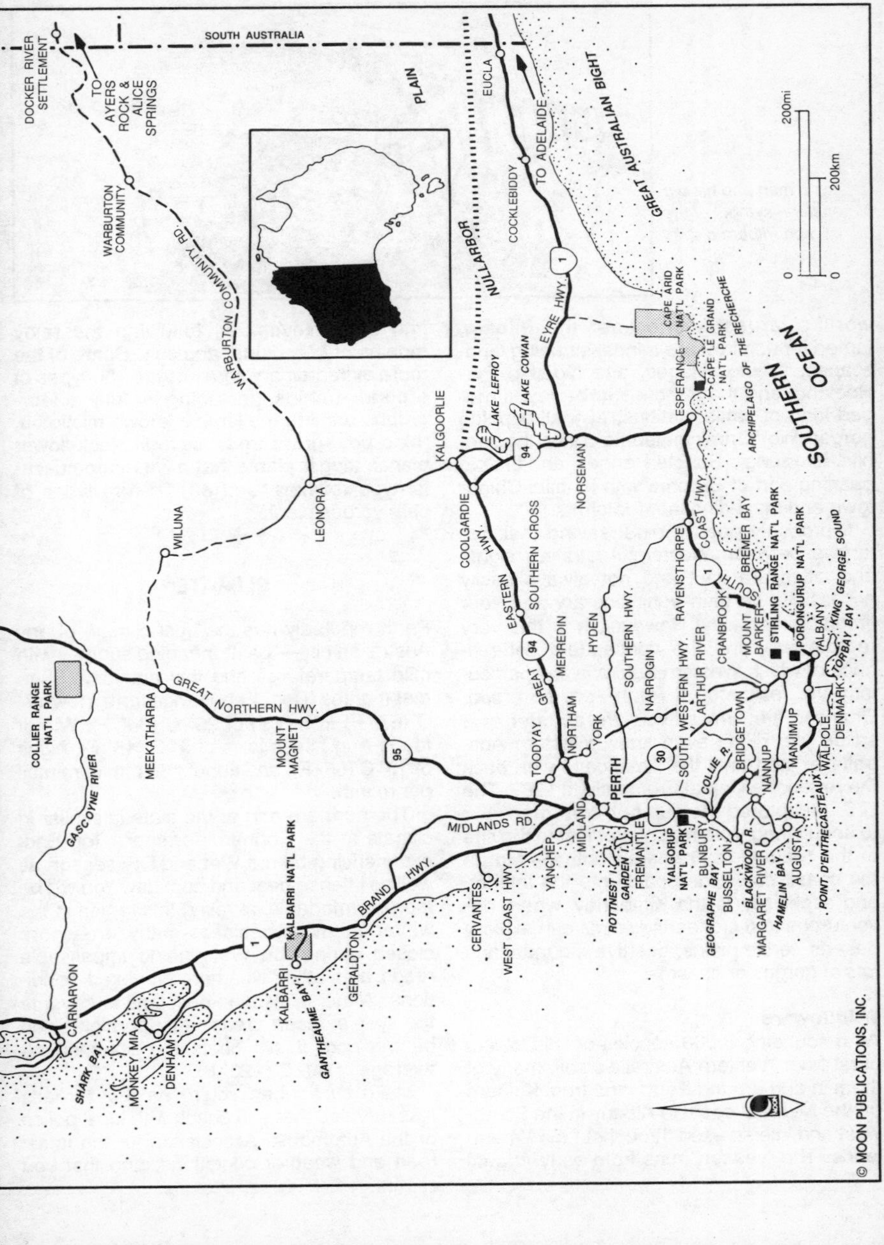

SOUTH AUSTRALIA
DOCKER RIVER SETTLEMENT
TO AYERS ROCK & ALICE SPRINGS
WARBURTON COMMUNITY
WARBURTON COMMUNITY RD.
NULLARBOR
PLAIN
EUCLA
TO ADELAIDE
COCKLEBIDDY
GREAT AUSTRALIAN BIGHT
EYRE HWY.
1
200mi
200km
0
CAPE ARID NAT'L PARK
CAPE LE GRAND NAT'L PARK
ARCHIPELAGO OF THE RECHERCHE
SOUTHERN OCEAN
ESPERANCE
LAKE COWAN
LAKE LEFROY
KALGOORLIE
NORSEMAN
94
COOLGARDIE
HWY.
LEONORA
WILUNA
SOUTHERN CROSS
EASTERN
GREAT
MERREDIN
RAVENSTHORPE
COAST HWY.
BREMER BAY
STIRLING RANGE NAT'L PARK
PORONGURUP NAT'L PARK
KING GEORGE SOUND
SOUTH
CRANBROOK
MOUNT BARKER
ALBANY
TORBAY BAY
DENMARK
WALPOLE
HYDEN
SOUTHERN HWY.
NARROGIN
ARTHUR RIVER
SOUTH WESTERN HWY.
BRIDGETOWN
MANJIMUP
NANNUP
COLLIE R.
30
YORK
NORTHAM
TOODYAY
PERTH
MIDLAND
FREMANTLE
YANCHEP
ROTTNEST I.
GARDEN I.
YALGORUP NAT'L PARK
BUNBURY
GEOGRAPHE BAY
BUSSELTON
BLACKWOOD R.
MARGARET RIVER
HAMELIN BAY
AUGUSTA
POINT D'ENTRECASTEAUX
COLLIER RANGE NAT'L PARK
MEEKATHARRA
GREAT NORTHERN HWY.
MOUNT MAGNET
95
GASCOYNE RIVER
MIDLANDS RD.
BRAND HWY.
CERVANTES
WEST COAST HWY.
KALBARRI NAT'L PARK
KALBARRI
GERALDTON
GANTHEAUME BAY
CARNARVON
SHARK BAY
MONKEY MIA
DENHAM
© MOON PUBLICATIONS, INC.

a man and his big monster—symbol of the rich Pilbara district

world's largest monocline; the **Pilbara,** famed for rich iron ore mines, stunning landscapes, fishing villages, and big-ship Port Hedland; and the remote **Kimberley,** a rugged land of cattle stations, eyeball-popping gorges, Wolf Creek meteorite crater, the beehive-ish Bungle Bungle Ranges, and the old pearling port of Broome with its mini-Chinatown and maxi-dinosaur footprints.

It probably goes without saying that distances between Western Australia's sights and cities are vast and not always easily accessible, so plan your itinerary and your timetable carefully. However, it is this very remoteness and the consequent self-reliance of which Western Australians—particularly the residents of Perth—are so proud. Chances are, unless you are a surfer or a sailor, you didn't even know Western Australia existed until the Americans won back the America's Cup at Fremantle in 1987. The U.S. recaptured the cup but W.A. managed to keep luring visitors, and not just to the site of the "victory" in Fremantle, either—but up the coast, down the coast, into the interior, and especially to the Kimberley, where adventurous and pioneering spirits can explore deserts, fertile plains, beehive mounds, and *lots* of gorges or chasms.

Wildflowers

An astounding 8,000 species of wildflowers burst from Western Australia's soil, many of them in and around Perth, and from Kalbarri on the Midwest coast to Albany in the Southwest and interspersed throughout the Wheatlands. The "season" runs from early August into early November, following the rainy months of May, June, and July. Some of the more extraordinary flora include 150 types of ground orchids (including a fully underground orchid), the largest known mistletoe, "blackboy" grass trees, several black-flower plants, trigger plants that have neuromuscular-type reflexes, and 80 different types of carnivorous plants.

CLIMATE

Perth reputedly has the best climate of any Australian city—"best" meaning sunny—with mild temperatures and low humidity. Summer months (Dec.-Feb.) range from a low 17° C (63° F) to a high of 29° C (84° F). Winter (June-Aug.) sees lows of 9° C (48° F), highs of 18° C (65° F), and about 166 mm of rainfall per month.

The northern part of the state is similar in climate to the Northern Territory's Top End, experiencing both a Wet and Dry season as well as intense heat and humidity. You will be more comfortable traveling this region in the winter months; besides, many areas are closed during the Wet due to impassable roads and other weather- provoked conditions. Winter is also the best time to traverse the state's desert areas—though nights can be freezing, it still beats the summertime average of 40° C (120° F).

Make sure when you're on those roads less traveled that you check with local police or the Automobile Association for the latest road and weather conditions, and that you and your vehicle are prepared for breakdowns and other emergencies. There will *not* be a McDonald's around the next bend!

HISTORY

In 1616 Dutchman Dirk Hartog and his fellow sailors rowed ashore from their vessel the *Eendracht,* making them the first acknowledged Europeans to land on Western Australia's coast. Between then and 1699 so many Dutchmen—traveling around South Africa on their way to Indonesia—sighted or alighted upon the shores that the region was dubbed "New Holland."

Buccaneer William Dampier landed near Broome in 1688, then again in 1699, but his findings went ignored by the British, who were none too impressed with his description of the area. Though Sydney was settled in 1788, the British showed little interest in extending their boundaries for another 38 years, when two important events took place: Matthew Flinders sailing round Australia in 1801 concluded that the east coast and New Holland were one and the same continent; *and* Britain got wind that the French—who'd been stirring about the local waters—might be planning to colonize. The usual barrage of dispatches, reports, and proposals were bandied about until, in 1826, Major Edmund Lockyer arrived from Sydney with a band of convicts and soldiers to settle a small penal colony at King George Sound (now Albany).

Shortly afterward, Captain James Stirling was dispatched by the governor of New South Wales to check out the Swan River region, already partially surveyed by the French, leading to the settlement of both Perth and Fremantle in 1829.

The new settlers soon became discouraged. The sandy soil rendered farming terrible and many of the newcomers scurried back to the east coast. Eventually the remaining colonists discovered fertile land at Guildford, between the Swan and Helena rivers, and began planting crops and raising livestock. Aside from devastating floods and droughts, there were occasional face-offs with local Aborginals who—a mite miffed with the whites for stealing their traditional lands, murdering their kinfolk, and contaminating them with heretofore unknown diseases—directed an occasional spear and ripped off the odd beast.

In 1850, the settlers were given a new lease on life when those workhorse convicts were brought in to build roads and bridges which would create vital links and replace the ferries thus far used to transport goods to and from Guildford. By the 1870s the area north of Perth was opened to grazing, followed by the eastern wheatlands, and cattle ranching up in the Kimberley region, but it was the 1892 gold rushes at Coolgardie and Kalgoorlie that helped the colony finally prosper and its population increase.

Western Australia achieved self-government status in 1890, but was left to fall by the wayside by the rest of the country during the Depression. This prompted a move in 1933 to secede from Australia—an effort knocked down by the British Parliament, then laid to rest during the subsequent postwar Good Times. (Though rumblings and grumblings of secession are still occasionally heard.) Today's Western Australia is the wealthiest state in the country, thriving on the Pilbara's incredibly rich iron-ore deposits, productive farm and wine-growing districts, and the tourism boom of Broome and the Kimberley.

PERTH

Small and tan and young and lovely—add to that remote and rich—and we ain't talkin' a midget "Girl From Ipanema" but Western Australia's sunny, snazzy capital city.

Isolated on the southwestern corner of the Australian continent, Perth is closer to Indonesia than to either Sydney or Melbourne. Nonetheless, this laid-back metropolis outdid its sister cities by once boasting the most millionaires in the country (though many of these are now bankrupt) as well as the fastest-growing population (in numbers, that is, not in age; approximately one-half of Perth's one million residents are under 30 years old).

As with the 1890s gold rush inland, the rich mineral deposits of the northern Pilbara region in the 1970s have filtered enormous wealth into the city and this shows no evidence of slowing. Add to that local entrepreneurs—such as Alan Bond of America's Cup fame—who have managed to wheel and deal mega-bucks from the east coast and other sources, parlaying them into an incredible variety of national and international conglomerates, resorts, and other enterprises (not all of which have done too well—and that goes for Big Boy Bond, too.)

Sitting on the banks of the Swan River (named in 1697 by Dutch navigators for its resident black swans), Perth was settled by Captain James Stirling and his colonists in 1829, and declared a city in 1856. In 1962, Perth achieved worldwide attention when just about every light in town was turned on for orbiting astronaut John Glenn, thus tagging it the "city of lights." Perth was "put on the map" again in 1980, when America's Skylab satellite smashed in smithereens over the eastern desert and, of course, in 1987, when the America's Cup was held in neighboring Fremantle. Perth today is a relaxed, beach- and boat-loving center of commerce, surrounded by a gorgeous coastline, striking wildflower meadows, and fertile vineyards and farmlands.

Compact and laid out in grids, Perth is a great city to get around in, particularly if you have no car—it's easy to walk just about anywhere. Both the bus and metropolitan railway stations are on Wellington St. just a few blocks from the city center, as are the General Post Office and tourist information center. Parallel to Wellington St., heading south, are Murray and Hay streets, the main shopping district, then comes St. George's Terrace, the major business street. Beyond St. George's Terrace is the Swan River and Barrack Street Jetty (with many of the big high-rise hotels sandwiched in between), and Kings Park sits at the west edge of town. North of the railway tracks is the suburb of Northbridge, home to many of the backpacker hostels, inexpensive ethnic eateries, chic cafés, and the Perth Cultural Centre.

Many books and brochures liken this city to California's San Diego or some place on the Mediterranean. Well, I've been to all three spots and, except for the climate (and tug o' war with the America's Cup), it looks just like Perth.

ST. GEORGE'S TERRACE

This tour of the city's main business thoroughfare—a mix of glitzy new banks and office buildings interspersed with historic structures—begins on the south side of Victoria Avenue and continues westward to Barracks Archway, then covers the north side of the street returning back to the government buildings.

Perth Concert Hall

Adjacent to Government House, this is the city's venue for folk music, orchestra recitals, and other year-round musical performances by both national and international artists. For information, phone (09) 325-9944.

Government House

This Gothic-revival-style residence complete with turrets and arches (à la the Tower of London), built between 1859 and 1864 at a

Perth's-eye view

cost of $30,000, still serves as the official home to the governor of W.A., as well as to visiting royalty. The public is welcome to visit the surrounding expansive gardens during special celebrations.

Council House
On the other side of Government House, Perth's civic administration center, opened by HRH Queen Elizabeth in 1963, houses five levels of offices, a circular council chamber, councillors' dining room, a large reception area, and a free public library. Hours are Mon.-Fri. 10 a.m.-2 p.m. (ground floor only). Guided tours are available Mon.-Fri. at 10:30 a.m. and 2:30 p.m. Admission is free. For information, phone 425-3333.

The Supreme Court
Just below Government House, the Supreme Court complex (Francis Burt Law Centre) includes the **Old Court House,** one of the city's oldest surviving colonial buildings (erected in 1836 with a few rear additions made in 1905), with many original details still intact. Presently serving as a legal history museum, the Old Court House includes a replica of an early legal office and related objects. An audiovisual presentation depicts the history of the law and the W.A. legal profession. The surrounding **Supreme Court Gardens,** sheltered by Norfolk Island pines, are a popular brown bag lunch spot for city workers. The **Barrack Street Jetty,** ferry and riverboat departure point, is just beyond the gardens.

The Old Court House hours are Tues. and Thurs. 10 a.m.-2 p.m. Admission is free. For information, phone 325-4787.

Alan Green Conservatory
Continuing west across Barrack St. along the green lawns of the Esplanade, you'll see this pyramid-shaped conservatory which houses a wide range of exotic tropical and semitropical plants within its controlled environment. Hours are Mon.-Sat. 10 a.m.-5 p.m., Sun. and public holidays 2-6 p.m. Admission is free. For information, phone 425-3153.

R And I Tower
Head north on William St. back to St. George's Terrace. The R and I Tower, at the corner, is home to both the beautifully restored, ornate old **Palace Hotel** (currently used as banking chambers) and Alan Bond's astounding collection of impressionist paintings. For information, phone 320-6206.

Old Perth Boys' School
Pointing west again, and situated along St. George's Terrace between William and Mill streets, this former government school (built in 1854) resembles a medieval church with

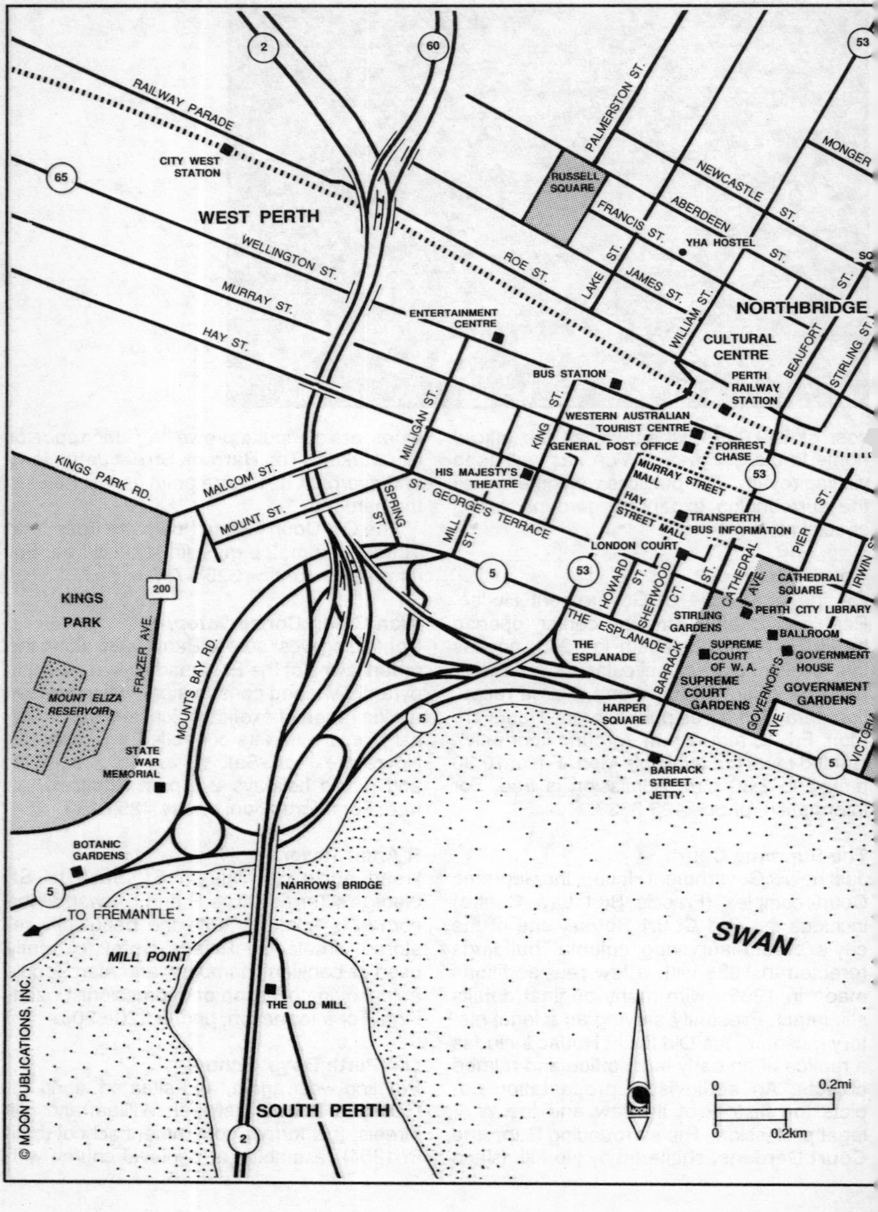
RAILWAY PARADE
CITY WEST STATION
WEST PERTH
WELLINGTON ST.
MURRAY ST.
HAY ST.
ROE ST.
PALMERSTON ST.
RUSSELL SQUARE
FRANCIS ST.
ABERDEEN
NEWCASTLE ST.
MONGER
YHA HOSTEL
LAKE ST.
JAMES ST.
WILLIAM ST.
NORTHBRIDGE
CULTURAL CENTRE
BEAUFORT
STIRLING ST.
PERTH RAILWAY STATION
ENTERTAINMENT CENTRE
BUS STATION
MILLIGAN ST.
KING ST.
WESTERN AUSTRALIAN TOURIST CENTRE
GENERAL POST OFFICE
FORREST CHASE
MURRAY STREET MALL
HAY STREET MALL
TRANSPERTH BUS INFORMATION
PIER ST.
KINGS PARK RD.
MALCOM ST.
MOUNT ST.
HIS MAJESTY'S THEATRE
SPRING ST.
MILL ST.
ST. GEORGE'S TERRACE
LONDON COURT
HOWARD ST.
SHERWOOD CT.
CATHEDRAL AVE.
CATHEDRAL SQUARE
IRWIN ST.
PERTH CITY LIBRARY
BALLROOM
STIRLING GARDENS
THE ESPLANADE
BARRACK ST.
SUPREME COURT OF W. A.
GOVERNMENT HOUSE
SUPREME COURT GARDENS
GOVERNOR'S AVE.
GOVERNMENT GARDENS
HARPER SQUARE
VICTORIA
BARRACK STREET JETTY
KINGS PARK
FRAZER AVE
MOUNT ELIZA RESERVOIR
MOUNTS BAY RD.
STATE WAR MEMORIAL
BOTANIC GARDENS
NARROWS BRIDGE
TO FREMANTLE
MILL POINT
THE OLD MILL
SWAN
SOUTH PERTH
0 0.2mi
0 0.2km
2
60
53
65
200
5
© MOON PUBLICATIONS, INC.

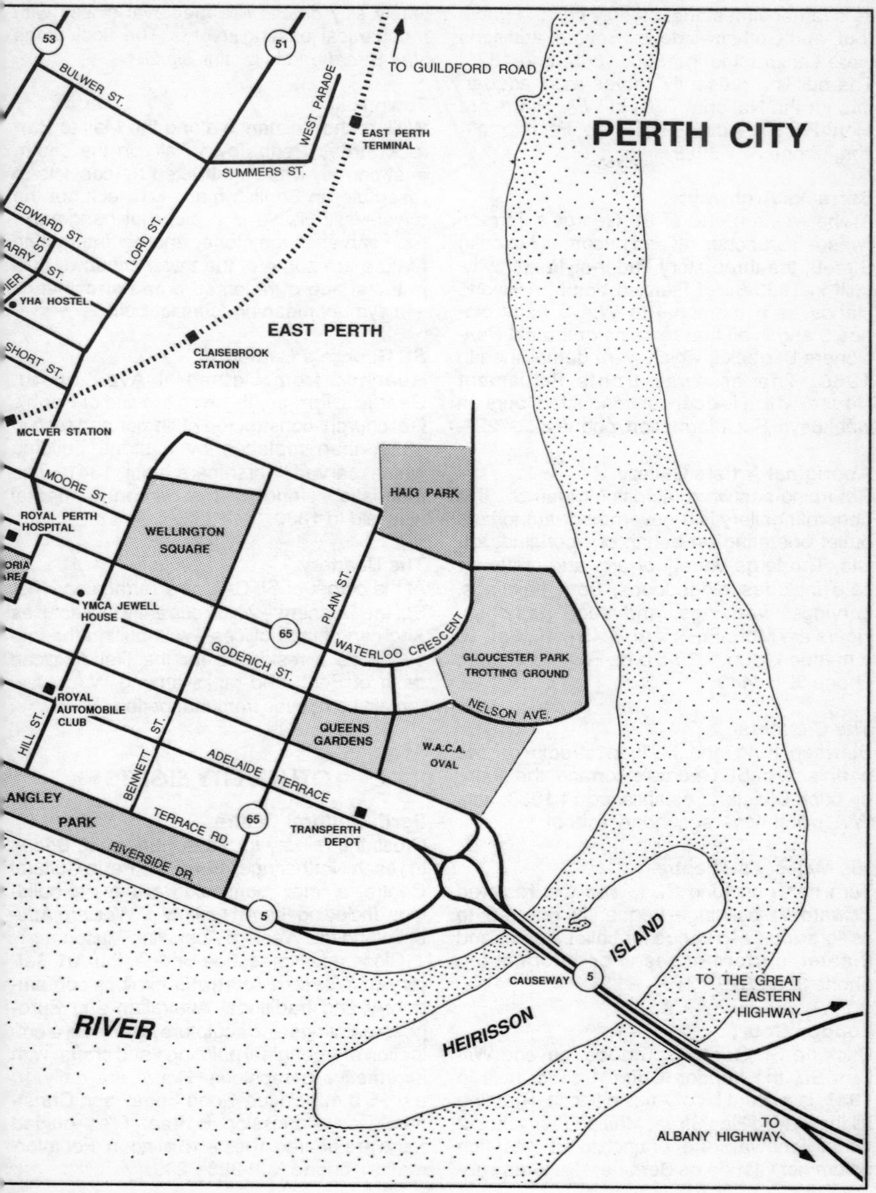
PERTH CITY
53
51
BULWER ST.
TO GUILDFORD ROAD
WEST PARADE
EAST PERTH TERMINAL
SUMMERS ST.
EDWARD ST.
LORD ST.
ARRY ST.
IER
YHA HOSTEL
EAST PERTH
SHORT ST.
CLAISEBROOK STATION
MCLVER STATION
MOORE ST.
HAIG PARK
ROYAL PERTH HOSPITAL
WELLINGTON SQUARE
ORIA ARE
PLAIN ST.
YMCA JEWELL HOUSE
65
WATERLOO CRESCENT
GLOUCESTER PARK TROTTING GROUND
GODERICH ST.
ROYAL AUTOMOBILE CLUB
NELSON AVE.
QUEENS GARDENS
HILL ST.
BENNETT ST.
W.A.C.A. OVAL
ADELAIDE TERRACE
ANGLEY PARK
65
TERRACE RD.
TRANSPERTH DEPOT
RIVERSIDE DR.
5
ISLAND
CAUSEWAY
5
TO THE GREAT EASTERN HIGHWAY
RIVER
HEIRISSON
TO ALBANY HIGHWAY

its quarried limestone, steeply pitched gable roof, and Gothic windows. Several additions were constructed in 1860, 1865, and 1876. The building presently serves as headquarters for the National Trust of W.A. Hours are Mon.-Fri. 9-5. Admission is free. For information, phone 321-6088.

Barracks Archway
At the western end of St. George's Terrace (where it branches off and becomes Malcolm Street), the three-story Tudor-style archway, built in 1863-66 of Flemish bond brickwork, stands as a memorial to W.A.'s early pioneers and is all that remains of the old Pensioners Barracks, which were demolished in 1966. The archway fronts **Parliament House,** which is open for conducted tours on weekdays. For information, phone 222-7222.

Aboriginal Artists Gallery
Returning eastward, across Milligan St., this nonprofit gallery is a government-authorized outlet operating on behalf of Aboriginal artists. The large variety of arts and crafts for sale includes didgeridoos, bark paintings, carvings, weavings, and sand paintings. Hours are Mon.-Fri. 9 a.m.-4:45 p.m., Sat. 10 a.m.-noon, Sun. 2:30-5 p.m. For information, phone 321-4440.

The Cloisters
Between King and Milligan streets on the north side of St. George's Terrace, the snappy brick Cloisters, established in 1858, was W.A.'s first boys' secondary school.

His Majesty's Theatre
Turn north on King St. to see this restored Edwardian building—frequently referred to as "gracious"—a venue for ballet, opera, and theater performances. For information, phone 322-2929.

London Court
Back on St. George's Terrace, beyond William St., the London Court Arcade, built in 1937, is a great bit of Aussie kitsch. Running all the way to Hay Street Mall, the *very* mock-Tudor laneway, the brainchild of hit-it-rich goldminer Claude de Bernales, features sublimely silly details like medieval clocks with mechanical jousting knights. The clock at the Hay Street end is a mini-Big Ben.

Town Hall
Walk a short distance along the Mall to Barrack Street. Perth Town Hall, on the southeast corner, was constructed by convicts to resemble an English market. Check out the tower—still visible is a piece of hangman's rope carved in the stone. Another interesting feature are some of the tower windows built in the shape of reversed broad arrowheads—a symbol meaning "convict-built."

St. George's Cathedral
Reached from Cathedral Ave., off St. George's Terrace, this was the site of Perth's first church, constructed of timber and rush in 1829, then replaced by a stone building which served worshipers until 1841. The foundation stone for the present cathedral was laid in 1880.

The Deanery
At the corner of St. George's Terrace and Pier St., the Deanery—which currently functions as Anglican church offices—was built in the late 1850s as a residence for the first Anglican dean of Perth and ranks among W.A.'s few remaining houses from that period.

OTHER CITY SIGHTS

Perth Cultural Centre
Cross the railway tracks at Horseshoe Bridge to reach Northbridge, site of the Perth Cultural Centre, a "mall" comprised of several buildings, including the Art Gallery of Western Australia and the Western Australian Museum.

Closest to Horseshoe Bridge, the **Art Gallery of Western Australia** exhibits contemporary and traditional Australian and European paintings and sculpture, including a collection of Aboriginal paintings and crafts (with informative pamphlets). Hours are daily 10 a.m.-5 p.m., closed Good Friday and Christmas Day. Admission is free. Free guided tours are offered Tues.-Fri. at noon. For information, phone (09) 328-7233.

Situated on the corner of the Mall and Beaufort St., the **Western Australian Museum** is centered on the **Old Gaol,** a restored, convict-built Georgian stone courthouse and gaol that served its purpose from 1856 to 1889 (the grounds were used for a number of public executions). Now serving as a museum, exhibitions feature W.A. historical and cultural memorabilia, including household items, political records, early mementos, a collection of meteorites (one weighs 11 tons!), a 25-meter blue whale skeleton, plus an outstanding Aboriginal gallery. Hours are Mon.-Thurs. 10:30 a.m.-5 p.m., Fri.-Sun. 1-5 p.m. Admission is free. For information, phone 328-4411.

More Museums

The **Mineral Museum of Western Australia,** 66 Adelaide Terrace (in Mineral House), features rocks, minerals, and special displays related to mining and geology. Hours are Mon.-Fri. 8 a.m.-5 p.m. Admission is free. For information, phone 325-0161.

Perth's oldest **fire station,** corner Irwin and Murray streets, serves as a museum which depicts W.A.'s firefighting techniques and machinery from 1901 to the present day. Hours are Mon.-Thurs. 10 a.m.-3 p.m. Admission is free. For information, phone 323-9468.

View antique telephones, Morse code equipment, stamp collections, and other related memorabilia at the **Post and Telecommunications Museum,** corner Murray and Pier streets. Hours are Mon.-Fri. 10 a.m.-3 p.m. Admission is free. For information, phone 420-7018.

At the northeast edge of the city, at the junction of Lord and Bulwer streets, the **Army Museum of Western Australia** houses uniforms, badges, medals, and other military items ranging from the colonial period to the present. Hours are Sun. and Thurs. 1-4:30 p.m. A donation is requested. For information, phone 328-0586.

Scitech Discovery Centre

Located at the corner of Railway Parade and Sutherland St., Scitech features entertaining hands-on experiments (for kids of all ages) on a variety of high-tech equipment. Hours are Mon.-Thurs. 10 a.m.-5 p.m., Fri. and Sat. 10 a.m.-9 p.m., Sun. 9 a.m.-6 p.m. Admission is $7. For information, phone 481-6295.

It's A Small World

See a huge museum collection of little things—miniature cars, rooms, trains, et cetera. Located at 12 Parliament Place, West Perth. Hours are Sun.-Fri. 10 a.m.-5 p.m., Sat. 2-5 p.m. Admission is $3. For information, phone 322-2020.

Old Mill

Perth's first flour mill, built in 1835, is situated at the southern end of the Narrows Bridge and displays many pioneering relics. Hours are Sun., Mon., Wed., and Thurs. 1-5 p.m., Sat. noon-4 p.m. A donation is requested. For information, phone 382-4144.

Perth Zoo

Across the Swan River (and beyond the Old Mill), at 20 Labouchere Rd., South Perth, the zoo is easily reached by bus or ferry from the city center. Noteworthy attractions include the great ape complex, nocturnal house, wallaby park, great cat enclosure, gibbon lake, and a walk-through aviary. Hours are daily 10 a.m.-5 p.m. Admission is $3. For information, phone 367-7988.

Parks And Gardens

Kings Park, at the west edge of the city, is Perth's park supreme—even though bushfires in 1989 burned nearly half of it. A short drive or easy walk from city center, its nearly 400 hectares consist mostly of natural bushland as well as a five-hectare **botanic garden** (noted for its spring wildflowers), natural trails, picnic areas, and paths for walking, jogging, and cycling. You'll catch some terrific views of the city, river, and surrounding countryside from a variety of perches and lookouts—especially from **Mount Eliza,** the park's most prominent knoll. Free guided tours are available. For information, phone 321-4801.

On the eastern edge of the city, **Queens Park,** corner Hay and Plain streets, is a quiet English-style park with a water garden. **Hyde Park,** corner William and Vincent streets,

WESTERN AUSTRALIA TOURISM COMMISSION

Cottesloe Beach, one of Perth's popular fun-in-the-sun spots

North Perth, caters to families with its adventure playground, and to birdwatchers with its ornamental lake. **Lake Monger,** in the close-by suburb of Wembley, is a popular spot for watching those seductive black swans, as well as wild ducks and other birdlife.

Beaches

Pick and choose from any of Perth's well-known beaches. For calm, Swan River swimming beaches, try **Crawley, Peppermint Grove,** and **Como.** If you'd rather tackle the surf, head for the beaches along the Indian Ocean—best bets are **Cottesloe, City Beach** (site of many national surfing contests), **Scarborough,** and **Trigg Island.** If you're looking for surf *and* you forgot your bathers, **Swanbourne** (north of Cottesloe) is a popular nude beach. Almost all beaches can be easily reached by bus.

SUBURBAN SIGHTS

Claremont Museum

Housed within one of W.A.'s oldest buildings (constructed by convicts in 1861-62), the museum's displays depict early settlement, convict and farming life, as well as replicas of bootmaker and barber shops. Located at 66 Victoria Ave., Claremont. Hours are Wed., Sat., and Sun. 2-5 p.m. Admission is $1. For information, phone (09) 386-3352.

Museum Of W.A. Sport

Inside the Superdrome, trophies and other memorabilia recall the good and not-so-good moments of Western Australian sports figures. Stephenson Ave., Mt. Claremont. Hours are daily 8 a.m.-8 p.m. Admission is free. For information, phone 387-8542.

Museum Of Childhood

Two buildings contain dolls (wax, wooden, and bisque), toys, photographs, literature, clothing, furniture, and other curios and playthings (almost 20,000 items) associated with W.A.'s pioneer children. Located at 160 Hamersley Rd., Subiaco. Hours are Mon.-Fri. 10 a.m.-3 p.m., Sun. 2-5 p.m. Admission is $1. For information, phone 381-1103.

Aviation Museum

Exhibits depicting the history of civil and military aviation from the origins up to the present (with an emphasis on W.A.) feature historic aircraft (such as the Lancaster heavy bomber and the Spitfire fighter), uniforms, medals, models, photos, and other aero-memorabilia. Bull Creek Dr., Bull Creek. Hours are daily 11 a.m.-4 p.m., closed Christmas Day and Good Friday. Admission is $3.50. For information, phone 332-7205.

Swan Brewery
Tour W.A.'s famed brewery and guzzle, er, *sample* some of the "homegrown" brews such as Swan Lager, Swan Draught, and Emu. Located at 25 Vaile Rd., Canning Vale. Tours last 1½-2 hours and are available Mon.-Thursday. Advance reservations are necessary. For information, phone 350-0222.

Cohunu Wildlife Sanctuary
Visit the Southern Hemisphere's largest aviary and see native animals in a "natural" environment. This is also the spot to have your photo taken with a koala. Mills Rd., Gosnells. Hours are daily 10 a.m.-5 p.m. Admission is $7.50. For information, phone 390-6090.

Elizabethan Village
Full-size re-creations of Shakespeare's birthplace and Ann Hathaway's cottage are furnished with 500-year-old antiques. Canns Rd., Armadale. Hours are Mon.-Fri. 10 a.m.-4 p.m., Sat.-Sun. 10 a.m.-5 p.m. Admission is $4. For information, phone 399-3166.

Pioneer World
This working model of a 19th-century gold miners' village allows visitors to pan for their own gold nuggets, filings, and dust (30-minute limit). Other attractions include working craftsmen, sing-alongs, silent movies, vaudeville shows, and other entertainment. Junction of South West and Albany highways, Armadale. Hours are daily 10 a.m.-5 p.m. Admission is $8.50. For information, phone 399-5322.

PERTH PRACTICALITIES

ACCOMMODATIONS

Perth's varied accommodations are as conveniently located as everything else in town. Older, cheaper hotels and some hostels are clustered in and around the city center, while others are just across the railway tracks in Northbridge. South Perth and several of the closer suburbs also provide motel and holiday flat units. Big spenders will find no shortage of luxury hotels, most of which are situated between St. George's Terrace and the Swan River.

Optimism over Perth's tourism boom in conjunction with the America's Cup race—and its accompanying groupies—saw upmarket accommodations increase by several thousand. Many of these hotels have been experiencing low occupancy, so it may be possible to strike a good deal on rates. Campgrounds and caravan parks are scattered 10-20 km from town.

As with all Australian cities and tourist centers, it's advisable to book rooms in advance. If you arrive without a reservation, contact the **Western Australian Tourist Centre,** Forest Place, corner of Wellington St. (tel. 09-483-1111).

City And Suburbs

Inexpensive (under $30): A well-recommended choice is **Jewell House,** 180 Goderich St. (tel. 09-325-8488), a YMCA-run establishment with clean, but basic, rooms. The reception office is open 24 hours, and guests have use of two TV rooms and a laundry room. Meals, weekly rates, and free baggage storage are available. **Downtowner Lodge,** 63 Hill St. (tel. 325-6973), opposite the Perth Mint, has 12 clean, quiet rooms, plus TV lounge and laundry facilities. The **Court Hotel,** 50 Beaufort St. (tel. 328-5292) offers inexpensive rooms near the Perth Cultural Centre.

Farther beyond the Cultural Centre, **Cheviot Lodge,** 30 Bulwer St. (tel. 227-6817), features modern kitchen and bathroom facilities, TV and games room, a laundry room, and free pick-up service from the bus station. **Mountway Holiday Units**, 36 Mount St. (tel. 321-8307), close to Kings Park, are self-contained one-bedroom flats with cooking facilities, full-size bathtubs, and TVs.

Moderate ($30-60): Make advance reservations for **The Adelphi,** 130A Mounts Bay Rd. (tel. 322-4666), situated at the base of Kings Park bluff. Rooms are bright and cheery (upper levels feature Swan River views), have air-conditioning, TVs, phones, and cooking facilities. Another popular choice is **City Waters Lodge,** 118 Terrace Rd. (tel. 325-1566), also with kitchens, phones, TVs, air-conditioning, and off-street parking.

Riverview Apartments, 42 Mount St. (tel. 321-8963), close to both Kings Park and city center, offer clean rooms in a good neighborhood, with all the conveniences of the other self-contained flats. **Airways Hotel,** 195 Adelaide Terrace (tel. 323-7799), located near the deluxe hotels, has many different sizes of rooms with cooking facilities plus a restaurant on the premises.

Also on the "good side" of town, with Swan River views, is the **New Esplanade Hotel,** 18 The Esplanade (tel. 325-2000), with room service, restaurant, bar, and a less-expensive "travelers' wing." At the high end of the moderate range **Miss Maud European Hotel,** 97 Murray St. (tel. 325-3900) is a small, friendly, centrally located establishment with Scandinavian decor, adjacent restaurant and bakery. Breakfast is included in the rates.

Expensive ($60 and way up): As you might imagine, with all the millionaires and money around, there is no shortage of luxury hotels in this city. Most are centrally located (i.e., near the banks) and all of them have the customary amenities such as restaurants, bars, room service, shops, health clubs, and

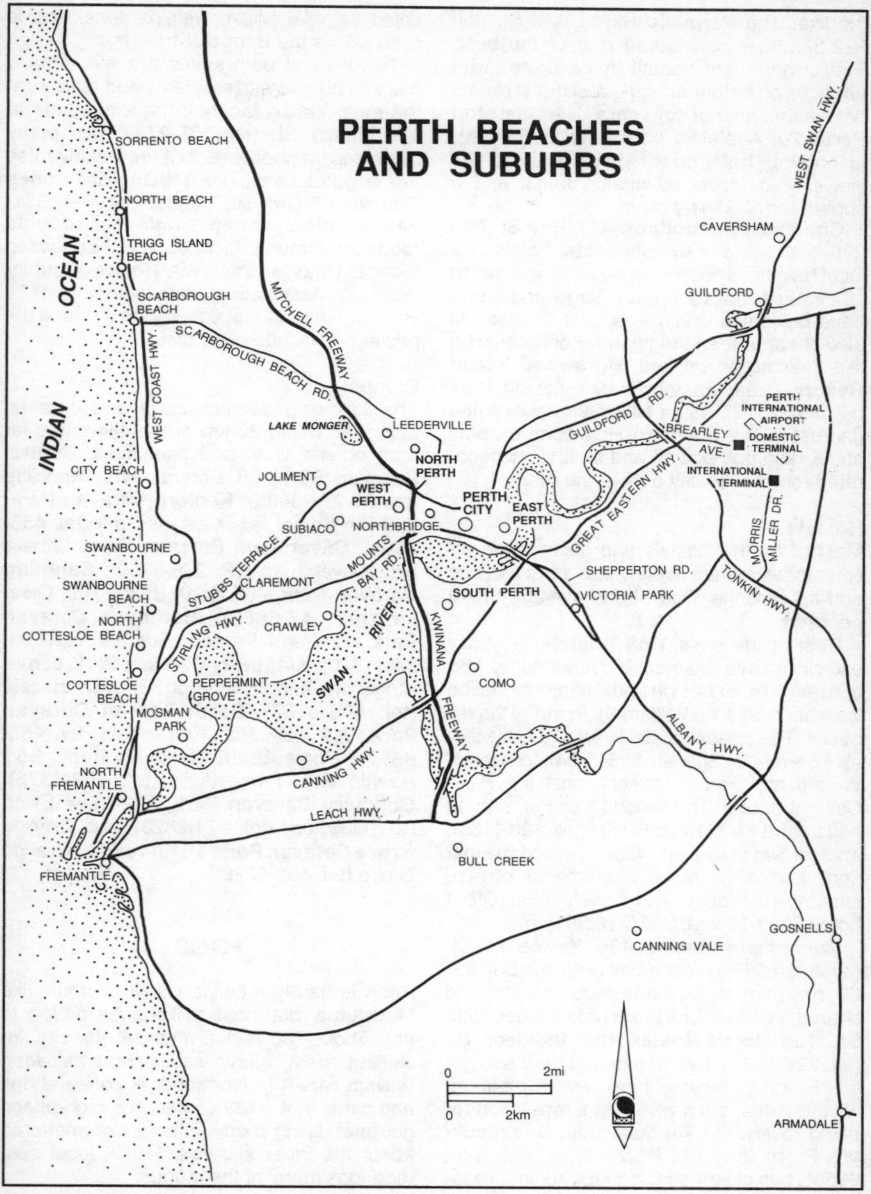
PERTH BEACHES AND SUBURBS
INDIAN OCEAN
SORRENTO BEACH
NORTH BEACH
TRIGG ISLAND BEACH
SCARBOROUGH BEACH
SCARBOROUGH BEACH RD.
WEST COAST HWY.
MITCHELL FREEWAY
LAKE MONGER
LEEDERVILLE
NORTH PERTH
CITY BEACH
JOLIMENT
WEST PERTH
PERTH CITY
EAST PERTH
SUBIACO
NORTHBRIDGE
SWANBOURNE
STUBBS TERRACE
MOUNTS BAY RD.
CLAREMONT
SWANBOURNE BEACH
NORTH COTTESLOE BEACH
STIRLING HWY.
CRAWLEY
SWAN RIVER
KWINANA FREEWAY
COTTESLOE BEACH
PEPPERMINT GROVE
MOSMAN PARK
NORTH FREMANTLE
CANNING HWY.
LEACH HWY.
FREMANTLE
SOUTH PERTH
COMO
BULL CREEK
CANNING VALE
SHEPPERTON RD.
VICTORIA PARK
ALBANY HWY.
GREAT EASTERN HWY.
GUILDFORD RD.
BREARLEY AVE.
TONKIN HWY.
MORRIS MILLER DR.
PERTH INTERNATIONAL AIRPORT
DOMESTIC TERMINAL
INTERNATIONAL TERMINAL
CAVERSHAM
GUILDFORD
WEST SWAN HWY.
GOSNELLS
ARMADALE
0 2mi
0 2km
MOON

the like. The **Parmelia Hilton,** Mill St. (tel. 322-3622), is considered one of the best. Public rooms are beautifully decorated with antiques and other artwork, and guest rooms have either river or city views. The **Sheraton Perth,** 207 Adelaide Terrace (tel. 325-0501), is another hefty-price winner with terrific views, well-decorated guest rooms, and a superb formal dining room.

Chateau Commodore, 417 Hay St. (tel. 325-0461), one of the city's older hotels, is a local favorite. Though the decor is somewhat . . . robust, the rooms are large and some have balconies with views. The Chateau is also cheaper than the others. For those who like their action packed, **Burswood Island Resort,** Great Eastern Hwy., Victoria Park (tel. 362-7777), has a full-on 24-hour casino (largest in the Southern Hemisphere), plus an 18-hole golf course and beautifully decorated rooms with city or river views.

Hostels

Most of Perth's hostels and backpacker accommodations are easy walks from the bus and rail stations. Dorm beds average $8-10 per night.

Both of the city's **YHA hostels** are busy establishments situated in Northbridge. You can reach either from the bus or railway station via a short walk up William St., north of the rail tracks. The closest hostel is an 87-bed facility at 42 Francis St. (tel. 328-7794), corner of William and Francis streets, past the Perth Cultural Centre. The second location, with 48 beds, is at 60 Newcastle St. (tel. 328-1135), another two blocks up William St. and make a right. Both sites have a communal kitchen, laundry, rec room, and bicycle hire. Office hours are 8-10 a.m. and 5-10:30 p.m.

Travelmate Hostel, 496 Newcastle St. (tel. 328-6685), reached by bus from Barrack St., has dorm beds, a few double rooms, and shared facilities. One block before Newcastle St., **Top Notch Hostel,** 194 Aberdeen St. (tel. 328-6667), has communal facilities, air-conditioning, bicycle hire, and discounted weekly rates, but it also has a reputation for being rowdy. On the quiet side, **Backpackers Perth Inn,** 194 Brisbane St. (tel. 328-9958), has clean, spacious rooms in a renovated colonial house with gardens, and is reached via the Barrack Street bus.

Travelers of both sexes are welcome to mix and mingle with residents and retirees at the main **YMCA** facility in the city center at 119 Murray St. (tel. 325-2744). It's pretty basic accommodations, but the weekly rates are a good deal. The **YWCA Rita Jones Centre,** 17 Ord St., West Perth (tel. 321-2479), offers cheap single and double rooms, communal facilities, a TV and video lounge. Ditto for the **CWA House** (Country Women's Association), well located at 1174 Hay St. (tel. 321-6081). Rooms are a bit pricier but include breakfast.

Camping

The following campgrounds and caravan parks fall within 20 km of the city and offer both on-site vans and campsites: **Central Caravan Park,** 38 Central Ave., Redcliffe (tel. 09-277-5696); **Kenlorn Caravan Park,** 229 Welshpool Rd., Queens Park (tel. 458-2604); **Caversham Caravan Park,** Benara Rd., Caversham (tel. 279-6700); **Careniup Caravan Park,** 467 North Beach Rd., Gwelup (tel. 447-6665); **Starhaven Caravan Park,** 18 Pearl Parade, Scarborough (tel. 341-1770); **Kingsway Caravan Park,** corner Kingsway and Wanneroo Rd., Landsdale (tel. 409-9267); **Perth Tourist Caravan Park,** 319 Hale Rd., Forrestfield (tel. 453-6677); **Forrestfield Caravan Park,** 351 Hawtin Rd., Forrestfield (tel. 453-6378); **Guildford Caravan Park,** 372 West Swan Rd., Guildford (tel. 274-2828); and **Orange Grove Caravan Park,** 19 Kelvin Rd., Orange Grove (tel. 453-6226).

FOOD

Perth is hardly a culinary *tour de force* like Melbourne, but those millionaires *do* like to eat. About 700 restaurants dot the city, including many ethnic establishments along William Street in Northbridge, coffee shops and cafés in the city center, and high-priced gourmet dining rooms in hotels or spattered about the inner suburbs. Fresh, local seafood tops many of the menus.

Inexpensive

The cheapest—and perhaps tastiest—places to eat at are the foodstalls and halls, where you can do a budget-type graze of many different types of food for less than a greasy spoon takeaway. The best food hall is the **City Centre Market,** near William St., in the Hay Street Mall. Select from a variety of ethnic goodies such as Indian, Indonesian, Chinese, and Mexican. Open for both lunch and dinner, this market puts on live entertainment Thursday-Saturday evenings. Other good choices are the **Sun Markets** Oriental foodstalls behind Myer Department Store, and the **Carillon Food Hall,** also in the Hay Street Mall.

The dining room at the YMCA-run **Jewell House,** 180 Goderich St., serves good-value hot lunches and dinners. Next to the YMCA's main building, **Jun and Tommy's,** 117 Murray St., offers inexpensive Japanese meals. Another choice is the **Hayashi Japanese BBQ,** 107 Pier St., with fixed-price lunches. **Fast Eddy's,** corner Hay and Milligan streets, is a 24-hour burger joint. **Cini Coffee Lounge,** 570 Hay St., dishes up cheap sandwiches, salads, and other light meals. **Crossways,** 129 Barrack St., is the Hare Krishna restaurant well known for its very reasonable vegetarian meals (and free reading material). Across the street, **Magic Apple,** 138 Barrack St., features healthy salads, smoothies, and sandwiches.

For cheap pub meals, try the **Railway Hotel,** 130 Barrack St., or the **Northbridge Hotel,** 198 Brisbane St., Northbridge (next to the Backpackers Perth Inn).

Moderate

Feast on satays, spicy curries, and noodles at **Katong,** 446 Murray Street. Open Wed.-Mon. for lunch and dinner. **Kings Park Garden Restaurant,** with city and river views, is a delightful spot for lunch and morning or afternoon teas. Dinner, with live music, is in the expensive range. Ethnic cafés and restaurants line William and surrounding streets in Northbridge. **Dim Sim House,** 309 William St., specializes in those delectable little dumplings and pastries, many containing some rather exotic fillings. Open daily, midmorning to midafternoon. Gorge on Lebanese favorites, fish, and vegetarian dishes at **Al Barakat,** 110 Aberdeen St.; open Tues.-Sun., lunch and dinner. **Quoc Nam,** 318 William St., is noted for its authentic Vietnamese meals and good service. Other recommended Vietnamese restaurants are **Kim Anh,** 178 William St. and **Café La Quan,** 175 William Street.

Hawkers Paradise, 234 William St., features Malaysian dishes and good service, while **Satay Inn,** 253 William St., offers a variety of satays and other Singaporean delights. Good Italian fare is served at **Nonnatina's,** 147 Beaufort St., and at **Mamma Maria's,** 105 Aberdeen Street.

Expensive

Inquire about dress codes and reserve tables well ahead, especially for weekends and holiday periods. **Lee Gardens,** 18 Plain St. (tel. 325-8906), is reputedly one of Perth's best Chinese restaurants featuring delectable, exotic menu offerings. Open Mon.-Fri. for lunch and dinner. And, for one of the best French restaurants, the prizewinner is **Pierre's,** 8 Outram St., West Perth (tel. 322-7648). Pierre's is elegant, formal, and *very* expensive. Open daily for lunch and dinner. **Timbuktu,** 620 Beaufort St., Mt. Lawley, has an eclectic, four-course prix fixe menu and a devoted following. Open daily for lunch and dinner. Expect candlelight, silver service, and a blend of international and contemporary cuisine at **The Plum,** 47 Lake St., Northbridge (tel. 328-5920).

ENTERTAINMENT AND EVENTS

Much of Perth's entertainment scene is geared toward its vibrant, young (or young at heart) residents. Check local newspapers, particularly the *Where To Go* entertainment guide in Friday's *West Australian* newspaper for current listings of arts and cultural events. You can also obtain a *What's On This Week* brochure at the Western Australian Tourist Centre, Forrest Place, corner of Wellington Street.

Cinemas

Perth has the usual round of commercial cinema complexes, most of the flicks months behind the U.S. Two movie houses that show more arty and/or cerebral films are the **Kimberley Cinema,** Barrack St., and the **New Oxford,** corner of Oxford and Vincent streets. There's a two-level wraparound **Omni Theater,** at the corner of Railway Parade and Sutherland St., West Perth (tel. 481-6481).

Pubs And Clubs

Plentiful clubs, pubs, and discos feature live music most nights of the week. Northbridge is the prime area for contemporary and casual venues, while discos and nightclubs in the big hotels cater to the yup-and-coming.

Hannibal's, 69 Lake St., is a popular disco where the disc jockey hangs suspended in a glass "cage." **River Cruise,** 230 William St., and **Aurora,** 232 William St., are the local meat markets. A bit more sophisticated are the **Brass Monkey Pub and Brasserie,** 209 William St., and the **Queen's Tavern,** 520 Beaufort St., Highgate. The **Shafto Lane Tavern,** corner Hay St. and Shafto Lane, is more down-to-earth and crowded, especially when the band's playing.

Dance to contemporary tunes at **Jules,** 104 Murray St., or listen to piano music and possibly watch a striptease at the **Old Melbourne Hotel,** corner Hay and Milligan streets (open 24 hours). Travelers frequent **Limbo's,** 232 William St., a venue for live music and graffiti lovers. Upmarket **Clouds,** in the Sheraton, is a huge disco with another meat market reputation. At the Parmelia Hilton, **The Adelphi** is a très chic wine bar.

For good old drinkin' pubs, try **Sherwood's Tavern,** 77 St. George's Terrace, **Milligan's,** 205 James St., and the **Northbridge Hotel,** 198 Brisbane Street.

The Casino

Burswood Island Resort, W.A.'s first casino, features more than 140 gaming tables, including roulette, baccarat, blackjack, craps, and Australia's own two-up. Restaurants, bars, and a cabaret are also part of this luxury resort complex on the banks of the Swan River, near the city. Open 24 hours a day except Christmas Day and Good Friday. For information, phone 362-7777.

Theater, Dance, And Concerts

The stunning **His Majesty's Theatre,** 825 Hay St. (tel. 322-2929), is home not just to many of Perth's theatrical productions but also to the **West Australian Ballet Company** and the **West Australian Opera Company.** Modern and traditional ballets are performed in February, May, June, and October, while the operatic season (April, August, and November) features classical works and operettas. For information, phone the theater or **Artsline** (tel. 484-1133).

The **Playhouse Theatre,** 3 Pier St. (tel. 325-3500), is headquarters of the Western Australian Theatre Company, which presents a number of classical and contemporary plays throughout the year. Other good local theaters include: **Dolphin Theatre,** University of Western Australia, Crawley (tel. 380-2432); **Regal Theatre,** 47 Hay St., Subiaco (tel. 381-1557); and **Hole in the Wall,** 180 Hamersley Rd., Subiaco (tel. 381-2733).

Perth Entertainment Centre, on Wellington near Milligan St., is where the big-name rock concerts and other major events are held. You can't miss the **Betts & Betts Walk of Fame** out front—a walkway of celebrities' autographed footprints. For information, phone 322-4766.

Folk music, orchestra recitals, and more "mellow" concerts are performed at **Perth Concert Hall,** 5 St. George's Terrace (tel. 325-9944). In summer, the band shell in the **Supreme Court Gardens** presents a variety of live music.

Theme Parks

Adventure World, 179 Progress Dr., Bibra Lake, is a family-oriented entertainment complex with an amusement park, native animals, waterways, and parklands. Hours are daily, Nov.-May and school holidays, 10 a.m.-5 p.m. Admission is $16.50, children $13.50. For information, phone (09) 417-9666.

Travel through an underground acrylic tunnel to view approximately 5,000 species of

WESTERN AUSTRALIA TOURISM COMMISSION

boat recreation

underwater life (such as starfish, crustaceans, and a small Port Jackson shark) at **Underwater World,** Hillary's Boat Harbour, West Coast Highway. Other attractions include Microworld, where you can watch seahorses, shellfish, and anemones through a video camera, plus a gift shop, and an underwater café that looks out on the Indian Ocean. Hours are daily 9:30 a.m.-6 p.m. Admission is $10.50. For information, phone (09) 447-7500.

Events

The city's big extravaganza is the annual **Festival of Perth** held in February and March. The festival showcases international and national big-name talents, as well as local joes, with a program roster which includes music, theater, dance, film, visual and literary arts, and a host of outdoor activities. For information, contact the University of Western Australia, Mounts Bay Rd., Crawley (tel. 09-386-7977).

SPORTS AND RECREATION

Great weather, great beaches, great park—it means Perth offers all types of land and water sports and year-round recreational opportunities. Call or drop by the **Western Australian Tourism Commission** on Hay St. for information on spectator and participant sports throughout the state.

Diving

A few scattered, centuries-old shipwrecks offshore should make things interesting for divers. Contact **Perth Diving Academy,** 281 Wanneroo Rd., Nollamara (tel. 344-1562), or the **Australasian Diving Centre,** 259 Stirling Highway, Claremont (tel. 384-3966).

Fishing

You'll luck out on the catch of the day at many coastal ports, particularly Fremantle, as well as along the Swan River banks. The prized fish in these parts is the blue marlin. Charter boats are available (check the yellow pages).

Swimming Pools

Not happy with the ocean or the river? A freshwater swimming pool is located at the **Superdrome,** Stephenson Ave., Mt. Claremont (tel. 387-8044).

Sporting Facilities

Tennis: Fees are reasonable at public tennis courts located within metropolitan and suburban parks. For sites and details, contact the **Western Australia Tennis Association** (tel. 09-481-0377).

Golf: Select from one of the city's many public golf courses after consulting with the **Western Australia Golf Association** (tel. 367-2490) or the tourist office. Some of Perth's country clubs are on the snooty side (but what else is new).

Other Participant Sports

Yachties should head straight for the tourism office. **Catamarans** and **sailboards** are available for hire at the Coode Street Jetty, South Perth (tel. 367-2988). They are popular on weekends and holidays, so book ahead. Depending on weather conditions, you can parasail on weekends at the South Perth foreshore. For information, contact **Flying High Parasailing** (tel. 446-1835).

Bushwalkers, cyclists, and **joggers** will find excellent trails throughout Kings Park and along the Swan River. The tourist office has maps and brochures, or contact the **Ministry of Sport and Recreation** (tel. 387-9700).

Spectator Sports

Aussie-rules football is the prime winter spectator sport, with games played every Saturday afternoon, March through September, at various league grounds throughout the city. For information, phone the **Western Australia Football League** (tel. 381-5599). In summer months, **cricket** is the buzz, with Sheffield Shield, Test, and one-day cricket played at the W.A.C.A. (Western Australia Cricket Association) grounds in Nelson Crescent, East Perth. For information, phone the **W.A.C.A.** (tel. 325-9800).

Other spectator sports include **rugby, soccer, basketball, baseball,** and **hockey.** Watch for details of all matches and sporting events in the Sports section of the Friday and Saturday newspapers.

Racing is a big-time favorite of Western Australians. For schedules and locales of **horse, trotting,** and **greyhound** racing, watch the Sports section of the morning newspapers. For **motor racing,** contact the W.A. Sporting Car Club (tel. 381-4432). For **motorcycle racing,** phone the Motorcycle Racing Club of W.A. (tel. 409-1002). On Friday nights throughout spring and summer months, the **RAS Showground** in Claremont hosts thriller speedcar and motorcycle races. Look for details in Friday's *West Australian.*

SHOPPING

Perth's main shopping district is the pedestrians-only Hay Street Mall and Murray Street Mall, both running parallel between William and Barrack streets, and the many arcades which branch off to St. George's Terrace and Wellington Street. Both major department stores, Myer and Aherns, are located here, as are Woolworth, Coles, scads of boutiques, specialty shops, bookshops, schlock and dime stores, cinemas, coffee lounges, and all kinds of general merchandise. Customary shopping hours are Mon.-Fri. 9 a.m.-5:30 p.m., Thurs. 9 a.m.-9 p.m., and Sat. 9 a.m.-noon.

Markets

Two of the better colorful, bargain-filled markets which offer a wide range of merchandise are **Beaufort Street Markets,** corner Greenway and Beaufort Street (Thurs. and Fri. 6 a.m.-9 p.m., Sat.-Sun. 10 a.m.-late), and **Midland Indoor Market,** 284 Great Eastern Highway (Sun. 8 a.m.-5 p.m.).

Crafts

For **Aboriginal handicrafts,** don't miss the **Aboriginal Artists Gallery** on St. George's Terrace (see "Sights," above). **Creative Native,** 36 King St. (tel. 322-3398), also sells and displays traditional and contemporary handmade Aboriginal art, including carved emu eggs and boomerangs.

Crafts Council Gallery, Wellington St., at the railway station (tel. 325-2799), exhibits crafts by leading Western Australians and also provides listings of other craft shops and outlets. For items constructed from native jarrah and blackboy wood, visit **Contempo Gallery,** 329 Murray St. (tel. 322-2306). Shop for contemporary crafts alongside colonial antiques at **Puritan Man,** 343 Stirling Highway (tel. 384-3434).

Other Shops

How about gems and money? See gems *before* they're turned into rings, pendants, and key chains at **Perth Lapidary Centre,** 58 Pier St. (tel. 325-2954). Purchase proof-issue coins, commemoratives and bank notes, coin jewelry, and books related to coin collecting and Western Australia's pioneering prospectors at **The Perth Mint,** 310 Hay St. (tel. 421-7277).

SERVICES

Branches of all the major national **banks** are located on or about St. George's Terrace, along with the ubiquitous automatic teller machines. You'll find **Bank of America Australia** at 28 The Esplanade (tel. 322-7555). Banking hours are Mon.-Thurs. 9:30 a.m.-4 p.m., Fri. 9:30 a.m.-5 p.m.

The **General Post Office,** 3 Forrest Place (tel. 326-5211), between the railway station and Hay Street Mall, is open for all postal services Mon.-Fri. 8-5.

For migrant information (employment, permits, etc.), see the **Immigration Office,** 12 St. George's Terrace (tel. 220-2311).

INFORMATION

As with all of Australia's capital cities, the state tourist office is chockablock with information, accommodations, and tour bookings. The **Western Australian Tourist Centre** (also known as Holiday W.A.) is on Forrest Place, at the corner of Wellington Street. Hours are Mon.-Fri. 8:30 a.m.-5:30 p.m., Sat. 8:30 a.m.-1 p.m. For information, phone 483-1111. A **Perth City Tourist Booth** is located along Hay Street Mall.

Info Link Government and Community Information and Inquiry Centre (tel. 427-3100) is housed within the Alexander Library Building at the James Street Mall.

The **ACROD Access Committee** (tel. 222-2961) provides **disabled visitors** with helpful brochures and information on accommodations, restaurants, theaters, and recreational areas within the state.

To obtain maps and touring advice, call in at the **Royal Automobile Club of W.A.,** (RAC), 228 Adelaide Terrace (tel. 421-4444). For motoring breakdowns, the number to phone is 325-0333.

In an emergency, dial 000 to summon **fire, police,** and **ambulance** services. Both **Royal Perth Hospital,** Wellington St. (tel. 224-2244), and **Sir Charles Gairdner Hospital,** Verdun St., Nedlands (tel. 398-3333), maintain 24-hour emergency rooms. For killer toothaches, go to **Perth Dental Hospital,** 196 Goderich St. (tel. 325-3452).

Other Information

The **Royal Automobile Club** on Adelaide Terrace stocks a good variety of local and national travel books. **Down to Earth Books,** 874 Hay St., and a branch of **Angus and Robertson,** 296 Murray St., are other good reading outlets.

The *West Australian* (morning) and the *Daily News* (evening) are Monday through Saturday papers, while the *Sunday Times* finishes the weekend. **Plaza Newsagency,** in the Plaza Arcade off Hay Street Mall, sells national and international newspapers, as do some of the large hotels.

GETTING THERE

By Air

If you're coming from Europe, Africa, or Southeast Asia, Perth will most likely be your Australian gateway city. **International carriers** include Qantas, Air New Zealand, British Airways, Malaysian Airlines, Thai Airways, Singapore Airlines, and Japan Airlines.

Domestic carriers that serve Perth from other Australian states are Australian Airlines (tel. 323-3333, or 13-1313, toll-free), Ansett (tel. 323-1111, or 13-1300, toll-free), and Compass, the new kid on the block that's giving the other guys a run for your money. Since the recent airline deregulation, competition has been keen and fares have fluctuated considerably (usually downward). For up-to-date prices and cheapest deals, consult the **YHA** office or **STA,** 426 Hay St., Subiaco (tel. 382-3977). Inquire into moneysaving **passes** before you leave home (or enter the country).

Perth International Airport is about 16 km northeast of the city center and the separate **domestic terminal** is about five km closer. Moneychanging and other customary big-city facilities are available.

The **Skybus** shuttle meets all incoming flights and drops passengers off at city airline offices and major hotels. Fare is $6 (international), $5 (domestic). **Transperth** city bus #338 operates between the domestic airport and city center. Services run daily, every 40-50 minutes, less frequently after 6 p.m. William Street, between St. George's Terrace and The Esplanade, is the main pick-up and drop-off spot. Fare is $1. **Taxis** are readily available and the 25-minute ride to city center should cost $10-15.

Don't forget to save ten bucks for **departure tax** if you're leaving the country.

By Train

Interstate trains arrive into and depart from the **East Perth Railway Terminal,** West Parade.

The fabled *Indian-Pacific* runs between Perth and Sydney. The 65-hour, three-night journey passes through Broken Hill and Adelaide and crosses the Nullarbor Plain on the world's longest straight stretch of railway line. Trains depart Sydney on Mon., Thurs., and Sat., and Perth on Sun., Tues., and Thursday. One-way fares are: $835, first-class berth with meals; $610, economy berth with meals; and $200, economy seat. The *Indian-Pacific* is included in the **Austrailpass,** which must be purchased outside the country.

The *Trans-Australian* connects Perth with Adelaide. Lasting 40 hours (two nights), trains leave from both cities on Wednesday and Saturday. One-way fares are: $540, first-class berth and meals; $400, economy berth and meals; $150, economy seat.

For information and bookings, phone **Westrail** (tel. 326-2222) or the Western Australian Tourist Centre.

By Bus

Main coach companies serving Perth daily from other Australian states are **Bus Australia** (tel. 277-1077), **Pioneer** (tel. 479-1600), and **Greyhound** (tel. 478-1122). Routes from the east coast usually travel via Adelaide, while the Darwin-to-Perth coaches journey across the Top End and down the west coast. Pioneer does the Ayers Rock-Perth run. Sample fares are: Sydney-Adelaide-Perth (61 hours) $210; Adelaide-Perth (37 hours), $156; Darwin-Perth (59 hours), $245. Inquire about stopover privileges and special passes for overseas visitors.

By Car

Western Australia is long, far, and wide. Sealed roads, suitable for conventional vehicles, are: Eyre and Great Eastern highways, from Adelaide (2,697 km); Eyre, South Coast, and South Western highways, from Adelaide (3,212 km); Stuart, Victoria, Great Northern, North West Coastal, and Brand highways, from Darwin (4,379 km); and Stuart, Victoria, and Great Northern highways, from Darwin (4,253 km). Make sure your vehicle and body are prepared for the arduous trek.

Though roadhouse facilities are available along the major byways, distances between them can be vast. The road from Ayers Rock is unsealed all the way to the goldfields, where it connects with the big highways. Carry plenty of spare everything—even passengers, to share the *very* long—and often boring—drive and expensive petrol costs. Also see "Crossing the Nullarbor" in the "South Australia" chapter.

Hitching

It's fairly cheap—and a lot less exhausting—to take the bus or share a ride (check the YHA bulletin boards). Waits of several days are not uncommon, plus who knows *where* you'll be waiting! There are some creepy stories about hitchhiking out there! Some friends once picked up a haggard old guy—who looked as if he hadn't eaten for a year—from the edge of the Nullarbor (and the middle of nowhere). He drove with them about 100 km—even *deeper* into nowhere, said, "This is where I get out," and wandered off into the proverbial sunset.

If you're dead set on thumbing it, hop a train to Midland if you're headed north or east, or Armadale if your direction is south. Women should be *especially* careful, and preferably travel with a male companion (or a pit bull).

GETTING AROUND

By Air

Ansett WA (tel. 323-1111, or 13-1300 toll-free), the regional carrier, provides scheduled service between Perth and Kalgoorlie, Paraburdoo, Karratha, Port Hedland, Broome, and Kununurra. **Skywest** (tel. 323-1188) and **Western** (tel. 277-4022), fly between Perth and smaller Western Australia towns and cities.

Buses And Trains

Transperth, the metropolitan transit district, operates free City Clipper buses approximately every 10 minutes, Mon.-Fri. 7 a.m.-5:30 p.m., Sat. 9-11:30 a.m. Routes are color-coded and circle the city center, covering most tourist attractions. Other buses connect the business center with suburban areas, and though not free, they're still good deals. Tickets, good for two hours from the time of issue, range from $1-1.50, depending on the number of zones you travel. (Fremantle, for example, is only two zones and it's about 20 km away!) You can also get an all-day ticket for five bucks, *plus* tickets are interchangeable on all Transperth buses, trains, and ferries.

If you're sticking around for a while, you might want to consider a **multirider ticket** which gives you 10 trips for the price of nine, or a five-day **sightseers ticket** that works out to under $4 per day. Buses operate Mon.-Fri. 6 a.m.-11:30 p.m., less frequently on weekends and public holidays. Obtain maps, schedules, tickets, and other information from **Transperth Information Services,** Perth Central Bus Station, Wellington St. (tel. 221-1211), or the head office at 10 Adelaide Terrace.

Transperth operates frequent rail service between the city center and Fremantle, Midland, Armadale, and points in between. Trains operate Mon.-Fri. 5:40 a.m.-11:30 p.m., not as often on weekends and public holidays. Westrail's *Australind* serves the south coast, down to Bunbury, twice a day. All departures are from the Central Railway Station, Wellington St. (next to the bus station). Contact Transperth Information Services, above, for details.

The Prospector makes one run daily to and from Kalgoorlie (eight hours). Fare is about $55 one way. Kalgoorlie trains, as well as Westrail country buses, depart from the East Perth Railway Station. For information, phone Westrail (tel. 326-2195), the railway station (tel. 326-2222), or the Western Australian Tourist Centre (483-1111).

Taxis

Meter-operated **taxis** can be hailed on city streets, plucked from taxi ranks around the central business district and Fremantle, or hired by phoning **Swan Taxis** (tel. 322-0111), **Black and White Taxis** (tel. 328-8288), or **Green and Gold Taxis** (tel. 328-3311). Cab fare begins at $1.80 plus $.66 per km, rising to an initial charge of $2.70 between 6 p.m.-6 a.m.

Car Rentals

The big-name **rental car** companies are located at both the domestic and international airports and in the city center. Charges range from $30-65, depending on size—some include unlimited kilometers while others give only the first 100-150 km for a free allowance. For information, contact **Avis** (tel. 325-7677), **Hertz** (tel. 321-7777), or **Budget** (tel. 322-1100).

Rent heartier vehicles for Outback travel from **South Perth Four Wheel Drive Rentals,** 80 Canning Hwy., Victoria Park (tel. 362-5444). Plenty of smaller rental companies are listed in the Yellow Pages—the tourist center also maintains current listings.

By Bike

Excellent trails and climate make Perth an ideal city for cycling. Rent **bicycles** for $10 per day from the YHA on Francis St. or from **Rideway Cycle Hire,** on the western side of the causeway (tel. 354-2393). **Koala Bike Hire,** in Kings Park (open daily) has hourly rates of about $3. For free brochures and trail maps, contact the Ministry for Sport and Recreation (tel. 387-9700).

Ferries

Transperth ferries depart from the Barrack Street Jetty to Mends St., across the Swan River in South Perth, daily 6:45 a.m.-7:15

p.m. One-way fare is under $1. Contact Transperth Information Services, above, for details. (Don't forget—your two-hour bus ticket is good on this ferry.)

Tours

The Western Australian Tourist Centre can help you plan and book organized tours within the city and state. Prices vary from $18-50, and include such destinations as wildflower-viewing (Aug.-Nov.), Swan Valley, El Caballo Blanco, the Darling Ranges, Wave Rock, Monkey Mia, Mt. Augustus, and Yanchep National Park. Longer three- to four-day treks up and down the coast average $300-450. Again, first check with YHA for the best deals with, possibly, more simpatico companions.

City Sights coach tours run about $15 for a half day, $28 for the full day-trip, but you can do it yourself on the **Perth Tram** (actually a bus in drag) which makes 1½-hour, commentator-assisted trips around the city sights. The tram operates daily 9:30 a.m.-6:30 p.m. Pick-up point is at 124 Murray St. (near Barrack St.).

Free guided **walking tours** of Kings Park are available from April through October. For information, phone 321-4801.

All **boat cruises** leave from Barrack Street Jetty. The bargain of the lot is Transperth's MV *Countess II,* which departs at 2 p.m. daily except Saturday, on a three-hour upstream Swan River cruise. Fare is $12. For information, phone 425-2651.

Boat Torque operates *Star Flyte* fast ferry to Rottnest Island, Perth's nearby holiday mecca. Tickets are about $60 and include a bus tour of the island. The *Lady Houghton* and *Miss Sandalford* vessels run Swan Valley River and vineyard cruises for $45. Day-cruises include morning tea, winetasting, lunch, entertainment, complimentary drinks, and commentary. The evening event features dinner, wine, and live entertainment. For information and reservations, phone 325-6033.

Five different boat trips, on the Swan River from Perth to the Indian Ocean at Fremantle, are offered by **Captain Cook Cruises.** For information and reservations, phone 325-3341.

Westrail offers a variety of rail excursions lasting from one day to one week, covering everything from coastal resorts and timber forests to wildflowers and goldfields. For information and bookings, contact the Western Australian Tourist Centre, or Westrail (tel. 326-2159).

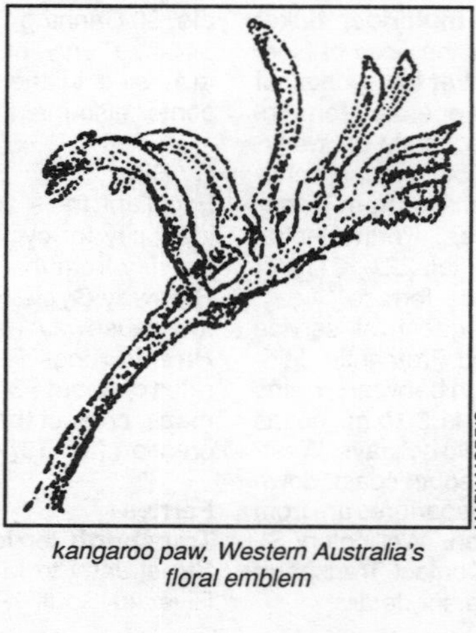

kangaroo paw, Western Australia's floral emblem

VICINITY OF PERTH

Even though this mega-state spans a third of the continent, you can still manage to get to some pretty interesting places in the course of a day or two.

FREMANTLE

You've heard of Fremantle—site of the 1987 America's Cup race where Kevin Parry lost the yachties' prized petunia to San Diego's Dennis Connor. Believe it or not, Fremantle actually existed *before* then!

Perth's port district (pop. 21,000), called "Freo" by the locals, sits 19 km southwest of Perth, where the Swan River kisses the Indian Ocean. Founded along with Perth in 1829, the city was named for Captain Charles Howe Fremantle, who claimed Australia's west coast for the British Crown. The settlement was practically dormant until those hard-working convicts were brought in to construct many of the town's buildings—including their own jail.

Though Fremantle is a modern port, much of the old district with its 19th-century buildings and shop fronts has been preserved and—thanks to the Cup race—spruced up and painted. It's an easy-stroll, a popular tourist town of historical sites, art galleries, and sidewalk cafés. The place is—dare I say it—"picturesque, charming, and quaint."

Historical Sights

If you arrive by train, you'll begin your tour at **Fremantle Railway Station,** Phillimore St., opened in 1907 to serve the harbor. Check out the cluster of black swans on the building's façade, as well as the **memorial water trough** in the park out front which commemorates the death of two Outback explorers (who died of thirst).

The **Round House** (1831) at Arthur Head, west end of High St., actually has 12 sides and is W.A.'s oldest remaining public building. Now roofless and empty, this was originally the colony's first gaol, site of its first hanging, and later a "holding tank" for Aborigines being shipped to Rottnest Island. Hours are daily 10 a.m.-5 p.m. Admission is free.

The convict-built **Western Australian Maritime Museum** (1850), corner of Cliff St. and Marine Terrace, was once a commissariat store. Exhibits include fascinating relics from a number of 17th-century Dutch ships wrecked off the coastline. One highlight is the ongoing reconstruction of the 1629 *Batavia* hull, a process which visitors can view as conservationists work. Hours are Mon.-Thurs. 10:30 a.m.-5 p.m., Fri.-Sun. 1-5 p.m. Admission is by donation.

Following Marine Terrace back toward town, you'll pass the **Old Court House** on your left, and a **statue** of C.Y. O'Connor (he's the bloke who built the artificial harbor here in the 1860s) off to the right. Continue on Marine Terrace, turning left at Essex Street which, as you cross South Terrace, becomes Henderson Street.

Fremantle Markets, on the corner, date from 1897. Reactivated in the mid-'70s (wasn't *everything?),* this is *still* the area's most lively weekly market. Approximately 150 stalls offer fruit, veggies, arts, crafts, and other market kitsch, bargains, and buskers. Shopping hours are Fri. 9 a.m.-9p.m., Sat. 9-5, Sun. 11 a.m.-5 p.m. The **Sail and Anchor** pub, across Henderson St., is a restored 1903 building that served as "command post" during the America's Cup trials and also houses a brewery (sheer coincidence, no doubt). This one-time site of the old Freemason's Hotel has housed pubs since the 1850s. Next to the markets, on South Terrace, **Scots Presbyterian Church** also dates from the 19th century.

The **Warders' Quarters** (1851), near the corner of William St., are stone terraces built by convicts to house their keepers at Fremantle Prison, and are still used today for the same purpose. Grim **Fremantle Prison,** on The Terrace off Fairburn St., was also con-

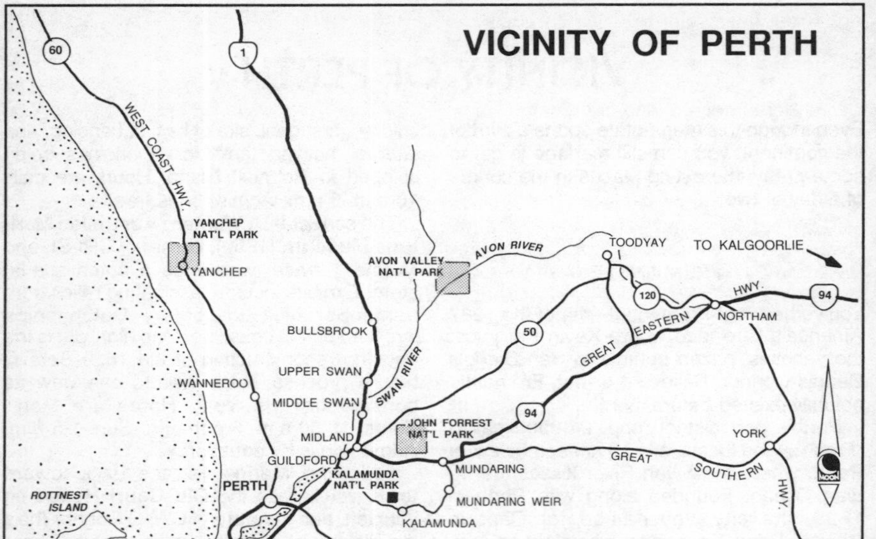

structed by convicts between 1851-59 and is still used today for the same purpose. A museum next to the prison gates depicts prison history and features prison memorabilia and other articles of bondage. Hours are Mon.-Fri. 9:30 a.m.-1 p.m., Sat. 1-4 p.m., Sun. 11 a.m.-5 p.m. Admission is free, and so are you.

Going left at William St., it's a two-block walk to St. John's Square. **Fremantle Town Hall** (1887), past the Information Centre, is an elegant structure opened in conjunction with Queen Victoria's Jubilee. Opposite the Town Hall, on William St., the **Federal Hotel** is another atmospheric pub that dates from 1887. **St. John's Anglican Church** (1881), next door, is a stone structure that took three years to complete.

Old **St. Patrick's Church** sits at the corner of Adelaide and Quarry streets. **Proclamation Tree,** across Quarry St., is a Moreton Bay fig tree planted around the turn of the century. On the opposite side of Adelaide St., the **Old Fremantle Boys' School** used to be guess what.

Fremantle Museum and Arts Centre, corner of Ord and Finnerty streets in Fremantle Park, served as the local lunatic asylum between 1861-65, a women's home (i.e., old ladies) in the early 1900s, and the 1942 headquarters for American Forces stationed in Western Australia. After a 13-year restoration, the Gothic-esque sandstone building reopened in 1972 as a museum and art center, which features changing exhibitions (with an emphasis on Western Australian artists), a museum wing with displays and mementos of Fremantle's history, a lecture room, and cloistered courtyard used for music and theatrical performances and crafts fairs. Hours are daily 10 a.m.-5 p.m., Wed. 7-9 p.m. Admission is free.

One block south, at the corner of Ord and Ellen streets, **Samson House** (1888) was and still is associated with a prominent Fremantle family (name of Samson). Contained within are historic photographs, antique furnishings, and a 20-meter-deep, in-house well. Hours are Sun. and Thurs. 1-5 p.m. Guided tours are available.

Other Sights

Down in the B Shed, at Victoria Quay, **Sails of the Century** boat museum features a wide range of vessels, including the America's Cup winner *Australia II*. Hours are daily 1-5 p.m. Admission is free. Watch as boatbuilders, using traditional 18th-century methods, construct a full-size replica of the *Endeavour,* the ship in which Captain James Cook discovered Australia. This ongoing (and *expensive)* project, at Fishing Boat Harbour, is Alan Bond's bicentennial gift to the nation. Hours are daily 10 a.m.-4 p.m.

Up Mews Road, toward the Esplanade, **Fremantle Crocodile Park** is home to more than 200 freshwater and saltwater crocs, living as they might in their Kimberley homeland. Viewing is from the safety of a raised metal walkway, enclosed with a tall chainlink fence. Education tours and a film document crocodile history and explain how the Aussie crocs were saved from extinction. Hours are daily 10 a.m.-5 p.m. Admission is $7.

Eyeball the terrific view of Fremantle Harbour from the **Observation Tower** of Fremantle Port Authority, 1 Cliff Street. Tours are available Mon.-Fri., hourly from 9:30 a.m.-3:30 p.m., and should be booked ahead.

The **Marine Museum,** 5 Beach St., displays Australian and international collections of shells, fossils, and gemstones. Open weekends. Admission is free. If you're into gas and electricity, you can study its local history at the **Energy Museum,** 12 Parry Street. Hours are Tues.-Thurs. 10:30 a.m.-4:30 p.m., Sat.-Sun. 1-4:30 p.m. Admission is free.

Arts And Crafts

Fremantle is a town filled with artisans, and their wares are on display and for sale. **Fremantle Art Gallery,** 43 High St., exhibits contemporary Western Australian paintings, prints, photography, and ceramics. Hours are daily 12-5 p.m. The **Artists Gallery Association,** an artists' co-op, features three galleries inside an old factory. Hours are Sat.-Sun. 2-5 p.m.

Bannister Street Craftworks, 8 Bannister St., is a converted warehouse which houses a variety of studios representing pottery, stained glass, fabric printing, leatherwork, woodwork, weaving, and gold- and silversmithing. Hours are Tues.-Fri. 10 a.m.-5 p.m., weekends and public holidays 12:30-5:30 p.m.

Praxis Gallery, 33 Pakenham St.; is comprised of three galleries exhibiting paintings, sculptures, photographs, prints, videos, and films by Australian and international artists. Hours are Tues.-Sat. 10 a.m.-5 p.m., Sun. 2-5 p.m. Nearby **Prism Gallery,** 23 Pakenham St., also specializes in works by local and overseas artists. Hours are Tues.- Fri. 10 a.m.-4 p.m., Sat.- Sun. 2-5 p.m.

See displays of Aboriginal arts including boomerangs, didgeridoos, bark paintings, and basketwork at **Gallery of Original Arts and Artifacts,** Cliff Street. Hours are Tues.-Fri. 10 a.m.-5 p.m., Sat.-Sun. 2-5 p.m. **Timothy's Toys,** Croke Lane, manufactures handmade wooden toys on the premises. Hours are Mon.-Sat. 9 a.m.-5 p.m., Sun. 1-5 p.m.

Accommodations

Fremantle YHA Hostel, 96 Hampton Rd. (tel. 09-335-3467), offers dorm beds inside a historic building for $10 per night. The **Freo 100 YHA,** 100 Hampton Rd. (tel. 336-2962) is only open 1 Dec.-31 March and has a one-week minimum, while **Freo 200 YHA,** 81 Solomon Rd. (tel. 335-3567), requires a minimum four-week stay. Weekly rates at both Freos run $45-70.

Inexpensive pub accommodations are available at two historic and well-located old-

Sailboats and surfboards are common coastal adornments.

timers: the **Federal Hotel,** 23 William St. (tel. 335-1645) and the **Norfolk,** 47 South Terrace (tel. 335-5405).

The **Fremantle Esplanade,** 46 Marine Terrace (tel. 430-4000), represents the big splurge ($110-250 per night), with all the goodies ("amenities," as they're known in the biz) that come with big bucks.

Food

You'll find plenty of reasonably priced pub meals and ethnic eateries in Fremantle, but fresh fish and seafood are the local specialties. **Lombardo's,** Mews Rd., Fishing Boat Harbour, is a waterfront complex with everything from takeaway fish and chips stalls and outdoor cafés to bistros and fine restaurants. **South Terrace** is another popular area lined with cappuccino bars and sidewalk cafés. One of Fremantle's ranking favorites is **Papa Luigi's,** 33 South Terrace, which serves coffee, cakes, and pasta dishes on a terrace overlooking the street. If there's a long wait, try the **Mexican Kitchen** next door, or—if you have your heart set on Italian—**Pizza Bella Roma** across the street.

Bengal, 48 High St., dishes up authentic Indian cuisine, along with some killer curries. Nearby **Koto,** 39 High St., is a small establisment which reputedly has the best Japanese food in the Perth area. **Vung Tau,** 19 High St., serves up Vietnamese and vegetarian dishes. **Gino's** not only has great food but is *cheap.*

Entertainment

High Street and South Terrace are where you'll find most of the live bands and a disco or two. Try **Clancy's** and the **Newport Arms** on South Terrace, and the **Exchange** and the **Auld Mug** on High Street.

A variety of regular **theatrical performances** are produced by the Harbour Theatre Company, Deck Chair Theatre Company, Spare Parts Puppet Theatre, and Fly By Night. For information, phone 335-7652.

Information

Pick up info, brochures, and walking tour maps at the **Fremantle Information Centre,** William St., near the Town Hall and mall (tel. 335-7652).

The **Wilderness Society,** 12 William St. (tel. 355-9512), stocks an array of "green" literature and products. Brochures and newsletters will inform you about numerous ecology-based groups, tours, and organizations.

Getting There

Frequent bus and train service connect Perth with Fremantle. **Transperth buses,** traveling various routes, depart from St. George's Terrace, while trains (traveling only one route) leave from Perth Central Station. In addition, some Rottnest Island ferries make a stop at Fremantle. For information, phone (09) 221-1211.

Getting Around

The **Fremantle Tram,** like the Perth Tram, makes frequent tours (with accompanying commentary) around the local sights. Cost is $4. For information, phone 367-8375.

ROTTNEST ISLAND

This sandy island resort—affectionately known as "Rotto,"—lies just 19 km off the Fremantle coast and is a favorite day excursion and holiday destination for Perth residents drawn to the bleached beaches, turquoise waters, and activities (or inactivity) that go with.

Rottnest translates to "Rat's Nest," a name bestowed upon it by Dutch mariner Willem de Vlamingh. Landing there in 1696, Willem mistook the native quokkas—a type of small marsupial—for a bunch of big, old rats. These days the quokkas are a protected species and one of the island's big tourist attractions.

Originally used as a prison settlement for mainland Aboriginals back in 1838, the prison was vacated in 1903, and 14 years later became a getaway spot for white society—and still is today. Thomson Bay is the main resort area of this tiny 11-km-long, five-km-wide island, and is one of the few shady spots. The rest of the landscape consists of sparse vegetation, a few low hills, some shallow salt lakes, plenty of white-sand beaches, and secluded rocky bays. Add to that the surrounding reef, protected lagoons, and some 12 shipwrecks to explore.

Sights

Get your bearings at **Rottnest Museum,** located at the main settlement. Exhibits and memorabilia cover convict history, wildlife, and shipwrecks. Walking-tour leaflets, including info and directions around the remaining convict-built buildings, are available. Hours are daily 10 a.m.-1:30 p.m. and 2:30-4:30 p.m. Dec.-Feb., daily 11 a.m.-1:30 p.m. and 2:30-4 p.m. other months.

Vlamingh Lookout, via Digby Dr., offers panoramic views of the island, surrounding ocean, and Gordon Lake. **Oliver Hill,** via Digby Dr., offers yet another dynamic island view and a leftover artillery battery.

Constructed of locally quarried limestone, **Rottnest Lighthouse,** Wadjemup Hill, in the center of the island, dates back to the mid-1800s. **Bathurst Lighthouse,** Gem Rd., Bathurst Point, the second of Rotto's lighthouses, was built in 1900.

Located in the island center east and northeast of the jetty are the small **salt lakes**—Government House, Serpentine, Herschell, Bagdhad, Pink, and Garden lakes. You'll see those quokkas (relatives of the wallaby) at the **Quokka Colony,** between Government House and Herschell lakes. This lot—used to having their faces stuffed by tourists—are quite tame.

Best **swimming beaches** include **Parakeet Bay,** at the northernmost tip of the island and **The Basin,** north of the main settlement. **West End,** the westernmost point on the island, is popular (and crowded) with hopeful **fishers. Shipwreck** sights are signposted along a marked trail around the island; however, snorkelers will need a boat to reach most of them. (Boats, and snorkeling and fishing gear, can be hired on the island.)

Accommodations And Food

If you want to make Rotto more than a day-trip, keep in mind that accommodations must be booked way in advance, particularly during holidays and summer months when the Perthos descend en masse. For information on rates and bookings, phone **Rottnest Island Board Booking** (tel. 292-5044).

Accommodations are concentrated around the Thomson Bay settlement and are comprised of cabins, hotel and motel rooms, a guesthouse, and campground. (Due to a water shortage, showers at Rotto accommodations are salt water; bring saltwater shampoo and soap with you as it's more expensive on the island.)

Moderately priced **Rottnest Hotel** (tel. 292-5011) overlooks the main beach and is Rotto's gathering spot. Built in 1864 as the summer residence of Western Australian governors, it was re-opened as a hotel in 1953. **Rottnest Island Board Cottages** (tel. 292-5044), sleep

Rotto—Perth's own offshore holiday island

four to eight people, at a cost of $270-500 per week. Campsites, tents, and cabins are available at **Tent-Land** (tel. 292-5033).

Food is relatively expensive, as on most tourist-type islands—even at the general store and fast-food center. **Rottnest Hotel** serves moderately priced steaks and salads in a casual environment, while the **Rottnest Island Lodge** is à la carte and expensive. Buy fresh bread and yummy baked goodies at the **Rottnest Island Bakery.**

Information

Tourist Information and walking and cycling maps are available at the **Tourist Information Centre,** at the end of the main jetty (tel. 292-5044).

Dial 000 to request **emergency assistance** or contact **Rottnest Medical Centre** (tel. 292-5030).

Getting There

Rottnest Airlines (tel. 09-478-1322) flies daily from Perth. A shuttle bus takes you from Rottnest Airport to the main wharf area.

Boat Torque Cruises operate a daily two-hour ferry service to the island aboard the MV *Rottnest Explorer* departing from Perth's Barrack Street Jetty and from Fremantle. Fare is $30 roundtrip from Perth, $25 roundtrip from Fremantle. *Star Flyte,* a new fast ferry and a more luxurious operation, also departs from both Perth and Fremantle. For information and bookings, phone 325-6033.

Getting Around

No cars are allowed on the island. Most visitors rely on bicycles—a round-the-island bike path covers 26 kilometers. Bring your own cycle on the ferry (an extra $5) or rent one from **Rottnest Bike Hire,** behind the Rottnest Hotel (tel. 292-5043). Rates run $7 per day.

If you'd rather not cycle, the Tourist Information Centre runs two-hour **Round the Island** bus tours from the main jetty and will get you back in time to catch Perth ferries. Highlights include convict-built architecture, the salt lakes, and WW II gun emplacements. The glass-bottom **Underwater Explorer** takes passengers on 45-minute boat tours over primitive corals, marinelife, and shipwrecks. Departures are from the main jetty. Fare is $10. For information on both tours, phone 292-5044.

YANCHEP NATIONAL PARK

Only 51 km north of Perth, Yanchep National Park is a 2,799-hectare, family-oriented coastal wonderland with bushland, caves, walking trails, a wildlife sanctuary, boating lake, swimming pool, golf course, footie ovals (football fields), limestone gorges, fauna exhibits, aviaries, a beer garden, and a museum. Despite all these attractions, 90% of the park has been maintained in its natural state.

Of the numerous caves set in the limestone hills, **Crystal Cave,** open to the public, features an underground stream in the main grotto, good examples of stalactites and stalagmites, and "fantasy lighting." Guided tours are offered several times daily.

Another favorite activity is the **Yaberoo Budjara Heritage Trail,** a 28-km walk through the Loch McNess wetlands, a refuge for waterfowl and other birds (and the Loch McNess monster?). Signs along the path—which follows the tracks used by the local Yaberoo Aborigines—explain the wetland ecology.

To reach Yanchep, follow the West Coast Highway north out of town, or catch a daily Transperth bus from Perth Central Bus Station.

Other Sights

Traveling the West Coast Highway from Perth, you'll pass through **Wanneroo,** another popular wine-producing area and a fast-growing artsy-craftsy-touristy center. The **Gumnut Factory,** 30 Prindiville Dr., Wangara Centre (tel. 09-409-6699), manufactures all types of gumnut creations and *you,* folks, can watch it happen. Don't miss Gumnutland, a model village with more than 30 handcrafted buildings, working railways, roads, and mini gumnut people—all crafted from timber, flowers, and gumnuts. Hours are daily 9-5.

If you're passing through Wanneroo on the weekend, stop at the **market** in the carpark at the corner of Prindiville Dr. and Ismail St., where 200 stalls offer a wide range of goods for sale.

Atlantis Marine Park, Two Rocks Rd., off Sovereign Dr. (tel. 561-1600), is located in the teeny township of Yanchep, a few kilometers before the national park. Watch, if you must, the dolphins and sea lions perform. Hours are daily 10 a.m.- 5 p.m., closed Christmas Day.

And then there's **Wild Kingdom Wildlife Park,** also on Two Rocks Rd. (tel. 09-561-1399), with wombats, dingoes, foxes, and other animals, as well as birdlife. Hours are daily 9:30 a.m.- 5:30 p.m.

Accommodations

The **Yanchep Inn** (tel. 09-561-1001), located within the park, has inexpensive to moderate rates for guest rooms and holiday units with two or three bedrooms. **Club Capricorn,** Two Rocks Rd. (tel. 561-1106), is an expensive beachfront resort with lodge and chalet accommodations, plus restaurant, swimming pools, and tennis courts.

Information

For info on **Yanchep National Park,** phone (09) 561-1004. In **Wanneroo,** the Tourist Information Centre is at 935 Wanneroo Rd. (tel. 405-4678).

SWAN VALLEY

The good news is that the scenic, fertile Swan Valley and its 20 or so wineries are a mere 20 km northeast of Perth—an easy car ride or river cruise away. The bad news is that the area is so close to the city and the city is expanding so rapidly that many of the rural communities are blending into urban-ity. The Swan River meanders the wide valley set at the foot of the Darling Ranges—a patchwork mix of small farms and award-winning wineries, stretching from Perth through historic Guildford to the Upper Swan, passing a number of interesting sights along the way.

Sights

The 1830 **Tranby House,** Peninsula Rd., Maylands, is Western Australia's oldest inhabited property. Hours are Mon.-Sat. 2-5 p.m., Sun. 11 a.m.-1 p.m. and 2-5 p.m. View nearly 30 locomotives (including steam, diesel, and electric), antique carriages, and other railway memorabilia, photos, and artifacts at the **Rail Transport Museum,** 136 Railway Parade, Bassendean (300 meters east of Ashfield Railway Station). Steam train tours are available May-October. Hours are Sun. and public holidays 1-5 p.m., Wed. 1-4 p.m. during school holidays. Admission is $2. For information, phone 457-3229.

In Guildford, situated at the rear of the historic 1840 Rose and Crown Hotel, 105 Swan St., the private **Hall Collection** consists of 40,000 antique and nostalgic artifacts

black swans meandering their namesake river

WESTERN AUSTRALIA TOURISM COMMISSION

including porcelain, paintings, glass, copper work, cameras, musical instruments, toys, and kitchen items. Hours are Tues.-Sun. 10 a.m.-4:30 p.m. Admission is $2.50. For information, phone 279-6542.

Woodbridge House, Third Ave., Guildford, is the National Trust-restored 1885 residence of Perth personality *extraordinaire* Charles Harper. Hours are daily, except Wed., 1-4 p.m., Sun. 11 a.m.-1 p.m. and 2-5 p.m. For information, phone 274-2432.

The **Mechanics Institute and Old Courthouse,** Meadow St., Guildford, exhibits period furnishings and clothing, blacksmithing tools and equipment, and bric-a-brac. Hours are 2-5 p.m. March to mid-December. For information, phone 279-1248.

Other 19th-century Guildford buildings are **St. Matthew's Church** in Stirling Square and the gaol, corner of Swan and Meadow streets. See local pottery at **Guildford Potters,** 105 Swan Street. Hours are daily 10 a.m.-3 p.m.

Caversham Wildlife Park and Zoo, corner of Arthur Rd. and Cranleigh St., West Swan, is a wildlife park featuring Australian and imported animals and birds. Hours are daily 10 a.m.-5 p.m. For information, phone 274-2202.

Gomboc Gallery, James Rd., Middle Swan, displays paintings, sculptures, and graphics by Western Australian artists. Hours are Wed.-Sun. and public holidays 10 a.m.-5 p.m.

Wineries

Swan Valley vineyards are sprinkled along the river, from the Guildford area to Upper Swan. Though vines were first planted in the 1830s, it's the Middle Swan district (with its more recent plantings) that is responsible for much of the high production. Most of the wineries welcome visitors for divine tastings.

Olive Farm Winery, 77 Great Eastern Hwy., South Guildford (tel. 277-2989), named for the olive trees planted along with the vines, is the region's oldest winery. Hours are Mon.-Fri. 10 a.m.-5:30 p.m., Sat. and public holidays 9 a.m.-3 p.m.

Some of the valley's currently renowned wineries include: **Houghton Wines,** Dale Rd., Middle Swan (tel. 09-274-5100); **Sandalford Wines,** corner West Swan and Middle Swan roads, Caversham (Tel. 274-5922); and **Westfield Wines,** Memorial Ave., Baskerville (tel. 269-4356).

For maps and information about all of the wineries plus other Swan Valley attractions, stop into the Western Australian Tourist Centre or the **Swan Valley Tourism Association,** Great Eastern Hwy., Midland (under the Town Hall clocktower), or phone 274-1522.

Getting There

Transperth buses and trains depart regularly for the Swan Valley. Trains stop at Guildford, then go on to the valley's gateway town of

Midland. Buses travel all the way to Upper Swan along Middle Swan Road. For information, phone Transperth (tel. 221-1211).

If you're traveling by car (30-40 minutes' drive), take Guildford Road or the Great Eastern Highway to Midland, then turn onto the Great Northern Highway through the valley's center.

THE DARLING RANGE

This range, full of wooded hills, valleys, and dams, runs east of the city and parallel to the coastline. It's a popular picnic, bushwalking, and weekend-away place for Perth dwellers, particularly from September to November when an astounding assortment of more than 4,000 wildflower species are a-blooming. You can take a number of different roads as far and flung as you like; one easy, close-to-Perth route is to catch Kalamunda Rd. from South Guildford, to Kalamunda sights, then pick up Mundaring Weir Rd., meeting the Great Eastern Highway back into Perth. Transperth buses journey to the Range on a variety of routes.

Sights

For some great coastal plain and city lights views, negotiate three kilometers of sharp hairpin and hair-raising turns on the one-way **Zig Zag Road** (formerly a railway line). Signs are posted off Kalamunda Road, Gooseberry Hill. You can also reach steep, 33-hectare, Gooseberry Hill via Gooseberry Hill Rd., Williams Rd., or Lascelles Parade.

Stirk Park and Cottage, 9A Headingly Rd., Kalamunda, is a restored 1881 cottage surrounded by a public reserve with scenic walks and waterways, an ornamental lake, model boat pond, and bowling greens. Hours are daily 9 a.m.-9 p.m. **History Village,** corner Railway and Williams roads, Kalamunda, is a museum on the site of the old railway station, plus the original state school building, post office, and a settler's cottage, transported to the site. Memorabilia and displays illustrate the area's early history. Hours are Thurs.-Sat. 9 a.m.-noon, Sun. 2-4:30 p.m.

Kalamunda National Park, via Kalamunda Rd., offers 375 hectares of forest scenery, granite boulder outcrops, seasonal wildflowers, wildlife, and birdlife. Visitors must carry their own water in hot weather.

Mundaring Weir, Mundaring Weir Rd., Mundaring, is the reservoir which provides water for the goldfields towns more than 500 km away. The **C.Y. O'Connor Museum,** named for the engineer who devised this system, features displays and exhibits relating to the complicated water system. Museum hours are Mon., Wed., Thurs., Fri., and public holidays 10:30 a.m.-3 p.m., Sat. 1-4 p.m., Sun. noon-5 p.m.

John Forrest National Park, reached via the Great Eastern Hwy., consists of 1,577 hectares of open forest and woodland, spring wildflowers, city and coastal views, and scenic walking trails. Western Australia's first national park was declared in 1895 and named for Lord John Forrest, the state's premier from 1890-1901.

Accommodations

The YHA operates **hostels** at Kalamunda (tel. 09-293-3869) and at Mundaring (tel. 295-1809). Both are on Mundaring Weir Rd. and offer dorm beds at $8 per night. **Campsites** are available at Mundaring Caravan Park, Great Eastern Hwy. (tel. 295-1125).

AVON VALLEY

Homesick English settlers fell in love with this lush, hilly valley which reminded them of their very own Avon—hence the name. Rainfall-green in winter and parched-sun brown in summer, this rural land—settled only one year after Perth—follows the course of the Avon River (an east- and southward branch of the Swan), running through the historic towns of Toodyay, Northam, and York.

Toodyay

Say "Two Jay" otherwise you'll be ignored—or worse. Toodyay (pop. 560) sits at the bend where the Avon River turns from east to south, and is the smallest of the river towns. There was an earlier Toodyay settled in the

1830s, some eight km downstream; *this* Toodyay—established in 1860 as Newcastle—was rechristened in 1910. The National Trust declared the town "historic" in 1980, and some 13 buildings have been classified as worthy of preservation.

Connors Mill, corner of Stirling Terrace and Piessa St., contains a steam engine, 1941 generator, and the **Moondyne Gallery,** which recounts the story of infamous bushranger Joseph Bolitho Jones (aka Moondyne Joe).

Trace the lives (and deaths) of 1800s pioneers and convicts at the **Old Gaol Museum and Police Station,** Clinton Street. The Old Gaol, an early stone and shingle-roofed structure, includes original cells. Hours are Wed.-Fri. 11 a.m.-3 p.m., Sat. 1-4 p.m., Sun. and public holidays 11 a.m.-4 p.m.

White Gum Company, Sandplain Rd., features commercially grown wildflowers, amid 283 hectares of white gum timberland. Hours are Wed.-Sun. 9 a.m.-5 p.m. Closed Christmas Day until the first Wednesday in March.

Avon Valley National Park, via Toodyay Rd. (make a left at Morangyup Rd. and follow posted signs), is a beautifully scenic 4,377-hectare park with valleys, slopes, woodlands, and open forest.

Northam

Believe it or not, Northam (pop. 6,800) is not only the largest Avon Valley town, but W.A.'s second-largest inland center (it's on the railway line to Kalgoorlie), notable for its black swans, white swans, and the whitewater Avon Descent Race.

See the **Avon Valley Arts Society,** 33 Wellington St., which is comprised of two historic structures—the Old Post Office (1892) and the Old Girls School (1877). The art center sells locally made arts and crafts. Hours are Tues.-Fri. 9 a.m.-4 p.m., Sat.-Mon. 10 a.m.-4 p.m.

The **Old Railway Station,** Fitzgerald St. West, contains early 1900s appliances and railway relics, plus renovated carriages and an old steam train. Hours are Sun. 10 a.m.-4 p.m.

Other historic sights are **Pioneer Graves,** Goomalling Rd.; **Morby Cottage** (1836), Avon Dr.; the **police station** (1866) and **courthouse** (1896), both on Wellington St.; **St. John's Church** (1890), Wellington St.; and **St. Saviour's Church** (1862), Toodyay Road.

York

Settled in 1830, this one-time commercial center for the Avon Valley declined when the railway passed it by in 1894 and it reverted to an agricultural community. In the 1970s, York (pop. 1,140) was rediscovered for its architectural delights and reputedly has more original buildings than any other town in Western Australia.

Avon Terrace, the main street, features buildings reflecting architectural styles ranging from the 1860s to the turn of the century. The **Old Police Station** complex is comprised of the old courthouse, troopers' cottage, stables, and cell blocks. Hours are Mon.-Fri. 11 a.m.-3 p.m., Sat.-Sun. and public holidays 10 a.m.-4 p.m. The **Post Office Museum** illustrates York's postal history beginning from 1840. Phone (096) 41-1301 to arrange admittance. Car lovers can rev their engines at the **Motor Museum,** where more than 100 veteran, vintage, classic, and racing vehicles are on display. Hours are daily 10 a.m.-5 p.m., closed Christmas Day and Good Friday. Trace printing history through commentary and demonstrations on a century-old letter press at **Sandalwood Press.** Hours are Tues.-Thurs., Sat.-Sun. 1-3 p.m.

The **Art Gallery,** Avon Terrace, exhibits locally crafted jarrah furniture, paintings, and stained glass. Hours are Sun. 1-3 p.m. The **Doll Museum,** also on Avon Terrace, features more than 1,000 doll babies representing all nationalities. Hours are Sat.-Sun. 10 a.m.-noon and 1-3 p.m.

One of York's oldest buildings is the **Residency Museum,** Brook Street. In a structure dating back to 1842, the museum displays photographs and artifacts of the town's early days. Hours are Tues.-Thurs., school and public holidays 1-3 p.m., Sat.-Sun. 1-5 p.m.

Balladong Farm, 5 Parker Rd., outside York on the way to Beverley, has been restored by the National Trust to show visitors what farm life was like in the 19th century. Displays include original breeds of stock and farm machinery, plus demonstrations of blacksmithing, milking, and wool spinning.

KAREN WHITE

Built in 1870, this information center was originally a flour mill.

Hours are Tues.-Sun. 10 a.m.-5 p.m. Guided tours can be arranged. For information, phone (096) 41-1279.

El Caballo Blanco

Located about halfway between Northam and Midland—reached via either Great Eastern Highway or Toodyay Road—El Caballo Blanco is one of Perth's major tourist attractions. The hordes trot forth to watch Spanish Andalusian dancing stallions perform, plus take tours of the car and carriage museum, horse stables, and animal nursery. Other amusements include two water slides, swimming pools, and a 200-meter "maxi" slide. Hours are Sat.-Wed. 10 a.m.-5 p.m. Admission is $10. For information, phone (095) 322-2087.

Accommodations

Toodyay: The **Old Toodyay Club YHA,** Stirling Terrace (tel. 09-574-2435), in the center of town, offers hostel accommodations for $6 per night. For inexpensive pub rooms, try either the **Victoria Hotel** (tel. 574-2206) or the **Freemasons Hotel** (tel. 574-2201). Both are on Stirling Terrace. **Appleton House,** Harper Rd. (tel. 574-2622) is a moderately priced, colonial-style B&B nestled in the hills. Campsites and on-site vans are available at both **Toodyay Caravan Park,** Railway Rd. (tel. 574-2612), and **Broadgrounds Park,** Stirlingia Dr. (tel. 574-2534). **Avon Valley National Park** (tel. 574-2540) has campsites with limited facilities.

Northam: The **YHA Hostel,** Fitzgerald St. (tel. 096-22-3323), is in the old railway station, and some dorms are inside railway carriages. Beds run $8 per night. Find basic pub rooms at **Avon Bridge Hotel,** Fitzgerald St. (tel. 22-1023), or the **Grand Hotel,** Fitzgerald St. (tel. 22-1024). **Buckland** country mansion, Buckland Rd., Irishtown (tel. 22-1130), offers stately—and moderately priced—accommodations in two upstairs rooms. The mansion is closed 23 Dec.-1 March. **Mortlock Caravan Park,** Great Eastern Hwy. (tel. 22-1620), has campsites and on-site vans.

York: Opposite the railway station, the **YHA Hostel,** South St. (tel. 096 41-1372), features dorm beds for $8 per night. The **Castle Hotel,** Avon Terrace (tel. 41-1007) is the recommended pub. Moderately priced **Hillside Homestead,** Forrest Rd. (tel. 41-1065) is an artist-owned, Edwardian residence with B&B accommodations, swimming pool, tennis court, and bicycles included in the price. Campsites and on-site vans can be rented at **Mt. Bakewell Resort and Caravan Gardens,** Eighth Rd. (tel. 41-1421).

Events

Avon Valley has two noteworthy events. Toodyay's **Moondyne Festival,** held annually in April, is a celebration of the colonial past including mock shoot-em-up holdups, jail breaks, coppers and convicts, plus an array of other fun sports and games.

The **Avon Descent,** begun at Northam each year on the first August weekend (when the river is full), features 800 or so canoeists in a fast-paced and furiously paddled whitewater race to Perth—a distance of 133 kilometers. The cheering crowds partying on the banks are just as much fun to watch—and join.

Information

The **area code** for Toodyay is 09; for Northam and York, 096. In Toodyay, the **tourist bureau** is on Stirling Terrace, in Connors Mill. Hours are Mon.-Sat. 9 a.m.-5 p.m., Sun. and public holidays 10 a.m.-5 p.m. For information, phone 09-574-2435.

The **Northam Tourist Bureau,** Beavis Place, Brabazon House, is open the same hours. For information, phone 22-2100. **York Tourist Bureau** is located at 105 Avon Terrace. For information, phone 096-41-1301.

Getting There

Westrail operates buses to Northam and York, departing Perth every morning. Fare is about $9 one way.

The Prospector rail service, also operated by Westrail, calls at Toodyay and Northam on its daily run to Kalgoorlie. Fares are a buck or two more than the bus. For information, schedules, and bookings, phone 09-326-2159.

It's about an hour-and-some's drive from Perth to any of the Avon Valley towns, and the distance between each of them averages 30 kilometers. The two main valley roads branch from Midland. Choose either the Great Eastern Highway to Northam and York or the Toodyay Road to Toodyay. If you're returning to Perth, take one route going and the other coming back.

THE SOUTH COAST

Below Fremantle the coastal road to Augusta, down in the southwest corner, passes nickel smelters, seaside resorts, industrial towns, established vineyards, and superb beaches (including W.A.'s best surfing spot). The inland route takes in some good bushwalking trails, dams and waterfalls, and a historic structure or two.

TO BUNBURY

Rockingham

Facing the Indian Ocean, Warnbo Sound, and Shoalwater Bay, Rockingham (pop. 25,000), 47 km south of Perth, once a major seaport from 1872-1908 (before Fremantle grabbed the honors), is now a favored holiday resort.

Rockingham Museum, corner Flinders Lane and Kent St., is a social history museum with memorabilia related to the district's early settlers. Hours are Tues.-Thurs. and Sat. 1-4:30 p.m., Sun. 10 a.m.- 4:30 p.m.

Safe **swimming beaches** are at the Foreshore Reserve, Rockingham Rd., and Point Peron, at the southern end of Cockburn Sound. Daily ferry service will transport you to **Penguin Island,** a colony of fairy penguins, and to **Seal Island,** with a colony of guess what.

A good Sunday **market** is held on Flinders Lane, 9 a.m.-4 p.m.

Good-value **accommodations** are offered at **CWA Rockingham,** 108 Parkin St. (tel. 527-9560). Two units house six to eight people. **Rockingham Ocean Clipper,** Patterson Rd. (tel. 527-8000), is a moderately priced hotel with room service, pool, TVs. Campsites and on-site vans are available at **Lakeside Caravan Park,** Mandurah Rd. (tel. 524-1182), and **Rockingham Palm Beach Holiday Village,** 37 Fisher St. (tel. 527-1515).

Yachties should note that the annual **Cockburn Sound Regatta,** W.A.'s largest, takes place here between Christmas and New Year's.

For local info (including ferry schedules), see the **Tourist Bureau,** 43 Kent St. (tel. 09-592-3464). Hours are Mon.-Fri. 9 a.m.-4:30 p.m., Sat.-Sun. 10 a.m.-4 p.m.

Transperth buses will get you here from Perth or Fremantle.

Mandurah

Another 29 km will bring you to Mandurah (pop. 11,000), one more beat-the-heat spot, situated at the entrance of Peel Inlet and at the mouth of Harvey Estuary (where dolphins are occasionally sighted).

Hall's Cottage, built in the early 1830s, is the local history museum. Hours are Sun. 2-5 p.m. Other historic structures are: **Christ Church** (1881), Scholl St. and Pinjarra Rd.; **Cooper's Cottage** (1845), Mandurah Terrace, near the bridge; **Eacott Cottage** (1842), Gibla St.; **Allandale** (1913), Estuary Rd., Dawesville (south of town); and **Hardy's Cottage** (built from local materials), Estuary Rd., Dawesville.

Kerryelle's Unique Collectors Museum, Gordon Rd. (tel. 09-535-1616), exhibits collections of gemstones, seashells, coins, banknotes, stamps, old bottles, dolls, and model cars. Hours are Mon.-Fri. 10 a.m.-4 p.m., Sat.-Sun. 10 a.m.-5 p.m. **House of Dunnies,** Henry Rd., Melros Beach (15 km south), features a series of handcrafted, folk dunnies (that means outhouses—a real Australian artform). **Threlfall Galleries,** Old Coast Rd. (tel. 534-2704), houses a collection of paintings and sketches depicting the local history.

Estuary Drive, a detour from the Old Coast Road, is the scenic route to Peel Inlet and Harvey Estuary, weaving through bushland and picnic spots. The **Foreshore Reserve,** in central Mandurah, is home to "Slim Jim," Australia's tallest cotton palm. More than 50 years old, Jim stands 39-plus meters high.

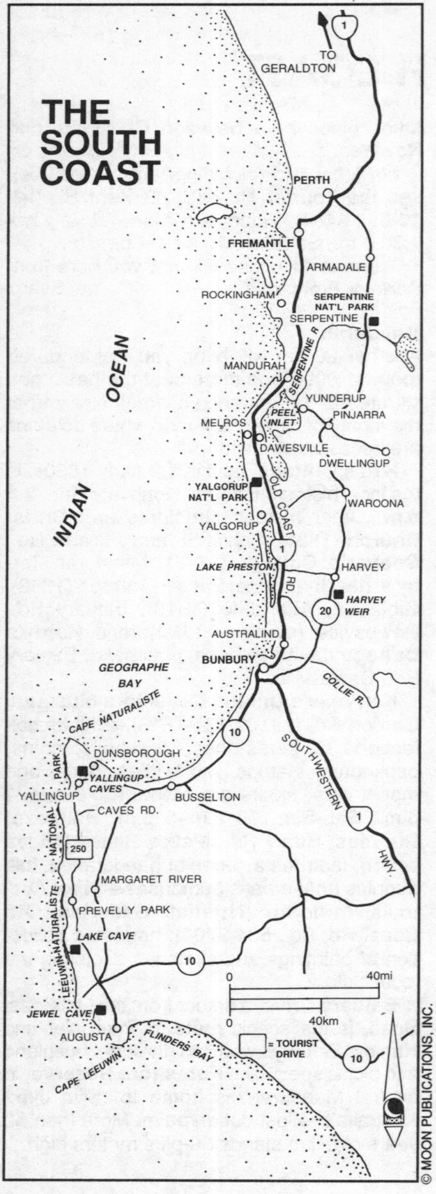

Marapana Deer Park, 13 Paganoni Rd. (tel. 537-1404), is W.A.'s first drive-through deer park and kangaroo sanctuary. Other wild things include donkeys, emus, and cockatoos. Visitors can feed the animals (food provided). Hours are daily 9 a.m.-4:30 p.m. See a large variety of Australian birds in natural bushland and water settings at **Western Rosella Bird Park,** Old Pinjarra Rd. (tel. 535-2104). Hours are daily 9:30 a.m.-5 p.m., closed Good Friday and Christmas Day.

Brighton Hotel, Mandurah Terrace (tel. 09-535-1242), has inexpensive pub rooms and counter meals. Also centrally located, the **Crabshell,** Gibson St. (tel. 535-5577), has motel rooms in the low-moderate range, plus air-conditioning, TVs, and a saltwater pool.

Some of the many camping and on-site van facilities are: **Peninsula Caravan Park,** Ormsby Terrace, at the entrance to Peel Inlet (tel. 535-2792); **Belevedere Caravan Park,** 153 Mandurah Terrace (tel. 535-1213); **Dawesville Caravan Park,** Old Coast Rd., Dawesville (tel. 582-1417); **Riverglen Caravan Park,** Pinjarra Rd. (tel. 535-1171); and **Timbertop Caravan Park,** Peel St. (tel. 535-1292).

For tourist info, contact **Mandurah Tourist Bureau,** 5 Pinjarra Rd. (tel. 535-1155). Hours are Mon.-Sat. 9-5.

Buses from Perth and Fremantle serve Mandurah.

Yalgorup National Park

About halfway between Mandurah and Bunbury, on a narrow coastal strip which includes Lake Clifton and Lake Preston, Yalgorup contains 11,545 hectares of heath, woodland, smaller lakes, interesting geological formations, and diverse bird- and wildlife (some birds migrate, visa-free, each year from the Soviet Union). Preston Beach, accessed through the park, offers good swimming and fishing.

Warning: Tiger snakes are known to inhabit the paperbark swamps and sedge lands; additionally, the lakes are *salty*—be sure to carry fresh water on long bushwalks during summer.

Australind

The name is a contraction of Australia-India, derived from an 1840s plan to colonize the area and breed horses for the Indian army. The ambitious venture never got off the ground, but the name sure stuck.

Located on the eastern bank of Leschenault Inlet, Australind (pop. 2,900), along with neighboring Bunbury, is famed for blue manna crabs—thousands of which are caught in the inlet each season.

The **Gemstone and Rock Museum,** 267 Old Coast Rd. (tel. 097-97-1401), contains displays of Bunbury agates and other Australian gemstones, natural crystals, as well as Aboriginal, American Indian, and English stone artifacts, *and* a cactus garden. Hours are Tues.-Thurs., Sat.-Sun. 10 a.m.-5 p.m.

St. Nicholas' Church (1860) Paris Rd., is supposedly the smallest church (four by seven meters) in Western Australia. **Henton Cottage** (1840), also on Paris Rd., once the Prince of Wales Hotel, is now an arts and crafts center.

The **scenic drive,** skirting the estuary, leads to crabbing and picnicking sites, while the **Collie River** offers recreational swimming, boating, and fishing.

Leschenault, 14 Old Coast Rd. (tel. 097-97-1352), on the estuary, is a moderately priced B&B with two guest rooms, TV lounge, and a pool. Campsites and on-site vans are available at **Leschenault Inlet Caravan Park,** Scenic Dr. (tel. 097-97-1095).

Most Bunbury-bound coaches from Perth call in at Australind.

The Inland Route

The South Western Highway runs from Perth, some 20 km inland, until it merges with the Old Coast Road at Bunbury. Various roads crisscross between the two highways, allowing travelers to venture inland through pine and jarrah forests or coastward en route.

Serpentine National Park (635 hectares), 52 km south of Perth, on the western edge of Darling Scarp, consists of lots of hills with steep gullies, granite outcrops and slopes, and the Serpentine River flowing through the middle. The park's most popular facility is its natural rock pool, ideal for swimming. Bushwalking is difficult due to steep trails, and rockclimbing is not recommended.

Pinjarra (pop. 1,340), 86 km south of Perth, was settled by farmers in 1830, making it one of W.A.'s oldest towns. Located on the estuary, this agricultural and timber-producing township features a number of historic structures. **Hotham Valley Tourist Railway** operates steam train journeys on the preserved 1913 railway line, May to October, between Pinjarra and the timber community of **Dwellingup.**

Waroona, 25 km south of Dwellingup, is the turnoff for Yalgorup National Park and Preston Beach. **Waroona Dam,** on Scarp Rd., is a power boating, water-skiing, and fishing area.

In 1916, the state's first controlled irrigation scheme was built at **Harvey** (pop. 2,480), 28 km beyond Waroona. If you drive out to **Harvey Weir,** three km east off Weir Rd., you can still see some of the workers' campsites. The 20-meter-tall **Big Orange** houses a small zoo, a miniature train, arts and crafts, and fruit and veggies.

Bunbury

Located 180 km south of Perth, on Koombana Bay, Bunbury (pop. 22,000) wears many hats—port, resort, industrial town, gateway to the Southwest, and blue-manna-crab-lovers' paradise.

King Cottage Museum, 77 Forest Ave., was built in the 1880s with bricks made from clay dug on the property. Examine pioneer memorabilia Sat.-Sun. 2-4 p.m. Other early structures are **St. Mark's Church** (1842), corner Flynn Rd. and Charterhouse St., and **St. Patrick's Cathedral** (1921), Parkfield Street. The **Cathedral Church of St. Boniface,** corner Parkfield and Cross streets, though only about 20 years old, is impressive for its interior built from native blackbutt wood.

The **Old Convent of Mercy** (1860s), Wittenoom St., has been turned into city and regional art galleries, and a community arts complex. Hours are Mon.-Fri. 10 a.m.-4:30 p.m., Sat.-Sun. 12-4:30 p.m. **Kelsue Arts Centre,** 60 Victoria St., exhibits regional paintings and crafts. Hours are Mon.-Fri. 9-5, Sat. 9 a.m.-noon.

The **Boyanup Transport Museum,** South Western Hwy. (20 minutes from Bunbury), houses the *Leschenault Lady* and *Koombana Queen,* two of Australia's oldest steam trains.

Catch some great views from: **Boulter Heights,** Withers Crescent; the **Lighthouse,** Apex Dr., off Malcom St.; **Marleston Hill Lookout Tower,** Apex Dr.; and along **Ocean Drive,** which follows the coastline for eight kilometers.

Big Swamp Bird Park, Prince Phillip Dr. (tel. 097-21-8380), has a walk-in aviary with 2,000 birds, a wildlife and waterfowl wetland, and a penguin pool and cave. Hours are Wed.-Fri. 1-5 p.m., Sat.-Sun. and holidays 10 a.m.-5 p.m.

Bunbury Backpackers, 22 Wittenoom St. (tel. 097-21-3359), offers hostel accommodations for $10 per night. **Prince of Wales,** Stephen St. (tel. 21-2016), has inexpensive pub rooms. **Clifton Beach Motel,** 2 Molloy St. (tel. 21-4300), and **Admiral Motor Inn,** 56 Spencer St. (tel. 21-7322), offer moderate rates and modern facilities.

WESTERN AUSTRALIA TOURISM COMMISSION

Cool dudes and hot surf mix on the South Coast.

Grab campsites and on-site vans at: **Bunbury Village Caravan Park,** corner Bussell Hwy. and Washington Ave. (tel. 95-7100); **Binningup Beach Caravan Park,** 31 Portland Dr. (tel. 20-1057); or **Punchbowl Caravan Park,** Ocean Dr. (tel. 21-4761).

For **food,** try the counter meals at the **Prince of Wales** on Stephen St. or the **Rose Hotel** on Victoria St.; also on Victoria Street is **Our Pancake Place.**

Tourist info can be obtained at the **Bunbury Tourist Bureau,** Carmody Place, in the old railway station (tel. 097-21-7922). Hours are Mon.-Fri. 8:30 a.m.-5 p.m., Sat. 9 a.m.-4 p.m., Sun. 9:30 a.m.-5:30 p.m.

South West Coachlines (tel. 09-324-2333) operate a daily Perth-Bunbury service, continuing to Busselton. Westrail's *Australind* makes the trip twice a day. **Westrail Coaches** meet the train at Bunbury and go on to Busselton and Margaret River. Augusta is its last stop.

FARTHER SOUTH

Busselton

Sheltered by Geographe Bay, Busselton (pop. 6,470) is a peaceful seaside resort not unlike Bunbury, 49 km to the north—a lazy place to fish, crab, and have beachy fun. It's also *real* close to **Yallingup,** which some say is Australia's very best surfing beach.

The **jetty,** two km long, used to be the longest wooden jetty in the Southern Hemisphere until 1978, when Cyclone Alby shortened its act. At the corner of Queen and Albert streets, see the *Ballarat,* a timber-hauling locomotive and W.A.'s first engine. Other historic sights are: **Wonnerup House and Old School** (1859), Layman Rd., Wonnerup; **Newtown House** (1851), Bussell Hwy., Vasse; and **St. Mary's Church of England** (1843), Queen St., the oldest stone church in the state.

The **Old Court House**, 4 Queen St., currently being restored, houses an art gallery, information center, book and craft shops, and artists' studios. Hours are Tues.-Sat. 10 a.m.-4 p.m. The **Old Butter Factory** (it's not "Ye Olde," but it has the same flavor), Peel Terrace, features 16 rooms of early pioneer furnishings, clothing, and artifacts, plus machinery and working models. Hours are Mon., Wed., Thurs., Sat.-Sun. 2-5 p.m., Fri. 9-11 a.m. **Bunyip Craft Centre,** Bunyip Rd., Wonnerup, exhibits the wares of more than 150 craftspeople. Hours are daily 9-5.

The **Oceanarium,** Geographe Bay Rd. near the jetty, displays local fish including a white pointer shark and stingrays. Hours are daily 9 a.m.-9 p.m. (Dec.-March), daily 9 a.m.-3 p.m. (April-Nov.).

Slightly north of Busselton, **State Tuart Forest,** Bussell Hwy. between Capel and the Sabina River, is the world's only natural tuart forest. Some trees are estimated to be 300-400 years old.

Dunsborough, 24 km west of Busselton, is a pretty holiday town. For an impressive view of the Indian Ocean, continue another 13 km to **Cape Naturaliste Lighthouse** at the tip of Geographe Bay.

Yallingup Beach, eight km southwest of Dunsborough, is surf heaven according to national and international sources. Follow Caves Road. **Yallingup Cave,** off Caves Rd. north of Yallingup, a limestone cave discovered in 1899, is highlighted with stalactites, stalagmites, pillars, columns, flowstone, cave crystals, helictites, and straws. Hours are daily 9:30 a.m.-3:30 p.m.

Hostel accommodations are available at **YHA,** 285 Geographe Bay Rd., Quindalup, two km south of Dunsborough (tel. 097-55-3107). Canoes, sailboards, and bicycles can be hired. The **YHA** in Yallingup, only two km from the beach, can be booked through the Dunsborough facility. Beds run $9 per night.

In Busselton, the **Geographe,** 28 West St. (tel. 52-1451), and **Villa Carlotta,** 110 Adelaide St. (tel. 52-1034), are inexpensive B&B guesthouses. The **Ship Resort,** 2 Albert St. (tel. 52-3611), offers moderately priced motel rooms. On the beachfront, **The Geographe Motor Inn,** Bussell Hwy., West Busselton (tel. 55-4166), is in the upper-moderate range.

This area has many caravan parks offering campsites and on-site vans. Some suggestions are: **Mandalay Caravan Park,** Bussell Hwy. (tel. 52-1328); **Acacia Caravan Park,** Bussell Hwy. (tel. 55-4034); and **Green Acres Beachfront Caravan Park,** 77 Gifford Rd., Dunsborough (tel. 55-3087).

For information, contact the **Busselton Tourist Bureau,** Southern Dr. (in the civic center), Busselton (tel. 52-1090), or the **Dunsborough Tourist Centre,** Naturaliste Terrace, Dunsborough (tel. 55-3517).

Margaret River

Midway between Yallingup and Margaret River, along Caves Road, is a cluster of wineries, with several more sprinkled around the Margaret River valley. Indeed, Margaret River (pop. 800), tiny though it may be, has come into its own as a wine-growing district that's giving the Swan Valley a run for the grapestakes.

The tourist-oriented township, 47 km south of Busselton, situated on the river of the same name, it is enticingly close to pounding surf beaches and calm swimming bays.

The **Old Settlement Craft Village,** on the banks of the Margaret River, depicts 1920s settlement life with period farm buildings and machinery, and crafts studios with gift items for sale. Hours are daily, except Christmas. View displays of seashells at **Bellview Shell Museum,** Bussell Highway. Hours are daily 8 a.m.-6 p.m. Interesting buildings include **St. Thomas More Catholic Church,** Mitchell St., and the **Greek Chapel,** Wallcliffe Road.

Set in bushland, **Eagle's Heritage,** Boodjidup Rd., boasts the largest collection of Australia's birds of prey. Hours are daily 10 a.m.-5 p.m. The **Marron Far,** Wickham Rd., 11 km south of town, produces thousands of the chestnut-like marron which can be seen in their various stages of development. Swimming and picnic facilities are provided. Hours are daily 10 a.m.-4 p.m. Guided tours are available several times each day.

Popular **Prevally Park,** south of the river-mouth, 10 km west of town, is known to have powerful surf. Follow Caves Rd. south through the lovely **Boranup Karri Forest.**

Mammoth Cave, 21 km south of Margaret River off Caves Rd., is noted for its fossil remains (including skeletons of Tasmanian

Margaret River vineyards welcome wineward travelers.

WESTERN AUSTRALIA TOURISM COMMISSION

tigers) and huge stalactites. **Lake Cave,** a few kilometers farther south, reached via a natural winding staircase down into a vast crater, contains an underground lake. The big bonanza, however, is **Jewel Cave,** eight km before Augusta, on Caves Road. Western Australia's largest tourist cave features one of the world's longest straws (5.9 meters long and more than 3,000 years old), as well as gigantic pillars, grotesque formations, and a mysterious underground river. All caves are open daily except Christmas, with guided tours available several times a day.

Margaret River Lodge, 220 Railway Terrace (tel. 097-57-2532), offers dorm and bunkhouse accommodations for $10 per night, plus use of swimming pool and TV lounge with open fireplace. If you've got four people to share with you, **Warrina Chalets,** Caves Rd. (tel. 57-2147), is a good deal. Self-contained chalets feature two bedrooms, cooking facilities, and log fireplaces. For campsites and on-site vans, contact **Margaret River Caravan Park,** 36 Station Rd. (tel. 57-2180), or **Riverview Caravan Park,** 8 Willmott Ave. (tel. 57-2270).

For cheap pub food, try the **Settler's Tavern,** Bussell Highway. The **Old Stone House,** Bussell Hwy., near the river, has steak, chicken, and fish on its menu, served in an atmospheric old house. Or pick your own strawberries (Oct.-April), raspberries, and boysenberries (Dec.-Jan.), and kiwi fruit (May-Aug.) at **Berry Farm Cottage,** Bessell Rd. (tel. 575-5054). Jams and wine are available for purchase. Hours are daily 10 a.m.-4 p.m.

Winery maps and other tourist information are available at **Margaret River Tourist Bureau,** corner Tunbridge Rd. and Bussell Hwy., Margaret River (tel. 097-57-2147).

Augusta

Situated near Australia's southwestern tip, Augusta (pop. 470) sits 320 km from Perth and is W.A.'s third-oldest settlement. Blue waters and white beaches, surfing and swimming sites, keep holidaymakers happy.

The **Augusta Historical Museum,** Blackwood Ave., displays early shipping relics and historical exhibits. Hours are Sat.-Thurs. 10 a.m.-noon and 2-4 p.m. (summer), Sat.-Thurs. 10 a.m.-noon (winter).

Hillview Lookout, Golf Links Rd. off Caves Rd., affords panoramic views and a directional plate to help you pick out nearby landmarks. **Cape Leeuwin Lighthouse,** at the end of Cape Leeuwin Rd., marks the junction of the Indian and Southern oceans and functions as an important meteorological station. Open to visitors Tues.-Sun. 9:30 a.m.-3:30 p.m. Nearby, see the waterwheel, built in 1895 to provide water for lighthouse builders, now encrusted in salt deposits.

The **YHA,** corner Bussell Hwy. and Blackwood Ave. (tel. 097-58-1433), has one cottage which accommodates eleven warm bodies. Beds run $8 per night. Inexpensive holiday flats with kitchen facilities are offered at **Calypso,** Ellis St. (tel. 58-1944). **Doonbanks Caravan Park,** Blackwood Ave. (tel. 58-1517), features a riverfront location with campsites and on-site vans.

If you're sick of counter meals, try the moderately priced **Colonial Restaurant,** Blackwood Avenue. The chow—I mean, *cuisine*—is French-influenced, despite the misleading name. Speaking of misleading names, the **Steak Cave,** corner Allnutt Terrace and Ellis St., serves inexpensive to moderate steaks and seafood in a *garden.*

Augusta Information Centre, 70 Blackwood Ave., Augusta (tel. 097-58-1695) assists with local inquiries.

THE SOUTHWEST

A few different routes will take you through W.A.'s Southwest to the coastal region, known as "The Great Southern," with glorious beaches, rugged ranges, capes and parks, holiday resorts, and historic settlements. The South Western Highway travels inland from Bunbury, meeting the coast (and the South Coast Highway) at Walpole. The Albany Highway runs *way* inland in a southeasterly direction from Perth, connecting with the coastal highway at Albany. Other itineraries include the Great Southern Highway from Perth, Vasse Highway (from Busselton), the Brockman Highway (north of Augusta), and the Muirs Highway (between Manjimup and Mount Barker).

THE SOUTH WESTERN HIGHWAY

Leaving Bunbury, you'll journey into **Donnybrook,** the center of W.A.'s oldest apple-growing region, where Granny Smith is queen of the crop (try to make this trip in late October when it's apple blossom time). Many artsy-craftsy shops and studios permeate this area. Farther along the landscape gives way to rolling hills, pine plantations, jarrah and karri forests, and—eventually—the big, blue sea.

One particularly scenic detour is the stretch from Balingup, 29 km beyond Donnybrook, to **Nannup,** an old timber town on the Vasse Highway. The narrow, winding, 45-km drive crosses, then follows, the Blackwood River.

Westrail buses serve South Western Highway towns and most Vasse Highway communities four times a week. Westrail's Bunbury-Albany bus travels to Denmark and Walpole/Nornalup once weekly.

Bridgetown

Settled in 1857, Bridgetown (pop. 1,520) is a peaceful little community 95 km south of Bunbury in the heart of jarrah land. Visit **Bridgedale,** 1 Hampton St., the town's oldest house, built in the 1860s and restored by the National Trust. Hours are Wed.-Sat. and Mon. 2-5 p.m., Sun. 11 a.m.-1 p.m. and 2-5 p.m.

The **Brierly Jigsaw Gallery,** Hampton St., is supposedly the country's only public jigsaw gallery. The collection includes puzzles from all over the world and visitors are invited to go to pieces over unfinished works. Hours are daily 9-5.

Good bushwalking and picnic spots are at **Bridgetown Jarrah Park** on Brockman Highway, and **Blackwood River Park** at the southern edge of town.

Carnaby Butterflies and Beetles, Bridge St., is 31 km northeast in Boyup Brook. The collection contains many rare specimens and is reputed to be the largest outside of the British Natural History Museum. Hours are daily 10 a.m.-4 p.m.

The **Bridgetown Hotel,** 38 Hampton St. (tel. 097-61-1641), offers inexpensive pub rooms which include breakfast. **Riverwood House,** South Western Hwy. (tel. 61-1862), is a moderately priced, no-smoking-allowed B&B. Campsites and on-site vans are available at **Bridgetown Caravan Park,** south Western Hwy. (tel. 61-1053).

Pick up tourist info at the **Bridgetown Tourist Bureau,** Hampton St. (tel. 61-1740). Hours are daily 9-5.

Manjimup

You can't miss the fact the Manjimup (pop. 4,150), 37 km from Bridgetown, is gateway to the Tall Timber Country—timber arches signal your arrival at both edges of town. Karri trees, more than a century old, can be seen in abundance.

Lumber up on the local timber industry at **Timber Park,** corner Rose and Edwards streets. The complex houses Timber Park Gallery, Bunnings' Age of Steam Museum, W.A.'s only timber museum, displays of vintage machinery and implements, and a variety of other attractions. For a *real* close-up look at the industry, put on a pair of sturdy shoes and visit the **Bunnings Diamond Mill,** Eastbourne Road. Tours are available Mon.-Fri. at 1, 2, and 3 p.m.

Seven kilometers down Seven Day Road, **Fonty's Pool,** once used to irrigate veggies, has been converted into a much-used swimming pool.

King Jarrah, three km along Perup Rd., is a 1,200-year-old tree with nearby walking trails. **Diamond Tree Tower,** 10 km south of town, sports a fire lookout atop a 51-meter karri tree.

A bit of log and decking is all that remains of **One Tree Bridge** on Graphite Rd., 22 km from town. A couple of kilometers from the bridge stand **The Four Aces,** 300- to 400-year-old giant karri trees.

Manjimup Caravan Park, Mottram St. (tel. 097-71-2093) has campsites and on-site vans, as well as a bunkhouse with dorm-type accommodations. **Fonty's Pool Caravan Park,** Seven Day Rd. (tel. 71-2105), is another option.

The **tourist bureau,** in Timber Park, provides the local skinny. Hours are daily 9-5. For information, phone 71-1831.

Pemberton

Set amid luscious karri forests, Pemberton (pop. 870) is reached via the Vasse Highway turnoff, 15 km south of Manjimup, or along the Vasse Highway from Nannup (76 km).

The **Pioneer Museum,** Brockman St., houses records, photos, and machinery from the early forestry settlement. Hours are daily 9-5. Restored **Brockman Saw Pit,** on the Pemberton-Northcliffe road, depicts lumber-cutting methods of bygone days. The **Pemberton Sawmill,** conversely, is highly automated and one of the largest in the Southern Hemisphere. The tourist bureau can arrange tours.

Follow the signs to **Gloucester Tree** off Brockman St., the world's highest fire lookout tree. The view from up top is great, but don't attempt the dizzying 60-meter climb unless you're in good shape and vertigo-free!

The **Rainbow and Tramway Trails** were the original 91-mm gauge railways which transported karri logs to the sawmill back in the 1920s. Sights along the Rainbow Trail include **Big Brook Arboretum** and **Big Brook Dam** (popular for fishing, canoeing, and sailboarding). Take a four-hour forest ride across rivers, streams, and old wooden bridges on the 1907 replica **Pemberton Tramway**. For bookings and information, phone (097) 76-1322.

Other pretty spots around Pemberton are **Beedelup Falls,** off Vasse Hwy., and the **Walk Through Karri,** in Beedelup National Park (this 400-year-old tree has a hole you can stand inside). **Warren National Park** also contains huge karri trees.

Trout lovers and fishers might want to visit **King Trout Farm,** Northcliffe Rd., or **Treenbrook Downs Trout Farm,** Old Vasse Highway. Both offer fishing gear rentals and cooking facilities. See how the fish you've just eaten breed at the **Trout Hatchery,** Pumphill Road. Hours are daily 9 a.m.-noon and 1-4 p.m.

Shops which sell local timbercrafts are: **Fine Woodcraft,** Dickenson St.; **Outpost Art and Crafts,** Brockman St.; **Warren River Arts and Crafts,** 63 Jamieson St.; and **Woodcraftsman's Studio,** Lot 6, Jamieson Street.

The **YHA Hostel,** Pimelea Rd. (tel. 097-76-1153), sits in the middle of the state forest, about 10 km northwest of town. Dorm beds run $8 per night. Moderately priced accommodations in town are available at **Gloucester Motel,** Ellis St. (tel. 76-1266), and **Tammeron Motor Lodge,** Widdeson St. (tel. 76-1019). Campsites with limited facilities are offered at **Pemberton Forest Camp** and **Warren National Park.** For information, phone 76-1200.

Tourist information is available at **Pemberton Tourist Centre,** Brockman St. (tel. 76-1133). Hours are daily 9-5.

Beyond Pemberton

Northcliffe, 28 km southeast of Pemberton, features more virgin karri forests. **Northcliffe Forest Park,** adjacent to town, is an ideal place to bushwalk, especially when the wild-

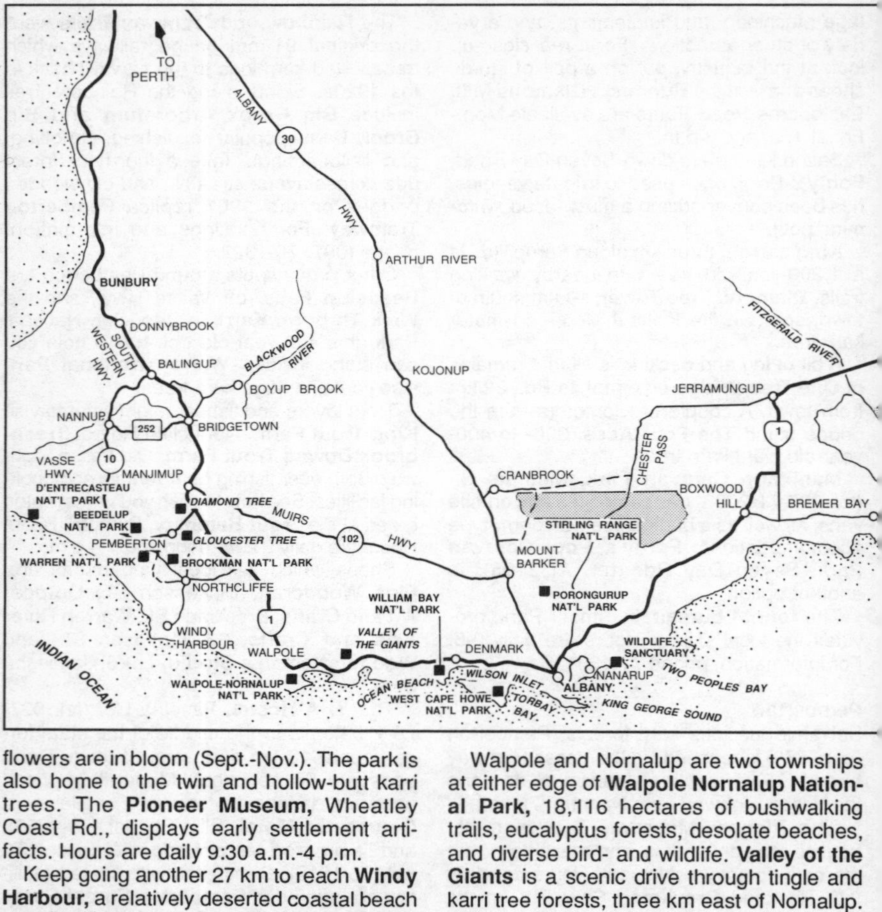

flowers are in bloom (Sept.-Nov.). The park is also home to the twin and hollow-butt karri trees. The **Pioneer Museum,** Wheatley Coast Rd., displays early settlement artifacts. Hours are daily 9:30 a.m.-4 p.m.

Keep going another 27 km to reach **Windy Harbour,** a relatively deserted coastal beach popular with rockclimbers for its huge D'Entrecasteaux Cliffs. Limited **camping** facilities (summer only, with a three-day max) are available at Windy Harbour Camping Area (tel. 097-76-7056).

Walpole/Nornalup

This coastal region with luscious bays, coves, and forests is reached via the South Western Highway, 119 km southeast of Manjimup. It marks the beginning of the South Coast Highway and the Rainbow Coast.

Walpole and Nornalup are two townships at either edge of **Walpole Nornalup National Park,** 18,116 hectares of bushwalking trails, eucalyptus forests, desolate beaches, and diverse bird- and wildlife. **Valley of the Giants** is a scenic drive through tingle and karri tree forests, three km east of Nornalup. Check out the view or stop for a picnic along **Knoll Drive,** also three km east of Nornalup in the park.

There's good fishing at **Walpole/Nornalup inlets, Mandalay Beach,** and on the **Frankland River. Deep River,** 36 km northwest of Walpole, is favored by canoeing enthusiasts.

Book ahead for dorm beds at the **YHA Hostel,** Dingo Flat Rd. off Valley of the Giants Rd. (tel. 098-40-8073). Beds are $5 per night; the property is on a beef and sheep station. **Tinglewood Homestead,** Walpole

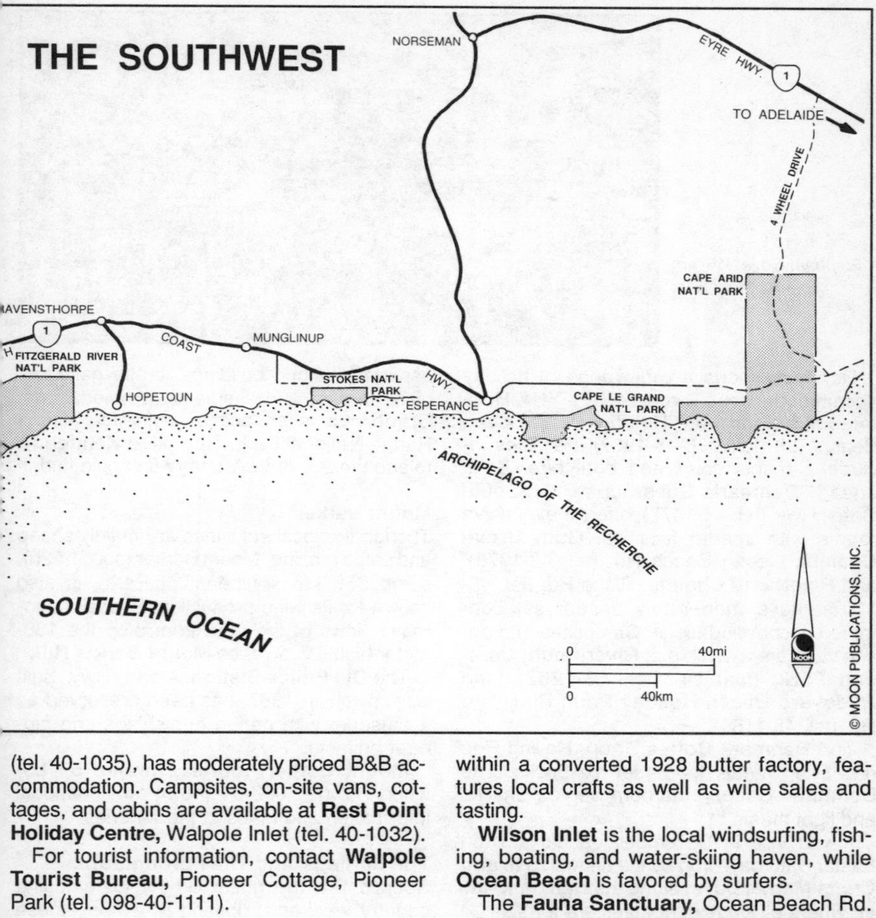

(tel. 40-1035), has moderately priced B&B accommodation. Campsites, on-site vans, cottages, and cabins are available at **Rest Point Holiday Centre,** Walpole Inlet (tel. 40-1032).

For tourist information, contact **Walpole Tourist Bureau,** Pioneer Cottage, Pioneer Park (tel. 098-40-1111).

Denmark

No, this is *not* a Danish settlement. Denmark (pop. 985), 66 km east of Nornalup, was named for Dr. Alexandra Denmark, an 1800s naval physician. Located on the Denmark River, recreational opportunities include surfing, swimming, fishing, water-skiing, bushwalking, and a couple of wineries.

In town, the **Denmark Gallery,** Scotsdale Rd., sells and exhibits local arts and crafts. **Groundrey Wines,** Mt. Shadforth Rd., housed within a converted 1928 butter factory, features local crafts as well as wine sales and tasting.

Wilson Inlet is the local windsurfing, fishing, boating, and water-skiing haven, while **Ocean Beach** is favored by surfers.

The **Fauna Sanctuary,** Ocean Beach Rd. adjacent to the caravan park, shelters a variety of marsupials including endangered species such as the tammar, woillie, darma, agile, and bettong. Hours are Tues.-Thurs. and Sat.-Sun. 2:30-4:30 p.m.

Best ocean and countryside views are from **Mount Shadford Scenic Drive** off South Coast Highway, along North St. to Mount Shadford Road. **William Bay National Park,** 15 km west of town, eight km off South Coast Highway, offers close-up views of rocks and reefs.

Elephant Cove, William Bay National Park

Denmark sports a wide range of holiday accommodations. The associate **YHA Hostel** is at **Wilson Inlet Holiday Park,** Ocean Beach Rd. (tel. 098-48-1267). Facilities include a tennis court and boat hire. Book ahead. **Denmark Guesthouse,** 31 South Coast Hwy. (tel. 48-1477), offers inexpensive rooms with shared facilities. **Gum Grove Chalets,** Ocean Beach Rd. (tel. 48-1378), and **Riverbend Chalets,** Riche Rd. (tel. 48-1107), have moderately priced, self-contained accommodations. Campsites and on-site vans are available at **Rivermouth Caravan Park,** Inlet Dr. (tel. 48-1262), and **Rudgyard Beach Holiday Park,** Rudgyard Rd. (tel. 48-1169).

The **Denmark Coffee Shop,** Holling Rd., has filling meals for under 10 bucks. The **Denmark Gallery** tearoom serves snacks and light meals.

If you visit in December, January, or on Easter Saturday, drop by the annual **Arts and Crafts Market Days,** along the Denmark River, where all kinds of goodies are for sale.

For tourist information, contact **Denmark Tourist Bureau,** Strickland St. (tel. 098-48-1265).

ALONG THE ALBANY HIGHWAY

From Perth, the Albany Highway passes through a hodgepodge of timber, sheep-farming, and mixed agricultural districts and small service towns. En route, **Williams, Arthur River,** and **Kojonup** are smattered with assorted historic buildings, crafts galleries, picnic areas, and simple accommodations. **Cranbrook** is an access point for Stirling Range National Park. Turn off at **Kendenup** to see the site of W.A.'s very first gold find.

Mount Barker

Though the local industries are mainly sheep and cattle grazing, Mount Barker (pop. 1,520), some 359 km southeast of Perth, is also known for its wine production. Eyeball panoramic views of the area from atop the 168-meter-high TV tower on **Mount Barker Hill.**

The **Old Police Station,** Albany Hwy., built by convicts in 1867, has been preserved as a museum with period furnishings and pioneer artifacts.

Mount Barker Tourist Bureau, 57 Lowood Rd. (tel. 098-51-1163), provides local information and maps to the wineries.

The Stirlings And The Porongurups

Sounds like the guest list for an amusing country weekend, doesn't it? Nope—these are two mountain ranges (and national parks) which rise dramatically from the surrounding flat agricultural plains. Both parks are close enough to Albany for a day outing.

Stirling Range National Park (115,671 hectares)—about 66 km long and 18 km wide —is filled with mountains, valleys, cliffs, delicate wildflowers, eucalyptus forests, rare plants, profuse bird- and wildlife, and moody mountain views. **Bluff Knoll** (1,073 meters) is W.A.'s third highest peak, and the park's most popular climb, followed by **Toolbrunup** (1,052 meters) and **Ellen Peak** (1,012 meters and a *hard* trek). You must obtain permission from the ranger on duty before embarking on any climb. If you don't feel like walking, a scenic drive will take you through the center of the park. For more information, phone (098) 27-9230.

Closer to Albany, **Porongurup National Park** (2,401 hectares) features karri forests, excellent birdwatching, panoramic views, easy walking tracks, and some of the world's oldest rock. Best bushwalks are to **Castle Rock** (570 meters), **Hayward's Peak** (610 meters), **Devil's Slide** (671 meters), **Nancy Peak** (662 meters), and **Morgan's View** (662 meters). For information, phone (098) 53-1095.

Campsites with limited facilities are available at Stirling Range National Park (tel. 098-27-9278). The **YHA,** Bluff Knoll turnoff (tel. 27-9229), has $10-per-night dorm beds within eight chalets. Campsites and on-site vans are also available at **Stirling Range Caravan Park,** Chester Pass Rd., South Borden (tel. 27-9229).

At Porongurup, **Karribank Guest House,** Main St. (tel. 098-53-1022), offers inexpensive rooms plus swimming pool, tennis court, and golf course. Adjacent to Karribank, **Porongurup Caravan Park,** Main St. (tel. 53-1022), rents campsites and on-site vans.

ALBANY

Albany (pop. 16,320) is Western Australia's oldest settlement and, because of its superb Princess Royal Harbour, it remained the state's principal port for years. Since its creation in 1826 as a military outpost to ward off French colonists, Albany (called Fredericks-town until 1832) has served as both a whaling port and coaling station. Situated 409 km southeast of Perth, this town is presently known as the Great Southern's commercial center as well as a tourist resort.

Historical Sights

Albany has preserved a number of its colonial buildings; most are on or around York St., Stirling Terrace, and the harbor foreshores.

The **Residency Museum,** Residency Rd., sits on the exact site where Major Edmund Lockyer and his merry band of convicts landed in 1826. Built in 1850, the museum was formerly the local magistrate's home and a naval training facility. Exhibits concern regional history as well as geography and environment. Hours are Mon.-Sat. 10 a.m.-5 p.m., Sun. 2-5 p.m. For information, phone (098) 41-4844.

Explore a full-scale replica of Lockyer's brig *Amity,* Port Rd., near the museum. You can go below deck and imagine how some 45 men and accompanying livestock survived in the cramped quarters. Hours are daily 9-5, closed Christmas Day. For information, phone 41-6885.

The one-time convict hiring depot and **Old Gaol** (1851) in Stirling Terrace now serves as a museum with WW I and II relics, pioneer tools and equipment, and Aboriginal artifacts. Hours are daily 10 a.m.-4:15 p.m. For information, phone 41-1401.

The restored **post office** (1870), Stirling Terrace, once housed the customs and bond store, court, holding cells, magistrate's and jury rooms. These days it's comprised of an Inter-Colonial Communications Museum and a restaurant. Hours are daily 10 a.m.-5 p.m.

Constructed of wattle and daub, **Patrick Taylor Cottage** (1832), Duke St., is thought to be Albany's oldest building. The cottage contains thousands of items, including early costumes, old clocks, and kitchenware. Hours are daily 2-4:15 p.m. For information, phone 41-6174.

Strawberry Hill Farmhouse, Middleton Beach Rd., built in 1836, is W.A.'s oldest farm. Originally the private home for the government resident, the two-story stone house has been restored by the National Trust. You can take tea in the adjoining miner's cottage. Hours are daily 10 a.m.-noon and 2-5 p.m., closed during July. For information, phone 41-3735.

Other historic structures include: **St. John's Church of England** (1848), York St., the first church consecrated in Western Aus-

Natural Bridge, near Albany

WESTERN AUSTRALIA TOURISM COMMISSION

tralia; **Albany Town Hall** (1888), refurbished in 1983 and converted into the Albany Town Theatre; **Vancouver Arts Centre** (1880s), used for regular arts and crafts exhibitions; and **Princess Royal Fortress** (1893).

Other Sights

Dog Rock, a huge granite outcrop near the corner of Middleton Road and Young Street, resembles the head of a big dog.

Emu Point, where Oyster Harbour enters the sea, is a favorite place for boating, swimming, and sailboarding. Other good swimming sites are **Middleton Beach, Ellen Cove,** and **Jimmy Newell's Harbour,** south of town.

Mount Clarence offers the best views plus a recast of the original Desert Mounted Corps memorial erected at Suez in 1932 (Gallipoli, remember?). You can see bullet marks in the granite blocks, transported from Suez. **Mount Melville** and **Marine Drive Lookout** offer other wide-eye panoramas.

On the coast, 21 km south of Albany, **Torndirrup National Park** affords a number of spectacular sights including the blowholes, Natural Bridge, and The Gap. To reach the park, follow Frenchman Bay Road.

At the end of Frenchman Bay Rd., **Whaleworld,** the former whaling station responsible for taking up to 850 whales each season (until operations ceased in 1978), now serves as a museum. Have a whale of a time learning the history of Albany's oldest industry. Hours are daily 9-5. For information, phone 44-4021.

Two Peoples Bay, 24 km east of Albany along Two Peoples Bay Rd., features more pretty beaches as well as a nature reserve which protects a small colony of noisy scrub birds. Believed to be extinct, the birds were rediscovered in 1961. Other nearby attractions are **Two Peoples Marron Farm,** Two Peoples Bay Rd., and **Valley Ponds Trout Farm,** Gull Rock Road.

Accommodations

The **YHA Hostel,** 49 Duke St. (tel. 098-41-3949), offers communal facilities and dorm beds for $8 per night, but fills up quickly. For inexpensive basic pub rooms, try the **Albany Hotel,** York St. (tel. 41-1031). Breakfast is included in the tariff. **Parkville Colonial Guesthouse,** 136 Brunswick Rd. (tel. 41-3704), and **Suffolk House,** 5 Harry St., Mount Melville (tel. 41-8571), are inexpensive B&Bs.

Moderately priced motels are the **Travel Inn,** 191 Albany Hwy. (tel. 41-4144); **Albany Dock Rock,** 303 Middleton Rd. (tel. 41-4422); and the **Albany Motel,** 270 Albany Hwy. (tel. 41-7399).

You'll find many caravan parks to choose from. Some which offer both campsites and on-site vans are: **Mount Melville Caravan Park,** 22 Wellington St. (tel. 41-4616); **Middleton Beach Caravan Park,** Flinders Parade, Middleton Beach (tel. 41-3593); **Panorama Caravan Park,** Frenchman Bay Rd. (tel. 44-4031); and **Emu Beach Caravan Park,** Medcalfe Parade, Emu Point (tel. 44-1147).

Food

The **London Hotel,** Stirling Terrace, and the **Premier Hotel,** York St., both offer pub meals. For burgers, pancakes, and other light meals, try **Dylan's on the Terrace,** 82 Stirling Terrace.

Earl of Spencer, Earl and Spencer streets, dates from the 1870s and is renowned for its ale, pasta, steaks, and great harbor view. Prices are inexpensive to moderate. The **Penny Post,** 33 Stirling Terrace, in the old Post Office, features moderately priced seafood specialties and cook-your-own steaks in a colonial atmosphere.

Kooka's, 204 Stirling Terrace (tel. 41-5889), offers excellent fresh and nouvelle-ish cuisine in a colonial cottage dominated by a kookaburra theme. Meals are in the expensive range and reservations are advised.

Information

For local information, contact the **Albany Tourist Bureau,** corner York St. and Peels Pl. (tel. 098-41-1088). Hours are Mon.-Fri. 8:30 a.m.-5:30 p.m., Sat., Sun., and public holidays 9 a.m.-4 p.m.

Pick up street maps and other road info at the **Royal Automobile Club,** 110 Albany Hwy. (tel. 41-1935).

Getting There

Skywest (tel. 09-323-1188) operates daily flights from Perth Airport to Albany.

Westrail provides daily coach service from Perth, traveling to Denmark once each week. Most of the national coach lines stop at Albany on their daily Adelaide-Perth run.

If you're driving, the Albany Highway from Perth (409 km) should get you here in under five hours. The South Western and South Coast highways from Bunbury (402 km, not counting detours) will take about the same time.

Getting Around

Love's Bus Service, the local transport company, travels weekdays and Saturday mornings to points along the Albany Highway, as well as to Middleton Beach, Spencer Park, and Emu Point.

Contact the **Albany YHA Hostel** for bicycle hire outfits (about $5 per day) and cheap tours into the Stirling Ranges or up and down the coast ($10-25). The **tourist bureau** can also arrange local tours.

THE WESTERN BIGHT

From Albany to Esperance, the South Coast Highway teases its way along the western end of the Great Australian Bight—a 480-km odyssey through capes and parks, bays and beaches.

Out Of Albany

Turn off at Boxwood Hill, 117 km northeast of Albany, and veer coastward another 63 km to **Bremer Bay,** a popular location for fishing, boating, water-skiing, and scuba diving.

Back on South Coast Highway, **Jerramungup** is about 60 km north of Boxwood Hill. The **Military Museum,** on the highway, features a large privately owned collection of fighting memorabilia including vehicles, badges, medals, guns, and swords.

Dog Rock, Albany's bow wow landmark

Ravensthorpe

A former gold and copper mining town, Ravensthorpe (pop. 330) is 114 km northeast of Jerramungup.

Cocanarup Homestead, classified as a historical site by the National Trust, is made up of several century-old stone buildings. The early 1900s Dance Cottage Museum is home to the local historical society's memorabilia collection. The old smelter sits three km from town, while ruins of a baked-out bakery and a played-out gold mine can be explored at **Kundip,** some 20 km farther. If you want to check out the **Raventhorpe Range** at the northern end of Foater Road, beware of the old mine shafts in that area!

Ravensthorpe Motel, junction Hopetoun and Esperance roads (tel. 098-38-1053), and **Palace Motor Hotel** (tel. 38-1005) both offer inexpensive to moderate accommodations. Campsites are available at **Ravensthorpe Caravan Park,** Morgan St. (tel. 38-1050).

Local info can be obtained at the **Ravensthorpe Tourist Information Centre,** Morgan St. (tel. 38-1163). Hours are Mon.-Fri. 8:30 a.m.-5 p.m.

Below And Beyond Ravensthorpe

Hopetoun, situated on the coast 50 km south of Ravensthorpe, offers more secluded bays, beaches, inlets, and fishing holes. Whales can often be seen near these shores in August and September.

Fitzgerald River National Park, accessed either from Hopetoun, Jerramungup, or Bremer Bay, features 240,000 hectares of sand plain, river valleys, narrow gorges, rugged ranges, coastal cliffs, sandy beaches, visible wildlife, and approximately 1,350 species of wildflowers and native plants. Check in with a ranger before you go bushwalking, and be sure to carry plenty of water. Swimmers should be aware of dangerous coastal rips. Some park areas are restricted at certain times of the year. For information, phone (098) 35-5043.

Stokes National Park (10,667 hectares), reached via gravel roads off the South Coast Highway east of Young River, is a coastal region for bushwalking, ocean fishing, inlet swimming, and birdwatching (seals have been sighted as well). Facilities are limited and you must carry your own water. For information, phone (098) 76-8541.

ESPERANCE

Beautifully situated across from the Recherche Archipelago, 730 km southeast of Perth, versatile Esperance (pop. 6,375) wears three hats—seaport, seaside resort, and agricultural center.

Named for the French frigate *L'Esperance* in 1772, the town was settled in 1863 when the Dempster brothers arrived with their families after an overland trek. Some 30 years later, with the advent of gold exploration, Esperance boomed as a port, then faltered again when the gold rush rushed out. Then, shortly after World War II *and* after a lot of research, it was discovered that trace elements were missing from the surrounding soil, which prohibited agriculture. The situation was remedied and *voilà*—a rich agrocenter and grain-loading port.

Sights

Esperance Municipal Museum, James St., features early machinery, tools, furnishings, and—best of all—a big Skylab display (Esperance was the lucky spot where Skylab decided to fall to earth in 1979). The museum park also houses **Craft Village,** where locally produced arts and crafts items can be purchased. Hours are daily 1:30-4:30 p.m. For information, phone (090) 71-1579.

Local crustaceans, fish, other marinelife, and shells are on view at **George's Oceanarium,** The Esplanade. Hours are Tues.-Sun. 10 a.m.-4 p.m., Sept.-May. For information, phone 71-2940.

The original Dempster Homestead, Dempster and Emily streets, is privately owned and can only be admired from the road.

The **Australian Parrot Farm,** Fisheries Rd., Yarrumun, exhibits a large number of parrots, pheasants, guinea fowl, and peafowl, plus a collection of more than 2,000 vintage bottles. Hours are daily 9-5. For information, phone 76-1284.

Salt-tolerant algae and salina are what makes **Pink Lake** pink—and sometimes pur-

look out over the astounding, pounding southern coast

ple. Some years, as much as 500,000 tons of salt are dredged from the lake, three km out of town, along Pink Lake Road.

Twilight Beach Scenic Drive leads from town up to Observatory Point and Lookout, then to Pink Lake. **Rotary Lookout,** on Wireless Hill, affords yet another town and bay vista.

Twilight Cove, near the town center, is a good safe swimming and fishing beach.

Islands And Parks

The **Recherche Archipelago,** also known as the Bay of Isles, is comprised of approximately 100 islands with sandy beaches, turquoise waters, plentiful water birds, and seal and penguin colonies. The MV *Grand* makes scenic two-hour cruises of the archipelago, or the MV *Sea Lion* will take you over to Woody Island—a wildlife sanctuary—for a five-hour picnic trip (Jan., Feb., and major holidays). Contact the tourist bureau for information.

Cape Le Grand National Park (31,390 hectares), 48 km southeast of Esperance, has some dynamite coastal scenery. Sand plains, freshwater pools, swamps, and massive granite outcrops (Mt. Le Grand, 353 meters, is the highest), make up the remaining terrain—home to birds, reptiles, grey kangaroos, possums, and bandicoots. A marked 15-km walking trail will lead you along the coast from Cape Le Grand to Rossiter Bay. Come September through November, when the wildflowers are in bloom. For information, phone (090) 75-9022.

Cape Arid National Park (279,415 hectares), 125 km east of Esperance, can be reached by conventional vehicle, but tracks within the park are only suitable for four-wheel-drive (weather permitting). Cape Arid also features splendid coastal scenery, granite outcrops, and excellent lookouts as well as diverse fauna. You must obtain permission from a park ranger before rockclimbing; swimmers should be wary of rips. Cape *Arid* also translates as bring your own water. For information, phone (090) 75-0055.

Accommodations

The **YHA Hostel,** Goldfields Rd. (tel. 090-71-1040), is two km east of the town center. Eight dorm and two twin rooms accommodate 110 happy hostelers. Dorm beds cost $8 per night.

Moderately priced self-contained holiday flats are available at: **Captain Huon,** 5 The Esplanade (tel. 71-2383); **Brighton Place,** 73 The Esplanade (tel. 71-2137); and **Esperance Beachfront Resort,** 19 The Esplanade (tel. 71-2513).

Rent a campsite or on-site van at **Bather's Paradise Caravan Park,** corner Westmacott and Chaplin streets., (tel. 71-1014); **Bush-**

land Caravan Park, Collier Rd. (tel. 71-1346); **Esperance Bay Caravan Park,** corner The Esplanade and Harbour Rd. (tel. 71-2237); or **Pink Lake Caravan Park,** Pink Lake Rd. (tel. 71-2424). Campsites with limited facilities are offered at both Cape Le Grand and Cape Arid national parks.

Information

For tourist and tour information, contact the Esperance Tourist Bureau, Dempster Street, in Museum Village (tel. 090-71-2330). Hours are daily, 9-5.

Getting There And Away

Skywest (tel. 09-323-1188) flies daily from Perth.

Three times each week the Prospector Perth-Kalgoorlie train connects with a Westrail coach to Esperance. If you'd rather take the bus all the way, Westrail coaches also depart Perth for Esperance three times a week. Some of the national bus companies stop at Esperance on the Perth-Adelaide route.

If you're heading up to the Goldfields, take the Coolgardie-Esperance Highway north out of town, straight up to Coolgardie (375 km north of Esperance and 39 km southwest of Kalgoorlie), or turn onto the Eyre Highway at Norseman (207 km) for the eastward trek across the Nullarbor Plain (see "Crossing The Nullarbor," in the South Australia chapter).

THE WHEATLANDS

Don't be shafted by the boring name—this agricultural heartland, stretching from Perth to Coolgardie and north of Albany to the Great Eastern Highway, has some wild rock formations, Aboriginal rock carvings, and worth-a-stop historical sights.

YORK TO HYDEN

Beginning at the Avon Valley, weave and wind your way through side-ways and by-ways to various Wheatlands attractions, ending at the simply *awesome* Wave Rock.

The Yoting-Kellerberrin Road, beyond the small wheaty township of Quairading (166 km east of Perth), accesses both **Kokerbin Rock,** with caves, a lookout, and a scenic drive, and Mount Stirling, a huge granite outcrop often climbed for the view.

Bruce Rock, 77 km east of Quairading, is another noteworthy outcrop. Bruce Rock Museum, 24 Johnson St., contains pioneering items.

Situated 68 km southwest of Bruce Rock, **Corrigin** (pop. 840) dates back to the 1880s. The **Pioneer Museum,** corner Kinjin Rd. and Kirkwood St., displays early machinery and pioneering memorabilia. Locally produced handicrafts can be purchased at the **Craft Cottage,** Walton Street.

Gorge Rock, 23 km southeast of Corrigin, is a swimming area created from a dammed gorge. **Jilakin Rock,** 50 km southeast, through Kulin, is a gray granite monolith overlooking a 1,214-hectare lake surrounded by bushland.

Wave Rock, three km outside Hyden and 108 km southeast of Corrigin, is the destination of most Wheatland travelers. This enormous 50-meter-high granite rock formation—shaped by wind and rain—is estimated to be 2,700 million years old. It resembles a huge curling wave made even more distinctive by vertical bands of color on its sloping face. A marked track will lead you around the base of Wave Rock over to **Hippo's Yawn,** another unique outcrop. **Bates Cave,** 21 km northwest of Hyden, features Aboriginal hand paintings.

Moderately priced accommodations in Hyden are offered at **Dieps B&B,** 17 Clayton St. (tel. 098-80-5179), and **Hyden Hotel,** 2 Lynch St. (tel. 80-5052). Campsites are available at **Wave Rock Caravan Park,** Wave Rock (tel. 80-5022).

The **Hyden Tourist Information Centre** is located on Lynch St. (tel. 80-5089).

THE GREAT SOUTHERN HIGHWAY

Situated on the Avon River, 66 km south of York, Beverley is known for its **Aeronautical Museum,** Vincent St., with displays of avia-

WESTERN AUSTRALIA TOURISM COMMISSION

Don't try riding this wave!

tion equipment, model airplanes, and the *Silver Centenary,* W.A.'s first privately made airplane. Historical buildings include **St. Paul's Church** (1862), Avon Dr., **St. John's in the Wilderness** (1895), Dale-Beverley Rd., and Beverley's oldest surviving building (and now a museum), **Dead Finish** (1872), 138 Vincent Street.

Narrogin (pop. 5,000), 137 km south of Beverley, is the commercial hub of this district. The **Court House Museum,** Norseman Rd., gives insight into early industry and society. **Albert Facey's Homestead,** on the road between Wickepin and Nomans Lake, was built by the colorful character of the same name. Facey's autobiography, *A Fortunate Life,* later became a miniseries. The homestead is open Tues.-Thurs. and Sat.-Sun. 9-5.

Attractions around **Wagin,** 50 km down the highway, include the **Giant Ram Tourist Park** (15 meters long and seven meters high —called the "largest ram in the Southern Hemisphere." Are there others?), **Wagin Historical Village,** and nearby **Mount Latham,** for rockclimbing and bushwalking. **Puntapin Rock** is another large and intriguing rock formation. **Lake Dumbleyung,** 39 kilometers east of Wagin, is the spot where Donald Campbell broke the world water speed record in 1964. Around a portion of the lake is a nature reserve with varied birdlife, a scenic drive, and lookout point.

Settled in the 1840s, **Katanning** (pop. 4,415) mixes a bit of history with modern services. The Old Mill (1889), Main St., houses early machinery and equipment, as well as a crafts shop. Hours are Mon.-Fri. 10 a.m.-4 p.m., Sat. 10 a.m.-12:30 p.m.

The Great Southern Highway joins the Albany Highway 85 km south of Katanning.

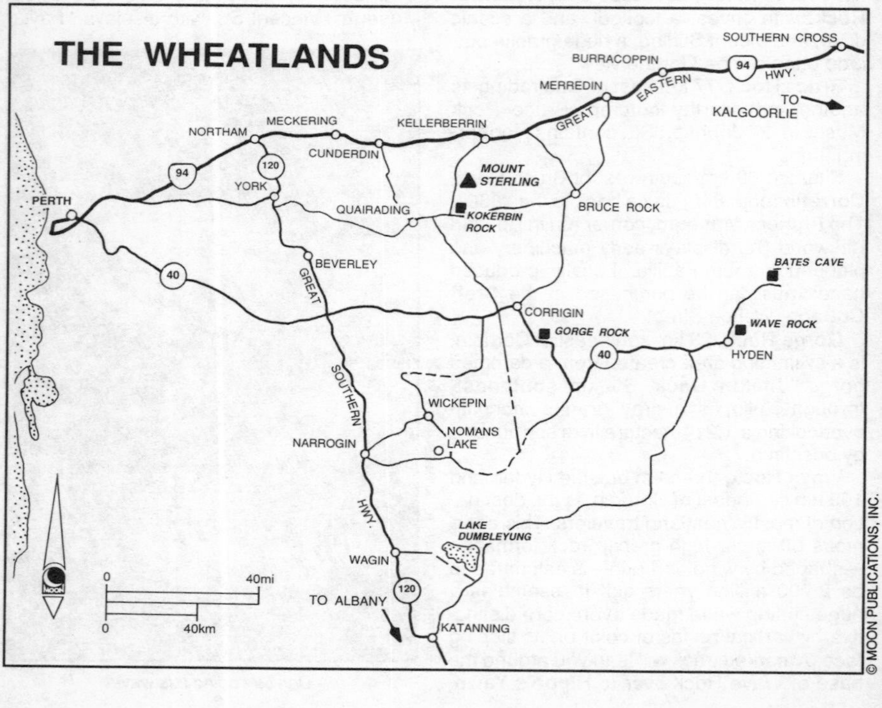

THE GREAT EASTERN HIGHWAY

The 500-km stretch from York to Kalgoorlie is also known as the Goldfields Heritage Trail and follows the original 1860s route established by surveyor Charles Hunt.

Meckering, a little rural town 133 km east of Perth, was severely damaged in a 1968 earthquake. Though the town was immediately rebuilt, you can see mementos of the destruction at the tourist center gazebo.

The Municipal Museum at **Cunderdin,** 24 km east, displays assorted vintage farm machinery, tractors, photos, and other relics. Hours are daily 11 a.m.-5 p.m. Cunderin Hill itself puts on a good spring wildflower show.

Kellerberrin, another 47 km eastward, is one of the route's oldest settlements. The District Museum displays yet more early implements. Kellerberrin Hill, north of the post office, is a good view spot. You can also turn off here for Mount Stirling and Kokerbin Rock.

Situated on both the Perth-Kalgoorlie railway line and the Great Eastern Highway, **Merredin** (pop. 3,520) represents the commercial center for this region. The **Old Railway Station** on the highway is a group of four 1920s buildings that now serve as a museum and arts center. Hours are daily 9 a.m.-3 p.m. Two walks which start off from the railway station are **Merredin Peak Heritage Trail,** an easy jaunt around the town's historic buildings, and a longer (six km) hike around the peak. **Burracoppin Rock,** 24 km east of Merredin, is a large rock outcrop popular with picnickers.

Merredin Oasis Hotel, 8 Great Eastern Hwy. (tel. 090-41-1133), has moderately priced, air-conditioned rooms with TVs, and a swimming pool. Campsites and on-site vans are available at **Merredin Travel Centre Caravan Park,** Great Eastern Hwy. (tel. 41-1535).

Western Australia's gold rush began in 1887 at **Southern Cross,** 109 km east of Merredin. Though the fever quickly moved east to Coolgardie and Kalgoorlie, Southern Cross (pop. 800) still retains its wide streets and historic buildings. **Yilgarn History Museum** (1892), Antares St., was originally the Mining Registrar's Office, then the town courthouse. Exhibits trace the town's early settlement and include mineral displays. Hours are Mon.-Sat. 9 a.m.-noon, 1:30-4 p.m. Other turn-of-the-century buildings are the **Forrester's Resource Centre** and **Lisignolis Shop,** both on Antares Street. **Wimmera Hill,** site of W.A.'s first major gold discovery, offers good views of the area.

Southern Cross marks the end of the Wheatlands and the beginning of the 188-km desert stretch to Coolgardie and the goldfields.

THE GOLDFIELDS

Western Australia's goldfields are hot, flat, and extremely arid, punctuated with deserted outposts, preserved ghost towns, and its semi-thriving hub, Kalgoorlie. The streets are wide, shoot-'em-out affairs (made that way so camel trains could turn around easily), and many of the buildings exude the wealth and opulence associated with gold frenzy. Try to ignore the cranes, conveyers, and tailings dumps, and envision the Golden Mile's hundred mines all flourishing simultaneously.

History

Until that 1887 gold strike in Southern Cross, Western Australia received merely poor-relative status from the eastern colonies. But what brings relatives flocking faster than gold? Though the Southern Cross find quickly ran dry, in 1892 prospector Arthur Bayley (acting on a hot tip given by a man he'd saved from death) staked a claim at Bayley's Reward, a huge gold reef about three km east of Coolgardie. By 1900, the town's population soared to 15,000, dropping considerably by 1905 when the rush rushed elsewhere. Bayley's Reward, however, continued to produce gold until 1963.

In 1893, Irish prospectors Paddy Hannan, Tom Flannigan, and Dan Shea found gold near the site of the present Mount Charlotte Mine. Though surface gold soon ran out, a bigger and deeper find was discovered along the Golden Mile (reputedly the world's richest square mile of gold-bearing earth), prompting companies and diggers to go underground. At one time, the Golden Mile boasted more than 100 working mines.

One enormous problem was the lack of water, or the pollution of what water there was: miners were dropping like flies from thirst and disease. Engineer C.Y. O'Connor came up with the perfect invention—a 563-km wood and pitch water pipe from Mundaring Weir, near Perth, to Kalgoorlie. Mocked and taunted by ignorant disbelievers, O'Connor nonetheless persevered with his pipeline. Unfortunately, three days after the water pumps were started and there was still nary a trickle, the despondent O'Connor shot himself to death—not realizing the water would take two weeks to travel such a distance. Dead or not, he'd solved the problem. By 1903 water began filling Kalgoorlie's new reservoir.

KALGOORLIE

"Queen of the Golden Mile," Kalgoorlie (pop. 20,000) sits 596 km east of Perth at the end of the Goldfields Heritage Trail.

Kalgoorlie goldfields continued to produce during the lean 1920s, ebbing and falling during depression and war. Just as the mines were faltering economically (Mount Charlotte Mine is the only big operation), the 1960s nickel boom brought renewed prosperity—and tourism—to town.

Sights

Kalgoorlie's biggest tourist attraction is **Hainault Tourist Gold Mine,** Boulder Block Rd., Fimiston (on the Golden Mile). See mining memorabilia and the inner (or under) workings. Visitors can take a 30-minute surface tour, 90-minute underground tour, or both. Tours depart several times daily and cost about $9 each, though you can explore the surface displays on your own, for free. For information, phone (090) 93-1065.

Learn the history and development of W.A.'s eastern goldfields at the **Golden Mile Museum,** 22 Outridge Terrace. This building is the former British Arms Hotel, supposedly the narrowest pub in Australia. Hours are daily 10:30 a.m.-4:30 p.m., closed Good Friday and Christmas Day. For information, phone 21-1419.

The **W.A. School of Mines and Mineral Museum,** Egan St., features displays of minerals, meteorites, gold nuggets, and gem-

WESTERN AUSTRALIA TOURISM COMMISSION

Kalgoorlie's architectural treasures

stones. Hours are Mon.-Fri. 9 a.m.-1 p.m. and 2-4 p.m. For information, phone 21-1800.

The 1903 **Town Hall,** Hannan St., houses historical memorabilia and an art gallery. Outside the building, a bronze statue of Paddy Hannan holding his waterbag, doubles as a drinking fountain.

Other architectural delights on Hannan St. are the **Post Office** and the **Exchange Hotel.**

Paddy Hannan's Tree, Outridge Terrace, near the head of Hannan St., marks the spot where Paddy found Kalgoorlie's first gold back in 1893.

Mount Charlotte Reservoir off Park St., near the end of Hannan St., is where C.Y. O'Connor ended his pipeline. The lookout gives a good town view.

Hammond Park, Lyall St., Lamington, is a flora and fauna reserve with tame emus and kangaroos and a detailed model of a Bavarian castle. Hours are daily 9 a.m.-4 p.m.

The **Arboretum,** adjacent to Hammond Park, features a marked walking trail to individual trees and a variety of birdlife.

Illegal And Legal

Amsterdam it ain't, but Hay Street is lined with brothels, à la Dutch treat, where costumed ladies of the night beckon the menfolk passing by. Though officialdom turns its eagle eye from this long-practiced local activity, it is not actually legal.

The **Two Up School,** Broad Arrow Rd., six km north of Kalgoorlie, is Australia's only legalized bush two-up school. This famous Aussie gambling game has been played in Kalgoorlie since the beginning of the gold rush. Hours are Mon.-Sat. 1:30 p.m.-dark, Sun. 11 a.m.-dark. Closed on race days and the mine's pay day. Don't bring alcohol and don't come if you're under 18 years old. For information, phone (090) 21-1413.

Accommodations

Would you want to stay anywhere but one of the classic old pubs? Find inexpensive to moderate rooms at: the **Exchange Hotel,** Hannan St. (tel. 090-21-2833); **York Hotel,** Hannan St. (tel. 21-2337); **Palace Hotel,** Hannan St. (tel. 21-2788); and **Surrey House,** 9 Boulder Rd. (tel. 21-1340). The **Star and Garter,** 497 Hannan St. (tel. 21-3004), has motel rooms in the expensive range, TVs, and a swimming pool.

Campsites and on-site vans are available at: **Golden Village Caravan Park,** Hay St. (tel. 21-4162); **Goldminer Tourist Caravan Park,** Great Eastern Hwy. (tel. 21-3713); and **Prospector Caravan Park,** Great Eastern Hwy. (tel. 21-2524).

Food

All of the pubs serve filling counter meals at reasonable prices. Hannan Street is lined with taverns and eateries. The **Exchange** and **York** hotels are especially recommended. **Matteo's,** 113 Hannan St., makes up good pizzas, and the **Victoria Cafè** is a popular local breakfast spot. The **Broccoli Forest Health Food Store and Kitchen,** at the top end of Hannan St., serves eat-in or takeaway vegetarian meals, and stocks bulk nuts, fruits, grains, and other natural foods.

If you've just hit gold, reserve a table at the very expensive **Amalfi,** 409 Hannan St. (tel. 21-3088). This long-established Italian restaurant is famous for its scaloppine.

Kalgoorlie brews its own beer, aptly named **Hannan's.**

Shopping

Got that gold fever? You can buy prospecting supplies and metal detectors at **International Lapidary,** 67 Hannan St. (tel. 21-3017).

Information And Services

For local information and tour bookings, contact **Kalgoorlie-Boulder Tourist Centre,** 250 Hannan St., Kalgoorlie (tel. 090-21-1413). Hours are Mon.-Fri. 8:30 a.m.-5 p.m., Sat.-Sun. 9 a.m.-5 p.m.

A branch of the **Royal Automobile Club** is at the corner of Hannan and Porter streets. For information, phone 21-1511.

For **emergencies,** phone 000, or the **Kalgoorlie Regional Hospital** (tel. 21-2222).

Getting There

Both **Ansett WA** (tel. 09-323-1111, or 13-1300 toll free) and **Skywest** (tel. 09-323-1188) fly to Kalgoorlie daily from Perth. **Goldfields Air Services** (tel. 090-93-2116) does the Esperance-Norseman-Kalgoorlie route several times each week.

The *Indian-Pacific* and *Trans-Australian* both stop at Kalgoorlie on their way to and from Perth several times each week. The *Prospector* leaves East Perth Rail Terminal every day except Saturday for the eight-hour trip. For information and bookings, phone Westrail (tel. 326-2159).

Greyhound and **Pioneer** coaches travel through Kalgoorlie on their Perth-Adelaide services.

Getting Around

The local **bus** operates regular runs between Kalgoorlie and Boulder for $1 each way. The tourist center has timetables.

Taxis are available 24 hours a day; a ride between the town and the airport is about $10. For bookings, phone 21-2177. All of the major car rental firms are located at Kalgoorlie Airport. Bicycles can be hired for $12 per day from **Johnston Cycles,** 76 Boulder St. (tel. 21-1157).

Goldrush Tours, Palace Chambers, Maritana St. (tel. 21-2954), offer a variety of guided tours and excursions including town tours ($17), gold detector tours ($20), Coolgardie ($24), and ghost towns ($29).

Tour the local **Royal Flying Doctor** base, 56 Piccadilly St., Mon.-Fri. at 2:30 p.m. For information, phone 21-2899.

VICINITY OF KALGOORLIE

Looking for gold? It's still out there. Grab a metal detector and join other weekend prospectors, but be sure you're well prepared—carry water, spare parts, and good maps. Check in with the tourist center and Royal Automobile Club before venturing out into this rugged, remote region. Both Boulder and Coolgardie are popular pit stops. Good luck.

Boulder

Boulder (pop. 5,600) is actually a satellite town of Kalgoorlie, built during the boom to service the Golden Mile. Boulder Block pubs used to see nonstop action but, alas, the town is much quieter these days.

The **Boulder Town Hall,** on Burt St., features an ornate clocktower and an exhibition of works by local artists. Next door, the **Goldfields War Museum** houses military artifacts and vehicles. Hours are Mon.-Fri. 9 a.m.-1 p.m. and 1:30-4:15 p.m., Sat. 9-11:30 a.m. The 1897 Boulder City Railway Station is home to the **Eastern Goldfields Historical Society** and its historical and pioneering exhibits. Hours are Mon.-Sat. 10 a.m.-12:30 p.m., Sun. 10 a.m.-4 p.m. The **Cornwall Hotel** is another gorgeous old grand dame.

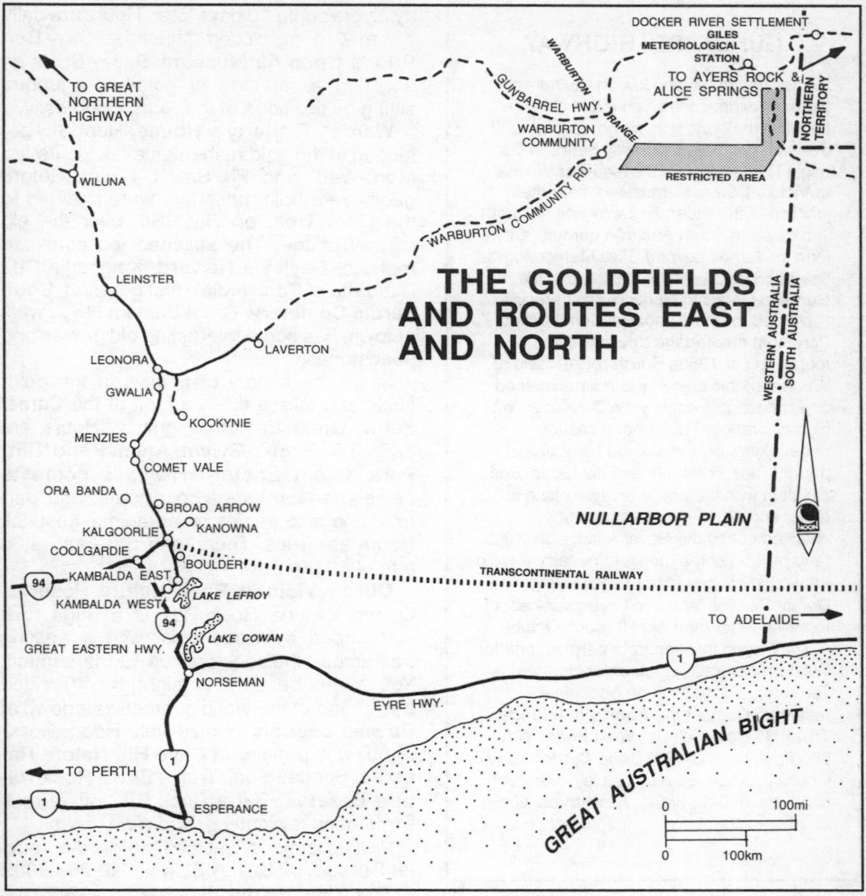

The **Boulder Tourist Information Centre** is inside the Goldfields War Museum—same hours, same phone.

The *Rattler* tourist train departs daily from Boulder Railway Station for a one-hour, commentary-accompanied journey of the entire Golden Mile. This is the train that originally linked Kalgoorlie with Boulder. Fare is $6. Departures are Mon.-Sat. 11 a.m., Sun. and holidays 1:30 p.m. and 3 p.m. For information and bookings, phone (090) 93-1157.

Coolgardie

You won't find the frenzied boom town of 1892. Settled into ghost-town retirement, Coolgardie (pop. 900), 40 km southwest of Kalgoorlie, is still a popular stopping place for gold-era aficionados. You'll easily get a sense of what this town was like in its glory just by the size of the streets and structures.

Details of Coolgardie's history can be gleaned from the 150 markers placed about town which recount the original use of each

GUNBARREL HIGHWAY

In case you're running low on "authentic" Outback experiences, you might consider traveling the *very, very* rough, rugged, and desolate Gunbarrel Highway between Carnegie Homestead (349 km east of Wiluna) to Victory Downs Homestead, near the junction of the Stuart Highway and Northern Territory and South Australia borders. Other than the turnoff beyond Giles Meteorological Station to Docker River Settlement, the Gunbarrel leads to plenty of nowheresville.

Named for the Gunbarrel Construction Party that created the track for the monitoring of 1950s British rocket tests at Woomera, this highway is *not* maintained and is passable only by 4WD vehicles with high clearance. This is not a casual undertaking. Be certain you have proper permits, are extremely well equipped, and check in with the police or shire office at either end. Also—have your vehicle checked out by the Royal Automobile Club (and pick up some maps, too), carry a radio transceiver linked to the Royal Flying Doctor Service, and don't even *think* about traveling other than April through October.

You'll need two separate permits (one for Western Australia, another for Northern Territory) to pass through Aboriginal reserves. Contact the **Aboriginal Lands Trust,** 35 Havelock St., West Perth, W.A. 6005 (tel. 09-483-1333); and **Central Land Council,** 33 Stuart Hwy., Alice Springs, N.T. 5750 (tel. 089-52-3800). Allow three weeks for processing.

building. An index to the markers is posted near the **Goldfields Exhibition** on Bayley Street. The exhibition relives Coolgardie's not-so-humble beginnings and includes goldfields memorabilia and a 35-minute video. Hours are daily 8-5, closed Christmas Day.

The **Old Railway Station,** Woodward St., serves as a transport museum which features a display of Modesto Varischetti's rescue. Name doesn't ring a bell? In 1907, Modesto became trapped by floodwaters while 300 meters underground and was rescued by divers some 10 days later. Hours are daily 7 a.m.-6 p.m., closed Christmas Day. **Ben Prior's Open Air Museum,** Bailey St., is an amazing assortment of gold-boom junque sitting by the edge of the road. Open daily.

Warden Finnerty's House, Hunt St., belonged to the gold rush rulemaker. Hours are Mon.-Wed. and Fri.-Sat. 1-4 p.m. Before gaols were built, prisoners were chained to the **Gaol Tree,** on Hunt St., over the old railway bridge. The attached leg irons are replicas. **Bayley's Reward,** Kalgoorlie Rd., is the site of Coolgardie's first gold find. **Coolgardie Cemetery,** Great Eastern Hwy., west of town, has some interesting old graves and headstones.

Learn the history of camels in the goldfields and take a ride yourself at the **Camel Farm,** Great Eastern Highway. Hours are daily 9-5. **Swn-Y-Gwynt Animal and Bird Park,** Great Eastern Hwy., is home to camels, emus, kangaroos, goats, and parrots, and also serves as an animal hospital. Hours are Tues.-Thurs. and Sat.-Sun. 9:30 a.m.-4:30 p.m.

Queen Victoria Rock Nature Reserve, Queen Victoria Rock Rd., is a huge rock surrounded by woodlands, with a walking trail across the rock and up to the summit. You might be able to sight the "freckled duck," one of the world's rarest waterfowl, at **Rowles Lagoon,** Bonnie Vale Road. Rock-climbing is popular at **Cave Hill Nature Reserve,** Sunday Soak Track. **Burra Rock Nature Reserve,** Burra Rock Rd., offers rock exploration, swimming, and wide views.

Pick up tourist info at the **Coolgardie Tourist Bureau,** 62 Bayley St. (tel. 090-26-6090).

The **YHA Hostel,** 56 Gnarlbine Rd. (tel. 090-26-6051), has dorm beds for $8 per night. The **Denver City Hotel,** Bayley St. (tel. 26-6031), one of the beautiful original hotels, offers inexpensive pub rooms. The **Golden Flag Motel,** Great Eastern Hwy. (tel. 26-6002), has moderate prices and a swimming pool. Campsites and on-site vans are available at **Coolgardie Caravan Park,** Bayley St. (tel. 26-6009).

The **Golden Flag** and **Golden Fleece** motels, both on Bayley St., serve good meals. For counter lunches, try the **Denver City**

Hotel. Pinky's Café in the Railway Lodge, Bayley St., is open daily for meals, snacks, and takeaways.

All of the interstate coaches stop in Coolgardie on the way to and from Kalgoorlie. **Bonnie Vale Station,** 12 km away, is a stop for Kalgoorlie-bound trains.

Kambalda

Kambalda, 55 km south of Kalgoorlie, was originally a gold-mining town called Red Hill (1897-1906). Regaining new importance—and a new name—when nickel was discovered in 1966, Kambalda continues to exist as a major mining center of the region. Situated on the shores of saltwater Lake Lefroy, Kambalda is a popular spot for weekend land yachting.

Red Hill Lookout offers vantage points of the town, lake, and surrounding countryside. **John Hill View Point** will give you a vantage point of the mine and slime dump.

Pick up permits to visit the mines at **Kambalda Tourist Bureau,** Irish Mulga Dr., Kambalda West (tel. 090-21-1446). Hours are Mon.-Fri. 9-5.

Norseman

Often called the "eastern gate to the western state," Norseman (pop. 1,900) sits at the western end of the Eyre Highway and is a major junction for travelers heading east across the Nullarbor Plain, south to Esperance (207 km) and the Rainbow Coast, or north to Coolgardie (also 207 km) and on to Perth. Since 1892, the Dundas Goldfields have been yielding gold from their super-rich quartz reef.

A collection of gold-rush tools and other items is on display at the **Historical and Geological Museum,** Battery Road. Contact the tourist bureau for hours.

Mount Jimberlana, seven km east of town, is an estimated 550 million years old—one of the oldest geological areas in the world. A walking trail to the summit takes about 30 minutes each way and affords great views of the hills, salt lakes, and mine operations. The **Heritage Trail** leads through bushland to **Dundas Rocks,** a popular picnic and bushwalk site 24 km south of Norseman.

MIKE WELLINS

the vintage Grand Hotel, in Kookynie, north of Kalgoorlie

If you want to try your luck fossicking in the **Western Gemstone Area,** first pick up a permit ($5) at the tourist bureau. Main gemstones to be found are moss agate, moss opalite, chrysophase, and jasper. Or, if you're more inclined toward panning for gold, get a permit for the **Gold Lease.**

Norseman Tourist Bureau is on Roberts Street (tel. 090-39-1071). Hours are daily 9-5. Free conducted tours of the mine workings depart the tourist bureau Tues.-Fri. at 9:30 a.m.

On Roberts St., the **Norseman Hotel** (tel. 39-1023) and **Railway Hotel** (tel. 39-1115) both offer inexpensive rooms. Campsites and on-site vans are available at **Norseman Caravan Park** (tel. 39-1262) and **Gateway Caravan Park** (tel. 39-1500), both on Prinsep Street.

NORTH OF KALGOORLIE

Be prepared for long, lonely stretches with no services or facilities. The road is sealed only up to Leonora, 237 km north of Kalgoorlie, and from Leonora to Leinster (131 km north) and Laverton (124 km northeast). This region of once-bustling gold towns harbors few reminders of the glory days (and *far* fewer residents).

Kanowna, 22 km along a dirt road northeast of Kalgoorlie, used to be filled with hotels, churches, and about 12,000 residents, but all that remains is the old railway station.

On the sealed road, **Broad Arrow** has held onto one turn-of-the-century hotel. The

1911 Ora Banda Hotel, along the dirt road west of Broad Arrow, has been restored since its 1960s movie debut in *The Nickel Queen*. Stone ruins are all that's left of **Comet Vale,** on the highway beyond Lake Goongarrie. **Menzies,** 132 km north of Kalgoorlie, managed to keep a number of buildings, including the Town Hall and Old Railway Station. The **Grand Hotel,** with its large rooms and wide verandas, lives on at **Kookynie,** 25 km along a dirt stretch east of the main road.

Forging northward another 105 km will bring you to **Leonora** (pop. 525) and its twin town, **Gwalia.** After gold was discovered in 1896, the Sons of Gwalia Mine claimed its fame as the largest underground mine outside the Golden Mile. And who do you suppose the mine's first manager was? Herbert Hoover—future president of the United States. Small world. Though the mine closed in 1963, much of it remains intact, as do many of the original structures. To get a feel for the place, see a historical display at the Gwalia Mine office, or walk the one-kilometer-long **Gwalia Heritage Trail.** Present-day Leonora serves as an administrative center for renewed gold-mining operations as well as the copper and nickel industries.

Turn-of-the-century, gold-boom life was *wild* at **Laverton** (pop. 875), 124 km northeast of Leonora, until the gold (and the town) died out in the early 1900s. The 1970s Poseidon nickel boom—and the huge Windarra Mine—have considerably revived Laverton, often used by visitors as a base from which to explore surrounding ghost towns and gold mines.

The sealed portion of the **Warburton Community Road** to Ayers Rock (1,033 km northeast) ends at Laverton. If you intend to travel this route, make sure you have a well-equipped 4WD or conventional vehicle with good ground clearance (the road is not suitable for caravans or trailers). You will also need permits to enter Aboriginal lands en route (see "Gunbarrel Highway" previous page), and enough fuel for a 600-km stretch. Check on current road conditions at the Laverton Shire Council and notify police of your intended departure and arrival times. Due to intense heat, travel is *not* recommended November through March. Fuel, food, supplies, and camping facilities are available at **Warburton Roadhouse,** 692 km from Leonora.

The road joins 45 kilometers of the Gunbarrel Highway near Giles Meteorological Station (230 km northeast of Warburton), crosses the Northern Territory border at Docker River Settlement, bringing you to Uluru (Ayers Rock) and Yulara another 233 km east. When you reach the border, you'll see the memorial plaque to Harold Lasseter (of Lasseter's Folly fame), who claimed to have found a magnificent gold reef out there and died trying to find it again.

North of Leonora, the sealed road ends 131 km away at Leinster, another nickel-producing town. Following the unsurfaced road 166 km northwest will take you to **Wiluna** (a has-been 1930s arsenic-mining community), and then to **Meekatharra** (183 km west), on the Great Northern Highway between Port Hedland and Perth.

WESTERN AUSTRALIA

No. 911

Fee—One Pound.

Yilgarn Goldfield.

MINER'S RIGHT.

Issued to Patrick Hannan

under the provisions of "The Goldfields Act, 1886;" to be in force until 10th August 1894.

Date of issue 11 Aug. 1893

[Not Transferable]

Warden.

THE NORTH COAST

The northern part of Western Australia has undergone so much expansion that, in 1976, the Brand Highway was opened to smooth the way for travelers who had previously relied on the Midlands Road up to Dongara (80 km longer and with many more stops). Above Geraldton the Brand becomes the North West Coastal Highway, linking with the Great Northern Highway from Port Hedland to Broome and through the Kimberley. Collectively, all of these roadways are still Highway 1, the sealed route that circles Australia.

It's a 1,780-km journey from Perth to Port Hedland, passing through the state's Midwest, Gascoyne, and Pilbara regions. The coastal road only *really* becomes coastal as it nears the Midlands Road junction; until then it runs about 40 km inland. Both the inland and coastal highways are *hot* during summer months.

PERTH TO GERALDTON

The Brand Highway cuts into the Great Northern Highway 55 km northeast of Perth. It's 150 km to the turnoff for Cervantes (pop. 240), a fishing town established in 1962, and the closest town to **Nambung National Park.** A spectacular site within the park is The Pinnacles, calcified spires of widely varying sizes and shapes, scattered eerily amid 400 hectares of yellow and ochre sand. Some of the long-eroded formations are thought to be 30,000 years old. Several lookouts over the desert and coast can be accessed via a 500-meter walking trail. The best time for Pinnacle viewing is sundown. Half-day tours depart Cervantes Service Station daily at 1 p.m. For information, phone (096) 52-7041. For park and Pinnacle information, contact the **Department of Conservation and Land Management** (tel. 096-52-7043).

To reach **Jurien,** a tiny rock lobster port on a sheltered bay, follow the side track 50 km north of Cervantes. Drovers Cave National Park, six km east of Jurien, has some good bushwalks, but all of the numerous caves have been locked up.

Greenhead, 56 km north of Jurien via the gravel Jurien Road or the sealed Brand Highway, features safe swimming, skin diving, and all kinds of fishing. **Leeman,** a short distance away, is also a relaxed fishing village.

Dongara (pop. 1,155) and neighboring **Port Denison** are holiday resorts and crayfish ports which touch the coast 359 km north of Perth. **Royal Steam Roller Flour Mill** is part of a restored village which includes the 1870 Old Dongara Police Station and tourist information center. Hours are Mon.-Fri. 10 a.m.-4 p.m., Sat. 10 a.m.-1 p.m. The 1870 **Russ Cottage,** Port Leander Dr., is furnished with period items. Hours are Sunday and public holidays 2-4 p.m.

The National Trust has classified a number of stone buildings at **Greenough,** an 1850s wheat-farming hamlet, 41 km above Dongara. The **Pioneer Museum,** Wonga Park, will fill you in on local folklore. Hours are Sat.-Thurs. 10 a.m.-4 p.m.

Midlands Road

The old Midlands Road begins 30 km farther up the Great Northern Highway, past the Brand Highway turnoff. This is well worth the drive in spring when the wildflowers put on a stupendous show.

At **Coorow,** you can detour 12 km west along Greenhead Road to Perth Basin, one of the world's deepest sedimentary basins. **Yarra Yarra Lakes,** between Carnamah and Three Springs, is a salty lake system with some wild color variations (red, green, and blue), plus prolific birdlife. Climb to the top of **Mingenew Hill** for excellent east and west views of the Irwin Valley.

Wildflower Way

One more alternate route to Geraldton is Wildflower Way, which runs parallel to the Midlands Road beginning at Wubin, off the

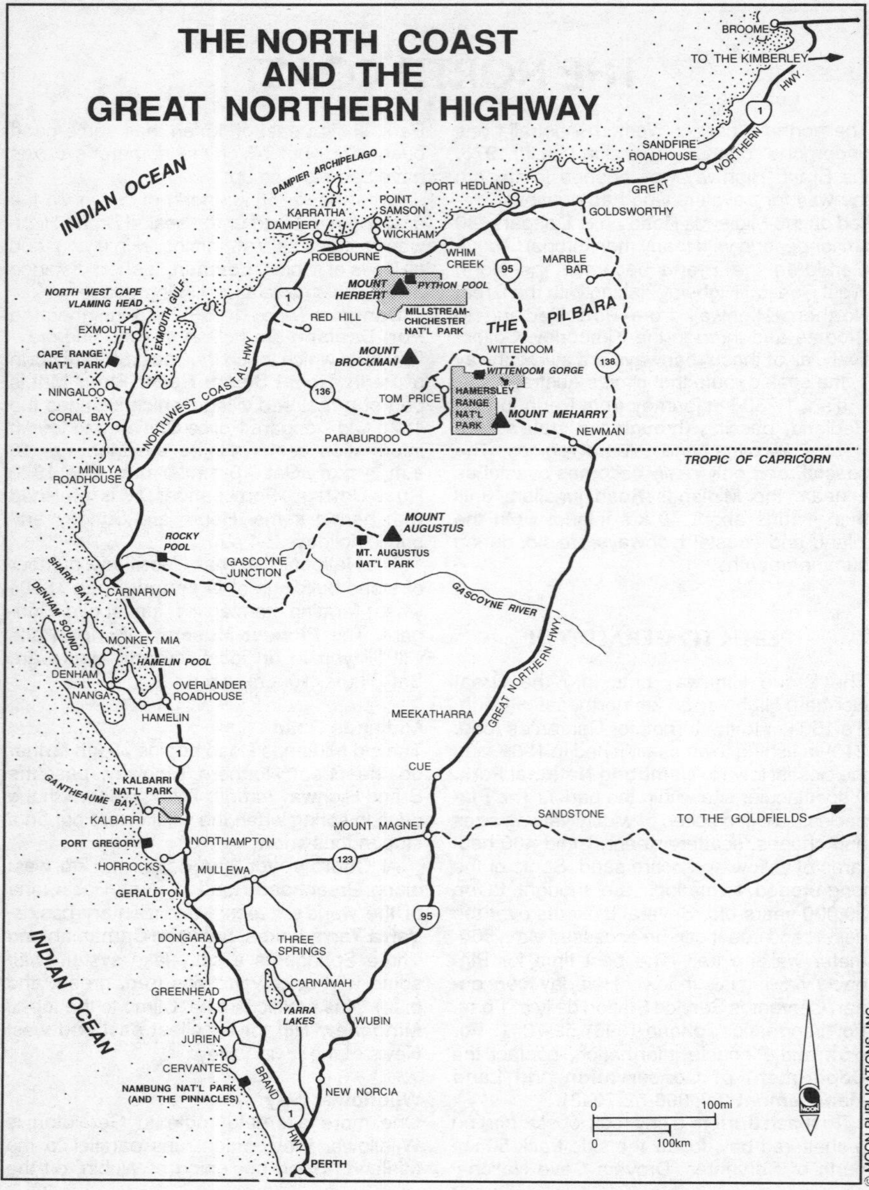

THE NORTH COAST AND THE GREAT NORTHERN HIGHWAY
BROOME
TO THE KIMBERLEY
HWY.
NORTHERN
GREAT
SANDFIRE ROADHOUSE
1
INDIAN OCEAN
DAMPIER ARCHIPELAGO
PORT HEDLAND
POINT SAMSON
KARRATHA
DAMPIER
WICKHAM
ROEBOURNE
WHIM CREEK
GOLDSWORTHY
MARBLE BAR
95
MOUNT HERBERT
PYTHON POOL
MILLSTREAM-CHICHESTER NAT'L PARK
NORTH WEST CAPE
VLAMING HEAD
EXMOUTH GULF
EXMOUTH
RED HILL
THE PILBARA
CAPE RANGE NAT'L PARK
MOUNT BROCKMAN
WITTENOOM
WITTENOOM GORGE
138
NINGALOO
NORTHWEST COASTAL HWY.
136
TOM PRICE
HAMERSLEY RANGE NAT'L PARK
MOUNT MEHARRY
CORAL BAY
PARABURDOO
NEWMAN
TROPIC OF CAPRICORN
MINILYA ROADHOUSE
MOUNT AUGUSTUS
ROCKY POOL
MT. AUGUSTUS NAT'L PARK
GASCOYNE JUNCTION
SHARK BAY
CARNARVON
GASCOYNE RIVER
DENHAM SOUND
MONKEY MIA
HAMELIN POOL
DENHAM
NANGA
OVERLANDER ROADHOUSE
HAMELIN
GREAT NORTHERN HWY.
MEEKATHARRA
CUE
KALBARRI NAT'L PARK
GANTHEAUME BAY
KALBARRI
SANDSTONE
TO THE GOLDFIELDS
MOUNT MAGNET
PORT GREGORY
NORTHAMPTON
123
HORROCKS
MULLEWA
GERALDTON
INDIAN OCEAN
DONGARA
THREE SPRINGS
GREENHEAD
CARNAMAH
YARRA LAKES
WUBIN
JURIEN
CERVANTES
BRAND
NAMBUNG NAT'L PARK (AND THE PINNACLES)
NEW NORCIA
HWY.
PERTH
0
100mi
0
100km
© MOON PUBLICATIONS, INC.

WESTERN AUSTRALIA TOURISM COMMISSION

the eerie Pinnacles in Nambung National Park

Great Northern Highway, and continuing 222 km to Mullewa, where you hook up to Highway 123 west. **Mullewa** (pop. 918), a sheep and wheat farming township, features a number of historical and natural sites. It should go without saying that Wildflower Way is a springtime bloom-a-thon that will knock your petals off.

GERALDTON

Established in 1849 as a major seaport for the Murchison lead mines (and later the Murchison Goldfields), Geraldton (pop. 20,895) is the major town of W.A.'s midwest region. Situated 424 km north of Perth, it is a leading winter holiday resort and renowned for its crayfish and rock lobster industry.

Sights

View 17th- and 18th-century Dutch shipwreck artifacts at **Geraldton Museum,** Marine Terrace. Other displays relate to the district's cultural and natural heritage. Hours are Mon.-Sat. 10-5, Sun. 1-5 p.m., closed Christmas Day and Good Friday. For information, phone (099) 21-5080.

Monsignor John Hawes, both a priest and architect, was responsible for the California mission-style **St. Francis Xavier Cathedral,** Cathedral Avenue. Building commenced in 1916 but was not completed until 1938.

Hermitage House, Cathedral Ave., was built to be Monsignor Hawes's retirement home. Hours are daily 9-5, holidays 10 a.m.-4 p.m., closed Good Friday. For information, phone 21-3999.

The Geraldton Historical Society headquarters is at the **Lighthouse Keeper's Cottage,** Point Moore Road. In continuous operation since 1878, the 35-meter-high lighthouse is banded in red and white stripes. Hours are Thursday 10 a.m.-4 p.m. For information, phone 21-2845.

Geraldton Art Gallery, corner Durlacher St. and Chapman Rd., exhibits regional artists. Hours are Mon.-Sat. 10 a.m.-5 p.m., Sun. 1:30-4:30 p.m., closed Christmas Day and Good Friday.

Mount Tarcoola, Sydney St., and **Separation Point Lookout,** Willcock Dr., both offer expansive views.

Most of the local beaches offer safe swimming. Lifeguards patrol **Mahomets Beach** on summer weekends.

Accommodations

The **YHA Hostel,** 80 Francis St. (tel. 099-21-2549), has six rooms for 33 people. Dorm beds run $8 per night.

Marine Terrace is the main drag for oldie-but-goodie seaside guesthouses with inexpensive lodging. Suggestions: **Bethel Guesthouse,** 311 Marine Terrace (tel. 21-4770);

Grantown Guesthouse, 172 Marine Terrace (tel. 21-3275); and **Sun City Guesthouse,** 184 Marine Terrace (tel. 21-2205).

Geraldton's Ocean West, corner Hadda Way and Willcock Drive, Mahomets Beach (tel. 21-1047), has moderately priced, self-contained cottages with TVs and cooking facilities. Motels in the same price range include **Hacienda Motel,** Durlacher St. (tel. 21-2155), and **Club Sun City Resort,** 137 Cathedral Ave. (tel. 21-6111).

Campsites and on-site vans are available at: **Separation Point Caravan Park,** corner Portway and Separation Way (tel. 21-2763); **Sun City Caravan Park,** Bosley St., Sunset Beach (tel. 38-1655); and **Belair Gardens Caravan Park,** Willcock Dr., Point Moore (tel. 21-1997).

Food

Marine Terrace is also the location for takeaways, cafés, pubs, cake shops, pizza places, and Chinese restaurants. **Golden Crust Bakery,** 36 Chapman Rd., bakes up fresh breads, pies, pasties, and cakes.

Entertainment And Recreation

The **Queens Park Theatre,** corner Cathedral Ave. and Maitland St., hosts nightly entertainment—either live or on cinema. For information, phone 21-5866 or 64-2047 (recorded info).

Sun City Scuba Club, Pace Sports Store, Marine Terrace (tel. 21-4229), organizes offshore reef tours and rents scuba equipment.

Information

The **Geraldton Tourist Bureau,** Chapman Rd. (in the Bill Sewell Community Recreation Centre), provides local and statewide information, as well as coach, tour, and accommodations bookings. Hours are Mon.-Sat. 9-5, Sun. and holidays 10 a.m.-4 p.m., closed Christmas Day and Good Friday. For information, phone (099) 21-3999.

Getting There

Both **Skywest** (tel. 09-323-1188) and **Ansett WA** (13-1300 toll free) fly between Perth and Geraldton. Fare is $130 one way. **Western Airlines** (tel. 09-277-4022) wings a Perth-Geraldton-Kalbarri-Useless Loop-Denham route three times a week for $120 one way.

Westrail, Bus Australia, and **Greyhound** provide regular coach service to and from Perth. Fare is in the $50 range one way. Northbound buses travel Highway 1 en route to Broome and Darwin. The coach terminal is in the same building as the tourist bureau.

Getting Around

Avis, Budget, and Hertz all have Geraldton agencies, but the best rates (from $25 per day) are at **Batavia Coast Hire Cars,** 25 Marine Terrace (tel. 21-2767). Hire bicycles for $10 per day from **Wheel Nuts Bicycle Hire,** Chapman Rd. (tel. 21-6600).

FARTHER NORTH

Beyond Geraldton

Leaving Geraldton, the Brand Highway metamorphoses into the North West Coastal Highway. **Northampton** (pop. 750), 50 km north, was a favorite Aboriginal site until lead and copper mines were established in the 1840s. Today the community prospers from the surrounding farmlands. Constructed of local sandstone, **Chiverton House Folk Museum** (1868-75), North West Coastal Hwy., houses a collection of early machinery and memorabilia. Hours are Sun.-Fri. 10 a.m.-noon and 2-4 p.m. For information, phone (099) 34-1215.

Horrocks Beach, 22 km west of Northampton, features a reef surrounding its five-km swimming beach, also good fishing (kingfish, whiting, herring, skippy, tailor, and rock lobster). The **Bowes River** turnoff, four km south of Horrocks, is the location for a number of ancient Aboriginal cave paintings. Bowes River is another jumpin' fishing spot.

Port Gregory, 43 km northwest of Northampton, is the midwest coast's oldest port, and nearby **Lynton** is a former convict-labor hiring depot. Though the town is defunct, many of the old ruins can still be seen.

From Lynton, follow Yerina Springs Rd. north, then turn east on Ogilvie West Rd. to

Hutt River Province, where self-appointed "Prince Leonard" is ruler. Having seceded from the Australian Commonwealth in 1970, Prince Leonard's kingdom rakes in revenue off special stamps, money, souvenir items, tearooms, a swimming pool, and other tourist snares.

Kalbarri

Situated where the Murchison River meets the Indian Ocean, Kalbarri (pop. 820) is a holiday resort famous for its gorgeous gorges and terrific fishing. This is also the area where the Dutch ship *Zuytdorp* was wrecked, *and* the long-ago home of a 400-million-old, two-meter-long scorpion known as the eurypterid.

Kalbarri National Park (186,096 hectares) features awesome sandstone cliffs and banded-in-red gorge walls (formed 400-500 million years ago). The fossil tracks of pre-vertebrate marine creatures have been located in the sandstone. The park also harbors a wide variety of wildlife and flora; try to come during the spring wildflower season. **Ross Graham** and **Hawk's Head** lookouts provide dynamic gorge views. A 35-km scenic drive leads to **The Loop** and **Z Bend,** two other spectacular viewing perches. Park facilities include short and long walking trails as well as picnic sites. Carry your own drinking water. For information, phone (099) 37-1140).

Jake's Corner, a few kilometers south of Kalbarri, has some of W.A.'s best surfing breaks. **Red Bluff,** just south, is where you can see tracks left by the ancient eurypterid (possibly the first creature to have walked on land) and explore frozen, tear-like threads of rock and other intriguing formations (also thought to be 400 million years old).

Rainbow Jungle, Red Bluff Rd., is lush with palms, ferns, tropical plants, rare and tropical birds, and fish. Open Tues.-Sunday; for information, phone 37-1248. **Fantasyland,** Grey St., combines collections of dolls, marinelife, fossils, and gemstones. Every morning at 8:45 a.m., the proprietor feeds pelicans on the foreshore opposite. Hours are Sun.-Fri. 9 a.m.-noon and 1:30-5 p.m., Sat. 9 a.m.-noon. For information, phone 37-1062.

Sailboats, canoes, surf cats, and pedal boats can be hired at **Kalbarri Hire Boats,** on the foreshore across from Murchison Caravan Park. **Kalbarri Sports and Dive,** Grey St. (tel. 37-1126), hires diving equipment and offers instruction.

Av-er-est, Mortimer St. (tel. 099-37-1101), offers inexpensive weekly rates on self-contained holiday units with TVs and cooking facilities. Holiday units in the moderate range include **Kalbarri Reef Villas,** Coles St. (tel. 37-1165), and **Sunsea Villas,** Grey St. (tel. 37-1187). Campsites and on-site vans are rented at **Kalbarri Tudor Caravan Park,** Porter St. (tel. 37-1077); **Murchison Caravan Park,** Grey St. (tel. 37-1005); and **Red Bluff Caravan Park,** Red Bluff (tel. 37-1080).

Western Airlines (tel. 09-277-4022) provides service between Kalbarri and Perth three times a week. Fare is $130 one way. **Westrail** coaches will take you to Kalbarri twice each week. Fare from Northampton is $55 one way. Rent bicycles at **Murchison Cycle Hire,** Porter St. (tel. 37-1105), for about $7 per day. For local tours (including a cruise up the Murchison River on the *River Queen,*) contact **Kalbarri Travel Service,** Grey St. (tel. 37-1104).

AROUND SHARK BAY

The Overlander Roadhouse (179 km north of Kalbarri) marks the turnoff from the North West Coastal Highway to Shark Bay, site of the first European landing on Australian soil (Dirk Hartog in 1616).

Stromatolites, among the world's oldest living fossils, can be seen in **Hamelin Bay's** clear, shallow waters. **Shell Beach,** near Nanga via Denham Rd., is created from billions of minute shells packed about 20 meters deep. Actual shell "blocks" (compacted by nature) have been constructed by locals along the Shark Bay foreshore. **Freshwater Camp,** Nanga's pioneer homestead, features the usual relics.

One-time pearling port **Denham,** 48 km northwest of Nanga, sits on the west side of Peron Peninsula (just above the 26th paral-

DOLPHIN ETIQUETTE

Please—Monkey Mia is *not* a dolphin Disneyland. These babies are not trained for your pleasure. When you're wading with the dolphins observe the following rules:

- wade about knee deep
- wait until the dolphins approach *you*
- never touch, or put anything into, the blowhole
- don't touch the head, dorsal fin, or tail (pat gently along the side of the body)
- do not scare the dolphins with loud noises
- don't try to swim with the dolphins, and don't reach over them for any reason
- check with rangers before feeding—the dolphins are fussy about their food
- if a dolphin gives you a fish, don't give it back. Accept it and say, "Thank you."

two of the untrained dolphins at Monkey Mia

MARK MORRIS

lel) and is Australia's westernmost town. Sightseeing **cruises** and fishing trips depart Denham Jetty. For cruise bookings and information on other local tours, contact **Shark Bay Visitors and Travel Centre,** Knight St. (tel. 099-48-1253). Hire **bicycles** ($10 per day) at **Shark Bay Recreation Centre** (tel. 48-1218).

Well-posted signs lead to **Monkey Mia,** one of the country's—and the world's—most unusual natural attractions, 25 km northeast of Denham. Since 1964, when a woman from one of the area's fishing camps began the practice, dolphins have regularly come up to these shores to be hand-fed by rangers and visitors. These sweet mammals will only accept whole fish, not any that has been gutted or gilled. Obey rangers' instructions on feeding and petting. There is no set feeding time —the dolphins are free to come and go as they please. An information center provides educational exhibits and videos on dolphin behavior. Fresh fish are sold for your feeding pleasure. Hours are daily 8:30 a.m.-4:30 p.m. For information, phone (099) 48-1366.

Bay Lodge, 109 Knight Terrace, Denham (tel. 099-48-1278), is a YHA associate. Backpackers' accommodations run $12 per night, while self-contained holiday units are in the moderate range. Other moderately priced, self-contained units are: **Denham Villas,** 58 Durlacher St. (tel. 48-1264); **Hartog Holiday Villas,** Denham-Hamelin Rd. (tel. 48-1323); and **Shark Bay Villas,** 92 Hartog Crescent (tel. 48-1264).

Campsites and on-site vans are available at: **Denham Seaside Caravan Park,** Knight Terrace (tel. 48-1242); **Shark Bay Caravan Park,** Spaven Way, off Durlacher St. (tel. 48-1387); **Blue Dolphin Caravan Park,** Hamelin Rd. (tel. 48-1385); and **Monkey Mia Dolphin Resort** (tel. 48-1320).

Local restaurants offer the usual counter meal and takeaway fare. The **Old Pearler Restaurant,** Knight Terrace, Denham (tel. 48-1373), is built out of shell blocks. Food is on the upmarket side and reservations are recommended.

Western Airlines (tel. 09-277-4022) operates a Perth-Denham service three times a week. Fare is $186 one way. Greyhound coaches will drop you at the Overlander; from there, a Denham Tourist Centre shuttle will transport you to to Denham and Shark Bay. Hire cars cost about $80 per day from **Budget** (tel 099-48-1247) and **Shark Bay Hire Cars** (tel. 48-1203), both in Denham.

CARNARVON

Positioned at the mouth of the Gascoyne River, Carnarvon (pop. 5,050) is known as the tropical gateway to the north. This seaside commercial center is famed for its tropical fruit plantations (particularly bananas) and its mile-long jetty, beloved by fishers. This was the also the spot about which Captain Dirk Hartog and various other explorers said such lousy things, but post-jetty, big-banana Carnarvon has redeemed itself. After all, the place can't be all bad if the fish come up to the foreshore to be hand-fed.

Carnarvon Museum, Robinson St., features historic displays and a shell collection. Hours are Mon.-Fri. 9-5, Sat.-Sun. 9 a.m.-noon and 2-5 p.m. For information, phone (099) 41-1146. Other local relics—including a whale bone arch—can be seen at **Pioneer Park,** Olivia Terrace.

Ponder trial plantings of tropical fruits and winter veggies at **Gascoyne Research Station,** South River Rd., North Carnarvon. Hours are Mon.-Fri. 8-5. For information, phone 41-8027.

Pelican Point is a good swimming and fishing site, just five kilometers from town. Other top fishing spots include **Dwyer's Leap** and **Prawn Jetty Beach.**

Practicalities

Carnarvon Accommodation Centre, 23 Wheelock Way (tel. 099-41-2511), is a YHA associate, with beds for $11 per night—and only two beds per room! Weekly rates are an even bigger bargain. **Carnarvon Backpacker's,** 46 Olivia Terrace (tel. 41-1095) has communal facilities, is centrally located, and charges $10 per night. Old-ish, cheap pub-hotels are: **Moir's Gascoyne Hotel,** Olivia Terrace (tel. 41-1412); **Port Hotel,** Robinson St. (tel. 41-1704); and the **Carnarvon Hotel,** Olivia Terrace (tel. 41-1181).

Carnarvon Close, 96 Robinson St. (tel. 41-1317) and **Carnarvon Beach Holiday Resort,** Pelican Point Rd. (tel. 41-2226), both offer moderately priced, self-contained holiday units.

Among the numerous caravan parks offering campsites and on-site vans are: **Plantation Caravan Park,** Robinson St. (tel. 41-8100); **Carnarvon Caravan Park,** Robinson St. (tel. 41-8101); and **Startrek Caravan Park,** North West Coastal Hwy. (tel. 41-8153).

The Gascoyne, Port, and Carnarvon hotels all have similar counter meals at reasonable prices. Robinson Street is the food strip: fish and chips, pizza, and the ubiquitous coffee lounge.

Tel-O-Mac, 280 Robinson St. (tel. 41-1873), sells fishing, camping, and diving gear. **Rosco's Sports Shop,** 11 Robinson St. (tel. 41-1385), rents diving equipment.

For local information, including tours and fishing charters, contact **Carnarvon District Tourist Bureau,** 6 Robinson St. (tel. 099-41-1146). Hours are Mon.-Fri. 9-5, Sat.-Sun. 9 a.m.-noon and 2-5 p.m.

Daily Perth-Carnarvon flights are operated by **Ansett WA** (tel. 13-1300 toll free). Fare is $212 one way. Carnarvon is a regular stop on the north-south **Bus Australia** and **Greyhound** coach routes. Fare from Perth is $92 one way.

The cheapest rental car firms are **Avis Australia,** Dempster Rd. and **Chippies Hire Cars,** West Street. Rates begin at $39 per day. Hire bicycles from **Rosco's Sports Shop** for about $5 per day.

VICINITY OF CARNARVON

Oyster-picking and crayfishing are specialties at the **Blowholes,** 70 km north of Carnarvon, via Pt. Quobba Road. Salt headed for Japan is loaded at **Cave Cuvier,** a deep natural port some 30 km north of the Blowholes.

Rocky Pool is a deep, freshwater swimming pool, on Gascoyne Junction Rd., 55 km inland. **Gascoyne Junction,** another 122 km east, is a gateway to the rugged Kennedy Range, full of wildlife, Aboriginal caves, rock paintings, and semiprecious gemstones. Gascoyne Junction Hotel, constructed of corrugated iron, is a famous old bush pub.

Mount Augustus, a 289-km gravel drive from Gascoyne Junction, is the world's largest monocline, measuring 717 meters above the surrounding plain (1,105 meters above sea level), and it remains one of Australia's best-kept secrets. Mount Augustus National Park, only just proclaimed in 1989, is also noted for Aboriginal rock paintings and unusual flora and fauna. Coach tours and scenic flights operate out of Carnarvon. **Mount Augustus Station Tourist Resort** (tel. 099-43-0527), at the foot of the rock, offers campsites and moderately priced units.

CONTINUING NORTH

The Ningaloo Reef

You'll be able to view everything from humpback whales to egg-laying turtles around this mini-Great Barrier Reef, one of the world's major reef systems. Running 260 kilometers along the North West Cape from Exmouth to Amherst Point, Ningaloo Reef—far more accessible than Queensland's Great Barrier—is fast becoming a snorkeling, scuba-diving, fishing, and boat-trip mecca. Get there before the developers do! The turnoff from North West Coastal Highway is just past the Minilya Roadhouse, 142 km north of Carnarvon.

Coral Bay, 78 km from the roadhouse (you'll cross the Tropic of Capricorn about midway), is the main entry point to **Ningaloo Marine Park,** just meters offshore. The reef covers more than 5,000 square kilometers of the Indian Ocean, is made up of almost 200 types of coral, and shelters incredibly diverse marinelife in its crystal waters—from teensy tropical fish to scary-looking whale sharks. Five shipwrecks around Ningaloo Station provide additional fun for divers. Sign up for a tour aboard the *Sub-Sea Explorer Coral Viewer* (tel. 099-42-5955), a semi-submersible viewing craft, or contact **Bay View Caravan Park** (tel. 42-5932) for a glass-bottom boat cruise. **Coral Dive** (tel. 42-5940) runs a full program of diving courses and rents necessary equipment.

At Coral Bay, **Bayview Holiday Village Caravan Park** (tel. 099-42-5932) offers campsites, cabins, chalets, and on-site vans. Rates run inexpensive to moderate. Self-contained holiday units are in the expensive bracket at **Coral Bay Lodge** (tel. 42-5932), but facilities include tennis courts and hire boats.

You'll need a 4WD to access most of **Cape Range National Park** and its 50,831 hectares of coastal scenery, limestone rocks, and gorges. Marked bushwalking trails lead to some of the gorges and lookout points. **Lightfoot Heritage Trail** is a seven-km walk through rugged limestone formations. First-come, first-serve campsites are available at selected locations. For information, phone (099) 49-1676.

Exmouth

Exmouth (pop. 2,590), at the tip of the peninsula and 155 km north of Coral Bay, is also popular for fishing, diving and other beach activities. The town originated, however, as late as the 1960s to service and house personnel at the joint U.S./Australian naval base at the top of the North West Cape. Used as an Allied base known as "Potshot" during WW II, the facility has ostensibly been used to maintain international contact with U.S. Navy vessels (including submarines) via 13 very low frequency radio transmitters. (At press time, this base was being turned over to Australian control.) Take steep **Lighthouse Drive** for panoramic views of the reef, cape, and communication towers.

King's Norcape Lodge Resort, Truscott Crescent (tel. 099-49-1334), offers lodge accommodations, family apartments, motel rooms, and campsites in every price range. For other campsites and on-site vans, contact: **Exmouth Cape Tourist Village,** corner Truscott Crescent and Murat Rd. (tel. 49-1101); **Lighthouse Caravan Park,** Vlaming Head (tel. 49-1478); or **Exmouth Accommodation and Caravan Park,** Yardie Creek Homestead (tel. 41-9389).

For reef dives and equipment hire, contact **Q Dive Exmouth Sales Hire and Service** (tel. 099-49-1662) or **Neilsen Diving** (tel. 49-1201).

Collect tourist information and book reef or fishing tours at **Exmouth Tourist Bureau,** Thew St. (tel. 49-1176).

Ansett WA flies every day except Saturday between Perth and Exmouth. Fare is

$264 one way. Daily Perth-Exmouth coach service is provided by **Bus Australia.** The fare is $110 one way.

Avis Australia (tel. 49-1014) and **Budget** (tel. 49-1052) rent cars for about $65 per day. Hire **bicycles** at King's Norcape Lodge (tel. 49-1334) or Exmouth Squash Centre (tel. 49-1149). Rates are $8 per day, $20 per week.

THE PILBARA COAST

The coastal portion of the Pilbara region is a cluster of early pioneering towns that are becoming fattened off their own natural resources and the rich inland mines. The Burup Peninsula area harbors some 10,000 ancient Aboriginal petroglyphs, most depicting the wildlife of the time.

Karratha (pop. 8,400), on Nickol Bay about 530 km northeast of Minilya Roadhouse, is a newish, rapidly expanding community, established mainly because of the Hamersley Iron Project. Additional growth can be attributed to the Woodside Petroleum Project, which is developing a gigantic natural gas reserve on the North West Shelf. The 3½ km **Jaburara Heritage Trail,** beginning at the water tanks, will lead you to Aboriginal carvings, grinding stones, shellfish middens, and spiritual taboo sites.

Up the road, **Dampier** (pop. 2,500) was built in the 1960s to serve as port facility for Hammersley Iron. The **Dampier Archipelago,** which the town faces, has a more exciting history of shipwrecks, whaling, and pearling. Boating and fishing these waters (with reefs containing more than 200 species of living coral) are primary pastimes.

Roebourne (pop. 1,700), 32 km southeast of Karratha, is known as "Gateway to the Pilbara." Established in 1864 along with the gold and copper mines, Roebourne is the oldest town in the northwest, as evidenced by its many remaining early stone buildings.

Aiming toward Cape Lambert, **Cossack,** the northwest's first port, once known as Tien Tsin Harbour, also has preserved its beautiful stone buildings. Nearby, Wickham is another iron ore company town. **Point Samson,** though modernized, is still a lovely little fishing village.

Accommodations in this area are on the expensive side. **King Bay Holiday Village,** The Esplanade, Dampier (tel. 091-83-1440), a YHA associate, is still in the moderate-expensive range. **Victoria Hotel,** Roe St., Roebourne (tel. 82-1001), has moderately priced pub rooms, and the least expensive motel is **Samson Accommodation,** Samson Rd., Point Samson (tel. 87-1052). Campsites and on-site vans, probably your best bet, are available at: **Karratha Caravan Park,** Mooligum Rd., Karratha (tel. 85-1012); **Harding River Caravan Park,** De Grey St., Roebourne (tel. 82-1063); and **Solveig Caravan Park,** Samson Rd., Point Samson (tel. 87-1414).

Forget the shopping center food and go to Point Samson for fresh fish 'n' chips and other seafood. **Moby's Kitchen** (tel. 87-1435) specializes in fresh local seafood in a garden setting overlooking the ocean, plus offers takeaways.

For Roebourne area tourist information, contact: **Norwest Tourist Centre,** Welcome Rd., Karratha City Shopping Centre, Karratha (tel. 091-85-2474); **Dampier Community Association,** High St. (tel. 83-1243); or **Roebourne Tourist Bureau,** Roe St., Roebourne (tel. 82-1060).

Ansett WA flies daily to Karratha from Perth. Fare is $300 one way. **Skywest** operates a weekly Karratha-Port Hedland service, $108 one way. **Bus Australia** and **Greyhound** serve Karratha and Dampier from Perth every day. Fare is $110 one way. The same coaches go into Roebourne for another 10 bucks.

Vicinity Of Roebourne

Traveling 60 kilometers on the Wittenoom Road will bring you to **Python Pool,** a former oasis for Afghan camel drivers *and* for the area's many pythons.

Millstream-Chichester National Park (199,710 hectares), 60 km farther, is an odd contrast to its semiarid surroundings, with natural springs, permanent river pools, lily ponds, and groves of date palms (thought to have been brought by the camel drivers). Carry your own food and water, and be pre-

WESTERN AUSTRALIA TOURISM COMMISSION

the Chichester Range

pared for heavy rain and rough roads. Camping is allowed in designated facilities. For information, phone (091) 84-5144.

Back on the North West Coastal Highway, 78 km east of Roebourne, the 1887 **Whim Creek Hotel** was a rowdy Outback pub, built to serve the Whim Well Copper Mine. Historic photos are on display and today's brew is on tap.

Port Hedland

Established originally as a service center for the surrounding cattle stations, Port Hedland (pop. 11,200), 1,762 km from Perth, is now the major deep-water port for the mega-buck Pilbara iron ore industry—visited by some of the world's biggest ships. By tonnage, it is Australia's biggest port. The entire town and **South Hedland,** its satellite, live and breathe for those rich inland mines. And, as if those miners aren't salty enough, the real stuff is produced a few kilometers away where huge salt dunes encrust the landscape.

Pretty Pool, behind Cooke Point Caravan Park, is a favorite spot for fishing and shell collecting. Wear sturdy shoes if you want to walk on the reef at low tide—these waters are full of venomous stonefish.

Backpacker's Hostel, 20 Richardson St. (tel. 73-2198), offers dorm rooms for $8 per night. Other than that, Port Hedland accommodations are expensive. **Pier Hotel,** The Esplanade (tel. 091-73-1488), in the upper-moderate range, is the best deal. Campsites and on-site vans are available at: **South Hedland Caravan Park,** Hamilton Rd., S. Hedland (tel. 72-1197); **Dixon's Port Hedland Caravan Park,** opposite the airport (tel. 72-2525); and **Cooke Point Ocean Beach Caravan Park,** Athol St. (tel. 73-1271).

Food is the usual coffee lounge, pub, and supermarket put-togethers. The **Hedland Hotel,** corner Lukis and McGregor, does the best counter meals. **Marg's Kitchen,** across from the tourist bureau, stays open late for good, simple meals.

For local information and tour bookings, contact **Port Hedland Tourist Centre,** 13 Wedge St. (tel. 091-73-1711). Hours are daily 9 a.m.-6 p.m.

Port Hedland Airport is an international gateway. **Garuda** provides service between Port Hedland and Bali.

Ansett WA operates daily flights to Port Hedland from Perth. Fare is $314 one way. Frequent flights serve Broome, Derby, and Darwin. **Bus Australia** and **Greyhound** coaches service Perth-Port Hedland daily. Fare is $125 one way.

Avis, Budget, and **Hertz** have agencies at Port Hedland Airport, but the cheapest rental cars are at **W.K. Motors,** Anderson St. (tel. 73-1729). Rates are from $20 per day.

Tours of the **Mount Newman Mining Company** depart the tourist bureau Mon.-Fri. at 10:30 a.m.

THE GREAT NORTHERN HIGHWAY

Though the coastal route to Port Hedland is more interesting, the inland Great Northern Highway is actually more direct. From Perth, the highway travels northeast through the Midwest and Pilbara regions, veers coastward at Newman, meeting up with the North West Coastal Highway 42 km south of Port Hedland.

Perth To The Pilbara

Up the highway, 132 km northeast of Perth, **New Norcia** is a strange contrast to other country towns. Founded in 1846 by Benedictine monks who came to inflict their gospel on the Aborigines, the Spanish village-esque monastic community consists of the monastery, church, old mill, jail, hotel, and the original boarding schools (now used as a Catholic college). The Benedictine monks still live and work there, much as they used to. The **Museum and Art Gallery** relate the town's history, and also houses a **tourist information center.** Hours are daily 10 a.m.-4:30 p.m., closed Christmas Day and Good Friday. For information, phone (096) 54-8056.

Mount Magnet, Cue, and **Meekatharra**—560, 640, and 760 kilometers respectively from Perth—are old Murchison River goldfields. Gold is still being mined at Mount Magnet. Nearby **ghost towns** include Austin (20 km south of Cue), Cuddingwarra (10 km west), Pinnacles (24 km east), Reedys (60 km northeast), and Tuckanarra (40 km north).

Prospecting for gold is *still* popular at **Sandstone,** 158 km east of Mount Magnet, which is also surrounded by a myriad of abandoned mining settlements. From Meekatharra, it's 183 km of unsealed road to Wiluna where the road turns south to Kalgoorlie, 534 km away (with the 166-km Wiluna-Leinster portion unsealed).

The Pilbara

This region encompasses 510,335 square km of isolated territory, rugged ranges, deep gorges, gigantic mining operations, company towns, and *enormous* wealth. Come see men and their ultra-big monsters rip the earth apart and extract its riches, then cart it off to Port Hedland for worldwide shipment.

More than 100,000 tons of iron ore are produced daily at **Newman,** 422 km north of Meekatharra, then shipped via private railway to Port Hedland and the big blue yonder. **Mount Newman Mining Company** operates free tours of its Mount Whaleback Mine (the world's largest open-cut mine). Tours depart Mon.-Fri., except public holidays, at 8:30 a.m. and 1 p.m. For information and bookings, phone (091) 75-1511.

WESTERN AUSTRALIA TOURISM COMMISSION

the monastery at New Norcia

Wittenoom

WESTERN AUSTRALIA TOURISM COMMISSION

Hamersley Range National Park is reached via unsealed road off the Great Northern Highway, 180 km west of Newman. The 617,606-hectare park encompasses a variety of spectacular gorges, stony watercourses, and permanent pools, as well as Mount Meharry (1,245 meters), Western Australia's highest mountain. Campsites with limited facilities are available. For information, phone (091) 89-8157.

I'll tell you the truth: I have not been to Wittenoom and I am *not* going—ever. And I'm not going to advise anyone else to go, either. Yes, I *know* it is the heart of the Pilbara, and that it sits at the mouth of the breathtaking Wittenoom Gorge. However, in this instance, the word "breathtaking" is given whole new meaning: asbestos. Wittenoom mined blue asbestos from 1937-66, when the mine closed and the population dropped from 1,500 down to 60. The fact is, microscopic asbestos fibers are still present in the Wittenoom tailings dumps and in the landfill used in and about town and the place continues to be a health risk. (An aside: a friend of mine who was previously unable to conceive immediately hatched twins after a visit to Wittenoom—and she was traveling *alone!)*

Tom Price, W.A.'s highest town, at 747 meters, and **Paraburdoo,** on the edge of the Hamersley Range, are two other company towns south of Wittenoom, that rail their ore production over to Dampier. Continuing along the Wittenoom Road (Highway 136) will take you to the North West Coastal Highway.

Another off-the-beaten path from Newman is along unsealed Highway 138. **Marble Bar** (pop. 357), 306 km north, is reputedly Australia's hottest place. It was hot gold-wise, too, with more than two million ounces produced since an 1891 discovery. The town was named for the Marble Bar, Australia's only jasper bar, easiest seen where it crosses the Coongan river, 10 km west of town. You're not allowed to chip at it, but you can get a sample at the jasper deposit on the road to Comet Mine. The **Comet Mine,** 10 km south of town, is still operating and features a souvenir shop with beautiful rocks, including the regional Pilbara jade. This whole area offers superb fossicking.

Goldsworthy, almost at the coast, was the Pilbara's first iron ore town and it thrived until mining shifted eastward to **Shay Gap.** Both towns took the brunt of Cyclone Enid when it hit in 1980.

As the Great Northern Highway merges with the North West Coastal Highway, south of Port Hedland, it remains the Great Northern Highway throughout the Kimberley region and almost to the Northern Territory border. It's 610 km from Port Hedland up to Broome. **Eighty Mile Beach** and several roadhouses are the diversions along the way.

THE KIMBERLEY

This is it, folks—the last outpost, the pioneer frontier, the place where Daniel Boone would give the coonskin off his cap for the chance to explore. Even with phones, faxes, and the sealed highway, this 350,000-square-km region is remote, rugged, and sparsely traveled (though this is destined to change now that it's hit the cover of *National Geographic).*

Though an 1885 gold find at Hall's Gap provided the first lure to this isolated area, it was soon supplanted by cattle ranching, and—thanks to the successful Ord River Irrigation Scheme—tropical fruit production for both domestic and worldwide markets.

The Kimberley is a magical haven of desert ranges, Outback stations, tropical forests, raging rivers, national parks, and more, more, more. The weather is a big drawback, however. It's best to travel here April to September, during the Dry. At other times of the year, not only do temperatures swelter above 40° C, but the very wet Wet swells rivers, floods roads, leaves settlements stranded, blackens tempers, and renders attractions inaccessible. Also common are bone-biting cold nights, May to July. You'll need a well- equipped 4WD for off-highway exploration.

BROOME

As the "gateway to the Kimberley," Broome (pop. 3,670) is one of the hottest (in both temperature *and* popularity) destinations in the country. Situated 2,353 km northeast of Perth, this dusty, cosmopolitan town is filled with boab trees, red dust, and oodles of character (and characters).

Pearls before swine—or at least cattle—certainly held true here. Beginning in the 1880s, the gung-ho pearling industry provided work for about 400 luggers (boats) and 3,000 men, contributing 80% of the world's mother-of-pearl until the advent of plastics. Now only a few luggers remain, in conjunction with newly established cultured pearl farming. But there's beef—and *plenty* of it as Broome's modern meatpacking industry is capable of processing some 40,000 head of cattle each season.

Though the Japanese targeted Broome during WW II, evidence of damage by both sides can be seen in the wrecked carcasses of Allied flying boats in Roebuck Bay, as well as the Japanese plane engines mounted near the Continental Hotel.

The Asian pearlers contributed to Broome's rich cultural mix, mini-Chinatown, and atmospheric appeal for a new breed of travelers.

Chinatown

Bounded by Carnarvon St. and Dampier Terrace, Short St. and Napier Terrace, "Chinatown" basically refers to Broome's older section—once alive with saloons, billiard parlors, boarding houses, and pearling sheds—now lined with restaurants, souvenir shops, and ubiquitous pearl purveyors.

The **Roebuck Bay Hotel** is *rowdy* most nights and weekends. Live bands play in the beer garden most Saturday afternoons, and you won't want to miss those arm wrestling and wet T-shirt contests!

Dating from 1916, **Sun Pictures,** near the corner of Short and Carnarvon streets, is one of Australia's few remaining open-air cinemas. Regular screenings of not-terribly-old releases are shown nightly. For program information, phone (091) 92-1677.

The glass-encased model of a **Chinese temple** sits on Dampier Terrace, near Short Street.

Other Sights

The **Broome Historical Society Museum,** Saville St. (in the old customs house), presents pearling-era items, historical displays, and a shell collection. Hours are Mon.-Fri. 10 a.m.-noon and 2-4 p.m., Sat.-Sun. 10 a.m.-noon. For information, phone (091) 92-1490.

The **Courthouse,** Frederick St., offers another sweep at Broome's past. Hours are Mon.-Fri. 9 a.m.-noon and 1-4 p.m.

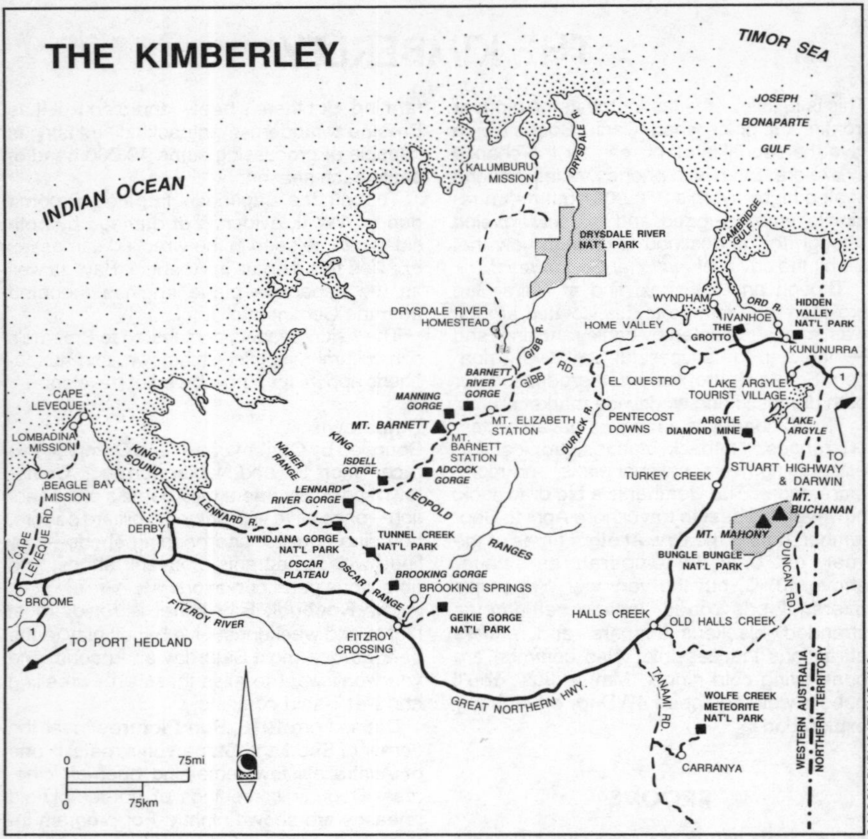

Horrie Miller (founder of Ansett WA) displays his Wackett aircraft outside the **Library and Art Gallery,** corner Mary and Hammersley streets.

The marble headstones with Japanese inscriptions and a commemorative column are the most interesting at the **cemetery** on Ann Street.

Buccaneer Rock, at the entrance to Dampier Creek, commemorates the visit by Captain William Dampier and the *Roebuck*.

The **Golden Staircase to the Moon** is an effect created by the full moon's reflection off the ocean bed during low tides. Check with the tourist bureau for dates and best vantagepoints.

Sights Near Broome

Popular **Cable Beach,** six km from town on Gantheaume Bay, is a white-sand and turquoise stretch for surfing, swimming, and sunning (nude, beyond the rock at the northern edge). Stingers invade these shores during summer months.

See some 100 crocs, ranging from babies to a six-meter-long adults, at **Broome Crocodile Farm,** Cable Beach Rd., Cable Beach. Primarily a research center, the farm also presents tours and video screenings. Hours are Mon.-Sat. 10 a.m.-noon and 2-3 p.m. For information, phone 92-1489.

Pearl Coast Zoological Gardens, Lullfitz Dr., Cable Beach (next to the crocodile farm), developed by British Lord McAlpine, is a bushland park with large aviaries, snake pits, a manmade lake, and lookout platform. Hours are daily 9 a.m.-5 p.m. For information, phone 92-1703.

Dinosaur footprints, 130 million years old, are visible at low tide at Gantheaume Point, seven km south of Broome, at the end of Cable Beach. If you're not able to see the real thing, cement casts are displayed near the beacon on the cliff. **Anastasia's Pool,** a manmade rock pool north of Gantheaume Point, fills up at high tide for those who want to take a dip.

Pearl Coast Aquarium, Port Dr., eight km from town at the deep-water port, supplies aquariums worldwide with local tropical fish. A pearling display explains modern farming techniques. Hours are daily 10-5. For information, phone 92-2443.

Birdwatchers can view more than 200 species of their feathered friends at the **Broome Bird Observatory,** 18 km east of town on Roebuck Bay. For information, phone 93-5600.

Cape Leveque Road, from Broome to Cape Leveque Lighthouse, spans a distance of around 200 km. Sites along the way include the Beagle Bay and Lombadina Aboriginal communities and their beautiful churches, plus another at One Arm Point, beyond Cape Leveque Lighthouse. Only the churches and souvenir shops welcome travelers.

Accommodations

The tourist influx has, unfortunately, driven accommodations rates way upward. It's best to book ahead, especially during Australian school holidays.

Broome Backpackers, Crocker Way (tel. 091-93-5050), offers dormitory accommodations and communal kitchen facilities for $10 per night. **Broome Bunkhouse,** Napier Terrace (tel. 92-1221), squashes 104 people into one bunkhouse. Rates are $15 per night, including breakfast.

Forrest House, 59 Forrest St. (tel. 93-5067), is a moderately priced guesthouse with breakfast included in the tariff. **Kimberley Holiday Home,** Herbert St. (tel. 92-1134), offers self-contained holiday units with cooking facilities in the upper-moderate range.

The **Continental Hotel,** Weld St. (tel. 92-1002) and **Roebuck Bay Hotel/Motel,** Carnarvon St. (tel. 92-1221) both have air-conditioning, TVs, and swimming pools, and are expensive. **Cable Beach Club,** Cable Beach Rd. (tel. 92-2505), with bungalows, suites, and studio units, is super-expensive and super-posh.

Campsites are located at: **Broome Vacation Village,** Port Dr. (tel. 92-1057); **Cable Beach Caravan Park,** Millington Rd. (tel. 92-2066); **Roebuck Bay Caravan Park,** Walcott St. (tel. 92-1366); and **Broome Caravan Park,** Great Northern Hwy., (tel. 92-1776).

Food

The sometimes-too-lively **Roebuck Bay Hotel** in Chinatown, serves a good range of counter meals for lunch and dinner. For Chinese in Chinatown, try **Wing's** on Napier Terrace, and **Weng Ho** on Dampier Terrace. For light meals in Chinatown, **Broome Burgers,** Napier Terrace, serves the obvious, while **Kool Spot,** Carnarvon St., is more of a sandwich, cake, and smoothy outlet.

Chin's Chinese Restaurant, Hamersley St., offers Asian specialties at moderate prices, plus takeaways. **Seaview Fine Food Takeaway,** Seaview Shopping Centre, packs to-go fish and chips, chickens, burgers, wienies, salads, and sandwiches.

Weld Street Bistro in the Continental Hotel offers daily changing menus, with emphasis on seafood, in the moderate-and-up price range.

For your splurge in fine dining, Broome's best is the **Club Restaurant** at Cable Beach Club, where only fresh ingredients are used. For reservations (required), phone 92-2505.

Shopping

Absolutely scads of shops will be happy to sell you **pearl jewelry** at expensive prices. Some high-quality (and high-priced) outlets are: Paspaley Pearling, Short St.; Linney's, Dampier Terrace; and the Pearl Emporium, Dampier Terrace.

WESTERN AUSTRALIA TOURISM COMMISSION

Pearl luggers once crowded Broome's shores.

Information And Services

For tourist information and local tour bookings, contact **Broome Tourist Bureau,** corner Great Northern Highway and Bagot St. (tel. 091-92-2222). Hours are Mon.-Fri. 9-5, Sat.-Sun. 9 a.m.-1 p.m.

Broome Hospital, Anne St. (tel. 92-1401), has a casualty department.

Getting There

Ansett WA offers scheduled service between Perth, Broome, and Darwin. Fare is $384 one way from Perth and $285 one way from Darwin. The local Ansett office is on the corner of Barker and Weld streets. For information and reservations, phone (091-92-1101, or 13-1300 toll free).

Bus Australia and **Greyhound** operate daily coaches to Broome from Perth (22 hours) and Darwin (11 hours). Fare is $160 one way, from Perth, and $150 one way from Darwin.

Getting Around

Broome Coachlines runs buses between Broome and Cable Beach. For schedules and information, phone 92-1068.

All of the major car rental firms are represented, with prices beginning at about $50 per day. For half that price, you can rent a VW at **Topless Rentals,** Hunter St. (tel. 93-5017).

Broome is an easy town for cycling. **Chinatown Bike Hire,** at Checkpoint Service Station, corner of Hamersley St. and Napier Terrace (tel. 92-1702), rents bicycles for $8 per day, with a break for weekly rentals. **Auski Tropical Resort,** 1298 Milner St. (tel. 92-1183) rents motorscooters, mokes, and jeeps.

Many local and extended tours depart Broome. Examples are: 4WD north coastal safari ($65); Koodarrawirn Aboriginal 4WD coastal tour ($70); Cape Leveque ($105); three- to four-day Kimberley camping safari ($345-$460). Book through Broome Tourist Bureau.

Kimberley Hovercraft will take you for a one-hour glide over Roebuck Bay for $28. For information, phone 93-5025.

DERBY

Broome may be the "gateway to the Kimberley," but Derby (pop. 3,000)—at the heart of many scenic attractions—has been dubbed "gateway to the gorges." Situated on the King Sound shore 220 km northeast of Broome, this port town was lively during the 1880s gold boom, until it, too, went the cattle route. More recently oil, diamonds, and, of course, tourism, have played an important role in the town's development as both an administrative center and a base for travel to some of W.A.'s most stunning gorges.

Sights

The **Derby Cultural Centre,** Clarendon St., exhibits Aboriginal artifacts, local arts and crafts, Jowlaenga sandstone, and a palm tree botanic garden. Hours are Mon.-Wed. and Fri. 10 a.m.-4 p.m., Thurs. 1-7 p.m., Sat. 8 a.m.-noon.

At the corner of Loch and Elder streets, the 1920s **Wharfinger's House,** built for the harbormaster, typifies tropical architecture.

The original **Old Derby Gaol,** dating from the 1880s, is situated next to the modern-day Derby Police Station.

The present **jetty,** constructed in 1963-64 to replace the original 1885 wooden structure, is used mainly for fishing, or observing the tidal movements (tides up to 11 meters give this the highest tidal range of any other wharf in the Southern Hemisphere).

Visitors are welcome to see Outback medical care in action (or about-to-be action) at the Kimberley headquarters of the **Royal Flying Doctor Service**, 60 Clarendon Street. For information, phone 91-1211.

Estimated to be 1,000 years old, the hollow **Boab Prison Tree,** seven km south of town, was used as an overnight "holding cell" for prisoners on their way to Derby.

Pigeon Heritage Trail details the adventures of an Aboriginal outlaw and folk hero named Pigeon who was shot and killed in 1887, following a three-year stand-off with police and white settlers. The self-guiding tour is presented in two stages—one from Derby, the other from Windjana Gorge. The tourist bureau provides brochures.

Events

The annual two-week **Boab Festival** in late June and early July presents a rodeo, mardi gras, street parties, arts and crafts exhibits, and mud football.

Accommodations And Food

Aboriginal Hostels Limited, Loch St. (tel. 091-91-1867), provides youth hostel accommodations for $14 per night.

West Kimberley Lodge, corner Sutherland and Stanwell (tel. 91-1031), offers inexpensive guesthouse lodging. On the expensive side are **Kimberley Motor Inn,** Delewarr St. (tel. 91-1166), and **Derby Boab Inn,** Loch St. (tel. 91-1044).

Derby Caravan Park, Rowan St. (tel. 91-1022), has campsites and on-site vans.

The **Spinifex Hotel,** Clarendon St., and the **Derby Boab Inn,** both serve moderately priced counter meals. **Wharf's Restaurant,** on the jetty, specializes in seafood.

Information

Walking maps, tourist literature, and tour bookings are available at **Derby Tourist Bureau,** Clarendon St. (tel. 091-91-1426). Hours are Mon.-Fri. 8:30 a.m.-4:30 p.m., Sat. 8:30-11:30 a.m.

For medical attention, contact **Derby Regional Hospital,** Loch St. (tel. 91-1426).

Getting There And Around

Daily flights from Perth or Broome are operated by **Ansett WA.** Fare from Perth is $387 one way (from Darwin it's only about $270 one way). One-way fare to Broome is $110. The airport is 42 km outside of town; a shuttle coach meets all flights and provides transport for $12.50 one way. The local An-

MARK MORRIS

methinks the boab tree is curious and curiouser

sett WA office is at 14 Loch Street. For information, phone 91-1266, or 13-1300 toll free.

Bus Australia and **Greyhound** run daily service from Perth for $190 one way. Fare from Broome is $35 one way; from Darwin, $140 one way.

Cars can be rented through Avis, Budget, or Hertz, and begin at $70 per day.

The tourist bureau can arrange scenic flights to Koolan and Cockatoo islands, as well as to some of the other Buccaneer Archipelago islands, but they start from $100 per person.

GIBB ROAD

This 705-km back road is used primarily to transport beef from the Kimberley's huge cattle stations to ports at Derby and Wyndham. It's also the most direct route over to Wyndham with convenient, if not always easy, access to the majestic gorge country and—for the well-prepared adventurer—to places where no one else has ever set foot! Although it's possible for conventional vehicles in excellent condition to negotiate this harsh road (a combination of bitumen, gravel, and natural earth, marked with some very large pits and pocks), a 4WD is advisable. Make this trip only April through November, and carry plenty of extra supplies. Petrol is available approximately midway at Mount Barnett Homestead.

The turnoff to Windjana and Tunnel Creek gorges kicks in 120 km east of Derby. **Windjana Gorge** features awesome multicolored cliffs that rise 90 meters above the Lennard River (which rages during the Wet, trickling down to a few pools during the Dry). **Windjana Gorge National Park** (2,134 hectares), part of the Napier Ranges, is home to a variety of native fauna—including crocodiles. Campsites with limited facilities are available May to October. For information, phone (091) 91-5121.

Pigeon's first victim, Constable Richardson, was killed at **Lillmooloora Police Station,** a couple of kilometers beyond Windjana Gorge.

Aptly named **Tunnel Creek,** about 35 km south, has cut a 750-meter-long tunnel through the Oscar Range. A central shaft exposes natural light. During the Dry the tunnel can be explored, but bring a torch or lantern, be ready for a short wade through cold water, and watch out for flying foxes. Aboriginal cave paintings can be seen near the tunnel's north end. From Tunnel Creek, it's 68 km to the Great Northern Highway and another 37 km to the roadhouse services at Fitzroy Crossing.

Back on Gibb Road, you'll mosey along the foothills of the King Leopold Ranges, a rugged area of tall granite outcrops. Then you'll pass through Ingliss Gap to the top of the range before dipping down to the Broome Valley. Along the way are sidetracks to **Lennard River Gorge, Isdell Gorge,** and **Adcock Gorge.**

Replenish petrol and other supplies at **Mount Barnett Station,** 308 km east of Derby, on the banks of the Barnett River. Campsites with limited facilities are available. For information, phone (091) 91-4652. **Manning Gorge,** on Mount Barnett Station, offers swimming, fishing, and a two-km walking trail to a waterfall.

Forging onward, the turnoff to **Barnett River Gorge** is another 22 km. Moderately priced accommodations are available at **Mount Elizabeth Station** (tel. 091-91-4644), 30 km off Gibb Road.

You must know where you are going, what you are doing, and—probably not a bad idea—who you are doing it with, before adventuring onto **Kalumburu Road.** This extremely isolated, rough, and rocky road is often closed. **Drysdale River Homestead,** 66 km from the Gibb-Kalumburu Road junction, is the last information center and service point. From there on out, you're on your own—*really* on your own. Many of the attractions, such as Mitchell Plateau and Drysdale River National Park, can only be accessed by foot. And, if you do make it to **Kalumburu,** at the end of the 276-km haul, you'll discover that Kalumburu Mission is an Aboriginal reserve, requiring an entry permit. (Apply through the Aboriginal Affairs Planning Authority, P.O. Box 628, West Perth, W.A. 6005, and allow four weeks for processing).

Next pit stop along Gibb Rd. is **Jack's** (or, sometimes, Joe's) **Waterhole** on the Durack

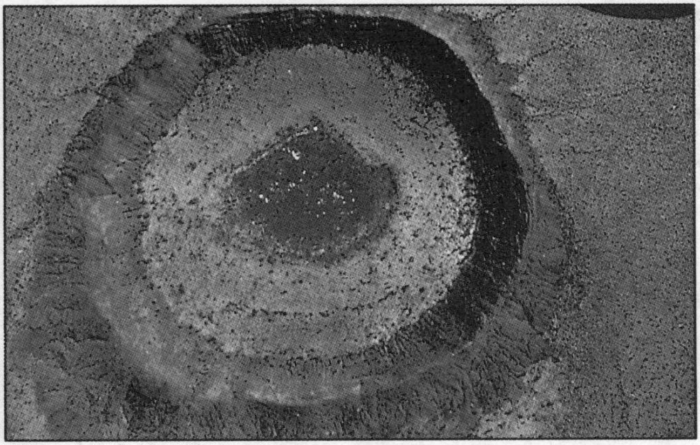

WESTERN AUSTRALIA TOURISM COMMISSION

Wolf Creek meteorite crater

River, a popular swimming, fishing, and camping stop. **Durack River Homestead** (tel. 091-61-4340) has moderately priced accommodations with all meals included. Four-wheel-drive tours of the region depart from here daily.

Home Valley Homestead (tel. 61-4322) is 56 km beyond Jack's (or Joe's). Accommodations, camping, and local tours are available here also. **El Questro Homestead** (tel. 61-4320), on the Pentecost River, has a fully self-contained stone cottage that accommodates six people. This is the last facility on Gibb Road. It's 33 km to the junction of the Great Northern and Victoria highways, where you go north to Wyndham or continue east to Kununurra.

THE GREAT NORTHERN HIGHWAY

Fitzroy Crossing And Vicinity

From Derby, it's 214 km to the gravel road north to Windjana Gorge and Tunnel Creek national parks, and another 42 km to **Fitzroy Crossing** (pop. 430) on the Fitzroy River. Basically a cattle town, this little township is enjoying the fruits of Kimberley popularity, providing services to travelers—either about to cross the river or stranded because of Wet season floods—as well as access to **Geikie Gorge National Park** (3,136 hectares), 21 km northeast. The 14-km-long gorge cuts through a fossilized "barrier reef" dating from the Devonian Period some 350 million years ago, and fossil deposits can be seen in the limestone cliffs. The park is filled with interesting vegetation and abundant wildlife including sawfish and stingers (usually found only near the sea), freshwater crocodiles, kangaroos, and wallabies. The park is open April to November (depending on the river's level). Boat tours of the gorge depart daily at 9:30 a.m. and 2 p.m.

During the Dry, campsites with limited facilities are available within the park; in Fitzroy Crossing, try the **Fitzroy River Lodge Caravan Park** (tel. 091-91-5141), **Fitzroy Crossing Caravan Park** (tel. 91-5080), or **Tarunda Caravan Park** (tel. 91-5004). The historic 1890s **Crossing Inn** (tel. 91-5080) offers moderately priced B&B rooms.

Brooking Gorge is also close to Fitzroy Crossing, but inquire first at Brooking Springs Station both for directions and permission to cross the privately owned land.

Fitzroy Crossing Information Centre is located at Fitzroy River Lodge, Great Northern Highway (tel. 091-91-5141).

Halls Creek And Vicinity

The turnoff to Tanami Rd. is 272 km beyond Fitzroy Crossing, and 16 km before Halls Creek—then it's another 114 km of unsealed road south to **Wolf Creek Meteorite Crater National Park** (1,460 hectares). Discovered in 1947, the crater measures 835 meters wide and 50 meters deep and is the second-largest meteorite crater in the world. The road is usually accessible May to November, but check at Halls Creek for current conditions. **Carranya Station** (tel. 091-68-0200), seven km south of the crater, provides limited supplies and camping facilities.

Western Australia's first gold rush took place in 1885 at **Halls Creek** (pop. 1,000), although the gold dried up just a few years later. Now the center of the vast East Kimberley beef lands, you can still see crumbling reminders of the old gold days at the town's original site, 15 km away along Duncan Road. **Mount Bradley Mine** off Duncan Rd. is one of the region's original mines (some shafts are still open—and deep—so take care when walking around). You can still see the rusting machinery left behind at the **Ruby Queen Mine,** abandoned in the 1970s.

Good local swimming and picnic spots are located at **Caroline Pool, Sawpit Gorge,** and **Palm Springs. China Wall,** on the way to old Halls Creek, is a natural white-quartz formation that resembles a mini-Great Wall of China.

Moderately priced, basic cabin accomodations (with air-conditioning) are available at **Swagman Halls Creek,** 31 McDonald St. (tel. 091-68-6060). Lodging in the expensive range is offered at the **Kimberley Hotel,** Roberta Ave. (tel. 68-6101), and **Halls Creek Motel,** Great Northern Hwy. (tel. 68-6001). **Halls Creek Caravan Park,** Robert Ave. (tel. 68-6169), has campsites and on-site vans. Fresh bread is baked Mon.-Sat. at **Halls Creek Bakery,** Great Northern Highway.

Halls Creek Information Centre, Great Northern Hwy. (tel. 091-68-6184), is open May to September. **Halls Creek Travel,** 78 Great Northern Hwy. (tel. 68-6107), provides tourist info and books bus and air transport (including scenic flights over Bungle Bungle).

One of Australia's greatest natural wonders is the 208,000-hectare **Bungle Bungle National Park,** with its amazing tiger-striped rock formations banded with black lichen and orange silica, plus thousands of low, domed beehive-appearing peaks. Though Bungle Bungle was only "discovered" in 1983, the place was no secret to the Kidja Aboriginals, who called the area "Purnululu." Vegetation is composed of everything from the Bungle Bungle fan palm to spiniflex and eucalpyts. Access to the park (a *very* rough 55 km from the Great Northern Highway, 108 km from Halls Creek) is difficult, limited only to 4WDs with good clearance, and only during April to October. Check on road and weather conditions beforehand. Daytime temperatures can be extreme and water must be carried.

Hikes can be taken to **Echidna Chasm** in the north, **Cathedral Gorge** in the south, and **Piccaninny Gorge,** an intense 18-km roundtrip. Entrance fee is $20 per vehicle. Due to the fragile ecology and travel difficulty, many visitors choose to take a scenic flight (departing from either Halls Creek or Kununurra) over the park. **Camping** is permitted at Belburn Creek. For information, phone the **Department of Conservation and Land Management,** Box 242, Kununurra, W.A. 6743 (tel. 091-68-0200).

The Great Northern Highway calls into **Turkey Creek Roadhouse** (tel. 091-68-7882), 53 km north of the Bungle Bungle turnoff. The roadhouse offers petrol, overnight accommodations, and 4WD Bungle Bungle tours.

Sorry, folks, they won't let you into the **Argyle Diamond Mine,** up the road from Turkey Creek, unless you fly in on an air tour from Kununurra. Discovered in 1979, this is supposedly the world's largest diamond deposit. It's annual production of 30 million carats includes white, champagne, and cognac diamonds, as well as rare and valuable pink diamonds.

From Turkey Creek, it's 151 km to the Great Northern and Victoria highways junction, from where you proceed north to Wyndham or east to Kununurra.

WYNDHAM

Western Australia's northernmost port welcomes you with a 20-meter-long concrete "Big Croc" sculpture at the town's entrance—a replica of the salties that inhabit its waters.

Situated on Cambridge Gulf, at the end of the Great Northern Highway, Wyndham (pop. 1,500) is nicknamed the "top town in the West." During the Halls Creek gold rush days the town prospered, then declined, made a comeback in 1919 when the Meatworks was established, then fizzled again after a 1985 fire closed the plant down. Today it survives mostly on tourism and as a service center for surrounding pastoral and Aboriginal communities.

Sights

What do you think about a spot called **Blood Drain Crocodile Lookout?** Located on the gulf side of the Meatworks complex, the adjacent creek once was used as a blood drain. Well, guess who came for dinner? And about 20 of them at a time! Since the Meatworks closed and the blood stopped flowing, fewer crocs dropped by until feeding began in 1987. Inquire at the tourist information center for feeding times and tide charts (they eat an hour before the full tide).

Five Rivers Lookout, at the top of the Bastion Range, offers magnificent views of the Forrest, Pentecost, Durack, King, and Ord rivers, as well as the port, Meatworks, surrounding gulf, and mudflats. Sunrise and sunset are the best viewing times.

Three Mile Valley, a miniature East Kimberley Range, is reached via Five Rivers Road. Rough gorges, splintered rocks, clear pools, and colorful vegetation closely duplicate the larger range. Walking trails lead to a variety of good sites.

Aboriginal rock paintings depicting spiritual figures and animals are located on the road to Moochalabra Dam. Built to provide the town's water supply, the dam is also a good picnic spot and fishing hole.

The **Grotto,** a rockbound waterhole off the Wyndham-Kununurra Road, is a favorite swimming spot. **Prison Tree,** King River Rd., is a huge boab tree lockup dating back to the 1890s.

Pay your respects to the historic dead at the **Gully, Bend,** or **Afghan** cemeteries.

Accommodations

It's sparse pickings up here. Least expensive motel units are at **Wyndham Roadhouse,** Great Northern Hwy. (tel. 091-61-1290). Accommodations in the expensive bracket are **Wyndham Town Hotel,** 19 O'Donnell St. (tel. 61-1202) and **Wyndham Community Club,** Great Northern Hwy. (tel. 61-1130). **Three Mile Caravan Park,** Baker St. (tel. 61-1064), offers campsites and on-site vans.

Information

Wyndham Tourist Information Centre, O'Donnell St. (in the Old Port Post Office), provides tourist literature. For information, phone (091) 61-1054.

Getting There And Around

Ansett WA has a daily Perth-Kununurra flight ($485 one way). From Kununurra, **I.J. and S.A. Thorley** (tel. 091-61-1201) provide daily coach transport to Wyndham. Fare is $20 one way.

Rental cars begin at about $65 per day and are available at Branko BP Motors, Great Northern Hwy. (tel. 61-1305).

KUNUNURRA

Where were *you* in the sixties? Kununurra (pop. 2,100) was just being born as center of the Ord River Scheme, the Kimberley region's successful irrigation project. Then, in 1979, it was a double whammy when the world's largest diamond deposit was discovered south of town at Smoke Creek. Surrounded by water, natural attractions, birds and wildlife, Kununurra is a travelers' stopover en route west to Broome (1,057 km) or east to Darwin (825 km).

Sights

Pandanus Palms Wildlife Park, Packsaddle Plains Rd., is a still-developing wildlife park with a range of native animals and birds. The **Zebra Rock Gallery** features displays of this unusual striped rock found only near Kununurra. Hours are daily 8 a.m.-6 p.m. For information, phone (091) 68-1114.

Collections of Aboriginal artifacts are displayed and sold at **Waringarri Aboriginal Arts,** Speargrass Road. This Aboriginal-run outlet offers boomerangs, didgeridoos, paintings, spears, fighting sticks, and many more

LOOKALIKES

The vicinity of Kununurra is inundated with lookalike rock formations:

- **Shark Fin Tree,** on Parker Road, looks like . . .
- **City of Ruins,** Weaber Plains Road, looks like . . .
- **Zebra rocks,** in the East Kimberleys, near Kununurra, look like . . .
- **Sleeping Buddha,** along the Ord River, on Victoria Highway, looks like . . .
- **Elephant Rock,** an end-on view of the Sleeping Buddha, looks like . . .
- **Sleeping Mummy** looks like **Sleeping Buddha** looks like **Elephant Rock** looks like . . . *you?*

crafts. Postcards, books, and music are also for sale. Hours are Mon.-Fri. 9-5 For information, phone 68-2212.

Nimberlee Art and Craft Cultural Centre, Poinsettia St., exhibits and sells locally produced paintings, photos, pottery, leatherwork, gemstones, and Aboriginal works. The complex also houses a woodturning workshop, aviaries, an orchid nursery, and a café. Hours are daily 8 a.m.-6 p.m. For information, phone 68-1425.

Kelly's Knob, near the town center, is a 191-meter-high viewpoint over the town, Ord River, and surrounding farmlands.

Adjacent to town, manmade **Lake Kununurra** has a wealth of wildlife and vegetation both on the lake and in the wetlands. Boat cruises are available.

The town fishing hole is **Ivanhoe Crossing,** a permanent waterfall on the Ord River near the Ivanhoe Station Homestead.

Hidden Valley National Park (1,817 hectares) near town is termed a "mini-Bungle Bungle." Features of this 300 million-year-old region include scenic gorges, rugged sandstone hills, Aboriginal rock art, abundant birdlife, and short walking trails.

Created by the Ord River dam, **Lake Argyle,** 72 km south of Kununurra along Parker Rd., contains nine times the water of Sydney Harbour. Rugged islands—which used to be mountain peaks—support a large number of birds and wildlife. Watch for Aboriginal rock paintings during the drive in. Boat cruises on Lake Argyle depart daily.

Moved from its original Lake Argyle site, the reconstructed **Argyle Homestead Museum,** Parker Rd., provides the history of early settlers' lives. Hours are daily 9 a.m.-noon and 2-4 p.m.

Accommodations

The centrally located **YHA Hostel,** Coolibah Dr., at the Uniting Church (tel. 091-68-1372), has dorm beds for $9 per night. **Desert Inn Backpackers,** Konkerberry Dr. (tel. 68-2702), has a/c dorms for $10 per night. **Travellers Guest House,** 111 Nutwood Crescent (tel. 68-1711), offers communal cooking facilities and moderate rates. The **Country Club Hotel,** Coolibah Dr. (tel. 68-1024), has a pool and a/c rooms, also in the moderate range.

Expensive digs are **Hotel Kununurra,** Messmate Way (tel. 68-1344), **Overland Motor Inn,** Duncan Hwy. (tel. 68-1455), and **Lake Argyle Inn** (tel. 68-7360).

Campsites are available at: **Hidden Valley Caravan Park,** Weaber Plains Rd. (tel. 68-1790); **Kimberleyland Holiday Park,** Duncan Hwy. (tel. 68-1280); **Town Caravan Park** (on-site vans, too), Bloodwood Dr. (tel. 68-1763); and **Lake Argyle Tourist Village** (tel. 68-7360).

Food

Gulliver's Tavern, corner of Konkerberry Dr. and Cotton Tree Ave., is a local drinking hole that also serves counter meals as well as more upmarket dinners in the dining room.

The **Kununurra Hotel** is another counter-meal establishment. A decent Chinese restaurant is housed inside the **Country Club Hotel,** on Coolibah Drive.

The **Bower Bird Café** at the Nimberlee Art and Craft Cultural Centre features light meals during the day and a smorgasbord at night.

Information And Services

For information on local attractions and tours, contact **Kununurra Visitors' Centre,** Coolibah Dr. (tel. 091-68-1177). Hours are daily 8-5.

For medical assistance, contact **Kununurra Hospital,** Coolibah Dr. (tel. 61-1104).

Getting There And Around

Ansett WA operates daily flights in and out of Kununurra. Sample one-way fares are: Perth, $485; Darwin, $180; Broome, $220; and Derby, $195.

Bus Australia and **Greyhound** come into Kununurra on the daily Perth-Darwin service. Sample one-way fares are: Perth, $255; Darwin, $95; Derby, $100.

Rental cars start at $60 per day and are available from **Avis,** Bandicoot Dr. (tel. 68-1258), **Budget,** Poinciana St. (tel. 68-2033), and **Hertz,** Poinciana St. (tel. 68-1257).

Travellers Guest House (tel. 68-1711) rents **bicycles** and **canoes,** and will send you off on two-day self-guided canoe tours.

A full range of **tours** depart from Kununurra to surrounding sights. Book with the visitor center or the YHA Hostel (you'll get a discount if you're staying there). **Wild Will and Sons Pony Treks** offer half-day ($30) and full-day ($60) horseback treks through the Kimberley Ranges. **Triangle Tours** (tel. 68-1272) will take you on a two-hour Ord River cruise ($20) or a full-day trip to Lake Argyle, including a two-hour cruise, for $60. **East Kimberley Tours** (tel. 68-2213) runs two-day 4WD Bungle Bungle camping trips for $240 (including camping gear and all meals).

Scenic flights over Bungle Bungle, Lake Argyle, and the Argyle Diamond Mine cost about $120 per person. Operators include Alligator Airways (tel. 68-1575), Ord Air Charter (tel. 68-1373), and Sling Air (tel. 68-1259). **Belray Diamond Tours** (tel. 68-1014) include a flight over Bungle Bungle and a three-hour tour of the diamond mine.

From Kununurra, it's 513 km along the Victoria Highway to Katherine, junction of the Victoria and Stuart highways. Proceeding 321 km north on the Stuart Highway (also called the Track) will bring you into Darwin—a kangaroo hop from Indonesia.

GLOSSARY

You only *think* they speak English down here. They don't—they speak "Strine" (Australian!). Also, they do *not* parlez français. Here is one linguistic idiosyncracy that will make beaucoup de fou: "ballet" is pronounced "bal-ette," "filet" is "fill-ette," "gourmet" is "gor-mette," and picturesque" is "picture-*skew.*" Another point to remember: many words are shortened by adding "y" or "ie" to them (e.g., brekkie for breakfast, telly for television), and an "o'" is often attached to the end of someone's name (as in "Johno" or "Bozo").

abo—derogatory term for "Aborigine," best avoided
amber fluid—beer
arvo—afternoon
avago—have a go, give it a try (also, **avagoyermug**)

back o'Bourke—in the middle of nowhere (also **back of beyond)**
banana bender—a Queenslander
barbie—put another shrimp on the . . .
barrack—to cheer on or root for a team
bathers—bathing suit (also **cozzie**)
battler—one who struggles
bikies—motorcyclists
billabong—pond or waterhole in an otherwise dry riverbed
billy—a tin can with a wire handle used for fixing "billy tea" over a campfire
bitumen—a sealed or surfaced road
black stump—the back o'Bourke begins at the black stump
bloke—a man
blowies—blow flies
bluey—swag
bonnet—the hood of a car
boot—the trunk of a car
booze bus—the Breathalyzer police van
brolly—umbrella
Buckley's—no chance
bush—the country, forest, or Outback (almost anyplace outside the city
bushrangers—Wild West-type outlaws (though some were good guys)

carn—rallying cry at football games (e.g., "carn the Magpies")
cheeky—sarcastic, insolent, rude (e.g., your irreverent author, Ms. Marael)
chunder—vomit
cobber—old-timer's term for "mate"
cockie—a farmer
come good—turn out okay
compo—compensation, such as worker's compo
corroboree—an Aboriginal meeting, usually with song, dance, and ceremonies
crook—sick

dag, daggy—a nerd, or nerd-like (actually the dirty wool lump on a sheep's bottom)
dero—derelict
didgeridoo—Aboriginal wind instrument
dilly bag—Aboriginal woven-grass carrying bag
dingo—a yellow dog
dinkum—honest, true (also **fair dinkum)**
dinky-di—genuine
donk—automobile engine
drongo—a stupid or worthless person
duco—automobile paint
dunny—an outhouse

earbash—nonstop chatter

fair go—an equal opportunity
fall pregnant—to get pregnant
financial—to be in good monetary condition
flat out—busy
footy—football
footpath—sidewalk
fossicking—gem- or rockhounding
galah—a fool or idiot (also a noisy parrot)

g'day—good day
gibber—stony desert
good on yer—good for you, well done
good oil—good information or ideas
grazier—big-time sheep or cattle farmer

hump—to carry something

icy pole—popsicle or ice cream on a stick

jackeroo—male ranch hand
jillaroo—female ranch hand
journo—a journalist
jumbuck—sheep
jumper—a sweater

Kiwi—a New Zealander
knock—to criticize
knockers—those who knock

lay by—lay away (to hold something in a store or shop)
loo—toilet

mate—friend
milk bar—the corner shop or convenience store
milko—milkman
mozzies—mosquitoes
muster—roundup sheep or cattle

never never—way out in the Outback
no worries—no problem
nought—zero

ocker—a brash, rude Aussie
offsider—an assistant
on the piss—out drinking
OYO—Own Your Own (flat, condo, apartment)
Oz—Australia

pastoralist—bigger big-time than a grazier
pom—an English person
postie—a mail person

randy—horny
ratshit—lousy
reckon—"I reckon that randy, ratshit ocker will push the milko down the loo."
rego—car registration
right—okay ("She'll be right, mate")
ripper—good, great, terrific
rubbish—garbage (also, to tease)

sandshoes—sneakers
see ya later—maybe you will, maybe you won't
sheila—archaic term for "girl"
she'll be right—no problem
shout—to treat or buy a round of drinks ("It's your shout")
spunk, spunky—good-looking ("He's a spunk")
station—a large ranch or farm
stuffed—exhausted, beat
sunbake—sunbathe
surfies—surfers
swag—possessions (often carried over your shoulder)
sweets—dessert

ta—thank you
tall poppies—successful people
taxi rank—taxi stand
thingo—you know, a *thing* (a-ma-bobby)
true blue—honest, real, dinkum
Two-up—Aussie gambling game

uni—university
ute—pickup truck
walkabout—a long walk away from civilization
whinge—whine or complain
wowser—a tightass, prude
wobbly—shaky behavior

yabbo—an unmannered, brash person
Yank—an American
yarn—a story or tale

BOOKLIST

The majority of books listed can be purchased at major bookshops in Australia, and many are available in the United States. Most Australian embassies and consulates feature libraries with a wide range of reference and reading matter. The most comprehensive collections are found at the Australian High Commission (London), the Australian Embassy (Washington, D.C.), and the Australian Consulate (New York).

The **Australian Book Source,** 1309 Redwood Lane, Davis, CA 95616, U.S.A. (tel. 916-753-1519), will send you an annual catalog of books in stock and, additionally, will try to fill special requests for Australian books (including used and antiquarian editions).

ABORIGINAL CULTURE, HISTORY, AND STUDIES

Berndt, Ronald, and Catherine Berndt. *The Speaking Land: Myth and Story in Aboriginal Australia.* New York: Penguin, 1989. Nearly 200 myths from a variety of Aboriginal societies and cultures are compiled in this first-of-a-kind anthology.

Broome, Richard. *Aboriginal Australians.* Winchester, MA: Allen and Unwin, 1982. A black response to the white invasion from 1788-1980.

Edwards, W.H. *An Introduction to Aboriginal Societies.* Social Science Press, 1988. Though mainly a college text, this volume is an excellent introduction to Aboriginal economic, social, religious, and political organization and values.

Herbert, Xavier. *Capricornia.* Sydney: Collins/Angus and Robertson, 1977. Originally published in 1938, this elaborate saga portrays the mistreatment of half-castes in Australia's north.

Isaacs, Jennifer. *Australian Aboriginal Paintings.* Weldons, 1989. A selection of traditional canvas and bark paintings from tribes of Arnhem Land and the western desert regions, including translated information from the artists.

———. *Bush Food.* Weldons, 1987. Bone up on Aboriginal bush tucker and herbal remedies.

Morgan, Sally. *My Place.* Fremantle Arts Centre Press, 1987. A powerful and poignant autobiography which traces three generations of Aborigines.

Neidjie, Bill, Stephen Davis, and Allan Fox. *Australia's Kakadu Man.* (Order through the Australian Book Source.) Bill Neidjie, one of the last of the Kakadu tribe, passes along some of his people's ancient wisdom through text and color photos.

Oodgeroo. *My People.* Jacaranda-Wiley, 1981. Formerly known as Kath Walker, Oodgeroo's provocative book of poems is now in its third edition.

Spencer, Sir Walter Baldwin. *The Aboriginal Photographs of Baldwin Spencer.* New York: Viking, 1987. A new coffee-table edition of the widely acclaimed Aboriginal photos, taken by Sir Walter from 1894-1927, on expedition in northern and central Australia.

Stewart, D., ed. *Burnum Burnum's Aboriginal Australia, a Traveler's Guide.* Sydney: Angus and Robertson, 1988. A large hardback volume that sets you exploring the country from an Aboriginal viewpoint.

BUSH AND OUTBACK

Bachman, Bill. *Off The Road Again.* Lothian, 1989. A terrific compendium of both quirky and mystical Outback photos.

Chatwin, Bruce. *The Songlines.* New York: Viking, 1987. The author chronicles his life with central Australian Aborigines.

Davidson, Robyne. *Tracks.* Winchester, MA: Allen and Unwin, 1982. An interesting tale of a determined woman who walks alone with her camels from Alice Springs to the Western Australia coast.

Ellis, G., and S. Cohen. *Outdoor Traveler's Guide: Australia.* Sydney: Collins/Angus and Robertson, 1988. This descriptive guide—containing many color photos and maps—embraces Australia's geography, vegetation, wildlife, parks, and natural areas.

McEnally, Lawrie, and Julie McEnally. *Going Bush.* (Order through Australian Book Source.) The guide for short or long bush adventures including preparation, survival, necessary gear, cooking tips, and critter warnings.

GENERAL INTEREST

Antipodes. American Association of Australian Literary Studies (190 Sixth Ave., Brooklyn, NY 11217). A twice-yearly Australian literary journal featuring Aussie poetry, fiction, essays, book reviews, and literary scene updates.

BP Touring Atlas of Australia. Viking O'Neil, 1990. This large-format, fully indexed road atlas contains easy-to-read maps, including key maps and capital city maps.

Dunstan, Keith. *The Amber Nectar.* Viking O'Neil, 1987. A book which celebrates the brewing and imbibing of Australian beer.

Granville, James. *Australia the Beautiful.* Weldons, 1983. This glossy volume of photography and text will take you on a pictorial journey of the continent and its inhabitants.

Hirst, Robin. *Pocket Guide to the Southern Skies.* Dynamo Press, 1985. Get your bearings on the Southern Cross, Magellan's Clouds, and other phenomena of the southern skies.

Johansen, Lenie. *The Dinkum Dictionary: A Ripper Guide to Aussie English.* Viking O'Neil, 1988. More than 16,000 entries of slang, usage, and Aussie vernacular.

Moult, Allan, and Leo Meier. *Australia the Beautiful Wilderness.* Weldons, 1983. Wilderness areas are described through lively chatter and beautiful photography.

HISTORY

Aitchison, Ray. *The Americans in Australia.* AEPress, 1986. Americans have exerted considerable influence in Australia, as far back as Captain Cook's landing.

Clark, Manning. *A Short History of Australia.* New York: Penguin, 1987. The acclaimed historian's abridged and accessible version of his five-volume *A History of Australia.*

Clarke, Marcus. *For the Term of his Natural Life.* Sydney: Collins/Angus and Robertson. An Australian literary classic depicting the gruesome life inside a penal colony.

Grant, Joan, ed. *The Australopedia.* McPhee Gribble/Penguin Books, 1988. Informative descriptions for young readers about the workings of Australia after 200 years of civilization.

Gunn, Aeneas. *We of the Never Never.* Random Century Australia, 1987. This turn-of-the-century account of Outback pioneer life and Aboriginal encounters is an Australian classic.

Hughes, Robert. *The Fatal Shore.* Collins, 1986. The best-seller that traces the country's convict origins, beginning with the 1788 arrival of the First Fleet.

Isaacs, Jennifer. *Pioneer Women of the Bush and Outback.* Weldons, 1990. Learn how ordinary bush and country women coped with daily life and hardships beginning from the last century onward.

Rajkowski, Pamela. *In the Tracks of the Camelmen.* Sydney: Angus and Robertson, 1987.

The lowdown on some of Outback Australia's most intriguing pioneers.

Sherington, Geoffrey. *Australia's Immigrants, 1788-1988.* Allen and Unwin Australia, 1990. This recently revised volume explores the role migration has played in Australian society.

Webby, Elizabeth. *Colonial Voices.* St. Lucia, Queensland: University of Queensland Press, 1989. An anthology which glimpses 19th-century historical events as well as daily life.

LITERATURE

Davis, Jack, Stephen Muecke, Mudrooroo Narogin, and Adam Shoemaker, eds. *Paperbark: A Collection of Black Australian Writing.* St. Lucia, Qld.: University of Queensland Press, 1989. More than 40 black authors have contributed oral literature, poetry, drama, novella, and other literary forms.

Facey, A.B. *A Fortunate Life.* New York: Penguin, 1988. An Australian bestseller, written by Bert Facey (published when he was 87 years old), describing the "ordinary" life of this extraordinary man.

Flood, Tom. *Oceana Fine.* Allen and Unwin Australia, 1989. An award-winning fantasy/thriller/whodunit novel set in Marvel Loch, Western Australia—a place of myth and mystery.

Franklin, Miles. *My Brilliant Career.* Sydney: Collins/Angus and Robertson. The novel-turned-film of a smarty-pants young woman coming of age in turn-of-the-century Outback Australia.

Gilbert, Kevin, ed. *Inside Black Australia: An Anthology of Aboriginal Poetry.* New York: Penguin, 1988. Diverse voices from riverbanks, universities, jail cells, urban ghettoes, campfires, and reserves.

Goodwin, Ken, and Alan Lawson, eds. *The MacMillan Anthology of Australian Literature.* New York: MacMillan, 1990. Thematically organized sketches, narratives, speeches, poems, historical and biographical material.

McCullough, Colleen. *The Thorn Birds.* New York: Avon Books. Be-still-my-heart saga (and miniseries), set in Western Australia, of lusty forbidden love between priest and parishoner.

Pritchard, Katharine Susannah. *Coonardoo.* Sydney: Collins/Angus and Robertson, 1975. This story of interracial love between a white station owner and his Aboriginal housekeeper was hot stuff in 1929 when it was first published.

NATURAL HISTORY

Cogger, Harold G. *Reptiles and Amphibians of Australia.* (Order through the Australian Book Source.) More than 800 species are featured in photos and line drawings.

Dangerous Australians: The Complete Guide to Australia's Most Deadly Creatures. Bay Books, 1986. Read up on venomous and dangerous wildlife, creepies, and crawlies.

Flood, Josephine. *The Riches of Ancient Australia.* (Order through the Australian Book Source.) Follow the continent's prehistoric heritage in this book complete with maps, photos, and drawings.

Longhurst, Peter. *Bush Strokes.* Bay Books, 1987. A full-color portfolio of 20 native Outback animals, combined with informative text.

MacKness, Brian. *Prehistoric Australia.* Golden Press, 1987. Catch up on 4,000 million years of the continent's evolution.

Slater, Peter. *The Birdwatcher's Notebook.* Weldons, 1989. A field notebook with useful sighting charts, birdwatching techniques, bird characteristics, and much more birding info.

INDEX

Page numbers in **boldface** indicate the primary reference. *Italicized* page numbers indicate information in maps, illustrations, callouts, or charts.
NT = Northern Territory; SA = South Australia; WA = Western Australia.

ABOUT THE AUTHOR

Marael Johnson divides her time between California and Australia, a country she has been exploring and writing about since 1983. She has freelanced as an area editor, researcher, and writer for a number of publications and has worked extensively on many Fodor's Travel Guides, specifically in the Australia, New Zealand, and South Pacific regions. In addition she has reviewed Australia's hotels and resorts for Star Service Worldwide Hotel Guide.

Before—and after—taking up travel writing full-time, the author designed and stitched clothing for rock stars, sold love beads outside American Express offices in Europe, and worked as a barmaid in Spain, an artist's model in California, a set dresser, an art catalog publisher, a vintage clothing collector, and a flea-market wheeler and dealer. She is also a published poet. She has lived in paisley-painted communes in Santa Cruz, elegant Victorians in San Francisco, squats in London, handmade tents in Spain, chateaus in France, monasteries along the Pacific Ocean, and owns a home in Yuppieville, California. She has completely disproven her mother's theory that "you can't run away," as well as Thomas Wolfe's, who swore "you can never go home again." She does both—very successfully.

Presently the author is working on a series of novellas.

SOUTHEAST ASIA HANDBOOK by Carl Parkes
Helps the enlightened traveler discover the real Southeast Asia. 16 color pages, 75 b/w photos, 11 illustrations, 169 maps, 140 charts, vocabulary and suggested reading, index. 873 pages. **$16.95**

BANGKOK HANDBOOK by Michael Buckley
Your tour guide through this exotic and dynamic city reveals the affordable and accessible possibilities. Thai phrasebook, color and b/w photos, maps, illustrations, charts, booklist, index. 214 pages. **$10.95**

PHILIPPINES HANDBOOK by Peter Harper and Evelyn Peplow
Crammed with detailed information, *Philippines Handbook* equips the escapist, hedonist, or business traveler with thorough coverage of the Philippines's colorful history, landscapes, and culture. Color and b/w photos, illustrations, maps, charts, index. 587 pages. **$12.95**

HAWAII HANDBOOK by J.D. Bisignani
Winner of the 1989 Hawaii Visitors Bureau's Best Guide Book Award and the Grand Award for Excellence in Travel Journalism, this guide takes you beyond the glitz and high-priced hype and leads you to a genuine Hawaiian experience. 12 color pages, 86 b/w photos, 132 illustrations, 86 maps, 44 graphs and charts, Hawaiian and pidgin glossaries, appendix, booklist, index. 879 pages. **$15.95**

KAUAI HANDBOOK by J.D. Bisignani
Kauai Handbook is the perfect antidote to the workaday world. 8 color pages, 36 b/w photos, 48 illustrations, 19 maps, 10 tables and charts, Hawaiian and pidgin glossaries, booklist, index. 236 pages. **$9.95**

MAUI HANDBOOK: Including Molokai and Lanai by J.D. Bisignani
"No fool-'round" advice on accommodations, eateries, and recreation, plus a comprehensive introduction to island ways, geography, and history. 8 color pages, 60 b/w photos, 72 illustrations, 34 maps, 19 charts, booklist, glossary, index. 350 pages. **$11.95**

OAHU HANDBOOK by J.D. Bisignani
A handy guide to Honolulu, renowned surfing beaches, and Oahu's countless other diversions. Color and b/w photos, illustrations, 18 maps, charts, booklist, glossary, index. 354 pages. **$11.95**

BIG ISLAND OF HAWAII HANDBOOK by J.D. Bisignani
An entertaining yet informative text packed with insider tips on accommodations, dining, sports and outdoor activities, natural attractions, and must-see sights. Color and b/w photos, illustrations, 20 maps, charts, booklist, glossary, index. 347 pages. **$11.95**

SOUTH PACIFIC HANDBOOK by David Stanley
The original comprehensive guide to the 16 territories in the South Pacific. 20 color pages, 195 b/w photos, 121 illustrations, 35 charts, 138 maps, booklist, glossary, index. 740 pages. **$15.95**

MICRONESIA HANDBOOK:
Guide to the Caroline, Gilbert, Mariana, and Marshall Islands by David Stanley
Micronesia Handbook guides you on a real Pacific adventure all your own. 8 color pages, 77 b/w photos, 68 illustrations, 69 maps, 18 tables and charts, index. 287 pages. **$9.95**

FIJI ISLANDS HANDBOOK by David Stanley
The first and still the best source of information on travel around this 322-island archipelago. 8 color pages, 35 b/w photos, 78 illustrations, 26 maps, 3 charts, Fijian glossary, booklist, index. 198 pages. **$8.95**

TAHITI-POLYNESIA HANDBOOK by David Stanley
All five French-Polynesian archipelagoes are covered in this comprehensive guide by Oceania's best-known travel writer. 12 color pages, 45 b/w photos, 64 illustrations, 33 maps, 7 charts, booklist, glossary, index. 225 pages. **$9.95**

NEW ZEALAND HANDBOOK by Jane King
Introduces you to the people, places, history, and culture of this extraordinary land. 8 color pages, 99 b/w photos, 146 illustrations, 82 maps, booklist, index. 546 pages. **$14.95**

OUTBACK HANDBOOK by Marael Johnson
Australia is an endlessly fascinating, vast land, and *Outback Handbook* explores the cities and towns, sheep stations and wilderness areas of the Northern Territory, Western, and South Australia. Full of travel tips and cultural information for adventuring, relaxing, or just getting away from it all. Color and b/w photos, illustrations, maps, charts, booklist, index. 370 pages. **$15.95**

BLUEPRINT FOR PARADISE: How to Live on a Tropic Island by Ross Norgrove
This one-of-a-kind guide has everything you need to know about moving to and living comfortably on a tropical island. 8 color pages, 40 b/w photos, 3 maps, 14 charts, appendices, index. 212 pages. **$14.95**

The Americas Series

NORTHERN CALIFORNIA HANDBOOK by Kim Weir
An outstanding companion for imaginative travel in the territory north of the Tehachapis. 12 color pages, b/w photos, 69 maps, illustrations, booklist, index. 759 pages. **$16.95**

NEVADA HANDBOOK by Deke Castleman
Nevada Handbook puts the Silver State into perspective and makes it manageable and affordable. 34 b/w photos, 43 illustrations, 37 maps, 17 charts, booklist, index. 400 pages. **$12.95**

NEW MEXICO HANDBOOK by Stephen Metzger
A close-up and complete look at every aspect of this wondrous state. 8 color pages, 85 b/w photos, 63 illustrations, 50 maps, 10 charts, booklist, index. 375 pages. **$13.95**

TEXAS HANDBOOK by Joe Cummings
Seasoned travel writer Joe Cummings brings an insider's perspective to his home state. 12 color pages, b/w photos, maps, illustrations, charts, booklist, index. 483 pages. **$11.95**

ARIZONA TRAVELER'S HANDBOOK by Bill Weir
This meticulously researched guide contains everything necessary to make Arizona accessible and enjoyable. 8 color pages, 194 b/w photos, 74 illustrations, 53 maps, 6 charts, booklist, index. 505 pages. **$13.95**

UTAH HANDBOOK by Bill Weir
Weir gives you all the carefully researched facts and background to make your visit a success. 8 color pages, 102 b/w photos, 61 illustrations, 30 maps, 9 charts, booklist, index. 452 pages. **$12.95**

ALASKA-YUKON HANDBOOK by Deke Castleman and Don Pitcher
Get the inside story, with plenty of well-seasoned advice to help you cover more miles on less money. 8 color pages, 26 b/w photos, 95 illustrations, 92 maps, 10 charts, booklist, glossary, index. 400 pages. **$13.95**

WASHINGTON HANDBOOK by Dianne J. Boulerice Lyons and Archie Satterfield
Covers sights, shopping, services, transportation, and outdoor recreation, with complete listings for restaurants and accommodations. 8 color pages, 92 b/w photos, 24 illustrations, 81 maps, 8 charts, booklist, index. 400 pages. **$13.95**

OREGON HANDBOOK by Stuart Warren and Ted Long Ishikawa
Brimming with travel practicalities and insider views on Oregon's history, culture, arts, and activities. Color and b/w photos, illustrations, 28 maps, charts, booklist, index. 422 pages. **$12.95**

IDAHO HANDBOOK by Bill Loftus
A year-round guide to everything in this outdoor wonderland, from whitewater adventures to rural hideaways. Color and b/w photos, illustrations, maps, charts, booklist, index. 275 pages. **$12.95**

WYOMING HANDBOOK by Don Pitcher
All you need to know to open the doors to this wide and wild state. Color and b/w photos, illustrations, over 60 maps, charts, booklist, index. 427 pages. **$12.95**

MONTANA HANDBOOK by W.C. McRae and Judy Jewell
The wild West is yours with this extensive guide to the Treasure State, complete with travel practicalities, history, and lively essays on Montana life. Color and b/w photos, illustrations, maps, charts, booklist, index. 393 pages. **$13.95**

COLORADO HANDBOOK by Stephen Metzger
Essential details to the all-season possibilities in Colorado fill this guide. Practical travel tips combine with recreation—skiing, nightlife, and wilderness exploration—plus entertaining essays. Color and b/w photos, illustrations, maps, charts, booklist, index. 550 pages. **$15.95**

BRITISH COLUMBIA HANDBOOK by Jane King
With an emphasis on outdoor adventures, this guide covers mainland British Columbia, Vancouver Island, the Queen Charlotte Islands, and the Canadian Rockies. 8 color pages, 56 b/w photos, 45 illustrations, 66 maps, 4 charts, booklist, index. 381 pages. **$11.95**

CATALINA HANDBOOK: A Guide to California's Channel Islands by Chicki Mallan
A complete guide to these remarkable islands, from the windy solitude of the Channel Islands National Marine Sanctuary to bustling Avalon. 8 color pages, 105 b/w photos, 65 illustrations, 40 maps, 32 charts, booklist, index. 262 pages. **$10.95**

BAJA HANDBOOK by Joe Cummings
A comprehensive guide with all the travel information and background on the land, history, and culture of this untamed thousand-mile-long peninsula. Color and b/w photos, illustrations, maps, charts, booklist, index. 400 pages. **$13.95**

YUCATAN HANDBOOK by Chicki Mallan
All the information you'll need to guide you into every corner of this exotic land. 8 color pages, 154 b/w photos, 55 illustrations, 57 maps, 70 charts, appendix, booklist, Mayan and Spanish glossaries, index. 391 pages. **$12.95**

CANCUN HANDBOOK and Mexico's Caribbean Coast by Chicki Mallan
Covers the city's luxury scene as well as more modest attractions, plus many side trips to unspoiled beaches and Mayan ruins. Color and b/w photos, illustrations, over 30 maps, Spanish glossary, booklist, index. 257 pages. **$10.95**

BELIZE HANDBOOK by Chicki Mallan
Complete with detailed maps, practical information, and an overview of the area's flamboyant history, culture, and geographical features, *Belize Handbook* is the only comprehensive guide of its kind to this spectacular region. Color and b/w photos, illustrations, maps, booklist, index. 212 pages. **$11.95**

JAMAICA HANDBOOK by Karl Luntta
From the sun and surf of Montego Bay and Ocho Rios to the cool slopes of the Blue Mountains, author Karl Luntta offers island-seekers a perceptive, personal view of Jamaica. Color and b/w photos, illustrations, maps, charts, index. 350 pages. **$12.95**

The International Series

EGYPT HANDBOOK by Kathy Hansen
An invaluable resource for intelligent travel in Egypt. 8 color pages, 20 b/w photos, 150 illustrations, 80 detailed maps and plans to museums and archaeological sites, Arabic glossary, booklist, index. 510 pages. **$14.95**

PAKISTAN HANDBOOK by Isobel Shaw
For armchair travelers and trekkers alike, the most detailed and authoritative guide to Pakistan ever published. 28 color pages, 86 maps, appendices, Urdu glossary, booklist, index. 478 pages. **$15.95**

MOSCOW-LENINGRAD HANDBOOK by Masha Nordbye
Provides the visitor with an extensive introduction to the history, culture, and people of these two great cities, as well as practical information on where to stay, eat, and shop. 8 color pages, 36 b/w photos, 20 illustrations, 16 maps, 9 charts, booklist, index. 205 pages. **$12.95**

NEPAL HANDBOOK by Kerry Moran
Whether you're planning a week in Kathmandu or months out on the trail, *Nepal Handbook* will take you into the heart of this Himalayan jewel. Color and b/w pages, illustrations, 50 maps, 6 charts, glossary, index. 450 pages. **$12.95**

NEPALI AAMA by Broughton Coburn
A delightful photo-journey into the life of a Gurung tribeswoman of Central Nepal. Having lived with Aama (translated, "mother") for two years, first as an outsider and later as an adopted member of the family, Coburn presents an intimate glimpse into a culture alive with humor, folklore, religion, and ancient rituals. B/w photos. 165 pages. **$13.95**

Moonbelts

Made of heavy-duty Cordura nylon, the Moonbelt offers maximum protection for your money and important papers. This all-weather pouch slips under your shirt or waistband, rendering it virtually undetectable and inaccessible to pickpockets. One-inch-wide nylon webbing, heavy-duty zipper, one-inch quick release buckle. Accommodates traveler's checks, passport, cash, photos. Size 5 x 9 inches. Black. **$8.95**

New travel handbooks may be available that are not on this list.
To find out more about current or upcoming titles,
call us toll-free at (800) 345-5473.

IMPORTANT ORDERING INFORMATION

FOR FASTER SERVICE: Call to locate the bookstore nearest you that carries Moon Travel Handbooks or order directly from Moon Publications:
(800) 345-5473 · Monday-Friday · 9 a.m.-5 p.m. PST · fax (916) 345-6751

PRICES: All prices are subject to change. We always ship the most current edition. We will let you know if there is a price increase on the book you ordered.

SHIPPING & HANDLING OPTIONS:

1) Domestic UPS or USPS first class (allow 10 working days for delivery): $3.50 for the first item, 50 cents for each additional item.

Exceptions:

- **Moonbelt** shipping is $1.50 for one, 50 cents for each additional belt.
- Add $2.00 for same-day handling.

2) UPS 2nd Day Air or Printed Airmail requires a special quote.

3) International Surface Bookrate (8-12 weeks delivery): $3.00 for the first item, $1.00 for each additional item. Note: Moon Publications cannot guarantee international surface bookrate shipping.

FOREIGN ORDERS: All orders which originate outside the U.S.A. must be paid for with either an International Money Order or a check in U.S. currency drawn on a major U.S. bank based in the U.S.A.

TELEPHONE ORDERS: We accept Visa or MasterCard payments. Minimum order is US $15.00. Call in your order: 1 (800) 345-5473. 9 a.m.-5 p.m. Pacific Standard Time.

ORDER FORM

Be sure to call (800) 345-5473 for current prices and editions or for the name of the bookstore nearest you that carries Moon Travel Handbooks • 9 a.m.-5 p.m. PST
(See important ordering information on preceding page)

Name:____________________ Date:__________

Street:______________________________

City:____________________ Daytime Phone:__________

State or Country:____________________ Zip Code:__________

Quantity	Title	Price

Taxable Total	
Sales Tax (7.25%) for California Residents	
Shipping & Handling	
TOTAL	

Ship: ☐ 1st class ☐ UPS (no P.O. Boxes) ☐ International Surface

Ship to: ☐ address above ☐ other____________________

Make checks payable to:
Moon Publications Inc., 722 Wall Street, Chico, California 95928 U.S.A.
We Accept Visa and MasterCard
To Order: Call in your Visa or MasterCard number, or send a written order with your Visa or MasterCard number and expiration date clearly written.

Card Number: ☐ **Visa** ☐ **MasterCard**

☐☐☐☐ ☐☐☐☐ ☐☐☐☐ ☐☐☐☐

Exact Name on Card: ☐ same as above expiration date:__________

☐ other____________________

signature____________________

79-4

THE METRIC SYSTEM

1 inch = 2.54 centimeters (cm)
1 foot = .304 meters (m)
1 mile = 1.6093 kilometers (km)
1 km = .6214 miles
1 fathom = 1.8288 m
1 chain = 20.1168 m
1 furlong = 201.168 m
1 acre = .4047 hectares (ha)
1 sq km = 100 ha
1 sq mile = 2.59 sq km
1 ounce = 28.35 grams
1 pound = .4536 kilograms (kg)
1 short ton = .90718 metric ton
1 short ton = 2000 pounds
1 long ton = 1.016 metric tons
1 long ton = 2240 pounds
1 metric ton = 1000 kg
1 quart = .94635 liters
1 US gallon = 3.7854 liters
1 Imperial gallon = 4.5459 liters
1 nautical mile = 1.852 km

To compute centigrade temperatures, subtract 32 from Fahrenheit and divide by 1.8. To go the other way, multiply centigrade by 1.8 and add 32.

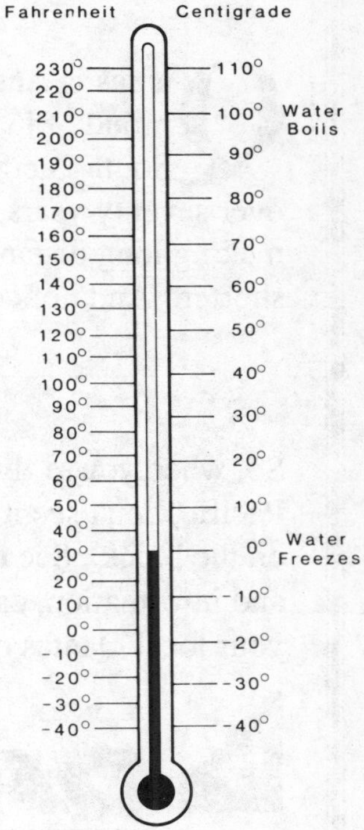

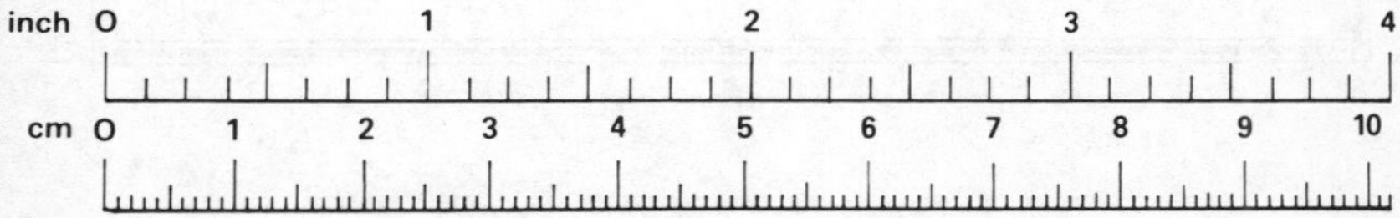